A Concise History of the American Republic

A CONCISE HISTORY

OF THE

Volume 2   Since 1865

An Abbreviated and Newly Revised Edition of

The Growth of the American Republic

NEW YORK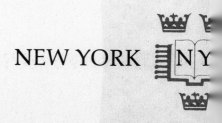

AMERICAN REPUBLIC

SAMUEL ELIOT MORISON

HENRY STEELE COMMAGER

WILLIAM E. LEUCHTENBURG

OXFORD UNIVERSITY PRESS   1977

Designed by
FREDERICK SCHNEIDER

Picture Adviser
JUDITH MARA GUTMAN

Copyright © 1977 by Oxford University Press, Inc.
A Concise History of the American Republic
is an abbreviated and newly revised edition of
The Growth of the American Republic,
Copyright © 1930, 1937, 1942, 1950, 1962, 1969 by Oxford University Press, Inc.
Library of Congress Catalogue Card Number: 76-40742
Printed in the United States of America

Samuel Eliot Morison

1887–1976

For the whole earth is the sepulchre of famous men, and their story lives on, woven into the stuff of other men's lives.

PERICLES, The Funeral Speech

Preface

A Concise History of the American Republic is a shortened and revised edition of *The Growth of the American Republic*, which first appeared in 1930. Over the next three decades, the two senior authors brought out four more editions. In the fifth edition, which appeared in 1962, Morison was responsible for the period up to the Civil War, and for the chapters on World War II; Commager for the period since 1860, except for the chapters on World War II. In the sixth edition, published in 1969, Leuchtenburg had the main responsibility for revision, and for writing new chapters on the recent period, but Morison and Commager also made revisions.

Leuchtenburg has written *A Concise History of the American Republic*, but the book draws largely upon the work of the two senior authors in *The Growth of the American Republic*. Furthermore, the senior authors made numerous editorial recommendations at different stages in the preparation of the manuscript. In particular, Leuchtenburg has closely followed Morison's suggestions for abridgment for the period up to the American Revolution and Commager's counsel on the most recent period. *A Concise History of the American Republic* aims to reach a wide audience that prefers a more compact historical account, but effort has been made to preserve the essence of *The Growth of the American Republic* and to maintain the stylistic integrity of those volumes. This new work also incorporates the most recent scholarship and carries the narrative down to the bicentennial year of 1976.

Our sincere thanks are extended to authors and publishers who have allowed us to quote passages from prose and poetry, to Esta Sobey for bibliographical assistance and to Delight Ansley, who prepared the index. We are especially happy to have an opportunity to acknowledge our debt to Judith Mara Gutman, whose contribution to illustrating this volume was indispensable, and to Byron S. Hollinshead, Jr., and the proficient staff of the Oxford University Press, especially Nancy Lane, Leona Capeless, and Joyce Berry.

We write for young men and women of all ages. We believe that history embraces the whole of a people's activity: economic and social, literary and spiritual, as well as political and military. We have endeavored therefore to give such stress to these different aspects that our story will be that of a growing and changing civilization in an expanding United States of America.

SAMUEL ELIOT MORISON
HENRY STEELE COMMAGER
April 1976　　　　　　　WILLIAM E. LEUCHTENBURG

The death of Samuel Eliot Morison on 15 May 1976 evoked widespread expressions of sorrow together with a sense of fulfillment for a life so rich in achievement. In his eighty-eight years Admiral Morison had written more than fifty books, taught with distinction at Harvard for four decades, served his country in two world wars, and, an accomplished mariner, had retraced the voyages of Columbus and Magellan. Born in the nineteenth century, with intimate associations with the world of eighteenth-century Boston, he embraced in his own life much of the history of the American republic about which he wrote with such felicity. In the last weeks of his life he was engaged in reading, with meticulous care, the manuscript of *A Concise History of the American Republic*, and we take pride in being associated with him in this, the final work of an illustrious career.

H.S.C.
W.E.L.

Contents

Maps

A Concise History of the American Republic

19

Reconstruction

1865–1877

The Prostrate South

Four years of warfare had devastated the South. Over large sections of the country, Union and Confederate armies had tramped and fought. From Atlanta to Savannah and from Savannah to Raleigh, Sherman had left a broad belt of blackened ruin: 'where our footsteps pass,' wrote one of his aides, 'fire, ashes, and desolation follow in the path.' Sheridan had swept down the fertile Shenandoah valley like an avenging fury. 'We had no cattle, hogs, sheep, or horses or anything else,' wrote a native of Virginia. 'The fences were all gone . . . the barns were all burned; chimneys standing without houses and houses standing without roofs, or doors, or windows . . . bridges all destroyed, roads badly cut up.' In the West, conditions were just as bad. The Governor of Arkansas wrote of his state: 'The desolations of war are beyond description. . . . Besides the utter desolation that marked the tracks of war and battle, guerilla bands and scouting parties have pillaged almost every neighbourhood.'

Some of the cities presented a picture as appalling as the countryside. Charleston had been bombarded and partially burned; a Northern visitor painted it as a city of 'vacant houses, of widowed women, of rotting wharves, of deserted warehouses, of weed-wild gardens, of miles of grass-grown streets, of acres of pitiful and voiceless barrenness.' The business portion of Richmond, the capital of the Confederacy, lay in ruins 'all up and down, as far as the eye could reach. . . . Beds of cinders, cellars half filled with bricks and rubbish, broken and blackened walls, impassable streets deluged with *débris*.' In Atlanta, brick and mortar, charred timber, scraps of tin roofing, engine bolts and bars, cannonballs, and long shot filled the ruined streets. Mobile, Galveston, Vicksburg, and numerous other cities of the South were in a similar plight.

With the collapse of the Confederacy, civil administration all but disappeared throughout the South. There was no money for the support of government and no authority which could assess or collect taxes. There were few courts, judges, sheriffs, or police officers with any authority, and vandalism went unrestrained except by public opinion or by lynch law. 'Our principal danger,' observed George Cary Eggleston, 'was from lawless bands of marauders who infested the country, and our greatest difficulty in dealing with them

Ruins of Charleston, South Carolina, 1865. (*Library of Congress, Brady Collection*)

lay in the utter absence of constituted authority of any sort.' Fraud and peculation added to the universal distress. United States Treasury agents seized hundreds of thousands of bales of cotton, and other property as well. The Federal Government subsequently reimbursed no fewer than 40,000 claimants because of illegal confiscation of their property.

The economic life of the South was shattered. Manufacturing had been all but destroyed. Few Southern banks were solvent, and it was years before the banking system was even partially restored. Confederate securities into which the people had sunk their savings were now as worthless as Continental currency. Shops were depleted of goods, and almost everything had to be imported from the North on credit. Even agriculture was slow to revive. Not until 1879 did the seceding states raise a cotton crop as large as that of 1860. In 1870 the tobacco crop of Virginia was one-third that of 1860, and the corn and wheat crop one-half. Farm land that had once sold for $100 an acre went begging at $5, and in Mississippi alone almost 6 million acres of land were sold for non-payment of taxes.

The transportation system had mostly collapsed. Roads were all but impassable, bridges destroyed or washed away, river levees broken. Railroad transportation was paralyzed, and most of the railroad companies bankrupt. Over a stretch of 114 miles in Alabama 'every bridge and trestle was destroyed, cross-ties rotten, buildings burned, water-tanks gone, ditches filled up, and tracks grown up in weeds and bushes.'

The cultural life of the South did not recover for over a generation. Schools, colleges, libraries, and churches were destroyed or impoverished, and the intellectual life of the South was paralyzed by the preoccupation with sheer survival and by obsession with the past and with defeat. 'You ask me to tell you the story of my last year,' wrote the poet Henry Timrod. 'I can embody it all in a few words: beggary, starvation, death, bitter grief, utter want of hope.' Young men of family who had interrupted their education to fight for Southern independence had to labor in the fields to keep their kinfolk from starving; and a planter's family which still had young men was deemed fortunate.

General Anderson worked as a day laborer in the yards of the South Carolina Railroad. George Fitzhugh, the philosopher of slavery, lived in a poor shanty among his former slaves. William Gilmore Simms, the South's leading man of letters, lost not only his 'house, stables, barns, gin house, machine and threshing houses, mules, horses, cattle, wagons, ploughs, implements, all destroyed' but what was probably the finest private library in the South. 'Pretty much the whole of life has been merely not dying,' wrote the Southern poet Sidney Lanier, himself dying.

The fall of the Confederacy dealt an extremely heavy blow to the planter aristocracy that had long guided the destinies of the South. Some of this class was excluded for a time from any participation in the government, and for such able leaders as Davis and Lee the disability was never removed. Slave property valued in 1860 at over $2 billion evaporated, and the savings and sacrifices represented by Confederate securities were lost. A labor system which was the very basis of the Southern economy was overthrown, the agricultural regime which it sreved was disarranged, and a new system, no less wasteful and scarcely less oppressive, was established in its stead.

The planter aristocracy suffered especially severely; for if the war had been 'a poor man's fight,' the poor white had nothing to lose, and his condition was no worse in 1870 than it had been in 1850. Many planters gave up the struggle to maintain themselves on the land. A few fled to England, Mexico, or Brazil; others migrated to the Northern cities or started life anew in the West; many moved to the towns and adapted themselves to business or professional life. The small farmers and poor whites took advantage of this exodus to enlarge their farms and elect men of their own kind to high office. A little while and the Tillmans, Watsons, and Longs would sit in the seats of the Calhouns, the Cobbs, and the Clays.

The Triumphant North

To the North the war brought not only victory but unprecedented prosperity, a sense of power, a spirit of buoyant confidence, and exuberance of energy that found expression in a thousand out-

The Richmond and Petersburg Railroad Depot, 1865. This Mathew Brady photograph of a demolished locomotive and a gutted station in the former Confederate capital of Richmond, Virginia, reveals how little was left of the railroad system of the South after the devastation of the Civil War. (*Brady Collection, Library of Congress*)

lets. To the generation that had saved the Union everything seemed possible. 'The truth is,' wrote Senator Sherman to his brother, the General, 'the close of the war with our resources unimpaired gives an elevation, a scope to the ideas of leading capitalists far higher than anything ever undertaken in this country before. They talk of millions as confidently as formerly of thousands.' Men hurled themselves upon the continent as if to ravish it of its wealth. Railroads were flung across mountain barriers, and settlers crowded into half a continent, while cattle swarmed over the grasslands of the High Plains. Forests were felled, the earth gutted of coal, copper, iron ore, and precious metals; petroleum spouted from untended wells. Telegraph wires were strung across the country and cables stretched from continent to continent; factories sprang up overnight; speculators thronged the floors of stock and produce exchanges, inventors flooded the patent office with applications for new devices with which to conquer nature and create wealth.

The census of 1870 revealed that, despite four years of war, the per capita wealth of the North had doubled in ten years. The war, while depressing some industries, created new opportunities for amassing private wealth. Supplying the armies with food and clothing and munitions proved immensely profitable. More profitable still was the business of financing the war, and many a fortune was founded upon speculation in government bonds and on the banking expansion encouraged by the National Banking Act. Banks which held government bonds received an estimated aggregate of 17 per cent interest annually upon their investment. The rewards of railroad organization, financing, construction, and operation were even greater. In the ten years after the war, the country doubled its railroad mileage, and the profits went, often by devious means, to establish the fortunes of Vanderbilt and Gould, Huntington and Stanford, and other multimillionaires.

No less spectacular was the exploitation of natural resources. After oil was struck in western Pennsylvania in 1859, thousands of fortune-hunters stampeded into the oil-soaked triangle between the Allegheny river and Oil Creek. During the war oil production increased from 21 mil-

lion to 104 million gallons, and the capitalization of new companies was not far from half a billion dollars. In 1860 silver production was a paltry $150,000; by the end of Reconstruction annual output had reached $38 million, and the silver barons of the West had come to exercise an influence in politics comparable to that of industrialists in the East. In the postwar years coal production trebled, and iron ore output in the Lake Superior region alone increased more than tenfold.

In the 1860's the number of manufacturing establishments increased by fully 80 per cent. Four times as much timber was cut in Michigan, four times as much pig iron was smelted in Ohio, four times as much freight was handled by the Pennsylvania Railroad, four times as many miles of railroad track were laid, in 1870 as in 1860. After the war, the woolens, cotton, iron, lumber, meat, and milling industries all showed a steady and even a spectacular development. And while property values in the South were suffering a cataclysmic decline, total property value of the North and West increased from $10 billion in 1860 to over $25 billion a decade later.

Accompanying this extraordinary development of business was a steady rise in the population of cities and in immigration. New York and Philadelphia, Boston and Baltimore, continued the growth which had begun back in the 'forties, and newer cities such as Chicago and St. Louis, Cleveland and Pittsburgh, St. Paul and San Francisco, more than doubled their population in ten years. Even during the war some 800,000 immigrants had entered the United States, and in the ten years after Appomattox some 3.25 million immigrants flooded into the cities and the farms of the North and the West.

These developments all contributed to the growth of income, and observers were already remarking upon the concentration of wealth in certain fortunate areas and favored groups. In 1870 the wealth of New York State alone was more than twice that of all the ex-Confederate states. Every business grew its own crop of millionaires, and soon the names of Morgan and Armour, Swift and Pillsbury, came to be as familiar to the average American as the names of his statesmen. A new plutocracy emerged from the war and Reconstruction, masters of money who were no less self-conscious and powerful than the planter aristocracy of the Old South.

While the old patterns were being rearranged in the South, a different kind of transformation was effected in the North. With the representatives of the planter class out of Congress, the spokesmen of industry, finance, and of free Western lands no longer had to contend with their most powerful opponent. During the war they pushed through legislation to fulfill the arrested hopes of the 'fifties, and after victory they garnered the fruits.

The moderate tariff of 1857 gave way to the Morrill tariff of 1861, and that to a series of war tariffs with duties scaling rapidly upward. By the National Banking Acts of 1863 and 1864, the Independent Treasury system of 1846 was swept away, and an act of 1865 imposed a tax of 10 per cent on all state bank notes, a fatal blow which none would regret. To ensure an ample labor supply, Congress in 1864 permitted the importation of contract labor from abroad, and though this act was soon repealed, the practice itself was not discontinued until the 'eighties. Internal improvements at national expense found expression in subsidies to telegraph and cable lines and in generous grants of millions of acres out of the public domain to railroad promoters.

Western farmers achieved a century-old ambition with the Homestead Law of 1862. This act, limited temporarily in its application to those who 'have never borne arms against the United States Government,' granted a quarter-section (160 acres) of public domain to anyone who would undertake to cultivate it. The Morrill Act, passed the same year, subsidized agricultural education through public lands. At the same time easier access to the West was assured through the government-subsidized railroads. By carrying out the promise of the Republican platform, this legislation strengthened that party in the agricultural West.

Finally, the Civil War had an important political consequence. The Republicans came out of the war with an aura of legitimacy, for they could claim to be the party that had saved the Union, while the Democrats had the odium of secession. For a generation Republican orators rang the changes on Fort Sumter and Andersonville prison, and 'waved the bloody shirt of the rebellion,' and presented themselves as the liberators and defenders of the former slaves.

The Freedman

In Reconstruction the Negro was the central figure. Upwards of a million blacks had in one way or another become free before the end of the war; victory and the Thirteenth Amendment liberated about 3 million more. Never before in the history of the world had civil and political rights been conferred at one stroke on so large a body of men. Many thought that freedom meant no more work and proceeded to celebrate an endless 'day of jubilee'; others were led to believe that the property of their former masters would be divided among them. 'Emancipation having been announced one day,' wrote Tom Watson about his Georgia home, 'not a Negro remained on the place the next. The fine old homestead was deserted. Every house in "the quarter" was empty. The first impulse of freedom had carried the last of the blacks to town.' Thousands took to the woods or to the road, or clustered around the United States army posts, living on doles or dying of camp diseases. As the most famous of colored leaders, Frederick Douglass, said, the black 'was free from the individual master but a slave of society. He had neither money, property, nor friends. He was free from the old plantation, but he had nothing but the dusty road under his feet. He was free from the old quarter that once gave him shelter, but a slave to the rains of summer and the frosts of winter. He was turned loose, naked, hungry, and destitute to the open sky.' Deaths among blacks from starvation, disease, and violence in the first two years of freedom ran into the tens of thousands. Yet despite the deprivations of a slave society, the freedmen contributed leaders who faced these harsh realities with uncommon good sense.

To the average Southerner emancipation changed only the legal position of the Negro. Few whites were willing to acquiesce in anything approaching race equality. Some of the former slaveholders tried sincerely and with some success

Frederick Douglass (1817–95). So eloquent was he as a speaker and so independent was his spirit that some who heard him on the lecture platform refused to believe that he had been reared as a slave. He married twice, the second time to a white woman. He answered critics of his second marriage by pointing out that his first wife 'was the color of my mother, and the second, the color of my father.' (*Art Museum, University of New Mexico*)

Freedmen in Richmond, Virginia. (*Library of Congress, Brady Collection*)

to assist the black in adjusting himself to his new status. But the small farmers and the poor whites were determined to 'keep the Negro in his place,' by laws if possible, by force if necessary. J. T. Trowbridge, writing shortly after the war, remarked that 'there is at this day more prejudice against color among the middle and poorer classes . . . who owned few or no slaves, than among the planters, who owned them by the hundred.'

Most planters sought to keep their former slaves as hired help or as tenant farmers, or on the sharecrop system, and every Southern state but Tennessee attempted to assure this by a series of laws collectively known as the 'black codes.' The codes of Virginia and North Carolina, where the whites were in secure control, were mild; those of South Carolina, Mississippi, and Louisiana, where blacks outnumbered whites, severe. These black codes conferred upon the freedmen fairly extensive privileges, gave them the essential rights of citizens to contract, sue and be sued, own and inherit property, and testify in court, and made some provision for education. In no instance, however, were the freedmen accorded the vote or made eligible for juries, and for the most part they were not permitted to testify against white men. Because of their alleged aversion to work they were required to have some steady occupation, and subjected to penalties for violation of labor contracts. The especially stringent vagrancy and apprenticeship laws lent themselves readily to the establishment of peonage. The penal codes provided harsher and more arbitrary punishments for blacks than for whites, and some states permitted individual masters to administer corporal punishment to 'refractory servants.' Negroes were not allowed to bear arms, or to appear in certain public places, and there were special laws governing their domestic relations.

Southern whites, who had never dreamed it possible to live side by side with free blacks, professed to believe that these laws were liberal and generous. But every one of the codes confessed a determination to keep the freedmen in a permanent position of inferiority. This Old South point of view was succinctly expressed in the most influential of Southern journals, *De Bow's Review*:

We of the South would not find much difficulty in managing the Negroes, if left to ourselves, for we would be guided by the lights of experience and the teachings of history. . . . We should be satisfied to compel them to engage in coarse common manual labor, and to punish them for dereliction of duty or nonfulfillment of their contracts with sufficient severity to make the great majority of them productive laborers. . . . We should treat them as mere grown-up children, entitled like children, or apprentices, to the protection of guardians and masters, and bound to obey those put above them in place of parents, just as children are so bound.

It was scarcely surprising that Northerners regarded the black codes as palpable evasions of the Thirteenth Amendment, which had abolished slavery, and conclusive evidence that the South was not prepared to accept the 'verdict of Appomattox.' In response to the black codes the North demanded that the Federal Government step in to protect the former slaves. This object, eventually embodied in the Fourteenth and Fifteenth Amendments and the various civil rights bills, was first pursued through the agencies of the Freedmen's Bureau and the military governments.

The Freedmen's Bureau of the War Department was created by Congress 3 March 1865, with powers of guardianship over Negroes and refugees, under General O. O. Howard, the 'Christian soldier.' The bureau extended relief to both races, administered justice in cases involving freedmen, and established schools for colored people. During its brief existence the Freedmen's Bureau set up over a hundred hospitals, gave medical aid to half a million patients, distributed over 20 million rations to the destitute of both races, and maintained over 4000 schools for black children. Yet, as the failure of the Freedmen's Bureau Bank—wiping out the savings of thousands of former slaves—revealed, the bureau also offered an opportunity for men of low character to enrich themselves.

The bureau's most important work was educational. As rapidly as schools were provided, the freedmen took advantage of them. 'It was a whole race trying to go to school,' wrote Booker T. Washington. 'Few were too young and none too old to make the attempt to learn. As fast as any kind of teachers could be secured, not only were day schools filled, but night schools as well. The great ambition of the older people was to try to learn to read the Bible before they died.' Most of these freedmen's schools were taught by Northern women who volunteered for what W. E. B. Du Bois called the Ninth Crusade:

Behind the mists of ruin and rapine waved the calico dresses of women who dared, and after the hoarse mouthings of the field guns rang the rhythm of the alphabet. Rich and poor they were, serious and curious, bereaved, now of a father, now of a brother, now of more than these, they came seeking a life work in planting New England schoolhouses among the white and black of the South. They did their work well. In that first year they taught one hundred thousand souls and more.

By the end of Reconstruction there were 600,000 blacks in elementary schools in the South; the Federal Government had set up Howard University in the national capital, and private philanthropy had founded industrial schools like

Freedman's Bureau, Memphis. A long line of blacks wait to hear their cases heard. This particular office of the Bureau distributed more rations than most. (*Library of Congress*)

Hampton Institute in Virginia and Fisk in Tennessee.

Progress in land-ownership, the other great ambition of the freedmen, proved slow and halting, one of the most egregious failures of reconstruction. Northern statesmen had encouraged the Negro to look to the Federal Government to provide 'forty acres and a mule.' But in the end nothing was done to help the black man become an independent landowner. The Federal Government still owned enough public land in the South to have given every Negro family a 40-acre farm,

while the cotton tax of some $68 million would have provided the mule. A Congress that was able to give 40 million acres of land to a single railroad might have done something to fulfill its obligation to the freedmen. Without effective assistance from federal—or state—governments, the vast majority of blacks could not purchase even small farms and were forced to lease land on such terms as whites were prepared to grant. And when the Negro did set up as an independent landowner he was severely handicapped by his unfamiliarity with farm management and marketing, and his lack of capital for farm animals and implements. In 1888 Georgia farmlands were valued at $88 million; the blacks, who were half the population, owned land to the value of $1.8 million.

Emancipation altered the form rather than the substance of the Negro's economic status for at least a generation after Appomattox. The transition from slave to independent farmer was long and painful, made usually through the medium of tenancy, and for many it was never completely made. Without the requisite capital, without credit except such as was cautiously extended by white bankers or storekeepers on usurious terms, and without agricultural skills, most freedmen were unable to rise above the sharecropper or tenant class. They continued to work in the fields, to live in the shacks provided by the former master or by his children, and to exist on credit provided by the same hands. A very few achieved something more—a business or a profession which brought them social standing as well as livelihood. After 1890 some blacks became laborers in the coal mines or steel mills or tobacco factories of the New South; others headed northward to work in industrial centers while their wives and daughters became 'domestics.' But the majority remained on land that belonged to others, plodding behind the plow in spring and picking cotton in the fall, reasonably sure of food and shelter and clothing, a Saturday afternoon in town, a Sunday at revival meetings, continuing in the ways of their fathers.

Reconstruction during the Civil War

Reconstruction had been debated in the North ever since the beginning of the war. As usual with American political issues involving sectional balance, the argument took place on the plane of constitutional theory. It turned largely on two questions: whether the seceded states were in or out of the Union when their rebellion was crushed and whether the prerogative of restoration lodged with President or Congress. From the Northern premise that secession was illegal, strict logic reached the conclusion that former states of the Confederacy had always been and were now states of the Union, with all the rights and privileges pertaining thereto. If, on the contrary, secession

was valid, the South might consistently be treated as conquered territory, without any legal rights that the Union was required to respect. Both sides adopted the proper deductions from the other's premise. Radical Republicans, the most uncompromising nationalists, managed to prove to their satisfaction that the Southern states had lost or forfeited their rights, while former secessionists insisted that their rights in the Union from which they had seceded were unimpaired!

But the question of the status of the Southern states was to be decided in accordance not with theory but with political necessities. Lincoln, with his customary clarity, saw this, and saw, too, how dangerous was any dogmatic approach. In his last speech, on 11 April 1865, he insisted that the question whether the Southern states were in or out of the Union was 'bad as the basis of a controversy, and good for nothing at all—a merely pernicious abstraction.... Finding themselves safely at home, it would be utterly immaterial whether they had ever been abroad.' Obviously, these states were 'out of their proper practical relation with the Union'; the object of all should be to 'get them into their proper practical relation' again.

Lincoln had been pursuing this eminently sensible policy since the beginning of the war. As early as 1862 he had appointed provisional military governors in Tennessee, Louisiana, and North Carolina whose duty it was to re-establish loyal governments. The North Carolina experiment came to naught, but in Tennessee Governor Andrew Johnson and in Louisiana General Banks made impressive progress toward restoring federal authority, and after the fall of Vicksburg, Arkansas was similarly reclaimed. Encouraged by this success, Lincoln, in a proclamation of 8 December 1863, formulated what was to be the presidential plan of reconstruction.

The object of this plan was to get the seceded states back into their normal relations with the Federal Government as quickly and as painlessly as possible; the means was the presidential power to pardon. The plan itself provided for a general amnesty and restoration of property other than slaves to most of those who would take a prescribed oath of loyalty to the Union. Furthermore, whenever 10 per cent of the electorate of 1860 should take this oath, they might set up a state government which Lincoln promised to recognize as the true government of the state.

This magnanimous 10 per cent plan was very promptly adopted in Louisiana and Arkansas. Thousands of voters, many of them cheerfully perjuring themselves, swore that they had not willingly borne arms against the United States; they were then duly registered. They held constitutional conventions, drew up and ratified new constitutions abolishing slavery, and their states then prepared to reassume their place in the Federal Union. But all was not to be such easy sailing. Congress, which was the judge of its own membership, refused to admit the representatives of these reconstructed states, and in the presidential election of 1864 their electoral votes were not counted.

The congressional leaders had a plan of their own which carefully retained control of the entire process of reconstruction in congressional hands. The Wade-Davis Bill of 8 July 1864 stipulated that Congress, not the President, was to have jurisdiction over the processes of reconstruction, and that a majority of the electorate, instead of merely 10 per cent, was required for the reconstitution of legal state governments. When Lincoln averted this scheme by a pocket veto, he brought down upon himself the bitter excoriation of the Wade-Davis Manifesto. 'The President . . . must understand,' said the two Congressmen, 'that the authority of Congress is paramount and must be respected . . . and if he wishes our support he must confine himself to his executive duties—to obey and execute, not make the laws—to suppress by arms armed rebellion, and leave political reorganization to Congress.' Here was the real beginning of the rift between the President and the Radicals. The term refers to those who were determined to employ the power of the national government to ensure the freedmen's rights and establish the supremacy of the Republican party in national politics and of Congress in the federal administration. Though at first small, the Radical faction included such formidable leaders as Thaddeus Stevens of Pennsylvania, Ben Wade of Ohio,

Zachariah Chandler of Michigan, and Charles Sumner of Massachusetts, and it would eventually come to dominate the Republican party.

With the publication of the Wade-Davis Manifesto, an issue had been raised that would not be settled until a President had been impeached, a Supreme Court intimidated, and the Constitution altered. Congressional opposition to Lincoln's plan was due in part to legislative *esprit de corps*, in part to concern for the black, in part to the hatreds engendered by the war, and in part to persuasive constitutional considerations, for it seemed only logical that Congress, which had the power to admit new states and was the judge of its own membership, should control reconstruction. Moreover, the Radicals thought it monstrous that traitors and rebels should be readmitted to full fellowship in the Union they had repudiated and tried to destroy. It would be the Union as in Buchanan's time, administered by 'rebels' and 'copperheads' for the benefit of an unrepentant slavocracy. Even Northerners who were quite willing to admit that Davis and Stephens were honorable men did not care to see them at their old desks in the Senate, shouting for state rights. Moreover, party interests were at stake. As Thaddeus Stevens put it, the Southern states 'ought never to be recognized as capable of acting in the Union, or of being counted as valid states, until the Constitution shall have been so amended . . . as to secure perpetual ascendancy to the party of the Union.' That was the nub of the matter. If the Southern states returned a solid Democratic counterpart to Congress, as appeared inevitable, a reunited Democratic party would have a majority in both houses of Congress. The amendment which Stevens had in mind was that providing for Negro suffrage, which would fulfill the moral obligation to the freedmen and create a flourishing Republican party in the South.

If the partisan considerations seem narrow, we should ask ourselves what other nation in history has ever turned over control of the government and of the spoils of victory to the leaders of a defeated rebellion.

For about six weeks after Lincoln's assassination there was a petty 'reign of terror,' directed by

Secretary Stanton and supported by President Johnson, who had always been in favor of hanging 'traitors.' Only the stern intervention of Grant prevented the seizure of Lee and other Confederate generals. Large rewards for the apprehension of Davis and his cabinet, as alleged promoters of the murder of Lincoln, resulted in their capture and temporary imprisonment. But the charge of complicity in the murder was quickly seen to be preposterous, and it was obviously impossible to get a Virginia jury to convict Davis of treason. Thirst for vengeance appeared to be slaked by the shooting or suicide of the assassin Booth, by hanging his three accomplices and the unfortunate woman who had harbored them, after an extra-legal trial by a military tribunal, and by hanging the miserable Henry Wirz, commander of the infamous Andersonville prison, for the 'murder' of Union prisoners.

All this was cause for shame, but no other great rebellion of modern times has been suppressed with so little loss of life or formal punishment of the vanquished. Not one of the rebel leaders was executed, none was brought to trial for treason. There were no mass arrests, not even of those officers of the United States who took up arms against their government. Even the civil disabilities imposed were mild; by 1872, only some 750 ex-Confederates were still barred from office-holding. For generations Southerners have rung the changes on the theme of Northern ruthlessness during the Reconstruction years, and many historians have concluded that the North imposed upon the South a 'Carthaginian peace.' Yet we have only to recall the suppression of the Peasants' Revolt in Germany in the sixteenth century, the ravages of Alva in the rebelling Low Countries, the punishments inflicted on the Irish by Cromwell and on the Scots after Culloden, or the Russian, Nazi, and Spanish revolutions of our own time, to appreciate how moderate was the conduct of the triumphant North after 1865.

Andrew Johnson Takes Charge

Lincoln's assassination and the accession to the presidency of Andrew Johnson drastically altered the political situation.[1] Like Tyler in 1841, Johnson was the nominal head of a party of which he was not really a member. Of origin as humble as Lincoln's, in early life a tailor in a Tennessee mountain village and unable to write until taught by his wife, he possessed many of Lincoln's virtues but lacked his ability to handle men. Self-educated and self-trained, he had a powerful though not well-disciplined mind. United with these intellectual qualities were the virtues of integrity, devotion to duty, and courage. But at a time when tact was called for, he was stubborn and inflexible; Johnson 'had no budge in him.' And he misunderstood the revolution brought by the war.

No President ever faced a more difficult situation. He had no personal following either in the South or in the North, none of the prestige that came to Lincoln from the successful conduct of the war, and no party organization behind him, for he had broken with the Democrats and had not been accepted by the Republicans. Seward and Welles were loyal to Johnson, but Stanton, with his customary duplicity, used the machinery of the War Department against him and kept the Radicals posted on cabinet secrets. Yet at the outset the Radicals were a minority, and they were generally well disposed toward him. It was Johnson's own blunders that isolated him not only from the Radicals but from the moderates.

At first Johnson appeared to be willing to cooperate with the Radicals. 'Treason is a crime and must be punished,' he said; 'treason must be made infamous, and traitors must be impoverished.' Bluff Ben Wade exclaimed exultantly, 'Johnson, we have faith in you. By the gods, there will be no trouble now in running this government.'

---

1. Some of the Radicals rejoiced in the removal of Lincoln and the accession of Johnson. 'I spent most of the afternoon in a political caucus,' wrote Representative George Julian of Indiana, 'and while everybody was shocked at his murder, the feeling was nearly universal that the accession of Johnson to the Presidency would prove a godsend to the country. Aside from Mr. Lincoln's known policy of tenderness to the Rebels ... his ... views of the subject of Reconstruction were as distasteful as possible to radical Republicans.'

But soon there was trouble enough. When Congress was not in session, Johnson swung around to a sharply different course. He proceeded to appoint provisional civil governors in all Confederate states where Lincoln had not already done so. These governors were enjoined to summon state constitutional conventions, which were to be elected by the 'whitewashed rebels'—former citizens of the Confederacy who took the oath of allegiance required by the presidential proclamation. Fourteen specified classes, assumed to be inveterate rebels, were excluded from this general amnesty and required to make personal application for pardon. Although many of those thus proscribed did receive special pardons from President Johnson, the general effect was to exclude many experienced statesmen from participation in the task of establishing the new state governments. The ensuing constitutional conventions invalidated the ordinances of secession, repudiated the state war debts—which they could not in any event have paid—declared slavery abolished, and wrote new state constitutions. Not one granted the vote to any class of blacks. Elections were promptly held under these new or amended constitutions, and by the autumn of 1865 regular civil administrations were functioning in all former Confederate states except Texas.

This speedy process of reconstruction excited distrust in the North. That distrust was exacerbated by the enactment of black codes, and by the understandable but impolitic alacrity with which Southern voters elected their former Confederate leaders to high offices. As James G. Blaine later wrote, 'If the Southern men had intended, as their one special and desirable aim, to inflame public opinion of the North against them, they would have proceeded precisely as they did.' Many Northerners came to believe that reconstruction had been accomplished before the South had either repented its sins or become reconciled to defeat. To meet this criticism Johnson, in the fall of 1865, sent a number of observers to survey conditions in the South. They returned with reports that the South had fairly 'accepted defeat,' but many continued to doubt that Southerners were willing to accord the Negro equal rights. 'Refusing to see that a mighty cataclysm had shaken the profoundest depths of national life,' says Professor Coulter, Southerners 'did not expect that many things would be made anew but rather looked for them to be mended as of old,—that Humpty Dumpty might after all be put back on the wall.'

Congress Intervenes

The Congress which met for the first time on 4 December 1865 appointed a joint committee of both Houses with authority to investigate and report on the title of Southern members-elect. This Joint Committee of Fifteen, a resurrection of the old Committee on the Conduct of the War, formulated the theory and set the pace of congressional reconstruction. The committee was not controlled by the Radicals, and many of the crucial measures came from moderates like Lyman Trumbull.

The most influential member of the committee was Thaddeus Stevens of Pennsylvania, leader of the Republicans in the House. A sincere democrat, lifelong spokesman for the poor and the oppressed, and tireless champion of public education, Stevens was now an embittered old man of seventy-four nursing an implacable enmity toward the Southern slavocracy and President Johnson, who, he thought, stood between them and their just deserts. 'The punishment of traitors,' he declared, 'has been wholly ignored by a treacherous Executive and a sluggish Congress. To this issue I desire to devote the small remnant of my life.' And he did. 'Strip a proud nobility of the bloated estates,' he demanded; 'reduce them to a level with plain republicans; send them forth to labor and teach their children to enter the workshops or handle a plow, and you will thus humble the proud traitors.' Partly out of passionate devotion to the Negro, partly out of conviction that the welfare of the Union was identical with the triumph of the Republican party, Stevens was determined to impose black suffrage on the South. 'I am for Negro suffrage in every rebel State,' he said. 'If it be just it should not be denied; if it be necessary it should be adopted; if it be punishment to traitors, they deserve it.' He insisted that Congress should treat the Southern states as nothing but conquered provinces.

Charles Sumner of Massachusetts, Republican leader in the Senate, was not on the Joint Committee, but next to Stevens he was the most powerful figure in congressional reconstruction. An idealist by conviction, and a reformer by training, he was a pedantic dogmatist, but in his way quite as sincere as Stevens. Against the ex-Confederates he held no vindictive feelings, but he was committed to giving Negroes the vote. Sumner advanced the theory that the Southern states had committed political suicide, had extinguished their standing as states, and were in the position of territories subject to the exclusive jurisdiction of Congress. Vain, humorless, and irritable, Sumner nevertheless had a distinguished record as a champion of good causes: the New England intellectuals looked to him for leadership, his polished orations impressed the commonalty, and he infused the Radical movement with altruism.

The Joint Committee propounded the theory of reconstruction upon which Congress ultimately acted. It announced that 'the States lately in rebellion were . . . disorganized communities, without civil government and without constitutions or other forms by virtue of which political relation could legally exist between them and the federal government,' that they had 'forfeited all civil and political rights and privileges under the federal Constitution,' and that they could be restored to their political rights only by Congress. In other words, the states were intact, but the state governments were, for most but not for all purposes, in a condition of suspended animation. Under this interpretation it was possible for Congress at once to deny representation to the Southern states and to accept the ratification of the Thirteenth Amendment by the legislatures of these same states.

The Radical program can be summarized:
1. To keep the ex-Confederate states out of the Union until they had set up governments that could be regarded as 'republican' in nature.
2. To require them, as prerequisites for readmission, to repeal their black codes, disqualify those who had been active in rebellion from holding state office, guarantee the Negro his civil rights and give him the right to vote and to hold office. Furthermore, they advocated constitutional amendments to protect the civil rights of the blacks.
3. To ensure a larger role for Congress in the process of reconstruction.

The Radicals did not, as is often said, share a common attitude on economic policy. They frequently held diametrically opposite views on currency and the tariff, and businessmen, who had diverse interests and attitudes, were as likely to be against them as for them. Some of the Radicals, however, wished to assure permanence to that body of tariff, agricultural, and money legislation which had been written into the statute books during the war years, and were prepared to exploit the Reconstruction crisis to achieve their ends.

The bitter conflict between the Radicals and President Johnson erupted over a proposal that represented the ideas not merely of the Radicals but of most Republicans and was, in fact, sponsored by the moderate Lyman Trumbull. Opposition to legislation to enlarge the scope of the Freedmen's Bureau bill centered in the Democrats, who exploited race prejudice; not one Democrat in either house of Congress voted for the bill. But on 19 February 1866 Johnson opened war on the advocates of civil rights by vetoing the measure.[2] In a shocking speech three days later, he denounced the campaign for Negro rights and cried that Stevens, Sumner, and Wendell Phillips were planning to assassinate him. Many Northern Republicans read Johnson out of the party.

Yet most Republicans still wanted conciliation with Johnson, and they hoped to win his approval for a second measure sponsored by Trumbull, a Civil Rights bill which sought to protect the rights of the freedman in the courts rather than through such institutions as the army. Congress enacted the bill, again without a single Democratic vote, but Johnson stunned his party by vetoing this measure too. The President announced that he opposed 'the Africanization of half the United States.' After this veto most Republicans broke with the President, and Congress passed the bill

2. A second Freedmen's Bureau bill was subsequently passed over the presidential veto, 16 July 1866.

Andrew Johnson had the misfortune to be the first political figure singled out by Thomas Nast, the greatest cartoonist of his day, for caricature. In this illustration (which depicts the atrocities suffered by blacks in the early Reconstruction period), Nast portrays the President as Iago and a wounded but proud black Union veteran as the scornful Othello. (*Harper's Weekly, 1 Sept., 1866*)

over his veto. Not Sumner nor Stevens but Johnson himself had turned the men of moderation in the party against the administration.

By now the Republicans were determined to write new guarantees into the Constitution and to insist that the Southern states accept them before they were readmitted into the Union. On 30 April 1866 the Committee of Fifteen reported the Fourteenth Amendment, the most important ever added to the Constitution. It was designed to guarantee the civil rights of the Negro against unfavorable legislation by the states, reduce congressional representation in proportion to the denial of suffrage to Negroes, disqualify ex-Confederates who had formerly held office, invalidate the Confederate debt, and validate the federal debt. Section I of the amendment was particularly significant. It first defined citizenship, and then provided that 'No State shall make or enforce any law which shall abridge the privileges or immunities of citizens of the United States; nor shall any State deprive any person of life, liberty, or property, without due process of law; nor deny to any person within its jurisdiction the equal protection of the laws.' It thus for the first time clearly threw the protection of the Federal Government around the rights of life, liberty, and property which might be invaded by the states, reversing the traditional relationships between these governments which had from the beginning distinguished our federal system. Designed to protect the Negro, this stipulation came increasingly to be construed as extending the protection of the Federal Government to corporations whose property rights were threatened by state legislation, although the framers of the amendment did not anticipate any such interpretation.

There was ample evidence that the freedman needed national protection. The conservative General Jefferson C. Davis reported that in Kentucky 19 blacks had been killed, 233 maltreated, and none of the offenders had been prosecuted. In Texas, one black was murdered for not doffing his hat; in Louisiana, a black who answered a white boy 'quickly' was 'taken thro' the town and across the Levee, and there stripped and terribly beaten, with raw-hides.' In May 1866 a mob of whites, aided by some of the police, burned and pillaged the Negro quarter of Memphis and killed 46 freedmen. In New Orleans on 30 July, a mob, numbering many police and former Confederate soldiers, assaulted a convention of Negroes and white Radicals, and killed and wounded scores in cold blood.

Everything now turned on the election of a new Congress in the autumn of 1866, one of the most critical contests in our history. A National Union Convention of moderates from both sections pledged support of the President but did not form a new party or create party machinery. Hence in most congressional districts in the North voters had to choose between a Radical Republican and a Copperhead Democrat. Faced with this prospect many moderate Republicans went over to the Radical camp. Johnson apparently sought a political realignment in which, with the Radicals driven from the party, he could lead a union of Republicans with War Democrats and Southern loyalists. Instead, he cut himself off from the mass of his own party. Southerners, he said, 'cannot be treated as subjugated people or vassal colonies without a germ of hatred being introduced, which will some day or other, though the time may be distant, develop mischief of the most serious character.' But the President proved to be an immoderate advocate of moderation. His 'swing around the circle,' a stumping tour of the Middle West, became in many instances an undignified exercise in vituperation. 'I would ask you,' the President shouted on 3 September 1866 in Cleveland, 'Why not hang Thad Stevens and Wendell Phillips?' The outcome was a smashing victory for the Republicans, who picked up a margin in Congress large enough to override a presidential veto.

Johnson saw himself as the champion of the Constitution, and he was a stubborn man, but Congress was no less determined. When ten of the former Confederate states refused to ratify the Fourteenth Amendment, they left Congress with no alternative save more drastic measures or acquiescence in denying equality to the Negro. In February 1867 Congressman James Garfield cried, 'The last of the sinful ten has, with contempt and scorn, flung back into our teeth the magnanimous offer of a generous nation. It is now our turn to act.'

Congressional Reconstruction

The Radicals took the results of the fall elections as a vindication of their 'thorough' policy, and under the implacable leadership of Stevens whipped through a series of measures of far-reaching importance. This program undid the whole of presidential reconstruction, placed the Southern states back where they had been in April 1865, and temporarily revolutionized the political system by substituting a quasi-parliamentary for a presidential system of government.

The most important legislation of the entire period was the First Reconstruction Act of 2 March 1867. This act declared that 'no legal government' existed in any Southern state except Tennessee, and divided the rest of the South into five military districts subject to army commanders. Escape from this military regime and restitution of state rights were promised on condition that a constitutional convention, chosen by universal male suffrage, set up governments based on black and white suffrage and that the new state legislatures ratify the Fourteenth Amendment. Johnson returned the bill with a scorching message, but to no avail.

In March 1867 military rule replaced the civil governments that had been operating in the South for over a year. The military governors ruled with a firm hand, sometimes with flagrant disregard for the rights of white inhabitants, at the same time that they secured rights for Negroes that these whites had denied them. Thousands of local officials were removed to make way for Northern 'carpetbaggers' or Negroes; the governors of six states were displaced and others appointed in their place; civil courts were superseded by military tribunals; the legislatures of Georgia, Alabama, and Louisiana were purged of conservatives; state legislation was set aside or modified; and an army of occupation, some 20,000 strong and aided by a force of Negro militia, kept order. The relatively brief rule of the major generals was harsh but had the merits of honesty and a certain rude efficiency. Particularly important were the efforts to cope with economic disorganization and to regulate the social life of their satrapies. Thus in South Carolina, General Sickles abolished imprisonment for debt, stayed foreclosures on property, made the wages of farm laborers a first lien on crops, prohibited the manufacture of whiskey, and softened racial discrimination.

The main task of the military commanders was to create new electorates and establish new governments. In each of the ten states they enrolled a new electorate; in South Carolina, Alabama, Florida, Mississippi, and Louisiana black voters outnumbered white. This electorate chose in every state a constitutional convention which, under the guidance of carpetbaggers, drafted new state constitutions enfranchising blacks, disfranchising ex-Confederate leaders, and guaranteeing civil and political equality to the freedmen.

These new state constitutions represented, in almost every instance, a definite advance upon the older constitutions. The Constitution of South Carolina, for example, set up a far more democratic, humane, and efficient system of government than that which had obtained during the antebellum regime. In addition to providing for universal manhood suffrage it abolished property qualifications for office-holding, reapportioned representation in the legislature, drew up a more elaborate Bill of Rights, abolished all 'distinctions on account of color,' reformed local government and judicial administration, outlawed dueling and imprisonment for debt, protected homesteads from foreclosure, enlarged the rights of women, and provided—on paper—for a system of universal public education.

By the summer of 1868 reconstructed governments had been set up in eight Southern states: the other three—Mississippi, Texas, and Virginia—were reconstructed in 1870. After the legislatures of the reconstructed states had duly ratified the Fourteenth Amendment, as well as the Fifteenth Amendment which stipulated that 'the right of citizens of the United States to vote shall not be denied or abridged by the United States or by any State on account of race, color, or previous condition of servitude.' Congress formally re-admitted them, seated their elected representatives and senators, and, as soon as the new governments appeared reasonably secure, withdrew the army.

Ambitious as their program for Reconstruction

was, the Radicals had an even larger ultimate aim—modifying the American governmental system by establishing congressional supremacy. The majority of Congress, not the Supreme Court, was to be the final judge of the powers of Congress; the President a servant of Congress. This new dispensation was implicit in the Reconstruction Act of 2 March 1867 and in two other pieces of legislation adopted the same day. First, the Command of the Army Act virtually deprived the Executive of control of the army by requiring that he issue all military orders through the General of the Army, who was protected against removal or suspension from office. Second, the Tenure of Office Act, by denying the President the right to remove civil officials, including members of his cabinet, without the consent of the Senate, made it impossible for him to control his own administration. The Radicals put it through in order to prevent Johnson from continuing to wield the patronage weapon against them and to stop him from ousting Secretary of War Stanton, the last Radical sympathizer left in the cabinet. The next move in the game was to dispose of Johnson by the impeachment process, whereupon Benjamin Wade, president *pro tem.* of the Senate, would succeed to his office and title.

Impeachment had been proposed by Benjamin Butler in October 1866, and all through the following year a House committee had been trying to gather evidence which might support such action, but without success. Now Johnson furnished the House with the excuse for which it had waited. Convinced that the Tenure of Office Act was unconstitutional, he requested and then ordered Secretary Stanton to resign. Stanton himself thought the act unconstitutional and had even helped write the veto message, but when General Lorenzo Thomas, the newly appointed Secretary of War, sought to take possession of his office, Stanton barricaded himself in the War Department. On 24 February 1868, the House voted to impeach the President for 'high Crimes and Misdemeanors,' and within a week eleven articles of impeachment were agreed upon by the Radicals. Ten of the articles dealt with the removal of Stanton; the other consisted of garbled newspaper reports from the President's speeches. A monstrous charge to

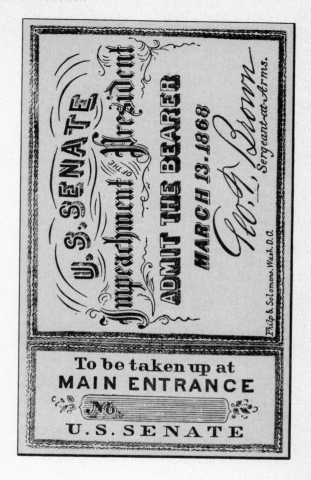

the effect that Johnson was an accomplice in the murder of Lincoln was finally excluded.

The impeachment of Johnson was one of the most disgraceful episodes in the history of the Federal Government, one that barely failed to suspend the presidential system. For had impeachment succeeded, the Radicals would have established the principle that Congress may remove a President not for 'high Crimes and Misdemeanors,' as required by the Constitution, but for purely political reasons. The managers of impeachment themselves admitted this; Johnson's crime, they asserted in their report, was 'the one great purpose of reconstructing the rebel states in accordance with his own will.' The President was defended by able counsel including William M. Evarts, leader of the American bar, and Benjamin R. Curtis, formerly a justice of the Supreme Court. These tore the allegations to shreds, and it was soon apparent to all but the most prejudiced that there was no valid case. Even the Tenure of Office Act charges proved groundless, for the law restrained a President from removing a cabinet officer he had appointed, and Stanton had been named not by Johnson but by Lincoln. Yet the Radicals would have succeeded in their object but for Chief Justice Chase, who insisted upon legal procedure, and for seven courageous Republican Senators who risked their political future by voting for acquittal.[3] One more affirmative vote and Ben Wade—who himself voted for conviction— would have been installed in the White House. Then, in all probability, the Court would have been battered into submission.

President Grant

Even as the Senate sat in solemn judgment on President Johnson, the triumphant Republicans met in party convention to nominate his successor, General Grant. Before the Civil War he had seldom taken the trouble to vote, and such political principles as he professed had inclined him toward the Democrats. He had been to Lincoln a faithful subordinate but to Johnson less than faithful, and after his break with Johnson he had been captured by the Radical politicians who saw in him an unbeatable candidate.

The campaign that followed was bitterly fought. To Republicans success promised an indefinite tenure of power, during which the party might be given a national basis through the extension of suffrage to the Southern blacks. To the Democrats, who nominated the former governor of New York, Horatio Seymour, whose wartime record had associated him with the Copperheads,

victory would spell the end of federal backing for the Negro, and the restoration of the remaining Southern states. The Republicans waved the 'bloody shirt of the rebellion' effectively. Grant carried all the states but eight, although his popular majority was only 300,000. The Negro vote of some 450,000 gave him his popular margin, and the exclusion of three Southern states (Mississippi, Texas, Virginia) and the control of six others assured him his large electoral college majority. With less equipment for the presidency than any predecessor save Harrison and a temperament unfitted for high political office, Grant was unable to overcome his deficiencies. Although a leader of men, he was not a good judge of men, and the very simplicity which had carried him safely through the intrigues of the Civil War exposed him to the wiles of politicians whose loyalty to himself he mistook for devotion to the public weal. It came as a shock that he seemed to have lost the qualities he had shown in the war—a sense of order and of command, resoluteness, and consistency. The magnanimous victor of Appomattox revealed himself in office petty, vindictive, and shifty. He was naïve rather than innocent, and his simplicity, as Henry Adams remarked, 'was more disconcerting than the complexity of a Talleyrand.' He regarded the presidency as a personal prerogative, a reward for services rendered rather than a responsibility.

Grant's only hope lay in the wisdom and integrity of his advisers, but his choices were bizarre. Altogether, during his eight years of office, Grant appointed no less than twenty-six men to his cabinet. Six—Hoar, Cox, Creswell, Jewell, Bristow, and Fish—proved to be men of intelligence and integrity, and of these Grant managed to dismiss all but one, Secretary of State Fish. It was fortunate that Grant was able to command, throughout the eight years of his administration, the talents of Hamilton Fish. A New York patrician, Grant's third choice for the State Department, and relatively unknown when he took office, Fish proved himself one of the shrewdest men who have ever directed the foreign affairs of the nation. He had what most of his colleagues in Grant's cabinet lacked—honesty, disciplined intelligence, learning, experience, urbanity, and a

---

3. Fessenden, Grimes, Trumbull, Ross, Van Winkle, Fowler, and Henderson. Fessenden died in 1869; none of the others was re-elected to the Senate; yet they did not suffer as severely as the legend of their martyrdom would suggest.

tact and patience sufficient to win and retain the confidence of his chief.

Yet for all his defects, Grant retained the devotion of millions. 'The plain man,' as Allan Nevins observes, 'had not elected Grant; he had elected an indestructible legend, a folk-hero.' It was well for Grant that he brought to the presidency this imperishable glamor, for he brought little else.

Radical Reconstruction in the South

The election of 1868 strengthened the position of the Radicals. To be sure, 'Let us have peace,' the concluding phrase of Grant's letter accepting the presidential nomination, had led the country to believe that Grant would abandon Radical reconstruction and adopt toward the white South a more conciliatory policy, and in the beginning this belief seemed justified. The President suggested to his cabinet a sweeping amnesty proclamation and urged Congress to complete the reconstruction process in Virginia, Mississippi, and Texas. By 1870 representatives from these states again sat in Congress. But it was soon clear that Grant was still in the Radical camp. He took the lead in a drastic reconstitution of the legislature of Georgia, and in South Carolina, Alabama, Mississippi, Louisiana, and Arkansas, he authorized the use of federal troops to overthrow duly elected Democratic governments and keep these states in the Radical Republican ranks.

Inevitably Radical reconstruction aroused determined opposition, which took both legal and illegal form. In states such as Virginia and North Carolina, where whites greatly outnumbered blacks, the Democrats recaptured control of the state governments by regular political methods almost at once. Elsewhere it was thought necessary to resort to a much greater degree of intimidation to destroy the combination that made Radical success possible. Whites who took part in Reconstruction soon felt the heavy weight of economic pressure or the sharp sting of social ostracism. Negroes were dealt with more ruthlessly, by employing terror.

Much of this violence was perpetrated by secret societies, of which the most famous, though not the largest, was the Ku Klux Klan. In 1867 a social

kuklos (circle) of young men in Pulaski, Tennessee, organized as the 'Invisible Empire of the South,' with elaborate ritual and ceremonial. The KKK described itself as an institution of 'chivalry, humanity, mercy and patriotism,' but it was in fact simply an institution for the maintenance of white supremacy. During the next three or four years the KKK and other secret societies—notably the Knights of the White Camellia and the White Leagues of Louisiana and Mississippi—policed 'unruly' Negroes in the country districts, discouraged blacks from serving in the militia, delivered spectral warnings against using the ballot, and punished those who disregarded the warnings. The Ku Klux Klan investigation of 1871 reported 153 Negroes murdered in a single Florida county that year; over 300 murdered in parishes outside New Orleans; bloody race riots in Mississippi and Louisiana; a reign of terror in parts of Arkansas; and in Texas, 'murders, robberies and outrages of all kinds.' Not all of this could be laid at the doors of the Klan or the White Leaguers, or even of the whites, but groups like the KKK were responsible for most of the violence that afflicted the South during these turbulent years. Under the impact of all this, Negro participation in politics declined sharply, and the Radical cause was put in jeopardy.

The Radicals had no intention of acquiescing tamely in the undoing of reconstruction. Their answer was first a series of state laws which sought to break up the secret societies and, when these proved unavailing, an appeal to Washington for help. The Grant administration responded with renewed military occupation of evacuated districts, the unseating of Democratic administrations on the ground of fraud, and a new crop of supervisory laws of which the most important were the Force Acts of 1870 and 1871 and the drastic Ku Klux Klan Act of 1871 authorizing the President to suspend the writ of habeas corpus and suppress violence by military force. Altogether some 7000 indictments and over 1000 convictions were found under these acts, but they did not fulfill their purpose. In large areas of the South—notably in South Carolina, Louisiana, and Mississippi—violence flourished throughout the entire reconstruction period.

From 1868 to 1877 the Radicals controlled, for

The KKK. This engraving is from a photograph of Mississippi Klansmen who were caught wearing these disguises after they attempted to murder a family. (*Library of Congress*)

varying periods, most of the reconstructed states of the South, but it was not, as it is sometimes called, 'Black Reconstruction.' In no state did the blacks ever control the government, and only in South Carolina—where blacks outnumbered whites four to three—did they have even a temporary majority in the legislature. There were no black governors, and very few Negroes in high positions in the executive branch or in administration. At no time did Negroes have a representation proportional to their numbers in any branch of any government.

Radical control of Southern states was exercised by an uneasy coalition of three groups—Negroes, 'carpetbaggers,' and 'scalawags.' Both of the latter words are heavily loaded. The one conjures up the image of an impecunious Yankee adventurer descending on a prostrate South with a carpetbag to be stuffed full of loot; the other was a word commonly applied to runty cattle and, by implication, to the lowest breed of Southerner. There were, in truth, disreputable adventurers among the carpetbaggers, but most were Union veterans who had returned to the South to farm, businessmen looking for good investments, government agents who for one reason or another decided to stay on in the South, schoolteachers who thought of themselves as a kind of 'peace corps' to the freedmen. As for the 'scalawags'—the largest single element in the Radical coalition—these were the men who had opposed secession in the first place and were now ready to return to the old Union and to take in the blacks as junior partners in the enterprise of restoration.

The Radical governments were, in many cases, incompetent, extravagant, and corrupt. The corruption was pervasive and ostentatious. In Florida, for example, the cost of public printing in 1869 exceeded the total cost for all of the state government in 1860; in South Carolina the state maintained a restaurant and barroom for the legislators at a cost of $125,000 for a single session, and under the head of 'legislative supplies' provided Westphalia hams, Brussels carpets, and ornamental cuspidors; and in Louisiana the youthful Governor Warmoth managed to garner a fortune of half a million dollars during four years of office, while bartering away state property and dissipating school funds. But corruption did not begin with the advent of the Radicals, nor did it cease when they were forced from office. The land and railroad legislation of some of the 'Redeemer' governments was no less corrupt and considerably more expensive than anything that the Radical governments achieved. Corruption was confined to no class, no party, and no section: larceny by the Tweed Ring in New York City and the Gas Ring in Philadelphia made the Southern Radicals look like feckless amateurs, as most of them were.

Radical reconstruction was expensive, and taxes and indebtedness mounted throughout the South, but we should keep in mind mitigating circumstances. The task of repairing the damages of the war was herculean and made unprecedented demands on government; with emancipation the population requiring public services had almost doubled and Radical governments for the first time tried to set up public schools for all children;

much of the property that had customarily borne the burden of taxation—banks, railroads, and industries—had been destroyed by the war, leaving almost the whole burden to fall on real estate. Some two-thirds of the total new indebtedness was in the form of guarantees to railroads and other industries. In this extravagant and often corrupt policy of underwriting railroads, the conservative governments which succeeded the Radicals spent, or pledged, more money than had the Radicals. Of the situation in Alabama, John Hope Franklin has observed, 'Corruption was bisectional, bipartisan and biracial.'

More important was the constructive side of Radical reconstruction—progressive legislation. In South Carolina the Radical legislature reformed the system of taxation, dispensed relief to the poor, distributed homesteads to Negroes, established numerous charitable and humane institutions, encouraged immigration, and, for the first time in the history of the state, provided free public schools and compelled attendance of all children from six to sixteen. It was in the realm of public education that the Radical governments made their most significant contribution. In general the Radical legislatures advanced political democracy and inaugurated social reforms, and these contributions go far to justify a favorable judgment upon them. So, too, does the consideration that the Radical legislatures enacted no vindictive legislation against the former slaveowners.

Notwithstanding these accomplishments, the Negro was unable to make any serious dent on Southern white hostility or prejudice. Convinced that he was incompetent politically, Southern whites blamed him for all the ills and burdens and humiliations of reconstruction. And because the experiment of black participation in politics had been associated with the Republican party, Southerners concluded that Democrats were the party of white supremacy and fastened upon the South a one-party system. Because some progressive laws were identified with carpetbag and Negro rule, they came to distrust such legislation. Because high taxes had accompanied Radical rule, they concluded that economy and good government were synonymous. Even many of their quondam

Northern champions reached the unhappy conclusion that black participation in politics had been premature.

Reconstruction and the Constitution

At no time in American history has the Constitution been subjected to so severe or prolonged a strain as during the era of reconstruction. There arose at once a number of knotty problems concerning the legal status of the seceded states after Appomattox and the status of persons who had participated in the rebellion. Throughout the war President Lincoln maintained the legal principle that the states were indestructible. This theory, though vigorously controverted by the Radical leaders, received judicial support in *Texas v. White* in 1869, in which Chief Justice Chase, speaking for the majority, said:

The Constitution, in all of its provisions, looks to an indestructible Union composed of indestructible States. . . . Considered, therefore, as transactions under the Constitution, the ordinance of secession . . . and all the acts of her legislature intended to give effect to that ordinance, were absolutely null. They were utterly without operation in law. The obligations of the State, as a member of the Union, remained perfect and unimpaired. . . . Our conclusion therefore is, that Texas continued to be a State, and a State of the Union.

Upon what theory, then, could reconstruction proceed? If the states were still in the Union, it was only the citizens who were out of their normal relations with the Federal Government, and these could be restored through the pardoning power of the President. This was Lincoln's theory, and Johnson took it over from him; when, in a series of proclamations, Johnson declared the insurrection at an end, the Supreme Court accepted his proclamations as legally binding.

But if the insurrection was at an end, by virtue of what authority did Congress proceed to impose military government upon Southern states and set up military courts? The Supreme Court had already passed upon the question of military courts in *ex parte Milligan*. In this case involving the validity of military courts in Indiana, the Court laid down the doctrine that 'martial rule can never exist where the courts are open, and in the proper

and unobstructed exercise of their jurisdiction'; and to the argument of military necessity the Court said, 'No doctrine involving more pernicious consequences was ever invented by the wit of man than that any of the [Constitution's] provisions can be suspended during any of the great exigencies of government. Such a doctrine leads directly to anarchy or despotism.' Yet within a year, in clear violation of this decision, Congress established military tribunals throughout the South; and when the validity of this legislation was challenged, in the McCardle case, Congress rushed through a law depriving the Court of jurisdiction over the case, while the Supreme Court sat idly by.

Radical leaders sought to legitimize their policies by relying upon the clause in the Constitution that 'the United States shall guarantee to every State a Republican Form of Government.' For three-quarters of a century this clause had been interpreted to mean that Congress would sustain the pre-existing governments, but now the Radicals insisted that—for the Southern states at least—a 'republican' form of government included Negro suffrage, despite the fact that at the beginning of the Reconstruction era only six Northern states permitted the black man to vote. The Court supported the Radicals to the extent of declaring that 'the power to carry into effect the clause of guarantee is primarily a legislative power, and resides in Congress.'

Some of the reconstruction acts were palpably unconstitutional, but the attitude of the Radicals was well expressed by General Grant when he said of this legislation that 'much of it, no doubt, was unconstitutional; but it was hoped that the laws enacted would serve their purpose before the question of constitutionality could be submitted to the judiciary and a decision obtained.' This hope was well founded, for the validity of some of the reconstruction measures never came before the courts, and others were not passed upon until long after they had 'served their purpose.' When Mississippi asked for an injunction restraining President Johnson from carrying out the reconstruction acts, the Supreme Court refused to accept jurisdiction. Georgia then brought suit against Secretary of War Stanton and General Grant, but once again the Court refused to intervene in what it termed a political controversy.

Individuals fared somewhat better. In *ex parte Garland* the operation of the federal test oath to exclude lawyers who had participated in the rebellion from practicing in federal courts was declared unconstitutional because *ex post facto;* and in *Cummings v. Missouri* similar state legislation was held invalid on the same grounds. For practical reasons it proved almost impossible to challenge the constitutionality of the confiscation of cotton or other property seized from those who were assumed to be rebels, but one notable case vindicated the right of the individual against lawless action even when committed in the name of the United States government. During the war Robert E. Lee's splendid estate at Arlington, Virginia, had been seized for nonpayment of taxes and bid in by the Federal Government, which then used it as a national cemetery. Long after the war the heirs of Lee brought suit. By a five to four vote the Supreme Court held that it would hear a suit against a sovereign—or its agents—and that the original seizure was illegal. Constitutionally, the significance of the decision lies in the assertion that no official of the government may cloak himself in the immunity of sovereignty for his illegal acts.

The Grant Administration

While Grant was wrestling with the difficult problems of Reconstruction he also had to concern himself with diplomatic and economic issues that were often altogether unrelated to the question of what policy to pursue toward the South. Thanks to Seward the Johnson administration was at its best in the realm of foreign affairs. Thanks to Hamilton Fish the Grant administration likewise won its most notable successes in this area. Both administrations had to cope with vexatious foreign questions which had grown out of the Civil War. Seward, by his firm attitude toward the French in Mexico and the Spaniards in Santo Domingo, sustained the Monroe Doctrine, and by strokes of diplomacy advanced imperialism in the Pacific. Spain's attempted conquest of Santo

Domingo broke down of its own accord, but the Spanish withdrawal from the island in 1865 appeared to be a diplomatic victory for Seward. Two years later Seward persuaded Napoleon III he must abandon the Mexican venture: in June 1867 the puppet-Emperor Maximilian slumped before a firing squad and the cardboard empire collapsed. Russia had long been eager to get rid of Alaska, and in 1867 Sumner in the Senate and a well-oiled lobby in the House permitted Seward to buy that rich domain, known at the time as 'Seward's Folly,' for $7,200,000. To round out his expansionist policy Seward annexed the Midway Islands west of Hawaii, and, with a view to the construction of an isthmian canal at some future date, acquired the right of transit across Nicaragua.

President Grant was enormously interested in another of Seward's projects—the annexation of Santo Domingo. This hare-brained proposal had originated with two Yankee fortune-hunters who planned to secure for themselves half the wealth of the island. They managed to draw into their conspiracy powerful economic interests and bought the support of such men as Ben Butler, John A. Rawlins, and Grant's personal secretary, Orville Babcock; these in turn won over the President. But when Grant submitted a treaty of annexation to the Senate, it encountered the implacable hostility of Charles Sumner and Carl Schurz and failed of ratification, a severe defeat for the administration.

The Santo Domingo episode, in itself minor, had important consequences. It revealed how easily Grant could be taken in and how naïve was his understanding of foreign affairs. It led to the deposition of Charles Sumner as chairman of the Senate Committee on Foreign Affairs, which widened the rift in the Republican party. And by distracting the attention of Grant and the Radicals from the Cuban situation, it enabled Fish to preserve peace with Spain.

A Cuban rebellion had broken out in 1868 and dragged on for ten dreadful years before it was finally suppressed. The sympathy of most Americans was with the rebels, but a movement to recognize Cuban belligerency encountered the firm opposition of Fish. Recognition would have been a serious mistake, for it would have gravely com-

A ripening pear. In this 1868 *Harper's Weekly* engraving, a covetous Secretary of State, William H. Seward, advocates annexation of Cuba, which had just raised the standard of rebellion against Spain, while a sage Uncle Sam counsels patience—but with the same end in view. Seward, who roved the Caribbean from Santo Domingo to the Danish West Indies in search of acquisitions, aimed at nothing less than 'possession of the American continent and the control of the world,' but Congress restrained his ambitions. From the presidency of James K. Polk to that of John Fitzgerald Kennedy, 'the Pearl of the Antilles,' only ninety miles off the Florida coast, tempted and vexed American administrations. (*Library of Congress*)

promised pending American claims against Great Britain for premature recognition of the belligerency of the Confederacy. As it was, the United States and Spain came to the very brink of war in 1873 over the curious *Virginius* affair. The *Virginius*, a ship flying the U.S. flag and carrying arms for the Cuban insurgents, was captured on the high seas by a Spanish gunboat; fifty-three of her seamen, including eight Americans, were summarily executed for 'piracy.' When Spain disowned the barbarous deed and paid an indemnity, and when it was discovered that the ship had no right to her American papers or to fly the American flag, the danger of war evaporated.

To the northward, too, relations were strained. During the war Canada had furnished a base for

Confederate raids on Vermont and New York. In time of peace the Fenians, or Irish Revolutionary Brother-Republics, took similar liberties in the United States. Two rival Irish republics were organized in New York City, each with its president, cabinet, and general staff in glittering uniforms of green and gold. Each planned to seize Canada with Irish veterans of the Union army, and hold it as hostage for Irish freedom. The first invasion, in April 1866, was promptly nipped by federal authorities at Eastport, Maine. But the ensuing outcry from Irish-Americans, who carried heavy weight at the polls, frightened the Johnson administration. Before it could decide who should take on the onus of stopping him, 'General' John O'Neil led 1500 armed Irishmen across the Niagara river. The next day, 2 June 1866, the Canadian militia gave battle, and fled; but the Fenians fled farther—to New York State, where they were promptly arrested and as promptly released. In the spring of 1870 tatterdemalion armies moved once more on Canada from St. Albans, Vermont, and Malone, New York. United States marshals arrested the Fenian leaders, and the armies disintegrated. Ridiculous as they were, the Fenian forays caused Canada much trouble and expense for which she was never reimbursed by the United States.

The greatest achievement of the Grant administration was the liquidation of outstanding diplomatic controversies with Great Britain. The sympathy of the English ruling classes for the Confederacy and the lax enforcement of neutrality by the British government had aroused deep resentment in the United States, and for some years no calm adjudication of American claims was possible. The most important of these claims had to do with the alleged negligence of the British in permitting the Confederate cruisers *Alabama*, *Shenandoah*, and *Florida* to be armed in, and escape from, British ports. Seward's persistent advocacy of these claims was finally rewarded in the last months of Johnson's administration by a convention for their adjudication. In April 1869 the Senate rejected this convention as insufficient, after Sumner had charged Great Britain with responsibility for half the total cost of the war: a mere $2,125 million! Sumner's speech shocked

his English friends who so faithfully had sustained the Union cause; nor were they much comforted by his explanation that the cession of Canada would be an acceptable form of payment.

After Sumner was eliminated as a result of his recalcitrance on Santo Domingo, negotiations went forward more successfully, for England was now ready to make amends. So the Canadian Sir John Rose staged with Hamilton Fish a diplomatic play of wooing and yielding that threw dust in the eyes of extremists on both sides. The covenant thus arrived at, the Treaty of Washington (8 May 1871), provided for arbitration of boundary disputes, the fisheries question, and the *Alabama* claims; determined rules of neutrality that should govern the arbitral tribunal (which subsequently assessed the British for damages wrought by the three cruisers); and contained an expression of regret for the escape of the *Alabama*.

Although the United States was thereby vindicated, the greater victory was for arbitration and peace. Never before had questions involving such touchy matters of national honor been submitted to a mere majority vote of an international tribunal. The English accepted the verdict with good grace. Charles Francis Adams never forgot that he was judge not advocate, and President Grant by his unwavering support of peaceful methods showed a quality not unusual in statesmen who know war at first hand. In a later message to the Arbitration Union of Birmingham, Grant set forth his guiding principle: 'Nothing would afford me greater happiness than to know that . . . at some future day, the nations of the earth will agree upon some sort of congress which will take cognizance of international questions of difficulty, and whose decisions will be as binding as the decisions of our Supreme Court are upon us. It is a dream of mine that some such solution may be.'

If the Grant administration, for all its shortcomings, was at its best in diplomatic affairs, the hero of Appomattox came off most poorly in coping with domestic issues such as the 'money question' and civil service reform. Like the Southern question, the money question was inherited from previous administrations. During the war the government had issued $450 million of legal tender notes, and at the close of the war some $400 million of these 'greenbacks' were still in circulation. The presence of greenbacks gave rise to two divisive issues. The first involved the medium of payment of the interest and principal of government bonds. Since these bonds had been purchased with depreciated greenbacks, farmers and workingmen reasoned that they should be redeemable in greenbacks unless otherwise specified, while bondholders insisted on payment in gold. The Democrats endorsed the proposal to redeem government securities in greenbacks, and Johnson went even further and urged that future interest payments be applied to liquidating the principal of the debt. But in his first inaugural address Grant committed himself to paying all government obligations in gold, and the first measure passed by the new Congress (18 March 1869) pledged the faith of the United States to such payment.

The second question concerned government policy toward the contraction of greenbacks and the resumption of specie payments. The inflation of the currency through greenbacks had tended to raise commodity prices, make credit easier and money cheaper. The farmer and the debtor therefore regarded with dismay any proposal to contract the currency by calling in these greenbacks. Business interests were divided; most wanted a stable currency, and hence opposed both currency expansion and abrupt resumption. But some businessmen, such as those who had gone into debt, favored expansion, while conservative bankers and others of the creditor class demanded that the government pledge itself to redeem greenbacks with gold and thus bring this paper currency to par.

A powerful argument for stabilizing the currency was that constant fluctuation in the value of greenbacks invited speculation. Because greenbacks were not legal tender for all purposes and because it was uncertain whether the government would ever redeem them in gold, they circulated at a discount which varied from month to month. In September 1869 two notorious stock gamblers, Jay Gould and Jim Fisk, took advantage of this fluctuation in the value of money to organize a 'corner' in gold. With the passive connivance of persons high in the confidence of the President and the Secretary of the Treasury, the nefarious scheme almost succeeded. On 'Black Friday,' 24 September 1869, the premium on gold rose to 162, and scores of Wall Street brokers faced ruin. Then the government dumped $4 million in gold on the market, and the 'corner' collapsed. 'The worst scandals of the 18th century,' wrote Henry Adams, 'were relatively harmless by the side of this which smirched executive, judiciary, banks, corporate systems, professions, and people, all the great active forces of society.' Yet the episode reflected not so much upon Grant's character as upon his judgment, which vacillated.

In 1870 the greenback question came before the Supreme Court. When Chief Justice Chase—who as Secretary of the Treasury had originally issued them—announced that greenbacks were not legal tender for obligations entered into prior to the emission of the notes, and even made the alarming suggestion that they were completely invalid,[4] the government promptly moved for a rehearing. Two vacancies on the Supreme Court afforded Grant a propitious opportunity. In Joseph P. Bradley and William Strong, Grant found jurists upon whose faith in the constitutionality of the greenbacks he could rely. He was not disappointed. In the second Legal Tender decision, *Knox v. Lee*, the Court in 1871 reversed itself and sustained the constitutionality of the Civil War greenbacks. Thirteen years later, in an even more sweeping decision, *Juilliard v. Greenman*, it proclaimed the government's right to issue legal tender even in time of peace. When, in 1874, Congress attempted to do this, Grant interposed his veto and the threat of inflation passed. In 1875 Congress finally provided for the resumption of specie payments on 1 January 1879. This act settled, for the time being, the legal tender question, but the money question remained to plague the next generation.

The tariff question also vexed the Grant administration. The skyhigh Civil War tariffs were originally accepted as emergency revenue measures; protected industries soon came to regard them as permanent. After Appomattox, Western farmers

4. *Hepburn v. Griswold* 8 Wallace 603 (1870).

and Eastern reformers joined hands in demanding tariff reduction, but the protected interests would not yield. The Grant administration set itself against tariff reform. Secretary Cox was forced out of the cabinet in part because of his sympathy for it, and David A. Wells, the able economist who was a special commissioner of revenue, had to resign for the same reason.

Nor did civil service reform fare better. In no area was the record of Grant's administration more discreditable. Grant's appointment of Jacob Cox to the Interior Department was a gesture toward reform, and when in 1871 a Civil Service Commission, headed by George William Curtis, submitted a list of desirable reforms, Grant promised a fair trial. But Cox was shoved out, and Grant soon scuttled the commission and packed the civil service with party henchmen. Curtis, wearied of shadow-boxing with the spoilsmen, resigned in disgust, and in 1875 the commission itself was discontinued.

The Liberal Republican Movement

Within less than a year after Grant's assumption of office, a revolt within the Republican party was in full swing. The full measure of administrative corruption was as yet unknown, but enough was suspected to outrage men who cherished standards of political decency. Grant's Southern policy was controversial, his Caribbean policy an affront, while his repudiation of reformers troubled even some of his own followers. Above all there was a growing distrust of Grant himself, which found expression in Senator Sumner's speech of May 1872 scoring him for taking and giving bribes, nepotism, neglect of duty, and lawless interference with the other departments of the government. Grant's abuse of the civil service alienated Cox and Schurz, his Southern policy antagonized Lyman Trumbull and Gideon Welles, his tariff policy cost him the support of David A. Wells, and such men as Chief Justice Chase, Horace Greeley, Charles Francis Adams, and E. L. Godkin came to regard the President as unfit for high office.

This revolt against Grant was started by liberals and reformers, but old-line politicians and disap-

pointed factional leaders soon flocked to it in embarrassing numbers. In the end it consisted of a group even more heterogeneous than usual in American parties. The one idea that animated them was distrust of President Grant. It was a movement of opposition rather than of positive reform; and therein lay its chief weakness. When the Liberal Republican convention met at Cincinnati 1 May 1872, this weakness became apparent. It was impossible for the discordant elements to agree upon a satisfactory platform or a logical candidate. The platform called for the withdrawal of troops from the South, civil service reform, and a resumption of specie payments; as for the tariff, the convention 'recognizing that there are in our midst honest but irreconcilable differences of opinion' remanded 'the discussion of the subject to the people in their congressional Districts.' Nor could the convention unite on a presidential candidate like Charles Francis Adams or Lyman Trumbull, the latter for almost 20 years one of the ornaments of the party. Intrigues and jealousies defeated them, and in the end the convention stampeded to Horace Greeley.

No man in the country was better known than Greeley, for over thirty years editor of the powerful New York *Tribune*, but he was renowned as an editor not as a statesman. A Vermont Yankee who had kept his homespun democracy and youthful idealism, Greeley persistently championed the cause of the underprivileged, the worker, and the farmer. Yet for all his intellectual abilities and idealism, Greeley lacked the first qualifications for responsible political position. He was impulsive, intriguing, vain, and vindictive, and his carefully cultivated idiosyncrasies laid him open to caricature. A familiar figure on the streets of New York, he wore a crumpled white coat, its pockets stuffed with newspapers, and crowning his bewhiskered face was a tall white hat. He reminded some of Mr. Pickwick, others of the Mad Hatter.

The nomination of Greeley came as a shock to the reformers who had organized the Liberal Republican movement. *The Nation* reported that 'a greater degree of incredulity and disappointment' had not been felt since the news of the first battle of Bull Run. But the discomfort of the reformers was as nothing to the dismay of Southern Dem-

Election Night, 1872. A New York City crowd peers up at the rooftop of a building at Broadway and 22nd Street where a stereopticon projects a bulletin showing Pennsylvania giving Grant a 100,000-vote lead. Final returns increased Grant's margin in the Keystone State to a whopping 138,000. Rock-ribbed Republican Pennsylvania voted for Buchanan in 1856 but did not wind up in the Democratic column again until Franklin D. Roosevelt's landslide in 1936. (New-York Historical Society, *Frank Leslie's Illustrated Newspapers, 23 Nov. 1872*)

ocrats. For thirty years Greeley had castigated the South and the Democratic party, and much of the responsibility for anti-slavery, and later for Radical reconstruction, could justly be laid at his door. Yet the Democrats had no choice but to make Greeley their nominee, for he offered the only alternative to the continuation of Radical reconstruction. But it was hard to work up enthusiasm for a candidate who had said: 'May it be written on my grave that I was never the Democratic party's follower and lived and died in nothing its debtor.'

Greeley proved himself an excellent campaigner, but the odds against him were insuperable. Grant could command the support of rank and file Republicans, veterans of the Union armies, the blacks North and South, and most of the German vote alienated by Greeley's temperance views. Grant carried all but six states; Greeley, with less than 44 per cent of the vote, failed to win a single state in the North or West. Three weeks later Horace Greeley died, broken-hearted. The Liberal Republican party did not long survive him, but many of the men who took part in that campaign would be active in the 'Mugwump' wing of the Republican party for the next generation.

Scandal and Stagnation

While the 1872 campaign was still under way, the country was startled by charges of wholesale corruption in connection with the construction of the Union Pacific Railroad, charges which reflected upon men high in Republican councils. The promoters of the Union Pacific, in order to divert the profits of construction to themselves, had organized a construction company, the Credit Mobilier of America. To this company the directors of the Union Pacific awarded fantastically profitable contracts. As a result of this corrupt arrangement the Union Pacific was forced to the verge of bankruptcy while the Credit Mobilier paid in a single year dividends of 348 per cent. Fearing Congress might interpose, the directors placed large blocks of Credit Mobilier stock 'where they would do most good.' Exposure of the scheme brought disgrace to a number of representatives, and to Vice-President Schuyler Colfax,

while others such as Henry Wilson of Massachusetts and James A. Garfield of Ohio were never able to explain away their connection with the unsavory affair.

Scarcely less excusable was the so-called Salary Grab. In 1873 Ben Butler pushed through a bill doubling the President's salary and increasing by 50 per cent the salary of Congressmen. This could be justified; what particularly affronted public opinion was that the increases granted to Congressmen were made retroactive for two years: thus each Congressman voted himself $5000 in back salary out of public funds. The bill was an evasion if not an outright violation of the Constitution, but Grant signed it without demur. A storm of indignation against this 'steal' swept the country, and in the following session Congress hastened to restore the old salary scale.

The Credit Mobilier and the Salary Grab were merely the most sensational of the exposures. In the Navy Department, Secretary Robeson accumulated a fortune of several hundred thousand dollars during his tenure of office. The Department of the Interior worked hand in glove with land speculators. The Treasury farmed out uncollected taxes to one J. D. Sanborn who promptly proceeded to highjack some $425,000 out of corporations, one-half of which he took for himself. The U.S. minister to England, Robert Schenck, lent his prestige to the Emma Mine swindle, and the minister to Brazil, J. W. Webb, defrauded the Brazilian government of $50,000 and fled to Europe, leaving the United States Government to refund the money, with apologies. The Custom House in New York was a sink of corruption, but when Collector Thomas Murphy was finally forced out, Grant accepted his resignation 'with regret.' In the national capital 'Boss' Shepherd ran up a debt of $17 million, a large part of which was graft, and found himself appointed by a grateful President to be chairman of the Board of Public Works. It was Shepherd, too, who was largely responsible for the failure of the Freedmen's Bank, a cruel hardship for thousands of trusting blacks.

Worse was still to come. After the Democrats carried the congressional elections of 1874, a Democratic House, the first since the Civil War, set

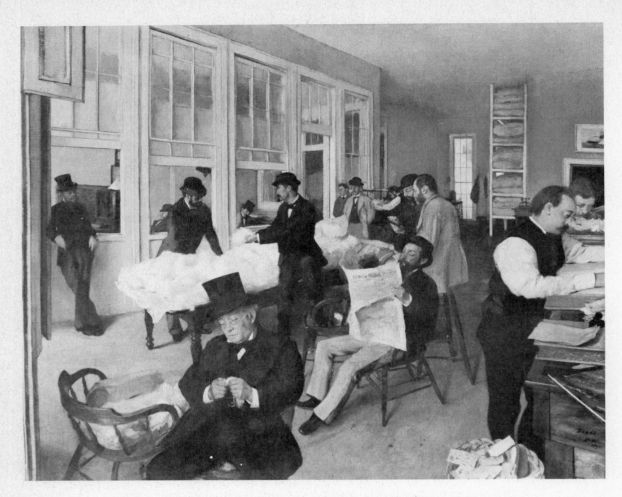

'The Cotton Exchange at New Orleans.' This painting by the French artist Edgar
Degas entitled 'Le Bureau de coton de la Nouvelle-Orleans' shows that though the
war devastated trade in the South, cotton continued to be 'King.' In 1872 Degas
visited the Crescent City, where his brothers were cotton brokers. 'One does
nothing here,' he wrote. 'It's in the climate, so much cotton, one lives for and by
cotton.' From the sketches he made he painted this picture on his return to France
in 1873. The following year he helped organize the first exhibition of the Impressionists. (*Musée des Beaux Arts, Pau. Photo Giraudon*)

The "Brains."

That achieved the Tammany victory at
the Rochester Democratic Convention.

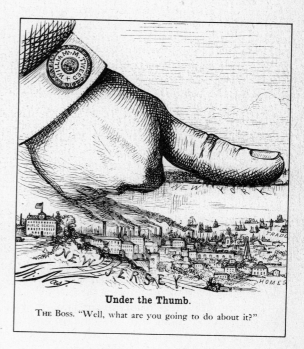

Under the Thumb.

THE BOSS. "Well, what are you going to do about it?"

The Tweed Ring. Nast, who invented the tiger as the symbol of Tammany Hall, caricatured the Tammany boss, William Marcy Tweed, so effectively that the Ring's lawyers offered him $500,000 to desist. New York voters might not be able to read, Tweed said, but they could 'look at the damn pictures,' in which he was depicted as obese and corrupt, wearing an ornate diamond stickpin. To evade imprisonment, Tweed, disguised as a sailor, fled to Spain, but he was identified from a Nast cartoon, arrested, and returned to America, where he died in a New York jail. (*Harper's Weekly,* 19 Aug. 1871)

353

afoot a series of investigations. In the Treasury and War departments, investigators uncovered sensational wrongdoing. For years a 'Whiskey Ring' in St. Louis had systematically defrauded the government of millions in taxes on distilled whiskey. The Ring had operated with the collusion of Treasury officials and of the President's private secretary, Babcock. When Grant was apprised of the situation he said, 'Let no guilty man escape.' But most of them did escape, Babcock with the President's connivance. No sooner had the 'Whiskey Ring' been exposed than the country confronted a new scandal. Secretary of the Treasury Benjamin H. Bristow found irrefutable proof that Secretary of War Belknap had sold Indian post traderships. Faced with impeachment, Belknap hurried to resign, and his resignation was accepted 'with great regret' by the President whom he had betrayed. Impeachment proceedings were instituted, but the Secretary was finally acquitted on the technical ground that the Senate no longer had jurisdiction over his case.

Corruption was not confined to the national government. It could be found in local governments, in business, and even in the professions. There was almost everywhere a breakdown of old moral standards. The industrial revolution, the building of transcontinental railroads, and the exploitation of new natural resources had called into existence a class of new rich untrained to the responsibilities of their position. Never before and only twice since—after World War I and in the 1970's—have public morals fallen so low.

State legislatures, too, were guilty of gross corruption. In the fierce struggle between Daniel Drew and Cornelius Vanderbilt for control of the Erie Railroad the legislature of New York State was auctioned off to the highest bidder, and both bar and bench proved that they too were for sale. In Pennsylvania the Cameron machine bought and sold legislation with bare-faced effrontery. In Wisconsin, Minnesota, and California, railroads controlled the legislatures; in Iowa the money for the Agricultural College realized from land-grant sales was stolen. Cities also presented a sorry spectacle. The brigandage of the Tweed Ring cost New York City not less than $100 million.

At a time when the Grant administration was reeling from reports of corruption, the panic of 1873 struck an even heavier blow. Reckless speculation and wholesale stock watering helped precipitate the panic. Other causes were perhaps equally important. Europe, too, felt the hard times, and overseas investors proceeded to call in their American loans. The unfavorable balance of trade, which had persisted all through the war and the postwar years, mounted during the early 'seventies. Too rapid expansion of the agricultural West produced surplus crops which could not be marketed abroad at satisfactory prices. Credit was overextended, currency inflated, and public finances deranged by the conflicting claims of greenbacks and of gold. With an immense self-confidence the country had mortgaged itself to the future; now it found itself unable to pay either interest or principal.

The crash came 17 September 1873 with the failure of the great banking house of Jay Cooke and Company—the house that had helped finance the war and the Northern Pacific Railroad. Soon one substantial business firm after another toppled, and the New York Stock Exchange took the unprecedented step of closing its doors for ten days. Industrial plants shut down, railway construction declined sharply, and over half the railroads defaulted on their bonds. Long bread lines began to appear in the larger cities, and tramps swarmed the countryside. Such a crisis was bound to have political consequences; it not only lead to the birth of a farmer-labor party, but put the chances of the Republicans in the 1876 election in serious jeopardy.

The Disputed Election of 1876

Republican defeat seemed certain in 1876 as the bankruptcy of the Grant administration became increasingly apparent. To give the party respectability, the Republicans chose the honest if uninspiring Rutherford B. Hayes, thrice Governor of Ohio. The Democrats, determined to make reform the issue of the campaign, nominated Samuel J. Tilden, who had broken the notorious Tweed Ring and then, as Governor of New York, smashed the 'Canal Ring.'

When the first reports came in, Tilden appeared

to have won a sweeping victory. He carried New York, New Jersey, Connecticut, Indiana, and apparently all the South while piling up a popular plurality of over 250,000. But, scanning the returns, the Republican campaign managers became convinced that the election might yet be swung to their candidate. Four states—South Carolina, Florida, Louisiana, and Oregon—were apparently in doubt. Without these states Tilden had only 184 electoral votes; 185 were necessary to win. On the morning after election Zach Chandler wired each of the doubtful states, 'Can you hold your state?'—and that afternoon he announced, 'Hayes has 185 electoral votes and is elected.'

The situation was highly precarious. In all three Southern states there had been intimidation and fraud on both sides. Hayes appeared to have carried South Carolina, but in Florida and Louisiana Tilden seemed to have a safe majority. Republican returning boards threw out about 1000 Democratic votes in Florida and over 13,000 in Louisiana, and gave certificates to the Hayes electors. In Oregon a Democratic governor had displaced a Republican elector on a technicality and appointed a Democrat in his place. From all four states came two sets of returns.

The Constitution provides that 'The President of the Senate shall, in the presence of the Senate and House of Representatives, open all the certificates, and the votes shall then be counted.' But counted by whom? If the Republican President of the Senate did the counting, the election would go to Hayes; if the Democratic House counted, Tilden would be President. And if the two houses could not agree on the procedure, there would be no President. Was the nation then to drift, distraught and confused, without a chief executive?

Conservatives, North and South, hastened to head off such a crisis. The solution was hinted at by Representative Garfield in a letter to Hayes. Some of the extremists on both sides, he wrote, were prepared to make trouble, but 'in the meantime two forces are at work. The Democratic businessmen of the country are more anxious for quiet than for Tilden; and the old Whigs are saying that they have seen war enough, and don't care to follow the lead of their northern associates.' Garfield suggested that 'if in some discreet way, these

southern men who are dissatisfied with Tilden and his violent followers, could know that the South is going to be treated with kind consideration,' they might acquiesce in Hayes's election. If Southern conservatives secured an end to military reconstruction, restoration of 'home rule,' some voice in the Hayes administration, and generous subsidies for internal improvements, particularly railroads, they were prepared to concede the presidency. The Hayes forces were prepared to make these concessions.

With this understanding and with Tilden's reluctant consent, Congress was able to act. On 29 January 1877 it set up an Electoral Commission of fifteen members (five from the House, five from the Senate, and five from the Supreme Court) to pass on the disputed credentials. It was originally planned to appoint to this committee seven Democrats and seven Republicans and, as the fifteenth member, the non-partisan Judge David Davis of Illinois. At the last moment, however—and not by inadvertence—the legislature of Illinois elected Davis to the U.S. Senate and, with the approval of both parties, Judge Bradley was named in his place. As it turned out it was Bradley who named the next President of the United States. For on all questions the Electoral Commission divided along strict party lines, and Bradley voted invariably with the Republicans. By a straight 8-7 vote the Commission awarded all four states to Hayes, and thus the presidency—electoral count: 185 to 184.

Would the Democrats accept a solution which seemed so partisan and so unfair? For a time it was touch and go. Northern Democrats were prepared to filibuster long enough to prevent Congress from opening and counting the votes. But in the end wiser counsels prevailed. With renewed assurances from Hayes that he would abide by the sectional understanding, enough Southern Democrats deserted the Northern intransigents to permit Congress to count the ballots, and on 2 March 1877, only two days before Inauguration Day, Hayes was declared elected. This compromise worked well for those who contrived it. The real victim of the compromise was the Southern Negro, for it had been made at his expense and delayed for three generations the enforcement of those guarantees written into the Fourteenth and Fifteenth Amendments.

The Undoing of Reconstruction

Even before the Compromise of 1877, the country had wearied of the 'Southern question.' No longer would opinion molders in the North sustain military rule. In 1874 the Democrats captured the lower house, and the repudiation of Radicalism was all but complete. Meantime all the Southern states had been readmitted, and by the Amnesty Act of 1872 almost all Southern whites who were still disfranchised were restored to full political privileges. When the Radicals, their power waning, called for more military intervention, Grant rebuffed them. 'The whole public,' he protested, 'are tired out with the annual autumnal outbreaks in the South, and the great majority are ready now to condemn any interference on the part of the government.'

In state after state conservative whites recaptured control of the political machinery, until by the end of 1875 only South Carolina, Louisiana, and Mississippi were still under Radical control, and even in these states that control was precarious. Negores were eliminated from politics, carpetbaggers scared out, scalawags won over— and 'home rule' was restored. The Redeemer governments then proceeded to reduce expenditures and taxes—often at the expense of school children—and to erase a good deal of progressive legislation from the statute books. Acting on the assumption that the Radicals had saddled their states with fraudulent debts, and on the fact that in some instances the railroads, for whose benefit the debts had been contracted, had not carried out their part of the bargains, the Redeemers proceeded to repudiate a good part of the state obligations. By this convenient method Southern states rid themselves of perhaps $100 million of debts.

When Rutherford B. Hayes was inaugurated President, 4 March 1877, the carpetbag regime had been overthrown in all the states save South Carolina and Louisiana, where it was still upheld by federal bayonets. In South Carolina Confederate veterans known as Red Shirts organized white voters, kept blacks away from the polls, and

elected the beloved Confederate General Wade Hampton governor and a Democratic legislature. A Republican returning board, however, sustained by federal soldiers, threw out the ballots of two counties, canceled thousands of others, and declared the carpetbag Governor D. H. Chamberlain duly re-elected. The Democratic members then organized their own House, and with Speaker, clerks, and sergeant-at-arms forced their way into the representatives' chamber where the Radicals were sitting. During three days and nights the rival Houses sat side by side, every man armed to the teeth and ready to shoot if the rival sergeant-at-arms laid hands on one of his colleagues. At the end of that time the Democrats withdrew, leaving Chamberlain in possession of the state house, but for four months the people of the state paid their taxes to Hampton's government. Chamberlain hastened to Washington to appeal for aid, but in vain. Faithful to the compromise by which he had been elected, President Hayes broke the deadlock by withdrawing the troops from Columbia, and the Democrats took possession. Two weeks later, when federal troops evacuated New Orleans, conservative white rule was completely restored throughout the South.

The withdrawal of troops by President Hayes in 1877 marked the abandonment not only of reconstruction, but of the Negro, who paid the price of reunion. There were three parts to the unwritten agreement: that President, Congress, and the North generally, would hereafter keep hands off the 'Negro problem'; that the rules governing race relations in the South would be written by whites; and that these rules would concede the Negro limited civil rights, but neither political nor social equality. The principle underlying this relationship was set forth succinctly by Henry Grady of the Atlanta *Constitution:* 'The supremacy of the white race of the South must be maintained forever, and the domination of the Negro race resisted at all points and at all hazards, because the white race is superior.' It was as simple as that.

The Negro's sole remaining hope lay with the courts. When, in 1873, the Supreme Court was called upon for the first time to interpret the phrases of the Fourteenth Amendment, Justice Samuel Miller, speaking for the Court, reviewed the history of the three Civil War Amendments and observed:

No one can fail to be impressed with the one pervading purpose found in them all, lying at the foundation of each, and without which none of them would have been even suggested; we mean the freedom of the slave race, the security and firm establishment of that freedom, and the protection of the newly made freedman and citizen from the oppressions of those who had formerly exercised unlimited dominion over him.

At the time this seemed the common sense of the matter, and no judge challenged this interpretation.

Each of these Amendments contained an unusual provision, 'Congress shall have power to enforce this article by appropriate legislation.' And, beginning with the ill-fated Civil Rights Act of 1866, Congress enacted a series of laws designed to do just that. The most important were the Enforcement Acts of 1870 and 1871 which threw the protection of the Federal Government over the Negro's right to vote; the Ku Klux Klan Act of 1871 which made it a federal offense to conspire to deprive Negroes of the equal protection of the laws; and the Civil Rights Act of 1875 which undertook to secure the Negro 'full and equal enjoyment of the accommodations, advantages, facilities, and privileges of inns, public conveyances on land or water, theatres, and other places of public amusement,' as well as the right to serve on juries.

Abandoned by Congress and the President, the Negro was now repudiated by the courts. If the 'one pervading purpose' of the Amendments was to protect the freedman, then it failed. Beginning with the Slaughterhouse case of 1873 the Supreme Court proceeded systematically to riddle the structure of Negro rights. In the Slaughterhouse case the Court asserted that all the important privileges and immunities derived not from national but from state citizenship and that the Fourteenth Amendment did not extend federal protection over these. The Cruikshank opinion of 1875, which involved a mob attack on blacks who were trying to vote, deliberately restricted the reach of the Fourteenth Amendment to state—not private—interference with rights, and to such interference as was clearly directed against blacks on account of

their race or color. When an election official in Kentucky refused to receive a black's vote, the Court held that Congress did not have authority to protect the right to vote generally, but only where that right was denied by the *state*, and on grounds of *race* or *color*. In 1878 the Court provided the legal foundation for segregation by striking down a Louisiana statute forbidding discrimination in transportation as an unlawful interference with congressional authority over interstate commerce! In the *United States v. Harris*, a case in which a Tennessee mob had lynched four black prisoners, the Court returned to the theme that the national government could protect the black only against acts by the state, and that for protection against violence by individuals or mobs the victim must look to state authorities. The crucial test came with the Civil Rights Cases of 1883, where the Court, in effect, wiped off the statute book the Civil Rights Act of 1875.

It would be running the slavery argument into the ground [said Justice Bradley] to make it apply to every act of discrimination which a person may see fit to make as to the guests he will entertain, or as to the people he will take into his coach or cab or car, or admit to his concert or theatre, or deal with in other matters of intercourse or business.

And the Court added, that

When a man has emerged from slavery and by the aid of beneficent legislation has shaken off the inseparable concomitants of that state, there must be some stage in the progress of his elevation when he takes the rank of a mere citizen, and ceases to be the special favorite of the laws, and when his rights as a citizen, or a man, are to be protected in the ordinary modes by which other men's rights are protected.

This was the thesis, too, of the crucial *Plessy v. Ferguson* decision of 1896 which, by accepting the doctrine of 'separate but equal accommodations,' threw the mantle of judicial approval over segregation.[5]

This jettisoning of the civil rights program did not go without protest from within the Court itself. Justice Harlan of Kentucky spoke for a con-

5. Reversed some sixty years later in the even more crucial decision of *Brown v. Board of Education of Topeka.*

'Twenty Years After Independence.' This photograph of a Fourth of July celebration in Richmond suggests that two decades after the Emancipation Proclamation blacks still had a long way to go, but it also indicates reverence toward the Great Emancipator. (*Valentine Museum, Richmond, Virginia*)

struction of the Constitution broad enough to embrace the rights of all citizens. And, observing that the 'separate but equal' doctrine of the Plessy case would, in time 'be quite as pernicious as the decision in the Dred Scott case,' Harlan wrote prophetically:

The destinies of the two races in this country are indissolubly linked together, and the interests of both require that the common government of all shall not permit the seeds of race hate to be planted under the sanction of law. What can more certainly arouse race hate, what more certainly create and perpetuate a feeling of distrust between these races, than state enactments which in fact proceed on the ground that colored citizens are so inferior and degraded that they cannot be allowed to sit in public coaches occupied by white citizens.

The end of Reconstruction and the nullification of the Enforcement Acts exiled the Southern Negro to a kind of no-man's land halfway between slavery and freedom. No longer a slave, he was not yet free. He was tied to the soil by the sharecrop and crop-lien systems, excluded from most

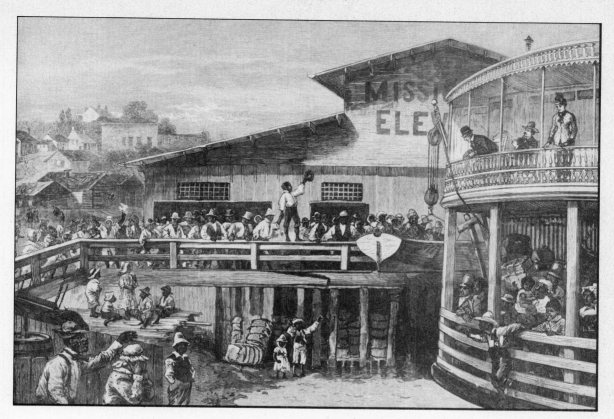

The Negro exodus. In 1879 some 50,000 blacks from Mississippi and other Deep South states migrated to the Western prairie out of discontent with the violent aftermath of Reconstruction, bad crops, and yellow fever, and with great expectations of 'sunny Kansas.' Many died during the bitter winter of 1879–80, and the 'Exodusters' found that racial discrimination was not confined to the South but was endemic in the old abolitionist havens too. This sketch by James H. Moser depicts a scene on the wharves at Vicksburg. (*Collection Judith Mara Gutman*)

professions and from many jobs, and fobbed off with 'separate' accommodations that were rarely 'equal.' He was expected not only to accept a position of social inferiority without protest, but to rejoice in it by playing the role of 'Uncle Tom.' At first gradually, then with dramatic speed, he was rendered politically impotent: 'grandfather' clauses, literacy tests, poll taxes, and—where these failed—naked intimidation, deprived him of the vote. In 1885 the Louisiana novelist, George Washington Cable, wrote:

One of the marvels of future history will be that it was counted a small matter, by a majority of our nation, for six millions of people within it, made by its own decree a component part of it, to be subjected to a system of oppression so rank that nothing could make it seem small except the fact that they had already been ground under it for a century and a half. . . . It heaps upon him in every public place the most odious distinctions, without giving ear to the humblest plea concerning mental or moral character. It spurns his ambition, tramples upon his languishing self-respect, and indignantly refuses to let him either buy with money or earn by any excellence of inner life or outward behavior, the most momentary immunity from these public indignities.

Southerners generally congratulated themselves that they had persuaded the North to concede them almost complete control of their domestic institutions. Yet the cost of the restoration of white rule was high, for white as well as for black. By sanctioning the use of fraud and coercion to deny the black his legal rights, they weakened moral standards. By restricting Negro voting they limited white suffrage, and thus struck a heavy blow at democracy. By identifying white supremacy with the Democrats they saddled a one-party system upon the South, and threw that party into the hands of the least enlightened elements of their society.

Reconstruction left deep physical and moral scars upon the South. A century later, the apostles of white supremacy were able to ring the changes on the evils of Reconstruction whenever even modest alterations in racial patterns were suggested. For decades after 1877, race relations were poisoned by an annual crop of outrages. Politics were forced into an unnatural groove, and the one-party system, a hostage to white supremacy, proved inhospitable to the introduction of new issues. Southern society remained relatively static, immune to modern movements in education and social regeneration. But Reconstruction also left another legacy: the civil rights amendments to the Constitution. In years to come, although much too tardily, Americans would begin to give to these provisions the meaning their framers intended.

20

The Economic Revolution

1865–1914

Industrial America

It was the dream of Jefferson that his country—'with room enough for our descendants to the hundredth and thousandth generation'—was to be a great agrarian democracy. 'While we have land to labor,' he wrote, 'let us never wish to see our citizens occupied at a work bench, or twirling a distaff,' for 'those who labor in the earth are the chosen people of God.' But within two generations of Jefferson's death the value of manufactured products was almost treble that of agricultural, and by 1910 the United States had progressed so far in the direction Alexander Hamilton wished that it had become the leading industrial power in the world. When the census of 1920 recorded over 9 million factory wage-earners producing commodities to the value of some $62 billion, and over 50 per cent of the population crowded into towns and cities, surely Hamilton was able to collect some bets from Jefferson in the Elysian Fields!

This economic revolution was a consequence of the creation of a national market, made possible by a railway network which linked farms to commercial centers and spurred the growth of cities.

As population tripled between 1860 and 1920, and incomes rose at an even more rapid pace, mass demand encouraged industrial expansion, which was further accelerated by the application of electric power and the introduction of the internal combustion engine. By the early 1900's many firms were operating on a national scale and not a few were turning out producers' goods for other industries rather than for the consumer. By then, too, the great corporation had established itself as the basic unit, and the main industries were dominated by a few huge enterprises which maintained extensive national organizations for buying and marketing.

This revolution enhanced national wealth, raised standards of living, and produced cycles of prosperity and depression with periodic unemployment. It speeded up urbanization, encouraged immigration, stimulated rapid growth of population, and modified social institutions such as the family. It helped plunge America into world affairs, shifted the balance of international payments, and made the United States a creditor nation. It led also to a concentration of wealth and control, creating, in a nation brought up on Jeffersonian principles, a whole series of difficulties which the teachings of the Fathers did little to illuminate.

The Age of Invention

The United States Patent Office was created in 1790 largely through the efforts of one of the greatest American inventors, John Stevens of Hoboken, New Jersey. So numerous were the patents granted to ingenious Americans in the following years that in 1833, it was said, the head of the Patent Bureau decided to resign because he felt that everything of importance had been invented! Yet the 36,000 patents granted before 1860 were but a feeble indication of the flood of inventions that was to inundate the Patent Office after the Civil War. From 1860 to 1890 no less than 440,000 patents were issued. The average number of inventions patented in any one year since 1900 equals or exceeds the total number patented in the entire history of the country before 1860.

Though the beginnings of many important inventions can be traced to the late eighteenth and early nineteenth centuries, their application on a large scale came only after the Civil War. In the eighteenth century Franklin, Galvani, and Oersted had experimented with electricity, and as early as 1831 Michael Faraday in England and Joseph Henry of the Smithsonian Institution had developed the principle of the dynamo. But it was not until after 1880 that the genius of Thomas A. Edison, William Stanley, Charles Brush, and a host of others put the dynamo to use on the streetcar, the elevated train, and the subway. Elias Howe invented the sewing machine in 1846, but it did not have general use until popularized by Isaac Singer after 1860, and was first applied to the making of shoes by Gordon McKay in 1862. Eli Whitney adapted for firearms the revolutionary principles of standardization and interchangeability of parts as early as 1798, but mass production did not come until after the achievements of Kelly, Holley, and Bessemer ushered in the age of steel. Dr. N. A. Otto of Germany invented the internal combustion engine in 1876, but it meant little to the average American until Henry Ford in 1908 placed a motorcar on the market that was not a rich man's toy but a poor man's instrument. By 1920 Ford was making more than 6000 cars a day in his Detroit factories, and the automobile industry ranked first in the country in value of finished products. Transportation was affected by invention in yet another way when around 1908 the vision of Samuel P. Langley and the perseverance of the Wright brothers and Glenn Curtiss lifted the airplane out of the experimental stage.

Invention radically changed communication too. In 1856 the Western Union Company was organized and soon the whole country was crisscrossed with a network of telegraph wires. In 1858 the duplex telegraph was invented, and in 1896 an Italian, Guglielmo Marconi, discovered the secret of wireless telegraphy. In the centennial year of 1876, Emperor Dom Pedro of Brazil, attending the Philadelphia Exposition, sauntered up to the booth of young Alexander Graham Bell; he picked up the cone-shaped instrument on display there, and as he placed it to his ear Bell spoke through the transmitter. 'My God, it talks!' exclaimed His Majesty; and from that moment the telephone became the central feature of the Exposition. Within half a century 16 million telephones had profoundly affected the life of the nation. The invention in 1867 of the typewriter by an erratic printer, Christopher Sholes, proved a boon to the writer as well as the business office. The linotype composing machine invented by Ottmar Mergenthaler, Hoe's rotary press, the web press, and folding machinery made it possible to print as many as 240,000 eight-page newspapers in an hour; and the electrotype worked a comparable change in printing magazines and books. This revolution—plus the benevolent policy of the postal authorities in allowing cheap postal rates—made it possible for new magazines to reach a mass market heretofore unsuspected.

Meantime a host of inventions were transforming daily life, especially in the towns. The 'Wizard of Menlo,' Thomas Edison, gave the world the incandescent lamp in 1880, and within a few years millions were supplied with better, safer, and cheaper light than had ever been known before. It was Edison, too, who perfected the talking machine—which was in time to become a music-

Glass Works, Wheeling, West Virginia. This lithograph is from *The Illustrated Atlas of the Upper Ohio River Valley*, published in 1877. (*Library of Congress*)

playing machine—and in conjunction with George Eastman developed the motion picture.

Machinery, science, and invention enabled man to increase his productivity a thousandfold. Under primitive conditions of weaving it required 5605 hours of labor to produce 500 yards of cotton sheeting; by 1900 manufacturers were able to turn out the same amount with only 52 hours of human labor. Two centuries ago Adam Smith celebrated the efficiency of machine production by observing that without machinery a workingman would need a full day to make a single pin, whereas machinery enabled him to manufacture 5000 pins in a day. A century later the great economist might have pointed his moral even more effectively, for by then a single worker could supervise the manufacture on automatic machines of 15 million pins each day.

The New South

Although the economic revolution continued to center in the Northeast, its impact was felt in every region, even the South. New cities like Birmingham, Chattanooga, and Durham sprang into existence, and Atlanta rose from her ashes to boast a population in 1880 four times as large as at the outbreak of the war. 'Chicago in her busiest days,' wrote a visitor, 'could scarcely show such a sight as clamors for observation here.' Here was the 'New South'—the South of cities, factories, and blast furnaces. 'Think of it,' said Henry Grady in a rapturous outburst—

In cotton a monopoly. In iron and coal establishing swift mastery. In granite and marble developing equal advantages and resources. In yellow pine and hard woods the world's treasury. Surely the basis of the South's wealth and power is laid by the hand of Almighty God!

Before the South could achieve wealth and power, it needed more capital and better transportation. Capital presented the more difficult problem. The South itself had no surplus, and the fiscal policies of the Reconstruction governments, Radical and Redeemer alike, were not calculated to inspire confidence in Northern or foreign investors. But gradually the South attracted, or accumulated, money. The Freedmen's Bureau and

the army spent large sums; the government appropriated millions for internal improvements; Northerners bought up farms and plantations, and Northern capital went into railroads, timberlands, coal and iron. Gradually, too, the South re-entered the world market with her exports, and lifted herself by her financial bootstraps. By the 'eighties money was pouring into the South from the North and from abroad. Much of this went to rebuilding the railroads. During the 'seventies the South added 5000 miles to her railroad network, and in the 'eighties no fewer than 23,000 miles.

For two generations Southerners had sent their cotton to the mills of Old and New England where the manufacturing establishments, labor, capital, and facilities for world marketing were well organized. The 'fifties had seen the beginnings of a textile industry in Georgia and South Carolina, but not until the 'seventies did the South seriously challenge the monopoly of New England mills. Proximity to raw materials and to water power, cheap labor, freedom from legal restraints, low taxes, and eager community support all gave Southern mills an advantage. By the end of Reconstruction over 100 Southern mills had almost half a million spindles; twenty years later some 400 mills boasted over 4 million spindles. Yet this was only a beginning. By 1920 the textile industry had moved south, and North Carolina, South Carolina, and Georgia ranked second, third, and fourth among the textile states of the nation.[1]

The pattern of the Southern textile industry differed in important ways from that of New England. Small mills sprouted on the outskirts of scores of little Carolina and Georgia towns, financed by local capital, managed by local enterprise, supported by local pride, and worked by white labor recruited from the neighborhood. The mill-workers, mostly from the poor-white class, welcomed the opportunity to exchange their drab and impoverished existence for the questionable attractions of the mill village. The great majority were women, and children between the ages of ten and fifteen; these worked an average of seventy hours a week for a wage of about three dollars. No

1. In 1957 each of these states had more spindles than all the New England states combined.

laws limited the hours of labor of women, and such child labor laws as were enacted remained unenforced.

The mill village gathered around the factory as a medieval village clustered about a feudal castle, and the mill manager ruled his community as a feudal lord ruled his manor. The company ordinarily owned the entire village—houses, stores, streets, the school, the church; needless to add, it effectively owned the workers, the shopkeepers, the teachers, and the preacher as well. Labor organizers could be denied access to the village, trouble-makers could be evicted, and teachers or preachers who indulged in criticism of the system could be sent packing. By the opening of the twentieth century the New South had gone a long way toward substituting industrial autocracy for the old agrarian feudalism.

The New South proved hospitable to a variety of industries. As with textile manufacturing, the tobacco industry enjoyed the advantages of the proximity of raw material, low transportation costs, and cheap labor; unlike textiles, it concentrated in large cities such as Richmond and Louisville, and used Negro labor. Two circumstances account in large part for its great prosperity: the invention, in 1880, of a cigarette-making machine by James Bonsack, and the organizing genius of James Buchanan Duke. Starting as a boy peddling his father's tobacco to North Carolina farmers, young Duke rose to be the Rockefeller of the tobacco industry, made his native town of Durham, North Carolina, the tobacco capital of the world, and in 1890 welded together the gigantic American Tobacco Company, whose operations—conducted in New York City—stretched from Southern tobacco fields to the Orient. The 'eighties saw, too, the beginnings of a flourishing coal and iron industry concentrated in Birmingham, Alabama, which quickly became the Pittsburgh of the South, and a lumber industry which exploited and devastated the pine forests of Louisiana and Mississippi. And after the opening of the new century the plains of Texas and Oklahoma, once the domain of Indians and cattlemen, became part of the empire of oil.

The industrialization of the South carried with it changes in political outlook. The 'Bourbons'

who ruled the South from Reconstruction to the turn of the century were committed to industrialization; before long the South, as well as the North, could boast its 'railroad Senators' and its 'coal and iron Senators.' The three men who controlled Georgia politics, General Alfred Colquitt, General John Gordon, and Governor Joseph E. Brown, were all deeply involved in railroad promotion, manufacturing, real estate, and speculation. Through Milton Smith and General Basil Duke the Louisville and Nashville Railroad manipulated Kentucky politics for over twenty years; when in 1900 a reformer, Governor William Goebel, threatened that control, he was assassinated.

Yet for all the talk of a 'New South,' old patterns persisted. The South of 1900 accounted for a smaller proportion of the total manufacturing product of the country than did the South of 1860. Far more than other sections, the South escaped those two concomitants of industry—urbanization and immigration. The South was still, in 1900 as in 1860, predominantly rural, and the population of the Southern states remained almost entirely native-born. Furthermore, the South continued to be almost wholly a staple-crop—and even a one-crop—section; if King Cotton had been deposed he was still a lively pretender. Nonetheless, the South was changing, and as, with the passing years, the contrast between the dream of the Old South and the reality of the New—between the myth of plantation and slavery and the reality of tenant-farming and the mill villages—became ever more visible, white Southerners grew more defiantly insistent upon the old magnolia legend. Perhaps most remarkable is that in the end the South imposed this myth not only on itself, but on the North as well.

Iron and Steel

'The consumption of iron,' wrote the great ironmaster, Abram S. Hewitt, 'is the social barometer by which to estimate the relative height of civilization among nations.' By this gauge, the progress of civilization in the United States from the Civil War to World War I was remarkable. The works of man in the United States of 1860 were constructed of wood and stone, with a little brick and iron; by 1920 America had become a nation of iron, steel, and concrete. The United States of 1860 produced less than one million tons of pig iron; 60 years later output approached 36 million tons and the United States easily led the world in iron and steel manufacturing. This transformation resulted from the exploitation of new resources of iron, the discovery of new processes for converting it into steel, the indirect subsidy that was contributed by the government in the form of a prohibitive tariff, and the rise of a group of ironmasters with a genius for organization and production.

In the late 1840's enormous iron-ore deposits were discovered in the northern Michigan peninsula, and the year of the rush to the California gold diggings witnessed a rush to the iron-ore fields around Marquette scarcely less spectacular. Superior, that greatest of lakes, proved to be rimmed by iron. In the mid-1880's Charlemagne Tower opened up the rich Vermilion iron range on the north side of the lake, pushed a railroad through from Duluth, and within a few years was shipping one million tons annually through the Soo Canal. To the west and north lay even richer fields. The Mesabi iron range west of the lake, the greatest ore producer in the world, made possible the supremacy of the American steel industry for half a century.

The ore fields of the Lake Superior region are hundreds of miles distant from coal deposits, but cheap lake and railway transportation brought the two together. Ore and coal met in smelters of Chicago where the first American steel rails were rolled in 1865, and in Cleveland, Toledo, Ashtabula, and Milwaukee. Much of the ore was carried to Pittsburgh, center of the great Appalachian coal fields and strategically located with reference to water and rail transportation. In the 'eighties the iron and coal beds of the southern Appalachians were first exploited, and soon Birmingham became a southern rival to Pittsburgh and Chicago; in the twentieth century Colorado with apparently inexhaustible resources of minerals emerged as the Western center of the steel industry.

The Bessemer and open-hearth processes were as fundamental to steel making as the new ore beds. The Bessemer process, which consists in blowing air through molten iron to drive out the impurities, was anticipated in America by William Kelly, a prophet without honor in his own country; for it was not until Henry Bessemer had demonstrated the utility of his method in England that American manufacturers adopted it. The Bessemer process gave U.S. steel producers one incalculable advantage: it was effective only where the phosphorus content of the iron ore was very low; comparatively little of the English iron ore was free from phosphorus, but practically all the Lake Superior ore was. By 1875 Andrew Carnegie had adopted the Bessemer process in his great J. Edgar Thomson steel works. Shortly after the Civil War, Abram Hewitt had introduced to this country the more costly Siemens-Martin open-hearth method of smelting, and the superiority of the steel it produced was soon apparent. In 1880 ten times as much steel was manufactured by the Bessemer as by the open-hearth process, but by 1910 the latter method accounted for twice the tonnage of the Bessemer process. The Bessemer and open-hearth processes not only made steel of fine quality and in enormous quantities but reduced the price from $300 to $35 a ton.

The application of chemistry to steel making introduced further economies and solved many technical problems. 'Nine-tenths of all the uncertainties were dispelled under the burning sun of chemical knowledge,' affirmed Andrew Carnegie. The introduction of electric furnaces made it possible to produce hard manganese steel for automobiles and machines and 'high-speed' steel for tools. By 1900 American furnaces turned out as much steel as those of Great Britain and Germany combined; and this supremacy in iron and steel manufacture, once attained, was never surrendered.

An important element in the growth of the iron and steel industry was the tariff, which enabled American manufacturers to compete successfully with their English and German competitors and to pile up fabulous profits. Abram Hewitt put the matter succinctly: 'Steel rails . . . were subject to a duty of $28 a ton. The price of foreign rails had advanced to a point where it would have paid [the

Andrew Carnegie (1835–1919). This painting by H. R. Butler suggests the benevolent serenity of the magnate who entered the mills at the age of thirteen, working from sunrise to sunset, and ended his days a multi-millionaire philanthropist. 'How much have I given away?' he asked his secretary. Informed that the sum had reached $324,657,399, Carnegie replied, 'Wherever did I get all that money?' (*Teachers Insurance and Annuity Association, Photo Jean Shapiro*)

manufacturer] to make rails without any duty, but of the duty of $28 a ton he added $27 to his price and transferred from the great mass of the people $50 million in a few years to the pockets of a few owners who thus indemnified themselves in a very short time, nearly twice over, for the total outlay which they had made in the establishment of their business.' Even Carnegie, when his company showed a profit of $40 million in a single year, felt that the time had come to abandon protection.

Andrew Carnegie was the greatest leader in the iron and steel industry and the archetype of the industrial age. A poor immigrant boy from Scotland, he followed and helped perpetuate the American tradition of rising from poverty to riches, and his success he ascribed entirely to the democracy which obtained in this country. By dint of unflagging industry and unrivaled business acumen, and especially through his extraordinary ability to choose as his associates such men as Charles Schwab, Henry Frick, and Henry

Phipps and to command the devotion of his workmen, Carnegie built up the biggest steel business in the world, and retired in 1901 to chant the glories of 'Triumphant Democracy' and to give away his enormous fortune of $450 million. This was made possible by the sale of his holdings to a rival organization, directed by the Chicago lawyer Elbert Gary and the New York banker J. Pierpont Morgan. The result was the United States Steel Corporation, a combination of most of the important steel manufacturers, capitalized at the colossal sum of $1400 million. Half of this capitalization was 'water,' but by 1924 the company had earned aggregate net profits of $2,108,848,640.

Trusts and Monopolies

The organization of U.S. Steel in 1901 brought to a climax a movement which had been under way for a generation: the concentration of business in large units—pools, trusts, corporations, and holding companies. Combination had many advantages. It tended to eliminate competition, diminishing the hazard that unregulated production would drive prices below costs and facilitating economies in manufacture, transportation, marketing, administration, and finance. Through combination, capital reserves could be built up to stabilize or expand industry. Where combination was along horizontal lines—the combination, for example, of all manufacturers of typewriters—it was easy to control production and price. Where combination was along vertical lines—the control, by one corporation, of the entire process from raw materials through manufacture to marketing of a single product, like the Ford car—it gave a degree of independence and power that no isolated industry could enjoy. In steel and oil, combination was both horizontal and vertical and created industrial sovereignties as mighty as states.

The primary legal instrument of combination was incorporation, which became widespread after the Civil War. Incorporation gives permanence of life and continuity of control, elasticity and easy expansion of capital, limited liability for losses in case of disaster, concentration of administrative authority with diffusion of responsibility, and the 'privileges and immunities' of a 'person' in law and in interstate activities.

The concentration of industry developed swiftly in the years after the Civil War and reached a climax around the turn of the century. The trust movement grew out of the fierce competition following hard upon the Civil War. Competing railways cut freight rates, in the hope of obtaining the lion's share of business, until dividends ceased and railway securities became a drug on the market. The downward trend of prices from 1865 to 1895 put a premium on greater units of mass production and led, in the 1870's, to pooling—'gentlemen's agreements' between rival producers or railroad directors to maintain prices and divide business, or even to pro-rate profits. But it was found so difficult to maintain these rudimentary oligopolies that a 'gentlemen's agreement' came to be defined as one that was certain to be violated.

In the 1880's pools were superseded by trusts—a form of combination in which affiliated companies handed over their securities to be administered by a board of trustees. The trust device was 'invented' by a Standard Oil lawyer in 1882; first adopted by the great oil combination, it quickly became the pattern others followed. The term itself shortly outgrew its purely technical meaning, and came to be used as a description of all large-scale combinations. According to the economist Eliot Jones, 'a trust may be said to exist when a person, corporation, or combination owns or controls enough of the plants producing a certain article to be able for all practical purposes to fix its price.' How much is 'enough' is something that not even the courts have been able to determine, and in some ways Mr. Dooley's definition of a trust is more accurate: 'A trust,' he said, 'is somethin' for an honest, ploddin', uncombined manufacturer to sell out to.'

The Standard Oil Company was not only the first trust and—as Allan Nevins observes—'the largest and richest industrial organization in the world'; it was also the most characteristic, and it provides the classic example of the advantages and dangers of this form of organization. It was built on the exploitation of a great natural resource; it prospered by the astute application of technology and of scientific management; it combined control of almost every activity that affected its welfare—raw material, transportation, wholesale and retail trade, and finances; it was deeply involved in overseas operations; it influenced, perhaps corrupted, political processes; it inspired, and frustrated, anti-trust legislation and litigation; and it piled up unparalleled fortunes for its founders and beneficiaries, most of which were poured back into philanthropy.

In 1858 Edwin Drake, prospecting along Oil Creek, near Titusville, Pennsylvania, sank a shaft some 70 feet into the ground and struck oil. The word echoed through the East like the cry of 'Gold' in 'forty-eight. Within two years tens of thousands of prospectors were sinking wells along the hillsides and in the gullies of the forsaken countryside. The life of the 'Regions' was like that of a Western mining camp. When a prospector struck oil at Pithole Creek, a town of almost 15,000 grew up overnight, with hotels, theaters, and concert halls, dance halls and brothels, newspapers and churches; five years more and the place was deserted. As prospectors denuded the hills of trees they erected a forest of derricks; the open wells sometimes caught fire, and a pall of smoke hung over the valley. Railroads pushed their way in, and enterprising oil men ran miniature pipelines to the swollen Allegheny, where the barrels were filled and floated down to Pittsburgh.

In nearby Cleveland a young commission-merchant, John D. Rockefeller—he was not yet twenty-five—watched the birth of the oil industry with shrewd understanding; in 1863 he sold out his commission business and acquired an oil refinery. Two years later his was the largest refinery in Cleveland, and in 1870 he and his partners incorporated as the Standard Oil Company of Ohio. Two years later he organized the South Improvement Company to do battle with, or absorb, his competitors in Pittsburgh and Philadelphia. With ample financial backing he bought up weaker competitors or forced them to their knees; entered into arrangements with shippers that put him in an invulnerable position; and achieved a virtual monopoly on the pipelines of the East. Within a decade he was master of the oil business of the nation.

What accounts for this spectacular achievement? Rockefeller's own explanation might apply to almost any one of the major monopolies of the day:

I ascribe the success of the Standard to its consistent policy to make the volume of its business large through the merits and cheapness of its products. It has spared no expense in finding, securing, and utilizing the best and cheapest methods of manufacture. It has sought for the best superintendents and workmen and paid the best wages. It has not hesitated to sacrifice old machinery and old plants for new and better ones. It has placed its manufactories at the points where they could supply markets at the least expense. It has not only sought markets for its principal products, but for all possible by-products.... It has not hesitated to invest millions of dollars in methods of cheapening the gathering and distribution of oil by pipe lines, special cars, tank steamers and tank wagons. It has erected tank stations at every important railroad station to cheapen the storage and delivery of its products. It has spared no expense in forcing its products into the markets of the world among people civilized and uncivilized. It has had faith in American oil, and has brought together millions of money for the purpose of making it what it is, and holding its markets against the competition of Russia and all the many countries which are ... competitors against American oil.

What Rockefeller failed to mention in this testimony was what made Standard Oil feared and hated. By playing competing railways one against another, he obtained rebates from their published freight rates, and even forced them to pay to the Standard rebates from competitors' freight payments. If competing oil companies managed to stagger along under such handicaps, they were 'frozen out' by cutting prices in their selling territory until the Standard had all the business.

The Standard Oil trust was soon followed by other combinations. The most important, besides Standard Oil and U.S. Steel, were the Amalgamated Copper Co., the American Sugar Refining Co., the American Tobacco Co., the United States Rubber Co., the United States Leather Co., the International Harvester Co., and the Pullman Palace Car Co., no one of which had a capitalization under $50 million. In no field was concentration more significant than in transportation and communication. By the turn of the century the major part of the railroad business was in the hands of six groups; the expressing business was apportioned between three companies which by their influence prevented the United States mails from taking parcels until 1912; the Western Union, until the rise of the Postal Telegraph, had a virtual monopoly on the telegraph business; and the American Telephone and Telegraph Company, capitalized in 1900 at one-quarter of a billion dollars, was already on its way to becoming the greatest of modern combinations.

The role of New York City bankers in putting together many of these combinations led to the fear that the most fearsome of all trusts was in the making—the 'money trust.' The House of Morgan was exhibit A in this concern. In 1864 Junius Spencer Morgan, long a leader in marketing U.S. securities in England, placed his son John Pierpont in charge of the American branch of the firm. Within a few years young Morgan had tied up with the old banking house of Drexel in Philadelphia, and soon was challenging the supremacy of Jay Cooke and Company. The failure of Cooke in the panic of 1873 put Morgan in a position of immense power. In the 1880's the House of Morgan formed a close association with the New York Central Railroad, and through that decade and the next organized and reorganized

J. P. Morgan (1837–1913). This 1903 portrait of the financial titan is by Edward Steichen, who over a lengthy career did so much to win recognition for photography as an art form. Steichen's picture of Morgan with his 'bead-bright eyes, ferocious eyebrows, and rubescent nose' conveys the enormous personal power of the man who ruled over the great house at Broad and Wall. It suggests what George Bernard Shaw meant in writing of the 'terrible truthfulness' of the camera. (*Metropolitan Museum of Art*)

railroads, extending its influence through the South and even into the Far West where, after the turn of the century, it formed an alliance with the Hill group. Meantime Morgan interests had spread into many other fields, until in the new century there was scarcely an important business which they did not touch except those in the orbit of the rival Rockefeller interests. In 1901 the House of Morgan put through the gigantic deal that created the United States Steel Corporation. Morgan brought together the warring manufacturers of agricultural instruments, and emerged with the International Harvester Company, and he helped finance American Telephone and Telegraph, General Electric, and a dozen other giants. The House of Morgan controlled a dozen large banks—Hanover, Chase, First National, Bankers' Trust, and others; more important, it had tied up with three of the greatest insurance companies—New York Life, Mutual Life, and Equitable.

Trust Regulation

In the 1880's the public began to demand effective regulation of the trusts; but the problem of regulation was seriously complicated by the federal form of government. Corporations are chartered by the states, not the nation. The constitutions of many states contained general prohibitions of monopolies or conspiracies in restraint of trade, but most state prohibitions were ineffective, especially after the federal courts began to interpret broadly the congressional authority over interstate commerce and to limit severely the kind of regulation permitted the states under the Fourteenth Amendment. A corporation chartered by one state has the right to do business in every other state. Hence it was easy for corporations to escape the restrictions or limitations of strict state laws by incorporating in states such as New Jersey, West Virginia, or Delaware where the laws as to issuing stock, accountability of directors, and the right to hold stock in other corporations were very lax.

To make up for the deficiencies of state legislation, Congress enacted the Sherman Anti-Trust Act in 1890. Its central provisions are found in the first two articles:

1. Every contract, combination in the form of trust or otherwise, or conspiracy, in restraint of trade or commerce among the several States, or with foreign nations is hereby declared to be illegal. . . .

2. Every person who shall monopolize, or attempt to monopolize . . . any part of the trade or commerce among the several States, or with foreign nations, shall be deemed guilty of a misdemeanor. . . .

It is difficult to determine the precise purpose of this law. At the time it was alleged that the act sought to give the federal courts common law jurisdiction over the crime of monopoly and conspiracy in restraint of trade; if so the law should have been interpreted in accordance with common law precedents to the effect that only *unreasonable* restraints of trade, or monopolies contrary to public interest, were illegal. But there were no such qualifications in the provisions of the act itself. Nor were there any definitions of the terms 'trust,' 'conspiracy,' and 'monopoly,' while the phrase 'in the form of trust or otherwise' left much to the imagination. In all probability the provisions of the law were purposely couched in indefinite terms, leaving to the courts the task of interpreting and applying them. By thus placing responsibility upon the courts the legislators evaded the problem, and put off its solution indefinitely, for judicial regulation proved singularly ineffective.

In *United States* v. *E. C. Knight and Company*, the Court in 1895 held that the mere control of 98 per cent of the sugar refining of the country did not in itself constitute an act in restraint of trade. In a vigorous dissenting opinion, Justice Harlan warned:

Interstate traffic . . . may pass under the absolute control of overshadowing combinations having financial resources without limit and audacity in the accomplishment of their objects that recognize none of the restraints of moral obligations controlling the action of individuals; combinations governed entirely by the law of greed and selfishness—so powerful that no single

State is able to overthrow them and give the required protection to the whole country, and so all-pervading that they threaten the integrity of our institutions.

This is just about what happened. Attorney-General Richard Olney wrote complacently, 'You will observe that the government has been defeated in the Supreme Court on the trust question. I always supposed it would be, and have taken the responsibility of not prosecuting under a law I believed to be no good.'

In case after case the courts emasculated or nullified the act; yet the disappointment of the anti-trust law should not be charged exclusively to the judiciary. The legislature failed to amend the act; the executive failed to enforce it. Altogether only seven suits under the Sherman Act were instituted by Harrison, eight by Cleveland, and three by McKinley, and all these suits were ineffective. More business combinations were formed during the McKinley administration than ever before. Only when the law was applied to labor unions—embraced in the ambiguous term 'or otherwise'—did the government win a series of victories.

The failure of the machinery of enforcement inevitably gave rise to the suspicion that the whole trust-busting movement was something of a sham. Americans were, in fact, caught on the horns of a dilemma. On the one hand their traditions exalted individualism and idealized the independent entrepreneur. On the other hand all those forces of technology which Americans so deeply admired advertised the advantages of large-scale organization. Had the people really wished to strike down trusts, they could have done so easily enough by taxing them out of existence. But wanting the best of both worlds—the pastoral world of the eighteenth century and the technological world of the twentieth, they contented themselves with ceremonial gestures. They satisfied their moral scruples by undertaking, from time to time, ritualistic skirmishes against the trusts.

Big Business and Its Philosophy

The age was memorable not for statesmen, as in the early years of the Republic, or for reformers and men of letters, as in the middle years, but for titans of industry. Schoolchildren today who have difficulty in remembering the names of any President between Grant and Theodore Roosevelt identify readily enough John D. Rockefeller. Few novelists of these years blunted their pens on the political scene, but the world of business was portrayed in distinguished novels, from Mark Twain's *The Gilded Age* and William Dean Howells's *The Rise of Silas Lapham* to Theodore Dreiser's *The Titan* and Henry James's *The Ivory Tower.*

Gold and silver, copper and oil, forest and stream, all the bounties of nature which in the Old World had belonged, as a matter of course, to crown or commonwealth, were allowed to fall into the hands of strong men. Willing legislators gave them first chance, and amiable judges confirmed them in what they had won or seized. No income tax impeded the swift accumulation of fortunes; no government official told them how to run their business; public opinion never penetrated the walls of their conceit.

Political power and social prestige naturally gravitated to the rich. They controlled newspapers and magazines; subsidized candidates; bought legislation and even judicial decisions. The greatest of them, such as J. P. Morgan, treated state governors as servants, and Presidents as equals. The new rich hired architects to build French châteaux or English country houses in Newport, Washington, New York, Cleveland, and San Francisco, and undertook to indulge themselves in luxuries which Thorstein Veblen designated as 'conspicuous waste.' They filled their houses with paintings and tapestries from the Old World; built enormous yachts; staffed their palaces with hordes of servants; gave parties which they imagined were like those of Versailles before the Revolution.

Business even fostered a philosophy which drew impartially on history, law, economics, religion, and biology to justify its acquisitiveness and its power. At its most full blown Social Darwinism was made up of four not wholly harmonious ingredients. First, the principle drawn from Jeffersonian agrarianism and Manchester liberalism, that that government was best which governed least, a doctrine vigorously enunciated by Professor William Graham Sumner of Yale. Second, the principle of the peculiar sanctity of property— including, of course, corporate charters and franchises. This principle, presumed to be written into the Fourteenth Amendment's prohibition of the deprivation of life, liberty, and property without due process of law, was applied with uncompromising rigor by jurists like Justice Stephen J. Field. Third, the principle that the acquisition of wealth was a mark of divine favor, and that the rich therefore had a moral responsibility both to get richer and to direct the affairs of society. Fourth, perhaps most persuasive of all, was the pseudo-scientific principle of 'the survival of the fittest,' derived from Darwinian biology and applied to the affairs of mankind by the English philosopher Herbert Spencer and his many American disciples. All this added up to the conclusion that America itself was a business civilization—and should be kept that way.

21
Workers and Immigrants

1865–1920

The Machine Tenders

During most of the nineteenth century the benefits of the mechanization of industry redounded to the advantage of society as a whole, but more especially to capital than to labor. Machinery made enormous savings in manufacturing costs, but only a small proportion of these savings was passed on to workers in the form of higher wages, and the decrease in hours of labor did not keep pace with the gains in productivity. In addition the workingman suffered from the fatigue and nervous strain of monotonous machine labor which devalued the experience of the skilled worker by eroding the creative instinct of craftsmanship.

As machinery represented a large part of capital investment, it was thought necessary to accommodate the worker to machinery rather than machinery to the worker. If efficiency required that machines be run twenty-four hours a day and seven days a week, workers were expected to adjust themselves. Furthermore machinery constituted a fixed capital charge which could not well

be reduced; when economies were necessary there was a temptation to effect them at the expense of labor. The introduction of machinery also resulted in throwing laborers out of work. While most were eventually absorbed in other industries, and while in the long run mechanization more than balanced losses in factory jobs by the growth of clerical and service positions, the process worked severe hardship on the individual employee. Moreover, the increasing efficiency of machinery sometimes resulted in the production of more commodities than the public could or cared to buy, leading to unemployment and lower wages. Industrial unemployment, a product of the machine age, grew proportionately with the development of the machine economy.

The rise of the giant corporation had consequences for labor almost as serious as those which flowed from mechanization. The fiction that a corporation was a person had a certain legal usefulness, but every worker knew that the distinguishing characteristic of a corporation was its impersonality. A person was responsible for his

'Bell-Time.' Winslow Homer's 1868 drawing shows workers, carrying their lunch buckets, streaming out of the mills in Lawrence, Massachusetts, at 7 p.m. at the end of a thirteen-hour day that began before dawn. Notice the range of ages and the large proportion of female employees. (*Library of Congress*)

acts to his own conscience; a corporation was responsible to its stockholders. As individuals, corporation directors might be willing to make concessions to labor, even at personal sacrifice; but as directors their first duty was to maintain dividends.

The change from individual employer to mammoth corporation sharply lessened the worker's bargaining power. It was one thing for an iron-puddler in the mid-nineteenth century to strike a bargain about wages and hours with the owner of a small ironworks; it was a very different thing for a 'roller' in the twentieth century to negotiate with the United States Steel Corporation. Theodore Roosevelt put the matter clearly:

The old familiar relations between employer and employee were passing. A few generations before, the boss had known every man in his shop; he called his men Bill, Tom, Dick, John; he inquired after their wives and babies; he swapped jokes and stories and perhaps a bit of tobacco with them. In the small establishment there had been a friendly human relationship between employer and employee.

There was no such relation between the great railway magnates, who controlled the anthracite industry, and the one hundred and fifty thousand men who worked in

374

'Steel Workers—Noontime.' This study by Thomas Anshutz, dated at about 1882, is said to be the first 'labor' painting in America. Anshutz, a pupil of Thomas Eakins, succeeded his mentor as director of the Pennsylvania Academy. Like Eakins, he anticipated twentieth-century artists in portraying urban America.

their mines, or the half million women and children who were dependent upon these miners for their daily bread. Very few of these mine workers had ever seen, for instance, the president of the Reading Railroad. . . . Another change . . . was a crass inequality in bargaining relation between the employer and the individual employee standing alone. The great coal-mining and coal-carrying companies, which employed their tens of thousands, could easily dispense with the services of any particular miner. The miner, on the other hand, could not dispense with the companies. He needed a job; his wife and children would starve if he did not get one. What the miner had to sell—his labor— was a perish-

able commodity; the labor of today—if not sold—was lost forever. Moreover, his labor was not like most commodities—a mere thing; it was part of a living, breathing human being. The workman saw that the labor problem was not only an economic but also a moral, a human problem.[1]

When in response to this situation laborers organized, giant corporations could afford to fight a strike for months, import strike-breakers, hire

1. *Theodore Roosevelt: An Autobiography*, Scribners, pp. 470–71.

Pinkerton detectives, carry their battle through the courts with highly paid lawyers, buy the press and influence politicians, and, if necessary, close down their plants and starve the workers into submission. In some places—Southern textile towns, Appalachian mining communities, lumber camps—industrial feudalism reigned. In 1914 a United States congressman testified that he had to have a pass to enter a Colorado town situated on the property of the Colorado Fuel and Iron Company.

The late nineteenth century had a double standard of social morality for labor and capital. Combination of capital was regarded as in accordance with natural laws; combination of labor as a conspiracy. Government had a duty to protect corporation interests, but government aid to labor was socialism. Appeals to enhance property interests were reasonable, appeals to protect labor interests demagogic. The use of Pinkerton detectives to protect business property was preserving law and order, but the use of force to protect the job was violence.

Corporations benefited, too, from widespread disapproval of the very idea of unionization, for in a land of equal opportunity, there were not and never would be classes, and any laboring man could rise by his own efforts. Even so openminded a man as President Eliot of Harvard could assert that the closed shop was un-American, and in 1886 the New York banker, Henry Clews, identified the strike with treason. 'Strikes may have been justifiable in other nations,' he said, 'but they are not justifiable in our country. The Almighty has made this country for the oppressed of other nations, and therefore this is the land of refuge . . . and the hand of the laboring man should not be raised against it.'

The Rise of Organized Labor

American labor failed to build a successful union movement during the years following the Civil War largely because it was unable to agree about the nature of industrial society. Throughout the nineteenth century and well into the twentieth, labor debated whether to accept or reject capitalism, whether to trust laissez-faire or seek government patronage, whether to organize on a broadly industrial or on a narrow craft basis, whether to embrace unskilled as well as skilled, black as well as white workers. Two rival approaches—reform unionism and trade unionism—vied for the allegiance of the workingman. The reform unionists rejected the factory system, with its division of labor and its sharp differentiation of interests of employer and employee, and sought to restore a society which valued the independent artisan. Determined not to become machine tenders assigned to a small part of the process of production, they strove to preserve their status as craftsmen. To safeguard equality of opportunity, they fought those forces of monopoly, especially in finance, which they believed aimed to shackle the worker. They viewed themselves as members of a 'producer class' which embraced master as well as journeyman, farmer as well as artisan. Yet as early as 1850, when the National Typographical Union was founded, some workers had abandoned the hope of escaping the factory system, or of becoming entrepreneurs, and accepted their role as wage-earners. Instead of looking for ways to be self-employed, they organized trade unions to bargain with employers, whose interests, they recognized, differed from their own. At the outset, the reform unionists had the larger following, but as the factory system colonized the city and the countryside, the trade union analysis came to seem more appropriate.

In 1866, under the guidance of William Sylvis of the iron molders, labor leaders set up the first national labor federation in America—the National Labor Union. Although it welcomed trade unions, the National Labor Union reflected the reform unionist outlook, for it included various middle-class reform organizations, including women's suffrage leagues. Moreover, it was hostile to the strike weapon and experimented with co-operatives as an alternative to the wage system. The National Labor Union also plunged into politics; in 1872, it sponsored the country's first national labor party, the Labor Reform party. But when both presidential and vice-presidential candidates turned down the nominations, the Labor Reform party looked ridiculous; that same year, the National Labor Union collapsed.

The fiasco of the Labor Reform party proved to

be only the first in a series of such episodes. In 1876, when Eastern labor reformers joined with Midwestern soft money men to create the National Independent party, more popularly known as the Greenback party, they chose, as their presidential candidate, Peter Cooper, who suffered the handicap of being 85 years old, and who attracted almost no working-class votes. In 1880, the Greenback-Labor party nominee, James Baird Weaver of Iowa, found little support in the factory towns of the industrial Northeast. In 1884, reform unionists sank to nominating the notorious Ben Butler on an Anti-Monopoly party ticket, although Butler may well have been in the race as an agent of the Republicans. Trade unionists concluded from these disasters that the attempts of reform unionists to find political solutions for the workers' problems were doomed to failure.

By far the most important organization of reform unionism was the Noble Order of the Knights of Labor, founded in 1869 by a Philadelphia tailor, Uriah S. Stephens, a Mason with a smattering of Greek who contributed his knowledge of ritual to the secret order. Native American in leadership and largely in personnel, it attempted to unite workers into one big union, under centralized control. Membership was open to men and women, white and black, skilled and unskilled, laborers and capitalists, merchants and farmers. Only liquor dealers, professional gamblers, lawyers, and bankers were excluded!

The growth of the Knights of Labor was phenomenal. When a Pennsylvania machinist, Terence V. Powderly, became Grand Master in 1878, the membership was under 50,000. A vain man, Powderly acted 'like Queen Victoria at a national Democratic convention.' Opposed to the tactics of combative unionism, he said: 'Strikes are a failure. Ask any old veteran in the labor movement and he will say the same. I shudder at the thought of a strike, and I have good reason.' Powderly emphasized co-operatives, and even more the land question, because 'we must free the land and give men the chance to become their own employers.' Yet under his leadership the Order made spectacular gains, especially after it shed its secrecy and thus overcame the hostility of the Catholic Church, and, ironically, after it won a great railroad strike on the Gould lines in the Southwest in 1885. Capital then, for the first time, met labor on equal terms, when the financier, Jay Gould, conferred with the Knights' leaders and conceded their demands. The prestige of this victory lifted the Order's membership to over 700,000 the following year, an increment of more than half a million members in 14 months.

In May 1886 local units of the Knights took part in a strike for the eight-hour day, which inadvertently associated the Order with violence. On 3 May Chicago police killed and wounded half a dozen labor demonstrators. The following day when the police broke up a protest meeting at Haymarket Square, someone threw a bomb into their midst; seven persons were killed and over sixty injured. Though the actual perpetrator of the outrage could not be found, a Cook County judge held that those who incited the deed were equally guilty with those who committed it. Under this ruling the jury found eight anarchists guilty of murder and sentenced one to imprisonment and seven to death. Of these seven, one committed suicide, four were executed, and the other two had their sentences commuted to life imprisonment. Six years later Governor John Peter Altgeld, alleging that 'the judge conducted the trial with malicious ferocity,' pardoned the three anarchists still in prison. Although these men were clearly innocent, Altgeld was denounced as an aider and abetter of anarchy. The Knights of Labor was in no way responsible for the Haymarket massacre and Powderly had even attempted to disassociate the Order from the eight-hour movement, but the revulsion against radicals embraced the Knights too. Indiscriminate strikes, all failures, mismanagement by Powderly, and the difficulty of holding skilled and unskilled labor in the same union also made serious inroads. By the end of the decade membership in the Order had dwindled to about 100,000, and the Knights soon all but disappeared.

As the Knights of Labor declined, its place in the van of the labor movement was usurped by a new organization, the American Federation of Labor. This body, which was to dominate the labor scene for the next half-century, rejected the idea of one big union in favor of craft unions of skilled workers. The two organizations differed in other respects as well: where the K. of L. had been idealistic and vague in its aims, the A.F. of L. was opportunistic and practical; where the old Order embraced farmer-labor parties and theoretically discouraged strikes, the new organization abjured third parties and relied on the strike and the boycott. The Knights had looked forward to a co-operative republic of workers, whereas the Federation accepted capitalism and chose to work within the established economic order.

The A.F. of L. issued from the brain of a foreign-born worker. In the late 'sixties a bullet-headed young man named Samuel Gompers, a London-born Jew of Flemish ancestry, was working in a highly unsanitary cigar-making shop in the Lower East Side, and speaking at union meetings. As he rose in the councils of his fellow workers, Gompers determined to divorce unionism from independent political action, which dissipated its energy, and from radicalism, which aroused the fear of the public and the fury of the police. By 1881 he and other local labor leaders had thought their way through to a national federation of craft unions, and five years later the A.F. of L. was established. Animated by the philosophy of the job, the Federation concentrated on tangible objectives like shorter hours and better wages. 'We have no ultimate ends,' testified one of Gompers's co-workers. 'We are going on from day to day. We are fighting only for immediate objects—objects that can be realized in a few years.'

By the turn of the century the A.F. of L. boasted a membership of over half a million; by 1914 it would reach 2 million. This rapid growth was in great part due to the leadership of Gompers who for 40 years guided its destiny, impressed it with his personality, permeated it with his ideas, inspired it with his stubborn courage, and held it steadily to the course of aggressive self-interest. The A.F. of L. opposed creating a separate labor party nor would it divide its ranks by giving allegiance to either of the major parties. Instead, it used its power to persuade legislators to adopt specific demands and judged them accordingly. It hewed to a simple line: 'Reward your friends and punish your enemies.' Nor did the A.F. of L. ever try to organize the great mass of unskilled workers in the factories.

The void was only partially filled by ragged unions that sprang up in the turbulent mining camps of the West and eventually coalesced in 1905 into the Industrial Workers of the World, the first labor organization formally committed to class warfare. The I.W.W. (or 'Wobblies,' as they came to be known) set out to organize the migratory farm workers of the Great Plains, lumbermen of the Far Northwest, copper miners in Arizona, and dock hands along the Pacific waterfront. In 1912 it ventured east to take charge of a textile strike in Lawrence, Massachusetts, where mill-owners had slashed wages. It won this strike, as well as an astonishingly large number of others. But when its activities threatened to interfere with the war in 1917 and 1918, it was destroyed.

Industrial Conflict

As labor shifted its objectives from social reform to the job, it resorted with increasing frequency to the strike and the boycott, and business retaliated with the lockout, the blacklist, the injunction, and company police or the National Guard. The result was uninterrupted industrial conflict, often violent, that assumed the ominous character of warfare.

The great majority of strikes after the 1870's involved hours or wages. As late as 1910, only 8 per cent of industrial workers were on an eight-hour day. In many industries hours were shockingly long: steel had a twelve-hour day and a seven-day week, a schedule maintained for many steel workers until 1923. Hours in textiles ranged from 60 to 84 a week, even for women and little children, who constituted a large part of the working force. Furthermore, from 1880 to 1910 the unskilled laborer commonly earned less than $10 a week and the skilled worker rarely more than $20, while earnings of women ranged from $3.93 a week in Richmond to $6.91 in San Francisco. During the whole of this 30-year period the average annual family income of industrial workers was never more than $650, or of farm laborers more than $400, sums considerably below a decent living standard. Moreover, unemployment averaged 10 per cent and was often higher, and even those employed rarely enjoyed continuous work, at a

The Great Strike of 1877. An angry mob watches Pittsburgh's Union Depot and Hotel go up in flames. Many workingmen and militia lost their lives in civil strife in which rioters raided the armory of the Pittsburgh militia, stole a cannon, marched on the gunshops, and set fires that razed large quantities of railroad property and nearly levelled the city. (*Library of Congress*)

time when with the growth of cities the vegetable garden, fruit trees, chicken-coop, and family cow disappeared.

The first great industrial conflict came in 1877 when the Eastern trunk railroads jauntily announced a wage-cut of 10 per cent, the second since the panic of 1873. Without adequate organization railway employees struck, and with the support of a huge army of hungry and desperate unemployed, the strike flared up into something that seemed to respectable folk like rebellion. During one week in July traffic was entirely suspended on the trunk lines, and every large industrial center was in turmoil. In Baltimore, Pittsburgh, Chicago, Buffalo, San Francisco, and elsewhere, there were battles between militia and the mob, and order was restored only by federal troops. Pittsburgh was terrorized for three days; fatalities ran into the scores, and a wall of three miles of flame destroyed every railroad car, including 160 locomotives, and every railroad building, and almost levelled the city.

Not until 1892 was the nation again to witness so menacing an outbreak. That year a strike in the Homestead works of the Carnegie Steel Company culminated in a pitched battle between infuriated strikers and an army of Pinkerton detectives hired by the president of the Carnegie Company, Henry C. Frick. The strikers won the sanguinary battle, but the attempted murder of Frick alienated public opinion and militia broke the backbone of the strike.

Two years later a strike erupted against the Pullman Palace Car Company in the model town of Pullman, Illinois. The strike resulted originally from the arbitrary refusal of Mr. Pullman to discuss grievances with representatives of his employees, but it came eventually to involve far larger issues. The cause of the Pullman workers was taken up by the American Railway Union, a powerful body under the leadership of the magnetic Eugene V. Debs. When this union voted to boycott all Pullman cars, the cause of the Pullman Company was championed by the newly organized General Managers' Association of Railroads. The result was paralysis of transportation throughout the North and widespread disorder. The railroads succeeded in enlisting the sympathies of President Cleveland and Attorney-General Olney, a former railroad lawyer. On 1 July, Olney appointed as special counsel for the United States a prominent railway attorney, at whose suggestion the federal circuit court at Chicago served on the officers of the American Railway Union a 'blanket injunction' against obstructing the railroads and holding up the mails. Hooligans promptly ditched a mail train and took possession of strategic points in the switching yards. Cleveland declared that he would use every dollar in the Treasury and every soldier in the army if necessary to deliver a single postcard in Chicago. On 4 July he ordered a regiment of regulars to the city. The effect was like that of sending British regulars to Boston in 1768.

Cleveland's antagonist in this conflict was not so much Debs as Governor John P. Altgeld. This honest and fearless statesman had already been marked for destruction by big business because he had helped Jane Addams to obtain factory regulations in Illinois and because he had pardoned the Haymarket prisoners. During the Pullman strike Altgeld was ready and able to maintain law and order with state militia. But his eloquent protest against gratuitous interference by the Federal Government and his demand for the withdrawal of U.S. troops were cavalierly disregarded. When Debs defied the injunction, he was given six months' imprisonment for contempt of court. By early August the strike was smashed.

The Supreme Court of the United States, to which Debs appealed his sentence, upheld the government, declaring that even in the absence of statutory law it had a dormant power to brush away obstacles to interstate commerce—an implied power that would have made Hamilton and Marshall gasp. Yet the whole affair was not without a certain educational value. Debs, in his prison cell, studied socialism and in time became the organizer and leader of the Socialist party; the workers learned the real meaning of the Sherman Anti-Trust Act; business awoke to the potentialities of the injunction; and the country at large was taught a new interpretation of the sovereign powers of the Federal Government. Only George Pullman emerged innocent of new ideas.

Scarcely less spectacular than the Pullman strike was the outbreak in Pennsylvania's anthracite coal fields in 1902. In 1898 the youthful John Mitchell had become president of the United Mine Workers, which then numbered some 40,000 members. Within two years he whipped it into shape, invaded the anthracite fields, where the railways controlled the operators, and wrested favorable terms from the powerful coal companies of eastern Pennsylvania. Two years later the operators abrogated this agreement, and the miners struck for recognition of their union, a nine-hour day, and a wage rise. For four tense months the strike dragged on while the strikers maintained an unbroken front. In the course of this struggle President George F. Baer of the Philadelphia and Reading Railroad announced that 'the rights and interests of the laboring man will be protected and cared for, not by the labor agitators, but by the Christian men to whom God in His infinite wisdom, has given control of the property interests of the country.' In October, with both a congressional election and a coal-less winter looming, Roosevelt brought pressure on miners and operators to arbitrate. The miners were willing, but not Mr. Baer, who rebuked the President for 'negotiating with the fomenters of anarchy.' Outraged, Roosevelt threatened to take over the mines and run them with militia. This

The Ludlow Massacre. In the winter of 1913–14 miners at the Rockefeller-owned Colorado Fuel and Iron Company in Ludlow, Colo., walked out of the pits and, abandoning the oppressive company town, set up tent colonies with their families. The worst episode of the prolonged and violent strike came when state militia machine-gunned the tent colony and set it afire; two women and eleven children burned to death or suffocated. (*State Historical Society of Colorado*)

threat, and the force of public opinion, persuaded the mine-owners to arbitrate, and the strike ended in a signal victory for the miners, enhancement of the prestige of John Mitchell and of President Roosevelt, and a triumph for the cause of arbitration.

Labor unrest in the coal industry was chronic. The murderous activities of the Molly Maguires in the eastern Pennsylvania coal fields in the early 'seventies had given the first premonition of class warfare. In 1903–04 came a violent outbreak in the Rockefeller-owned coal fields of Colorado which was crushed by the military. Ten years later the United Mine Workers tried to unionize the Colorado Fuel and Iron Company; armed guards broke up the miners' camps, and the militia attacked a tent village in the 'Ludlow massacre,' which took the lives of several men, women, and children. The ensuing battle between outraged miners and soldiers plunged parts of Colorado into something like civil war, aroused nation-wide sympathy for the strikers, and led, eventually, to far-reaching reforms.

Labor Legislation and the Courts

Until the 1930's American social legislation lagged a generation behind that of European states like Denmark and Germany and such Commonwealth nations as Australia and New Zealand, for the role of the Federal Government was sharply circumscribed. Yet as early as 1868 Congress established an eight-hour day on public works, and in 1892 an eight-hour day for all government employees; the Adamson Act of 1916 extended this boon to all railway workers. In 1898 Congress passed the Erdman Act providing for arbitration of labor disputes on interstate carriers, and in 1908 an Employers' Liability Act, likewise confined to railway employees. A Bureau of Labor, created in 1884, was elevated to cabinet rank in 1913. The La Follette Seaman's Act of 1915 gave seamen for the first time the full status of free men. Twice Congress attempted to outlaw child labor—in 1916 under the guise of a regulation of commerce, and again in 1919 through the medium of taxation, but both laws were nullified by the Court.

Before the 1930's, most social legislation lay in the domain of the states, but progressive reforms ran the constant danger of judicial nullification. It is forbidden in most state constitutions and in the Fourteenth Amendment to deprive persons of liberty or property without due process of law. As no reform can be effected without depriving someone of something he may deem a liberty or a property right, American courts (following English precedents) early elaborated the doctrine of a superior 'police power'—the reserved right of the state to protect the people's health, safety, morals, and welfare. However, when labor laws began to appear on the statute books, corporation lawyers persuaded courts that such laws were not a proper exercise of the police power but a violation of the 'due process' clause of the Fourteenth Amendment.

For half a century after Reconstruction judges such as Field and Sutherland, and their disciples in the state courts, turned the bench into a dike against the surging tides of welfare legislation. They interpreted the Constitution as a prohibition rather than an instrument, and, insisting that they were without discretion and that their functions were purely mechanical, struck down hundreds of state police laws. In truth, the judges were writing into law their fears that labor statutes constituted 'the first step towards socialism.' In 1913 Justice Holmes observed, 'When twenty years ago a vague terror went over the earth and the word socialism began to be heard, I thought and still think that fear was translated into doctrines that had no proper place in the Constitution or the common law.' In 1905 the Supreme Court drew a vigorous dissent from Holmes in *Lochner* v. *New York* when in a split decision it invalidated a New York law prescribing hours of labor in bakeries. 'The Fourteenth Amendment does not enact Mr. Herbert Spencer's *Social Statics*,' Holmes protested.

Yet the conservatives did not always prevail. As early as 1898 the Supreme Court, in *Holden* v. *Hardy*, accepted a Utah law limiting to eight the hours of labor in mines. An Oregon Act of 1903 limiting to ten the hours of employment for women was upheld by the Supreme Court in 1908 in the notable case of *Muller* v. *Oregon*—notable especially because the mass of sociological, economic, and physiological data introduced by the counsel for Oregon, Louis D. Brandeis, was admitted as evidence. Thus the principle was established that the courts could take cognizance of the circumstances that demonstrated the reasonableness of the exercise of the police power. Following Australian and British precedents, fifteen states, beginning with Massachusetts in 1912, enacted minimum wage laws for women and children, and in 1916 Brandeis and Felix Frankfurter persuaded the Supreme Court to accept the Oregon act.[2] Seven years later, however, in a remarkable reversal, the Court, in the *Adkins* case, found a District of Columbia minimum wage law unconstitutional, and on this rock of judicial intransi-

2. *Stettler* v. *O'Hara* 243 U.S. 629 (1916). On this case the Court divided four to four, thus sustaining the act.

gence the campaign for minimum wage legislation was temporarily grounded.

In no other industrial nation were the hazards of industry so great. In 1917 fatal accidents in manufacturing establishments amounted to 11,338 and non-fatal to the astonishing total of 1,363,080. Statutes required the installation of safety devices and provided for sanitary and fire inspection, but not until inspection was entrusted to civil servants was there any perceptible improvement. To secure compensation for the injured or incapacitated victims, it was necessary to get rid of the monstrous common law doctrines which stipulated that if the worker had willingly assumed the risks of his job, if his accident resulted from his own negligence or that of a fellow worker, the company was not responsible. Alone of major industrial nations the United States lacked workmen's compensation legislation at the turn of the century. Congress provided workmen's compensation for interstate railroad workers, but when the states enacted similar laws, the courts declared them void. Not until 1917 when the Supreme Court sustained New York's new compensation act were the states able to go ahead. Within a few years most states outside the South had legislated workmen's compensation. Advanced European countries also provided unemployment and old-age pension programs, but here, too, the United States lagged behind. Although a few companies experimented with pension plans and Wisconsin adopted pathbreaking unemployment insurance, not until the New Deal did the nation begin to take appropriate action.

A Nation of Nations

Unionists viewed with alarm the tidal wave of immigration which spilled almost 18 million persons on American shores in the single generation from 1880 to 1910. When unions attempted to organize these 'new' immigrants, as the United Mine Workers did, they succeeded. But in part because of ethnic and religious antagonisms, partly because much of organized labor was by this time committed to the craft principle, most unions made no serious effort to enlist the immigrants. Almost inevitably labor experienced its most serious difficulties in those industries where

the proportion of foreign-born workers was highest—meat-packing, iron and steel, and mining. Although some of the most important labor leaders were foreign-born, many unions became champions of immigration restriction.

The transfer of peoples from the Old World to the New was the most extensive and successful experiment of its kind in history, carried out on a larger stage and over a longer period and with fewer convulsive reactions than any comparable enterprise. The disruptive agricultural revolution in Europe, persistent poverty for the peasants, recurrent hard times for workers, war and the constant threat of military service for young men, political oppression, religious persecution, a class system which closed the door of opportunity to the vast mass of the poor and denied education to their children—these were, for 200 years, the main motivations for the emigration of 40 million Europeans to the United States. As for the magnetic attraction of America, that is even more easily explained: open land, work for almost all who were willing to work, a higher standard of living for ordinary folk than was known in Europe, religious freedom, political democracy, greater social equality, a second chance for the young.

Men and women foregathered in the mill towns of Scotland or the fishing villages of Norway, or along the sanguinary banks of the Danube, to sing some new ballad about America or listen to the latest America-letter: in America you eat meat every day; in America you do not pull your forelock to the priest or take your hat off to the mayor—he takes his hat off to you; in America women do not work in the fields; in America all the children go to school; in America no one makes you serve in the army. When Andrew Carnegie was a little boy in Dumfermline, Scotland, he used to hear his father and mother sing

To the West, to the West, to the land of the free,
Where the mighty Missouri rolls down to the sea;
Where a man is a man if he's willing to toil,
And the humblest may gather the fruits of the soil;
Where children are blessings, and he who hath most
Has aid for his fortune and riches to boast.
Where the young may exult and the aged may rest,
Away, far away, to the land of the West.

It was this song that induced the elder Carnegie to

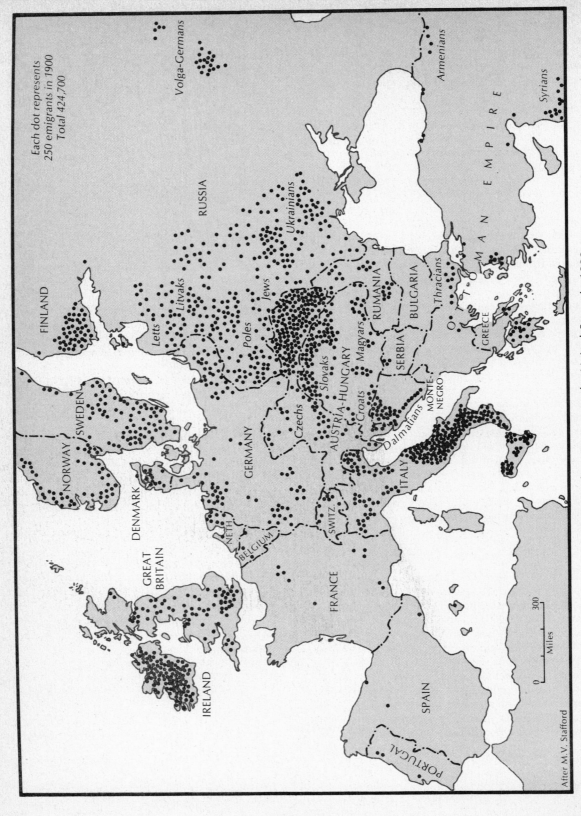

Each dot represents
250 emigrants in 1900
Total 424,700

Volga-Germans

Armenians

Syrians

O T T O M A N   E M P I R E

RUSSIA

Ukrainians

Thracians

FINLAND

Letts

Litvaks

Poles

Jews

BULGARIA

GREECE

RUMANIA

SERBIA

SWEDEN

NORWAY

Czechs

Slovaks

AUSTRIA-HUNGARY

Magyars

MONTE-
NEGRO

DENMARK

GERMANY

Croats

Dalmatians

ITALY

GREAT
BRITAIN

NETH.

BELGIUM

SWITZ.

IRELAND

FRANCE

PORTUGAL

SPAIN

300

Miles

0

After M. V. Stafford

Emigration from Europe to the United States in 1900

'In the Land of Promise—Castle Garden.' Charles Ulrich painted this scene of the entrance way for throngs of Hungarians, White Russians, Croats, and other 'New Immigrants' from the European continent in 1884. This picture has a saccharine quality typical of much of American art in the Gilded Age. (*Corcoran Gallery of Art*)

migrate to America, where his son amassed a fortune.

In the three-quarters of a century after Appomattox some 33 million emigrants sought American shores, swarming out onto the rich prairie lands of the West, transforming the cities into enormous cosmopolitan beehives, performing the back-breaking labor that made possible the economic expansion of the nation, creating new problems of assimilation and adaptation, and bringing to the United States the richest cultural heritage vouchsafed any modern nation—though one all too often dissipated. After a century and a half of colonization and unprecedented natural increase, the population of the English colonies in America was but slightly over 2 millions; every decade from 1850 to 1930 witnessed an immigration large enough to replace this entire population.

In attempting to interpret the significance of the greatest folk movement in history, it may be well to dispose of certain misconceptions. Neither immigration nor racial heterogeneity is a recent development; immigration was as large, proportionately, in the later colonial period as in the latter part of the nineteenth century, and the population of the colonies on the eve of the Revolution, though predominantly English and African, represented six or seven nationalities and three or four languages. Nor was there ever any ground for fearing that the 'native stock' would succumb to the alien invasion. Despite the fecundity of many of the immigrant groups, the number of Americans of foreign or mixed parentage constituted only one-fifth of the population in 1920, and declined steadily thereafter. And though the number of foreign-born in the country more than doubled in the 50 years after 1880, so, too, did the population, and the foreign-born made up a smaller percentage of the population in 1930 than in 1880.

Of the 35 million who migrated to America between 1850 and 1930, the largest number were from the United Kingdom—some 8.5 million in all—of whom over 4.5 million came from Ireland. Germany accounted for approximately 6 million, Canada for almost 3 million, and the three Scandinavian countries for 2.25 million. The largest number of immigrants from northern and western Europe arrived in the generation immediately after the Civil War—there was a notable decline in immigration from Germany and the United Kingdom after 1890 and from Scandinavia after 1910.

The ingredients that made up the American population in 1870 did not differ markedly from those which had made up the population a century earlier, but in the 1870's there began to appear new types among the thousands who swarmed in at Castle Garden, New York: Austrians and Hungarians from the valley of the Danube, Bohemians from the river Moldau, Poles from the Vistula, and Serbs from the river Save, blue-eyed Italians from the banks of the Arno and olive-skinned Italians from the plains of Campania or the mountains of Sicily, Russian Jews from the Volga and the Dnieper and the steppes of Ukraine. By the 'eighties this trickle from southern and eastern Europe had become a stream, by the 'nineties a torrent, and in the early years of the new century a veritable flood. Altogether in the 50 years between 1880 and 1930, Italy sent over 4.5 million emigrants, Austria, Hungary, and the succession states over 4 million, Russia and Poland perhaps another 4 million—a total from these countries alone of 13 million. In 1860 southern and eastern Europe made up only 1 per cent of the foreign-born population; in 1910, 38 per cent. While the 'old' immigration was predominantly Protestant, the 'new' arrivals were for the most part Catholic, Greek Orthodox, or Jewish. The United States, in short, had become a much more heterogeneous country.

Immigrants from northern Europe tended to go west and take land. Though numbers of Germans congregated in cities such as Cincinnati, St. Louis, and Milwaukee, Norwegians and Swedes showed a marked tendency to go out to the land. The great agricultural states of Minnesota, Illinois, North and South Dakota, Nebraska, and Iowa still have substantial Scandinavian population, and Minnesota displays no less than 400 Swedish place names, while the influence of these industrious and intelligent farmers was felt south to Texas and west to California. However, most of the Irish remained in the cities of the Eastern seaboard, where their group loyalty and talent for politics in a democratic medium made them the first and most enduring of ethnic blocs in American politics.

Like the Irish, the immigrants from southern and eastern Europe chose the cities. Most of them were far too poor to buy a farm or invest in the machinery and stock necessary for modern agriculture, and peoples whose language, customs, and religion were very different from those of the older stock naturally tended to live together in colonies rather than isolate themselves on farms or in small towns. For many, too, migration to America was their urban movement—inspired by the same notions that took native Americans from the farms to the cities. In 1900 two-thirds and in 1930 three-fourths of the foreign-born were liv-

Immigrants arriving, New York harbor. This picture was taken about 1900 by Frances Benjamin Johnston, one of several distinguished women photographers whose work, long neglected, is now highly valued. (*Coll. Judith Mara Gutman*)

ing in towns and cities. The proportion of foreign-born in such large cities as New York and Detroit was impressive, but the concentration in the smaller industrial cities, such as Paterson, New Jersey, or Fall River, Massachusetts, was even more notable. American cities came to have their 'ghettos,' their 'little Italy' or their 'China-town,' and 'slum' became a familiar word in the American vocabulary. In 1890 two-thirds of the population of New York City was crowded into tenements. Desperately poor, without industrial or mechanical skills, the immigrants from southern and eastern Europe became, for the most part, unskilled laborers in mine, in factory, or on the railroad. Jews congregated in the garment trade, Finns in mining, Portuguese in the textile towns.

Two other groups of immigrants came in increasing numbers after the turn of the century: Canadians and Mexicans. It was easy for Canadians to drift into the United States, and after the

Civil War many found their way to northern New England, the Great Lakes states, and the Far Northwest. Canadian immigration first took on major proportions after 1910; in the next 20 years 1.5 million Canadians, one-third French and about two-thirds English-speaking, crossed the border, cementing the strong ties already binding the two neighboring democracies. The census of 1930 revealed that not far from 750,000 Mexicans were domiciled in the United States, the majority of them in the border states of Texas, New Mexico, Arizona, and California. For the most part poor and illiterate, these casual laborers worked under shocking conditions in the cotton, rice, and beet-sugar fields of Colorado and the Southwest.

Toward the assimilation of these millions of immigrants, the United States held inconsistent attitudes. The predominant expectation was that the newcomer, no matter what his place of origin, would conform to Anglo-Saxon patterns of behavior and cherish those institutions transported to the New World from the British Isles. Competing with this view was the conviction that in this hemisphere a new type was being fused out of a variety of ethnic elements. In 1845 Emerson predicted:

In this continent,—asylum of all nations,—the energy of Irish, Germans, Swedes, Poles, and Cossacks, and all the European tribes,—of the Africans, and of the Polynesians,— will construct a new race, a new religion, a new state, a new literature, which will be as vigorous as the new Europe which came out of the smelting-pot of the Dark Ages.

Still a third conception came from the experience of the settlement-house workers: respect for the cultural heritage of the new arrivals. Those who saw at first hand the tragic alienation of first from second generation Americans feared that attempts to 'Americanize' the immigrants would lead to ethnic self-hatred and would deprive the country of a variety of distinct cultural contributions.

Most newcomers were quick to abandon their Old World loyalties and profess those of the New. Everything conspired to root out old attachments and supplant them with new: the vastness of the country which broke up compact settlements; the economy which rewarded speedy acquisition of the American language; the political system which encouraged naturalization and voting; the habit of voluntary association which welcomed most newcomers into political parties, granges, and a hundred other organizations; and perhaps most effective of all, the public schools. The Russian Jew, Mary Antin, recalled:

Education was free. That subject my father had written about repeatedly, as comprising his chief hope for us children, the essence of American opportunity, the treasure that no thief could touch, nor even misfortune or poverty. It was the one thing that he was able to promise us when he sent for us; surer, safer than bread or shelter. On our second day I was thrilled with the realization of what this freedom of education meant. A little girl from across the alley came and offered to conduct us to school. My father was out, but we five between us had a few words of English by this time. We knew the word school. We understood. This child, who had never seen us till yesterday, who could not pronounce our names, who was not much better dressed than we were; was able to offer us the freedom of the schools of Boston! No application made, no questions asked, no examinations, rulings, exclusions; no machinations, no fees. The doors stood open for every one of us. The smallest child could show us the way.[3]

The immigrant contribution of muscle and brawn is obvious; the contribution to public affairs, industry and labor, science and education, arts and letters, is scarcely less apparent. To remember the achievements of Carl Schurz and John Peter Altgeld in politics, Jacob Riis in social reform, E. L. Godkin in journalism, Andrew Carnegie, James J. Hill, and Henry Villard in business, Samuel Gompers in unions, Alexander Graham Bell in the field of invention, Louis Agassiz in science, Augustus Saint-Gaudens in sculpture, and Jascha Heifetz in music, is to realize the extent to which the foreign-born have enriched American life.

Putting Up the Bars

Despite these contributions, many Americans took a hostile attitude toward the newcomers and demanded that immigration, especially of Orientals, be restricted or ended altogether. For well-

3. Mary Antin, *The Promised Land*, Houghton Mifflin Co.

nigh a century, Congress had left the regulation of immigration to the states, but in the 1880's it felt called upon to act, largely because California settlers expressed alarm over the mass migration of Chinese coolies. The discovery of gold in 1849 and the consequent demand for cheap labor had first brought the Chinese to California, and their numbers were augmented in the 'sixties by the demand for laborers on the Central Pacific Railroad; by the end of the 'seventies there were almost 150,000 Chinese in California alone. Their low standards of living, long hours of labor, and tractability were said to constitute a serious menace to native labor. At the same time they aroused racial prejudice by their exotic appearance, customs, religion, and language, and their obvious intention to return to China with their savings. As a result an anti-Chinese movement developed in the 'seventies under the leadership of an Irish agitator, Denis Kearney. Taken up by the California Workingmen's party, it culminated in discriminatory legislation and a demand for the prohibition of further Oriental immigration. In response to this demand Congress, in 1882, enacted a law excluding Chinese laborers for a period of ten years—a prohibition that was extended in 1890 and again in 1902 until it became permanent.

By then the West Coast was demanding that the policy of exclusion be extended to embrace the Japanese, who arrived in large numbers in the first decade of the twentieth century. To avoid an international crisis, President Roosevelt, in 1907, reached a 'gentlemen's agreement' with the Japanese government whereby it pledged itself to continue 'the existing policy of discouraging emigration of its subjects of the laboring classes to continental United States.' Despite this agreement a small stream of Japanese continued to trickle in, and between 1911 and 1913 California and other Western states enacted a series of laws designed to prevent Japanese from owning or even leasing real estate. In 1924 Congress went out of its way to ban Japanese immigration completely, a deliberate affront to a wartime ally. 'Our friends in the Senate have in a few minutes spoiled the work of years,' said Secretary of State Charles Evans Hughes, 'and done lasting injury to our

common country.' By its long record of racial prejudice, segregation in schools, prohibition of land-holding, and discrimination in immigration, the United States managed to stockpile for itself a formidable arsenal of ill-will among the Japanese people.

Once embarked upon a policy of regulation, Congress faced two basic alternatives: selection or exclusion. The first general immigration law, that of 1882, was based upon the theory of selection; it imposed a head tax of 50 cents on each immigrant admitted, and excluded convicts, idiots, and persons likely to become public charges. From this time on a long series of federal acts elaborated the policy of selection; Congress increased the head tax, prohibited contract labor, and considerably extended the classes excluded. The new statutes excluded the sick and diseased, paupers, polygamists, prostitutes, anarchists, alcoholics, and—by the Act of 1917—persons with constitutional inferiority complexes!

Though this policy of selection afforded protection against some unwelcome additions to the population, it made no response to the rising clamor for a plan designed to reduce the total number who would be admitted and to select those thought to be best. Agitation came from three disparate groups. First, and most powerful, was organized labor, which had long looked upon the immigration of unskilled workers as a major threat. Second were social reformers who had come to the conclusion that there could be no solution of the problems of slums, public health, and the exploitation of the poor as long as illiterate immigrants poured into the great cities. Third were the traditionalists who had been taken in by the doctrines of Nordic supremacy and who deplored the

> Accents of menace alien to our air,
> Voices that once the Tower of Babel knew.[4]

The criterion of selection was to be literacy, and an historic battle was waged over this issue. A bill incorporating a literacy test passed one of the two Houses of Congress no less than 32 times, and on four occasions it was approved by both Houses and

4. Thomas Bailey Aldrich, 'Unguarded Gates.'

went to the President, only to be vetoed each time. In 1917, however, a bill was enacted over Wilson's veto. By its terms no alien over 16 years of age who could not read English or some other language was to be admitted to the United States. Since in the first decade of the century less than 3 per cent of the 'old' immigrants were illiterate, but over half of those from Sicily and southern Italy, the literacy test provided a method of discrimination on ethnic lines.

After the First World War a new wave of immigration led Congress to abandon the policy of selection for one of absolute restriction. By the Immigration Act of 1921, the number of aliens admitted from any European, Australasian, Near Eastern, or African country[5] was to be limited to 3 per cent of the total number of that nationality residing in the United States in 1910, a system designed to reduce the proportion of immigrants from southern and eastern Europe. The act also severely restricted the total number that could be admitted in any one year. In 1924 Congress

5. The Act of 1917 created a Barred Zone, including India, Siam, Indo-China, and other parts of Asia, from which no immigrants were to be admitted.

framed a new law which provided for parcelling out the immigration quotas from the various European countries in proportion to the 'national origins' of the American people. Immigration from Western Hemisphere nations was left undisturbed, except by a Department of Labor ruling that no immigrants should be admitted who might become public charges.

The enactment of the first quota law of 1921 ended an era. In a hundred years the tide of immigration had risen to a flood, engulfing the whole country and depositing millions of people from every land and the cultural accretions of centuries. Then suddenly it ebbed. The Statue of Liberty still stood guard over New York harbor, its beacon light held proudly aloft, the inscription on its base not yet erased:

Give me your tired, your poor,
Your huddled masses yearning to breathe free,
The wretched refuse of your teeming shore,
Send these, the homeless, tempest-tost to me:
I lift my lamp beside the golden door.

But it was a symbol of things strange, and faintly remembered.

22

The Passing of the Frontier

1865–1890

The Last West

The roaring vitality, the cascading energy of the American people in the postwar years, is nowhere better illustrated than in the history of the West. The generation after the Civil War witnessed the most extensive movement of population in our history; a doubling of the settled area; rapid transition from primitive society to contemporary civilization; the subjugation of the Indian; the rise and fall of the mineral empire and of the cattle kingdom; the emergence of new types of economic life articulated to the geography of the High Plains and the Rocky Mountains; and the organization of a dozen new states with a taste for political experiment.

The most notable of these developments was the conquest of the Great Plains—that region extending from about longitude 98 to the Rocky Mountains, and from Texas to the Canadian border. This vast area, comprising roughly one-fifth of the United States, had long interposed a hazardous barrier to settlement. In the 1840's the frontier had reached the edge of the Plains. Then, instead of moving progressively westward as it had always done, the frontier leaped 1500 miles to the Pacific coast. For 30 years the intervening territory was practically uninhabited except by Indians and Mormons; not until the decade of the 'seventies did settlers begin to close in on the Plains and Mountain regions; then the process went on with unprecedented rapidity until by 1890 the frontier line had been erased.

The environment of the Great Plains required a radical readjustment. Here was an immense grassland, sparsely wooded, with few navigable streams, and with a rainfall seldom sufficient for farming as practiced in the East. When pioneer farmers tried to apply here the experience they had gained and the tools they had developed in the wooded East, they failed. Before white settlers could establish themselves permanently on the Plains, four things were necessary: the suppression of the Indian; new methods of farming to cope with inadequate rainfall; a substitute for traditional wooden fencing; and transportation to take the crops to market. The army and the destruction of the buffalo undid the Indian; barbed wire solved the fencing problem; the windmill, dry farming, and irrigation went far to overcome the effect of insufficient rainfall and intermittent droughts; and the railroad furnished transportation. In the course of this arduous struggle with the Plains environment, the miner, the cattleman, and the farmer evolved institutions that differed markedly from those which had obtained in the woodlands of the East—a modification not only of the tools and methods of farming, but of social attitudes, economic concepts, and political and legal institutions as well.

The Railway Key

For almost fifty years after the Civil War the railroad dominated industry and politics. There were 35,000 miles of steam railway in 1865, practically all east of the Mississippi; during the next eight years the country doubled its rail network. By 1900, with just under 200,000 miles, the United States had a greater railway mileage than all Europe. Railroad expansion touched American life at countless points. It closely interacted with western migration, with iron and steel, and with agriculture; it greased the way for big business and high finance, helped pollute politics, and gave birth to new problems of constitutional law and government policy. By widening the market for manufactured goods, it helped trigger a revolution in the economy.

Immediately after the war came mechanical improvements such as the coal-burning expansion-cylinder locomotive, the Pullman sleeping car (1864), and the safety coupler. The Westinghouse air brake (1869) did more than any other invention to transform the original string of boxes on tracks into the modern train and to make possible safe operation at high speeds. But it was the old wood-burning, spark-belching 'bullgine,' gay with paint and sporting a name instead of a number, tugging unvestibuled coaches with swaying kerosene lamps and quid-bespattered wood stoves, which first wheezed across the Great Divide and linked the Atlantic to the Pacific.

On 1 July 1862 President Lincoln signed the first Pacific Railway Act. This law provided for the construction of a transcontinental railroad by two corporations—the Union Pacific which would build westward from Council Bluffs, Iowa, and the Central Pacific, which was to build eastward from Sacramento, California. It pledged liberal aid in the form of alternate sections of public lands to the depth of ten miles (and later twenty) on either side of the road, and loans ranging from $16,000 to $48,000 for every mile of track completed. Active construction, which began in 1865, confronted almost insuperable obstacles, including the constant struggle with mountain blizzard and desert heat, and—in the mountains—with the Indians as well. That the obstacles were overcome must be attributed not only to the indomitable perseverance of engineers like the U.P.'s General Grenville Dodge and of entrepreneurs like the C.P.'s Collis Huntington but also to the endurance of the thousands of laborers—ex-soldiers, Irish immigrants, and Chinese coolies—upon whose brawny shoulders the heaviest part of the task rested.

When I think [wrote Robert Louis Stevenson] of how the railroad has been pushed through this unwatered wilderness and haunt of savage tribes . . . ; how at each stage of construction, roaring, impromptu cities full of gold and lust and death sprang up and then died away again, and are now but wayside stations in the desert; how in these uncouth places pigtailed Chinese pirates worked side by side with border ruffians and broken men from Europe, talking together in a mixed dialect mostly oaths, . . . how the plumed hereditary lord of all America heard in this last fastness the scream of the 'bad medicine wagon' charioting his foes; and then when I go on to remember that all this epical turmoil was conducted by gentlemen in frocked coats, and to nothing more extraordinary than a fortune and a subsequent visit to Paris, it seems to me . . . as if this railway were the one typical achievement of the age in which we live.[1]

Both the Union and the Central Pacific roads were pushed forward in record time, 20,000 laborers laying as much as eight miles of track a day in the last stages of the race. When, amidst universal rejoicing, the two sets of rails were joined with a golden spike at Promontory Point, Utah, 10 May 1869, the Union Pacific was regarded as the winner, but the Central Pacific promoters had made enough to enable them to buy the state government of California.

Within a few years Congress chartered and endowed with enormous land grants three other

1. *Across the Plains*, pp. 50–52.

'The First Transcontinental Train Leaving Sacramento, California—May 1869.'
This rare example of Western folk art, painted by Joseph Becker in 1869, shows
snow still on the tracks, though the month is May, and Chinese workmen waving
the train through. The 'C.P.R.R.' on the coal car stands for Central Pacific
Railroad. (*The Thomas Gilcrease Institute of American History and Art, Tulsa*)

lines: (1) the Northern Pacific—from Lake
Superior across the Badlands of Dakota to the
headwaters of the Missouri, and by an intricate
route through the Rockies to the Columbia river
and Portland; (2) the Southern Pacific—from
New Orleans across Texas and through the territory of the Gadsden Purchase to Los Angeles, up
the San Joaquin valley to San Francisco; (3) the
Sante Fe—following closely the old Santa Fe Trail,
from Atchison, Kan., to Sante Fe and Albuquer-
que, through Apache and Navajo country and

across the Mojave desert to San Diego. By 1883 all
three links had reached the Pacific. Thus within 20
years of the Pacific railway legislation there were
four transcontinentals; a fifth, the Great Northern, was pressed through in the next decade by the
dynamic James J. Hill.

The transcontinental railways drastically altered population patterns in the West. At the
end of the Civil War, the Plains and the Rocky
Mountain regions were virtually unpeopled, and
the Overland Stage Line required at least five days

Slaughtering buffalo. This scene along the line of the Kansas-Pacific Railroad appeared in Frank Leslie's illustrated periodical in 1871. It has been estimated that sixty million bison roamed the land in 1800; by 1895, there were fewer than a thousand. (*Library of Congress*)

to transport passengers and mails from the Missouri river to Denver, where potatoes sold for $15 a bushel. The railways brought a dramatic change. They pushed out into the Plains far in advance of settlers, advertised for immigrants in the Eastern states and Europe, transported them at wholesale rates to the prairie railhead, and sold them land at from $1 to $10 an acre. Henry Villard of the

Northern Pacific employed almost a thousand agents in England and continental Europe, and the Union Pacific's advertising painted the Northwest in such roseate colors that U.P. lands were popularly known as Jay Cooke's banana belt. The Santa Fe Railroad attracted to Kansas, in 1874, 10,000 German Mennonites whose ancestors had colonized the Ukraine, and these brought with them not only piety and industry but the Red Turkey wheat which made Kansas prairies bloom like a garden. Thousands of section-hands entered a free homestead right, saved their wages to buy farm equipment and a team of horses, built a sodhouse or cabin, and became permanent settlers. The termini and eastern junction points of these lines—like Omaha, opposite the old Council Bluffs of the Indians; Kansas City, hard by the former jumping-off place for the Oregon Trail; Duluth, the 'Zenith City of the Unsalted Seas'; Oakland on San Francisco bay; Portland, Oregon; Seattle, Washington—places non-existent or mere villages before the Civil War—became in thirty years metropolitan cities.

The new Northwest was the domain of James J. Hill, the 'Empire Builder,' and the Great Northern Railway his path of empire. St. Paul was a small town on the edge of the frontier when he migrated thither from eastern Canada just before the Civil War, and Minneapolis a mere village at the Falls of St. Anthony on the Mississippi. Such importance as they had was due to their position at the end of a trail from the Red river of the North, which connected Winnipeg with the outside world. Long trains of two-wheeled ox-carts transported the peltry and supplies in 40 or 50 days' time. In the winter of 1870 Donald Smith, resident governor of the Hudson's Bay Company, started south from Winnipeg, and James J. Hill north from St. Paul, both in dog-sleds. They met on the prairie and made camp in a snowstorm; from that meeting sprang the Canadian Pacific and the Great Northern railways. In the panic of 1873 a little Minnesota railway with an ambitious name, the St. Paul and Pacific, went bankrupt. Hill watched it as a prairie wolf watches a weakening buffalo, and in 1878, in association with two Canadian railway men, wrested it from Dutch bondholders by a mere flotation of new securities.

The day of land grants and federal subsidies was past, and Hill saw that the Great Northern Railway, as he renamed his purchase, could reach the Pacific only by developing the country as it progressed. So he introduced scientific farming, distributed blooded bulls free to farmers, supported churches and schools, and assisted in countless ways the development of the communities of the 'Hill country.' In constructing his railroad Hill showed equal forethought and shrewdness, and by 1893 the Great Northern had reached tidewater at Tacoma. Ten years more, and Hill had acquired partial control of the Northern Pacific, had purchased joint control of a railway connecting its eastern termini with Chicago, and was running his own fleets of steamships from Duluth to Buffalo, and from Seattle to Japan and China.

The Indian Barrier

The Indians of the Great Plains and the Rocky Mountains, perhaps 225,000 in number, presented a formidable obstacle to white settlement. Strongest and most warlike were the Sioux, Blackfeet, Crow, Cheyenne, and Arapahoe in the north; the Comanche, Kiowa, Ute, Southern Cheyenne, Apache, and Southern Arapahoe in the south. Mounted on swift horses, admirably armed for Plains warfare, and living on the millions of buffalo that roamed the open range, these tribes for generations had successfully resisted white penetration.

The fate of the California Indians after the gold rush was prophetic of what was to happen elsewhere. There were 100,000 Indians in California in 1850, ten years later only 35,000; the Commissioner of Indian Affairs wrote that 'despoiled by irresistible forces of the land of their fathers; with no country on earth to which they can migrate; in the midst of a people with whom they cannot assimilate; they have no recognized claims upon the government and are compelled to become vagabonds—to steal or to starve.' The advance of the miners into the mountains, the building of the transcontinental railroads, and the invasion of the grasslands by cattlemen threatened other tribes with the same fate. Most serious was the wanton destruction of the buffalo, indispensable not only for food but for hides, bowstrings, lariats, fuel, and a score of other purposes. Scarcely less ruinous were two other developments: the perfection of the Colt repeating revolver, fearfully efficient in Plains warfare, and the spread of smallpox, cholera, and venereal diseases among the Indians.

The story of Indian relations from 1860 to 1887, the year of the passage of the Dawes Act, is a melancholy tale of intermittent and barbarous warfare, greed, corruption and maladministration, of alternating aggression and vacillation on the part of the whites, of courageous defense, despair, blind savagery, and inevitable defeat for the Indians. President Hayes observed in his annual message of 1877, 'Many, if not most, of our Indian wars have had their origin in broken promises and acts of injustice on our part.'

Until 1861 the Indians of the Plains had been relatively peaceful, but in that year the invasion of their hunting grounds by thousands of ruthless miners, and the advance of white settlers along the upper Mississippi and Missouri frontier, together with dissatisfaction at their treatment by the government and the breakdown of the reservation system, resulted in numerous minor conflicts. In 1862 the Sioux of the Dakota region devastated the Minnesota frontier and massacred and imprisoned almost a thousand white men, women, and children. Retribution was swift and terrible and fell indiscriminately upon the innocent and the guilty. For the next 25 years warfare was constant, each new influx of settlers driving the Indians to acts of desperation which brought on renewed outrage and punishment. In 1864 the Cheyenne, banished from their hunting grounds to the wastes of southeastern Colorado, attacked Ben Halliday's stages and harried mining settlements to the north; they were persuaded to abandon their depredations and concentrate at Indian posts, and at one of these posts Colonel Chivington ordered a savage slaughter of the Indian men, women, and children which sent a thrill of horror through the nation. General Nelson Miles called the Sand Creek Massacre the 'foulest and most unjustifiable crime in the annals of America,' but Denver hailed Chivington, a former Methodist minister, who exhibited his collection of a hundred scalps at a local theater. Two years later a small force under Colonel Fetterman was in turn massacred by the embittered Sioux. The climax came in 1876 when gold-seekers overran the Sioux reservation in the Black Hills. Under Sitting Bull and Crazy Horse the Sioux ambushed the impetuous 'glory-hunter,' General George Custer, on the Little Big Horn, and annihilated his whole command of 264 men. Punishment was quick; the Sioux were scattered and Crazy Horse captured and murdered by his guard.

In the mountains, as on the plains, the Indians were driven from their ancient homes. In Montana the Crow and the Blackfeet were ejected from their reservations; in Colorado the vast holdings of the Utes were confiscated and opened to settlement; in the Southwest the Navajo were herded onto a bleak reservation, and ten years of warfare ended in the capture of the intractable Geronimo and the practical destruction of the Apache. The discovery of gold on the Salmon river in western Idaho precipitated an invasion of the country of the peaceful Nez Percés. Chief Joseph struck back, but in vain, and in 1877 there began a retreat eastward over 1500 miles of mountain and plain that remains the most memorable feat in the annals of Indian warfare. In the end the feeble remnant of the Nez Percé tribe was captured and exiled to Oklahoma. Chief Joseph spoke for all his race:

I am tired of fighting. Our chiefs are killed. Looking-Glass is dead. Too-hul-hut-sote is dead. The old men are all dead. It is the young men now who say 'yes' or 'no.' He who led the young men is dead. It is cold and we have no blankets. The little children are freezing to death. My people, some of them, have run away to the hills and have no blankets, no food. No one knows where they are, perhaps freezing to death. I want to have time to look for my children and see how many of them I can find. Maybe I can find them among the dead. Hear me, my chiefs. My heart is sick and sad. I am tired.

Authority over Indian affairs was divided between the Departments of War and of the Interior, and both departments vacillated, the one failing to live up to treaty obligations, the other failing to protect the Indians on their reservations from the aggressions of white settlers. By fraud and chicanery large areas of Indian lands were alienated by 'treaty' or by 'sale.' One railroad acquired 800,000 acres of Cherokee lands in southern Kansas by methods that the governor of the state denounced as 'a cheat and a fraud in every particular,' but nothing was done to cancel the arrangement, and the railroad resold the lands to settlers at 100 per cent profit.

If most frontiersmen believed that the only good Indian was a dead Indian, Easterners, removed by a century from the Indian menace, had a different attitude. Statesmen like Carl Schurz, religious leaders such as Bishop Whipple, and

Major-General George Armstrong Custer (1839–76). Only two years after graduating from West Point in 1861, he was brevetted major-general and during the Civil War he earned a brilliant reputation as a cavalry officer. 'Custer's Last Stand' at the Battle of the Little Big Horn, 25–26 June 1876, was one of the memorable episodes in the waning years of the Wild West. Vain, cocksure, Custer has been denounced as a glory-hunter who led his men into a massacre, but more recent scholarship has placed the blame for the disaster on his subordinate commanders and on a feckless policy toward the Indians. (*Library of Congress*)

Sioux Indian camp. This photograph of the Villa of Brule, 'the great hostile Indian Camp' on the River Brule near Pine Ridge, South Dakota, was taken in about 1891, shortly after the appalling 'Battle' of Wounded Knee of 29 December 1890 in which United States troops killed two hundred Dakota Sioux, including women and children. (*Library of Congress*)

literary figures like Helen Hunt Jackson, whose *A Century of Dishonor* stirred the nation's conscience, effected important changes in Indian policy.

In 1887 Congress adopted the Dawes Severalty Act, which set Indian policy for the next half-century. The Dawes Act was the first serious attempt to teach Indians the practices of agricul-

ture and social life and merge them in the body politic of the nation. It provided for the dissolution of the tribes as legal entities and the division of tribal lands among individual members. To protect the Indian in his property the right of disposal was withheld for 25 years; upon the expiration of this probationary period, the Indian was to become the unrestricted owner and to be admitted to full citizenship in the United States. In October 1901 the Five Civilized Nations of Oklahoma, already well assimilated, were admitted to citizenship and in 1924 Congress granted full citizenship to all Indians.

The Dawes Act was hailed at the time as an Indian Emancipation Act; it might better have been compared to Appomattox. Under the operation of this misguided law, Indian holdings decreased in the next half-century from 138 to 48 million acres, half of these arid or semi-arid. Whites deprived Indians of their lands by various kinds of deceit and even by murder, in one case the bombing of two sleeping children. Indian timber land was seized by speculators; in 1917 the Indian commissioner explained that 'as the Indian tribes were being liquidated anyway it was only sensible to liquidate their forest holdings as well.' Tribal funds amounting to more than $100 million were diverted from their proper use to meet the costs of the Indian Bureau—including the costs of despoiling the Indians of their lands. Not until the New Deal did the government adopt a more responsible policy, and even then glaring injustices remained.

The Mining Frontier

The vast territory between the Missouri and the Pacific, first explored by fur traders, had been crossed and recrossed by emigrants along the great trails, but it was the miners who first revealed the possibilities of this country. In 1849 the lure of gold had drawn to California a heterogeneous throng of miners who later formed the nucleus of a large permanent population and who developed the varied agricultural resources of the state. This process was to be repeated time and again in the 'sixties: in Colorado, Nevada, Arizona, Idaho, Montana, and Wyoming. In each state precious metals attracted the first settlers; then, as the big pay dirt was exhausted, the mining population receded, and its place was taken by ranchers and farmers who established, with the aid of the railroads and the government, the permanent foundation of the territory.

In 1859 the discovery of gold in the foothills of the Rockies, near Pike's Peak, drew thousands of eager prospectors. Denver City, Golden, Boulder,

and Colorado City arose almost overnight, and the Territory of Jefferson—changed later to Colorado—was organized. The mining boom soon spent itself; not until the silver strikes of the 1870's, the advent of the railroads, and the influx of farmers was the basis for a sounder development laid. By 1880 Leadville, the second city of Colorado, had 13 schools, 5 churches, and 28 miles of streets; its annual silver production soon outdistanced that of any foreign country save Mexico.

In the same year that gold was discovered in Colorado came the announcement of a rich strike of silver on the eastern slopes of the Sierra Nevada. Here was located the Comstock Lode, one of the richest veins in the world. Within a year roaring towns like Virginia City sprang up in the desert waste, the Territory of Nevada was carved out of Utah, and 10,000 men were digging frantically in the bowels of the earth for the precious ore. Nevada furnishes the most extreme example of a mining community; nowhere else in history do we find a society so completely and continuously dependent upon minerals. However, very little of the enormous riches remained there. The change from placer mining to more efficient quartz mining required expensive machinery, engineering skill, and the organization of mining as a big business. So outside capital took over; the miners became day laborers working for wages, and the profits went to stockholders scattered throughout the United States and Europe. Mining added nothing to the wealth of the state. It did not create permanent industries or cities, nor provide foundations for healthy growth. This was the history of Comstock, and to a greater or less extent of most of the mines of the West in the following decade.

The story of Idaho runs parallel to that of Nevada. After gold was discovered in 1860 on the Nez Percé reservation in the extreme eastern part of Washington Territory, a wave of prospectors rolled in. Lewiston and Boise City sprang into existence, and in 1865 the Territory of Idaho was carved out of Washington and Montana. But mining furnished a most insubstantial foundation, and the census of 1870 showed a population of only 15,000. Gold was discovered east of the Con-

Albert Bierstadt, 'Storm in the Rocky Mountains—Mt. Rosalie' (1866). Bierstadt (1830–1902) was the most successful member of the second generation of the Hudson River school, painters of grand landscapes in the romantic tradition. Born in Germany, Bierstadt painted Rocky Mountain vistas out of memories of the Swiss and Italian Alps. (*The Brooklyn Museum*)

tinental Divide, too, but the mines along the Sweetwater were soon played out, and after 1865 the future of Wyoming Territory depended almost wholly upon cattle and sheep.

Although Montana produced over $100 million in precious metals in the first decade, the mining kingdom was short-lived and scarred by violence. For a brief time the notorious Henry Plummer and his gang of cutthroats threatened the prosperity of the Montana camps, and it required a vigilante organization such as that which had arisen in California fifteen years earlier to restore law and order. Virginia City, Montana, which typified the mining towns of the West, was thus described by N.P. Langford in his book *Vigilante Days and Ways:*

This human hive, numbering at least ten thousand people, was the product of ninety days. Into it were crowded all the elements of a rough and active civilization. . . . Nearly every third cabin in the town was a saloon where vile whiskey was peddled out for fifty cents a drink in gold dust. Many of these places were filled with gambling tables and gamblers, and the miner who was bold enough to enter one of them with his day's earnings in his pocket, seldom left until thoroughly fleeced. Hurdy-gurdy dance-houses were numerous, and there were plenty of camp beauties to patronize them. . . . Not a day or night passed which did not yield its full fruition of fights, quarrels, wounds, or murders. The crack of the revolver was often heard above the merry notes of the violin. Street fights were frequent, and as no one knew when or where they would occur, everyone was on his guard against a random shot.

But it would be a mistake to picture the mining camps as mere nests of lawlessness. They had, to be sure, few of the institutions taken for granted in the East—churches, schools, newspapers, theaters—but they hastened to establish these institutions as quickly as they could. Moreover, they showed ingenuity in developing a legal system appropriate to their circumstances. Each miners' camp was an administrative and a judicial district. It had its own executive officers, judges, recorders; voted laws and regulations suited to its own peculiar needs; and enforced these laws through public opinion and police officers. The legal codes and practices of these mining communities were eventually recognized in the American courts and incorporated into U.S. statutes and the constitutions and laws of the western states.

Not gold and silver but copper proved the chief resource of Montana, and of Arizona too. In the 1870's Marcus Daly, once an impoverished Irish immigrant, bought an option on a small silver mine in Butte, the Anaconda. In the next half-century he and his associates took over two billion dollars' worth of copper out of this 'richest hill in the world.' To control this and other mines, Daly, William Clark, and other 'copper kings' corrupted the public life of the state for a generation. Clark got a senatorship, $100 million, and a mansion on New York's Fifth Avenue with 121 rooms and 31 baths. After the turn of the century, copper mining shifted to Arizona where the Phelps-Dodge interests dominated the economy of the state, and where a single copper mine at Bisbee yielded more money than all the gold and silver mines of the Territory.

The gaudy last gold rush belongs as much to Canadian as to American history. The discovery of gold along the Klondike, which flows from Yukon into Alaska, came in 1896; soon 30,000 fortune-hunters were washing the icy waters of the Klondike and its tributaries. The Klondike strike furnished material for a dozen red-blooded novels which gave Jack London an international reputation; inspired Robert Service to write and a million hams to recite 'The Shooting of Dan McGrew'; and provided the background for Charlie Chaplin's wonderful movie *The Gold Rush.*

More important, it marked the beginnings of modern Alaska.

Ephemeral as it was, the mining frontier had a great impact. The miners forced a 'solution' of the Indian 'problem,' dramatized the need for railroads, and laid the foundations for a permanent farming population. Out of the necessities of their situation they contributed much of value to the legal and political institutions of the West. They produced, in the 30 years from 1860 to 1890, $1,241,827,032 of gold and $901,160,660 of silver, enabled the government to resume specie payments, and precipitated 'the money question' which was for well-nigh twenty years the main political issue before the country. They added immeasurably to folklore, enriched the American idiom, and in the stories of Bret Harte and Mark Twain inspired lasting contributions to literature.

The Cattle Kingdom

One of the most dramatic shifts in the screen-picture of the West was the replacement of millions of buffalo that had roamed the Great Plains by cattle, and of the Indian by the cowboy and the cattle king. The territory between the Missouri and the Rockies, from the Red river of the South to Saskatchewan—an area comprising approximately one-fourth of the United States—was the cattle kingdom, the last American frontier. Here millions of cattle—Texas longhorns, full-blooded Herefords, Wyoming and Montana steers—fatted on the long luscious grasses of the public lands, and cowboys and their liege lords, the cattle barons who ruled this vast domain, developed a unique society.

The emergence of the cattle industry on a large scale was due to a combination of causes: the opening up of the public domain after the Civil War, the elimination of the Indian danger and the annihilation of the buffalo, the extension of railroads into the High Plains, the decline in cattle-raising in the Middle West and the East, increased consumption of meat here and abroad, the invention of the refrigerator car, and the growth of great packing centers.

Since the days when the American Southwest belonged to Spain, the sturdy Texas longhorn, descendant of Spanish *toros* from the plains of Andalusia, had grazed on the limitless prairie, but not until the middle 'sixties did the 'long drive' north to the region of rich grasses and good prices cease to be an experiment. On the first of the organized long drives, 35,000 longhorns pounded up clouds of dust all along the Chisholm Trail, across the Red and Arkansas rivers and into the land of the Five Nations, to Abilene, Kansas. Two years later no less than 350,000 longhorned kine made their way along the Chisholm and Goodnight trails to fatten on the tall northern grasses and find a market at one of the several roaring cattle towns on the Kansas and Pacific Railroad: Abilene, Dodge City, or Newton. Later the 'long drive' extended north to the Union Pacific and even to the Northern Pacific.

In after years [writes the historian of the cattle kingdom] the drive of the Texas men became little short of an American saga. To all who saw that long line of Texas cattle come up over a rise in the prairie, nostrils wide for the smell of water, dust-caked and gaunt, so ready to break from the nervous control of the riders strung out along the flanks of the herd, there came a feeling that in this spectacle there was something elemental, something resistless, something perfectly in keeping with the unconquerable land about them.[2]

Between 1866 and 1888, cowboys, who first learned their art from Mexican *vaqueros*, drove some 6 million cattle from Texas to winter on the High Plains of Colorado, Wyoming, and even Montana. Every spring they rounded up the herds in designated areas, all the way from Texas to Wyoming and the Dakotas, identified their owners' cattle by the brands, and branded the calves, dividing up pro rata the strays or 'mavericks.' The breeding cattle were then set free for another year while the likely three- and four-year-olds were driven to the nearest cow town on a railway. Each 'outfit' of cowboys attended its owner's herd on the drive, protecting it from wolves and rustlers, sending scouts ahead to locate water and the best grazing.

The long drive seems romantic in retrospect, but to the cowboys it was hard and often hazardous work. Andy Adams, later one of the cattle

barons of Texas, describes a dry drive along the Old Western Trail:

Good cloudy weather would have saved us, but in its stead was a sultry morning without a breath of air, which bespoke another day of sizzling heat. We had not been on the trail over two hours before the heat became almost unbearable to man and beast. Had it not been for the condition of the herd, all might yet have gone well; but over three days had elapsed without water for the cattle, and they became feverish and ungovernable. . . . We threw our ropes in their faces, and when this failed, we resorted to shooting; but in defiance of the fusillade and the smoke they walked sullenly through the line of horsemen across their front. Six-shooters were discharged so close to the leaders' faces as to singe their hair, yet, under a noonday sun, they disregarded this and every other device to turn them, and passed wholly out of our control. In a number of instances wild steers deliberately walked against our horses, and then for the first time a fact dawned upon us that chilled the marrow in our bones—*the herd was going blind.*[3]

In Wyoming, where cattlemen seized most of the public and much of the Indian lands, the great cattle companies ruled supreme. For almost 20 years the Wyoming Stock Growers' Association was the *de facto* government of the Territory; it formulated laws and regulations governing land and water rights, the round-up, and similar matters, and enforced them on members and nonmembers alike; it agitated ceaselessly for revision of the land laws and for recognition of the prior rights of cattlemen; it attempted, by fraud, intimidation, and violence, to keep Wyoming the exclusive preserve of the ranchers.

This proved impossible. The most dangerous threat to the cattle kingdom, in Wyoming as elsewhere through the West, was not, at first, the farmer but the lowly sheepherder. Sheep, like cattle, could graze free on Uncle Sam's inexhaustible lands; labor costs were negligible; and the wool clip, protected by high tariffs, was increasingly valuable. The cattlemen, convinced that sheep ruined the grass by close cropping, waged open war on their rivals. The Tonto Basin War in northern Arizona, like Kentucky feuds, dragged on for years and ended only when ranchers and

2. E. S. Osgood, *The Day of the Cattleman*, p. 26.

3. Andy Adams, *The Log of a Cowboy*, Houghton Mifflin Co., pp. 63–64.

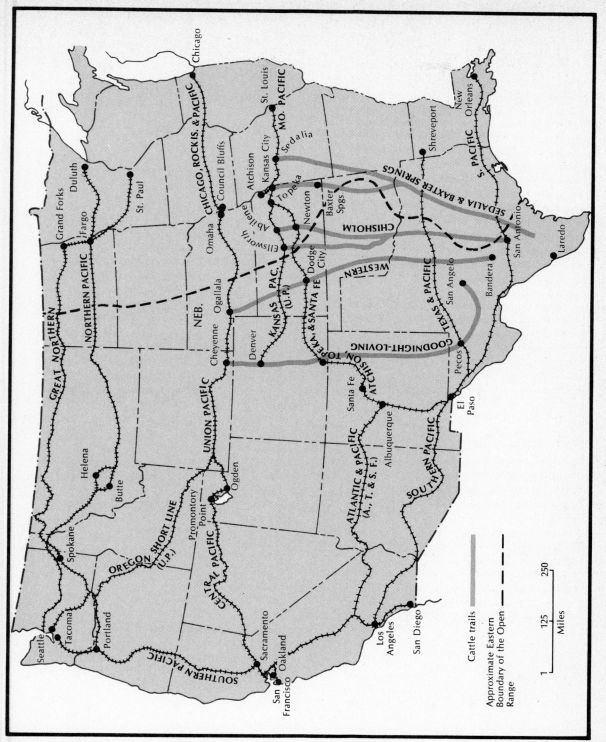

Railroads and Cattle Trails, 1850–1900

sheepherders had wiped each other out. But in the end the sheepmen triumphed, even in Wyoming where sheep came to outnumber cattle ten to one. Oddly enough, though the sheepherder is an older and more beloved figure than the rancher, and one with many Biblical associations, sheep raising never caught the American imagination or acquired a folklore or a literature.

The cattle boom reached its height about 1885. By that time the hazards of ranching had increased enormously. The appearance of cattle diseases and the enactment of state quarantine laws, the conflict between cattlemen and sheepherders, between northern and southern cattlemen, and between cattlemen and homesteaders, the decline of prices because of overproduction, the destruction of the range by overgrazing, and the determination of the Federal Government to enforce its land laws—all these presaged the decline of the cow kingdom. Then came the two terrible winters of 1885–86 and 1886–87 which almost annihilated the herds on the open ranges. Cattle owners began to fence off their lands. Almost in a moment the cattle range replaced the open ranges. The cowboy, now a cattleman or ranch employee, was penned in behind wire and no longer knew the joys and dangers of the long drive.

The Disappearance of the Frontier

The picturesque 'Wild West' fell before the pressure of farmers, swarming by the hundreds of thousands onto the High Plains and into the mountain valleys. During the Civil War, dangers and uncertainties, especially in the border states, induced many to try their luck in the new regions, while the liberal provisions of the Homestead and later land acts, the low cost of railroad lands, and the high rewards of farming proved an irresistible magnet for thousands of others. From Council Bluffs, Iowa, eastern terminus of the Union Pacific, the Reverend Jonathan Blanchard wrote in 1864:

When you approach this town, the ravines and gorges are white with covered wagons at rest. Below the town, toward the river side, long wings of white canvas stretch away on either side, into the soft green willows; at the ferry from a quarter to a half mile of teams all the time await their turn to cross. Myriads of horses and mules drag on the moving mass of humanity toward the setting sun; while the oxen and cows equal them in number.

All this seems incredibly remote from Shiloh and the Wilderness; one of the great pulses of American life went on beating amid the din of arms.

The close of the war brought a sharp acceleration of this movement. It was in part the absorbing power of the West that enabled a million soldiers to resume civilian life without serious economic derangements. Southerners by the tens of thousands, despairing of recouping their fortunes in the war-stricken South, migrated westward although excluded temporarily from the privileges of the Homestead Act. Immigrants, mostly from northern Europe, found their way to the prairies of Iowa and Minnesota and eastern Dakota by the hundreds of thousands. The railroads provided transportation, ensured markets, and were active colonizing agents.

But it was not enough to provide land and transportation for the migrants. Some method had to be found to overcome the natural handicaps to agriculture in the semi-arid Plains. In the Plains, where lumber had to be imported, the cost of timber-fencing a quarter-section of land was prohibitive. Yet if cattle were to be controlled, crops protected from the ravages of cattle, and water holes preserved, fencing was essential. In 1874, J. F. Glidden discovered a solution: barbed wire. By 1883 Glidden's company was turning out 600 miles of barbed wire daily, and fencing had been reduced to a mere fraction of its former cost. The importance of barbed wire to the development of the Great Plains was comparable to that of the cotton gin in the South.

Fencing made farming on the High Plains possible, but not necessarily profitable. There was still the menace of drought. For a time irrigation promised to solve the problem. The Pueblo Indians were familiar with irrigation, and the Mormons had reclaimed millions of acres by this ancient method. In 1894 the Carey Act turned over to the Western states millions of acres of public lands to be reclaimed through irrigation. When the law proved ineffective, the Federal Government took charge; under the Reclamation

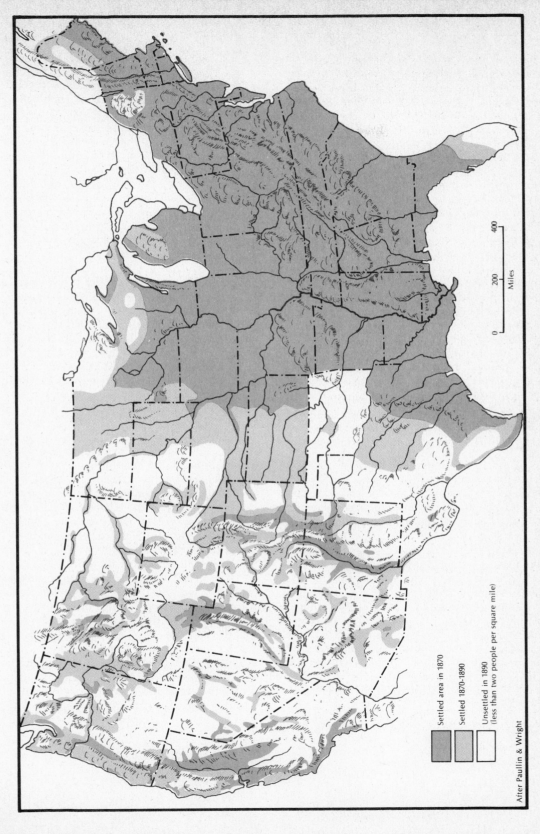

The Passing of the Frontier

Settled area in 1870

Settled 1870–1890

Unsettled in 1890
(less than two people per square mile)

0   200   400

Miles

After Paullin & Wright

Act of 1902 acreage under irrigation was multiplied fourfold. Yet irrigation was not an unqualified success, and its effects were limited to a comparatively small area of the mountainous West and to California.

Far more effective was the use of deep-drilled wells and of the windmill, and the practice of dry farming. By drilling from 100 to 500 feet below the surface it was possible to tap ground water and bring it to the surface in slender metal cylinders lowered and raised by never failing windmills. Dry farming—the conservation of moisture in the soil by creating a dust blanket to prevent evaporation—made it possible to grow cereal crops successfully over large parts of the Plains.

As a result of all these factors—transportation, immigration, the growth of domestic and foreign markets, new methods of fencing and of cultivation—the settlement of the last West went on with unprecedented rapidity. In the 20-year period from 1870 to 1890 the population of Nebraska increased eightfold, Washington fourteenfold, and Dakota Territory fortyfold. In his annual report for 1890, the Superintendent of the Census made an historic announcement:

Up to and including 1880 the country had a frontier of settlement, but at present the unsettled area has been so broken into by isolated bodies of settlement that there can be hardly said to be a frontier line.

The 'disappearance of the frontier' was shortly marked by a great historian, Frederick Jackson Turner, as the close of a movement that began in 1607 and the start of a new era in American history.

Yet if the frontier line had been obliterated, Western settlement continued at a brisk pace. Indeed, more land was patented for homestead and grazing purposes in the generation after 1890 than in the previous generation. The westward movement of population, too, continued unabated. While from 1890 to 1930 population grew in the flourishing Middle Atlantic and North Central States by about 90 per cent, in the Mountain and Pacific States it increased threefold, and the greatest era in the westward movement was still to come.

Political Organization

In 1860 something over one-third of the area of the United States consisted of Territories. From Minnesota to Oregon, from Texas to the Canadian border, there were no states. Nevada was admitted in 1864 to obtain its three electoral votes for Lincoln, and Nebraska in 1867 over President Johnson's veto (in time to cast its vote for his impeachment), but few of the remaining Territories showed promise for early admission into the Union. Yet within a generation all this region, comprising something over a million square miles, was organized politically, and the major part included in states.

The transcontinental railroads proved crucial to state-making in the West, for they brought to the Territories a permanent farmer population and a solid economic foundation. This became apparent first in the northernmost tier. In 1870 the population of the Dakota, Idaho, and Washington Territories was only 75,000; by 1890, after the Northern Pacific had been completed and the Great Northern almost finished, their population had increased to one million. However, statehood was held up for a full decade by political differences in Congress. The decisive influence of Colorado, admitted in 1876 as the Centennial State, in the disputed presidential election of that year brought the statehood question into party politics. Furthermore, there was fear in the East of Western radicalism, and resentment over the repudiation of railway bonds. By playing politics with the futures of the Territories, both parties forfeited the confidence of these embryo states and made them the more willing to follow the banner of Populism in the early 1890's.

The so-called blockade came to an end abruptly in 1888, with the prospect of complete Republican control of the government. Both parties and both Houses then strove to get credit for the admission of the Western states. Hence, the Omnibus Bill of 1889 provided for the admission of North and South Dakota, Montana, and Washington. No provision was made for Wyoming and Idaho, but in both Territories constitutional conventions met without specific authority, and a few months later

Cherokee Strip. At high noon on 22 April 1889 Oklahoma 'Boomers' race to stake their claims. By nightfall nearly two million acres had been settled in a madcap fashion, and Oklahoma City boasted a population of 10,000. (*Oklahoma Historical Society*)

both were admitted by a debate-weary and vote-hungry Republican Congress.

With the admission of these six states there existed for the first time a solid band of states from the Atlantic to the Pacific, but not for another two decades would the rest of the continental United States achieve statehood. The same year that the Omnibus Bill passed, the government purchased a large part of the lands of the Five Civilized Tribes and threw Oklahoma open to settlement under the homestead laws. At high noon on 22 April 1889 a gun was fired, and settlers raced pell-mell across the prairie to stake their claims. By November, Oklahoma had 60,000 settlers; within a decade almost 800,000, and in 1907 Oklahoma and Indian Territory were admitted as one state. When in 1890 the Mormon government in Utah promised to abandon polygamy, it removed the last objection to its admission to statehood. Under the able administration of the Mormon Church the Latter-day Saints had prospered amazingly, and when Utah was finally admitted in 1896, it was with a flourishing population of some 250,000. In 1912 Arizona and New Mexico entered the Union too.

Thus was completed a process inaugurated by the Northwest Ordinance of 1787. Since then the United States had grown from 13 to 48 states, embracing the whole continental domain.[4] Texas came in as an independent republic; Maine and West Virginia were separated from other states; Vermont and Kentucky entered without previous Territorial organization. But all the others, after passing through a Territorial stage, were admitted as states in a Union of equals, in the greatest experiment in colonial policy and administration of modern times.

4. The non-contiguous Territories of Alaska and Hawaii achieved statehood half a century later.

23

The Politics of Dead Center

1877–1890

Masks in a Pageant

There is no drearier chapter in American political history than that which records the administrations of Hayes, Garfield, Arthur, Cleveland, and Harrison. Civil War issues were dead, though politicians continued to flay the corpses. National politics became little more than a contest for power between rival parties waged on no higher plane than a struggle for traffic between rival railroads. 'One might search the whole list of Congress, Judiciary, and Executive during the twenty-five years 1870–1895 and find little but damaged reputations,' wrote Henry Adams. 'The period was poor in purpose and barren in results.'

At first glance it would appear that this was an era of Republican supremacy. No Democrat had entered the White House with as much as 50 per cent of the vote since Franklin Pierce in 1852, and none would again until Franklin D. Roosevelt 80 years later. The Republicans came out of the war as the party of the Union, while the Democrats were tarred with secession and even treason. As the Grand Old Party that had stood by the flag, Republicans for a generation counselled: 'Vote

the way you shot.' The Grand Army of the Republic, the leading veterans' organization, mobilized the vote of old soldiers for the Republicans, and for nine of ten campaigns beginning in 1868 the G.O.P. chose a military figure as their presidential nominee; during that same period, the Democrats did so only once. The G.O.P.'s stronghold was New England and the belt of New England migration across northern New York, the Old Northwest, and sweeping west to Oregon, the region which had been the center of anti-slavery sentiment. Since this sector was rural and Protestant, the party was strongly inclined toward temperance, nativism, and anti-Catholicism.

As a legacy of the Civil War era, the Republicans won the allegiance of black voters, but this did not prevent the party from playing a double game in the South. Some leaders wanted to use federal force to protect the freedman's right to vote, either out of solicitude for the black or in order to prevail at the polls. But others attempted to create a 'lilywhite' Republican party in the South. This policy was pressed by Northern industrialists, who hoped to find allies in the New South for their tariff policies; by merchants in border cities like Cincinnati who feared that agitating the Negro question jeopardized North-South trade; and by publicists who had come to share the racial outlook of the old slavocracy. Neither strategy succeeded in breaking the Democratic hold on the South, and after the abortive attempt to push through a Force bill in 1890, most Republicans gave up. By the end of the century, the South, with Northern acquiescence, had virtually completed black disfranchisement.

Outside the South, the Republicans commanded the support of the wealthy and were accepted by many others as the party of culture and respectability. Along the elm-lined streets of New England and the Old Northwest, not a few thought of the Democratic party as an almost illegitimate organization. Frederic Howe recalled: 'There was something unthinkable to me about being a Democrat—Democrats, Copperheads and atheists were persons whom one did not know socially. As a boy I did not play with their children.'

Despite these disadvantages, the Democrats showed impressive strength, largely because they were less of a sectional party than the Republicans. Powerful not only in the 'Solid South' but in the border states and the Southern belt of migration in the Midwest, the Democrats could capitalize, too, on their following in Northern cities. In 1880 the Democrats had a plurality of 24,000 in the twelve largest cities; by 1892, the margin had reached 145,000. The Democrats enlisted the support of most Irish Catholics, while the Republicans recruited the natural enemies of the Irish, especially British immigrants and French Canadians. Burton K. Wheeler remembered that to win Democratic nomination in Butte 'it was best to claim nativity in County Cork and second best to claim birth in some county in Ireland with slightly less prestige in Montana.'

By 1874 the two parties had struck an equilibrium, and for the next two decades each election turned on a very few votes. In the five presidential contests from 1876 to 1892, the Republicans failed to win a popular majority even once, and in three of these elections the difference between the major party candidates was less than 1 per cent. From 1877 to 1897 the Democrats controlled the presidency and Congress at the same time for but two years; the Republicans achieved this for four years, but in only two did they have a working majority.

Since the parties were roughly equal, political leaders were wary about introducing disturbing new issues that might break up their coalitions. In the South, Democrats agitated the race question and clamped a lid on economic questions that might prove divisive. In the North, Republicans kept alive Civil War memories to distract attention from economic difficulties that could split their party. 'Our strong ground,' Hayes wrote Blaine when he was campaigning for the presidency, 'is the dread of a solid South and rebel rule. I hope you will make these topics prominent in your speeches. It leads people away from hard times, which is our deadliest foe.'

During this entire period the electorate played a game of blind man's buff, for no consequential issue divided the major parties. Questions of currency and the tariff broke on sectional rather than party lines. Although America was emerging from her isolation, there was little appreciation of world responsibilities. Big business was growing bigger, and thoughtful men recognized the conflict of 'wealth against commonwealth' which Henry D. Lloyd would soon dramatize; but political leaders showed little awareness of the implications. The farmer was threatened by forces over which he could exercise no effective control; but politicians lacked the imagination to understand even the existence of a farm problem until it was called to their attention by political revolt.

Behind the colorless titular leaders were the real rulers—men who sat in committee rooms listening to the demands of the lobbyists, 'boys' who 'fried the fat' out of reluctant corporations. At the head of their ranks were great bosses such as Roscoe Conkling of New York. Next were the representatives of special interests—Standard Oil, sugar trust, steel, and railroad men known by business rather than political affiliations. Yet there was always a small group who preserved integrity and a sense of responsibility, men such as Lyman Trumbull of Illinois.

James G. Blaine of Maine, Congressman, Senator, twice Secretary of State, and perpetual aspirant to the presidency, typified this era, as Calhoun and Webster did an earlier one. A man of intellectual power and personal magnetism, Blaine was the most popular figure in American politics between Clay and Bryan. Year after year thousands marched, shouted, and sang for 'Blaine of Maine' pictured as the 'Plumed Knight,' defender of the true Republican faith. A magnificent orator, he could inspire a frenzy of enthusiasm by twisting the British lion's tail or solemnly intoning the platitudes of party loyalty. Yet he made no impression upon American politics except to lower its moral tone. He was assiduous in cementing a corrupt alliance between politics and business and in fanning the flames of sectional animosity. His name is connected with no important legislation; his sympathies were enlisted in no forward-looking causes. Nevertheless, he was rewarded with votes, office, power, and almost with the presidency.

Business had no party favorites except insofar as it preferred to invest in successful rather than unsuccessful candidates. Democratic senators such as Gorman of Maryland could command business support quite as effectively as Republicans like Cameron of Pennsylvania. In a number of states, a single corporation dominated political life; as in Montana under Anaconda Copper. The California railroad king, Collis Huntington, conceded: 'Things have got to such a state that if a man wants to be a constable he thinks he has first got to come down to Fourth and Townsend streets to get permission.' But even when party leaders were most sympathetic to business, they frequently had institutional interests which were not identical with those of the corporations. Politicians, far from being unfailingly subservient to business, often preyed on merchants and importers; and in cities like New York, businessmen played a prominent role in the campaign for civil service reform to curb the spoilsmen.

Glimmerings of Reform

In an era of generally issueless politics, one group sought to introduce reforms: the patrician dissenters who advocated a civil service system. Members of the older gentry who were being pushed aside by the newly rising industrialists resented a rude new world which did not accord them the deference they had been led to expect. Henry Adams later wrote of the return of his family to the United States in 1868 after a decade abroad: 'Had they been Tyrian traders of the year 1000 B.C., landing from a galley fresh from Gibraltar, they could hardly have been stranger on the shore of a world, so changed from what it had been ten years before.' They looked back to a golden age just beyond their memory. Charles Eliot Norton thought the ideal community 'New England during the first thirty years of the century, before the coming in of Jacksonian Democracy, and the invasion of the Irish, and the establishment of the system of Protection.' They loathed the industrialization of America and what it was doing not only to politics but to culture. 'Between you and me and the barber, I like it not,' wrote Richard Watson Gilder. 'The steam whistle attachment which you can see applied nowadays even to peanut stands in the winter streets; the vulgarizing of everything in life and letters and politics and religion, all this sickens the soul.'

These genteel reformers sought to emulate the British M.P. and were disappointed that America would not afford them the same recognition their friends in Parliament enjoyed. They were convinced that the hope of the republic lay in the conquest of politics by an educated elite. Like classic British liberals, they favored free trade, hard money, and civil service reform, and opposed both business and labor union monopolies. Most were Republicans, but they had bolted their party in 1872 to help launch the Liberal Republican movement and in 1884, as 'Mugwumps,' would leave their party again. In 1876, they found the Republican choice, Rutherford B. Hayes, acceptable, chiefly because they knew him to be honest. Joseph Pulitzer of the Democratic New York *World* cried: 'Hayes has never stolen. Good God, has it come to this?'

A well-educated lawyer, Union officer, twice elected to Congress and for three terms governor of Ohio, Hayes was experienced and able, but he was seriously handicapped as President in his efforts to effect constructive measures. Not only the Democrats but even many of his own party re-

The assassination of James A. Garfield. On 2 July 1881, the President went to the Baltimore and Potomac Railroad Depot in Washington, D.C., to board a train that would take him to a college reunion in Williamstown, Mass. At the station he was fatally wounded by a political factionalist, Charles A. Guiteau. On 19 September 1881, Garfield died, and on 30 June 1882, Guiteau was executed. (*Library of Congress*)

fused to recognize his election as legitimate; they referred to him as 'His Fraudulency.' Factional disputes also plagued him. Hayes incurred the animosity of Blaine, leader of the 'Half Breeds,' and the implacable hostility of Conkling, chieftain of the 'Stalwarts.' The 1876 elections had preserved Democratic control of the House, and two years later the opposition party captured the Senate too. At one point Haye was reduced to the sorry state of having only three supporters in the Senate, and one of these was a relative. In such circumstances it is a tribute to Hayes that his administration was not a total failure.

That it was not a complete failure can be credited to the courage with which Hayes set out to cleanse his party of the corruption which had so seriously damaged it during the Grant administrations. He named a cabinet of moderates: as Secretary of State, William Evarts of New York who had defended Andrew Johnson at the impeachment trial; the able John Sherman as Secretary of the Treasury; the paladin of the patrician reformers, Carl Schurz, to be Secretary of the Interior. He broke with the principle of vindictive sectional rule by appointing a former Confederate officer, David Key of Tennessee, Postmaster General. Hayes also tried, somewhat quixotically, to reform the party system and lessen the control by local politicians of the national government. He issued an executive order which forbade federal office-holders to manage politics. 'Party leaders,' said Hayes to the astonishment of the politicians,

412

'should have no more influence in appointments than other equally respectable citizens.' Hayes was combatting a system under which senators, responsive to local machines, controlled the national party and in turn the Federal Government.

But Hayes quickly found that if he was to govern he also had to be a leader of his party. He was soon dispensing patronage to the men who had put him in office like any other politician; especially scandalous was the way he rewarded every member of the notorious Louisiana returning board which had been instrumental in giving him the presidency. John Hay commented acidly: 'Not Pomeroy or Butler or Boss Tweed himself ever attempted to run an administration in the interests of his own crowd as this model reformer has done.' Although he thereafter removed some of Grant's most offensive appointees and cleaned up the New York custom house, he was never able to win the full confidence of the civil service reformers.

Indecisive as it was, Hayes's struggle with the spoilsmen had considerable consequence. That encounter was precipitated by Hayes's ouster of Chester A. Arthur and Alonzo B. Cornell from the New York custom house, which was mismanaged and corrupt. Senator Conkling, alarmed at the assault on his organization, persuaded the Senate to reject the nominations of those whom the President appointed to succeed Arthur and Cornell. This squabble involved not merely a falling-out between two Republican factions and 'Senatorial courtesy,' but a larger issue of the form of government. By such devices as the profligate use of legislative riders, Congress, since the Civil War, had so largely eaten into the presidential prerogative that the chief executive was by way of becoming a mere figurehead. The Republican Senate sought, as one writer noted, to turn the presidency 'into an office much like that of the doge of Venice, one of ceremonial dignity without real power.' President Hayes took up this challenge, and in the end, with the support of the Democrats, he won out. His appointees were renominated and confirmed, and the normal constitutional relationship between President and Congress began to be restored.

For the larger task of articulating the government to new economic forces, Hayes was not prepared. He responded to the 'Great Strike' of 1877 by sending troops to put down the strikers. When Congress approved the Bland-Allison Silver Act in 1878, Hayes interposed his veto unsuccessfully. To the problems of railroad malpractices, trusts, and land frauds he gave no attention. He later confessed that 'the money-piling tendency of our country . . . is changing laws, government and morals, and giving all power to the rich, and bringing in pauperism and its attendant crimes and wickedness like a flood,' but when President he did not even hang out danger signals. His administration, for all its political drama, was largely negative.

As the election of 1880 approached, the Stalwarts proposed Grant for a third term, but he was blocked by the Half Breed leader, Blaine. One of the 306 Stalwarts who stood by Grant to the end had 306 medals struck bearing the legend, 'The Old Guard,' thereby coining a new name for Republican regulars. A 'dark horse' from Ohio, General James A. Garfield, got the nomination, and to placate Conkling, who had supported Grant, the convention named his henchman, Chester A. Arthur, to the vice-presidency. The Garfield-Arthur ticket won with a popular plurality of less than 10,000 in a total of over 9 million votes.

Four months after his inauguration, at the climax of another bitter patronage struggle with Conkling, Garfield was shot in the back by a disappointed office-seeker who boasted, 'I am a Stalwart and Arthur is President now.' After a gallant struggle, Garfield died on 19 September 1881. The murder of Garfield, and the assassin's admission he killed the President in order to replace him with a factional leader, brought the nation to its senses on the extremism of spoils politics and promoted a civil service reform law.

Yet politicians fought the bill sponsored by 'Gentleman' George Pendleton of Ohio bitterly, some out of desire to preserve their control of patronage, others from a Jacksonian fear that a permanent civil service would produce an overbearing Prussian bureaucracy or haughty Mandarins. Others objected that a competitive examination was a class device which would discriminate against those too poor to afford a college educa-

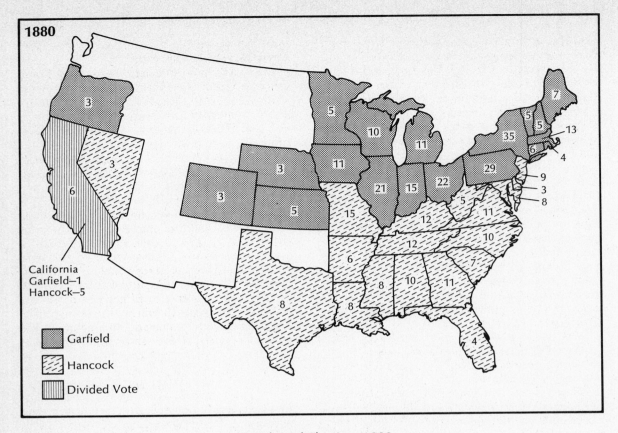

1880

California
Garfield—1
Hancock—5

Garfield
Hancock
Divided Vote

Presidential Election, 1880

tion. Restricting entrance to college graduates, observed one critic, would open doors to a Pierce but exclude a Lincoln, while a Mississippi Congressman objected that if government jobs were to be based on competence, his constituents would not qualify. Under other circumstances, such appeals would have carried the day. But the country had had enough of unrestrained factionalism. A rapidly industrializing society wanted to place government on a more businesslike basis. In enacting the Pendleton bill in 1883, Congress wrote the demands of the patrician reformers, the protests of the importers, and the public outcry at Garfield's death into law.

The Pendleton Act created a Civil Service Commission to administer a new set of rules which required appointments to be made as a re-

sult of open competitive examinations and prohibited assessments on office-holders for political purposes. By law these new rules were applied only to some 14,000 positions, about 12 per cent of the total, but the President was empowered to extend them at his discretion. At the turn of the century there were not far from 100,000 in the classified civil service; at the end of Theodore Roosevelt's administration the number had more than doubled, and when Wilson left the White House it had increased to almost half a million. At the same time most states were passing civil service laws. It was fortunate that the merit principle was adopted before the twentieth century when administrative expansion greatly increased the need for honest and expert service.

To the surprise of many, civil service reform had

414

the ardent support of Garfield's successor, Chester A. Arthur. A satellite of the corrupt Conkling, the new President had nothing in his record to justify the hope that he would make more than a mediocre executive and much to arouse fear that he would be a very bad one. Unexpectedly he developed genuine independence. He severed his connections with the worst of the spoilsmen, vetoed a lavish river and harbor bill, and prosecuted, with some vigor, the 'Star Route' frauds in the Post Office Department. The Arthur administration brought one other change too. The War of the Pacific involving Peru, Bolivia, and Chile, and the rising interest in an isthmian canal, awakened the nation to a realization of the decrepitude of its navy,[1] inferior to that of Chile, and in 1882 Congress authorized 'two steam cruising vessels of war . . . to be constructed of steel of domestic manufacture.' The *Chicago* and the *Boston* entered active service in 1887, and a new era in U.S. naval history began.

The Administrations of Cleveland and Harrison

Arthur's placid administration ended in the most exciting presidential campaign since the Civil War, although the only real issue between the parties was possession of the government. The Republicans, disappointed in Arthur, turned to the magnetic Blaine. But Blaine was more than conscientious Republicans could swallow. The principal charge against him was prostitution of the speakership to personal gain; in that connection he could not explain his missive to a certain Fisher with the damning postscript, 'Burn this letter.' Even Conkling, when asked to campaign for Blaine, replied, 'I don't engage in criminal practice.' Under the leadership of Carl Schurz and George William Curtis the reform wing bolted from the convention, promised to support any decent nomination the Democrats might make,

and proudly accepted the name 'Mugwump' which was given them in derision.[2]

With the Promised Land in sight, the Democrats nominated Grover Cleveland, a self-made man who as reform mayor of Buffalo and governor of New York had distinguished himself for firmness and integrity, to the disgust of Tammany Hall. 'We love him for the enemies he has made,' said General E. S. Bragg. Powerful journals such as *Harper's Weekly*, with Nast's telling cartoons, shifted over to Cleveland, as did the Mugwumps.

The 1884 campaign was noisy and nasty. Cleveland was charged, among other things, with fathering an illegitimate child, which he admitted, to the consternation of his supporters. But, as one of them concluded philosophically, 'We should elect Mr. Cleveland to the public office which he is so admirably qualified to fill, and remand Mr. Blaine to the private life which he is so eminently fitted to adorn.' Democratic torchlight processions paraded the streets, shouting,

> Blaine, Blaine, James G. Blaine,
> The continental liar from the State of Maine
> *Burn this letter!*

To which Republican processions retorted: 'Ma! Ma! Where's my pa?' The contest was bitterly fought throughout the North, but New York was the decisive state. Here Blaine had a strong following among Irish-Americans, which was weakened at the eleventh hour by the tactless remark of a supporter, a hapless parson named Burchard, who described the Democracy as the party of 'Rum, Romanism, and Rebellion.' Blaine neglected to rebuke this insult to the faith of his Celtic friends; Cleveland carried New York by a plurality of 1149 in a vote of over a million; and New York's electoral votes gave him the presidency. Yet the crucial point about the 1884 outcome is that the net shift compared to the previous election was the smallest of any in American history. The politics of dead center had reached almost exact equilibrium.

For a person of such generous bulk, Grover

---

1. '"I don't think I should like America."—"I suppose because we have no ruins and no curiosities," said Virginia, satirically.—"No ruins! no curiosities!" answered the Ghost; "you have your navy and your manners."' Oscar Wilde, *The Canterville Ghost*.

2. Mugwump, a term applied on this occasion by the New York *Sun*, is the word for 'great captain' in Eliot's Indian Bible.

Grover Cleveland (1837–1908). This etching by Anders Zorn suggests the hefty bulk of the twenty-second and twenty-fourth President of the United States. (*National Portrait Gallery, Smithsonian Institution*)

Cleveland was remarkably ungenial. He showed steadfast devotion to duty, but was singularly lacking in imagination and in understanding of the problems of farmers and urban workers. Cleveland hated paternalism in all forms: the tariff, land grants to railroads, pensions, social welfare legislation. He reflected his party's suspicion of strong government, a consequence in part of Southern resentment of Reconstruction, in part of the long period out of power which taught the Democrats to act as opposers. They were so much the party of state rights and limited government that Republican Tom Reed asked: 'Are they but an organized "no"?'

416

Cleveland's attitude toward government action is exemplified by his veto of the Texas Seed bill in 1887, with a message that was frequently quoted later by opponents of the Welfare State. In reply to requests from sufferers of a severe drought, Congress had voted the small sum of $10,000 for seed grain. When Cleveland vetoed the measure, he declared:

I do not believe that the power and duty of the General Government ought to be extended to the relief of individual suffering which is in no manner properly related to the public service or benefit. Though the people support the Government, the Government should not support the people. Federal aid in such cases encourages the expectation of paternal care on the part of the Government and weakens the sturdiness of our national character. The friendliness and charity of our countrymen can always be relied upon to relieve their fellow-citizens in misfortune.

Character made Cleveland's administration the most respectable between Lincoln's and Theodore Roosevelt's. He alone of the titular leaders had sufficient courage to defy the groups that were exploiting the government and to risk his career in defense of what he thought right. He advanced civil service reform, challenged the predatory interests that were engrossing the public lands, denounced the evils of protection, and called a halt to raids on the Treasury by veterans. If the total achievements of his administration were negative, even that was something of a virtue at a time when too many politicians were saying 'yes' to the wrong things.

The main drama of Cleveland's first term centered on the tariff problem. The high tariff contributed, in Cleveland's opinion, not only to increases in the prices of protected goods, but to the development of trusts. Furthermore, when government revenues showed a consistent surplus over ordinary expenses of almost $100 million annually all through the 'eighties, this surplus offered a standing temptation to extravagance of the pork barrel and pension grab variety. In 1887, Cleveland, despite warnings to avoid the explosive subject, startled the nation by devoting his annual message exclusively to the tariff. 'Our progress toward a wise conclusion,' he wrote, 'will not be improved by dwelling upon theories of protection

and free trade. It is a condition which confronts us, not a theory.' The *Nation* called the message 'the most courageous document that has been sent from the White House since the Civil War.' But Blaine denounced it as pure 'free trade,' and the Republicans prepared joyously to make capital out of it in the forthcoming campaign. Cleveland, though, had accomplished his purpose. He had brought the tariff question sharply to the attention of the country, and he had forced his own party to espouse tariff reform as the paramount issue.

In 1888 the Democrats renominated Cleveland, and the Republicans picked the grandson of the hero of Tippecanoe, Benjamin Harrison of Indiana. In a campaign marked by pronounced ethnic appeals, the Irish vote was turned against Cleveland. A naturalized Anglo-American was inspired to inquire of the British Minister, Sir Lionel Sackville-West, how he should vote in order to serve the mother country. Sir Lionel, with incredible stupidity, advised him by letter to vote for the Democrats, a piece of counsel that hurt Cleveland with the Anglophobic Irish. Though Cleveland's popular vote exceeded Harrison's by 100,000, the Republicans carried New York State by a few thousand votes, and again New York was decisive. Harrison made a dignified figurehead in the presidency. Honest and conscientious, he lacked the insight to comprehend the problems of a new day.

With the autocratic 'Czar' Thomas B. Reed as Speaker of the House, and with a majority in both Houses, the Republicans used their newly regained power to benefit their followers. Within a year Postmaster-General Wanamaker had removed over 30,000 postmasters, more than twice as many as Cleveland had dismissed in the same period. The McKinley tariff bill of October 1890 was pushed through as the result of a bargain between Western Republicans who wanted silver legislation and Eastern Republicans who wanted a high tariff.[3] Its provisions were formulated chiefly by William McKinley of Ohio and Nelson W. Al-

3. The year 1890 saw the passage of the McKinley tariff, the Sherman Silver Purchase bill, the Sherman Anti-Trust Act, the Disability Pension Act, and the admission of the last of the 'omnibus' states.

Benjamin Harrison (1833–1901). Eastman Johnson's charcoal drawing heightened with chalk is believed to have been executed in 1889, the year Harrison entered the White House. Johnson (1824–1906) was one of the leading portrait and genre artists of the day. In 1849 he had gone to Europe to study, and he proved so successful that he was invited to be court painter at The Hague. His best known work is 'Old Kentucky Home.' (*National Portrait Gallery, Smithsonian Institution*)

drich of Rhode Island, but the important schedules were dictated by such interested groups as the National Association of Wool Manufacturers.[4] During his campaign Harrison had announced that 'it was no time to be weighing the claims of old soldiers with apothecary's scales,' and he lived up to the implications of that statement. 'God help the Surplus,' said Harrison's Pension Commissioner, whose openhandedness cost the Treasury millions. The total expenditures of the Fifty-first Congress, 2 December 1889 to 3 March 1891, reached the unprecedented sum of almost a billion dollars. 'This is a Billion Dollar country,' was the retort attributed to 'Czar' Reed.

Government and the Railroads

At a time when railroads were looked upon as an unmixed blessing and their promoters were regarded as public benefactors, the Federal Government aided them with a liberality which at the time seemed commendable but which a later generation came to regard as excessive. Besides granting charters and rights of way across the territories, Congress gave land, loans, subsidies, and tariff remission on rails. The Northern Pacific alone obtained the enormous total of 44 million acres of public lands, an area equal to the entire

4. The unpopularity of the McKinley tariff was largely responsible for the big turnover in the congressional elections of 1890. Only 88 Republicans were elected to the new House, as against 235 Democrats and nine Populists; McKinley himself failed of re-election.

state of Missouri. Altogether the Federal Government gave the railroads 131,350,534 acres. Furthermore, the states—notably Texas and Minnesota—granted the railroads an additional 48,883,372 acres.

While disposing briskly of their agricultural and grazing lands to obtain ready cash, the railroads reserved mineral and timber lands and potential town sites for speculative purposes, a policy encouraged by amiable interpretations of the law by successive land commissioners. Some of these holdings proved fabulously rich. It cost about $70 million to build the Northern Pacific, but in 1917 that road reported gross receipts from land sales of over $136 million, with substantial valuable acreage still unsold.

The Federal Government received substantial benefits in return for its largess. Land-grant railroads were required to carry government mail at a reduced price, and also to transport military personnel and supplies at less than normal charges, an arrangement of considerable importance during the First World War. Spokesmen for the railroads estimated the accumulated value of these benefits at more than the total worth of the land grants, but those who have ventured into the labyrinths of this accounting have never been known to emerge. However one may assess such claims, it does seem that short of government construction and operation—something unimaginable to Americans of that generation—subsidy was probably the only way to get the Western railroads built, and for all its shortcomings the system did achieve its purpose of spanning a continent. Yet, given all the chicanery in which the railroads indulged, it is not surprising that many Americans were more shocked by the corruption than impressed by the achievements.

Within a few years after the extension of the railroads, the Western farmers, who had initially welcomed them as an unmitigated boon, now blamed them for the hard times of the 1870's, which they traced to abuses by the railroads. To the farmer the most grievous abuses were the high freight rates charged by the Western roads, rates so exorbitant that the farmers at times burned their corn for fuel rather than ship it to market. The railway masters argued that they were barely

able to maintain dividend payments, and it is true that in periods of depression, such as those following upon the panics of 1873 and 1893, a good many roads went into receivership. Furthermore, on some routes vigorous competition drove rates below cost. Yet it is equally true that profits were often exorbitant, and that both the extortionate freight rates and the financial troubles of the roads were traceable to excessive construction costs, fraudulent purchase of other properties at inflated prices, stock manipulation, and incompetent management.

Construction costs ran so high chiefly because costs were artificially increased by dummy construction companies in order to provide profits for the directors. In the East, Jay Gould and Jim Fisk systematically milked the Erie Railroad, which did not finally recover until the 1940's. This technique of using dummy construction corporations is illustrated by the short-lived Southern Pennsylvania Railroad, a little road started by Vanderbilt in order to force the Pennsylvania Railroad to buy it. A contractor offered to construct it for $6.5 million, but instead Vanderbilt organized a corporation consisting of his clerks, which received $15 million to build the road; the syndicate who furnished this money was paid with $40 million in railroad shares. The Pennsylvania, which eventually had to buy this property, not unnaturally expected to earn dividends on the cost of acquiring all this. No wonder Poor's Railroad Manual for 1885 estimated that approximately one-third of all railroad capitalization that year represented water.

Complaint was loud and persistent against other abuses too. Railroad 'pools' eliminated competition in large areas by fixing prices and dividing up profits. By granting secret rebates to powerful shippers, railroads put small shippers at a hopeless disadvantage. The Standard Oil Company was granted a rebate on each barrel of oil shipped to Cleveland, and an additional drawback on each barrel shipped by a competitor. The long-and-short-haul evil consisted in slashing freight rates at competitive points and making up the losses at noncompetitive points. Goods traveling from Boston to Denver direct paid $1.70 a hundredweight, but if they traveled from Boston to San Francisco

'The Senatorial Round-House.' Thomas Nast's satirical cartoon, which appeared in *Harper's Weekly* in 1886, depicts a Senate so dominated by special interests that the nation has been reconstituted as 'The Rail-Road States of America.' As he blows off steam, the filibustering Senator treads on a copy of a bill 'to prevent members of Congress from accepting fees from subsidized railroads.' In the very next year Congress instituted the first federal regulation of railroads. (*Coll. Judith Mara Gutman*)

and then back to Denver, they went for $1.50. Farmers bridled also at railroad domination of all the great grain elevators in Chicago; through them the roads fixed the price they would pay for wheat from the hinterland. Railroads also owned the Union stockyards which enabled them pretty well to determine the price of beef in the Mid-West. Protests were voiced as well against the corrupt activities of railroads in politics. In New Hampshire, as in California, a 'railroad lobby,' ensconced in an office near the state capitol, acted as a chamber of initiative and revision; and, as the novelist Winston Churchill tells us in his *Coniston* and *Mr. Crewe's Career*, few could succeed in politics unless by grace of the Boston and Maine.

A movement to curb these abuses gained new strength during the postwar deflation and the panic of 1873. Centered in the Mid-West, it won support from Massachusetts to California. It took several forms: denial of further state aid, as in the constitutions of California, Kansas, and Missouri; recovery of land grants; prohibition of practices such as rebates and passes; and regulation of rates and services. The Eastern state governments inclined to supervision by special railway commissions, and that of Massachusetts, under the leadership of the gifted Charles Francis Adams, Jr., became the conservative model for numerous states.

The Mid-Western states adopted more direct methods. The Illinois Constitution of 1870 instructed the legislature to 'pass laws to correct abuses and to prevent unjust discrimination and extortion in the rates of freight and passenger tariffs.' Pursuant to this charter the legislature outlawed discrimination, established a maximum rate, and created a Railway and Warehouse Commission to regulate roads, grain elevators, and warehouses. At the demand of farmers, and of businessmen who had suffered from railroad discrimination, the example of Illinois, denounced as socialist in the East, was followed in 1874 by Iowa and Minnesota, and by Wisconsin with its drastic Potter law. Within a few years the railroads of the Middle West found their independence severely circumscribed by a mass of restrictive legislation.

The Supreme Court validated this legislation in the 'Granger' cases. The first and most important of these, *Munn* v. *Illinois* (1876), involved the constitutionality of a statute regulating the charges of grain elevators. In one of the most far-reaching decisions in American law, Chief Justice Morrison R. Waite, pointing to the historical right of the state in the exercise of its police power to regulate common carriers, announced:

When private property is affected with a public interest it ceases to be *juris privati* only.... When, therefore, one devotes his property to a use in which the public has an interest, he ... must submit to be controlled by the public for the common good, to the extent of the interest he has created.

The warehouse owners not only challenged the right of the state to regulate their business but contended further that rate-fixing by a legislative committee violated the Fourteenth Amendment by denying 'due process of law.' To this contention the Court responded:

The controlling fact is the power to regulate at all. If that exists, the right to establish the maximum charge, as one of the means of regulation is implied.... We know that this is a power which may be abused; but that is no argument against its existence. For protection against abuses by legislatures, the people must resort to the polls, not to the courts.

On the same day that the Court validated the Illinois statute, it handed down decisions on Granger laws establishing maximum rates in the important cases of *Peik* v. *Chicago & Northwestern R.R.*, *Chicago, Burlington & Quincy R.R.* v. *Iowa*, and *Winona & St. Peter R.R.* v. *Blake*. The Court sustained these laws against charges that they violated not only the Fourteenth Amendment but the exclusive authority of Congress over interstate commerce. The railroad, said the Court,

is employed in state as well as interstate commerce, and until Congress acts, the State must be permitted to adopt such rules and regulations as may be necessary for the promotion of the general welfare of the people within its own jurisdiction, even though in so doing those without may be indirectly affected.

Thus the Court announced three major principles: first, the right of government to regulate all business affected with a public interest; second, the

Union Stockyards, Chicago, 1889. Above is the main portal and below are the cattle pens. At a time when litigation over the regulation of marketing facilities provided the most important items on the docket of the Supreme Court, farmers and ranchers focused much of their attention on these huge stockyards, covering 360 acres and with 40 miles of railway track linked to all of the railroads entering the great city. One awe-struck observer wrote: 'If for ten hours of every working day in the year, a constant stream of cattle at the rate of ten per minute, of hogs at the rate of thirty per minute, with the small addition of four sheep every minute, passed through these yards, it would fall short of the actual numbers brought to this market for sale, slaughter, or distribution!' (*Chicago Historical Society*)

right of the legislature to determine what is fair and reasonable; third, the right of the state, in areas of concurrent authority, to act where Congress has failed to act.

Within a decade the composition of the Supreme Court became more conservative, and two of the three Granger principles were duly modified. In 1886, in the Wabash case, the Court retreated from the third principle by holding invalid an Illinois statute prohibiting the 'long-and-short-haul' evil, on the ground that it infringed upon the exclusive power of Congress over interstate commerce. That same year, in *Stone* v. *Farmers' Loan Co.*, the Court intimated that the reasonableness of the rate established by a commission might be a matter for judicial rather than legislative determination. Three years later, in *Chicago, Milwaukee and St. Paul Railroad Co.* v. *Minnesota*, this obiter dictum became the basis for a decision invalidating rate regulation by a legislative commission. These decisions dealt a heavy blow to state regulation of roads and rates, and placed the burden squarely upon the Federal Government.

Congress responded with the Interstate Commerce Act of 1887, which represented a compromise between the Massachusetts or supervisory type of regulation and the Granger or coercive type of regulation. It specifically prohibited pooling, rebates, discrimination of any character, and higher rates for a short haul than for a long haul. It provided that all charges should be 'reasonable and just' but failed to define either of these ambiguous terms. Perhaps most important, it established the first permanent administrative board[5] of the Federal Government, the Interstate Commerce Commission, to administer the law. Enforcement was left to the courts, but a large part of the burden of proof and prosecution was placed upon the commission. Although the bill was popularly regarded as a victory for the public, it had the support of the railroads, and railway stocks rose in the market upon its passage.

Administrative regulations were still so foreign to the American conception of government that the federal courts insisted upon their right to review orders of the Interstate Commerce Commission, and by a series of decisions took the teeth out of the act. In the *Maximum Freight Rate* case (1897), the Supreme Court held that the commission did not have the power to fix rates, and in the *Alabama Midlands* case of the same year it practically nullified the long-and-short-haul prohibition. It was found almost impossible to require agents of the railroads to testify about railroad malpractices, and witnesses would introduce into the court new testimony which had been withheld from the commission, thus requiring an entirely new adjudication. Reversals of the commission's rulings were frequent; by 1905 fifteen of the sixteen cases appealed to the Supreme Court had been decided adversely to the commission. Furthermore, down to 1897 shippers had succeeded in collecting refunds from recalcitrant roads in only five out of 225 cases. Indeed, the roads evaded the provisions of the act so successfully that Justice Harlan declared the commission to be a 'useless body for all practical purposes,' and the commission itself, in its annual report for 1898, confessed its failure. Nevertheless, the principle of federal regulation of railroads had been established, and the machinery for such regulation created. It remained for a later administration to apply the principle and make the machinery effective.

5. The Civil Service Commission, established in 1883, came four years earlier, but it was not involved directly in regulation of the economy.

24

The Embattled Farmer

1860–1897

The Agricultural Revolution

While manufacturing was advancing rapidly in the half-century following the Civil War, agriculture remained the basic industry, the one which engaged the largest number of people. But agriculture itself was undergoing a revolution, featuring expansion of its domain, application of machinery and science to farming, use of modern transportation to convey products to world-wide markets, and intervention by the Federal Government. This revolution exposed the farmer to the vicissitudes of the industrial economy and the world market and brought a vast increase in productivity which did not always yield comparable returns. From 1860 to 1910 the number of farms in the United States and the acreage of improved farm land trebled. More land was brought under cultivation in the 30 years after 1860 than in all the previous history of the nation. Yet in 1900 the farmers' share of the national wealth was less than half that of 1860. Farm population grew absolutely, but the proportion of people living on farms declined; while the agricultural domain expanded, the relative political and social position of the farmer contracted.

In the half-century after the Civil War farming was subjected to a series of shocks. First, war and its aftermath partially destroyed the plantation system and fostered the crop-lien and sharecrop systems. Second, opening up the High Plains and the West depressed farming in the Middle West and the East and required drastic readjustments. In 1860 Ohio led the nation in the production of wool; by 1900 Wyoming and New Mexico were the leading woolen states. A third shock was the rapid growth of world markets, and of world competition, as the productivity of the American farm outstripped the nation's capacity to consume. American wheat competed with the wheat of the Argentine, Australia, and Russia; beef and wool with the products of Australia, New Zealand, and the Argentinian pampas; cotton with Egypt and India. Fourth, and scarcely less disturbing to the agricultural equilibrium, was the impact of new machinery, new crops, and new techniques. Except in isolated regions like the Southern highlands or the rich Pennsylvania and Maryland country, the average farm ceased to be a self-sufficient unit, where a man and his family raised most of what they needed, and became instead a cog in an industrial system.

Residence of Mr E. R. Jones. Town Dodgeville. Wis. 1881.

'Residence of Mr. E. R. Jones,' Dodgeville, Wisconsin, 1881. This watercolor and tempera rendering of a Midwestern farm was done by the self-taught 'naïve' artist Paul Seifert, who revealed a talent for composition and precise detail and who achieved unusual shading by painting on colored paper. The Dodgeville area had been settled sixty years earlier by lead miners, and as farmers tilled the soil they could hear 'the rumble of blasts deep beneath the earth' under their furrows. (*New York State Historical Association*)

One thing, however, did not greatly change. American agriculture continued to be extensive rather than intensive, robbing the land of its fertility and leaving desolation behind. Not until the sharp rise in farm land values in the early years of the new century dramatized the passing of cheap good land did the government realize the need for conservation, or the farmer the necessity for scientific farming. Then it was almost too late. When economists came to count the cost, they found that 100 million acres—an area equal to Illinois, Ohio, North Carolina, and Maryland— had been irreparably destroyed by erosion; that another 200 million acres were badly eroded; that over large areas the grasslands of the Great Plains had been turned into dust, and that the forest resources of the Eastern half of the country were rapidly disappearing.

The Use and Abuse of the Homestead Act

Under the Homestead Act any citizen, except one who had served in the Confederate army, could obtain 160 acres on the public domain by living on it or cultivating it for five years. Recognizing that the neat little rectangular farm of the East was not really suitable to the West, Congress added a complex series of other laws: the Timber Culture Act of 1873, the Desert Land Act of 1877, the Timber and Stone Act of 1878, the Carey Irriga- tion Act of 1894, and the Enlarged Homestead Act of 1909. These statutes broadened the areas that could be patented, facilitated entry and final ac- quisition, and provided government aid to enter- prises like reclamation.

All of this should have meant that the immense public domain—perhaps 1 billion acres in 1860— would go into the hands of the independent yeoman. In fact, only one-sixth to one-tenth of the public domain went to Homesteaders, and the rest was not given away but sold—or held off the market by speculators, or by the government it- self. By the end of the century Homesteaders had patented about 80 million acres, but the railroads had received—from federal and state govern- ments—180 million acres, the states had been given 140 million acres, and another 200 mil- lion acres—much of it Indian lands—had been

put up for sale to the highest bidders. The Home- stead policy was never suited to the needs of the landless workingman or immigrant; after all, how was he to move himself and his family to the West, build a house and barn, buy farm equip- ment and cattle, and keep going for a year until the money for his crops came in? Moreover, for all their professed concern for the independent yeoman, Congress and the states proved far more interested in satisfying the demands of business and speculator groups. Railroads and lumber companies, ranchers' associations, emigration and colonization companies, and individual specu- lators like Ezra Cornell of New York or Amos Lawrence of Boston got princely domains.

The disposition of public lands in the South illustrates the unhappy history of the Homestead Act. In 1866 Congress set aside some 47 million acres of public lands in five Southern states for 80-acre homesteads. Ten years later the pressure of Northern lumber interests forced a repeal of these arrangements, and the land was thrown open to purchase by speculators. One con- gressman acquired 111,000 acres in Louisiana; a Michigan firm got 700,000 acres of pine lands. One English company bought 2 million acres of timberland in Florida, and another got 1.5 million acres in Louisiana for 45 cents an acre. In 1906 a government expert concluded that the exploita- tion of the South by these and other companies was 'probably the most rapid and reckless destruc- tion of forests known to history.'

Cleveland instituted some far-reaching re- forms, and these were carried further under Har- rison. An act of 1889 put an end to all cash sale of public lands, and the next year the government limited land acquisitions to 320 acres; in 1891 came the first act setting aside forest reservations on public lands. But these modifications were both too little and too late.

Machinery and Scientific Agriculture

The application of machinery to agriculture lagged fully a century behind the application of ma- chinery to industry. Mechanization of agriculture began in the 'thirties and 'forties, when Obed Hussey and Cyrus McCormick experimented

The 'Holt combine.' Drawn by thirty-three mules, this harvester, which first appeared in 1886, marked the culmination of the era of animal power just before the gasoline engine revolutionized agricultural machinery. (*Caterpillar Tractor Co.*)

with a reaper, A. D. Church and George Westinghouse with a thresher, and John Lane and John Deere with a chilled plow. Agricultural machinery, however, remained relatively unimportant before 1860. The Civil War, robbing farms of their laborers and raising grain prices, induced farmers to adopt machines such as the reaper, which enabled a woman or a boy to perform the work of several men. Over 100,000 reapers were in use by 1861 and during four years of war the number grew by a quarter of a million. After the war almost every operation in the North from seeding to harvesting was mechanized. The Oliver chilled plow, perfected in 1877, meant an enormous saving in time and money; within a few years the wonderfully efficient rotary plowed and harrowed the soil and drilled the grain in a single operation. George Appleby's twine binder greatly increased the amount of grain a farmer could harvest, and the steam threshing machine was perfected. Within twenty years the bonanza farms of California were using 'combines' which reaped, threshed, cleaned, and bagged the grain in a single operation. During these same years the mowing machine, the corn planter, corn binder, husker and sheller, the manure spreader, the four-plow cultivator, the potato planter, the mechanical hay drier, the poultry incubator, the cream separator, and innumerable other machines entirely transformed the ancient practices of agriculture. It took 21 hours to harvest a ton of timothy hay in 1850; half a century later, four hours. This vast saving in labor made it possible for a proportionately smaller number of farmers to feed an ever-increasing number of city-dwellers and have a surplus left for export.

In the twentieth century came the application of steam, gasoline, and electricity to the farm. Huge combines, formerly drawn by 20 or 30 horses, were propelled by gasoline tractors. The value of farm implements and machines increased from about $246 million in 1860 to $750 million in 1900, and then, swiftly, to $3595 million in 1920. This growth was distinctly sectional. Mechanization did not profit much of New England, with its rolling topography and little specialties, or the South where cotton and tobacco farming did not take readily to machines. But the Middle West and the Far West absorbed reapers, mowers, tractors, harvesters, and threshers at a great rate. In 1920 the average value of farm implements and machinery on each South Dakota farm was $1500; on each farm in the Cotton Belt $215.

Farming as a way of life gave way to farming as a business. The small diversified farm of the 1860's, with fields of grain, orchard and vegetable garden, pasture mowing and woodlot, gave way to the large farm specializing in staple crops which could be produced with one kind of machinery and sold for cash. Rising land values, heavy costs of machinery, and the substitution of chemical fertilizer for manure required capital and commonly involved the farmer in heavy indebtedness. One result was an ominous increase in farm mortgages and in tenancy: by 1930 almost every second farmer was a tenant, and one-fifth of the total value of farms was mortgaged.

As long as there was abundant cheap land and a shortage of labor, conditions which obtained until some time after the Civil War, it was more economical for farmers to abandon wornout soil and move on to virgin land than to cultivate intensively and invest in expensive fertilizers. It was the passing of these conditions that led to scientific agriculture, conservation, and reclamation. Scientific agriculture in the United States has depended largely upon government aid. A number of states subsidized agriculture even before the Civil War, and as early as 1839 Congress made its first appropriation, $1000, for agricultural research, although the Constitution gives Congress no explicit jurisdiction over farming. In 1862 Congress created a Department of Agriculture, under the direction of a commissioner with the happy name of Isaac Newton, and in 1889 this department was raised to executive grade with a secretary of cabinet rank. The Department of Agriculture grew steadily until by 1930 it embraced some 40 subdivisions and bureaus and spent almost $100 million.[1] Its Bureau of Plant Industry introduced over 30,000 foreign plants including alfalfa from Liberia, short-kernel rice from Japan, seedless grapes from Italy, and grass from the Sudan to cover the High Plains; its Bureau of Entomology fought plant diseases; its Bureau of Animal Husbandry conquered hog cholera, sheep scab, and Texas fever in cattle. The first government department to undertake extensive research, it was, for a time, the country's leading research institution.

The Morrill Land-Grant College Act of 1862 not only had a great impact on education but was the most important piece of agricultural legislation in American history. This far-sighted law, which provided for the appropriation of public land to each state for the establishment of agricultural and industrial colleges, discriminated heavily in favor of the more populous states of the

1. In 1968 the Federal Government spent $5.9 billion on agriculture. In 1973 the Federal Government spent $6.2 billion on agriculture.

Winslow Homer, 'Country School,' 1871. Homer's painting, though realistic in its portrayal of peeling walls and cracked floorboards, conveys a romantic innocence of the rural setting and the idealized young woman teacher. Through such a scene, writes Marshall Davidson, move 'Whittier's barefoot boys and Howells' summertime idlers.' Though the locus of the painting is interior, one has a pervasive awareness of nature immediately beyond the sun-bright windows. (*City Art Museum of St. Louis*)

East—where farming was of less importance—and against the agricultural states of the West. New York State got almost a million acres of Western lands, while Kansas, which depended entirely on agriculture, got 90,000 acres. Seventeen of the states, including Illinois, Wisconsin, and Minnesota, turned the Morrill land-grant money over to the existing state universities; others, like Iowa, Indiana, and Oregon, chose to set up independent agricultural and mechanical colleges. At first agricultural colleges were looked upon by the farmer with suspicion, but in time farmers learned their value and came to take pride in them. Scarcely second to the Morrill Act in importance was the Hatch Act of 1887. Influenced by the valuable work performed by the experimental station of Wesleyan University in Middletown, Connecticut, Congress provided in this act for agricultural experiment stations in every state; since that time Congress has steadily expanded the work of education and experimentation in agriculture.

Scientific agriculture has its roll of heroes. Mark Alfred Carleton, who experienced on the Kansas plains the devastations of wheat rust and rot and the vagaries of Kansas weather, scoured Asia for a wheat strong enough to withstand the rust, the droughts, and the frosts of the Middle West. He returned with the Kubanka wheat and later introduced the Kharkov wheat to the American farmer; by 1919 over one-third of U.S. wheat acreage was sown with Carleton's varieties. Niels Ebbesen Hansen of the South Dakota Agricultural College brought back from the steppes of Turkestan and the plateaus of inner Mongolia a yellow-flowered alfalfa that would flourish in the American Northwest. From Algeria and Tunis and the oases of the Sahara came white Kaffir corn, introduced by Dr. J. H. Watkins, and admirably adapted to the hot dry climate of the great Southwest. Dr. Stephen M. Babcock saved the dairy farmers of the nation millions of dollars through the Babcock milk test, which determined the butter fat content of milk; he gave the patent to the University of Wisconsin. Seaman Knapp found in the Orient varieties of rice wonderfully adapted to the Gulf region today. Luther Burbank, in his experimental garden at Santa Rosa, California, created a host of new plants by skillful crossing, and George Washington Carver of the Tuskegee Institute developed hundreds of new uses for the peanut, the sweet potato, and the soy bean.

The Agricultural Revolution in the South

The Civil War and Reconstruction shattered the old plantation regime in the South and brought about a widespread redistribution of land and revolutionary patterns of land-tenure. The crippling of the planter class led to the most far-reaching transfer of land-ownership since the Revolution, as yeoman farmers, small merchants and businessmen, Northern soldiers, carpetbaggers, and investors snapped up what looked like bargains in land. On the surface this meant the breakup of plantations into small farms and a striking increase in land-ownership. In 1860 there were 55,128 farms in Alabama; twenty years later there were 135,864. Between 1860 and 1880 in nine cotton states the number of farms under ten acres jumped almost twentyfold.

But these figures are misleading. The years after the war saw a revolution not in land-ownership but in farm labor. The number of large farms (or plantations) remained about the same, but now they were divided up into small 'holdings' and farmed not by slaves but by sharecroppers and tenants. In Louisiana the percentage of farms over

100 acres actually went up in the two decades after secession from 34 to 70. As C. Vann Woodward concludes, 'The evils of land monopoly, absentee ownership, soil mining, and the one-crop system, once associated with and blamed upon slavery, did not disappear, but were instead, aggravated, intensified, and multiplied.'[2]

The explanation was to be found in the sharecrop and crop-lien systems. These twin evils emerged as a response to the breakdown of the old labor system and the collapse of credit after the war. Sharecropping was an arrangement whereby planters could obtain labor without paying wages and landless farmers could get land without paying rent. Instead of an interchange of money, there was a sharing of crops. The planter furnished his tenant with land and frame cabin, and, generally, with seed, fertilizer, a mule, a plow, and other implements; in return he received at the end of the year one-half of the crop which the tenant raised. The tenant furnished his labor, and got, in return, the rest of the crop as well as whatever he could raise for himself in his vegetable garden. At the end of the war most freedmen and many poor white farmers entered into such an arrangement. This system, which appeared at first to be mutually advantageous, was really injurious to all. The sharecropper was rarely able to escape into the farm-owning class; the planter could seldom farm efficiently with sharecrop labor. With every year the number of tenant farmers increased, farm profits and soil fertility decreased. In 1880, one-third of the farmers of the Cotton Belt were tenants; forty years later, two-thirds.

The crop-lien system was perhaps even more disastrous. Under this system the farmer mortgaged his ungrown crop in order to obtain supplies for the year. Rates of interest were usurious, and the merchant who supplied food, clothing, seed, and other necessities customarily charged from 20 to 50 per cent above the normal price. Because cotton and tobacco were sure money crops, creditors generally insisted that most of the land be planted to one of these, which accelerated soil exhaustion. As early as 1880 two-thirds of the farmers of South Carolina had

2. *Origins of the New South*, pp. 179–80.

mortgaged their ungrown crops, and by 1900 this proportion was applicable to the entire cotton belt. Sharecrop and crop-lien systems served to keep the poorer farmers of the South in perpetual bondage to the large planters, country storekeepers, and bankers—a condition from which few were ever able to extricate themselves. For when the farmer's share failed to meet the inflated charges against him at the country store, he was forced to renew the lien on next year's crop to the same merchant—and often on more onerous conditions. The result was increasing impoverishment of the farm population, growing class stratification, and a determination to seek political redress.

The 'Farm Problem'

When we've wood and prairie land,
Won by our toil,
We'll reign like kings in fairy land,
Lords of the soil.

So sang Richard Garland and the 'trail-makers of the Middle Border' as they pushed hopefully westward from the forests of Maine to the coulees of Wisconsin, the prairies of Iowa, and the sunbaked plains of Kansas, Nebraska, and the Dakotas. They won their wood and prairie land, but often won it for others—for absentee landlords, railroads, banks, and mortgage companies, who became the real lords of the soil. Within a generation the 'marching song of the Garlands' gave way to a different tune:

There's a dear old homestead on Nebraska's fertile plain,
There I toiled my manhood's strength away:
All that labor now is lost to me, but it is Shylock's gain,
For that dear old home he claims today.

And when young Hamlin Garland wrote his *Main-Travelled Roads* he dedicated it to 'my father and mother, whose half-century of pilgrimage on the main travelled road of life has brought them only pain and weariness.'

The conquest of a continent had resulted not in the realization of Jefferson's dream of a great agrarian democracy but in a 'farm problem.' There was the physical problem of soil exhaustion and erosion, drought and frost and flood, plant and animal diseases; the economic problem of rising costs and declining returns, exploitation in the domestic market and rivalry in the world market, mortgages and tenancy; the social problem of isolation and drabness, inadequate educational, religious, medical, and recreational facilities, narrowing opportunity and declining prestige. Finally, there was the political problem of wresting remedial legislation from intransigent governments, which were much more responsive to the demands of business than to the appeals of the farmer.

Of all these problems, the physical difficulties were the most intractable. By 1930 almost 100 million acres in the South—approximately onesixth of the total—had been hopelessly lost or seriously impaired through erosion, and in some sections of the Piedmont as much as half of the arable land had been swept of its topsoil. Early travelers in the South recorded that the streams were as clear as those of New England, but by the twentieth century the rivers of the South, which every year carried to the ocean over 50 million tons of soil, were mud-black or clay-red. Southern farmers tried to replenish their worn-out soil with fertilizer, but that meant an intolerable financial burden. Not until the Tennessee Valley Authority began to produce cheap fertilizer and the New Deal to provide low-cost farm loans was the South able to inaugurate a program of restoration.

In the grasslands of the West, too, the farmer confronted the ravages of insect pests. Before the attack of the chinch bug and the corn borer, the boll weevil and the alfalfa weevil, the average farmer was all but helpless, and what reader of Rölvaag's *Giants in the Earth* can forget how the grasshoppers destroyed not only the wheat but the morale of the farmers of the West:

And now from out the sky gushed down with cruel force a living, pulsating stream, striking the backs of the helpless folk like pebbles thrown by an unseen hand.... This substance had no sooner fallen that it popped up again, crackling and snapping—rose up and disappeared in the twinkling of an eye; it flared and flittered around them like light gone mad; it chirped and buzzed through the air; it snapped and hopped along the ground; the whole place was a weltering turmoil of raging little demons.... They whizzed by in the air; they literally

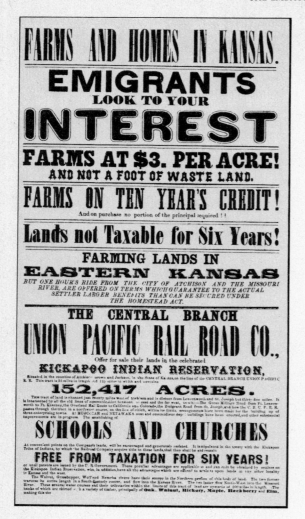

FARMS AND HOMES IN KANSAS.
EMIGRANTS
LOOK TO YOUR
INTEREST
FARMS AT $3. PER ACRE!
AND NOT A FOOT OF WASTE LAND.
FARMS ON TEN YEAR'S CREDIT!
And on purchase no portion of the principal required ! !

Lands not Taxable for Six Years!
FARMING LANDS IN
EASTERN KANSAS
BUT ONE HOUR'S RIDE FROM THE CITY OF ATCHISON AND THE MISSOURI RIVER, ARE OFFERED ON TERMS WHICH GUARANTEE TO THE ACTUAL SETTLER LARGER BENEFITS THAN CAN BE SECURED UNDER THE HOMESTEAD ACT.

THE CENTRAL BRANCH
UNION PACIFIC RAIL ROAD CO.,
Offer for sale their lands in the celebrated
KICKAPOO INDIAN RESERVATION,
Situated in the counties of Atchison, Brown and Jackson, on the line of the CENTRAL BRANCH UNION PACIFIC R. R. This tract is 22 miles in length and 11½ miles in width and contains
152,417 ACRES.

SCHOOLS AND CHURCHES
FREE FROM TAXATION FOR SIX YEARS!

Railroad lands for sale, May 1867. This poster announces the availability of a huge tract in northern Kansas purchased by the Union Pacific from the Kickapoo Indians. The placard boasts of the presence of coal and points out that the land, bisected by the old Overland Mail Route to California, is watered by tributaries of the Kansas and Missouri rivers along which are stands of oak, walnut, hickory, maple, hackberry, and elm. (*Union Pacific Railroad Museum*)

covered the ground; they lit on the heads of grain, on the stubble, on everything in sight—popping and glittering, millions on millions of them. The people watched it stricken with fear and awe.[3]

More complex, but more susceptible to remedial action, was the farmer's economic problem: rising costs and falling prices, a situation exacerbated by the rapid expansion of the agricultural domain. This expansion westward brought ruin to the farmers of New England and the seaboard South and placed the Western farmer in a precarious position, because his future rested on unrealistic assumptions about the land, the weather, the market, and the credit system. Even official reports of the Kansas Board of Agriculture told prospective settlers: 'Kansas agriculture means a life of ease, perpetual June weather, and a steady diet of milk and honey.' One Kansas newspaper urged:

Do not be afraid of going into debt. Spend money for the city's betterment as free as water. Too much cannot be spent this year, if properly applied. Let the bugaboo of high taxes be nursed by old women. Do all you can for Belle Plaine regardless of money, and let the increase of population and wealth take care of the taxes. Double, treble, quadruple our expenditures, and do it in the right manner, and before the year 1886 is passed Belle Plaine will be able to pay them and much more—and Belle Plaine will boom with a double pica black face B.

This boom spirit was exacerbated by the eagerness of Eastern banks and loan companies to lend money without discretion. *Rhodes Journal of Banking* estimated that the savings banks of New Hampshire and Vermont had invested 40 per cent of their funds in Western mortgages. So great was the desire of Easterners to speculate that competition existed not among borrowers but among lenders. The manager of one loan company reported: 'During many months of 1886 and 1887 we were unable to get enough mortgages for the people of the East who wished to invest in that kind of security. My desk was piled high every morning with hundreds of letters each enclosing a draft and asking me to send a farm mortgage from Kansas or Nebraska.'

This feverish optimism overlooked the fact that

3. *Giants in the Earth*, Harper & Bros., pp. 342–43.

the opening up of the West was paralleled by a no less remarkable expansion of the agricultural domain of Canada, the Argentine, Australia, Russia, and Brazil. When the American farmer grew more than the American market could absorb—a condition with which the cotton planter was long familiar—he had to sell his product in the world market, which determined the price he received, at home as abroad. Industry, which could regulate its production and which operated behind tariff walls, bought in a world market and sold in a protected market; agriculture, which could not effectively regulate its production and had little to gain from tariffs, bought in a protected market and sold in a world market. The cost of the farmer's transportation was fixed by the railroads, his manure by a fertilizer trust, his farm implements by the McCormick Harvester Company, his fencing by a barbed wire trust. The prices he paid for daily necessities—for furniture and clothing, for lumber and leather goods—were artificially raised by the operation of protective tariffs.

The expansion of agriculture into the West meant an absolute dependence upon railroads, and freight charges came to consume an increasingly large share of the farmer's income. The *Prairie Farmer* asserted in 1867 that Iowa corn cost eight or ten times as much at Liverpool as the farmer received for it at the local grain elevator. In 1880 wheat fetched almost a dollar in the Chicago pit, but it cost 45 cents to ship a bushel of wheat from central Nebraska to Chicago. Furthermore, railroads came to control the warehouse facilities of the West, fixed the price for storage, and controlled grading.

Above all, the price the farmer paid for money was prohibitively high. Some states attempted, through usury laws, to fix low interest rates, but such laws were flouted or evaded, and interest rates in the farm belts of the South and West were seldom below 10 per cent and in the 'nineties much higher. Inadequate banking facilities were in part responsible. In 1880 the per capita banking power of the Eastern states was $176, of the Central states $27, and of the Southern states $10. Furthermore, with the rise in the value of money after the Civil War, the farmers' debt appreciated steadily. It took about 1200 bushels of wheat, corn, oats, barley, and rye to buy a $1000 mort-

gage in the years 1867 to 1869; between 1886 and 1888 it required approximately 2300 bushels to repay that mortgage.

During most of the thirty years after the Civil War the farmer of the South and West was the victim not only of rising costs but of falling prices. Wheat which netted the farmer $1.45 a bushel in 1866 brought only 49 cents in 1894. Corn which brought 75 cents at Chicago in 1869 fell to 28 cents in 1889. Cotton sold at 31 cents a pound in 1866 and 6 cents in 1893. Agriculture, which represented not quite half of the national wealth in 1860, accounted for but one-fifth half a century later. The value of manufactured products was 50 per cent higher in 1870 than the value of all farm products; by 1910 it was over twice as large. The farmer received 30 per cent of the national income in 1860, 19 per cent in 1890, 13 per cent in 1920, and after the collapse of the early 'thirties, 7 per cent in 1933.

Farming yielded not only decreasing economic returns but also decreasing social returns. Before the coming of the automobile, the telephone, and the radio, the isolation of the farm was fearful. Thousands of families were cut off from companionship and conviviality, church and school. Thousands of mothers died in childbirth, thousands of children died through lack of simple medical care. It was the women who suffered most from the narrowness of farm life. The confession of Benét's John Vilas might have been that of a whole generation of pioneers:

> I took my wife out of a pretty house,
> I took my wife out of a pleasant place,
> I stripped my wife of comfortable things,
> I drove my wife to wander with the wind.[4]

No wonder the wives and the mothers inspired the revolt against the farm, and encouraged their sons and daughters to try their fortunes in the cities.

City life offered opportunities and conferred a social prestige that no longer attached to farm life. The farmers, who had once been regarded as 'the chosen people of God,' came to be looked upon as 'hayseeds' and 'hicks,' fit subjects for the comic strip or the vaudeville joke. An ever increasing number of young people, unwilling to accept the

4. *John Brown's Body*, p. 143.

Sod-house frontier. In this photograph, taken about 1886, the Chrisman sisters pose in their finest before their sod home on Lillian Creek north of Broken Bow, Custer County, Nebraska. In *Old Jules*, Mari Sandoz has written a moving memoir of the experiences of a girl raised in a sod house in Nebraska's Niobrara river country northwest of Broken Bow. (*Nebraska State Historical Society*)

drudgery and frustration that their parents had suffered, left the farms for the cities. Between 1870 and 1930 the rural population declined from over 80 to less than 40 per cent of the total, and the drop in the actual farm population was even more precipitous.

It must not be supposed that the farmer made no effort to save himself. For almost every problem he had a solution, one that was usually reasonable and intelligent. But solutions generally required legislative action, and the farmer was

seldom in a position to obtain such action. From Jefferson to Jefferson Davis the politics of the nation had been guided chiefly by those who were responsible to the farmers. But with the shift in population from the farm to the city, the rise of giant corporations, and the concentration of financial power in the East, this situation changed. Farmers wanted railroad regulation, but the railroad interest was too powerful, except for the brief Granger interlude. The vast majority of farmers wanted cheap money and a more flexible banking system, too, but they got neither. Farmers still constituted the largest single economic group in 1870, but they could not bridge the sectional gulf. Although the Southern planter and the Middle Western farmer shared similar problems, they failed to forge an effective alliance. Nor were the farmers successful in placing their representatives in state legislatures or in Congress. Lawyers and businessmen constituted the majority of the legislatures even in such states as Georgia and Nebraska, while in the halls of Congress a 'dirt' farmer was something of a curiosity.

Agrarian Revolt

When the bubble of Civil War prosperity burst in 1868, the collapse of crop prices resulted in the first agrarian revolt, which featured the organization of farmers' societies. The first of the societies was the Patrons of Husbandry, commonly known as the Grange. In 1866 President Johnson sent Oliver H. Kelley, a clerk in the Bureau of Agriculture, on a tour of investigation through the South. Kelley returned deeply impressed with the poverty, isolation, and backwardness of the farmers of that section, and determined to establish a farmers' society which might ameliorate these evils. In 1867 he and a group of government clerks in Washington, D.C., founded the Patrons of Husbandry, and in the following year the first permanent Grange of this society was born in Fredonia, New York. When the panic of 1873 burst, the Grange had penetrated every state but four. Two years later it boasted a membership of over 800,000 in some 20,000 local Granges, most of them in the Middle West and the South. The major function of the Grange was social. One secret of its success was that it admitted women to membership, and for farmers' wives the Grange, with its meetings and picnics, lectures and entertainments, offered an escape from the loneliness and drudgery of the farm.

The Grange was formally non-political, but almost from the beginning the movement took on a distinctly political character. In Illinois, Iowa, Wisconsin, Minnesota, Kansas, California, and elsewhere, the farmers elected their candidates to legislatures and judgeships, and agitated for regulatory statutes. The result was the so-called Granger laws limiting railroad and warehouse charges and prohibiting some of the grosser railway abuses.

The Grangers also embarked upon business ventures. To eliminate the middleman, they established hundreds of co-operative stores on the Rochdale plan, whereby profits were divided among shareholders in proportion to their purchases. They set up co-operative creameries, elevators, and warehouses, organized farmers' insurance companies, and constructed their own factories, which turned out excellent reapers, sewing machines, and wagons for half the price charged by private concerns. But owing to relentless opposition by business and banking interests, the individualism of the farmers, overexpansion and mismanagement, most of the co-operative enterprises failed. Yet some good resulted. Prices were reduced, thousands of farmers saved money, and with the establishment of Montgomery Ward and Company in 1872 specifically 'to meet the wants of the Patrons of Husbandry' the mail-order business came into existence. By 1880 Grange membership had fallen to 100,000. Chastened, the Grange confined itself thereafter largely to social activities.

The Grange gave way to the more aggressive Farmers' Alliances, and the history of farm revolt during the 'eighties and 'nineties is largely that of the Alliance movement. There were, at the start, several Alliances, but by the late 'eighties consolidation had resulted in the creation of two powerful groups, the Northwestern Alliance, and the Farmers' Alliance and Industrial Union, commonly known as the Southern Alliance. The Northwestern Alliance was particularly strong in Kansas, Nebraska, Iowa, Minnesota, and the Dakotas, and during the hard times of the late 'eighties it became a major influence in the politics of the Middle Border. The Southern Alliance dated back to a cattlemen's association in Lampasas County, Texas, in the middle 'seventies. By the early 'nineties the Southern Alliance boasted a membership of from one to three million and was the most powerful farmers' organization in the country. It had three times as many members as the Northwestern Alliance, and was much more

Granger meeting. This engraving is of a gathering near Winchester in Scott County, Illinois, in 1873. Notice the presence of women, who were organized in Grange auxiliaries. One placard protests against a scandal of the Grant administration, 'No More Mobilier Swindle,' while another reads, 'President $50,000 a Year, Congressmen $7000 a Year, Farmers 75 cts. a Week?' (*Library of Congress*)

radical. Despite an obvious community of interest between the Northwestern and the Southern Alliances, all efforts to amalgamate the two organizations foundered on the rocks of sectionalism.

The activities of the Alliances were more diverse than those of the Grange. Social affairs included not only the customary meetings and picnics, but farmers' institutes, circulating libraries, and the publication of hundreds of farm newspapers and dozens of magazines, so that the Alliance became, in the words of one observer, a farmers' national university. The economic enterprises of the Alliance were more substantial than those of the Grange. The North Dakota Alliance underwrote co-operative insurance, the Illinois Alliance organized co-operative marketing, and thousands of farmers' 'exchanges' were established; it was estimated that in 1890 the various Alliances did a business of over $10 million.

But historically the significance of the Alliance lies in its political rather than its social and economic activities. From the first the Alliances entered more vigorously into politics than had the Grange. Their programs embraced demands for

436

strict regulation or even government ownership of railroads and means of communication, currency inflation, abolition of national banks, prohibition of alien land ownership and of trading in futures on the exchange, more equitable taxation, and progressive political reforms. An original contribution was the sub-treasury scheme, which provided for government warehouses where farmers might deposit non-perishable produce, receiving in exchange a loan of up to 80 per cent of the market value of the produce, which might be redeemed when the farmer had sold his produce. This scheme had the triple advantage of enabling the farmer to borrow at a low rate of interest, sell his produce at the most favorable market price, and profit by an expanded and flexible currency. When first advanced, it was regarded as a socialistic aberration, but the Warehouse Act of 1916 and the Commodity Credit Corporation of 1933 adopted a similar proposal as national policy. By 1890, the Alliances, with an ambitious set of legislative demands, were prepared to plunge into national politics to launch the Populist movement, the most far-reaching farm protest in the history of the nation.

Populism

In 1890 American politics lost its steady beat and began to dip and flutter among strange currents of thought that issued from the caverns of discontent. Many Americans had come to feel that something was radically wrong and groped for a remedy. Industrial unrest was acute; 1890 witnessed the most strikes in any one year of the nineteenth century. Money was tight, credit inflexible, and banking facilities inadequate. Vital political institutions were undemocratic: the Senate, chosen not by popular vote but by state legislatures, was a stronghold of special interests; the Supreme Court increasingly reflected the ideas of the privileged.

Dissatisfaction was most acute on the farms of the South and the West. The Middle Border was suffering the devastating effects of deflation following a land boom. After several years of excessive rainfall there came in 1887 a summer so dry that crops withered all along the border of the

Plains. Eight of the next ten years in western Kansas and the Dakotas were too arid, and the region suffered also from chinch bugs, high winds, and killing frosts. From 1889 to 1893 more than 11,000 farm mortgages were foreclosed in Kansas alone and in fifteen counties of that state over three-quarters of the land fell into the hands of mortgage companies. The West was literally in bondage to the East. During these years the people who had entered that El Dorado trekked eastward again; on their wagons they scrawled, 'In God we trusted, in Kansas we busted.' Whole sections of the West were left without a single person. Half the people of western Kansas deserted the country between 1888 and 1892. Little wonder that Oliver Goldsmith's 'The Deserted Village' was the favorite work of Populist orators. The misery of the Middle Border was more than matched in the South where cotton growers struggled from year to year against a falling market, while mortgage indebtedness and tenancy grew at an ominous rate.

In the 1890 elections the angry farmer struck back. The Southern Alliance, spurning third party tactics, launched a campaign to capture the Democratic party, and scored a series of stunning victories. It won control of the legislatures in eight states, and elected six governors and more than 50 Congressmen. In South Carolina, 'Pitchfork Ben' Tillman pushed a series of reforms through the legislature and created a political machine to do his bidding. That same year the Alliance helped launch a series of state third parties in the West. These new parties elected five of seven Congressmen and a U.S. Senator in Kansas and won the balance of power in South Dakota and Minnesota. Kansas called its organization the People's party, which two years later was to be the name of the national party. A generation which knew its Latin found it an easy transition from People's party to calling its followers Populists.

The new party had some remarkable leaders. Davis H. Waite, Governor of Colorado, friend of all the underprivileged of the earth, was called by his admirers the 'Abraham Lincoln of the Rockies' and by his critics 'Bloody Bridles Waite' because he had said it was better 'that blood should flow to the horses' bridles rather than our national liber-

'I Feed You All!' This lithograph perceives the farmer as the fulcrum of American society as the nation celebrates its centennial. The other figures—the lawyer, the statesman, the soldier, the preacher—are peripheral while the broker, who appears over the caption 'I Fleece You All,' is viewed with contempt. The picture suggests, not altogether correctly, a society still pre-industrial—the age of sail rather than steam, the noble yeoman not at his tractor but at his plow. (*Library of Congress*)

ties should be destroyed.' Minnesota boasted the inimitable Ignatius Donnelly, discoverer of the lost Atlantis, advocate of the theory that Bacon wrote Shakespeare's plays, author of the prophetic *Caesar's Column*, undismayed champion of lost causes and desperate remedies. Kansas, where, as William Allen White remembered, the

farm revolt became 'a religious revival, a crusade, a pentecost of politics in which the tongue of flame sat upon every man and each spake as the spirit gave him utterance' was most prolific of leadership. Here the sad-faced Mary Lease went about advising farmers to 'raise less corn and more Hell.' Here Jerry Simpson, the sockless Socrates of the prairie, espoused the doctrines of Henry George and exposed the iniquities of the railroads. Here Senator William A. Peffer of the hickory-nut head and long flowing beard, whom Roosevelt denounced as 'a well-meaning, pin-headed, anarchistic crank,' presented with logic and learning *The Farmer's Side, His Troubles and Their Remedy.*

The Populist convention that met in Omaha on Independence Day of 1892 approved a platform, drawn up by the eloquent Ignatius Donnelly, that raked both the major parties and painted a melancholy picture of the American scene:

We meet in the midst of a nation brought to the verge of moral, political, and material ruin. Corruption dominates the ballot-box, the legislatures, the Congress, and touches even the ermine of the bench. The people are demoralized; . . . The newspapers are largely subsidized or muzzled; public opinion silenced; business prostrated; our homes covered with mortgages; labor impoverished; and the land concentrating in the hands of the capitalists. The urban workmen are denied the right of organization for self-protection; imported pauperized labor beats down their wages; a hireling standing army, unrecognized by our laws, is established to shoot them down, and they are rapidly degenerating into European conditions. The fruits of the toil of millions are boldly stolen to build up colossal fortunes for a few, unprecedented in the history of mankind; and the possessors of these in turn, despise the republic and endanger liberty. From the same prolific womb of governmental injustice we breed the two great classes—tramps and millionaires.

Specifically, the platform demanded the free and unlimited coinage of silver; a flexible currency, controlled by the government and not by the banks, with an increase in the circulating medium; a graduated income tax; the sub-treasury scheme; postal savings banks; public ownership and operation of railroads, telegraph, and telephones; prohibition of alien land ownership and reclamation of railroad lands illegally held; immigration restriction; the eight-hour day for labor; prohibition of the use of labor spies; the direct election of Senators, the Australian ballot, the initiative and referendum. The platform was regarded throughout the East as little short of communism, yet within a generation almost every one of the planks was enacted in whole or in part. The People's party was a seed-bed of American politics for the next half-century.

The Populist standard bearer, James Baird Weaver, received over a million popular votes, better than 8 per cent of the national total, and 22 electoral votes, all west of the Mississippi. The Populists were the only third party to break into the electoral column between 1860 and 1912. Save for the Republicans, no new party had ever done so well in its first bid for national power. The Populists ran reasonably well in the Middle Border, where they elected governors in North Dakota and Kansas, but their new stronghold was the Mountain states, where they captured almost twice as many counties as both major parties combined, and in a single election established themselves as the majority party. However, this new strength threatened to drive the Populists even farther in the direction of an obsession with one issue, silver.

No party could hope to forge a winning combination if its sectional alliance was limited to the sparsely populated Middle Border and Mountain West. In 1892 the Populists failed completely to crack the South, where Alliance leaders were reluctant to divide the white vote by abandoning the one-party system. In Tillman's South Carolina, the Populists fielded no candidates at all, and Weaver, as a former Union general, was, as Mrs. Lease observed wryly, 'made a regular walking omelet by the Southern chivalry of Georgia.' The new party made almost no impression on the Old Northwest. The Populists took only one county north of the Ohio and east of the Mississippi. Weaver, a native son of Iowa, got only 5 per cent of the vote of that state. Donnelly, who ran third as Populist candidate for governor of Minnesota, wrote in his diary: 'Beaten! Whipped! Smashed! . . . Our followers scattered like dew before the rising sun.'

In a three-cornered race, Cleveland rolled up the biggest victory for the Democrats in forty years. But the outcome proved deceptive, for it encouraged Cleveland and his supporters to adopt policies which would lead to the disruption of their party.

The Money Question

Grover Cleveland, a little stouter and more set in his ideas, was inaugurated President on 4 March 1893, and promptly confronted the money question. Investor classes entertained the classical bullion theory, which held that the value of money was determined by the bullion which was held as security for its redemption. It required that all money in circulation have behind it some substantial metallic value, and that government confine itself to issuing money on security of bullion actually in the treasury vaults, either directly or indirectly through banks. As long as the ratio between gold and silver remained relatively stable, the bullion theorists accepted a bimetallic standard; when the decline in the value of silver disrupted that long-established ratio, orthodox economists turned to the single gold standard.

This classical view was disputed by those who regarded money as a token of credit rather than of bullion, and maintained that it was the proper business of the government to regulate money in the interests of society. They pointed out that bullion, especially gold, did not provide a sufficiently large or flexible basis for the money needs of an expanding nation, and that tying the whole monetary system to gold placed it at the mercy of a fortuitous gold production. They insisted that bullion security for money was unnecessary or necessary only in part; that the vital consideration was the credit of the government, and that 'the promise to pay' of the United States was sufficient to sustain the value of any money issued by that government. These proponents of credit money demanded that currency be expanded whenever essential to meet the needs of the country. Enthusiastic support for this viewpoint came from the farmers of the South and the West and from debtor groups everywhere—groups who had favored easy money since the days of Shays's Rebellion.

After the middle 'seventies the inflationists transferred their zeal from greenbacks to silver. Silver satisfied the requirement that there should be some substantial security behind money. Furthermore, dependence upon both silver and gold would ensure a reasonable expansion of the currency but guard against any such reckless inflation as might result from the use of mere legal tender notes. Silver had behind it, too, the powerful silver-mine owners and investors. In 1861 the mines had produced approximately $43 million worth of gold but only $2 million of silver. The coinage ratio between silver and gold of 15.988 to 1 undervalued silver, and in consequence silver was sold for commercial purposes and only gold was carried to the mints for coinage. But as the result of the discovery of immense deposits of silver in the West, by 1873 the value of silver mined had increased to $36 million while the value of gold had declined to the same figure; the price of silver had consequently slumped to approximately the legal ratio. The next year, for the first time since 1837, it fell below that ratio, and it became more profitable to sell silver to governments for coinage than to sell it for commercial purposes.

But when the silver-mine owners turned to governments, they found their market gone. Germany in 1871 had adopted a gold standard, and the rest of Europe hastened to suspend the free coinage of silver. Still worse, from the point of view of the silver interests, the United States had, by the Coinage Act of 1873, demonetized silver by the device of omitting from the act any specific provision for coining silver dollars. Silverites hotly charged a trick, and the act became known as 'the Crime of '73.' The schoolmaster in *Coin's Financial School*—a book which was to the free silver crusade what *Uncle Tom's Cabin* was to the anti-slavery crusade—wrote:

> It is known as the crime of 1873. A crime, because it has confiscated millions of dollars worth of property. A crime, because it has made tens of thousands of tramps. A crime, because it has made thousands of suicides. A crime, because it has brought tears to strong men's eyes and hunger and pinching want to widows and orphans. A crime because it is destroying the honest yeomanry of the land, the bulwark of the nation. A crime because it has brought this once great republic to the verge of ruin, where it is now in imminent danger of tottering to its fall.

From the middle 'seventies to the middle 'nineties, silver interests and inflationists joined in demanding the free and unlimited coinage of silver. In 1878 the silverites pushed through, over a presidential veto, the Bland-Allison Act which required the government to purchase each month not less than $2 million nor more than $4 million worth of silver, to be coined into silver dollars at the existing legal ratio with gold. Successive secretaries of the treasury chose the minimum amount, and the addition to the currency was not sufficient to increase appreciably the per capita circulation of money. The hard times of the late 'eighties intensified the silver agitation. Domestic and world production of the white metal soared, further depressing the price of silver. At the same time per capita circulation of money barely held its own, and in some sections declined sharply. The connection between low commodity prices and high gold prices, between low per capita circulation of money and high interest rates, was not lost upon the farmers.

Yet silver agitation might have come to nought had it not been for the admission of the 'omnibus' states. When the enabling acts of 1889 and 1890 brought into Congress representatives from six new Western states, the Senate at once became the stronghold of silver sentiment. The result was the Sherman Silver Purchase Act of 1890. This measure stipulated that the Treasury Department purchase each month 4.5 million ounces of silver at the market price, paying for such silver with Treasury notes of the United States. It contained further the fateful provision that 'upon demand of the holder of any of the Treasury notes . . . the Secretary of the Treasury shall . . . redeem such notes in gold or silver coin, at his discretion, it being the established policy of the United States to maintain the two metals on a parity with each other upon the present ratio.'

The Sherman Act proved a futile and dangerous compromise. It neither raised the price of silver, nor increased the amount of money in circulation, nor halted the steady decline in crop prices. The failure of the Sherman Act to effect these ends was variously explained by two opposing schools of thought. Gold monometallists insisted that the act demonstrated that the price of silver could not be raised artificially by government action. Silverites argued that the law proved the futility of compromise and the necessity for free and unlimited

coinage. The act provided, to be sure, for the purchase of practically the entire domestic production of silver. But the world output was almost three times the domestic production, and as long as there were huge quantities of silver seeking a market, the price would be sure to slump. The solution, said the gold forces, was to abandon silver to its fate and return to the gold standard. The solution, said the silverites, was to open our mints to unlimited coinage of silver, and peg the price at the traditional ratio of 16 to 1. The bimetallists reasoned that if the United States stood ready to exchange, with all comers, one ounce of gold for sixteen ounces of silver, no one would sell silver for less than that sum. That is, if the United States could absorb all the silver that would be brought to her mints, she could peg the price, and bimetallism would be an established fact. But that if was crucial. The success of the operation depended upon the ability of the United States to pay out gold for silver until speculators were convinced of the futility of trying to break the price, or until the increased demand for silver raised its commercial value.

The silver question aroused intense emotions. 'Gold-bugs' smugly denounced their opponents as cheats, while silverites branded the monometallists as 'Shylocks.' We can see now that the issue was both deeper and less dangerous than contemporaries realized. It was deeper because it involved a struggle for the ultimate control of government and economy between the business interests of the East and the agrarian interests of the South and the West. It was less dangerous because none of the calamities so freely prophesied would have followed the adoption of either the gold or the silver standard. When the country committed itself to the gold standard in 1900, the event made not a ripple. When the gold standard was abandoned a full generation later, the event led to no untoward results.

The President and the Panic

The Cleveland administration was just two months old when it was struck by the panic of 1893. The agricultural depression which began in 1887 had seriously curtailed the purchasing power of one large group of consumers, and had similarly affected railway income. The collapse of markets abroad, owing to business distress in Europe and Australia, had serious repercussions on American trade and manufacturing. Overspeculation attendant upon the organization of trusts endangered stability, while industrial disorders like the Homestead strike reduced profits and cut purchasing power. Finally the Government's silver policy impaired business confidence and persuaded European creditors to dump American securities on the market and drain the nation of its gold.

By midsummer of 1893 the panic was in full swing. The Reading Railroad had failed in the spring. In July came the failure of the Erie, and soon the Northern Pacific, the Union Pacific, and the Santa Fe were all in the hands of receivers. Banks everywhere called in their loans, often with consequences fatal to firms and individuals unable to meet their obligations; over 15,000 failures were recorded for the year 1893. 'Men died like flies under the strain,' wrote Henry Adams, 'and Boston grew suddenly old, haggard, and thin.' In rural areas banks toppled like card-houses; of the 158 national bank failures in 1893, 153 were in the South and the West. By the summer of 1894, four million jobless walked the streets of factory towns in a vain search for work.

Convinced that monetary uncertainty was the chief cause of the panic, President Cleveland summoned a special session of Congress to repeal the Sherman silver law and enact legislation which should 'put beyond all doubt or mistake the intention and the ability of the Government to fulfill its pecuniary obligations in money universally recognized by all civilized countries.' Cleveland's discreet manipulation of the patronage provided enough Democratic votes to help the Republicans repeal their own silver-purchase act at the request of a Democratic President and a bimetallist Secretary of the Treasury! Wall Street breathed more freely, but the farmers cried betrayal, and 'Silver Dick' Bland warned the President that Eastern and Western Democrats had finally come to 'a parting of the ways.'

Nor did repeal of the Sherman Act bring about that restoration of prosperity so confidently predicted. The Treasury was freed of its obligations to purchase silver but Secretary of the Treasury John Carlisle's troubles had just begun. Distrust of the monetary policy of the government was by no means allayed, and there began a steady raid on the gold reserves of the Treasury. Holders of silver certificates, fearful for the future, began to bring them to the Treasury and ask for gold. The resultant drain on the gold reserve not only carried that reserve below the established mark of $100 million, but threatened to wipe it out altogether. To the frightened President it seemed that the hour was fast approaching when the government would be unable to meet its legal obligations in gold and would therefore be pushed onto the silver standard. Hence he decided to sell government bonds for gold; in desperation he turned to a banking syndicate headed by the House of Morgan. This bond sale did not permanently help the Treasury, because purchasers of the bonds simply drew from it the gold with which to pay for their bonds, thereby depleting the gold supply of the Treasury at one end as fast as it was replenished at the other. More bond sales thus became inevitable, and twice again Cleveland turned to the bankers. This convinced the farmers that there was a traitor in the White House and a Judas in the Treasury Department. Finally in 1896, the Treasury floated a $100 million bond issue through popular subscription. With the success of this fourth and last bond issue, the crisis passed.

The financial difficulties of the government were ascribable not only to the gold drain, but to a sharp decline in revenues. The McKinley tariff had actually reduced income from customs duties, and the depression cut into internal revenues, while the 'billion dollar Congress' had committed the government to heavy expenditures. As a result the surplus of 1890 became a deficit of $70 million by 1894. In the face of this situation Cleveland tried to force the Democratic party to redeem its pledge of tariff reduction. But vested interests had been built up under Republican protection, and Democratic Senators from the East were no less averse to tariff reduction than their Republican colleagues. The Wilson tariff in the House sought to reduce duties, but when it emerged from the joint committee of the House and Senate the

Coxey's army. Leading the marchers on horseback is Carl Browne, a religious mystic who believed that he and Coxey shared an unusually large quantity of the soul of Christ. A painter of Western panoramas, Browne designed a banner for the army with a picture of the head of Christ (who, it was remarked, bore a striking resemblance to Browne) and with the inscription: 'Peace on Earth Good Will to Men. He Hath Risen, but Death to Interest on Bonds.' (*Library of Congress*)

reduction was no longer recognizable. Protectionist Democrats like Gorman of Maryland had introduced no fewer than 634 changes, most of them upward. Cleveland, who had insisted that 'a tariff for any other purpose than public revenue is public robbery,' denounced the bill as smacking of 'party perfidy and party dishonor.' Believing, however, that the Wilson-Gorman tariff was some im-

provement on the McKinley Act, he allowed it to become law without his signature.

Since the sponsors of the Wilson bill anticipated a reduction in customs receipts, they had wisely added a provision for a tax of 2 per cent on incomes above $4000. However, this tax was declared unconstitutional by a five to four decision of the Supreme Court which fifteen years earlier had unanimously validated the war income tax. As some of the opinions, notably that of Mr. Justice Field, were characterized by gross prejudice and as one judge had changed his mind at the eleventh hour, the Pollock decision seemed further proof to farmers and workingmen of the class bias of the government.

While Congress was making futile gestures toward tariff reform and free silver, a more constructive proposal came from 'General' Jacob Coxey, a wealthy quarry owner of Massillon, Ohio, who with his wife and infant son, Legal Tender Coxey, would shortly lead an army of unemployed on a march to Washington. Coxey's legislative attack on the depression and the money question was double-barreled. One bill authorized any county or town desiring to undertake public improvements to issue non-interest-bearing bonds which should be deposited with the Secretary of the Treasury in exchange for legal tender notes. Public improvements thus financed were to guarantee employment to any jobless man at not less than $1.50 for an eight-hour day. The Good Roads bill called for $500 million of legal tender notes to construct a county road system throughout the country at the same rate of pay. These measures were designed to inflate the currency, bring down interest rates, inaugurate much-needed public improvements, and provide work for the unemployed. The program was not unlike that later inaugurated by Franklin D. Roosevelt, but at the time it excited only contempt or amusement.

This year, 1894, was the darkest that Americans had known for thirty years. Everything seemed to conspire to convince the people that democracy was a failure. Ragged and hungry bands of unemployed swarmed over the countryside, the fires from their hobo camps flickering a message of warning to affrighted townsfolk. Coxey's army of broken veterans of the armies of industry, inspired by the pathetic delusion that a 'petition on boots' might bring relief, marched on Washington, only to be arrested for trespassing on the Capitol grounds. When Pullman workers struck for a living wage, every agency of government was enlisted to smash the strike. When Congress passed an anti-trust law, it was enforced not against the trusts but against labor unions. When Congress enacted an income tax, it was voided in the highest court. Tenant farmers cheered lustily as 'Pitchfork Ben' Tillman demonstrated how he would stick his fork into the ribs of Grover Cleveland, and on the plains the 'Kansas Pythoness' Mary Lease warned the East that 'the people are at bay, let the bloodhounds of money beware.' There was intellectual ferment too. Everywhere people were discussing the revelations of Lloyd's *Wealth against Commonwealth*, the first great broadside against the trusts, and Edward Bellamy's Utopian novel, *Looking Backward*; while Jacob Riis told the sordid story of *How the Other Half Lives*.

Bryan, Bryan, Bryan, Bryan

The party in power is always blamed for hard times. The 1894 elections, in which the G.O.P. won over numbers of urban voters who had previously been in the Democratic camp, ended the 20-year period of party equilibrium and began an era of Republican supremacy. For the next 16 years the Republicans would control both houses of Congress, and during the next 36 years, the Democrats would win only three Congressional elections.

The silver issue portended still more trouble for the Democratic party. Either the silver forces would capture control of the party, or the silverites would secede and make the lusty young Populists one of the great major parties. In 1893–94 silver Democrats effected a fusion with the Populists, and in many Western states it was difficult to distinguish between the two parties. But the silver leaders were unwilling to abandon the Democrats without a final effort to seize control of the party organization, and a fierce struggle ensued.

While the Democratic party was being torn apart, the Republicans concluded that in 1896 any Republican could be elected—a boast that Mark Hanna made a prophecy. Marcus Alonzo Hanna was a businessman satiated with wealth but avid for power, naturally intelligent though contemptuous of learning, personally upright but tolerant of corruption, cynical in his management of

'A Man of Mark!' This 1896 cartoon in William Randolph Hearst's New York *Journal* shows McKinley, wearing a syndicate collar, dangled by his sponsor, Marcus Alonzo Hanna (1837–1904). Hearst had hired the cartoonist Homer Davenport for his San Francisco *Examiner* and brought him to New York for the 1896 campaign, during which Davenport created his image of Hanna covered with dollar signs, an impression that 'Uncle Mark' was not able to shake off for the rest of his life. (*Library of Congress*)

men but capable of abiding friendships; he was the nearest thing to a national 'boss' that had ever emerged in this country. Convinced that the business interests should govern the country, Hanna believed ardently in the mission of the Republican party to promote business activity, whence prosperity would percolate to the farmers and wage-earners. Since 1890 he had been grooming for the presidency his friend William McKinley, and at the 1896 G.O.P. convention McKinley was nominated on the first ballot. Only one untoward event marred the jollity of the occasion: as the convention committed itself to the gold standard, the venerable Senator Henry Teller of Colorado bade

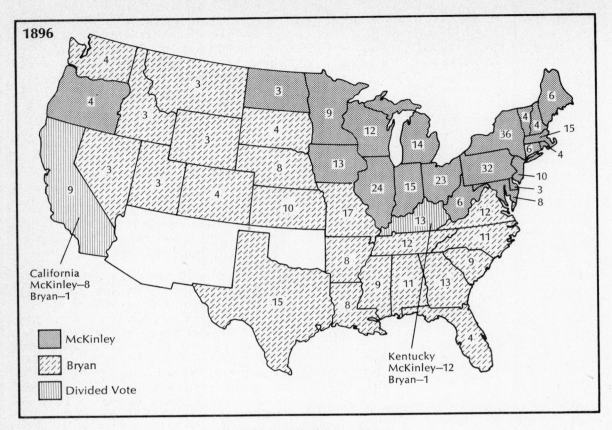

1896

California
McKinley—8
Bryan—1

Kentucky
McKinley—12
Bryan—1

■ McKinley

▨ Bryan

▥ Divided Vote

Presidential Election, 1896

farewell to the party which forty years earlier he had helped to found. And up in the press gallery William Jennings Bryan looked on with palpitating interest as Teller led a grim band of twenty-two silver delegates from the convention hall.

Three weeks later, when the Democratic convention met at Chicago, the silverites, instead of going over to the Populists, captured control of the party organization. Trainload after trainload of enthusiastic delegates swarmed into the streets of the Windy City, silver badges gleaming from their lapels. 'For the first time,' wrote one Eastern delegate, 'I can understand the scenes of the French Revolution!' The Democratic party had been taken over by spokesmen for the farmers of the South and the West who had long since decided to repudiate their own President. Champ

Clark of Missouri called Cleveland one of the three great traitors of our history, linking him with Benedict Arnold and Aaron Burr, while Altgeld had put it even more bluntly: 'To laud Clevelandism on Jefferson's birthday is to sing a Te deum in honor of Judas Iscariot on Christmas morning.'

'All the silverites need,' said the New York *World* on the eve of the Convention, 'is a Moses. They have the principle, they have the grit, they have the brass bands and the buttons and the flags, they have the howl and the hustle, they have the votes, and they have the leaders, so-called. But they are wandering in the wilderness like a lot of lost sheep, because no one with the courage, the audacity, the magnetism and the wisdom to be a real leader has yet appeared among them.' The lament was premature. In the person of William

Jennings Bryan of Nebraska, the silver forces found their leader. Only 36 years of age, Bryan had already distinguished himself as the most aggressive and eloquent spokesman of silver in the country.

Bryan's opportunity arrived with the debate on the platform. The champions of gold had made impressive appeals, 'Pitchfork Ben' Tillman had failed to do justice to silver, and the sweltering throng of 20,000 was anxious and impatient. Bryan's was the closing speech, and as he made his way nervously down the aisle a great shout went up. The silver forces came, he said, not as petitioners, but as a victorious army.

We have petitioned, and our petitions have been scorned; we have entreated and our entreaties have been disregarded; we have begged, and they have mocked when our calamity came. We beg no longer; we entreat no more; we petition no more. We defy them.

The delegates had found their champion, and every sentence was received with a frenzied roar of applause. Bryan's rousing peroration drew the class and sectional lines:

You come to us and tell us that the great cities are in favor of the gold standard; we reply that the great cities rest upon our broad and fertile prairies. Burn down your cities and leave our farms, and your cities will spring up again as if by magic; but destroy our farms and the grass will grow in the streets of every city in the country.... Having behind us the producing masses of the nation and the world, supported by the commercial interests, the laboring interests and the toilers everywhere, we will answer their demand for a gold standard by saying to them: You shall not press down upon the brow of labor this crown of thorns, you shall not crucify mankind upon a cross of gold.

Bryan's 'Cross of Gold' speech helped make him the choice of the Democrats to wage the Battle of the Standards.

Not only on silver, but on banks, trusts, the injunction, and other issues, the Democrats had stolen the Populist thunder, although they failed to adopt the full Populist program. When the People's party met, the fusionists were in complete control, to the distress of those like Henry Demarest Lloyd who charged that the social emphases of their party were being superseded by the single questionable issue of silver. The

Populists endorsed Bryan, but balked at accepting the Democratic vice-presidential nominee, a banker, and named the Georgia firebrand Tom Watson instead, thereby giving Bryan two different running mates. Within a short time silver Republicans bolted to Bryan; Gold Democrats named a separate ticket but actually threw their support to McKinley. For the first time in 30 years the country divided roughly along class and sectional lines, and the electorate was confronted with a clear-cut choice.

In Bryan the agrarians had an ideal leader:

Prairie avenger, mountain lion,
Bryan, Bryan, Bryan, Bryan,
Gigantic troubadour, speaking like a siege gun,
Smashing Plymouth Rock with his boulders from the
    West.[5]

Radical only on economic questions of money, banks, and trusts, strictly orthodox in matters of morality and religion, Bryan justified his title, 'the Great Commoner.' Born in a small farming town in southern Illinois, he came from mixed Scotch, Irish, and English stock from both North and South. One of his parents was Baptist, one Methodist; he himself joined the Presbyterian church. For generations his family had participated in the westward movement—from the Virginia tidewater to the Mississippi valley; he continued the process by moving out to the frontier in Nebraska. He attended a small denominational college, studied law, dabbled in politics, and finally became champion of a great popular cause. He was well equipped for politics, but it was qualities of character rather than of mind that won for him such loyalty as no other leader of his generation could command. Conservatives responded as though the Hun were thundering at the gates. The New York *Tribune* denounced 'the wretched rattle-pated boy, posing in vapid vanity and mouthing resounding rottenness.' But this seems not to have disturbed Bryan. Mark Sullivan wrote: 'Bryan used to repeat what his enemies said, with a smile and manner that was subtly designed as half-way between Christ forgiving his

5. Vachel Lindsay, 'Bryan, Bryan, Bryan, Bryan,' *Collected Poems*, Macmillan.

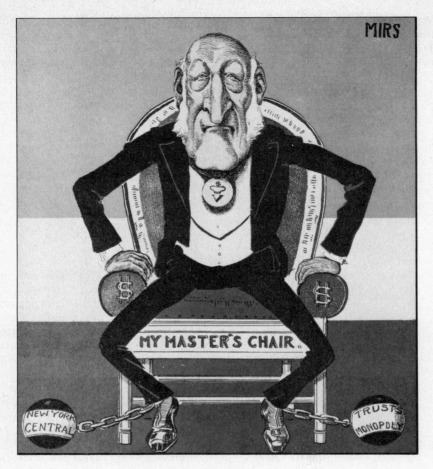

The railroad Senator. This caricature shows Chauncey Depew (1834–1928) wearing the ball and chain of the New York Central. In 1866, after being confirmed as the first United States minister to Japan, Depew was offered a place as attorney for the Vanderbilt interests. When he wavered, Commodore Vanderbilt told him: 'Railroads are the career for a young man; there is nothing in politics. Don't be a damned fool.' Depew resigned his ministerial appointment to accept Vanderbilt's offer, and by 1885 was president of the New York Central and Hudson River lines. But he did not have to give up his political aspirations. In 1899, when this caricature appeared, the New York legislature sent him to the U.S. Senate where progressive reformers immediately branded him a lackey of the special interests. (*Library of Congress*)

persecutors and John L. Sullivan showing himself a good sport.'

In the 1896 election Bryan received more votes than had ever before been cast for a presidential candidate and more than any Democratic nominee would get for another twenty years. But McKinley not only outpolled him by half a million but won a big edge in the Electoral College. Bryan carried the late Confederacy and most of the Middle Border and the Mountain West; but the electoral votes of the populous East and the Middle West together with five trans-Mississippi states gave McKinley an emphatic victory. In the silver region, Bryan won by prodigious margins—Montana, 4–1; Colorado, 6–1. In the East, he met disaster; he lost every county in New England, all but one in New York. The Eastern worker was repelled by a Western rural movement which, by spurring inflation, threatened his real wages. As Daniel De Leon said, labor feared it might be crucified 'upon a cross of silver.' McKinley ran so well in the cities that the Democratic plurality of 145,000 in the twelve largest cities in 1892 became a Republican advantage of 352,000 in 1896.

But Bryan lost chiefly because he failed to carry the old Granger areas. The more settled the Midwestern states became, the less they were dependent on outside forces they could not control. Since farmers there had nearby city markets for many of their crops, which were carried by a well-developed railroad system, they were not as subject to the whims of the world market and their operations were less speculative than they had been at the outset. Furthermore, this section was much more industrialized and urbanized. The election demonstrated that the industrial Northeast had extended its empire to embrace all of the Old Northwest, and the Republicans would hold this region for most of the next generation.

The election of McKinley constituted a triumph for a manufacturing and financial rather than an agrarian order. 'For a hundred years,' Henry Adams observed, 'the American people had hesitated, vacillated, swayed forward and back, between two forces, one simply industrial, the other capitalistic, centralizing, and mechanical. . . . The issue came on the single gold standard, and the majority at last declared itself, once and for all, in favor of a capitalistic system with all its necessary machinery. All one's friends, all one's best citizens, reformers, churches, colleges, educated classes, had joined the banks to force submission to capitalism; a submission long foreseen by the mere law of mass.'

McKinley left no doubt that he regarded the election as a mandate for the policies industry wanted. He named a lumber baron Secretary of War, the president of the First National Bank of Chicago Secretary of the Treasury, a New York banker Secretary of the Interior, a post that had been conceded to the West. He summoned Congress into special session to rush through the mountain-high Dingley Tariff Act. In the 1898 elections the Populists were all but wiped out. 'For the first time in twenty years the silver menace is cleared away from the financial horizon,' wrote *The Nation*. With the silver forces routed, McKinley was able to push through the Gold Standard Act of 1900, and the enormously increased production of gold in Australia and the Klondike soon muted the cry for free silver. Yet Bryan's campaign had significance not only as the last protest of the old agrarian order against industrialism, but as the first attempt to create a new order. Bryan was the bridge between Andrew Jackson and Franklin D. Roosevelt.

25

The American Mind

1865–1910

The Gilded Age

Historians agree that the Civil War and its aftermath devastated Southern culture and coarsened Northern society. Of the destructive impact on the South, there can be no doubt. The Kentucky-born scientist, Nathaniel Shaler, wrote:

Not only did the Civil War maim the generation of Kentuckians to which I belonged, it also broke up the developing motives of intellectual culture of the commonwealth. Just before it I can see that while the ideals of culture were in a way still low and rather carnal, there was an eager reaching-out for better things; men and women were seeking, through history, literature, the fine arts, and in some measure through science, for a share in the higher life. Four years of civil war, which turned the minds of all towards what is at once the most absorbing and debasing interest of man, made an end of all this. . . .[1]

Many of the South's intellectual leaders—the novelist Simms, the poet Paul Hamilton Hayne, the sociologist George Fitzhugh—retired to live with poverty and bitterness for the rest of their lives. Others fled the South for the more prosperous or hospitable North and West: Frederick Barnard left the University of Mississippi to become president of Columbia University; the LeConte brothers gave up their scientific work in South Carolina and went to the new University of California; the novelist George W. Cable of Louisiana took refuge in Massachusetts; the brilliant young architect, Henry Hobson Richardson, moved from New Orleans—via Paris—to Boston and New York.

Such intellectual energies as the South was able to summon up went chiefly into the elegiac celebration of the Lost Cause. The dream of the Old South was a phantasmagoria of the wide-spreading plantation and the white-pillared manor house, of families always old and distinguished, of aristocratic colonels and great ladies and girls who were lovelier and purer than girls elsewhere, of happy slaves singing in the cotton fields or dancing in the quarters on Saturday nights, of an independent yeomanry and picturesque mountaineers given to Elizabethan speech, of a special grace, a special hospitality, and sense of chivalry and code of honor, a Cause forever right

1. Shaler, *Autobiography*, pp. 76–77.

and forever Lost. The Old South was, in short, mankind before the Fall, but it was Southern mankind, not Yankee—a unique experience which Providence had vouchsafed to Southerners and which set them apart.

In the meantime a lusty and arrogant North, its wealth enhanced by the war, was pushing forward to ever greater power. The decade after Appomattox was a period of relentless tawdriness and vulgarity. It was the era of lachrymose novels and the pious tales of Horatio Alger; of Rogers's plastercast statues and Currier and Ives lithographs and massive choruses of 10,000 voices shouting the Anvil Chorus to the accompaniment of cannon fired by electricity. The editor of *The Nation*, E. L. Godkin, called this a 'chromo civilization,' and in 1871 in *Democratic Vistas* Walt Whitman pronounced it:

Cankered, crude, superstitious, and rotten. . . . Never was there, perhaps, more hollowness of heart than at present, and here in the United States. . . . I say that our New World democracy . . . is so far an almost complete failure in its social aspects, and in really grand religious, moral, literary and esthetic results.

All true enough, yet we must not accept these verdicts uncritically. Next year after *Democratic Vistas* came Whitman's 'Thou Mother with Thy Equal Brood'—the most exultant tribute to America that any poet has ever penned:

Thou wonder world yet undefined, unform'd, neither do I define thee, . . .
Land tolerating all, accepting all, not for the good alone, all good for thee,
Land in the realms of God, to be a realm unto thyself,
Under the rule of God to be a rule unto thyself.

Whitman had recognized that along with so much that was vulgar there was, in these years, an immense vitality. For if the war had coarsened the characters of some, it had refined the spirits of others, and there was truth in the noble words of Justice Oliver Wendell Holmes, who bore the wounds of three battles:

The generation that carried on the war has been set aside by its experience. Through our great good fortune, in our youth our hearts were touched with fire. It was given to us to learn at the outset that life is a profound and passionate thing. . . . We have seen with our own eyes, beyond and above the gold fields, the snowy

heights of honor, and it is for us to bear the report to those who come after us.

Literary Currents

And bear the report they did. The literary record of the war was varied and rich. No public man of the nineteenth century wrote more eloquently than Lincoln, and a handful of his public papers can be ranked as world literature. The memoirs of the great captains like Grant and Longstreet are unfailingly interesting but rarely possess the literary qualities found in the recollections of some of the lesser figures: Joshua Chamberlain's *The Passing of the Armies,* or Thomas W. Higginson's *Army Life in a Black Regiment,* or General Taylor's brilliant *Destruction and Reconstruction.* Nor has any American war produced more memorable poetry. In Walt Whitman's poems we can read much of the history and meaning of the war, from 'Eighteen Sixty-one':

Arm'd year—year of the struggle,
No dainty rhymes of sentimental love verses for you terrible year, . . .

to the lovely elegy for President Lincoln: 'When Lilacs Last in the Dooryard Bloom'd.' Whitman spanned the whole period from the 'fifties to the 'eighties, linking the romanticism of the Golden Day and the naturalism of the Gilded. In the years after the war he wrote many of his greatest poems.

These years, too, saw the emergence of three great writers who were to dominate the literary scene for almost half a century—Mark Twain, William Dean Howells, and Henry James—as well as Emily Dickinson, whose exquisite genius awaited later recognition. Though Twain, Howells, and James had very different backgrounds, they had much in common: a revolt against the pervasive romanticism which plagued so much of the style of the time; an obsession with the relations between the New World and the Old—all three lived much of their lives abroad; disillusionment with many aspects of American society; and a common concern for moral values.

Born in frontier Missouri where North meets South and East meets West, Sam Clemens spent his boyhood on the banks of the river whose epic he was to write under the name Mark Twain. Before he was twenty-five he had served an apprenticeship as a Mississippi pilot, learning the great river and the varied country it traversed and the society that floated on its muddy waters. When the war came he enlisted, briefly, in a volunteer Confederate company, then—like his own Huck Finn—lit out for the Territory. It was there, in Nevada and California, that he found the material for *Roughing It*, the first full-length novel about the Far West. In 1867 he sailed to the Mediterranean and the Holy Land. *Innocents Abroad* (1869), which gave him a reputation as a 'humorist' which he never quite lived down, struck the familiar note of American innocence and Old World corruption. *The Gilded Age* (1874) drew on his acquaintance with the frontier and with the Washington of Grant's administration. Thereafter it was the Mississippi that provided inspiration for his greatest books. From the steamboat leadsmen's cry at two fathoms, 'by the mark, twain!' he took his literary name, and on the river were born his three immortal characters, Tom Sawyer, Huck Finn, and the Negro Jim. These early books—*Roughing It, Innocents Abroad, Old Times on the Mississippi* (later *Life on the Mississippi*), and *Tom Sawyer,* all written before 1877—were, as Van Wyck Brooks observed, 'germs of a new American literature with a broader base in the national mind than the writers of New England had possessed. By his re-creation of the frontier life in the great central valley, by his skill in recapturing its speech and its turns of mind, Mark Twain pre-empted for later writers a realm that was theirs by right of birth but might never have been theirs for literature if he had not cleared the way.'[2]

Mark Twain published *Tom Sawyer* in 1876; thereafter he entered into the era of his greatest productivity and his highest achievement. In the course of the following twenty years he wrote *The Prince and the Pauper*, an enlarged version of *Life on the Mississippi, A Connecticut Yankee in King Arthur's Court, Pudd'nhead Wilson, Joan of Arc,* and, of course, the immortal *Adventures of Huckleberry Finn*.

2. *The Times of Melville and Whitman*, p. 297.

Huckleberry Finn (1884) is, by common consent, the greatest of Mark Twain's books and one of the two or three greatest of American novels. The wonderful device of the raft floating down the Mississippi through the heartland of America enabled Mark Twain to pass in review American society at mid-century. All modern American literature comes from *Huckleberry Finn*, said Ernest Hemingway, for it is the first novel so unmistakably American in subject matter, setting, characters, idiom, and style that it could not have been written elsewhere. 'Emerson, Longfellow, Lowell, Holmes, I knew them all, and all the rest of the sages, poets, seers, critics, humorists,' said Howells. 'They were like one another and like other literary men. But Mark Twain was sole, incomparable, the Lincoln of our literature.'

William Dean Howells wrote, at the age of 23, an undistinguished campaign biography of Lincoln and was rewarded with the consulship at Venice. There he had time to immerse himself in European letters, and to study America from the vantage point of the Old World. Returning home at the close of the war, he wrote critical essays for *The Nation* and in 1871 the Ohio printer's devil became editor-in-chief of the *Atlantic*, that house-organ of the Brahmins. Somehow he found time to carry on his editorial and critical work, while a steady stream of novels and stories flowed from his pen. As with Mark Twain's, Howells's early books anticipate his later themes: the conflict in manners, and in standards, of Boston and the hinterland (*A Chance Acquaintance*, 1873), the impact of the Old World on unsophisticated Americans (*A Foregone Conclusion*, 1875, and *The Lady of the Aroostook*, 1879), and the morality of the commonplace and the immorality of what passed for 'romance.'

The first major critic to recognize that Mark Twain was not just a humorist but an authentic genius, just as he was the first to recognize talent in his young friend Henry James, Howells functioned for almost half a century as Dean—or Pope—of American letters. Not the greatest novelist of his generation, nor the most profound critic, nor the most talented editor, nor the most perspicacious biographer, he combined these roles more successfully than any other individual. In

Mark Twain [Samuel Langhorne Clemens] (1835–1910). He appears here in his Connecticut home dressed in the robe he wore when he was awarded an honorary degree from Oxford in 1907. On that occasion a large cheering crowd escorted him from the site of the ceremony to the college gates. 'I came in with Halley's Comet in 1835,' he said, 'and I expect to go out with it.' And so he did—with the reappearance of the comet in 1910. (*Mark Twain Memorial, Hartford, Conn.*)

some forty novels, thirty plays, a dozen books of criticism, and a score of biography and travel recording 'the more smiling aspects of American life,' Howells provided the most comprehensive description of middle-class Victorian America to be found in our literature. Howells was the American Balzac, fascinated by the homely details of social relationships. *The Rise of Silas Lapham* drew a classic portrait of the self-made man; *A Modern Instance* interpreted a Victorian marriage and its breakdown; *A Hazard of New Fortunes* dramatized industrial conflict in New York City; and *Dr. Breen's Practice* dealt with the new woman. In all of this, as James wrote, 'he adores the real, the natural, the colloquial, the moderate, the optimistic, the domestic, and the democratic.'

Gradually the 'optimistic' note died out as Howells came up against 'the riddle of the painful earth.' More and more he got caught up in the conflicts of the day. 'After fifty years of optimistic content with civilization and its ability to come out all right in the end,' he wrote, 'I now abhor it, and feel that it is coming out all wrong in the end, unless it bases itself anew on a real equality.' Yet while Howells criticized the America of his day more sharply than did Mark Twain, he never suffered the desperate bitterness that ravaged the author of *The Man that Corrupted Hadleyburg.* Thus, Howells wrote *A Traveller from Altruria* to show what men could do to save themselves, while Mark Twain wrote *The Mysterious Stranger* to show that man was not worth saving. Still, if realism triumphed over romanticism, much of the credit goes to Howells. He did more than anyone else to obtain a hearing for the rebellious younger novelists who were coming to the fore: he found a publisher for Stephen Crane's *Maggie, A Girl of the Streets*, wrote an introduction to Hamlin Garland's *Main-Travelled Roads*, championed Thorstein Veblen and Edward Bellamy, and welcomed a host of European naturalists like Émile Zola.

Where Mark Twain wrote of rivermen and miners and smalltown boys and slaves, and Howells of the proper middle classes, Henry James took for his theme the sophisticated relationships of an aristocratic—or sometimes merely a very rich—international society. Unlike the Old World, America he found thin and arid, lacking color, drama, intensity, and the marrow of literature. After 1875 James lived mostly abroad, and though a few of his novels—*The Bostonians*, for example—have an American setting, generally he set his stories in the great houses, the hotels, or the boulevards of London, Paris, and Rome. He was fascinated by the trappings and machinery of society—houses, gardens, teas, ceremonies—but only because these reflected, or concealed, values with a deeper moral significance. A long shelf of novels and stories—and James wrote almost as voluminously as Howells—elaborates on two basic themes. The first of these—the interaction of New World innocence and Old World sophistication—is the theme of the greatest of his books—*The American* (1877), *The Portrait of a Lady* (1881), *The Ambassadors* (1903), *The Wings of the Dove* (1903), *The Golden Bowl* (1904). The second—the interaction of the artist and fashionable society—permeates much of these books as well as *Roderick Hudson* (1876), *The Aspern Papers* (1888), and others. Because James wrote of subjects and characters far removed from the interest of the average American, and in an intricate style, he had few readers in his own lifetime. Like Melville, he has been rediscovered in our time, and is now generally acknowledged to be one of the great masters of the modern novel.

These three novelists grew to literary maturity during the period of the Darwinian controversy, but their writings do not reflect the new philosophy, which had a much greater impact on younger men of letters, born after the Civil War. These were especially fascinated by the principle of the survival of the fittest. In Frank Norris's *Vandover and the Brute*, the central character reverts to a kind of animal brutality, and Jack London's Wolf Larsen argues crudely 'that life is a mess' in which 'the strong eat the weak.' In Theodore Dreiser's writings, man was less animal than fool, victim of his own vagrant impulses, pitiful vanities, insatiable lusts and greeds. Dreiser was obsessed with power; the city provided his background, and his characters pitted their cunning and ruthlessness against their fellow men in the desperate battlefields of business or of love. Frank Cowperwood, the protagonist of *The Titan* and *The*

Financier, is a far more sophisticated creature than Wolf Larsen, but not therefore more admirable. Through a quarter-century of writing, from *Sister Carrie* (1900) to *An American Tragedy* (1925), Dreiser played variations on the theme of determinism, a salient feature of Darwinian thought. The Norwegian-American O. E. Rölvaag, in *Giants in the Earth* (1927), wrote the epic story of the immigrant farmer in the Dakota country. *Giants in the Earth* caught the spirit of the westward movement, but instead of being the proud story of man's conquest of the earth, it is the record of earth's humbling of man.

Philosophy and Religion

The year 1859, when Darwin published his *Origin of Species*, began a revolution in thought as in science. The leaders of practically every Christian sect fought hard for the book of Genesis and special creation, and Louis Agassiz of Harvard University attacked evolution of species on scientific grounds. But with the support of scientists like Asa Gray and of popularizers like Edward Youmans and John Fiske, the doctrine of evolution spread rapidly, and by the 'eighties had triumphed in most intellectual circles, and was making heavy inroads on the popular consciousness.

This doctrine of evolution was chiefly responsible for the abandonment of transcendentalism and the formulation of pragmatism. Rooted in the eighteenth century, transcendentalism celebrated many things dear to the romanticists: Nature, individualism, spontaneity, the imagination. It rested upon primal intuitions not susceptible to proof, such as the benevolence of God and of Nature, and preferred *a priori* principles to the findings of the laboratory. Such a philosophy was clearly irrelevant to the kind of universe unveiled by Darwin. Truth could no longer be something plucked from the inner consciousness of man, nor yet what God revealed to man; any hypothesis must stand up under laboratory tests. Moral standards, when discovered to be the product of social evolution and environment, could no longer be thought absolute. Laws, by the same test, were neither eternal nor cosmic; they derived from the social needs of the day. Fixed ideas were as out of place in politics and economics as in science and religion.

Pragmatism was elaborated by a remarkable group of philosophers who came to maturity in the last third of the nineteenth century: Chauncey Wright, Charles Peirce, William James, and John Dewey—all from New England. Although European philosophers cried out that its concern with consequences was a piece of American sordidness, it may yet be admitted that pragmatism was one of the really important innovations in the history of thought through the ages. It is not easy to define pragmatism; the Italian Papini observed that pragmatism was less a philosophy than a method of doing without one. James certainly, and Dewey probably, would have conceded this, for they insisted that pragmatism was less an independent system of thought than a way of thinking about philosophical questions. They intended pragmatism not for the schoolroom but for the world of affairs. 'Better it is,' wrote Dewey, 'for philosophy to err in active participation in the living struggles and issues of its own age and times than to maintain an immune monastic impeccability.' The pragmatists regarded truth not as an absolute, but as something that each society and each thinking individual had to make for himself. 'The truth of an idea,' wrote James, 'is not a stagnant property inherent in it. Truth *happens* to an idea. It becomes true, it is *made* true by events.' The test of truth was to be found in its consequences; the business of the philosopher was to find out what worked best. 'The ultimate test of what a truth means,' wrote James, 'is the conduct it dictates or inspires.' The pragmatists conceived of our world as still in the making, a conception admirably suited to a nation so oriented to progressive changes as the United States.

The effect of such an attitude on politics, law, economics, social institutions, education, art, and morals was little less than revolutionary. Progressive teachers abandoned the idea that education consisted of acquiring a body of information, and tried to make it a function of society. Political scientists talked less about abstractions such as 'sovereignty' and more about the political process. Jurisprudents ceased to regard the law as a body of

William James (1842–1910), in a portrait by Ellen Emmet. Few thinkers had a greater influence on his age than this Harvard philosopher who pioneered in making psychology a laboratory science, expanded on C. S. Peirce's conception of pragmatism, and in works like *The Varieties of Religious Experience* (1902) sought to harmonize faith and science. (*Houghton Library, Harvard University*)

changeless truth and accepted the doctrine that every generation must make its own precedents. Economists reluctantly surrendered 'laws' which they had long regarded as inviolable, and sociologists came to reject the dour doctrine that man is the creature of his environment, and taught instead that man could transform his environment. Even historians submitted that historical truth was relative to each generation.

Protestant fundamentalism suffered most from the new philosophy. Theological scholars applied to the Bible critical standards long accepted in other fields of scholarship, testing the Scriptures by the facts of history, philology, geology, archaeology, and other sciences, but the Protestant churches were more afraid of Darwinism than of the 'higher criticism,' and several Southern states actually passed laws forbidding the teaching of evolution. Orthodox defenders of the faith quoted with approval Disraeli's declaration, 'Is man an ape or an angel? I, my Lords, am on the side of the angels.' Stout champions of science countered with vigorous attacks upon what they denominated religious bigotry: John William Draper's *History of the Conflict Between Religion and Science* (1874) and Andrew D. White's 'Warfare of Science' (1876)[3] ran through innumerable editions, while the professional agnostic, Colonel Robert Ingersoll, lectured on 'Some Mistakes of Moses' to rapt audiences.

Moderates on both sides, meantime, attempted to effect a reconciliation. John Fiske, a very behemoth of a scholar, who wrote on history, ethnology, and sociology, expounded a reconciliation of science and religion as early as the 'sixties, published his elaborate *Outlines of Cosmic Philosophy* in 1874, and thereafter, by books and lectures, spread his message that evolution was simply God's way of doing things. Soon the most popular of American preachers, Henry Ward Beecher, announced his conversion, and shortly thereafter such distinguished clergymen as President McCosh of Princeton came over to the side of the evolutionists.

While 'higher criticism' and Darwinism caused

---

3. Elaborated later (1896) into the two-volume *History of the Warfare Between Science and Theology*.

some churchmen to do battle for their faith, others chose to meet a third challenge, that of the industrial revolution which was making it increasingly difficult for people to lead the life that Christ commanded. They were troubled by the conviction that class divisions had fractured the nation and atrophied the capacity of people of different social groups to feel toward one another, and they were especially concerned that the ministers had become alienated from the poor in the great cities. The social gospel movement discarded all but the essentials of the gospel and concentrated on making the Church an instrument of social reform. From his parsonage in Columbus, Ohio, Washington Gladden championed the cause of industrial peace, and millions of copies were sold of Charles Sheldon's *In His Steps*, describing a congregation which followed consistently the teachings of Jesus.

Probably the most influential books came from the pen of the gifted Walter Rauschenbusch. Upon graduation from seminary, he was sent to the Second German Baptist Church of New York, a small, impoverished congregation on the fringe of Hell's Kitchen. Here, in the depression of the 1890's, he saw good men go 'into disreputable lines of employment and respectable widows consent to live with men who could support them and their children. One could hear human virtue cracking and crumbling all around.' This experience convinced Rauschenbusch that evil was the consequence not of individual frailty but of environment. When Rauschenbusch went as professor to the Rochester Theological Seminary, it was to train a generation of preachers in the social gospel and to produce a series of books, the most notable of which was *Christianity and the Social Crisis* (1907).

While many of the Protestant churches sought to come to terms with the new forces, the Roman Catholic Church was under no pressure to conform to the new science. It specifically repudiated 'modernism' in the papal encyclical *Pascendi Dominici Gregis* of 1907, although in the encyclical *Rerum Novarum* of 1891 the Church had sharply attacked the evils of unregulated capitalism and encouraged far-ranging reforms.

Perhaps in the long run the most important

religious development of these years was the growth of Catholicism. In 1890 the Roman Catholic Church counted some 9 million communicants in the United States; thirty years later the number had doubled, and every sixth person and every third church member was Catholic. This growth resulted in large part from the flood of immigration which brought 16 million people to the New World during these years; well over half came from the Catholic countries of central and southern Europe. No church that had been in the Americas a century before the Jamestown plantation could be called an immigrant church, but probably the majority of Catholic communicants were first- or second-generation Americans, while the Church hierarchy was long dominated by the Irish—thus Cardinal Gibbons of Baltimore and Archbishop Ireland of St. Paul. As in the past the growth of Catholicism gave rise to anti-Catholic movements. Most prominent of these was the American Protective Association which flourished, chiefly in the Middle West, during the 'nineties. Like the Know-Nothings of the 'fifties and the Klan of the 1920's, the A.P.A. was wholly negative in character; unlike them it did comparatively little damage.

Social and Legal Thought

Though Darwinism deeply affected social and legal thinking, a number of theorists challenged the view that progress could come only as a result of the survival of the 'fittest' at the end of a struggle that would require several thousand years to work itself out. Frank Lester Ward, the father of American sociology, formulated a philosophy which, while fully accepting Darwinian evolution in the realm of Nature, resolutely rejected its authority in the realm of human nature. Man, he argued—and he was a distinguished zoologist and paleontologist—is not subject to the same iron laws that govern the animal world, for while environment, or Nature, masters and transforms the animal world, man masters and transforms Nature. What is more, he does this not by a blind struggle for existence, but by co-operation and applied intelligence. In book after book—*Dynamic Sociology, Applied Sociology, Psychic*

Factors in Civilization—Ward emphasized that survival of the fittest required the application of organized intelligence, and the institution best qualified to organize man's intelligence was government.

The same forces that shaped sociology shook the study of economics to its foundations. Economists, like sociologists, had acquiesced passively in a series of iron laws that were said to control the economy. The full-throated attack upon this notion came from a new generation of academic economists, most of them trained in Germany where they were taught that the State should be an agency to produce a more humane social order. In 1885, a group of young men, all of whom had studied in Germany—Simon Patten, Herbert Baxter Adams, John Bates Clark, Edwin James, and E. R. A. Seligman—founded the American Economics Association. They boldly asserted: 'We regard the state as an educational and ethical agency whose positive aid is an indispensable condition of human progress. . . . We hold that the doctrine of laissez faire is unsafe in politics and unsound in morals.'

Men such as these wished to place the American university at the service of government. At the University of Wisconsin, they played an important role in aiding the administration of Governor Robert M. La Follette. The university, especially the School of Economics, Politics and History under Richard T. Ely, trained students for careers in public administration; it even offered a course in bill drafting. Wisconsin is only the most spectacular example of what was happening across the country in these years. A similar relationship existed in New Jersey between Governor Woodrow Wilson and a group of reformers with close ties to Princeton and Columbia. On the national level, government commissions looked into problems of conservation, rural life, and industrial strife. By the time America entered World War I, it was accepted as a matter of course that professors like Felix Frankfurter would man the wartime agencies.

No economist did more to change old ways of viewing society than Thorstein Veblen. A Norwegian farm-boy who had grown up in the Middle West, Veblen was all his life something of an outsider, and able therefore to look at institutions and practices of the American economy without emotional or intellectual commitments. This he did in *The Theory of the Leisure Class* (1899), *The Theory of Business Enterprise* (1904), and a long series of other volumes. Veblen emphasized the irrational element in the economy; the role of conspicuous leisure, conspicuous consumption, and conspicuous waste; the conflict between the instinct for craftsmanship and the instinct for pecuniary gain, the engineer and the price system. He called for an economy which would be controlled by engineers, subject to the discipline of tools and the machine, rather than by businessmen, who valued profits rather than production.

Evolution and pragmatism profoundly affected the interpretation of politics and history as well. There was a widespread revolt against Newtonian concepts of government—against the tyranny of abstract concepts like the state, and the illusion that there could be such a thing as 'a government of laws and not of men.' Instead scholars turned to the analysis of constitutions and governments as they actually functioned: to the Constitution as a mechanism that often broke down and had to be tinkered with rather than as a sacred Covenant. They analyzed what presidents and judges did rather than abstractions called The Executive Power or The Judiciary; explored the battlefields of party politics or the misty fogs of public opinion rather than the formal documentary record. Woodrow Wilson, who was a professor of politics at the time, explained:

Government is not a machine but a living thing. It falls not under the theory of the universe, but under the theory of organic life. It is accountable to Darwin, not to Newton.

History, in many ways closer to literature than to the social sciences, responded somewhat more sedately to the new teachings. In the 'nineties the elder statesmen who had dominated the historical stage for two generations were passing from the scene. The venerable George Bancroft completed the Author's Last Revision of his great history just in time to have it go out of date on publication. In 1892 the indomitable Francis Parkman published the final panel of his great historical series on the struggle between the French and English for the control of North America—the most impressive achievement of the era of historical romanticism. With the death of Bancroft in 1891 and of Parkman in 1893 the golden age of American history came to an end and the iron age set in. Three names dominate the new generation. In 1890 Captain Alfred Mahan published the remarkable *Influence of Sea-Power upon History*; the next year Henry Adams completed his brilliant nine-volume study of the administrations of Jefferson and Madison and turned to the study of historical forces; in 1893 young Frederick Jackson Turner announced a frontier interpretation that was to bemuse the imagination of American historians for another half-century. Turner and Charles A. Beard both were deeply influenced by the Populist revolt and the Progressive movement, but they developed very different formulas. Turner argued that what chiefly differentiated America from the Old World was the frontier, which took a European and transformed him into an American. Beard's emphasis, too, was environmental; in a prodigious flow of books and articles he read an economic interpretation into much of American history from the making of the Federal Constitution to American participation in two world wars. A crusader as much as an historian, Beard used scholarship as a weapon in the struggle for Progressivism and reform, and eventually for isolationism.

Of all the social sciences, the study of law responded most decisively to evolution and pragmatism. Under the compelling pressures of the new exegesis Natural Law gave way to historical jurisprudence, and this in turn to sociological jurisprudence. The concept of the law as a living, growing organism owes much to the most distinguished American jurist of his generation, Oliver Wendell Holmes, Jr., who sat on the Supreme Courts of Massachusetts and the United States for half a century, from 1882 to 1932. A product of Harvard and of the Union Army, Holmes had early associated with members of the Metaphysical Club of Cambridge, and he took in pragmatism as naturally as his father, the famous Dr. Holmes, accepted the new teachings about antisepsis. From

Oliver Wendell Holmes, Jr. (1841–1935). For half a century, from 1882 to 1932, 'the Great Dissenter' graced the bench first of the Massachusetts Supreme Court, then of the U.S. Supreme Court. 'If there is any principle of the Constitution that more imperatively calls for attachment than any other it is the principle of free thought—not free thought for those who agree with us but freedom for the thought that we hate,' he said. This portrait by Charles Hopkinson was painted a few years before Holmes retired in 1932. Presidents never pay calls, but in 1933 the newly elected Franklin D. Roosevelt courteously broke precedent to visit the former judge. 'Why do you read Plato, Mr. Justice,' FDR asked. 'To improve my mind, Mr. President,' the ninety-two-year-old man replied. (*Photograph by ACKAD, Washington, D. C.*)

the beginning he confessed the pragmatist's distrust of absolutes. 'The life of the law has not been logic,' he wrote in *The Common Law*, which he published in 1881, 'it has been experience. The felt necessities of the time—the prevalent moral and political theories, intuitions of public policy, avowed or unconscious, even the prejudices which judges share with their fellow men—have had a good deal more to do than the syllogism in determining the rules by which men should be governed. The law embodies the story of a nation's development through many centuries and cannot be dealt with as if it contained only the axioms and corollaries of a book of mathematics.'

Scientific Interests

Tocqueville observed that a democracy almost inevitably addressed itself to what was practical and immediate in science, a generalization largely valid for this period. These years witnessed a series of ambitious explorations of the Far West; the organization of research at the Lawrence and Sheffield scientific schools and at government bureaus; far-reaching developments in geology, paleontology, botany, and ethnology; and the popularization of science by men like John Fiske and Edward Youmans.

With settlement ready to penetrate the Last West, the need for knowledge of its geology and geography, its flora and fauna, was urgent, and in the decade after the war the Federal Government undertook to fill the need. The Wilkes Exploring Expedition of the 'forties, the Railroad Surveys and Boundary Surveys and Coastal Surveys of the 'fifties, provided the pattern. First in the field was the army-sponsored Geological Survey of the Fortieth Parallel led by the gifted Clarence King of the Sheffield Scientific School, whom John Hay called 'the best and brightest man of his generation.' Meanwhile the Corps of Engineers launched a large-scale expedition to explore the territory west of the 100th meridian, which yielded 40-odd volumes of scientific reports of immense value. The Hayden Geological Survey of the Territories mapped much of the *terra incognita* of the Far West. Easily the most dramatic of the expeditions were those headed by the remarkable John Wesley Powell, a one-armed veteran of the Civil War who

had already piloted four boats down the 900 miles of the Green and Colorado rivers. Out of all this came not only discoveries but, in 1879, the creation of the United States Geological Survey headed first by Clarence King and then by Powell.

A more scientific interest in native races emerged. Lewis Morgan, having led the way with his work on the Iroquois, turned his attention to the Indians of the West and the Southwest, and in 1877 published *Ancient Society*, an argument for the common origin and evolution of all races which owed a great deal to Darwin. During these same years Hubert Howe Bancroft published his five-volume *History of the Native Races of the Pacific Coast*, and the Swiss-born Adolphe Bandelier launched his pioneering studies of the archaeology of the pueblo Indians of the Southwest which led to his fascinating novel, *The Delight Makers*. The year 1879 saw both the establishment of the United States Bureau of Ethnology and the founding of the Archaeological Institute of America.

Notable contributions were also coming from the universities. At Harvard Asa Gray completed his *Flora of North America*. In the midst of the war James Dwight Dana, dean of academic geologists, published his *Manual of Geology*, which reflected the evolutionary findings of Charles Lyell in England. Dana's Yale colleague, the paleontologist Othneil Marsh, organized a series of scientific expeditions into the West and published his *Vertebrate Life in America*, which placed the study of fossils on a scientific basis. At the Smithsonian Institution the zoologist Spencer Baird brought to completion his *History of North American Birds*.

All this work revealed the urgent need to conserve resources. Pioneer in alerting the American people was the versatile George Perkins Marsh, diplomat, historian, philologist, and scientist. From observing the waste of soil and forest in his native Vermont, and from experience in Turkey and Asia Minor, he came to appreciate the consequences of these violations of nature's laws. In 1864 he published his masterpiece, *Man and Nature* (later published as *The Earth as Modified by Human Action*), the most influential American geographical work of the nineteenth century. It dealt with 'man as a disturbing agent,' described the destruction of animal and vegetable life by men, and emphasized the need to conserve forests. John Wesley Powell applied Marsh's central thesis to the problem of land and water on the High Plains. In 1878 Powell's memorable *Report on the Arid Regions of the West* warned against using Eastern techniques of farming on the High Plains, argued for farm units of not less than 2500 acres, stressed the paramount importance of water and access to water supplies, and insisted that the right to water should inhere in the land.

These fermenting years were distinguished by contributions to both pure and popular science. In 1876 Edward Pickering, director of the astronomical observatory at Harvard, began a photographic record of the stellar universe. At Yale Willard Gibbs, the most gifted mathematician of his generation, made fundamental advances in mathematical physics with papers on the equilibrium of heterogeneous substances. William James opened America's first psychological laboratory in the early 'seventies, and there began studies that culminated in his epoch-making *Principles of Psychology*. In the meantime, John Fiske was engaged in reconciling Darwinian evolution, Spencerian sociology, and liberal religion in the *Outlines of Cosmic Philosophy*, a work that sprawled through four volumes, and Edward Youmans fed it to the public through the *Popular Science Monthly* and the many volumes of his International Scientific Series.

Journalism

In the eighteen-sixties and 'seventies New York City was the newspaper center of the nation. Although local papers such as the *Springfield Republican*, *Boston Transcript*, *Toledo Blade*, and *Cincinnati Commercial* were influential, the great New York dailies—the *Tribune*, *Sun*, *Evening Post*, and *Times*—held a commanding position.

William Cullen Bryant, since 1826 editor of the *Evening Post*, was dean of America's journalists. Few more vigorous, discriminating, and far-sighted critics have dealt with the American scene than this poet-editor who combined respectability with a zeal for righteousness. He lifted American

journalism to a higher literary and ethical plane than it had heretofore occupied, and gave not only his editorial column but his entire paper a dignity that assured it the leading place in American journalism. But he lacked the talent to appeal to a broad popular audience, and his following was limited almost entirely to the intellectual elite.

Horace Greeley of the *Tribune*, greatest of American editors, was spokesman for the plain people, of the entire North. Practical, liberal, open-minded, fearless, and with boundless faith in democracy, he was a social reformer who fashioned a great paper as an instrument for social purposes. He founded the *Tribune* in 1841, drove its circulation up over the hundred thousand mark, and until the close of the Civil War exerted a larger influence over public opinion north of the Mason-Dixon Line than any other editor—and possibly than any other private citizen in the country. Throughout a long career Greeley found room in his paper for the liveliest literary intelligence, the most varied points of view, and the most extreme reforms. His thirty years' editorial leadership of the *Tribune* still constitutes the greatest achievement of personal journalism in our history.

A very different paper was *The Sun*, after 1868 under the control of Charles A. Dana, graduate of Harvard College and of Brook Farm. Dana had been trained to journalism under Greeley; he had seen service in the war under Grant, and was close to the center of power. By attracting to his staff some of the most skillful journalists of the day, he made *The Sun* the most popular paper in the country. With the passing of years, however, Dana grew increasingly cynical and even capricious, equally hostile to corruption and to civil service reform, to organized capital and to organized labor; in the end he frittered away his influence and condemned his paper to sterility.

The most powerful newspaper in the country outside New York City was probably the *Springfield Republican*, edited from 1844 to 1915 by three generations of Samuel Bowleses. Like the *Tribune*, the *Republican* issued a weekly edition, which had a much wider circulation, spreading liberal principles throughout New England and into the Ohio and Mississippi valleys. The second

Samuel Bowles advocated a magnanimous policy toward the defeated South, fought corruption under Grant, and held fast to principles of independence and honesty.

More powerful than many daily papers were weekly journals of opinion such as *The Nation*, *The Independent*, and *Harper's Weekly*. Of these *The Nation*, under the Irish-born E. L. Godkin, was for the thirty years after 1865 easily the most influential. A great editor, incisive and vigorous, with high literary and intellectual standards, Godkin enlisted the best minds in the country: Henry James and William James, Henry Adams, James Russell Lowell, William Dean Howells, C. W. Eliot and Daniel C. Gilman, Asa Gray and John Fiske. Yet for all his high-mindedness, Godkin found himself increasingly out of touch with the political and economic realities of his adopted country. His liberalism was doctrinaire; he had no understanding either of the farmer or the working-man. 'He couldn't imagine a different kind of creature from himself in politics,' wrote William James shrewdly, and it is significant that the most fervent appreciation of Godkin came from his New England and English friends who, like him, often mistook good taste for good sense.

Securely in the American tradition was *Harper's Weekly*, long edited by the versatile and scholarly George William Curtis. A family magazine, designed for entertainment rather than agitation, it was a force for political decency, and Curtis came in time to occupy the position previously held by Bryant. *Harper's Weekly* is chiefly remembered for its lively coverage of the Civil War, Winslow Homer's early drawings, and Thomas Nast's political cartoons.

The *Atlantic* and *Harper's Monthly*, high-minded but somewhat parochial, had for some time almost pre-empted the field of the monthly magazine. After the war they were joined by a number of newcomers. First arrival was *The Galaxy*, designed to compete with the *Atlantic* and ultimately absorbed by it. Mark Twain, Henry James, and many of the most popular English authors wrote for the new magazine, and it gave extensive space to new developments in science. More interesting was California's bid for literary attention, the *Overland Monthly*, edited

by Bret Harte, whose 'Luck of Roaring Camp' and 'Outcasts of Poker Flat' first appeared in its pages. Harte abandoned the magazine at the end of a year, and it never lived up to its initial promise. A happier fate was reserved for that best of all children's magazines, the beloved *St. Nicholas*. Founded in 1873 by Mary Mapes Dodge who had already written *Hans Brinker and the Silver Skates*, *St. Nicholas* managed to attract to its pages almost every distinguished author on both sides of the Atlantic, and many of the most talented artists and engravers as well.

The late eighteen-seventies and 'eighties marked a dividing line in American journalism. First there developed the subordination of politics to 'news,' with a consequent development of the highly efficient machinery of reporting and news-gathering, and the organization of news-gathering agencies like the United Press and the Associated Press. Second, we note the passing of the personal element in journalism and the growth of editorial anonymity. Third, the creation of chains, with elimination of competition, and the use of syndicated material. Fourth, an enlargement and improvement in the appearance of the newspapers, accomplished in large part through the immense growth of advertising, which gave newspaper-owners the money to install expensive machinery like the linotype. And last, the Federal Government co-operated by providing low postal rates for newspapers and magazines, and rural free delivery.

No one better represented the new journalism than Joseph Pulitzer. A Hungarian-German Jew, trained under Carl Schurz, he first made a respectable newspaper of the St. Louis *Post-Dispatch*, which he took over in 1878, then moved on to New York where he acquired the almost defunct *World* from the speculator Jay Gould. By elaborating on the sensationalism of James Gordon Bennett, Pulitzer pushed the circulation of the *World* up to unprecedented figures, passing the million mark during the hectic days of the Spanish-American War. His paper, popular in appeal, played up sensational news in screaming headlines and illustrations, while its bold political program recommended it to the poor. Yet the *World* under Pulitzer was never merely a 'yellow' journal.

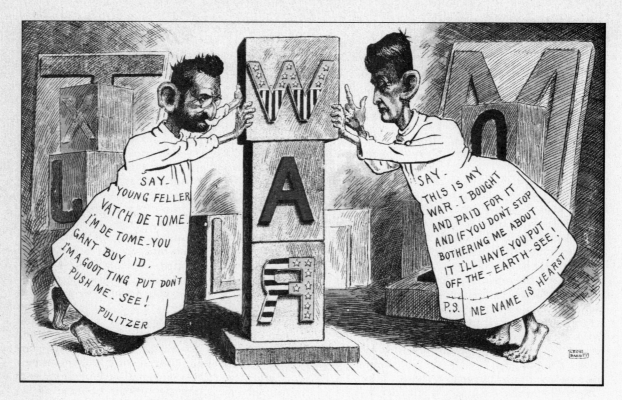

'The Yellow Kids.' This savage cartoon depicts the publishers Joseph Pulitzer and William Randolph Hearst in 1898 as childish irresponsibles playing at war. Two years earlier they had brawled over a comic strip character, 'The Yellow Kid,' who gave the name of 'yellow journalism' to the sensationalist press. The cartoonist, in a heavy-handed way, represents the Hungarian-born Pulitzer as talking with a thick Continental accent. 'Vatch de Tome' translates as 'Watch the Dome,' symbol of Pulitzer's newspaper, the New York *World*. (*Library of Congress*)

There was a wide gap between the news stories and the editorial page, conducted on a high intellectual and moral plane. After the retirement of Pulitzer and the accession of Frank I. Cobb to the editorship, the *World* became the leading Democratic organ in the country, a position which it maintained under the able direction of Walter Lippmann until its demise in 1931.

The success of Pulitzer in tapping substrata of newspaper readers was contagious. William Randolph Hearst, who had inherited a vast mining fortune, bought the New York *Journal* in 1896. Soon Hearst was outsensationalizing Pulitzer, and there ensued a fierce struggle which sent the circulation of both papers soaring, but degraded the press. Hearst, in the *Journal* and in the nationwide chain of papers he acquired, brought 'yellow' journalism to its most extreme development, but without the editorial compensations offered by the *World*. Lavish use of enormous black leaders, colored paper, blaring full-page editorials, and colored cartoon strips assured the Hearst papers an extraordinary popularity, but sensationalism became a national menace when, in order to boost circulation, Hearst whipped up popular demand for war with Spain. E. L. Godkin, in one of his last editorials, hotly denounced 'a regime in which a blackguard boy with several millions of dollars at his disposal, has more influence on the use a great nation may make of its credit, of its army and navy, of its name and traditions, than all the statesmen and philosophers and professors in the country.'

Pulitzer and Hearst, for all their faults, were real journalists; not so Frank A. Munsey, who in 1882 came to New York City from Portland, Maine, and began to deal in magazines and newspapers the way Daniel Drew had dealt in stocks. An entrepreneur, who at one time owned more valuable newspaper properties than anyone else in the country, Munsey subscribed to no ascertainable policies beyond an uncritical attachment to the status quo and recognized no responsibility to the public.

At one time or another Munsey owned six New York papers, two in Baltimore and one each in Philadelphia, Washington, and Boston; most of these he merged or killed, for he believed in the survival of the fittest, by which he meant, of course, the most profitable. 'Frank Munsey,' wrote William Allen White in one of the bitterest of obituaries, 'contributed to the journalism of his day the talent of a meat packer, the morals of a money changer, and the manners of an undertaker. He and his kind have about succeeded in transforming a once-noble profession into an eight per-cent security.'

Despite this vulgarization of the press, the professional standards and ethics of journalism were on the whole improving as a result of the establishment of schools of journalism—of which those at Columbia and the University of Missouri were the most influential—and the example of such papers as the *New York Times*. When Ochs bought the *Times* in 1896, it was on the verge of collapse; by printing only the news 'that's fit to print,' and building up a staff of skillful correspondents, Ochs made the *Times* the American counterpart of *The Times* of London. The vigorous growth of such papers as the St. Louis *Post-Dispatch*, the Baltimore *Sun*, and the Chicago *Daily News* also helped to offset the low standards of the mass circulation press.

The 'eighties saw something of a revolution in magazines as well. The magazine field had long been dominated by respectable family journals like *Harper's*, content with a modest circulation and catering to middle-class readers whose tastes were primarily literary. In 1886 came the *Forum*, designed—as its title announced—for discussion of controversial issues. Three years later Benjamin Flower launched the lively *Arena*, which opened its pages to radicals, reformers, and heretics of all stamps. Then came a flood of weekly and monthly magazines devoted to agitation rather than to entertainment—Bryan's *Commoner*, for example, and *La Follette's Weekly*. In 1912 Oswald Garrison Villard obtained control of *The Nation*, and transformed it into a radical weekly. The *New Republic*, launched two years later under the auspices of Herbert Croly, and with an editorial staff that included Walter Lippmann and Randolph Bourne, was designed 'to start little insurrections,' and assumed at once a commanding position among the magazines of opinion.

Education

The effect of the war on education in the South was disastrous. Schoolhouses had fallen into ruin; teachers were killed or scattered; the impoverished South, less able to bear heavy taxes than at any time, now faced the additional burden of providing a public education for white and Negro alike. The University of North Carolina closed its doors for some years during reconstruction; the University of Louisiana was kept alive only by the heroic self-denial of a few professors who refused to abandon the stricken institution. Southern education did not fully recover until the twentieth century.

In the North, by contrast, education progressed at almost every level. By mid-century the responsibility of the community to provide schooling for all its children was generally acknowledged, but that obligation was faithfully discharged only in elementary education. In 1870 there were only 200 public high schools in the entire country; a decade later the number had increased to some 800. As late as the 1870's it was still possible to challenge the legality of public support to high schools; not until 1874 was this question forever laid to rest by Justice Thomas Cooley of the Michigan Supreme Court in the Kalamazoo case.

During the decades after Reconstruction, education made even more spectacular gains. No nation was ever more fully committed to the ideal of education, free, universal, and comprehensive, than the United States. Yet in 1870 there were only 6,871,000 pupils enrolled in the public schools of the country, and of these only 80,000 were in the high schools.[4] By 1920, however, enrollment had leaped to 21,578,000,[5] of whom over two million were in the high schools. In the same half-century the percentage of children between five and seventeen who were in school increased from 57 to 78, while the average daily attendance grew fivefold. In 1870 Americans spent some $63 million on their public schools; by 1920 expenditures had passed the billion mark.

Most pupils went to a 'little red schoolhouse'—more picturesque than efficient—where some student working his way through a nearby college, or a girl too young to marry, taught all subjects and all grades, largely by rote. Discipline was capricious but severe, corporal punishment taken for granted, and extracurricular activities were limited to marbles or crack-the-whip on a muddy school ground. The backbone of the curriculum was the 'three R's'—reading, 'riting, and 'rithmetic. Children learned spelling, and many other things, out of Noah Webster's Blue Backed Spellers, which had already done service for three generations, and 'spelling-bees' were as exciting a part of school life as basketball games today. McGuffey's Readers, which sold over 100 million copies between 1836 and the end of the century, introduced children to 'selections' from the best of English and American literature. The novelist Hamlin Garland, who went to country schools in Iowa during these years, remembered that 'from the pages of McGuffey's Readers I learned to know and love the poems of Scott, Byron, Southey, Wordsworth, and a long line of English masters, and got

my first taste of Shakespeare.' The McGuffey Readers, with their pious axioms and their moral tales, made a somewhat heavy-handed contribution, too, to 'molding character.'

By 1870 almost two-thirds of public school-teachers were women—a number which increased through the rest of the century. With only twelve normal schools in the country at the outbreak of the Civil War, the great majority of teachers were untrained, and it was generally supposed that any respectable girl was competent to teach school. In due course states created boards of education designed to establish minimum requirements, and gradually teaching took on some of the characteristics of a profession. During the reconstruction years nine states provided for compulsory school attendance for at least part of the year, and some even enforced these laws.

In 1867 Congress created the office of United States Commissioner of Education to 'collect statistics and facts concerning the conditions and progress of education' and 'to diffuse information regarding the organization and management of schools and methods of teaching.' Though the office was reduced to the status of a bureau and systematically starved by Congress, it managed nevertheless to attract distinguished educators: first Henry Barnard, founder and editor of the *American Journal of Education*; then the learned philosopher, William T. Harris, for a long time superintendent of schools of St. Louis. Under Harris's auspices the first public kindergarten was opened in 1873, and it was Harris, too, whose long series of annual reports on public schools did for his generation what Horace Mann's reports had done for an earlier generation, providing a rationalization of public education in an industrial age.

What was later known as 'progressive' education received its formulation and earliest application during these years. The doctrines of the Swiss Johann Pestalozzi and of the German Friedrich Froebel had been introduced to America just before the war; now they triumphed in the work of Edward A. Sheldon of the Oswego State Normal School, whose graduates carried the new gospel throughout the East and the Middle West. Almost equally important was the work of Colonel Francis

4. Compare, however, Great Britain, which had a population roughly two-thirds that of the United States; only 1,450,000 children were enrolled in schools, and the number who attended was much smaller.

5. Non-public school enrollment for 1900 was 1,334,000 and for 1920 was 1,700,000.

Parker who had studied pedagogy in Germany, returned to be the superintendent of schools in Quincy, Massachusetts, where he quietly carried through a revolution in education whose philosophy and techniques anticipated, and deeply influenced, John Dewey two decades later.

In the next generation progressive education came into its own. The leaders in the transformation of the school were Lester Ward, who thought education the mainspring of progress; William James, whose *Principles of Psychology* provided inspiration for the new dispensation; G. Stanley Hall, first professional psychologist in America, the author of a pioneer work on *Adolescence*; Edward L. Thorndike of Columbia University's new Teachers' College, whose experiments shattered orthodox assumptions about the learning process; and above all John Dewey, philosopher and symbol of the whole progressive education movement. Dewey believed that the school was a legatee institution which had to carry on functions previously attended to by other groups in the community. In *The School and Society* (1899) he wished to use the school as a lever for reform to make society more 'worthy, lovely, and harmonious.' In *Democracy and Education* (1916) he argued that in an 'intentionally progressive' society, culture could not be divorced from vocation.

The 'revolution' that these men and their disciples carried through involved a shift in emphasis from subject matter to learning by experience, from education as a preparation for life to education as life itself. It called for participation in the learning process by the children themselves—the original principle of the *Kindergarten*—through such activities as woodworking and cooking; did away with much of the formality of the classroom; greatly broadened the curriculum, often at the expense of thoroughness and discipline; encouraged children to play an active role in such affairs as student government; and attempted to make each school, in the words of Dewey, 'an embryonic community life, active with types of occupations that reflect the life of the larger society.' Within a short time Dewey and his associates at Teachers' College succeeded in imposing their educational outlook on much of the country.

Higher education in the North, meantime, experienced a renaissance which can be traced to a number of factors: the Morrill Land-Grant Act of 1862; the demand of business and the professions for specialized knowledge and skills; new pressures for educational facilities for those heretofore neglected; and the emergence of a remarkable group of educational statesmen, most of them deeply influenced by German ideas and practices.

Agitation for the Morrill Act began as early as 1850, and in 1859 a bill looking to federal support for agricultural education passed both houses of Congress only to be vetoed by Buchanan. Three years later Lincoln gladly signed a more generous bill sponsored by Justin Morrill of Vermont. The Morrill Land-Grant Act of 1862 gave each state 30,000 acres of public land for each Congressman, to be used as endowment or support of a college of agricultural and mechanical arts. Under provisions of the Morrill Act, undoubtedly the most important piece of educational legislation in nineteenth-century America, land grant colleges were founded in every state. Some states gave their lands to existing institutions; others to private universities; most established new agricultural and mechanical schools.

The scientific revolution and the growing complexity of economic life resulted in the encouragement of the natural sciences and the establishment of numerous professional and vocational schools. Soon schools of law, medicine, architecture, and engineering were turning out graduates fitted by special training to meet the demands of the economy. Some of the older states assigned their Morrill funds to schools of science or engineering at existing institutions: Massachusetts turned her money over to the new Institute of Technology, and New York's princely grant of one million acres provided a large part of the endowment of the new Cornell University. Private philanthropy created a series of engineering schools: Columbia's School of Mines in 1864, Lehigh University in 1865, Stevens Institute in 1870, and a School of Mines in Colorado as early as 1874—two years before that Territory was admitted as a state.

In these years, too, educational leaders sought to provide in America the kind of facilities for graduate study that had long flourished abroad.

Ever since George Ticknor and George Bancroft had led the way to Göttingen University in the second decade of the century, eager graduates of American colleges had streamed to Berlin, Jena, Halle, Leipzig, and Munich, bringing back with them admiration for German scholarship, the seminar, and the Ph.D. degree. Yale awarded the first Ph.D. granted in America in 1861 and ten years later organized a graduate school; Harvard followed in 1872; and President Andrew D. White, who had studied at Berlin, made provision for graduate studies on the German model at Cornell. With the opening of the Johns Hopkins University in 1876 the German model was firmly transplanted in the New World.

The third influence—a quickened sense of equalitarianism—required provision for higher education for women and for Negroes. Wesleyan Academy for girls had opened at Macon, Georgia, as early as 1836, and the gallant Mary Lyon had persevered against heavy odds to found Mount Holyoke College at South Hadley, Massachusetts, in 1837, while Oberlin—pioneer in this as in so many things—adopted coeducation in the late 1830's. The postwar years saw the founding of Vassar, the gift of a rich brewer of Poughkeepsie, New York, which opened its doors in 1867; Wellesley College and Hunter College in 1870 and Smith College in 1871. Meantime Iowa led the way among state universities in adopting coeducation, and most of the state and municipal universities in the North followed its example. At a time when Englishmen were debating the propriety of establishing their first college for women, the United States could boast a dozen flourishing women's colleges, and a growing acceptance of coeducation as the common sense of the matter.

Oberlin College had admitted blacks almost from the beginning, and before the Civil War blacks had founded a university of their own at Wilberforce, Ohio. Institutions for blacks in the South were largely industrial training colleges. General Clinton Fisk, who had been a colonel of a black regiment during the war, opened a training school for blacks in Nashville in 1866 which eventually evolved into Fisk University. In 1868 General Samuel Armstrong, who also had led a black regiment, established Hampton Institute in Virginia; a few years later its most distinguished graduate, Booker T. Washington, was to found Tuskegee Institute in Alabama.

A fourth contribution to the educational renaissance was the emergence of the most remarkable group of statesmen in the history of American higher education. In 1869 Harvard elected a 35-year-old chemist, Charles W. Eliot, to the presidency. Eliot, who had spent some time observing German universities, was a scientist prepared to accept the teachings of Darwinian evolution, and he was peculiarly sensitive to the changes brought about by the industrial revolution. He signalized his advent to the presidency by a revolution in academic policies. Though Eliot was not the first to advocate the elective system, his tireless championship of freedom of choice helped popularize the system. Of greater ultimate significance was Eliot's rehabilitation of the schools of law and medicine, which he placed upon a sound professional basis. So significant was his achievement and so widespread his influence that he came to be regarded as the first citizen of his country.

While Eliot was transforming Harvard, Andrew Dickson White was pioneering far above Cayuga's waters, at Ithaca, New York. The new Cornell University, based on income from the Morrill Land Grant and on gifts from the industrial philanthropist Ezra Cornell, was both public and private and thus established a new pattern of higher education. Graduate of Yale, student at Paris and Berlin, professor at the University of Michigan, chairman of the New York State committee on education, White had long dreamed of a university that should be the equal of those of Germany and France, and now he had his chance. He decided that Cornell would have no barriers of color, sex, or faith; it would treat students like adults, encourage mature scholarship, maintain professional standards for the study of engineering and agriculture, and be a stronghold of academic freedom. Opened in 1868, Cornell set a pattern, later followed by Hopkins and Chicago, of springing to life full-panoplied in academic armor.

An even more important educational statesman was Daniel Coit Gilman, who had helped found the Sheffield Scientific School at Yale, and in 1871 became president of the new University of California. In 1874 a Baltimore philanthropist, Johns Hopkins, left $7 million to found a university and a hospital; when the trustees of the university turned to Eliot of Harvard, White of Cornell, and Angell of Michigan for advice, each recommended that they make Gilman president and give him a free hand. They did. Gilman created a university largely on the German model, with emphasis on graduate study and scholarship. He put his money in men, not buildings, and collected not only a distinguished faculty but an exceptional group of younger 'Fellows'—among them the future President Woodrow Wilson, Josiah Royce and John Dewey, leaders of two schools of philosophy, J. Franklin Jameson and Frederick Jackson Turner, historians, Walter Hines Page and Newton D. Baker, prominent in the public life of the next generation. Wilson said later of Gilman that he was 'the first to create and organize in America a university in which the discovery and dissemination of new truth were conceded a rank superior to mere instruction.'

In the half-century after the Civil War, higher education underwent an immense expansion: the 52,000 students who attended some five hundred colleges in 1870—all of them financially and most of them intellectually impoverished—increased to 600,000 students in 1920—more than in all the universities of the Old World. The habit of building new universities overnight, from the ground up, proved contagious. In 1889 John D. Rockefeller made his first munificent gift to create the new University of Chicago, which promptly took its place among the foremost institutions of learning. In the 1880's, too, the railroad magnate, Leland Stanford, endowed a university at Palo Alto, California, in memory of his son. Supported by an initial gift of some $20 million, this Stanford University became at once the leading private institution of learning west of the Mississippi. A third major creation of private benevolence was Clark University in Worcester, Massachusetts, which, under the guidance of the eminent psychologist G. Stanley Hall, undertook to be a New England version of the Johns Hopkins University. From these new universities came many innovations: the quarter system, the summer session,

extension divisions, the university press, and above all the creation of new graduate and professional schools. More prophetic of future developments was the rapid growth of state universities after the turn of the century; California, which attracted only 197 students in 1885, enrolled over six thousand in 1915. Many of the best state institutions, such as Michigan, Wisconsin, Illinois, and California, could hold their own academically with the older private universities.

New educational statesmen came to the fore. William Rainey Harper, a Hebrew scholar from Yale, gathered about him on Chicago's Midway perhaps the most remarkable group of scholars to be found in America in the 1890's and inaugurated far-reaching experiments that contrasted sharply with the traditional Gothic architecture of the institution. Nicholas Murray Butler was elected president of Columbia University in 1901, and for over forty years directed the destinies of that institution, changing it from a small residential college to the leading center for graduate research in the country. Influenced by the German example, these men were interested primarily in graduate and professional training and in the university as a center for research. Woodrow Wilson, who came to the presidency of Princeton just as Butler took over the helm at Columbia, preferred the English model. He toughened the intellectual fiber of the college and introduced something like the Oxford tutorial system, with marked success; when he was defeated in his attempt to add on top of this a great graduate school, he resigned to become Governor of New Jersey.

An essential instrument of education, and of popular culture, was the library. The first of the great modern public libraries was founded in Boston in the 'fifties, and soon attracted both public support and generous private bequests. The Chicago Public Library was developed around the gift of 7000 volumes presented after the great fire of 1871 by Thomas Hughes of England, author of *Tom Brown at Rugby*, the New York Public Library, which quickly became the largest of its kind in the Western world, was formed by the merger of three privately endowed libraries with the library resources of the city, while the Library of Congress, built around the nucleus of Thomas Jefferson's private library, is the largest and most effective library in the world. The major impulse to the public library movement came from the generosity of Andrew Carnegie. Inspired by a passion for education, persuaded that the public library was the most democratic of all highways to learning, and mindful of his own debt to books and his love of them, the Pittsburgh iron-master devoted some $45 million of his vast fortune to the construction of library buildings throughout the country. By requiring a guarantee of adequate support to the libraries he built, he laid the foundation for healthy growth of library facilities after his own gifts had served their initial purpose.

If, as most Americans from Jefferson to John Dewey confidently believed, education could be counted on to provide a sound basis for 'a happy and a prosperous people,' Americans at the turn of the century had reason to be cautiously optimistic. The principle of universal free public education from kindergarten through the university had been established; it would take only another half century or so for the practice to catch up with the principle.

The Fine Arts

Even before the Civil War the architectural renaissance sponsored by Thomas Jefferson and Benjamin Latrobe, and its offspring the Greek Revival, had petered out, and the most promising architects, James Renwick and Richard Upjohn, had turned to Gothic. Renwick's Grace Church and St. Patrick's Cathedral, and Upjohn's Trinity Church and Church of the Ascension, all in New York City, gave promise of a Gothic revival like that which flourished in the England of Ruskin and Gilbert Scott. What came instead was pseudo-Gothic. Used in many large public buildings, such as the Smithsonian Institution in Washington, it had a peculiar fascination for college trustees, who littered the academic landscape with grotesque structures. The enraptured John Fiske of Harvard urged that 'we honestly confess our stupidity and show some grain of sense by copying the Oxford and Cambridge buildings literally.' Harvard did not accept this advice but Trinity College in Hartford, Connecticut, did, and Knox College on the Illinois prairie; and a few years later the new

University of Chicago reproduced Oxford, 'battlemented towers' and all. Spires and buttresses, stained glass windows and gargoyles, jig-saw scroll work, endless bric-a-brac—all of this proclaimed the emptiness and insincerity of the architects and confessed the decline in taste since the simplicity and dignity of Jefferson and Bulfinch.

Out of all this welter two distinguished architects emerged: Henry Hobson Richardson and Richard Morris Hunt. As a student in Paris, Richardson fell under the influence of the medievalist Viollet-le-Duc, and he set out to transplant Romanesque architecture to the United States. Such was Richardson's power that he enjoyed a success greater than any other architect before Frank Lloyd Wright. 'To live in a house built by Richardson,' wrote one art historian, 'was a cachet of wealth and taste; to have your nest-egg in one of his banks gave you a feeling of perfect security; to worship in one of his churches made one think one had a pass key to the Golden Gates.' Richardson's greatest monuments were Trinity Church, Boston, for which John La Farge did the stained-glass windows, and the fortresslike Marshall Field warehouse in Chicago. Although it was these public buildings that contemporaries most prized, later critics have been more impressed by Richardson's influence on domestic architecture, particularly his use of shingles to create low, rambling houses which adapted to the landscape of the New England seacoast, and anticipated some of the innovations of Frank Lloyd Wright.

Contemporary with Richardson was Richard Morris Hunt, the favored architect of the plutocracy. He introduced to America the beauty and lavishness of the French Renaissance and built for millionaires magnificent country houses patterned after châteaux, or palatial town houses that resembled hôtels-de-ville. Viollet-le-Duc had prophesied an architecture of metal and glass, and even as Richardson and Hunt wrought in their derivative styles, these materials were working a revolution in architecture, notably in the work of the bridge-builders, John Roebling and his son Washington, who all through the 'sixties and 'seventies supervised the construction of that *stupor mundi*, the Brooklyn Bridge.

These years saw the beginning also of the pro-

Stanford University. Opened at Palo Alto, California, in 1891 with an initial gift of $20,000,000, the Leland Stanford Junior University erected twenty-seven buildings of buff sandstone and red tile connected by long colonnades in a Romanesque mode around two quadrangles. In the beginning, Stanford had more female students than male, until Mrs. Stanford limited the number of women to five hundred. (*Los Angeles County Museum*)

fessionalization of art and architecture. The American Institute of Architects had been founded in the late 'fifties, and the National Academy of Design in the early 'sixties when the Massachusetts Institute of Technology, and then Cornell University, offered the first formal training for architects. In the early 'seventies Boston opened her Museum of Fine Arts; a group of New York philanthropists chartered the Metropolitan Museum of Art; and in the national capital William Corcoran—son of an Irish immigrant—built and endowed the gallery that bears his name. Important, too, was the development of landscape architecture and of city planning associated so largely with the work of Frederick Law Olmsted. He laid out Central Park, Prospect Park in Brooklyn, the Capitol grounds in Washington, the park system of Boston and, eventually, the Chicago

World's Fair of 1893, and was chiefly instrumental in preserving Yosemite valley as a national park and in protecting Niagara Falls from the worst ravages of commercialization.

The advance in American aesthetics in the post-Reconstruction era might be measured by comparing the buildings of the Centennial Exposition of 1876 with those of the Columbian Exposition at Chicago in 1893. The first had been a helter-skelter of frame and iron structures without either design or harmony—doubtless the ugliest collection of buildings ever deliberately brought together at one place in the United States. The Chicago Exposition, by contrast, was elaborately designed by Richard Morris Hunt, who enlisted the most distinguished artists and architects in the country: Daniel Burnham of Chicago, Stanford White, and Louis Sullivan among the architects; Augustus Saint-Gaudens, Daniel Chester French, and Frederick MacMonnies among the sculptors; Mary Cassatt as one of the painters; while Frederick Law Olmsted was put in charge of landscaping.

Though these artists created along the shores of Lake Michigan the best designed and most beautiful exposition of modern times, the design was conventional and the beauty mostly derivative, for the overall plan was classical. Hunt's Administration Building was a brilliant copy of St. Paul's Cathedral in London; Charles Atwood's Art Building had been unequalled—so Burnham said—since the Parthenon. Louis Sullivan's exquisitely decorated Transportation Building did reveal originality, but almost everything else reminded the visitor of something he had read about or heard about. Americans had not yet developed an indigenous architectural style.

To the despair of Louis Sullivan, the classical style spread over the whole United States. Washington adopted the classical as the official style; soon most public buildings, railroad stations, libraries, banks, and college dormitories were being constructed in this mode. Sullivan resisted the vogue. The most gifted architect of his generation—he built the great Auditorium Building in Chicago, and the Carson, Pirie, and Scott store with its daring use of glass and metal and its rich ornamentation—Sullivan failed in the end to sustain this early promise. It remained for his student and disciple, Frank Lloyd Wright, to vindicate his philosophy and realize his vision.

Trained in the architectural office of Adler and Sullivan, Wright had taken to heart Sullivan's guiding principle that function determines form and form follows function. He conceived a building not as something superimposed upon the landscape, but as part of an organic whole embracing the structure and its furnishings, the grounds and gardens about it, the people who use it or live in it. He began to apply these ideas in the 'nineties as soon as he set up on his own, in such early prairie-style buildings as the Isabel Roberts House at River Forest, Illinois, as well as in the first Taliesin House at Spring Green, Wisconsin, where he worked and taught. In 1906 he built the Unity Temple in Oak Park, Illinois, which helped to revolutionize ecclesiastical architecture in the United States. At the same time he was putting up office buildings and factories, among them the dazzling Larkin Building in Buffalo. Later there came masterpieces—houses like Falling Waters near Pittsburgh where the rocks and waterfalls were incorporated into the house itself; the Imperial Hotel in Tokyo, built to withstand earthquakes; office buildings such as the futuristic Johnson Wax works in Racine, Wisconsin; desert residences like his own Taliesin West in Arizona. Wright's artistic life spanned two generations; he tied together the world of Louis Sullivan and the world of Mies van der Rohe and Walter Gropius.

Three major figures dominated American painting during the transition years: Winslow Homer, Albert Ryder, and Thomas Eakins.

Homer was a product of the Civil War. Trained as a lithographer, he had been sent to the battle lines by *Harper's Weekly*; his work was the best to come out of the war—'Prisoners from the Front' and 'The Sharpshooter,' or some of his Negro sketches. In the postwar years Homer lifted genre painting to the highest level it had attained in America: 'Morning Bell' (1866), 'High Tide at Long Branch' (1869), the beloved 'Snap-the-Whip' (1872), 'The Carnival' (1875). Homer's greatest period, however, was still ahead. In one great canvas after another—'The Life Line, 'Fog Warning,' 'Lost on the Banks,' 'The Undertow,'

Portrait of Walt Whitman by Thomas Eakins. A splendid teacher who stressed anatomical study, a gifted mathematician, a pioneer in photography, Eakins (1844–1916) was above all the greatest American painter of his age. As early as 1871, the Philadelphia artist had painted 'Max Schmitt in a Single Scull,' and in 1875 he did his stark 'The Gross Clinic.' But Eakins's uncompromising naturalism proved unacceptable. At the Centennial Exhibition of 1876, 'The Gross Clinic' was hung in the medical display rather than with art works, and when in 1886 he stripped the loincloth from a male model in a class that included female students, he was forced out of the Pennsylvania Academy. The following year he met Walt Whitman (1819–92), who was living out his days, a crippled man, across the Delaware in Camden, and Eakins painted this classic portrait of 'the Good Grey Poet.' (*Pennsylvania Academy of the Fine Arts*)

John Singer Sargent (1856–1925) in his Paris studio. The painting is his full-length portrait of 'Madame X,' who was, in fact, Mme. Gautreau, the wife of a French banker. Sargent's oil, exhibited at the Paris Salon of 1884, shocked the *haute monde* because of his candid rendering of the décolletage, the lavender make-up, and scarlet hair of the free-living New Orleans-born beauty. So great was the outcry that Sargent had to relocate in London, where his stylish, and more circumspect, portraits earned him fat fees and comparison to Reynolds and Gainsborough. Sargent himself, however, regarded 'Madame X' as his masterpiece. (*Archives of American Art, Smithsonian Institution*)

'Eight Bells,' and 'Gulf Stream'—he was to portray the struggle of man against the elements.

Ryder, like Herman Melville, lived obscurely in New York. Like Melville, too, he lived, as Lewis Mumford has observed, 'in a dark, moon-ridden world, stirring with strange beauty that indicated unexplored realities, deeper than the superficial levels of being.' Ryder's imagination was lyrical and mystical. He transferred to his varnish-covered canvases a mysterious world of clouds flitting across the moon, ships forever lost scudding before the wind, dim figures out of the mythological past—thus his 'Death on a Pale Horse,' 'The Flying Dutchman,' 'Jonah,' 'Siegfried and the Rhine Maidens,' which make us fancy for a moment, in Justice Holmes's phrase, 'that we heard a clang from behind phenomena.'

In these years, too, the most original genius among American painters was experimenting with new techniques and new subjects. Thomas Eakins had studied at the École des Beaux Arts, but that artistic finishing school left little impression on him. Back in Philadelphia in 1870 he began to turn out pictures whose unashamed realism forfeited the popularity his talent merited: paintings of swimmers, fishermen, oarsmen, and professional men and women busy with their work. A kind of Thorstein Veblen among artists, Eakins had no use for the salon or the academy; he brought to his art a scientific knowledge of the human body and portrayed it with an intimacy that shocked many of his contemporaries. When he painted President Hayes it was at his desk, working, and in shirt sleeves; as Presidents were not supposed to have shirt sleeves, the painting was rejected. 'I never knew but one artist, and that's Tom Eakins, who could resist the temptation to see what they think ought to be rather than what is,' said Walt Whitman, whose portrait is one of Eakins's masterpieces.

In the first decade of the new century, a group of Eakins's disciples launched the 'Realistic' movement. Robert Henri, George Luks, Everett Shinn, William Glackens, and John Sloan had all studied at the Philadelphia Academy under Eakins's disciple, Thomas Anshutz. Most of them had worked as pictorial reporters on the old Philadelphia *Press*, where they had come to know the seamy side of life in the great city, and most had studied in Paris. During the 'nineties they drifted to New York where they formed a loose-knit brotherhood joined by other young rebels and independents like George Bellows and Maurice Prendergast. The leader of the group was the gifted Robert Henri. Affectionately and sensitively they painted the color of the great city—McSorley's Bar, boys swimming off East River piers, children dancing in the teeming streets of the Five Corners; Bowery bums lounging under the 'El'; Yeats dining at Petipas; girls drying their hair on the roofs of tawdry tenements; a prize-fight at Sharkey's; the Staten Island ferry. In 1908 these Manhattan realists gave their first exhibition and were promptly dubbed the 'Ash-Can School.' When two years later they presented an exhibition, two thousand visitors tried to crash the gates on opening day. These exhibits mark the beginnings of modern art in America as truly as the Armory Show of 1913.

In the meantime another group of painters took up impressionism, that new technique, vision, and philosophy of painting which artists like Monet were revealing to an astounded world. The most distinguished landscape painter of the prewar era, George Inness, had anticipated something of impressionism, and so, too, John La Farge, who was equally talented in oils, water colors, murals, and stained glass. He returned from Paris in the 'sixties determined that his paintings 'indicate very carefully in every part the exact time of day and circumstance of light.' In 1874 Mary Cassatt settled in Paris, where she studied with Degas, exhibited with the Impressionists, bought their paintings, and herself experimented both with impressionism and with techniques of Japanese art with notable success. Others who revealed the influence of Impressionists were Childe Hassam, who painted the New England countryside in shimmering light and New York City in its gayer and more colorful moods, and the frail Theodore Robinson, who had studied with Monet and whose early death deprived his country of its most promising Impressionist.

Modern American sculpture begins with Augustus Saint-Gaudens, who for a generation towered over all of his artistic contemporaries. Born in Ireland of Irish and French parentage, he nevertheless recorded the American genius with rare sympathy and understanding. His Lincoln, in Lincoln Park, Chicago, with its intuitive comprehension of the combination of rugged shrewdness and spirituality, is so convincing that 'no one, having seen it, will conceive him otherwise thereafter.' The Farragut Monument (1881), its base executed by Stanford White, and the Shaw Memorial (1897) in Boston established him as the foremost monumental sculptor of his day. But the loveliest of Saint-Gaudens's statues is the figure he made for the tomb of Mrs. Henry Adams. 'From Prometheus to Christ, from Michael Angelo to Shelley,' wrote Henry Adams, 'art had wrought on this eternal figure almost as though it had nothing else to say.'

26

Imperialism and World Power

1876–1906

The United States in World Affairs

Writing in 1889 Henry Cabot Lodge observed that 'our relations with foreign nations today fill but a slight place in American politics, and excite generally only a languid interest.' From the settlement of the *Alabama* claims and the successful weathering of the *Virginius* affair to the eruption of the Hawaii and Venezuela crises, foreign relations were singularly placid. The change came in the 1890's, and it synchronized with the passing of the frontier, the shift from the 'old' to the 'new' immigration, the rise of the city, and the coming of age of our industrial system. Almost every year before 1876 the United States suffered an unfavorable balance of trade; almost every year thereafter the balance was decidedly in its favor. In 1865 foreign trade had been $404 million; by 1890 it had reached $1635 million.

America's longstanding interest in the Pacific came increasingly to center on the Hawaiian islands, 2300 miles southwest of California. Hawaii, or the Sandwich Islands, had been discovered by Captain Cook in 1778, and early served as a convenient port of call in the China trade and

recruiting station for Yankee whalers. By 1840 Honolulu, with whalemen and merchant sailors rolling through its streets, shops filled with Lowell shirtings, New England rum, and Yankee notions, missionaries living in frame houses brought around the Horn, and a neo-classic meeting house built of coral blocks, was a Yankee outpost. In the 1850's and 1860's efforts toward annexation aborted, but in 1875 the United States concluded with the Hawaiian monarch a reciprocity treaty which granted exclusive trading privileges to both nations and guaranteed the independence of the islands against any third party; twelve years later the Senate approved a treaty renewing these privileges and ceding Pearl Harbor on the island of Oahu to the United States.

These treaties greatly stimulated the sugar industry, which the sons of thrifty missionaries had established in Hawaii. American capital poured in, sugar production increased fivefold within a decade, and by 1890, 99 per cent of Hawaiian exports went to the United States. Native Hawaiians became increasingly disturbed by the growing determination of the American government to establish a protectorate, the ambitions of American

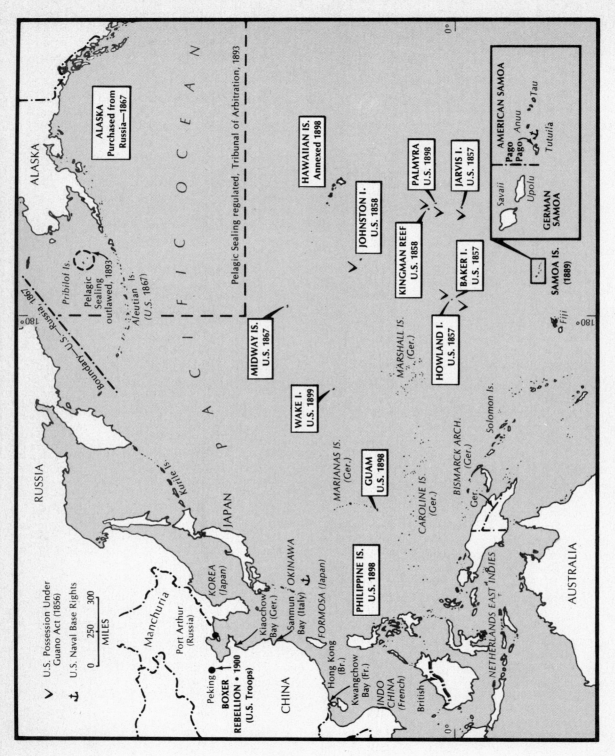

United States in the Pacific

settlers, and the overdependence on the American economy. Then came the McKinley tariff of 1890, which by providing a bounty of 2 cents a pound to domestic sugar dealt a catastrophic blow to the Hawaiian economy; sugar fell overnight from $100 to $60 a ton, and property values collapsed. American planters and industrialists who had opposed annexation out of fear that it would hamper their importation of Asiatic labor, now concluded that only annexation could restore to sugar interests in Hawaii their American market on equal terms.

They were even more alarmed when, in 1891, Queen Liliuokalani inaugurated a policy looking to the elimination of American influence and the restoration of autocracy. This threat excited a prompt counteroffensive. After marines had been landed from the U.S.S. *Boston* with the connivance of the American minister John L. Stevens, a Committee of Safety consisting largely of missionaries' sons deposed the hapless Queen on 17 January 1893. A provisional government under Chief Justice Sanford B. Dole promptly opened negotiations for annexation to the United States. 'I think we should accept the issue like a great Nation,' wrote Minister Stevens, 'and not act the part of pigmies nor cowards.' President Harrison, in full sympathy with this 'white man's burden' attitude, precipitately accepted a treaty of annexation on 14 February; but before the Senate got around to it, Grover Cleveland became President and hearkened to the appeal of 'Queen Lil.' 'I mistake the Americans,' he said, 'if they favor the odious doctrine that there is no such thing as international morality; that there is one law for a strong nation and another for a weak one.' He withdrew the treaty from the Senate and sent out a special commissioner to investigate. When the commissioner reported that the Hawaiian revolution was the work of American interests, aided by Minister Stevens, he denounced the affair. But the provisional government would not step down, and Cleveland was forced to recognize the Republic of Hawaii.

Between 1893 and 1898 two developments in the Far East sharpened the demand to annex the Hawaiian islands. The first was the rise of Japan to world power, and the fear of a Japanese inundation of the islands; the second was the prospective annexation of the Philippines, which gave Hawaii new significance as a naval base. Toward annexation McKinley had no such scruples as had animated his predecessor, but there was still sufficient opposition in the Senate to necessitate action by a Joint Resolution, on 7 July 1898, instead of through the normal method of a treaty. An organic act of 1900 conferred American citizenship on all subjects of the short-lived republic and the full status of a Territory of the United States, eligible for statehood, on the islands.

The Samoan, or Navigators', Islands were to the South Pacific what the Hawaiian were to the North Pacific, and from the 1830's on they had offered refuge to whalers and a virgin field for missionaries. In 1878 a treaty granted the United States trading privileges and the right to build a coaling station at Pago Pago in the island of Tutuila. Shortly thereafter Great Britain and Germany secured comparable concessions, and there followed ten years of ridiculous rivalry for supremacy among the three powers, each supporting a rival claimant to the native kingship. The danger of involving the United States in serious international complications was averted by the establishment in 1890 of a tripartite protectorate guaranteeing the independence and neutrality of the islands and confirming American rights to Pago Pago. Unimportant as this episode was, it constituted nevertheless, in the words of Secretary of State Gresham, 'the first departure from our traditional and well established policy of avoiding entangling alliances with foreign powers in relation to objects remote from this hemisphere.' After another embarrassing native civil war, and intensified bad feeling between the United States and Germany, the tripartite agreement was abrogated in 1900, and the islands divided between Germany and the United States, Great Britain obtaining compensation elsewhere.

Well before, this policy toward Latin America took a new direction under the vigorous leadership of Secretary of State James G. Blaine. Since 87 per cent of Latin American exports to the United States entered duty free, Blaine threatened to clamp a tariff on them unless the Latin American countries lowered their duties on U.S. prod-

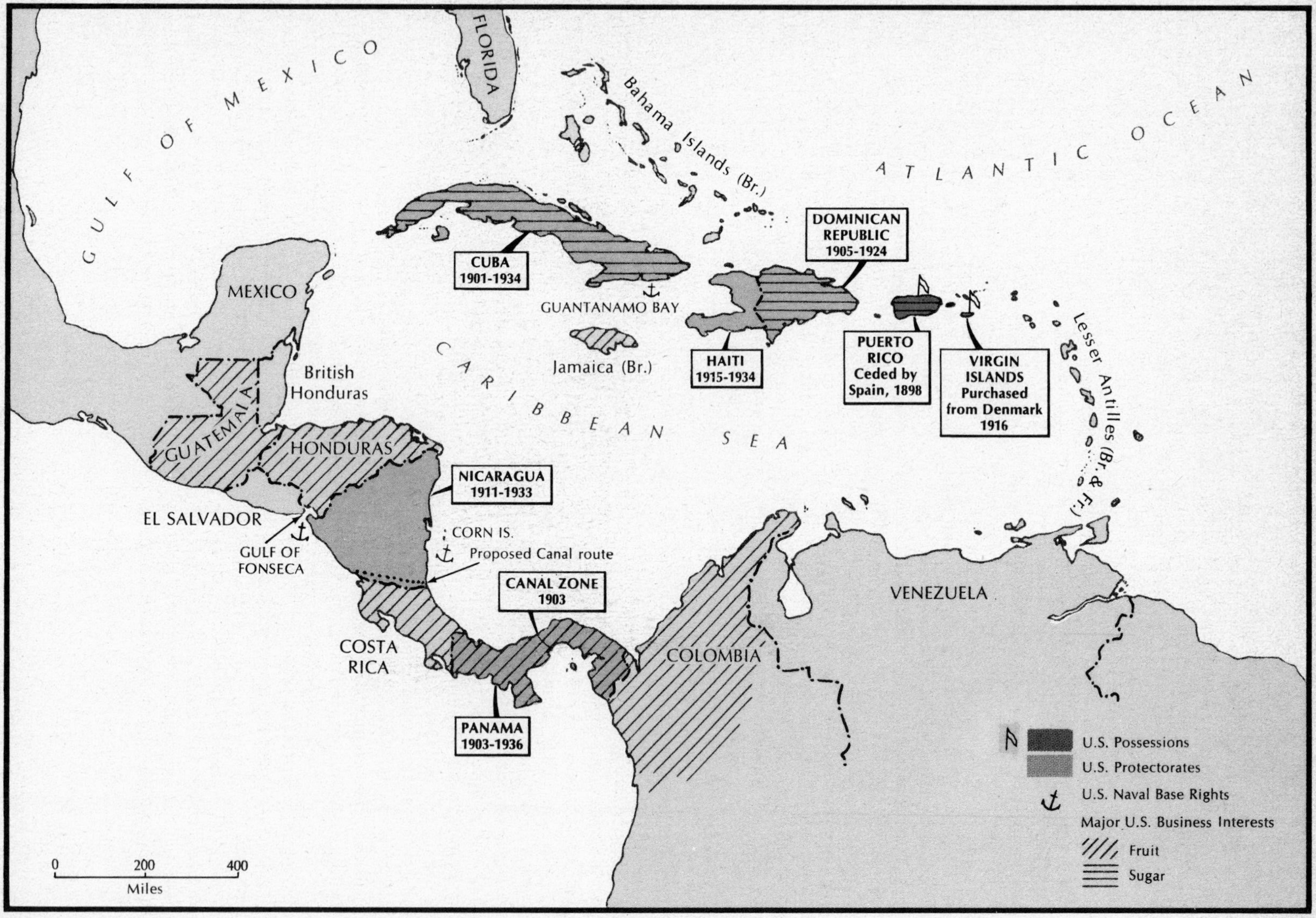

United States in the Caribbean

Map labels:

ATLANTIC OCEAN

GULF OF MEXICO

CARIBBEAN SEA

Lesser Antilles (Br. & Fr.)

VENEZUELA

COLOMBIA

VIRGIN ISLANDS Purchased from Denmark 1916

PUERTO RICO Ceded by Spain, 1898

DOMINICAN REPUBLIC 1905–1924

HAITI 1915–1934

Bahama Islands (Br.)

Jamaica (Br.)

GUANTANAMO BAY

CUBA 1901–1934

FLORIDA

MEXICO

British Honduras

GUATEMALA

HONDURAS

EL SALVADOR

GULF OF FONSECA

NICARAGUA 1911–1933

CORN IS.

Proposed Canal route

CANAL ZONE 1903

PANAMA 1903–1936

COSTA RICA

Legend:

U.S. Possessions
U.S. Protectorates
U.S. Naval Base Rights
Major U.S. Business Interests
Fruit
Sugar

0   200   400
Miles

ucts. To promote a Pan-American customs union, a series of uniform tariffs which would give reciprocal preference to American products or goods in all American countries, he called a Pan-American Conference in 1881. President Garfield's death was followed by a change in the State Department, and President Arthur revoked the invitations. Eight years later President Harrison placed Blaine once more in a position to advance his cherished project. In October 1889 the first International American Conference, representing eighteen countries, convened at Washington to consider Blaine's proposals for a Pan-American customs union and the arbitration of international disputes. To the Latin Americans both seemed like the invitation of the spider to the fly, and were politely rejected. But the Conference resulted in the creation of a Commercial Union of American States, renamed the Pan American Union in 1910, which served as a clearinghouse for the dissemination of scientific, technical, and economic information and set a precedent for future interhemispheric meetings.

Although the Pan-American Conference did not accept arbitration as a formal policy, American statesmen served as arbiters of several boundary disputes in Latin America, and the principle of arbitration won a notable victory in the Bering Sea controversy. Eager to prevent extermination of the seal in Alaskan waters, mainly by Canadian sealers, Blaine proclaimed American jurisdiction over the Bering Sea, and excluded all Canadian fishing vessels from these waters. The controversy took an ugly turn, but in 1891 the United States and Great Britain had the good sense to resort to arbitration. The tribunal decided all points of law adversely to the United States, but implicitly admitted the wisdom of Blaine's efforts by drawing up regulations to save the seal.

Far more dangerous was a boundary dispute in South America. British Guiana and Venezuela had long quarreled over their boundary line, a disagreement that suddenly took on new importance with the discovery of gold in the hinterlands of both countries. Both Britain and Venezuela advanced ambitious claims, but Venezuela's was especially extravagant; Lord Salisbury, refusing to submit the question to arbitration be-

cause, not unreasonably, he feared arbiters would split the difference, sent troops to the disputed area. Secretary of State Olney promptly dispatched a note which gave a definition of the Monroe Doctrine that alarmed Latin America, insulted Canada, and challenged England:

Today the United States is practically sovereign on this continent, and its fiat is law upon the subjects to which it confines its interposition.... Distance and three thousand miles of intervening ocean make any permanent political union between a European and an American state unnatural and inexpedient.

Lord Salisbury allowed four months to go by before acknowledging this cheeky note—and rejecting it. On 17 December 1895 President Cleveland informed Congress of Salisbury's refusal, asked it to set up a commission to determine the proper boundary line, and added that any attempt by Britain to assert jurisdiction beyond that line should be resisted by every means in the nation's power. No facts of the controversy could justify these extreme claims and provocative language, but Olney and Cleveland had become disturbed by British encroachments in Latin America, including the seizure of Belize (British Honduras), and Congressmen had put Cleveland on the defensive by insisting that after having refused to take a strong line on Hawaii and Samoa he could not permit an Old World monarchy to discipline a New World republic.

Only the felt necessity for friendship with the United States induced the Salisbury government to let this challenge lie. The British navy's numerical strength over the American was at least five to one, but Britain, as Bayard wrote, 'has just now her hands very full in other quarters of the globe.' In early January 1896 came Jameson's raid in the Transvaal and Kaiser Wilhelm's congratulatory telegram to the Boer leader Kruger. The South African crisis reinforced Britain's determination to avoid war. After some secret diplomacy at London and Washington, Great Britain and Venezuela concluded a treaty submitting the boundary question to an arbitral tribunal, to be governed by the rule that 'adverse holding or prescription during a period of fifty years shall make a good title.' Thus Cleveland and Olney

Twisting the lion's tail. In this 1888 cartoon, which appeared in *Judge*, Cleveland, by his tariff policies, is depicted as a pawn of England, an allegation designed to appeal to both American nationalists and Irish-American Anglophobes. As the President kneels before John Bull, he is joined by Secretary of State Thomas Bayard, Speaker of the House John Carlisle, and Rep. Roger Q. Mills, sponsor of tariff reform legislation. Behind them George William Curtis, the patrician editor of *Harper's* magazine, surrenders American prosperity while 'Marse Henry' Watterson, editor of the Louisville *Courier-Journal*, strikes the colors. (*Library of Congress*)

secured their principle that the whole territory in dispute should be subject to arbitration, and Salisbury his, that the British title to *de facto* possessions should not be questioned. The tribunal, which included the Chief Justices of Great Britain and the United States, gave a unanimous decision in 1899, substantially along the line of the original British claim. So the Monroe Doctrine was vindicated, arbitration triumphed, and Anglo-American friendship was restored.

Manifest Destiny and Cuba Libre

In the eighteen-nineties, the spirit of 'manifest destiny,' long dormant, was once more abroad in the land. Captain A. T. Mahan, the naval philosopher of the new imperialism, demonstrated in his brilliant series on the history of sea power that not the meek, but those who possessed big navies, inherited the earth, and his teachings were heeded. The Reverend Josiah

Strong, author of the enormously popular tract, *Our Country*, asked rhetorically, 'Does it not look as if God were not only preparing in our Anglo-Saxon civilization the die with which to stamp the peoples of the earth, but as if he were massing behind that die the mighty power with which to press it?' The Washington *Post* stated on the eve of the Spanish War:

We are face to face with a strange destiny. The taste of Empire is in the mouth of the people even as the taste of blood in the jungle. It means an Imperial policy, the Republic, renascent, taking her place with the armed nations.

In 1880 the U.S. Navy ranked twelfth in the world; by 1900, with 17 battleships and 6 armored cruisers, it was third.

The Cuban revolution of 1895 brought this latent imperialism to a head. From the days of Jefferson, Cuba had been regarded as properly within the American sphere of influence, and the possibility of ultimate acquisition was never out of the minds of American statesmen. Yet curiously enough, when the opportunity came, during the Ten Years' War of 1868–78, the United States was coy. That Ten Years' War was characterized by all the disorder, cruelty, and affronts to American interests and honor that later marked the course of the revolution of 1895. However, in the first instance the murder of the crew of the *Virginius* in 1873 did not create a demand for war, while the explosion of the *Maine* in 1898 was followed by a wave of war hysteria.

How did it happen that the destiny which necessitated American control of the Caribbean in the eighteen-nineties was not manifest in the eighteen-sixties? Americans of the eighteen-nineties had come to share with the British, Germans, and French a willingness to take up 'the white man's burden.' Editors of journals like the New York *World* and *Journal* found that circulation responded to atrocity stories. For three years, from 1895 to 1898, mongering of sensations went on until the country was brought to the point where it demanded intervention on behalf of 'humanity.' The economic stake of the United States in Cuba had increased enormously during these thirty years. As the American minister to Spain said, 'The sugar industry of Cuba is as vital to our people as are the wheat and cotton of India and Egypt to Great Britain.' Even more important than the $50 million invested in Cuban sugar and mining was trade with Cuba, which by 1893 had passed the $100 million mark, and the business and shipping interests dependent upon that trade. Finally, the United States had developed world interests which made it seem necessary to control the entire Caribbean. American interests in the Pacific enhanced the importance of an isthmian canal and made the islands that guarded the route to the canal strategically important, especially to provide harbors and coaling stations for a big navy.

These concerns would lead the United States in 1898 to fight a war to liberate Cuba, but by then the Cubans had already struggled three years for their own liberation. The fundamental cause of the revolution which broke out in 1895 was Spanish oppression; the immediate cause was the prostration of the sugar and tobacco industries which resulted from tariffs, both American and Spanish. The price of sugar which had been 8 cents per pound in 1884 fell to 2 cents in 1895. The consequent misery furnished the impetus for revolution. From the beginning the United States was inextricably involved in the revolution. When, within a fortnight of the outbreak of war, a Spanish gunboat fired upon an American vessel, an outburst of jingoism revealed the temper of the country. 'It is time,' said Senator Cullom, 'that some one woke up and realized the necessity of annexing some property.' In the face of a mounting demand for intervention, President Cleveland remained imperturbable. When Congress, in April 1896, passed a concurrent resolution recognizing the belligerency of the Cubans, Cleveland ignored it, and in the summer of 1896 he confessed that 'there seemed to be an epidemic of insanity in the country just at this time.' Yet by the end of that year even Cleveland's patience had been strained well-nigh to the breaking point by Spain's refusal to conciliate the rebels.

McKinley had been elected on a platform calling for Cuban independence, but at first he, too, moved with circumspection. 'You may be sure,' he confided to Carl Schurz, 'that there will be no

The sinking of the *Maine*, Havana harbor, 15 February 1898. This chromolithograph portrays vividly the violent explosion that took 260 lives and made a national catchphrase of 'Remember the *Maine*!' The small portraits are of Admiral Montgomery Sicard, commander of the North Atlantic Squadron, and Captain Charles Sigsbee, who survived the blast. (*Chicago Historical Society*)

jingo nonsense under my administration.' In September 1897 McKinley tendered the good offices of the United States to restore peace to Cuba, but even though a more liberal government had come to power in Spain, the American overture was rejected. Nevertheless, the Spanish government did inaugurate some long overdue reforms. General Weyler, who had earned the unenviable title of 'Butcher Weyler,' was recalled; the policy of herding Cubans into concentration camps, where many died of disease and mistreatment, was disavowed; all political rights enjoyed by peninsular Spaniards were extended to the Cubans; and a program looking to eventual home rule was inaugurated.

Home rule no longer satisfied the Cubans, who were increasingly confident that the United States would intervene. They would accept nothing but independence, the one demand Madrid felt it could not grant. Reforms which might have headed off the revolution had they been offered in 1895 had come too late, and the war of extermination went on. Yet the sincere desire of the Spanish government for peace did much to moderate the attitude of the American government if not of the American people. In his annual message of December 1897 McKinley repudiated the idea of intervention and urged that Spain 'be given a reasonable chance to realize her expectations and to prove the asserted efficacy of the new order of things to which she stands irrevocably committed.' But neutrality was not to the interest of the Cuban junta, and on 9 February 1898 the *Journal* printed a private letter to Washington from the Spanish minister, Enrique de Lôme, which had been stolen from the Havana post office. 'McKinley's message,' wrote the tactless minister, 'once more shows what McKinley is, weak and a bidder for the admiration of the crowd, besides being a would-be-politician who tries to leave a door open behind himself while keeping on good terms with the jingoes of his party.'

At this juncture the nation was horrified by the news that in the night of 15 February 1898 the battleship *Maine* had blown up in Havana harbor with the loss of 260 lives. 'Public opinion,' Captain Sigsbee wired, 'should be suspended until further report,' but when a naval court of inquiry reported that the cause of the disaster was an external explosion by a submarine mine, 'Remember the *Maine*!' went from lip to lip. Without a dissenting vote Congress rushed through a bill appropriating $50 million for national defense. McKinley continued to exercise restraint, but war fever was mounting. Redfield Proctor, a fair-minded Vermonter who had opposed war, gave the Senate on 17 March a vivid description of the horrors of the concentration camps he had seen in Cuba. Still Spain procrastinated. On 25 March McKinley sent Madrid what turned out to be his ultimatum: immediate armistice, final revocation of the concentration policy, American mediation between Spain and Cuba, and, ambiguously, independence for Cuba. Spain's formal reply was unsatisfactory, but Madrid, anxious to avoid war, moved toward peace with unusual celerity. Orders were given revoking the concentration policy and a desperate effort was made to persuade the Pope to request a suspension of hostilities—a request to which Spain could agree without loss of face. But McKinley's reply was non-committal. On 9 April the Spanish government accepted every demand but Cuban independence, and Woodford, the American minister at Madrid, thought, perhaps too optimistically, even that might be worked out. Hostilities were suspended, and Woodford cabled that if nothing were done to humiliate Spain further the Cuban question could be settled in accordance with American wishes. Any President with a backbone would have seized this opportunity for an honorable solution.

But by now McKinley's course was set. He had lost faith in Spain's ability to resolve the conflict. Nor did he have the courage to withstand public sentiment. Although Mark Hanna, much of big business, and the Republican Old Guard wanted peace, Congress, the press, and much of the country were clamoring for war. Theodore Roosevelt wrote in a private letter, 'The blood of the murdered men of the *Maine* calls not for indemnity but for the full measure of atonement, which can only come by driving the Spaniard from the New World.' By going to war, McKinley would silence such critics within his own party, and deny the Democrats the opportunity to campaign for Free Silver and Free Cuba. On 11 April the President, making only casual reference to the fact that Madrid had capitulated on almost every point at issue, sent Congress a message which could have only one consequence: war.

Exit Spain

Lightheartedly the United States entered upon a war that brought quick returns in glory, but new and heavy responsibilities that were to grow all through the next century. Although imperialistic in result, the war was not so in motive, as far as the vast majority were concerned. To the Joint Resolution of 20 April 1898, authorizing the use of armed forces to liberate Cuba, was added the self-denying Teller Amendment, declaring that 'The United States hereby dis-claims any disposition or intention to exercise sovereignty, jurisdiction or control over the said Island, except for the pacification thereof, and asserts its determination, when that is accomplished, to leave the government and control of the Island to its people.'

With what generous ardor the young men rushed to the colors to free Cuba, while the bands

Off to war. In Washington, D.C., the 1st Regiment D.C. volunteers depart for Camp Alger, May 1898. (*Library of Congress*)

crashed out the chords of Sousa's 'Stars and Stripes Forever!' And what a comfortable feeling of unity the country obtained at last, when William J. Bryan got himself commissioned Colonel and donned a uniform alongside the irrepressible T. R.; when Joe Wheeler, the gallant cavalry leader of the Confederacy, became a high commander of the United States Army in Cuba! To most Americans, the war arrayed hip-hip-hurrah democracy against all that was tyrannical,

treacherous, and fetid in the Old World. And what heroes the war correspondents created—Lieutenant Rowan who delivered the 'message to Garcia,' Commodore Dewey ('You may fire when ready, Gridley'), Captain Philip of the *Texas* ('Don't cheer, boys, the poor fellows are dying'), and Teddy Roosevelt with his horseless Rough Riders!

Prince Bismarck is said to have observed, just before his death, that there was a special prov-

Frederic Remington, 'Captain Grimes's Battery Going Up El Poso Hill,' 1898. 'It was a fine sight to see the great horses straining under the lash as they whirled the guns up the hill,' wrote Teddy Roosevelt of this episode in the battle for San Juan Hill. But hardly had the Americans opened fire, he went on, when 'there was a peculiar whistling singing sound in the air, and immediately afterward the noise of something exploding over our heads.' Shrapnel from Spanish batteries wounded several of his regiment, grazed Teddy's wrist, and routed Remington, the noted Western illustrator who had been sketching Grimes's horses. Remington reported: 'It was thoroughly evident that the Spaniards had the range of everything in the country. Some gallant soldiers and some as daring correspondents as it is my pleasure to know did their legs proud there. The tall form of Major John Jacob Astor moved in my front in jack-rabbit bounds. Prussian, English, and Japanese correspondents, artists, all the news, and much high-class art and literature, were flushed, and went straddling up the hill.' (*New-York Historical Society*)

idence for drunkards, fools, and the United States of America. While Spain had almost 200,000 troops in Cuba before the war, the American regular army included less than 28,000 officers and men, scattered in small detachments from the Yukon to Key West. The American Commissary Department was disorganized, and soldiers complained that they were fed on 'embalmed beef.' Volunteers neglected even such principles of camp sanitation as were laid down in Deuteronomy, and for every one of the 286 men killed or mortally wounded in battle, 14 died of disease. Yet the little

U.S. expeditionary force was allowed to land on the beach at Daiquiri without opposition (20–25 June), and the Captain-General of Cuba, with six weeks' warning was able to concentrate only 1700 on the battlefields of Las Guasimas, El Caney, and San Juan, against 15,000 Americans.

It was the navy, however, that clinched the conquest of Cuba. On 19 May the Spanish admiral, Cervera, with four armored cruisers and three destroyers, slipped into the narrow land-locked harbor of Santiago Bay and was promptly bottled up by the American navy under Admiral Sampson and Commodore Schley. With the army closing in on Santiago, Cervera had no alternatives but surrender or escape. On 3 July the Spanish battlefleet sailed forth from Santiago Bay to death and destruction:

> Haste to do now what must be done anon
> Or some mad hope of selling triumph dear
> Drove the ships forth: soon was *Teresa* gone
> *Furór, Plutón, Vizcaya, Oquendo,* and *Colón.* [1]

Not since 1863 had there been such a Fourth of July as that Monday in 1898 when the news came through. Santiago surrendered on the 16th and except for a military promenade in Puerto Rico, which Mr. Dooley described as 'Gin'ral Miles' Gran' Picnic and Moonlight Excursion,' the war was over. Ten weeks' fighting and the United States had wrested an empire from Spain.

The most important event of the war had occurred not in the Caribbean but in the Far East. As soon as war was declared, Commodore Dewey, commander of the Asiatic Squadron, set out under full steam for the Philippines, and on the night of 30 April he entered Manila Bay, where a Spanish fleet was anchored. Gridley fired when ready; they all fired; and the Spanish fleet was utterly destroyed. But not until 13 August—one day after the signing of the peace protocol—did an American expeditionary force, with the support of Aguinaldo's Filipino army, take the city of Manila.

The collapse of her military and naval power forced Spain to sue for peace. McKinley dictated

terms on 30 July—immediate evacuation and relinquishment of Cuba, cession of Puerto Rico and an island in the Ladrones (Guam, as it turned out), and American occupation of Manila pending final disposition of the Philippine Islands. Spain signed a preliminary peace to that effect on 12 August, sadly protesting, 'This demand strips us of the very last memory of a glorious past and expels us . . . from the Western Hemisphere, which became peopled and civilized through the proud deeds of our ancestors.' John Hay wrote his friend Theodore Roosevelt in a very different vein: 'It has been a splendid little war; begun with the highest motives, carried on with magnificent intelligence and spirit, favored by that fortune which loves the brave.'

The Fruits of Victory

In the formal peace negotiations which began at Paris on 1 October 1898, only the question of the disposition of the Philippines offered serious difficulties. If they had been contented under Spanish rule, there would have been no question of annexing them. However, an insurrection had just been partially suppressed when the Spanish War broke out, and Dewey had encouraged Emilio Aguinaldo, leader of the *insurrectos*, to return from exile after the battle of Manila Bay. Upon the fall of Manila the Filipino leader had organized the 'Visayan Republic' and made a bid for foreign recognition. The obvious thing to do was to turn the Philippines over to the Filipinos, as Cuba to the Cubans. But Dewey cabled that the 'republic' was only a faction, unable to keep order within its nominal sphere. Still, Aguinaldo represented government in the islands, and if the United States expected to retain the Philippines, it would first have to conquer them.

McKinley was in a quandary. In his message of December 1897 he had laid down with respect to Cuba the rule that 'forcible annexation . . . can not be thought of. That, by our code of morality, would be criminal aggression.' Did the same rule hold good for the Philippines? Already navalists were emphasizing the military importance of the islands and suggesting the danger should Germany or Japan annex them. Senator Beveridge

---

1. 'Spain in America' in *Poems* by George Santayana, Scribners, p. 118.

An expansive Uncle Sam. In this cartoon, which appeared in *Puck* in 1900, the anti-imperialist Carl Schurz offers anti-expansion elixir, as Joseph Pulitzer of the New York *World* and the reform Democrat Oswald Ottendorfer, proprietor of the German-language newspaper, the *New-Yorker Staats-Zeitung*, back him up, but Uncle Sam, having become accustomed to his portly shape, will have none of it. (*Library of Congress*)

was speaking hopefully of 'China's illimitable markets' and Whitelaw Reid wrote that the Philippines would 'convert the Pacific ocean into an American lake.'

Yet there were still several choices. The United States might simply guarantee the independence of the Philippines as it was to do in Cuba. It might take only the island of Luzon, leaving the rest of the archipelago to the Filipinos. It might take the Philippines in trust, as it were, with a promise of independence—the principle of the Bacon bill that was defeated only by the casting vote of the Vice-President in the Senate. Or it might annex all the Philippines.

McKinley hesitated long and prayerfully, but finally concluded to fulfill manifest destiny by taking them all. 'One night late it came to me this way,' he told his Methodist brethren, '(1) That we could not give them back to Spain—that would be cowardly and dishonorable; (2) that we could not turn them over to France or Germany, our commercial rivals in the Orient—that would be bad business and discreditable; (3) that we could not leave them to themselves—they were unfit for self-government—and they would soon have anarchy and misrule over there worse than Spain's was; and (4) that there was nothing left for us to do but take them all, and to educate the

489

Filipinos, and uplift and Christianize them.' So Spain was required to part with the islands for $20 million, and on 10 December 1898 the Treaty of Paris was signed and the United States became, officially, a world power.

However, the prospect of the annexation of an alien people without their consent aroused the fierce indignation of many Americans who thought it a monstrous perversion of the ideals which had inspired the crusade for Cuba. Old-fashioned Senators like Hoar of Massachusetts girded on their armor to fight for the principles of the Declaration of Independence, while others pointed out that the conquest, defense, and administration of the Philippines would cost far more than the islands would ever bring in return. Opponents warned that flouting the principles of democracy in the Philippines would impair the vitality of democracy at home. Some, though, who opposed the creation of an American empire did so out of dislike of incorporating other races and cultures in white American society. Tillman cried: 'Coming . . . as a Senator from . . . South Carolina, with 750,000 colored population and only 500,000 whites, I realize what you are doing, while you don't; and I would save this country from the injection in it of another race question.' Finally they argued that the Constitution did not permit the acquisition of extraterritorial possessions and the government of alien peoples without their consent. For two months the fate of the treaty hung in suspense. But on 6 February 1899 the necessary two-thirds majority for ratification was obtained, after what Lodge called 'the hardest fight I have ever known.'

McKinley, in 1897, had rejected a proposal to buy Cuba because he did not care to buy an insurrection; the United States now found that it had purchased, for $20 million, a first-class Filipino insurrection. The Filipinos, who had been good Catholics for over three centuries, did not wish to be 'uplifted and Christianized' by the Americans; but when, on 4 February 1899, Aguinaldo's troops disregarded the command of an American sentry to halt, the United States Army undertook to 'civilize them with a Krag.' Before the Philippine insurrection was stamped out it had cost the United States almost as many lives as the Spanish War, in hellish fighting between white soldiers and men of color. Colonel Frederick Funston boasted he would 'rawhide these bullet-headed Asians until they yell for mercy' so they would not 'get in the way of the bandwagon of Anglo-Saxon progress and decency.' The United States did in the Philippines precisely what it had condemned Spain for doing in Cuba. Soon stories of concentration camps and 'water-cures' began to trickle back to the United States, and public opinion became inflamed.

To the banner of anti-imperialism rallied people of the most diverse views. Republicans like Speaker Reed joined hands with Democrats such as Cleveland and Bryan; Samuel Gompers spoke for labor, and Andrew Carnegie paid the bills. Editors like E. L. Godkin of *The Nation*, college presidents like David Starr Jordan of Leland Stanford, philosophers like William James, clergymen like Henry Van Dyke, social workers like Jane Addams, all worked together for a common cause. Mark Twain, deeply embittered by the conquest of the Philippines, suggested that Old Glory should now have 'the white stripes painted black and the stars replaced by the skull and cross bones.' The most powerful indictment came from the young poet William Vaughn Moody in 'An Ode in Time of Hesitation':

Tempt not our weakness, our cupidity!
For save we let the island men go free,
Those baffled and dislaureled ghosts
Will curse us from the lamentable coasts
Where walk the frustrate dead . . .
O ye who lead,
Take heed!
Blindness we may forgive, but baseness we will smite.[2]

In 1900 the Democrats, determined to make imperialism the 'paramount' issue, once again named Bryan, who also got the nominations of the Silver Republicans and one wing of the Populists. Their platform warned: 'The Filipinos cannot . . . be citizens without endangering our civilization; they cannot be subjects without imperiling our form of government.' But Bryan had played such

2. William Vaughn Moody, *Selected Poems*, Houghton Mifflin, 1931.

Bryan campaign poster, 1900. This elaborate chromolithograph, by its reference to 'No Crown of Thorns' and 'No Cross of Gold,' joins the anti-trust and free silver emphases of the Commoner's 1896 campaign with the newer issue of 'No Imperialism.' (*Library of Congress*)

491

an ambiguous role in the treaty debate that he obscured the imperialism issue. Moreover, during the campaign he insisted that silver was still the nation's chief concern; as Tom Reed remarked, 'Bryan would rather be wrong than President.' The Republicans held all the trump cards and played them well. The end of the economic crisis that had begun in 1893 appeared to justify the claim that McKinley was the 'advance agent of prosperity.' McKinley's running mate, Colonel Theodore Roosevelt, stormed through the West crying, 'Don't lower the flag,' and even referred to Bryan as 'my opponent.' By sweeping all of the agricultural West, including the Middle Border, McKinley improved on his performance in 1896; Bryan won only the South and four silver states. Henceforth, for good or evil, America was a world power with an overseas empire.

The Open Door

Many Americans feared that the annexations of the year 1898 were only a beginning; that the United States was destined to become a great colonial power. Imperialism in the Roman sense did not, however, appeal to the American people. But if the United States had no more than a passing desire to acquire an overseas empire, the country had an avid interest in developing foreign markets not only in Latin America but in Asia, where the partition of China jeopardized American prospects. The Japanese victory in the War of 1894–95 had revealed to the world the weakness of China: to forestall the Japanese, the European powers hurried to obtain spheres of influence in China. 'The various powers,' said the Dowager Empress of China, 'cast upon us looks of tiger-like voracity, hustling each other in their endeavors to be the first to seize upon our inner-most territories.' Japan had already acquired Formosa (Taiwan) and established ascendancy in the 'Hermit Kingdom' of Korea; in 1897 and 1898 Russia took Port Arthur and the Liaotung Peninsula, which gave access to the interior of Manchuria; Germany seized Kiaochow in Shantung, France consoled herself with a lease to Kwangchow bay, adjoining Indo-China; Italy got Sanmun bay, south of the Yangtze; and England added to her holdings the port of Wei-hai-wei. Along with these leases went valuable railway concessions, which promised to give European powers all but complete control over China's internal trade.

The carving up of China appeared to threaten American trade and to nullify part of the value of the Philippines. Interested parties drafted a proposal urging all the major powers to accept the principle of trade equality in China, and to refrain from violations of Chinese territorial integrity. Hay accepted these proposals and incorporated some of them into his own 'open door' policy for China. In a circular note of 6 September 1899, Hay, while recognizing the existence of 'spheres of influence,' requested from each major European power a declaration that, in its respective sphere, it would maintain the Chinese customs tariff, and levy equal harbor dues and railway rates on the ships and merchandise of all nations. The powers made ambiguous replies, with Britain most favorable, Russia least, but Hay promptly announced the agreement of all the powers as 'final and definitive.'

The 'open door' policy originally aimed solely at safeguarding American commercial interests in China, but within less than a year it was given a new and far-reaching interpretation. The brazen exploitation of China by the great powers had created deep antipathy to foreigners, and in June 1900 a secret organization called the Boxers tried to expel the 'foreign devils.' Within a short time the Boxers had massacred some 300 foreigners, mostly missionaries and their families; others were driven into Peking, where they took refuge in the British legation. An expeditionary force to rescue the beleaguered Europeans was hurriedly organized; the United States contributed some 5000 soldiers. Concerned that the situation might deteriorate into general war, Hay bent his energies to localizing the conflict. On 3 July, in a circular note to all the powers, he tried to limit the objectives of the joint intervention:

The policy of the government of the United States is to seek a solution which may bring about permanent safety and peace to China, preserve Chinese territorial and administrative entity, protect all rights guaranteed to friendly powers by treaty and international law, and safeguard for the world the principle of equal and impartial trade with all parts of the Chinese Empire.

These were not the objectives entertained in the chancelleries of Berlin, St. Petersburg, and Tokyo, but these powers, fearful of each other and of war, concurred. The danger of war subsided, and the Chinese government permitted the joint expedition to save the legations. Punishment, however, was visited upon the guilty Boxers, and China was saddled with an outrageous indemnity of $333 million. Of this some $24 million went to the United States; half of it was eventually returned to the Chinese government which established therewith a fund for sending Chinese students to American colleges.

Now the United States was committed to maintain not only an 'open door' to China but the political integrity of that decrepit empire. Yet what did the commitment mean? Only by alliance with some European power like England could the United States have enforced this policy, and at no time did the exigencies of American politics permit an open alliance. Americans rejoiced in the spectacle of the United States teaching a moral lesson to the wicked imperialists of the Old World, but as Secretary Hay said, 'the talk of the papers about our pre-eminent moral position giving us the authority to dictate to the world, is mere flap-doodle.' And when, in 1901, Japan made cautious inquiries about the American reaction to Russian encroachments in Manchuria, Hay assured them that the United States was not prepared 'to attempt singly, or in concert with other Powers, to enforce these views in the east by any demonstration which could present a character of hostility to any other Power.' In short the United States wanted an 'open door' but would not fight for it.

Yet we cannot dismiss the 'open door' policy quite this easily. It faithfully expressed America's sentimental interest in China; delayed for a time the attack on China from Japan; and probably enhanced American prestige in China and other parts of the globe. And, like the Monroe Doctrine, it came in time to be a hallowed principle: that America would have no part in imperialistic designs on China and would discourage such designs in others. It helped build up popular support for resistance against Japan's aggression in China, and this in turn exacerbated Japanese resentment toward the United States.

The American Colonial System

The annexation of extra-continental territory, already thickly populated by alien peoples, created new problems in government. The petty islands and guano rocks that had already been annexed had never raised, as Puerto Rico and the Philippines did, the embarrassing question of whether the Constitution followed the flag. Opinions of the Supreme Court in 1901 in the 'Insular Cases,' a muddle of split decisions, left the status of the new possessions very unclear, but eventually, as in the British Empire, a theory was evolved from practice. Insular possessions are of two categories: incorporated and unincorporated; and the question of what constitutes incorporation is revealed in congressional legislation. Alaska was held to be incorporated, but Puerto Rico was unincorporated, despite the fact that after 1917 the inhabitants of the island became citizens of the United States. Unincorporated territories are not foreign, however, and their exports are not controlled by American customs duties unless by special act of Congress. But Congress may, nevertheless, impose such duties as it sees fit. This meant, according to a dissenting opinion by Chief Justice Fuller, that

if an organized and settled province of another sovereignty is acquired by the United States, Congress has the power to keep it like a disembodied shade, in an intermediate state of ambiguous existence for an indefinite period: and more than that, after it has been called from that limbo, commerce with it is absolutely subject to the will of Congress, irrespective of constitutional provisions.

Thus the country was able to eat its cake and have it; to indulge in territorial expansion and yet maintain a tariff wall against such insular commodities as sugar and tobacco which might compete with home-grown products.

The question of the civil and political rights of the inhabitants of these new possessions proved even more perplexing. Organic acts of Congress became the constitutions of the Philippines, Hawaii, and Puerto Rico, but to what extent was Congress bound, in enacting these laws, and the courts, in interpreting them, by the provisions of the United States Constitution? How far, in short, did the Constitution follow the flag? To this question the Court returned an ingenious answer. It distinguished between 'fundamental' rights and 'formal' or 'procedural' rights. Fundamental rights are extended to all who come under the sovereignty of the United States, but mere procedural rights, such as trial by jury, extend to the inhabitants of unincorporated territories only if Congress so chooses. Like eighteenth-century London, the government at Washington was reluctant to admit the existence of an empire. Despite the legitimization of this vast accretion, no colonial office was established or colonial secretary appointed, and the imperial administration was characterized by diversity and opportunism.

Cuba was not a colony, but until 1902 the island was ruled by the United States Army, with General Leonard Wood as military governor. This regime conducted a remarkable clean-up of Havana under the direction of Major William C. Gorgas which halved the average annual death rate. In 1900 came one of the worst yellow-fever epidemics in years. A commission of four army surgeons under Dr. Walter Reed investigated the cause. Working on the theory advanced by a Cuban physician, Dr. Carlos Finlay, they proved that the pest was transmitted by the stegomyia mosquito; and two of them, Dr. James Caroll and Dr. Jesse W. Lazear, proved it with their lives. Major Gorgas then declared war on the mosquito; and in 1901 there was not a single case of yellow fever in Havana. One of the greatest scourges of the tropics was at last under control.

By the Teller Amendment the United States had disclaimed any intention of exercising sovereignty over Cuba. On the conclusion of the war General Wood provided for the calling of a constitutional convention, which drafted a constitution modeled upon that of the United States. But the American government applied discreet pressure to induce the Cubans to add a series of provisions known collectively as the Platt Amendment. The Amendment gave the United States an ultimate veto over Cuba's diplomatic and fiscal relations with foreign powers, recognized the right of the United States to intervene to preserve Cuban independence and to protect life and property, and committed Cuba to sell or lease a naval base.

Under terms of the Platt Amendment the United States leased and built a naval base at Guantánamo, which was retained even after the Amendment itself was abrogated. The right of intervention was first exercised in 1906, at the request of Cuba. President Theodore Roosevelt[3] sent his Secretary of War, William Howard Taft, to take charge of the island. When peace and stability were restored, the United States withdrew, leaving the affairs of Cuba in sound condition. At the same time Roosevelt warned the islanders that 'if elections become a farce and if the insurrectionary habit becomes confirmed . . . it is absolutely out of the question that the Island remain independent; and the United States, which has assumed the sponsorship before the civilized world for Cuba's career as a nation, would again have to intervene.'

The Philippine Islands presented peculiar difficulties, especially since from the beginning it was supposed that American tenure was temporary. The Filipino Insurrection dragged on until 1902, but as early as 1900 military government gave way to a civil Philippine Commission under William Howard Taft, first Governor-General of the islands. The Commission, entrusted with executive, legislative, and judicial powers, was authorized to reconstruct the government of the islands from the bottom up. Enlarged by the addition of three Filipinos, the Commission was instructed to 'bear in mind that the government which they are establishing is designed . . . for the happiness, peace and prosperity of the people of the Philippine Islands, and the measures adopted should be made to conform to their customs, their habits, and even their prejudices' so far as was consistent with the principles of good government. The Organic Act of 1902 recognized the islands as unincorporated territory of the United States and the inhabitants as 'citizens of the Philippine Islands' entitled to the protection of the United States, and provided for the ultimate creation of a legislature.

The United States gave the Philippines as enlightened an administration as is possible in an imperial system which, no matter how well

---

3. Theodore Roosevelt's accession to the presidency in 1901 is discussed in the next chapter.

intentioned, is inevitably paternalistic and self-interested. Under American rule the Filipinos made remarkable advances in education, well-being, and self-government. Through Taft's diplomacy at Rome, the United States acquired title to vast areas of agricultural land from the religious orders, and sold them on easy terms in small holdings to the peasants. 'Uncle Sam' provided the islands with honest, intelligent, and sympathetic administrators such as Taft and W. Cameron Forbes; with schools, sanitation, good roads, a well-trained native constabulary, a representative assembly, and baseball. The number of pupils attending school rose from 5000 in 1898 to over a million in 1920. The infant death rate in Manila declined from 80 to 20 per thousand between 1904 and 1920; and smallpox and cholera were practically stamped out. Although the islanders defrayed the entire cost of civil administration, their per capita taxation in 1920 was only $2.50, and their per capita debt, $1.81. But American economic policy left the islands at the mercy of the U.S. market, and as late as 1946 Congress required the Filipinos to grant special privileges to American businessmen. From the outset the islands were an American hostage to Japan, and the Filipinos sensed that some day their country might have the unhappy fate of serving as a battleground for imperial powers.

The Big Stick

'There is an old adage that says, "speak softly and carry a big stick."' This familiar quotation, from one of Theodore Roosevelt's earlier speeches, provided cartoonists with a vivid image to depict the President's aggressive foreign policy. Yet, paradoxically, it was Roosevelt who gave the Hague Tribunal its first case (a dispute with Mexico), who instructed his delegation at the second Hague Conference to work for the restriction of naval armaments, who was responsible for the return of the Boxer indemnity, who smoothed over a dangerous controversy with Japan, participated in the Algeciras Conference, and won the Nobel peace prize for successful mediation between Russia and Japan.

Roosevelt inherited from McKinley a Secretary of State, John Hay, whose experience as ambas-sador in London made him eager to meet halfway the new British policy of friendship. There was, in fact, an Anglo-American understanding during the entire progressive era. Downing Street readily conceded to Washington a free hand in the New World; and in return the State Department refrained from any act or expression that would unfavorably affect British interests, and supported British diplomacy in the Far East. The entente, if we may so call it, was consummated by the appointment of the author of *The American Commonwealth*, James Bryce, to the Washington embassy in 1907.

A first fruit of this understanding was the Panama Canal. The 1898 voyage of the U.S.S. *Oregon*, steaming at full speed round the Horn to be in time for the big fight, touched the popular imagination; and new island possessions in the Caribbean and the Pacific made an interoceanic canal appear vital. The Clayton-Bulwer Treaty of 1850 stood in the way of its realization, but not the government of Lord Salisbury. The Hay-Pauncefote Treaty of 1901 abrogated the earlier agreement, permitted the United States to construct a canal and control it, and provided that the canal would be open to all nations on equal terms.

The project for an isthmian canal had captivated the United States since Polk's administration. In 1876 French interests purchased from Colombia the right to build a canal across Panama, but De Lesseps, engineer of the Suez canal, failed to cut a canal through the mountains and jungles of Panama. When his company was forced into bankruptcy, a new organization was set up for the sole purpose of selling the dubious assets of the old to the United States.

With the quickening of interest in the canal project Congress became a battleground of rival groups: the Panama Canal Company, which wished to sell its concession on the Isthmus, and an American syndicate which had purchased a concession from the Republic of Nicaragua. McKinley appointed a commission to investigate the merits of the rival routes and the commission, finding that the Panama Company wanted $109 million for its concession, reported in favor of the Nicaraguan route, which had the added advantage of sea-level rather than lock construction. The

Panama Company countered by reducing its price to a mere $40 million and by engaging the services of a prominent New York lobbyist, William Nelson Cromwell, who tactfully contributed $60,000 to the Republican campaign fund and enlisted the powerful support of Senator Hanna. Heaven itself came to the aid of the Panama Company; in May 1902, while Congress was considering the rival routes, Mont Pelée in Martinique erupted with a loss of 30,000 lives. Mount Monotombo in Nicaragua followed suit, and when the Nicaraguan government denied that an active volcano existed in that republic, the Panama lobbyists triumphantly presented each Senator with a Nicaraguan postage stamp featuring a volcano in full action. Under these genial auspices Congress on 28 June 1902 passed the Spooner Act authorizing the President to acquire the French concession for $40 million if Colombia would cede a strip of land across the Isthmus of Panama 'within a reasonable time' and upon reasonable terms; if not, the President was to open negotiations with Nicaragua. On 22 January 1903 Secretary Hay induced the Colombian chargé at Washington to sign a treaty granting the United States a hundred-year lease of a ten-mile wide canal zone, for the lump sum of $10 million and an annual rental of $250,000.

The Colombian government procrastinated about ratifying the treaty in spite of a truculent warning from Hay that something dreadful would happen in case of amendment or rejection. Roosevelt was outraged. 'I do not think the Bogotá lot of obstructionists should be allowed permanently to bar one of the future highways of civilization,' he exclaimed to Hay. Neither did Cromwell nor a revolutionary Panama junta, dominated by Philippe Bunau-Varilla, a former agent for the French canal company. In July 1903 at New York an informal meeting of Panama businessmen, agents of the Panama Company, and United States army officers agreed on a way out: the secession of Panama from the Republic of Colombia. Without making any promise or receiving any of the plotters, Roosevelt and Hay let their intentions become so notorious that Bunau-Varilla advised the junta to proceed in perfect assurance of American assistance.

The revolution came off according to schedule. The Governor of Panama consented to being arrested, the Colombian admiral on station was bribed to steam away, and United States warships prevented troops from being landed by the Colombian government to restore authority. Three hundred section hands from the Panama Railroad and the fire brigade of the city of Panama formed the nucleus of a revolutionary army commanded by General Huertas, former commander in chief of Colombian troops. On 4 November a Declaration of Independence was read in the Plaza, and General Huertas addressed his soldiers. 'The world,' he said, 'is astounded at our heroism. President Roosevelt has made good.' Two days later Secretary Hay recognized the Republic of Panama, which by cable appointed Bunau-Varilla its plenipotentiary at Washington. With him, twelve days later, Hay concluded a treaty by which the Canal Zone was leased in perpetuity to the United States. As Roosevelt afterwards declared, 'I took Panama.' Colombia was hit by the big stick, but all Latin America trembled. Subsequently, in 1921, the United States paid $25 million to hush Colombia; it would have been better to have paid the sum eighteen years earlier.

Open to commercial traffic in August 1914, and formally completed six years later, the Panama Canal was a triumph of American engineering. No less remarkable was the sanitary work of Colonel Gorgas, which gave one of the world's worst pestholes a lower death rate than any American city, while Colonel George Goethals converted the spot described by Froude as 'a hideous dung-heap of moral and physical abomination' into a community of healthy workers.

Roosevelt's intervention in Santo Domingo produced the 'Roosevelt corollary' to the Monroe Doctrine. The financial affairs of that republic were in a desperate state, and in 1904 the government appealed to Roosevelt 'to establish some kind of protectorate' over the island and save it from its European creditors. Roosevelt had no desire to get involved in the affairs of the Republic—'about the same desire,' he said, 'as a gorged boa constrictor might have to swallow a porcupine wrong-end-to'—but he agreed that something had to be done to avoid anarchy and

'The Conquerors: Culebra Cut, Panama Canal.' To link the two oceans, American engineers had to create artificial lakes by damming two rivers and then connect them by wedging out an eight-mile gorge (Culebra Cut) through the Continental Divide. Despite the frustration of slides into the Cut, the Panama Canal was nearly finished when Jonas Lie (1880–1940) painted this picture in 1913. A series of paintings of the Canal by the Norwegian-born artist was presented to the U.S. Military Academy at West Point as a memorial to General Goethals. (*Metropolitan Museum of Art, George A. Hearn Fund, 1914*)

European intervention. He set forth his views in an open letter to Elihu Root: 'If a nation shows that it knows how to act with decency in industrial and political matters, if it keeps order and pays its obligations, then it need fear no interference from the United States. Brutal wrongdoing, or an impotence which results in a general loosening of the ties of civilizing society may finally require intervention by some civilized nation; and in the Western Hemisphere the United States cannot ignore this duty.' In February 1905 he signed a protocol with the Dominican Republic placing an American receiver in charge of its customs, and arranging that 55 per cent of customs receipts should be applied to the discharge of debts and 45 per cent to current expenses. The Senate refused to ratify the protocol, but Roosevelt went ahead anyway, and in 1907 the Senate came around. In little more than two years Santo Domingo was transformed from a bankrupt island to a prosperous and peaceful country, with revenues more than sufficient to discharge its debts and pay its expenses. But a dangerous precedent had been established, and within a decade the United States was deeply involved in the affairs of other Latin American nations. So burdensome did this responsibility become that a quarter-century later the Department of State officially repudiated the 'Roosevelt corollary.' But in the 1960's the United States was still meddling in Dominican affairs.

Elsewhere in the Caribbean Roosevelt moved with more restraint. In 1902 a crisis arose over the question of international intervention to collect Venezuelan debts. Great Britain, Germany, and Italy established a blockade to force the dictator, General Castro, to come to terms. Castro appealed to Roosevelt to arbitrate the claims, but inasmuch as no American rights were involved, Roosevelt properly refused. Yet he deprecated the use of force to collect debts, and looked askance at the potential threat to the Monroe Doctrine. A crisis was avoided when Germany, breaking away from the lead of Great Britain, agreed to submit her claims to arbitration. The Hague Tribunal settled the dispute satisfactorily, scaling down the demands and accepting the doctrine of the Argentinian jurist Luis Drago which denied the propriety of coercion for the collection of claims.

For the first time the United States had a President the rulers of Europe looked upon as one of themselves. In the Russo-Japanese War, the President, at the suggestion of the Japanese and the German Emperors, negotiated directly with premiers and crowned heads. He brought the two belligerents together and broke the deadlock, from which the Treaty of Portsmouth emerged. Roosevelt preserved for the time being the integrity of China, but the Treaty of Portsmouth merely substituted Japan for Russia in Manchuria and embittered the Japanese, although Roosevelt's action had been dictated by friendship for Japan.

By the conclusion of the Treaty of Portsmouth, Roosevelt established for his country a right that she did not at that time want—to be consulted in world politics. Again, in the Moroccan crisis of 1905–6, he quietly intervened to preserve peace with justice. French policy of hegemony in Morocco threatened a war with Germany that might easily have become a world conflagration. At the suggestion of the German Emperor, Roosevelt urged France to consent to a conference on the North African question, and the American representative, Henry White, was in large part responsible for the Algeciras Convention which, whatever its inadequacies, did keep peace for several years. The Senate ratified the Convention, but with the qualifying amendment that ratification did not involve any departure 'from the traditional American foreign policy which forbids participation by the United States in the settlement of political questions which are entirely European in their scope.'

27

The Progressive Era

1890–1916

The Promise of American Life

At the turn of the century, Americans could look back over three generations of unparalleled progress. The nation had advanced, in Jefferson's prophetic words, to 'destinies beyond the reach of mortal eye.' The continent was subdued, the frontier gone, and already Americans were reaching out for new worlds to conquer. The institution of slavery, which had threatened to destroy not only the Union but democracy, had been itself destroyed. The ideal of free public education had been substantially realized; the ideal of a free press maintained; the ideal of religious freedom cherished. Population had increased from 5 to 76 million, and in the half-century from 1850 to 1900 national wealth had grown from $7 to $88 billion. When, in 1888, James Bryce finished his survey of *The American Commonwealth,* he concluded that life was better for the common man in America than elsewhere on the globe.

Yet thoughtful Americans did not look with complacency upon their institutions. The continent had been conquered, but the conquest had been attended by reckless abuse of soil, forest, and water. The greatest of manufacturing nations, the

United States permitted the exploitation of women and children and neglected the aged, the incompetent, and the infirm; cyclical depressions plunged millions into want. Wealth was gravitating rapidly into the hands of a few, and the power of wealth threatened the integrity of the Republic. In the great cities the slums grew apace. The Civil War had ended slavery but the degradation of the Negro was a blot on American civilization. Corruption poisoned the body politic. Against these crowding evils there arose a full-throated protest which demanded extension of the power of government over industry, finance, transportation, agriculture, labor, and even morals, a protest which gave to these times the name, 'the progressive era.'

The first of the many problems reformers faced on the threshold of the new century was the ethical confusion which resulted from attempting to apply the moral code of an individualistic, agrarian society to a highly industrialized and integrated social order. In a simple village society, personal and social morals were much the same, and the harm that a bad man could do was pretty well limited to crimes directly inflicted on other individuals. But in a complex industrial society personal crimes and social sins were very different. Society could be hurt in a thousand new ways, many of them not recognized by the Ten Commandments or the law codes. Those guilty of the new sins against society were often upright and well-intentioned gentlemen. The impersonality of 'social sin,' the diffusion of responsibility through the use of the corporate device, required reformers to formulate a new social ethics and to educate the people to that new code, and much of the work of the 'muckrakers' was directed toward this end. They also had to devise new administrative machinery for discovering the consequences of industrial malpractices and new legal machinery for fixing responsibility, and the effort to do this can be read in the struggle over trust, factory, pure food, and similar legislation.

A second problem—the rise of big business, the growth of trusts and monopolies—greatly concerned reformers because so many difficulties flowed from the new industrial order—unemployment, exploitation of workers, the use of natural resources for corporate aggrandizement. Political reformers learned that to cleanse politics it was necessary to regulate the business interests that controlled politics; social reformers found that to eliminate child labor or the sweatshop or the slums it was essential to curb the industrial interests that profited from these evils. Henry Demarest Lloyd concluded his analysis of *Wealth Against Commonwealth* with the observation: 'The word of the day is that we are about to civilize industry.'

No less serious was the problem of the maldistribution of wealth. Benjamin Franklin had found 'a general happy mediocrity.'

There are few great proprietors of the soil [he wrote] and few tenants; most people cultivate their own lands, or follow some handicraft or merchandise; very few are rich enough to live idly upon their rents or incomes or to pay the high prices given in Europe for Paintings, Statues, Architecture, and other works of Art, that are more curious than useful.

The first half of the nineteenth century saw the rise of a few large fortunes, most of them either in land or in shipping, but when Moses Yale Beach of the New York *Sun* published in the 1850's a pamphlet on 'Wealthy Men of New York,' he discovered only nineteen who could be called millionaires, and the richest, John Jacob Astor, boasted a fortune of only $6 million. The industrial revolution changed all this. Men discovered a hundred new ways of making money, and many of the new fortunes carried with them no sense of responsibility. In 1896 Charles B. Spahr concluded that 1 per cent of the population owned over half the total national wealth, and that 12 per cent owned almost nine-tenths. When in 1892 the New York *Tribune* compiled figures on the millionaires, it discovered that almost 1000 had earned their fortunes in 'merchandising and investment,' over 600 in manufactures, over 300 in banking and brokerage, over 200 in transportation. The *Tribune* counted 178 millionaires in the lumber industry, 113 in coal and lead mining, 73 in gold and silver mining, and 72 in oil.

Another problem which challenged the progressives was the rise of the city. By 1890 nine of every ten people in Rhode Island clustered in towns, and Massachusetts had a larger proportion of people in towns of 10,000 than any nation in Europe. One district of New York's Eleventh Ward, with a density of 986 per acre, was probably the most crowded spot on earth; even the notorious Koombarwara district of Bombay had but 760 persons per acre. In the twenty years from 1880 to 1900 the population of New York City increased from a little less than two to almost three and a half millions; Chicago grew from half a million to a million and a half, to become the second city in the nation; such cities as Detroit, Cleveland, Buffalo, Milwaukee, Indianapolis, Columbus, Toledo, Omaha, and Atlanta more than doubled. In 1880 there were 19 cities with a population of 100,000 or more; by 1910, there were 50. Those who came to the great cities, either from the farms or from foreign lands, had to tear up their roots, and the process of transplantation was often painful.

The rapid and unregulated growth of cities created perplexing questions. How should the teeming thousands be housed? What provision could be made to guard against the diseases and epidemics that resulted from filth, congestion, and poverty? What measures should be adopted to control crime and vice; what measures to prevent the recurrence of fires such as those which devastated Chicago in 1871 and Boston in 1872? Could the cities build enough schools for their children and find room between the crowded streets for playgrounds? The burden of finding answers for these questions devolved upon the city governments, and in no field was the progressive movement more vigorous than in municipal reform, where it borrowed liberally from English and German experience. The cities were the experimental laboratories in which many of the new progressive ideas were tested.

Working within the framework of municipal, state, or federal government, reformers frequently confronted a further problem—the prevalence of corruption. Although not unique to America, corruption flourished more shamelessly in the United States than in other democratic nations. This resulted in part from America's tradition of lawlessness; in part from the unstable character of social life, especially migration from country to city, and from Old World to the New; in part from the absence of a 'patriciate'—a class with the leisure and skill for public service. Fundamentally there was a deep-rooted belief, inherited from the Jacksonian period, that any honest man could fill any office, and the fear of a permanent bureaucracy, which kept the expert out of politics. Thus incompetents brought the prestige of office so low that 'gentlemen' did not go into politics.

Too often, the fight against corruption yielded disappointing results. After the reformers had won a victory over the local 'ring' or the state 'boss,' the public lost interest in the housecleaning that followed, and permitted corrupt groups to regain lost ground. The exposure of the 'Shame of the Cities' or of dishonesty in state politics loomed large at the time, but was actually of little importance. Far more significant was the effort of progressives to devise new techniques and administrative agencies to ensure better government.

Finally, there was the race question. Since the Civil War the position of the freedman had steadily worsened. The vast majority of Southern blacks were every year more deeply sunk in the tenancy-mortgage morass, and as late as 1900 only some 8000 Negro boys and girls attended high schools in the entire South. Political and civil rights presumably guaranteed by the Fourteenth and Fifteenth Amendments were eroded. There had been little separation of the races in public facilities in the 70's and 80's, but after *Plessy* v. *Ferguson* in 1896 'Jim Crow' became almost universal. With the rise to power of the classes represented by men like Vardaman of Mississippi, racial violence became the order of the day: in the fifteen years after 1885 almost 2500 blacks were lynched. In the North, blacks were herded into ghettos, segregated in most public places, fobbed off with inferior schooling, cold-shouldered by labor unions, and consigned to the most menial and ill-paid jobs.

The Era of Muckrakers

In 1906 President Roosevelt applied to those engaged in uncovering corruption in American society the epithet 'muckrakers':

In Bunyan's *Pilgrim's Progress*, you may recall the description of the Man with the Muck-rake, the man who could look no way but downward with the muck-rake in his hands; who was offered the celestial crown for his muck-rake, but would neither look up nor regard the crown he was offered, but continued to rake the filth of the floor.

Like many other epithets—Puritan, Quaker, Democrat—the term became in time a title of approbation. For the muckrakers exposed iniquities and stirred public opinion to the point where it was willing to support men like Roosevelt and Wilson in their reform programs.

Actually the literature of protest began some two decades earlier, the work of philosophers, and social scientists, such as Lester Ward, Thorstein Veblen, Henry George, and Edward Bellamy.[1] George's *Progress and Poverty*, published in 1879, resulted from his effort to resolve the paradox of progress and poverty through a 'formula so broad as to admit of no exceptions.' The

1. Ward and Veblen are discussed in the chapter entitled 'The American Mind.'

An escaped convict is treed and captured. (*Department of Archives and Manuscripts, Louisiana State University, Baton Rouge*)

formula which he found was the Single Tax—a tax which would wipe out unearned increment on land, ensure equal access to the land and its resources, and thus destroy monopoly, eliminate speculation, and restore equality. George's diagnosis of the causes of poverty and inequality was more profound than his single-tax cure, and a whole generation of progressives confessed their indebtedness to this 'Bayard of the Poor'—men like Hamlin Garland, Tom Johnson, Clarence Darrow, and Brand Whitlock in the United States, Sidney Webb, H. G. Wells, and Bernard Shaw in England, Tolstoy in Russia, and Sun Yat-sen in China. Nor was George's influence confined to the intellectuals. Over two million copies of his book were sold in America alone, and on the dusty plains of Kansas, in the slums of Liverpool and of Moscow, on the banks of the Ganges and of the Yangtze, poor men painfully spelled out its message. While *Progress and Poverty* envisioned a single action by the State that would liberate the forces of individual enterprise, the utopia of Edward Bellamy's *Looking Backward, 2000–1887* was a co-operative industrial society, where not only profit but even money was eliminated. The book enjoyed an enormous popularity, and hundreds of Nationalist Clubs, dedicated to the nationalization of industries and natural resources, were established.

Though late nineteenth-century periodicals also published articles of exposure, historians usually date the start of muckraking with Lincoln Steffens's 'Tweed Days in St. Louis,' in the October 1902 issue of *McClure's*, for not until then did such writing captivate the nation. By January 1903, *McClure's* was publishing an installment in Ida Tarbell's series on Standard Oil, Ray Stannard Baker's indictment of labor violence, and Steffens's 'The Shame of Minneapolis.' 'Shame' suggests that muckraking was a kind of secular Great Awakening, for, with imagery borrowed from Protestant evangelism, the journalists sought to arouse the country to a consciousness of guilt. Muckraking could not have succeeded without a public eager to hear the worst. By the end of 1903, newsstands were covered with magazines featuring muckraking articles, and the demand had not begun to be sated. 'Time was,' Mr. Dooley remarked to his friend Hennessy, when the magazines 'was very ca'ming to the mind.' But no more:

Now whin I pick me fav-rite magazine off th' flure, what do I find? Ivrything has gone wrong. . . . All th' pomes by th' lady authoresses that used to begin: 'Oh, moon, how fair!' now begin: 'Oh, Ogden Armour, how awful!' . . . Graft ivrywhere. 'Graft in th' Insurance Companies.' 'Graft in Congress,' 'Graft be an Old Grafter,' 'Graft in Its Relations to th' Higher Life,' be Dock Eliot. . . .

Exposure of malpractices by corporations and the wealthy was a characteristic form of muckraking. Ida Tarbell's free-lancing for *McClure's* resulted in her classic *History of the Standard Oil Company*, which analyzed the methods whereby Standard Oil had crushed competitors, seized natural resources, and purchased legislative favors. Within a few years appeared a whole cluster of books of this type: Charles Edward Russell's *Greatest Trust in the World*, an attack on the beef trust; Thomas Lawson's *Frenzied Finance*, an exposé of Amalgamated Copper by a Wall Street insider; Burton J. Hendrick's *Story of Life Insurance*, which did much to create public demand for regulation of that business; and Gustavus Myers's *History of the Great American Fortunes*, which concluded that many fortunes were based on fraud or favor. Works like Myers's and Russell's series, 'Where Did You Get It, Gentlemen?', by taking much of the respectability away from accumulated wealth aided the movement to redistribute income.

The muckrakers also leveled their guns at political corruption and the alliance between corporations and politics. In a notable series published as *Shame of the Cities*, Lincoln Steffens, greatest of the muckrakers, exposed 'Philadelphia: Corrupt and Contented'; 'Pittsburgh, a City Ashamed'; and 'The Shamelessness of St. Louis.' In Minneapolis, Steffens achieved one of the great coups in the history of reporting. He obtained the ledger in which graft collectors had entered their accounts and the names of the persons to whom money was paid, and photographed its pages. In *McClure's*, he told how, under a mayor who had been elected twice by the Republicans, twice by the Democrats, the chief of detectives, an ex-gambler, had invited criminals to Minneapolis, fired 107 honest policemen, and freed prisoners to collect revenues for the gang. Steffens's writings helped Joseph Folk win the governorship of Missouri and Robert La Follette to gain re-election as governor of Wisconsin. Steffens worked out a law of municipal government: privilege controlled politics. In Colorado, Judge Ben Lindsey found the same rule applicable to state politics, and in *The Beast* told with compelling fervor the story of corporation control of the Centennial State. Nor were national politics immune from the muckraker's rake; in 'The Treason of the Senate' the novelist David Graham Phillips called the roll of Senators he found loyal to their business masters but traitors to their constituents: Depew of New York, Aldrich of Rhode Island, and others of the same stamp.

For every volume by a muckraking journalist there was a companion volume of fiction. Theodore Dreiser's *The Financier* and *The Titan* made it easier to understand *Frenzied Finance*. Frank Norris's *The Octopus* complemented Bryan's attacks on the railroad monopolies, and Norris's picture of wheat speculation in *The Pit* explained much of the agrarian protest. Russell's exposure of the meat trust was not nearly as effective as Upton Sinclair's account of life in the stockyards, *The Jungle*—a book which contributed directly to the enactment of meat inspection legislation. David Graham Phillips's best novel, *Susan Lenox: Her Fall and Rise*, found many readers for an exposure of the white slave traffic. And the story of corruption in politics was never better told than in the American Winston Churchill's *Coniston* and *Mr. Crewe's Career*.

Humanitarian Reform

Inspired by the example of Toynbee Hall in London, social workers established settlement houses in the slums of the great cities. In 1886, Stanton Coit set up the first American settlement house in New York City, and by the turn of the century almost a hundred such settlements had been founded, including the Henry Street Settlement in New York, the South End House in Boston, and Hull House, established by Jane Addams in Chicago in 1887. Designed originally to end the estrangement between social classes, they became in time elaborate social service agencies and foci for social reforms. Hull House, with its day nursery, gymnasium, drama school, handicrafts shop, and many other activities, quickly became a laboratory for social work. Jane Addams and associates like Dr. Alice Hamilton spearheaded drives for regulation of the labor of women and children, the establishment of the first juvenile court, protection for immigrant girls, improved sanitary inspection, and better schools. The proposal for a federal Children's Bureau originated with Lillian Wald of Henry Street, and social workers also helped launch city surveys modeled on Charles Booth's study of London. Presidents listened to what these women had to say, and legislatures did their bidding. Hull House became a world institution, and Jane Addams more nearly a world figure than any other woman of her day.

Settlement workers early engaged in a 'battle with the slums,' especially with the malodorous tenement house—a huge, compact structure of five or six stories, with scores and often hundreds of rooms and apartments. The rooms were small, dingy, airless, and sunless; the halls long and dark; the sanitation shockingly primitive; and many of the tenements were fire traps. By 1890 over a million New Yorkers were packed into 32,000 tenements; some of these were decent apartment houses, but many were 'crazy old buildings, rear yards, dark, damp basements, leaking garrets, shops, outhouses, and stables converted into dwellings though scarcely fit to shelter brutes.' That year a Danish immigrant, Jacob Riis, published *How the Other Half Lives*, which depicted the horrors of tenement blocks like Blind Man's Alley, Murderers' Alley, Poverty Gap, Misery Row, and Penitentiary Row. Riis sketched vividly the lives of the poor in New York's East Side:

Cherry Street. Be a little careful, please! The hall is dark and you might stumble over the children pitching pennies back there. Not that it would hurt them; kicks and cuffs are their daily diet. They have little else. Here where the hall turns and dives into utter darkness is a step, and another, another. A flight of stairs. You can *feel* your way, if you cannot see it. Close? Yes! What

Ferreting out evil. For the progressives, the phrase had more than metaphorical significance. This nattily dressed city employee demonstrating a rat-catching ferret is the personification of the middle-class urban reformer. (*Library of Congress*)

would you have? All the fresh air that ever enters these stairs comes from the hall-door that is forever slamming, and from the windows of dark bedrooms that in turn receive from the stairs their sole supply of the elements God meant to be free, but man deals out with such niggardly hand.

Theodore Roosevelt, after reading *How the Other Half Lives*, stopped by at Mulberry Street and left his card, saying: 'I have your book and I have come to help.'

The country responded to such accounts with an outburst of humanitarian activity of a sort that had not been seen since before the Civil War. The American people suddenly discovered the poverty in their midst, for in the United States each generation has to discover all over again, with innocent surprise, that we have poor among us. Others came to feel that if they did not reform the city, it would threaten their own safety. 'The city has become a serious menace to our civilization,' warned Josiah Strong. 'Not only does the proportion of the poor increase with the growth of the city, but their condition becomes more wretched. Dives and Lazarus are brought face to face.' Even when doing humane errands at considerable personal sacrifice, some reformers were awed by an apocalyptic vision of an uprising of the ignorant poor. Riis wrote of 'the sea of a mighty population, held in galling fetters, heav[ing] uneasily in the tenements.' Many of the reformers responded to such warnings by seeking to impose upon the immigrants in the slums the middle-class way of life; their interest in tenement house legislation represented less humanitarianism than an effort at social control.

Despite opposition from vested interests, public opinion rallied to the reformers. A tenement house commission appointed by Governor Theodore Roosevelt recommended a series of changes, and most of these were incorporated in the model tenement house law of 1901 which did away with the old 'dumbbell' tenements and ensured more decent housing for the poor. State after state followed the example of New York, and by 1910 most of the great cities had inaugurated housing reform. Yet though the worst conditions were eliminated, new slums constantly replaced the old.

This same period witnessed the climax of the movement for the organization of charity. Almost every large city in the country had a Charity Organization Society similar to that founded in New York in 1882, designed to introduce efficiency into the haphazard administration of charity by scores of private agencies. These societies maintained shelters for homeless men, undertook the care of dependent children, 'rescued' delinquent girls, provided legal aid to the poor, fought loan sharks, and attempted in scores of ways to alleviate the burden of poverty. Professional social work started with Mary Richmond of Baltimore, who trained young women prepared to make social service a career. In 1909 the Russell Sage Foundation established a clearing house for this work and inaugurated a series of far-reaching investigations into the causes of poverty, crime, and disease.

Social workers paid particular attention to children. John Spargo, echoing *The Bitter Cry of the Children*, told of little girls toiling 16 hours a day in factories and nine-year-old 'breaker boys' working ten hours a day picking slate out of moving coal. Jane Addams, who had created the first summer camp for poor children, wrote in *The Spirit of Youth and the City Streets* the best argument yet made for playgrounds and parks. By 1915 over 400 cities had community playgrounds. Baby clinics and day nurseries were established; free milk was distributed; Visiting Nurses' Associations gave medical care to children; and eventually medical and dental examination became routine at most public schools.

Juvenile delinquency was especially vexatious. At common law, children above seven were held capable of crime, and those above fourteen had the same responsibility as an adult; as late as 1894 these common law principles were incorporated into the penal code of New York. Children were tried by the same laws as were applied to adults and, when convicted, were jailed with adult offenders, and thus schooled in a career of crime. In 1899 Miss Addams persuaded Illinois to establish special courts for children, and soon the institution spread throughout the country. Most notable of those who labored for a more humane attitude toward the juvenile delinquent was Judge Ben Lindsey of the Denver Juvenile Court, whose judicial practices and writings commanded international attention.

Everywhere efforts were made to improve prison conditions, mitigate the penalties of the law, and humanize the administration of justice. Under the leadership of Frederick Wines, the Cincinnati Prison Conference of 1870 inaugurated a new era in penal and prison reform, and within a generation many of the recommendations of that conference had been incorporated into law. Altgeld had written a slashing attack on *Our Penal Machinery and Its Victims* as early as 1884; as Governor of Illinois he did much to reform that machinery and rescue its victims. It was reading Altgeld's book that started Clarence Darrow on his life-long career as champion of the underdog. The fundamental idea that 'the supreme aim of prison discipline is the reformation of criminals' was acknowledged in principle, though rarely in practice. Reformatories were established for juvenile delinquents; first offenders were separated from hardened criminals; the indeterminate sentence and the parole system were widely adopted; state prison farms were established; convict labor and the lease system were outlawed in some states at least; some of the most barbarous features of the penal codes were repealed; and several states abolished capital punishment.

The 'emancipation' of women had proved a mixed blessing; for many, emancipation from the drudgery of the home meant a change to the worse drudgery of the sweatshop. The shift from the country home to the city apartment and the declining size of the family circumscribed the domestic activities of women, but when they turned their energies and talents into business or the professions, they encountered discrimination. Moreover, in few states did married women enjoy the same property rights as men; marriage and divorce laws worked to their disadvantage; and they were denied participation in politics where they might better their position. Furthermore, strict codes imposed a double standard of morality. But during these years the women's rights movement achieved equality in the schools, improvement in legal status, reform of marriage and divorce laws, regulation of hours and conditions of female labor, prenatal care and maternity aid,

and, in 1920, the Nineteenth Amendment granting woman suffrage.

Most importunate of all the crusades was that against 'Demon Rum,' a movement which dated to the early days of the Republic. By 1851 temperance forces had established prohibition in Maine and won minor victories in other states, but between 1860 and 1880 the liquor business increased almost sevenfold, and by the end of the century large cities with heavy Irish and German populations contained about one saloon for every 200 inhabitants. Old stock, Protestant middle-class Americans, especially in rural areas and small towns, waxed indignant at the mores of urban immigrants, who flouted such values as self-control and sobriety. The churches denounced drinking as a sin; women attacked the saloon as a menace to the home; reformers exposed the unholy alliance of the liquor business with crime and the connection between intemperance and poverty; businessmen discovered that drinking affected the efficiency of workingmen and increased the dangers of industrial accidents; while Southern whites insisted on denying liquor to the Negro. For many of the progressives, prohibition was as crucial a reform as social welfare legislation. As Andrew Sinclair has written, they looked forward to 'a world free from alcohol and, by that magic panacea, free also from want and crime and sin, a sort of millennial Kansas afloat on a nirvana of pure water.'

Prohibition was furthered by three well-organized agencies: the Women's Christian Temperance Union, founded in 1874 and long dominated by Frances Willard; the Anti-Saloon League, founded in 1895; and the Methodist Church. By the turn of the century these organizations had succeeded in drying up five states, all predominantly rural. In the first fifteen years of the new century prohibition advanced with rapid strides, and by the time the United States entered World War I over two-thirds of the states were dry, and almost three-fourths of the population lived under 'local option' dry laws. The large cities, however, continued to be wet and from them supplies of liquor flowed unimpeded into thirsty dry areas. During World War I, Congress, allegedly for reasons of economy and efficiency,

Woman's suffrage day. In St. Louis on 16 May 1911, a speaker in a stylish suit, shirtwaist and rakish bonnet addresses the predominantly male crowd. (*Missouri Historical Society*)

prohibited the wartime manufacture or sale of intoxicants. While this law was still in force Congress wrote prohibition into the Constitution in the form of the Eighteenth Amendment.

The achievements of the humanitarians were impressive, yet much that they did was only palliative, as the reformers themselves recognized. Josephine Shaw Lowell, founder of the New York Charity Organization Society, active in work for dependent children, for delinquent girls, and for the insane, decided finally to withdraw from much of this work. She explained:

If the working people had all they ought to have, we should not have the paupers and the criminals. It is better to save them before they go under than to spend

your life fishing them out when they're half drowned and taking care of them afterwards.

As a result of this more realistic attitude, progressives then turned from organized charity and humanitarianism to political and legislative action.

Progressivism in Politics

The progressives achieved their most notable results in state and municipal politics. State constitutions were thoroughly revised or liberalized by amendments, over 900 of which were adopted in the first two decades of the new century. South

508

'McSorley's Bar.' To the prohibitionists, the saloon was the epitome of evil, but to artists like John Sloan this males-only bar was a convivial gathering place for ale-drinkers. Sloan (1871–1951) was a disciple of Robert Henri, who in 1908 formed 'the Eight,' a group of painters of the urban scene dismissed by critics as the 'Ash-Can School.' (*Detroit Institute of Arts, Gift of the Founders Society*)

Dakota in 1898, Utah in 1900, and Oregon in 1902 adopted the initiative and referendum, and by the First World War over 20 states had provided for these devices. In 1908 Oregon committed itself to the recall, and within six years its example was followed by ten states, all but one west of the Mississippi. At first confined to executive officers, the recall was extended by Arizona to judges, and by Colorado to judicial decisions. Governor La Follette, who had been twice defeated for the governorship by a boss-ridden convention, persuaded Wisconsin to adopt the direct primary in 1903; within a decade two-thirds of the states had enacted direct primary and presidential preference laws. Yet the direct primary often proved disappointing, for professional politicians found ways to control the primaries; by 1912 one advocate of the plan confessed that 'some bosses are wondering why they feared the law, and some reformers why they favored it.' No such dissatisfaction followed adoption of the Australian or secret ballot, which soon became universal. More popular still was the demand for direct election of Senators. As early as 1899 Nevada formulated a method for circumventing the constitutional requirement of election by state legislatures, and by 1912 some thirty states had provided for the expression of popular opinion in the choice of Senators. The Seventeenth Amendment, ratified in 1913, was therefore rather a recognition of an accomplished fact than an innovation.

From New York to California reform governors gave their support to enlarging the scope of government control over business. Charles Evans Hughes, elected Governor of New York after exposing spectacular corruption in the great insurance companies, obtained the establishment of a public utilities commission. In Wisconsin Robert La Follette regulated public utilities, reorganized the tax system, established an industrial commission, and made the state university an effective instrument of the regeneration of the state. Hazen Pingree in Michigan, Albert Cummins in Iowa, and Hiram Johnson in California shattered railway domination over state politics. In the South, Charles B. Aycock changed North Carolina into the most progressive of Southern commonwealths, Charles A. Culberson brought Texas into the main current of the reform movement, and 'Alfalfa Bill' Murray made Oklahoma for a brief period an experimental laboratory of Bryan democracy.

The progressives also scored gains in municipal politics. Tom Johnson, a wealthy manufacturer who had come under the influence of Henry George, rescued Cleveland from the grip of the utilities and the domination of Mark Hanna and made it, for a time, the best governed city in the country. In Toledo, 'Golden Rule' Jones guided the city in accordance with his interpretation of the Golden Rule, and after his death Brand Whitlock carried on the work of reform—including municipal ownership of public utilities—in the same spirit and with even more acute understand-

ing. Emil Seidel, Socialist mayor of Milwaukee, gave that city efficient and honest government, and in San Francisco, Fremont Older exposed the skulduggery of a political ring controlled by the president of the Union Pacific. Even New York, under mayors like Seth Low and John Purroy Mitchel, lapsed into respectability, only to repent and reinstate the Tammany Tiger.

The reformers also tried to find permanent solutions to the vexatious problems of city government. The commission plan grew out of the Galveston flood of 1900; adopted with modifications by Houston and Des Moines, it was soon widely copied. The council-manager plan resulted from a similar crisis—the Dayton flood of 1913. By 1940, some 332 cities had adopted the commission form, and 315 cities the council-manager.

Much of this progressive zeal was naïve, some of it was misguided. Fundamentally moralists, the reformers assumed that most of the failings of government could be ascribed to Bad Men—bosses, vested interests, 'malefactors of great wealth'—and assumed, too, that if only Men of Good Will would devote themselves to public service, all would be well. Progressivism had a touching faith, too, in mechanical contrivances; Wilson once said that the 'short ballot was the key to the whole problem of the restoration of popular government in this country.' Yet progressives like Jane Addams, Louis Brandeis, and Robert La Follette were as hard-headed as any of their successors. If their faith failed to move mountains, it did eliminate many of the obstacles in the way of effective popular government. Insofar as politics was more honest, society more enlightened, in 1914 than in 1890, much of the credit goes to the indefatigable progressives.

The Struggle for Negro Rights: Washington and Du Bois

The most conspicuous failure of the progressive movement was in race relations. Many Northern liberals had wearied of the Negro issue. Worse yet, Southern progressives themselves often exploited racial prejudice; men like Josephus Daniels of North Carolina, who on most matters went along with Bryan and La Follette, readily

Booker T. Washington (1856–1915). Born into slavery, he had gone to work in a salt furnace after the Civil War, gained a hard-earned education, and built Tuskegee Institute in Alabama into a college with one hundred buildings and a two-million-dollar endowment. Yet despite all of his accomplishments, when he dined at the White House with Theodore Roosevelt in 1901 (a year before this photograph was taken), the Southern press denounced this violation of racial taboos as 'a crime equal to treason.' 'Entertaining that nigger,' said Senator Tillman of South Carolina, would 'necessitate our killing a thousand niggers in the South before they will learn their place again.' (*Library of Congress*)

511

sacrificed the Negro to their political ambitions. Daniels stated, 'We abhor a northern policy of catering to Negroes politically just as we abhor a northern policy of social equality.'

Left to fend for themselves, blacks developed two conflicting approaches: one represented by Booker T. Washington of Tuskegee Institute in Alabama, the other by the Massachusetts-born W. E. B. Du Bois of Atlanta University. The issues these two towering figures raised, the programs they sponsored, have dominated black thought and thought about blacks. Born in slavery, raised in abject poverty, catching an education as best he could at the new Hampton Institute in Virginia, Booker T. Washington came to be the most distinguished leader of his race after Frederick Douglass. When *Up From Slavery* appeared in 1901, William Dean Howells called Washington 'a public man second to no other American in importance.' Persuaded that blacks must win economic independence before they could expect to command social or political equality, Washington opened the Tuskegee Normal and Industrial School for Negroes in 1881, with the object of teaching students habits of work, thrift, and good citizenship.

Over a period of almost forty years Washington counseled progress by evolution rather than by violence, temporary acquiescence in policies of segregation, and co-operation with the ruling white class. 'In all things that are purely social,' he said, in a speech of 1895, 'we can be as separate as the fingers, yet one as the hand in all things essential to mutual progress.' 'The wisest among my race,' he insisted, 'understand that the agitation of questions of social equality is the extremest folly.' To win his immediate objective of economic gains, Washington told blacks to shun politics and scolded them not to forget that they were to work with their hands. This philosophy of accommodation delighted the white community, relieved to hear a Negro leader consign his brethren to an inferior status. Washington won the confidence of Presidents, influenced newspaper editors, and persuaded Northern white philanthropists to pour money into Tuskegee and other projects that had his blessing. But at the same time that Washington was playing the public role of 'Uncle Tom,' he

was acting in a very different fashion behind the scenes. He lobbied against discriminatory legislation and financed litigation against disfranchisement laws, and advised Presidents Roosevelt and Taft on patronage; at his suggestion, Negroes were named to such posts as collector of internal revenue in New York and assistant attorney general, appointments not to be matched or surpassed by a black until after World War II.

Despite his dedication Washington fought a losing battle, in part because his program was irrelevant to the urban black. He trained Negroes for jobs on the land and in handicrafts at a time when America was rapidly industrializing. He told the black man to stay in the rural South, but by 1910 Washington and New York each had more than 90,000 Negroes. In the city the Negro met discrimination from most unions, an ever-tightening cord of residential segregation, and a pattern of legitimized violence. The new century began with the lynching of more than 100 Negroes in its first year, and in 1909 a Memphis newspaper reported that no white man had been hanged in Shelby County since 1890, but noted, 'Since then we have had a hanging of negroes pretty much regularly every year.'

At the beginning of the century the young W. E. B. Du Bois, trained at Harvard and Berlin, challenged the Washingtonian program of compromise and concession. Negroes, said Du Bois, could never win economic security without the vote, or achieve self-respect if they acquiesced in a position of inferiority, or attain true equality if they preferred vocational to intellectual training. Du Bois argued in *Souls of Black Folk* that the Negro would be raised by the 'Talented Tenth' who had a liberal arts education. In 1905 he and his followers met at Niagara Falls, Canada, to inaugurate what came to be called the Niagara Movement. The Niagara platform, as elaborated at subsequent meetings, called for evenhanded enforcement of the laws, and Congressional action to ensure that the Fourteenth Amendment would be carried out 'to the letter.'

This movement made slow progress until white reformers who had previously backed Washington decided that more militant action was needed. Moved by an ugly race riot in Lincoln's town of

The Niagara Movement. In this photograph of black leaders silhouetted against a backdrop of Niagara Falls, W.E.B. Du Bois is second from the right in the second row. Du Bois (1868–1963) spoke for more militant blacks who challenged Booker T. Washington's leadership. Their meeting near Niagara Falls in 1905 helped lead to the founding of the NAACP. (*Schomburg Center for Research in Black Culture, New York Public Library*)

Springfield, Illinois, in 1908, William English Walling wrote in the *Independent*: 'Either the spirit of the abolitionists, of Lincoln and of Lovejoy, must be revived and we must come to treat the Negro on a plane of absolute political and social equality or Vardaman and Tillman will soon have transferred the Race War to the North. . . . Yet who realizes the seriousness of the situation and what large and powerful body of citizens is ready to come to their aid?' Stirred by Walling's challenge, a group of Northern whites sent out a call for a National Negro Conference in 1909; the call was written by the publisher of the New York *Evening Post*, Oswald Garrison Villard, the grandson of William Lloyd Garrison. To the conference came many of the Niagara Movement participants as well as such luminaries as Jane Addams, William Dean Howells, and John Dewey.

The conferees' plans for a permanent organization led to the creation of the National Association for the Advancement of Colored People with Moorfield Storey of Boston as president, Walling chairman of the executive committee, and Du Bois director of publicity and research. The strength of the Association lay in its college-educated Negro members. With Du Bois as editor, the NAACP organ, the *Crisis*, reached a circulation of 100,000 a month by 1918. Under the leadership of Arthur B. Spingarn, white and black lawyers carried out a successful strategy of litigation. In 1915, the Supreme Court invalidated the grandfather clauses in the Oklahoma and Maryland Constitutions, and in 1917 the Court ruled unconstitutional a Louisville ordinance imposing residential segregation.

Unlike Walling and Storey, most white progressives were either indifferent to race or shared in the prejudices of their day. Theodore Roosevelt's administration was marred by an ugly episode of discrimination against black troops, and in 1912, Roosevelt, who had outraged the South by inviting Booker T. Washington to dine at the White House, insisted that the Progressive party be a lily white organization in the South. Woodrow Wilson's administration, largely Southern, appointed whites to posts previously granted to blacks and imposed racial segregation on the national government. Not until the 1940's would civil rights for the Negro take a prominent place on the agenda of American liberalism.

Theodore Roosevelt and the Square Deal

In September 1901, President McKinley was murdered by an anarchist, and Theodore Roosevelt became President of the United States. Not yet forty-three, Roosevelt was the youngest by several years in the line of Presidents; but few have been better equipped to administer the office.

He had already achieved prominence as a naturalist, a man of letters, a soldier, and a statesman. He had served as a member of the New York State Assembly and as Civil Service Commissioner, and in between had found time to write the four-volume *Winning of the West*, and to win a bit of it himself as a Dakota ranchman. In 1895 he had accepted the thankless post of Police Commissioner of New York City, a post which threw him into intimate contact with social reformers. Two years later McKinley appointed him Assistant Secretary of the Navy, but this office proved too confining for his ebullient energies and with the outbreak of the Spanish War he organized the Rough Riders and fought his way to glory at San Juan Hill. Elected Governor of New York in 1898 on his return from war, he had struck at corruption with such vigor that in self-defense Boss Platt and the machine politicians had boomed him for the vice-presidency. His accession to the presidency, regarded with dismay by conservatives,[2] inaugurated a new era in American politics.

People everywhere knew Teddy as a red-blooded, democratic American of enormous vitality. Henry Adams said: 'Roosevelt more than any other man living, showed the singular primitive quality that belongs to ultimate matter—the quality that medieval theology ascribed to God—he was pure act.' He could lasso a bucking steer, turn out an historical essay, hunt lions, run a political convention, play tennis, lead a regiment, and hypnotize an audience with equal facility; he could hold his own in the company of cowboys, ward politicians, Methodist clergymen, reporters, and diplomats. Like Bryan and Wilson, Roosevelt was a moralist. It was almost impossible for him to think of a political question except in moral terms. 'Theodore,' Tom Reed said to him, 'if there is one thing more than another for which I admire you, it is your original discovery of the ten commandments.' His morality was positive, but not

2. H. H. Kohlsaat tells of riding in the McKinley funeral train with Mark Hanna. 'He was in an intensely bitter state of mind. He damned Roosevelt and said, "I told William McKinley it was a mistake to nominate that wild man at Philadelphia. I asked him if he realized what would happen if he should die. Now look, that damned cowboy is President of the United States,"' *McKinley to Harding*, p. 101.

Theodore Roosevelt as Hamlet. So irresolute was the President on the tariff issue, which he thought a matter of 'expediency and not morality,' that in this caricature in *Puck*, entitled 'Tedlet's Soliloquy,' Joseph Keppler, Jr. portrays him as the melancholy Dane. Borrowing and modifying a line from Shakespeare's drama, Keppler has T. R. saying, as in Hamlet's soliloquy, 'Thus the Tariff does make cowards of us all.' Roosevelt professed to believe in tariff reform, but no time ever seemed right for it; before an election was perilous and after an election was no better. In the end he bequeathed the whole problem to his successor, who was not so agile at evasion. Keppler, whose father, the founder of *Puck*, was an even more noted cartoonist, sold the magazine in 1914, and from then until his death in 1956 devoted himself to the cause of the American Indian. (*Library of Congress*)

subtle; and he regarded those who differed with him as either scoundrels or fools.

Roosevelt believed that as President he had two important functions: to serve as moral leader and to enforce the national interest against special interests. The country, he thought, faced two great dangers: the mob, which might be whipped up by demagogues, and the plutocracy, which, by its excessive greed, incited the mob. He sought to strengthen the government as a mediating force, for he had, as he once said, a horror of extremes. He aimed to carry out a program that would be neither populistic nor representative of the men he called 'malefactors of great wealth.'

Roosevelt's commitment to change was always qualified by his distaste for most reformers. He demanded a 'square deal' for labor, but no one in the country was more vitriolic in denouncing men like Altgeld, Debs, and Bryan who tried to inaugurate the 'square deal.' He avoided dangerous issues such as tariff and banking reform; and even on those issues he did pursue, he was usually ready to compromise rather than risk a break with the Old Guard. His chief service to the progressive

cause was to dramatize the movement and make it respectable. Yet Roosevelt's dramatics often distracted attention from the big tent to the side shows. After the seven years of tumult and shouting had passed, many reformers felt they had been fighting a sham battle and that the citadels of privilege were yet to be invested.

Roosevelt believed in executive leadership and gave an exhibition of it that recalled Andrew Jackson and anticipated his cousin Franklin. According to his conception of stewardship, 'it was not only his right but his duty to do anything that the needs of the Nation demanded, unless such action was forbidden by the Constitution or by the laws,' and he soon indicated his conviction that the needs of the nation were multifarious.

Yet he responded to the outcry for regulation of corporations with circumspection. He knew he had come to power not by choice of the people but 'by act of God'; Roosevelt had the common sense to see that the problem was complicated. However, he knew, too, that the country was ready for action. At Roosevelt's behest Congress in 1903 established a Department of Commerce and Labor and authorized a Bureau of Corporations to investigate interstate corporations. At first the new bureau was innocuous, but eventually it investigated the oil, packing, tobacco, steel, and other industries and furnished material for prosecution under the anti-trust laws.

More dramatic was Roosevelt's decision to reinvigorate the Sherman law. In 1902 he shocked Wall Street by instructing his Attorney General to enter suit against the Northern Securities Company, a consolidation of the Hill-Morgan and the Harriman railways which embraced the Northern Pacific, the Great Northern, and the Chicago, Burlington and Quincy systems. By a 5–4 vote the Supreme Court in 1904 sustained the government and overruled its previous decision in the E. C. Knight case, thereby stopping a process of consolidation that Harriman proposed to continue until every important railway came under his control. Roosevelt asserted: 'It was necessary to reverse the Knight case in the interests of the people against monopoly and privilege just as it had been necessary to reverse the Dred Scott case in the interest of the people against slavery.'

In part as a consequence of the Northern Securities suit, the President grew steadily in popularity. Merely by being himself—greeting professors and pugilists with equal warmth, teaching his boys to ride and shoot, leading major-generals on a point-to-point ride, exercising with his 'tennis cabinet,' praising the good, the true, and the beautiful and denouncing the base, the false, and the ugly—Roosevelt became an institution. In 1904 the Republicans nominated Roosevelt by acclamation. When the Democrats discarded Bryan and put up a conservative New York judge, Alton B. Parker, Roosevelt polled a stunning 56.4 per cent of the vote, the greatest proportion any Republican had ever received, and on 4 March 1905 became 'President in his own right.'

Encouraged by this mandate, Roosevelt turned with new enthusiasm to the enforcement of his trust policies. Altogether there were forty-five prosecutions, and in notable instances they were successful. But they simply punished the grosser mischief after it had been committed and did not always do that. As early as 1905, Roosevelt had reached an informal gentleman's agreement with

the House of Morgan. He left the impression that he would avoid court action against Morgan companies in return for their co-operation. Roosevelt came to conclude that the mere size and power of a combination did not necessarily render it illegal; there were 'good trusts' such as the International Harvester Company, another Morgan firm, which traded fairly and passed on their economies to consumers; and there were 'bad trusts,' which did not. The Supreme Court raised this moral distinction to the dignity of a legal one when, in the Standard Oil case of 1911, it accepted the common-law doctrine that only those acts or agreements of a monopolistic nature 'unreasonably' affecting interstate commerce were to be construed as in restraint of trade. Justice Harlan, in a vigorous dissent, denounced this 'rule of reason' as 'judicial legislation' and a 'perversion of the plain words of an Act in order to defeat the will of Congress.' But the 'rule of reason' became the guiding rule of decision, notably in the United States Steel Corporation case in 1920.

Roosevelt did, however, expand government supervision over business in other fields, such as labor relations. His intervention in the coal strike of 1902 revealed his determination to make full use of the authority of the Chief Executive. It was his initiative, too, that led Congress to enact factory inspection and child labor laws for the District of Columbia, and safety appliance legislation for interstate carriers. Yet despite his enthusiasm for the 'square deal,' Roosevelt failed to support Senator Beveridge in his struggle to outlaw child labor.

Government supervision of railways furnished the fireworks for the second Roosevelt administration as the trusts had for the first. Abandoned by Congress, ignored by Presidents Harrison, Cleveland, and McKinley, and emasculated by court decisions, the Interstate Commerce Act of 1887 had proved all but useless. Nonetheless, the necessity for regulation remained urgent. The railroads themselves were anxious to make the prohibition of rebates effective, and in 1903 they supported the Elkins Act, which made the published freight rates the lawful standard, substituted civil for criminal penalties, and provided that shippers were equally liable with the railroads

'Manchester Valley.' This painting by Joseph Pickett (1848–1919), a self-taught artist, indicates the centrality of the railroad to the life of the American small town. Pickett, who started his brief career in his middle years using house paint, worked very deliberately (sometimes spending years on a single canvas) behind his general store in New Hope, Pennsylvania. Only four of his paintings survive, but he was known to have done more, for he painted backdrops for his shooting gallery in the period when he traveled with a carnival. (*Museum of Modern Art, Gift of Abby Aldrich Rockefeller*)

for obtaining rebates. Under this act the Attorney General instituted prosecutions against the Chicago & Alton and the Burlington for granting rebates and against Chicago packing houses for accepting them. Soon the government went after bigger game. In 1907 Judge Kenesaw Mountain Landis assessed a fine of $29,240,000 against the Standard Oil Company for accepting rebates, but the sentence was set aside by a higher court.

In 1904 Roosevelt pronounced railway regulation the 'paramount issue,' and in 1906 Congress responded with the Hepburn Act, which made rate regulation for the first time possible. The act authorized the ICC to determine and prescribe maximum rates. The railroads could appeal, but the burden of proof was now on the carrier, not the commission. Regulation was extended to include storage, refrigeration, and terminal facilities, sleeping car, express, and pipeline companies, and in 1910, telephone and telegraph companies. The law prohibited free passes for other than railroad employees, and required the railroads to disgorge most of the steamship lines and coal mines they had bought up to stifle competition—a requirement which they managed to evade. The Hepburn Act represented a substantial advance in railway regulation; within two years the commission heard almost twice as many complaints as in the previous nineteen years, and by 1911 it had reduced almost 200,000 rates by as much as 50 per cent. Yet the act did not get to the heart of the matter, for it failed to empower the commission to evaluate railroad properties and the cost of service by which alone it could determine reasonable rates. Not until 1913 was provision made for valuation, and another decade was to elapse before that valuation came to be used for rate-making.

Another step toward federal centralization was the extension of governmental supervision over foods and drugs. Investigations of Dr. Harvey Wiley, chief chemist of the Department of Agriculture, revealed almost universal use of adulterants and preservatives in canned and prepared foods, while the Ladies' Home Journal campaigned against poisonous patent medicines and misleading advertising and Samuel Hopkins Adams exposed 'The Great American Fraud.' In 1905 Roosevelt asked Congress to act, and, with the support of the American Medical Association and despite the frantic efforts of the Liquor Dealers' Association and the patent-medicine interests, Congress adopted in 1906 a Pure Food and Drugs Act, amended in 1911 to forbid misleading labeling of medicines.

The main spur for a pure food and drugs bill came from a book which, ironically, was written for a very different purpose. In March 1906 Upton Sinclair published The Jungle, a novel which made a frankly Socialist appeal and included an introduction by Jack London, who assured readers that the book was 'straight proletarian.' A story of the tribulations of a Lithuanian immigrant and his conversion to socialism, The Jungle was a startling success; but not, in Sinclair's view, for the right reasons. Instead of rising to indignation about the exploitation of the workers, the American public focused on a dozen pages vividly describing the processing of diseased cattle. When men who worked in the tank rooms fell into open vats, Sinclair wrote, 'sometimes they would be overlooked for days, till all but the bones of them had gone out to the world as Durham's Pure Leaf Lard.' As Mr. Dooley said, it was 'a sweetly sintimintal little volume to be r-read durin' Lent.' The public outcry against poisoned meat not only rescued the pure food and drugs bill from defeat but led to the adoption of federal meat inspection. Though this legislation still left much to be desired, it did give American consumers better protection than the laws of any other country then afforded.

Unquestionably Roosevelt's most important achievement came in the conservation of natural resources. As early as 1873 the American Association for the Advancement of Science had called attention to the reckless exhaustion of forest resources, but not until 1891 did Congress pass a Forest Reserve Act authorizing the President to set aside timber lands. Under this authority Harrison withdrew some 13 million, Cleveland 25 million, and McKinley 7 million acres of forest from public entry. Nevertheless, exploitation was still outpacing conservation when Roosevelt assumed office. Taking advantage of the 1891 law, Roosevelt set aside almost 150 million acres of unsold government timber land as national forest reserve, and at the suggestion of Senator La Follette withdrew from public entry some 85 millions more in Alaska and the Northwest, pending a government study of their resources. The discovery of a gigantic system of fraud by which railroads, lumber companies, and ranchers were looting and devastating the public reserve enabled the President to obtain authority to transfer the national forests to the Department of Agriculture, whose forest bureau, under the far-sighted Gifford Pinchot, administered them on scientific principles.

Realizing the necessity for arousing the public

Seeing the West. In California, this group of tourists was photographed making a pilgrimage to the natural wonders of Yosemite. This spectacular region on the western slope of the Sierra Nevada played an important part in the history of the conservation movement. As early as 1864 Congress granted land there for a state park, and in 1890 it created the Yosemite National Park, which in 1906, in Theodore Roosevelt's presidency, also acquired the state park. Under the authority of the secretary of the interior, the U.S. Army operated the park until 1916, when the National Park Service was established. The name 'Yosemite,' meaning 'grizzly bear,' derives from the clan totem of the Indians who dwelled there. (*Los Angeles County Museum*)

to the imperative need for conservation, Roosevelt took a great variety of different initiatives. He secured wide publicity for the work of the Forest Service. In 1907 he appointed an Inland Waterways Commission to canvass the whole question of the relation of rivers and soil and forest, of water-power development, and of water transportation. That same year the President invited all the state governors, cabinet members, justices of the Supreme Court, and other notables to a White House conference which focused attention upon conservation and gave the movement an impetus and a prestige that enabled it to survive later setbacks.

By sponsoring an ambitious irrigation program Roosevelt helped bring new life to barren regions of the West. The Newlands Reclamation Act of 1902 provided that irrigation should be financed out of the proceeds of public land sales under federal supervision and established a Reclamation Service. Over the next generation, the government constructed Roosevelt dam in Arizona, Hoover dam on the Colorado, Grand Coulee on the Columbia, and a dozen others. Roosevelt also put an end to the acquisition of water-power sites by private utilities and created five national parks, four game preserves, and over fifty wild bird refuges. Alone of our Presidents up to this time, Theodore Roosevelt grasped the problem of conservation as a whole. Unfortunately, until the accession of Franklin D. Roosevelt, none of his successors had the breadth of vision to carry on the work he so hopefully inaugurated.

Taft and the Insurgency

Strong-willed Presidents have generally managed to nominate their successors, and Roosevelt bequeathed his office to William Howard Taft, a man he loved as a brother and believed the ideal person to carry out his policies. In the 1908 election, Taft overwhelmed Bryan, who, in his third try for the White House, made the poorest showing, save for Parker's race, of any Democrat since the party split in 1860. Many progressives welcomed the change from Roosevelt to Taft, for except in the realm of conservation the last year of T.R.'s administration was without achievement;

as soon as the Republican leaders in Congress learned that Roosevelt would retire in 1909, they had ignored alike his recommendations and his threats. 'Big Bill' Taft, it was hoped, would apply the emollient of his good nature to the wheels of legislation.

If Roosevelt appeared to be less conservative than he really was, Taft seemed more so. Roosevelt was primarily a man of action, Taft of inaction. As a constitutional lawyer Taft did not share Roosevelt's view that the President could do anything not forbidden by law; rather, the executive could do only those things for which he had specific authority under the Constitution. Taft was by instinct cautious, by training 'regular.' Roosevelt had given the presidency an organic connection with Congress; under Taft the initiative passed to Old Guard leaders like 'Uncle Joe' Cannon of Illinois in the House and Nelson W. Aldrich in the Senate who thought reform had gone far enough, if not too far. And when Roosevelt sailed to Africa in March 1909, he left his successor with many critical problems, especially the tariff and the trusts, unsolved.[3]

The Republican platform of 1908 pledged to revise the tariff: an issue that Roosevelt had gingerly avoided. Revision was popularly understood as reduction, and Taft had specifically committed himself to this interpretation. A student of William Graham Sumner's at Yale, Taft had thereafter opposed high protection. 'Mr. Taft is a very excellent man,' wrote Senator Foraker in 1909, 'but there never was a minute since I first knew him when the tariff was not too high to suit him.' For downward revision there was, by 1909, pressing demand, especially in the Midwest, which exported many of its commodities. The tariff was blamed for the rising cost of living and was thought to be 'the mother of trusts.' In his inaugural address the new President asked that 'a

3. In August 1908, he explained, 'Well I'm through now. I've done my work. People are going to discuss economic questions more and more: the tariff, currency, banks. They are hard questions, and I am not deeply interested in them; my problems are moral problems, and my teaching has been plain morality.' John Hay noted in his diary: 'Knox says that the question of what is to become of Roosevelt after 1908 is easily answered. He should be made a bishop.'

Campaigning for the Socialist ticket, the Lower East Side, New York City, 1908.
J. G. Phelps Stokes, the millionaire Socialist candidate for the state legislature,
appeals to the crowd to vote for the Socialist slate headed by Eugene V. Debs.
Though the Socialists had their greatest numerical strength in districts peopled by
'New Immigrants,' the party found its greatest following in proportion to popula-
tion in rural Oklahoma. (*Museum of the City of New York*)

tariff bill be drawn in good faith in accordance with
the promises made before the election,' and he
summoned Congress into special session to act.

When Congress assembled, Sereno Payne of
New York was ready with a tariff bill which placed
iron ore, flax, and hides on the free list and reduced duties on steel, lumber, and numerous
other items. The bill promptly passed the House,
but in the Senate representatives of interested
industries fell upon it. When it emerged as the
Payne-Aldrich tariff, it was seen that of the 847

changes, some 600 were upward and that the free
list was a joke. Accused of violating the party's
promise to revise the tariff, Aldrich retorted:
'Where did we ever make the statement that we
would revise the tariff *downward*?' Progressive
Republicans were outraged, and La Follette,
rapidly emerging as their leader, organized the
Midwestern Senators to fight the proposed measure item by item. In a stirring debate La Follette
attacked the woolens schedule, Beveridge the tobacco, Cummins the steel, Bristow the sugar, Dol-

William Howard Taft (1857–1930). Robert Lee MacCameron's oil portrait was painted in the year Taft became President. The new Chief Executive's girth provided the subject for jokes at his expense. Taft, it was said, once got up in a streetcar and offered his seat to three ladies. (*National Portrait Gallery, Smithsonian Institution*)

liver the cotton, and if in the end they failed, they did at least enlighten the country on the connection between tariffs and trusts, and laid dynamite for the political explosion of 1910. The insurgents urged Taft to veto the bill for violating party pledges, but after painful vacillation he signed it.

To heal this deep sectional wound in the party would require deft diplomacy. But the President promptly made a bad situation worse by deciding to tour the Middle West in the summer of 1909, to 'get out and see the people and jolly them.' He began his trip by paying tribute to Aldrich in the East; in Winona, Minnesota, in the heart of progressive discontent, he enraged insurgents by calling the Payne-Aldrich measure 'the best tariff bill that the Republican party has ever passed, and therefore the best tariff bill that has been passed at all'; and he capped the tour by having himself photographed with his arms around Speaker Cannon.

Progressive Republicans, already uneasy about Taft's performance, came to suspect him of playing traitor to Roosevelt on conservation. James R. Garfield, Roosevelt's lieutenant in conservation, was supplanted in the Interior Department by R. A. Ballinger, who was presently accused by Chief Forester Gifford Pinchot of letting a Morgan-Guggenheim syndicate obtain reserved coal lands in Alaska. The President then fired Pinchot, an act interpreted as a dramatic reversal of Roosevelt's program. Actually, Taft was not unfriendly to conservation. He was the first President to withdraw oil lands from public sale, he obtained from Congress authority to reserve the coal lands which Roosevelt had set aside without specific authority, and he made the Bureau of Mines guardian of the nation's mineral resources. Pinchot was replaced by the head of the Yale School of Forestry, and his policy was continued by the purchase, in 1911, of great timbered tracts in the Appalachians. But the Ballinger-Pinchot affair served further to alienate the insurgents from Taft.

The progressives directed their indignation not only against the President but against the Old Guard upon whom he depended. In the Senate, La Follette, Beveridge, and Dolliver excoriated Aldrich to such effect that he decided not to stand for re-election. In the House, insurgency took the form of a revolt against Speaker Cannon, 'a hard,

narrow old Boeotian,' who controlled a well-oiled legislation mill which rejected progressive grist. In March 1910 George Norris offered a resolution depriving the Speaker of membership on the powerful Committee on Rules and making that committee elective, and Democrats joined with progressive Republicans to put it through. If the progressive cause gained, legislative efficiency lost. Authority was needed to enforce party discipline in a body so unwieldy as the House. Some progressives denied any right of party leaders to regularize the flow of legislation. Victor Murdock later described his attitude as 'merely reflecting Jonathan Edwards' philosophy that nothing should come between God and man, in maintaining that nothing should come between the people and their representatives.' Cannon bridled at such notions: 'The Speaker does believe and always had believed that this is a government through parties, and that parties can act only through majorities.' Although at the time the defeat of Cannon struck a blow for progressivism, many modern-day liberals find the Speaker's concept of party government more appropriate to liberal democracy than that of the insurgents who spoke for the autonomy of the Congressman.

The fights over Payne-Aldrich, Ballinger-Pinchot, and Cannonism caused an irrevocable split between Taft and the progressive Republicans, and in the 1910 campaign the President attempted to drive the insurgents out of office. Taft sent the Vice-President to campaign against La Follette in Wisconsin, and worked with the Southern Pacific crowd against Hiram Johnson in California. But the progressives handed him and the Old Guard a stunning set of defeats. Iowa Republicans howled down a resolution to endorse Taft; Johnson, who said his Republicanism came not from Washington but from Iowa and Wisconsin, overwhelmed the Taft Republicans; and La Follette won impressively. This factionalism in the primaries proved devastating for the Republicans in November. The Democrats captured the governorships of Massachusetts, Connecticut, and New York; sent Dr. Woodrow Wilson, lately president of Princeton University, to the State House in New Jersey; and won control of the House for the first time since 1894.

Taft's political ineptitude must not blind us to

'Catching the Limited,' 1910. William Harnden Foster's oil is one of the earliest paintings of the exciting new invention, the aeroplane. But unwittingly it demonstrates that the railroad still dominated American transportation, for the purpose of the flight is to enable the straw-hatted passenger with his satchel to catch up with the express train that will carry him to his destination. (*Berry-Hill Galleries*)

his achievements. The Mann-Elkins Act of 1910 strengthened the Interstate Commerce Commission by empowering it to suspend rate increases until and unless their reasonableness was ascertained, and created a Commerce Court to hear appeals from the ICC. The Department of Commerce and Labor, established in 1903, was wisely divided; and Congress set up a Children's Bureau in the new Department of Labor. A postal savings bank and a parcel post—conveniences long overdue—were provided. Approximately twice as many anti-trust prosecutions were instituted during Taft's four years as in Roosevelt's seven. The Sixteenth, or income-tax, Amendment and the Seventeenth Amendment, which transferred the election of United States Senators from state legislatures to the people, were adopted by Congress in 1909 and 1912 respectively and ratified in 1913. Alaska, peevish and discontented since the collapse of the Klondike gold bubble, at last obtained full territorial government in 1912, the same year that New Mexico and Arizona became the forty-seventh and forty-eighth states of the Union. Here again Taft antagonized the progressives by refusing to certify the admission of Arizona until it expunged from its constitution a provision for the popular recall of judges; once admitted as a state, Arizona promptly restored the device.

Even developments in foreign affairs served to lessen Taft's popularity and tear his party asunder, despite the fact that the unlucky President's foreign policy was often more sensible than Roosevelt's had been. When Japan began to consolidate her position in Manchuria, Secretary Knox countered by proposing, in 1909, that the United States and European powers lend China sufficient money to buy back all the railroads controlled by foreign interests. But his plan was rejected somewhat contemptuously by Russia and Japan. Failing in this effort to assist China, Taft insisted that American bankers be allowed to participate in a four-power consortium to finance railway construction in the Yangtze valley, 'in order that the United States might have equal rights and an equal voice in all questions pertaining to the disposition of the public revenues concerned.' But this plan, innocent enough in purpose, was repudiated by Wilson within two weeks of his accession to office.

It was fear of Japan, too, which provoked the so-called Lodge corollary to the Monroe Doctrine. In 1911 an American company proposed to sell Magdalena Bay in Lower California to a Japanese fishing syndicate. On hearing of the proposal, Senator Lodge, suspicious that the syndicate might be a cover for the government itself, introduced and the Senate passed a resolution that the purchase or control by any non-American government of any part of the American continents which had a potential naval or military value would constitute an unfriendly act. Though Taft declared that he was not bound by the resolution, it further aggravated Latin American opinion. The doctrine was strictly a one-way affair; designed to prevent foreign establishments in the Western hemisphere, it did not limit American expansion to other continents.

A comparison of the Roosevelt and Taft policies recalls the old adage that some persons can make off with a horse, while others cannot look over the stable wall. Secretary Knox signed treaties with Nicaragua and Honduras similar to Roosevelt's pact with Santo Domingo, underwriting American loans by guaranteeing bankers against revolution and defalcation. But the Knox treaties were rejected by the Senate, and Taft's policy both in Central America and the Far East was denounced as 'dollar diplomacy.' In 1911 Taft, a warm friend to international peace, concluded treaties with both England and France for the arbitration of all disputes, including those involving 'national honor.' The German-American press and professional Irish-Americans broke out into shrieks of dissent. A presidential election was approaching, and the Senate rejected the treaties.

Again it was Taft's misfortune, not his fault, that tariff reciprocity with Canada failed. In November 1910 three United States commissioners concluded with two members of the Dominion Parliament a reciprocity agreement to be adopted by identical legislative acts. The agreement provided free trade in primary food products, which would naturally flow from Canada southward, and a large reduction on manufactures, which would obviously go the other way. It was a sincere effort by Taft to cement friendly relations, but bad politics. Insurgent Republicans, most of whom represented Western

President Taft and Colonel Goethals in Panama. In 1907, two years before William Howard Taft entered the White House, George Washington Goethals (1858–1928) was appointed chief engineer of the Panama Canal. He proved a brilliant choice. By his accessibility and his grasp of detail, he created such an *esprit de corps* among his motley work crew of 30,000 that he was able to complete his arduous assignment ahead of schedule. In 1915 Congress rewarded him with an expression of gratitude and elevation to the rank of major-general. (*Library of Congress*)

agrarian states, were able to argue that reciprocity was a good bargain only for the trusts, which would gain a new market and free raw materials at the farmer's expense; yet many Eastern industrialists opposed it too. Democratic votes pushed the bill through Congress, but in the debate, Champ Clark, the new Democratic Speaker, said, 'I am for it because I hope to see the day when the American flag will float over every square foot of the British North American possessions clear to the North Pole.' Clark's words infuriated Canadians, and Sir Wilfrid Laurier, the Canadian Prime Minister, was forced to appeal to his country. Canadian manufacturers, who feared to lose their protected home market, financed the opposition, and in September 1911 the treaty and Sir Wilfrid went down to defeat.

Taft's foreign policy also widened the division between the President and his predecessor. Roosevelt disliked Taft's Latin American policy, and he fiercely denounced the President's proposal for blanket arbitration treaties as 'maudlin folly' and the product of 'sloppy thinking.' Stung by Roosevelt's attack, Taft commented privately: 'The truth is that he believes in war and wishes to be a Napoleon and to die on the battlefield.'

The Campaign of 1912

In the summer of 1910, Theodore Roosevelt, recently returned from his African safari and a triumphal progress through Europe, embarked on a speaking tour in the West which showed that shooting lions and dining with crowned heads had not dulled his fighting edge for reform. His ideas, systematized as the 'New Nationalism,' included not only the old Roosevelt policies of honest government, regulation of big business, and conservation, but a relatively new insistence on social justice. This principle led to vigorous criticism of recent Supreme Court decisions which had nullified social legislation in the states. He urged the country to rely not on the courts but on a Chief Executive who would be 'the steward of the public welfare,' and he boldly asserted the rights of the community over 'lawbreakers of great wealth.' At Osawatomie on 31 August 1910, T.R. stated: 'The man who wrongly holds that every human right is

secondary to his profit must now give way to the advocate of human welfare, who rightly maintains that every man holds his property subject to the general right of the community to regulate its use to whatever degree the public welfare may require it.'

Conservative Republicans shuddered at the 'New Nationalism' and feared a split in the party. Taft was worried. 'I have had a hard time,' he confessed to his old friend. 'I have been conscientiously trying to carry out your policies, but my method of doing so has not worked smoothly.' Although still friendly, the two men were being pulled apart. Insurgents were continually telling Roosevelt that the President had surrendered to the Old Guard, and entreating him to run in 1912. Taft, on the other hand, was surrounded by friends and relatives whose advice resembled that of George III's mother: 'George, be a King!'

Roosevelt had declared in 1904 that 'under no circumstances' would he again be a Presidential candidate. Moreover, Taft was his friend and his own choice. But Roosevelt, who despised Taft's foreign policy and was uneasy about his domestic program, was infuriated when in October 1911 the Taft administration filed an anti-trust suit against U.S. Steel which, by implication, impeached Roosevelt's judgment in sanctioning a special dispensation when he was President. On 21 February 1912, Roosevelt announced, 'My hat is in the ring.' That same day, in an address which opened his campaign, he spoke of big business as 'inevitable and desirable,' but also insisted that the rich man 'holds his wealth subject to the general right of the community to regulate its business use as the public welfare requires,' and urged that the police power of the state be broadened. Further, he advocated not only the initiative and the referendum, but the recall of decisions by state courts. His radicalism alienated thousands of Republican voters, cost him the support of friends like Lodge, and made his nomination by the Republicans extremely improbable.

The contest for the Republican nomination became unseemly and bitter. In the Ohio primary campaign, Taft and Roosevelt called one another Jacobin, apostate, demagogue, and fathead. In the thirteen states which chose their delegates to party

Theodore Roosevelt on the way to the Progressive party convention, 6 August 1912. As his demeanor suggests, the Colonel was in a heroic mood. The leader of a secession from the Republican party, T.R. knew his chances for victory were slim, but he claimed that the only alternative to a triumph for progressivism was 'a general smash up of our civilization,' and he refused to let Taft have the better of him. 'I wish to Heaven I was not in this fight,' the former President wrote to Ambassador Jusserand, 'and I am in it only on the principle, in the long run a sound one, that I would rather take a thrashing than be quiet under such a kicking.' (*Chicago Historical Society*)

conventions through popular primaries, Roosevelt won 278, Taft 46, and La Follette 36 delegates. Roosevelt had the overwhelming support of rank and file Republicans, but the bosses were with Taft. Where delegates were chosen by conventions, the President was almost uniformly successful, and the Southern districts, the Republican rotten boroughs, returned a solid block of Taft delegates who represented little more than the federal office-holders in that region. With the credentials of some 200 delegates in dispute, Roosevelt, who charged that his legitimate majority was being stolen, told his enraptured followers, 'We stand at Armageddon and we battle for the Lord.' When the party organization awarded practically all the contested seats to Taft men, Roosevelt instructed his delegates to take no further part in the proceedings; and Taft was renominated easily.

Roosevelt and his followers at once took steps to found a new party. In August 1912 the first Progressive party convention met at Chicago amid scenes of febrile enthusiasm. The delegates paraded around the convention hall singing 'Onward Christian Soldiers' and

> Follow! Follow!
> We will follow Roosevelt,
> Anywhere! Everywhere,
> We will follow on.

The Progressive party welcomed social workers like Jane Addams, municipal reformers like Harold Ickes of Chicago, as well as moneyed men like George Perkins, known as Secretary of State for the House of Morgan. The new party equivocated on its trust plank, but the rest of the platform, which reflected the social justice aspirations of leaders like Jane Addams, was so radical that Gene Debs declared that the red flag of socialism had been replaced by the red bandannas of the Progressives. The convention nominated Roosevelt by acclamation, and a phrase of the beloved leader, 'I am feeling like a bull moose,' gave the new party an appropriate symbol, beside the Republican elephant and the Democratic donkey.

In the perspective of history the formation of the Progressive party appears to have been a mistake for the reformers. The bolt lost many good men their political careers and ended all chance of liberalizing the Republican party. Roosevelt's error was so contrary to his long-settled principles of party regularity that one naturally asks whether appetite for power was not his moving force. Like the elder Pitt, Roosevelt believed that he, and he alone, could save the country; unlike Pitt, he did not win the opportunity to justify his faith.

The year before Roosevelt entered Harvard and the year after Taft entered Yale, Woodrow Wilson, son and grandson of Scots Presbyterian ministers, came up to Princeton. Wilson was remembered at Whig Hall, Princeton, for having lost an interclub debating contest rather than defend protection against free trade. Before graduating from Harvard, Roosevelt wrote his first book, *The Naval History of the War of 1812*, which sounded the note of preparedness for war upon which his life closed. In his last year at Princeton, Wilson published an article exposing the irresponsibility of congressional government, which he later did so much to remedy. Roosevelt entered public life in 1881; Wilson, after a brief and unprofitable practice of law, took his doctorate at Johns Hopkins, and began a quiet career of teaching and scholarship. In 1890, the year after Roosevelt was appointed to the Civil Service Commission, Wilson became a professor of political science at Princeton; and in 1902, the year after Roosevelt became President of the United States, Wilson was chosen president of Princeton University.

As a scholar, publicist, and leader in education Wilson enjoyed a national reputation; but active politics was considered a closed sphere to professors. However, George Harvey, the arch-conservative editor of *Harper's Weekly*, was attracted by Wilson's views; an anti-Bryan Democrat, Wilson had denounced 'the crude and ignorant minds of the members of the Farmers Alliance,' and deplored the 'passion for regulative legislation.' Harvey's suggestion in 1906 that Wilson was presidential timber was greeted skeptically, but the college president took it to heart. In 1910 the Democrats of New Jersey—an amorphous state, half bedroom to New York and half to Philadelphia, under the control of corporations attracted by the laxity of its laws—thought their unsavory reputation might be sweetened by a scholar. At Harvey's suggestion the bosses nominated Wilson, and the people elected him governor. Within a year Wilson had repudiated the bosses, broken the power of the sinister 'Jim' Smith, and written more progressive legislation into the statute books than had been enacted in the previous half-century. He split with Harvey, but a silent politician from Texas, Colonel Edward M. House, took him up; and Wilson became a leading candidate for the presidential nomination. At the Democratic convention in 1912, Champ Clark of Missouri had a majority of the delegates, but, unable to muster the necessary two-thirds, on the forty-sixth ballot he lost to Wilson.

The presidential election became a three-cornered contest between Taft, Roosevelt, and Wilson; but really between the last two. Roosevelt ran on a more advanced program of social reform, while Wilson opposed both a national child labor law and minimum-wage legislation. Roosevelt believed that big business was inevitable and that it should be regulated. Wilson subscribed rather to the doctrine of Louis Brandeis that bigness was a curse and government had a responsibility to break it down. The solution, as Brandeis saw it, was regulated competition instead of regulated monopoly. While Roosevelt's 'New Nationalism' borrowed from continental experience with a directive state, Wilson's 'New Freedom' derived from British liberalism. 'The history of liberty,' Wilson asserted, 'is the history of the limitation of governmental power.' Roosevelt, with biblical imagery and voice like a shrilling fife, stirred men to wrath, to combat, and to antique virtue; Wilson, serene and confident, lifted men out of themselves by phrases that sang in their hearts, to a vision of a better world.

Wilson polled less than 42 per cent of the vote, but he won an overwhelming victory in the Electoral College. Roosevelt, with 27 per cent, carried six states. Taft, with 23 per cent, took only Utah and Vermont. Nine hundred thousand voted for the Socialist nominee, Eugene Debs. Progressives thought of 1856 and looked toward 1916. The Grand Old Party, as they saw it, had gone the way of the Whigs—killed by a great moral issue it would not face, and another bland Buchanan was in the White House. But the Old Guard neither died nor surrendered. And Woodrow Wilson, instead of playing the part of Buchanan, welded his party into a fit instrument of his great purpose 'to square every process of our national life again with the standards we so proudly set up at the beginning and have always carried at our hearts.'

Wilson and the New Freedom

Woodrow Wilson came to power at a propitious time. The progressive movement was nearing its culmination, and new men in the Democratic party were eager to transform it from a diffuse alliance of rural Southerners and machine bosses into a modern national organization. It was one of those moments in history when the situation called for a particular kind of man, and the man was there. Wilson, who had minimized the importance of the presidency in his *Congressional Government in the United States*, had come to think of the Chief Executive as 'the only national voice in affairs.' A month before his inauguration he wrote that the President 'must be prime minister, and he is the spokesman of the Nation in everything.' And more perhaps than anyone who had ever held the office Wilson understood the force of words as a political weapon. In 1909 he had cried: 'I wish there were some great orator who could go about and make men drunk with this spirit of self-sacrifice . . . whose tongue might every day carry abroad the golden accents of that creative age in which we were born a nation.'

The Democratic party for which he was now the spokesman had undergone little change since Andrew Jackson's time. The elements in it that counted were the emotional and somewhat radical Western wing represented by Bryan; Irish-Americans of the industrial states, who wanted the power and office denied them during the Republican dynasties; a large segment of labor; and the Solid South, including almost every white man in the late Confederacy, and many in the new Southwest—Oklahoma, New Mexico, and Arizona. Tradition, habit, and common suspicion of Big Business and Wall Street held these groups together. Though the Democrats had enough popular appeal to poll a plurality in five of the ten presidential elections since Reconstruction, the party wanted leadership. Cleveland's victories had proved barren, Bryan had thrice failed, and the majority leaders in Congress were elderly and timid. For the task of leadership Wilson proved himself peculiarly equipped. He had inherited a Calvinistic philosophy which placed the halo of moral necessity on expediency, and he had developed an intellectual arrogance which inclined him to rely largely upon his own judgment, while from a prolonged professional study of the science of government he had learned the necessity of executive direction of the modern state.

Portrait of Woodrow Wilson (1856–1924) by Sir William Orpen. (*White House Historical Association*)

Wilson's inaugural address, striking a note of high idealism and couched in words reminiscent of Jefferson's first inaugural, aroused hope and enthusiasm.

We have been proud of our industrial achievements, but we have not hitherto stopped thoughtfully enough to count the human cost of lives snuffed out, of energies over-taxed and broken, the fearful physical and spiritual cost to the men and women and children upon whom the dead weight and burden of it all has fallen pitilessly the years through. The groans and agony of it all had not yet reached our ears, the solemn, moving undertone of our life, coming up out of the mines and factories and out of every home where the struggle had its intimate and familiar seat. . . . The great Government we loved has too often been made use of for private and selfish purposes, and those who used it had forgotten the people.

No administration of modern times has been inaugurated with more passionate eloquence, but Wilson was neither a fighting progressive like La Follette, nor a spokesman for agrarian and labor discontent like Bryan. He was rather a nineteenth-century liberal, suspicious of special interests whether they were of Wall Street or of the Grange or the labor union, and distrustful of the new breed of intellectuals who were calling for government to intervene directly in the economy. 'I don't want a smug lot of experts to sit down behind closed doors in Washington and play Providence to me,' he said. Wilson's beliefs, noted Walter Lippmann, were 'a fusion of Jeffersonian democracy with a kind of British Cobdenism. This meant in practical life a conviction that the world needs not so much to be administered as to be released from control.' Wilson spoke for 'the man on the make,' the risk-taking entrepreneur who asked only a fair chance to gain his fortune. To foster the interests of the small capitalist, the new President offered a three-point program: a lowered tariff to deny the trusts an unfair advantage; a changed banking structure to make credit more available to the small businessman; and trust legislation to prevent big business from squeezing out the small competitor.

Wilson, who had entered politics as an admirer of J. P. Morgan, had become increasingly critical of financial interests which he believed were crushing the independent businessman. Even before he took office, Wilson attempted to build up public support by a blunt attack on Wall Street. If any tycoon dared to frustrate his program, he warned, 'I promise him, not for myself but for my countrymen, a gibbet as high as Haman—not a literal gibbet, because that is not painful after it has been used, but a figurative gibbet, upon which the soul quivers as long as there are persons belonging to the family who can feel ashamed.' Yet however radical his rhetoric, Wilson proposed to do little to disturb vested interests, and his program ignored many of the realities of life in industrial America.

On 8 April 1913, hardly more than a month after he was inaugurated, Wilson made the dramatic move of coming before Congress in person to deliver his message on tariff reform. Not since John Adams had a President appeared before Congress. One Democratic Senator protested: 'I am sorry to see revived the old Federalistic custom of speeches from the throne.... I regret all this cheap and tawdry imitation of English royalty.' But Wilson was determined to seize the initiative in law-making by narrowing the distance between 'the two ends of Pennsylvania Avenue.' A slight thing in itself, this act caught the popular imagination.

On the very day he took office, Wilson had summoned Congress into special session to revise the tariff. It was a dangerous issue; in the preceding twenty years only one tariff revision had not resulted in defeat at the polls. But Wilson did not hesitate. 'The tariff duties must be altered,' he said. 'We must abolish everything that bears even the semblance of privilege, or of any kind of artificial advantage, and put our business men and producers under the stimulation of a constant necessity to be efficient, economical and enterprising.' After a brief debate, the Underwood tariff, as it came to be known, passed the House by a strict party vote. The real struggle, as everyone anticipated, came in the Senate, which prepared to exercise its ancient prerogative of rewriting a House measure. In May Wilson lashed out at the sinister activities of lobbyists for special interests, and through the hot months of a Washington summer, held Congress to its appointed task. He himself set an example of ceaseless vigilance, scrutinizing every section of the measure and appearing with embarrassing frequency at Senate committee rooms. Through such adroit personal leadership, Wilson secured enactment of the measure with almost unanimous Democratic support.

The Underwood tariff was far from a free-trade measure, but it did reverse a tariff policy which had prevailed for fifty years. A London editor called it 'the heaviest blow that has been aimed at the Protective system since the British legislation of Sir Robert Peel.' The act lowered average duties from some 37 per cent to some 27 per cent; more important were reductions in specific schedules and additions to the free list. Duties were decreased on 958 articles, raised on 86, and maintained on 307. Reductions embraced important commodities such as iron and steel, while wool, sugar, coal, and many other products were to enter duty free. To meet the anticipated reduction in customs revenues, Representative Cordell Hull of Tennessee added a provision for a graduated tax on incomes of $4000 and over, ranging from 1 to 6 per cent.

While Congress was still wrestling with the Underwood tariff, Wilson presented a proposal to reorganize the banking system. The need for a thorough overhaul was almost universally recognized. The 'bankers' panic' of 1907 reflected no basic unsoundness in the economic system, but a ruinous shortage of currency and inelasticity of credit; only by hasty importations of gold from abroad and by resort to extra-legal forms of currency was business able to weather the crisis. The final report of a National Monetary Commission, created by Congress, listed no less than seventeen serious defects in the American banking system, among them the concentration of financial power in New York. The extent of that concentration was emphasized by the Pujo Committee of 1912, which revealed that the firm members or directors of two sets of New York banks, controlled by the Morgan and Rockefeller interests, held '341 directorships of 112 corporations having aggregate resources of capitalization of $22,245,000,000.'

If all agreed to the necessity of reform, they disagreed vigorously about what shape it should take. Conservatives wanted a central bank like the old Bank of the United States without its branches, with control of credit in the hands of the bankers, whereas Bryan's followers insisted that control of the new banking system should be exclusively governmental and that the system should be decentralized. In June Wilson appeared before Congress to outline his own program.

We must have a currency, not rigid as now, but readily, elastically responsive to sound credit. . . . And the control of this system of banking and of issue which our new laws are to set up must be public, not private, must be vested in the Government itself, so that the banks may be the instruments, not the masters of business and of individual enterprise and initiative.

Carter Glass was ready with a bill which carried out these general principles, and for six months

Congress wrangled over this administration measure which metropolitan bankers and Western farmers criticized with equal severity. Wilson had little to fear from the opposition of the bankers, but he could not afford to forfeit the support of Bryan and his followers. In the end the provisions of the new law recognized both of Bryan's demands: that there should be no active banker representation on the banking board and that all Federal Reserve currency should be governmental obligations. So disciplined had the party become under Wilson's leadership that not a single Democratic Senator voted against the bill.

The Federal Reserve Act of December 1913 created a new national banking system upon regional lines. The country was divided into twelve districts, each with a Federal Reserve Bank owned by the member banks, which were required to subscribe 6 per cent of their capital. These regional banks acted as agents for their members. All national banks were required to join these regional banks and state banks were permitted to join; within a decade one-third of the banks, representing 70 per cent of the banking resources of the country, were members of the Federal Reserve system. A Federal Reserve Board, consisting of the Secretary of the Treasury, the Comptroller, and six others appointed by the President, supervised the business of the regional banks. The law authorized a new type of currency: Federal Reserve notes secured by short-term commercial paper and backed by a 40 per cent gold reserve. The new system was designed to develop more elastic credit, a sounder distribution of banking facilities, and more effective safeguards against speculation. In time the bankers themselves admitted that the Federal Reserve system had added immeasurably to the financial stability of the country.

The Federal Reserve Act also aimed to provide easier credit for farmers, but the law did little to bring down farm interest rates or ease farm credit. These objects were partially achieved, however, by the Federal Farm Loan Act of May 1916 which created a Federal Farm Loan Board and 12 regional Farm Loan banks authorized to extend loans on farm property. A further step toward better credit facilities for farmers was taken in the Warehouse Act of 1916, which authorized licensed ware-

Marcel Duchamp, 'Nude Descending a Staircase, No. 2.' In 1913 the Association of American Painters and Sculptors sponsored an exhibit at the 69th Regiment Armory in New York City that turned out to be the most momentous event in the history of twentieth-century art in the United States. Nearly 300,000 people in New York, and in other cities when it went on tour, came to see the work not only of Americans like 'the Eight' but of European Post-Impressionists, Fauves, and Cubists, and often went away bewildered. The prominent critic Royal Cortissoz derided 'Ellis Island art,' and at the Art Institute of Chicago students hanged Matisse in effigy. The greatest sensation of the Armory Show was created by Duchamp's *'Nu descendant un escalier.'* The *American Art News* ran a contest challenging its readers to locate the nude, and one observer captioned the picture 'An explosion in a shingle factory.' (*Philadelphia Museum of Art, The Louise and Walter Arensberg Coll.*)

'Tariff Descending Downward.' This clever political cartoon takes advantage of the stir created by Duchamp's 'Nude Descending a Staircase' to depict President Wilson as a 'near-Futurist' artist. Looking on are the sponsors of the tariff bill, Representative Oscar W. Underwood of Alabama and Furnifold M. Simmons of North Carolina. John McCutcheon's cartoon appeared in the Chicago *Tribune* on 3 April 1913; exactly six months to the day later, Congress enacted the tariff revision Wilson sought. (*Library of Congress*)

houses to issue against farm products warehouse receipts which might be used as negotiable paper. Thus were the Populists vindicated a quarter-century after their sub-treasury scheme had been rejected with contempt.

As soon as the tariff and banking reform bills were disposed of, Wilson appeared before Congress to ask for legislation on trusts and monopolies. His address of 20 January 1914 included five recommendations: prohibition of interlocking directorates of corporations, banks, railroads, and public utilities; authority for the Interstate Commerce Commission to regulate the financial operations of railways; explicit definition of the anti-trust laws; creation of a federal interstate trade commission to supervise and guide business; and penalization of individuals, not business, for violations of the anti-trust laws. Congress responded with two bills: the Clayton bill, which prohibited numerous forms of unfair trade practices, and a measure to set up a commission with limited authority. When the Clayton bill was denounced as inadequate, Wilson embraced a proposal from Brandeis to establish a strong regulatory commission, although this was an idea that the New Nationalists had advanced and Wilson opposed in 1912. The Federal Trade Commisssion Act replaced Roosevelt's Bureau of Corporations with a new non-partisan commission. The act outlawed unfair methods of competition and authorized the commission to issue 'cease and desist' orders against any corporation found guilty of violations, and, if this failed, to bring the accused firm into court.

Once Wilson accepted the FTC approach, he lost interest in the Clayton bill, which emerged as a weak law. Senator Jim Reed complained: 'It is a sort of legislative apology to the trusts, delivered hat in hand, and accompanied by assurances that no discourtesy is intended.' The Clayton Act prohibited discriminations in price which might tend to lessen competition or create monopoly and 'tying' agreements limiting the right of purchasers to deal in the products of competing manufacturers. It forbade corporations to acquire stock in competing concerns, and outlawed interlocking directorates in large corporations and banks. In keeping with the President's recommendation, officers of corporations were made personally responsible for violations of the law.

Wilson, who opposed grants of special privilege to any group, set himself stiffly against a demand to exempt unions and farm organizations from anti-trust prosecutions. Faced by a party revolt, he agreed only to a provision that such organizations were not, per se, in restraint of trade. Unions were exempted from the terms of the act as long as they sought legitimate objectives, and the use of the injunction in labor disputes 'unless necessary to prevent irreparable injury to property . . . for which there is no adequate remedy at law' was explicitly forbidden. Samuel Gompers hailed

these provisions as 'labor's charter of freedom,' but the act proved to be a good deal less than that.

'With this legislation,' said Wilson optimistically, 'there is clear and sufficient law to check and destroy the noxious growth [of monopoly] in its infancy.' But the courts reserved to themselves the right to determine what constituted 'unfair methods of competition' just as they reserved the right to interpret the phrase 'irreparable injury to property,' and in the war and postwar years judicial rulings became increasingly conservative. The effort to enforce the provision making directors responsible for corporation malpractices broke down when the government failed to prove its case against the directors of the New Haven Railroad. During the war the Clayton Act was tacitly suspended, and in the postwar period of Republican ascendancy the Federal Trade Commission, by encouraging the formulation of codes of trade practices, entered into something suspiciously like an alliance with the trusts. Two decades after the enactment of the Wilsonian anti-trust legislation, the trusts were as powerful as ever. Perhaps all this merely demonstrates the validity of Thurman Arnold's theory that the function of anti-trust agitation and legislation is purely ceremonial— that it provides us the satisfaction of declaiming against the 'evil' part of a 'necessary evil' while retaining what is necessary about it. Still, if the legislation did not curb monopolies, it may well have imposed on them a pattern of good behavior.

In pushing through his three-point program, Wilson had demonstrated that he was a great leader: of his party, of Congress, of the nation. He had held the 63rd Congress in Washington for over a year and a half, the longest session in history, and he had kept relentless pressure on its members. The *New York Times* commented: 'President Cleveland said he had a Congress on his hands, but this Congress has a President on its back, driving it pitilessly. . . . Never were Congressmen driven so, not even in the days of the "big stick."' Above all, Wilson had proven what many reasonable men had long doubted—that the Democratic party could govern.

Yet by the autumn of 1914 Wilson was content to call a halt to further reforms. As spokesman for the Democratic party's Jeffersonian equal rights tradition, he rejected three types of legislation: social welfare innovations that sought to hurdle constitutional barriers; proposals aimed at benefiting special interests, including workers; and measures which reflected the New Nationalist approach of reconciling business and government. He blocked a bill to provide long-term rural credits, refused to support a woman's suffrage amendment, opposed child labor legislation, and in March 1915 almost vetoed the La Follette Seamen's bill. Until alarmed by the storm of liberal disapproval, he permitted members of his cabinet to practice racial discrimination. For all his rhetoric against big business, his appointments to government agencies were so conservative that one Senator said of his selections for the Federal Reserve Board that they looked as though they had been chosen by the head of the National City Bank.

Wilson might have continued his cautious drift to the right had it not been for the collapse of the Progressive party, which carried the threat that Roosevelt's ardent following might move back into the Republican fold. Having won less than 42 per cent of the vote in 1912, Wilson was doomed to defeat in 1916 if a reunited Republican party polled its full strength. To attract voters of a progressive inclination, Wilson decided to turn to the left. Moreover, just as his views in New Jersey had shifted, Wilson's convictions were no doubt changing as the result of his White House experience. He began the transformation with the appointment in January 1916 of the distinguished reformer, Louis D. Brandeis, to the Supreme Court, a selection that was confirmed despite an appalling outburst of anti-Semitism. In rapid succession he reversed himself to support social welfare measures, including a law excluding the products of child labor from interstate commerce and a Workmen's Compensation Act for federal employees. He gave his blessing to special interest legislation for farmers and workers, including the Rural Credits Act, which provided long-term farm loans, and the Adamson Act, imposing an eight-hour day on all interstate railways. The New Nationalist program of business-government cooperation won a partial victory with the creation of a tariff commission and the exemption of exporters from the anti-trust laws.

In four years Wilson had reasserted presidential leadership, converted a state-rights party to enlightened nationalism, and made clear that progressivism transcended party lines. If Wilson had not accepted the idea that the national government would play a directing role in the economy, or the conception of a managerial class ruling in the national interest, he could nonetheless boast that the Democrats had 'come very near to carrying out the platform of the Progressive Party' as well as their own.

28

Wilsonian Diplomacy
and World War I

*

1913–1920

Moralistic Diplomacy

Wilson had not mentioned foreign affairs in his inaugural address; yet his first administration was concerned largely, his second almost exclusively, with international relations. He approached the world with the same high-mindedness with which he advanced the New Freedom, and in his two terms he succeeded in moderating American imperialism in China, the Philippines, and the Caribbean, in achieving a less vindictive peace after World War I than many wanted, and in launching an association of nations. Yet he would also learn that good intentions were not always enough. To ensure the independence of Mexico, he would intervene in that country's affairs. To achieve a peaceful world, he would lead his country into war. And, in the end, his hopes for a new world order, in which the United States would play an active role, would be shattered.

In principle and to a lesser extent in practice, Wilson reversed much of the foreign policy of his predecessors. The first hint of that reversal was a statement in March 1913 withdrawing support from the proposed bankers' loan to China as in-

compatible with Chinese sovereignty. This was widely interpreted as a formal repudiation of 'dollar diplomacy.' At the same time Secretary Bryan launched a program of conciliation treaties in whose success he had a touching faith. Altogether Bryan concluded thirty agreements submitting all disputes—including those involving questions of 'national honor'—to arbitration, and providing a 'cooling-off' period of one year before resort to arms; of the major powers only Germany refused to sign.

Bryan had long favored independence for the Philippines, and in 1914 a Bryan follower, Representative Jones of Virginia, introduced a bill granting immediate self-government to the Filipinos and promising complete independence in the near future. Under pressure from the War Department, which was alive to the strategic importance of the Philippines, and from Catholics who feared confiscation of church property, Wilson maneuvered for a less drastic measure, which would not stipulate a specific time-limit on American control. The Jones Act, passed in 1916, formally pledged the United States to withdraw from the Philippines 'as soon as a stable government can be established therein,' and inaugurated far-reaching political and administrative reforms, including a popularly elected legislature. At the same time Governor-General Harrison filled the civil service with native Filipinos and encouraged the Philippine government to establish state-controlled railroads, banks, mines, and industries. Under these auspices the Filipinos made such progress that President Wilson, in his last annual message, reminded Congress that the time had come to fulfill the promise of the Jones Act. But the incoming Republican administration had no sympathy with such a program, and reversed practically all of Harrison's enlightened policies. Not until 1934 did Congress finally provide for Philippine independence; not until 1946 did the law take effect.

Wilson showed even more high-mindedness in his reaction to two Panama Canal problems that he had inherited. The first was the long-standing dispute with Colombia, which still bitterly resented the part that President Roosevelt had played in detaching Panama. In 1914 Bryan negotiated a treaty with Colombia which expressed 'sincere regret' for whatever injury the United States might have inflicted, paid an indemnity of $25 million, and granted Colombia free use of the Panama Canal. That a powerful nation should apologize to a weak one was something new in international relations. To Roosevelt it was nothing less than an outrage, and his friend Senator Henry Cabot Lodge led a successful fight against ratification of the treaty, thus delaying for seven years the restoration of good relations with Colombia and getting in some practice for his more ambitious battle against the Versailles treaty a few years later. The second dispute grew out of the special exemption which Congress had granted American coastwise shipping from paying tolls on the canal. The British protested this as a violation of earlier treaty agreements. Convinced that the British were right, and anxious to have British support in Mexico, Wilson persuaded Congress to repeal the exemption.

Within two weeks of his inauguration Wilson announced that one of the chief objects of his administration would be to cultivate the friendship of Latin America. A few months later, he promised that the United States would 'never

again seek one additional foot of territory by conquest.' Yet despite such sincere protestations of altruism, Wilson and Bryan continued many of the Caribbean policies of Roosevelt and Taft. Marines remained in Nicaragua, and in 1914 Bryan negotiated a treaty which so seriously infringed on Nicaraguan sovereignty that it was denounced by the Central American Court of Justice. In Santo Domingo Bryan authorized 'an enlargement of the sphere of American influence beyond what we have before exercised'; and as minister to that hapless republic he sent an ex-pugilist named James Sullivan who introduced the worst Tammany methods into Dominican politics, exploited his office for personal profit, and in the end helped precipitate a revolution. In 1916 Wilson ordered a military occupation of the Dominican Republic, which lasted for eight years. A year earlier, after civil strife had taken over 2000 lives, the United States Marine Corps occupied Haiti. Under the terms of the treaty the Wilson administration dictated to the Haitians, American control was continued until 1930.

Elsewhere in the Caribbean, relations were less troubled. Despite some mistrust, Wilson avoided any critical difficulty in Cuba. Puerto Rico, like Cuba, was governed for a time by the United States military, but in 1900 the Foraker Act had established civil government of the old crown colony type: an elective assembly, with an executive council appointed by the President acting as an upper house. This, too, was contrary to the Wilsonian philosophy, and in 1917 Congress enacted a law granting American citizenship to the inhabitants of the island, and a semi-responsible government. Not until 1947 were the islanders permitted to elect their own Governor, but in 1952 the island achieved Commonwealth status, whatever that term might mean in American constitutional law. Intervention in Nicaragua, Santo Domingo, and Haiti, then, were balanced, in a sense, by a more enlightened policy toward Cuba and Puerto Rico.

Mexico presented the real test of Wilson's policy toward Latin America. In 1911 a revolution had overthrown Porforio Díaz, dictator of Mexico for thirty-five years, during which Indian lands had been seized, peons exploited, and the masses

Bluejackets with rifles picking off snipers, Vera Cruz, 1914. Wilson, who thought that the Mexicans would welcome the American forces as liberators, was shocked at the bloodshed. When the President met with reporters, he seemed to Senator Lodge to be 'pale, parchmenty,' and 'positively shaken,' and Wilson told Admiral Grayson, 'The thought haunts me that it was I who ordered those young men to their deaths.' (*Library of Congress*)

reduced to desperation. The revolution was conducted by a small doctrinaire middle class under Francisco I. Madero, but supported by the peons in the hope of recovering their lands. Installed as constitutional President in 1911, Madero neither kept order nor satisfied the aspirations of the landless. A counter-revolution of the landowners, backed by foreign investors, displaced him by assassination in February 1913, and installed Victoriano Huerta as President. Although unable to exert his authority over the greater part of the country, which was fast falling into anarchy, Huerta was promptly recognized by Great Britain and most of the Powers. Strong pressure on President Wilson to do the same was exerted by the American ambassador and by American business

interests which owned 78 per cent of the mines, 72 per cent of the smelters, 58 per cent of the oil, 68 per cent of the rubber plantations, and some two-thirds of the railroads of Mexico.

President Wilson refused to be moved by the importunities of business, for he would not recognize a government that did not rest upon the consent of the governed. Such a policy, importing moral considerations into the realm of international law, departed from the traditional practices of the United States as well as of other nations. The easier course would have been to accord the Huerta government *de facto* recognition, and leave to the Mexicans the solution of their problems of constitutional law and democracy. Wilson's policy was fraught with peril, for it placed upon the United States the responsibility of deciding which government was moral, and there was no assurance that the decision would be disinterested. Furthermore in the event that Huerta did not back down, Wilson faced the awkward alternatives of some kind of intervention or of a serious loss of prestige.

Wilson moved to a showdown with Huerta. In February 1914 he permitted American arms to go to the leader of the Constitutional forces, Venustiano Carranza. But the landed aristocracy and the Catholic Church rallied to Huerta, and the situation seemed as unsolvable as ever. At this point the zeal of a Mexican colonel made history. When the crew of an American warship landed, without permission, at Tampico, they were arrested. The Mexican commander instantly apologized and returned the men, but Admiral Mayo demanded not only an apology but a salute to the American flag, and Wilson, eagerly looking for an excuse to intervene, backed him up. On 21 April American marines landed at Vera Cruz, which they took with slight loss to themselves but at the cost of several hundred Mexican casualties. However, war with Mexico did not begin, partly because Wilson realized that his legal case was ridiculous, since he was demanding acknowledgment from a government he did not recognize, and his moral case far from strong, but chiefly because he wished above all to help the people of Mexico find themselves.

At this acute juncture, Wilson was rescued by a proposal from Argentina, Brazil, and Chile for a joint mediation, an offer the President gladly accepted, especially as he was confident that he could control the proceedings. A conference with these 'A.B.C.' powers at Niagara Falls in May 1914— the first of its kind in the history of the Americas—averted war and proposed a new constitutional government for Mexico. Huerta stood out stiffly against the terms of the mediation, but he was forced out of office, and in August, Carranza, leader of the Constitutional party, became President. Unhappily, there was to be no peace for stricken Mexico. No sooner had Carranza won Mexico City than his ablest lieutenant Francisco ('Pancho') Villa, raised the standard of revolt. With incomparable ineptitude the Wilson admin-

istration decided to back Villa, mistakenly supposing him more tractable than Carranza. But when Carranza shattered the Villa forces, the United States had no alternative save to accord him recognition.

During the five years that followed there were occasional outbreaks of peace in Mexico. The main trouble was that the underlying force of the revolution—the land hunger of the peasants— was unable to find a leader determined to adopt fundamental reforms. Meantime, Wilson adopted a policy of 'watchful waiting,' while endeavoring, without much success, to create a Pan-American machinery for dealing with a situation that was taking a heavy toll of the lives and property of both American civilians in Mexico and of Mexicans. Defeated by Carranza and abandoned by the United States, Villa resorted to banditry. Early in 1916, he took Americans from a train in Mexico and murdered them, then crossed the border in raids that, in Columbus, New Mexico, left nineteen Americans dead. Wilson, in retaliation, sent an expeditionary force under General John Pershing that pursued Villa deep into the interior of Mexico. It failed to capture him, and in violating Mexican soil, outraged Carranza and aroused the suspicion of much of Latin America. Yet, although Wilson had, as his biographer Arthur Link observes, 'embittered Mexican-American relations, for many years to come,' he had also,

almost alone, stood off Europe during the days of the Huertista tyranny, withstood the powerful forces in the United States that sought the undoing of the Revolution, and refused to go to war at a time when it might have insured his re-election.

In Latin America, Wilson had pursued a policy of evangelical diplomacy without engaging the nation in a major war; in Europe, the difficulties in such a course were more numerous, the risks infinitely more grave.

The Struggle for Neutral Rights

On 28 June 1914 a shot was fired that closed an era of progress, liberalism, and democracy and inaugurated an age of warfare, destruction, revolutionary upheavals, and dictatorships, which is not yet ended. Archduke Franz Ferdinand, heir to the throne of Austria-Hungary, was assassinated at Sarajevo in the province of Bosnia. A month later Austria declared war on Serbia, and by early August all of the great powers of Europe were embroiled in what has come to be known as the First World War. President Wilson at once proclaimed the neutrality of the United States, and in 1914 there was an almost universal determination on the part of the American people to stay out of the European conflict, which did not appear to involve any American interests.

Nonetheless, from the very outset, American public opinion predominantly favored the Allies. It matters little how much this was due to Allied propaganda, since propaganda can be effective only on receptive minds. The majority of Americans were English-speaking, and regarded some part of the British Empire as their mother country, with whom war would have seemed immoral. Ties of language and literature, law and custom, as well as those of a more personal character, bound America to the British in a hundred ways. With France our relations were more sentimental than intimate, but the tradition of Franco-American friendship went back to the Revolution. With Germany and her allies, on the other hand, American relations were amicable but not cordial. To many Americans the posturings and saber-rattlings of William II were ridiculous when they were not odious. Suspicion was intensified by Germany's cynical violation of Belgian neutrality. Wilson himself illustrated these attitudes. Of mixed Scots and English ancestry, steeped in English literature and history, and an admirer of British political institutions, he was willing to endure almost any provocation rather than risk war with England. Though Wilson tried to be neutral, Bryan was right in protesting that the President was quicker to hold Germany than England to 'strict accountability' for violations of neutral rights.

The United States also developed an economic stake in the war. Even before 1914 a large part of American trade had been with the Allied nations, and when the Allies blockaded the Central Powers, United States trade with Germany became negligible, while trade with Great Britain and France

'Portrait of a German Officer,' 1914. This painting by Marsden Hartley (1877–1943) is suggestive of what many associated with Prussian militarism, including the emblem of the Iron Cross. Hartley, who had his first one-man show at Stieglitz's '291' gallery in 1909, painted it while he was living in Berlin, where he exhibited with the *Blaue Reiter* group at the First Autumn Salon in 1912. The initials in the lower left corner are those of a German friend. (*Metropolitan Museum of Art, Alfred Stieglitz Collection, 1949*)

mounted impressively. This increase in foreign trade, in full swing by the middle of 1915, rescued the United States from a commercial depression that had lasted a year. Within a year after the outbreak of war the whole fabric of American economic life was so closely interwoven with the economy of the Allies that any rupture would have been ruinous. It was the realization of this, in addition to sympathy for the Allies, that persuaded Wilson and his cabinet to reject an embargo on munitions of war.

Countenanced by international law, the munitions trade was theoretically open to all belligerents. In fact, Allied sea power prevented the Central Powers from procuring American munitions; the Allies got all they wanted; and American munitions exports increased in value from some $40 million in 1914 to $1290 million in 1916, and total trade to the Allies from $825 million to $3214 million. Germany never officially denied the legality of this trade, but protested bitterly that its one-sided nature violated the spirit of neutrality. To the suggestion that the United States place an embargo upon munitions exports, Washington replied that it could not change the rules of neutrality to the advantage of one belligerent while the war was in progress. As a technical defense this was sound; but both belligerents were changing the rules of war, and it was within the rights of Congress to stiffen neutrality requirements as the Dutch had done, by treating armed merchantmen as warships and interning them. But neither Congress nor most of the nation wished to do so.

Without credit the belligerents could not buy American goods. At the beginning of the war the United States was a debtor nation: this situation was promptly reversed as foreign investors dumped their securities on the American market. Soon the Allies found it advisable to finance their purchases in the United States through loans floated in Wall Street, a scheme Bryan opposed. 'Money,' he said, 'is the worst of all contrabands because it commands everything else.' In August 1914 the State Department announced that 'in the judgment of this Government, loans by American bankers to any foreign nation which is at war are inconsistent with the true spirit of neutrality.' Yet within a month this position was modified to permit bank credits to belligerents; by the late summer of 1915 Bryan was out of the cabinet; and in September 1915 the State Department withdrew altogether its opposition to loans. By the time the United States entered the war, over $2 billion had been lent by the American public to the Allied governments, as opposed to only $27 million to the Central Powers.

Though America's economic stake in an Allied victory no doubt inclined some people toward war, it was not the crucial consideration. The financial community as a whole preferred American neutrality, which afforded Wall Street all the profits of war without the corresponding sacrifices and taxation. Furthermore, most of the loans were secured by pledged collateral which would be unaffected by the outcome of the war. To be sure, the Wilson administration saw Germany as a threat to a stable world order in which American interests, including those of American capital, would thrive. But it was neither trade, nor munitions, nor loans, nor propaganda that persuaded the administration of the necessity of war; it was the German submarine policy.

From the beginning the United States waged a losing struggle to preserve her rights as a neutral. There were two fundamental difficulties: lack of international law to deal with unforeseen circumstances, and the immense stakes and savage fighting which made the belligerents ready to flout law or morality if that was necessary for their survival. America's first and most prolonged dispute came with Great Britain. Promptly upon the outbreak of the war, Britain instituted a new type of blockade that extended considerably the contraband list; expanded the 'continuous voyage' doctrine to justify confiscating cargoes of enemy destination in neutral ships, even when billed for neutral ports; and declared all of the North Sea and the English Channel 'military areas.' American direct trade with the Central Powers was entirely, and indirect trade largely, cut off. In addition, the Allies employed such questionable devices as rationing trade to neutrals and blacklisting firms suspected of trading with the Central Powers.

Against these palpable violations of its neutral

rights, the United States protested in vain. At any time after the middle of 1915 a real threat of an American embargo on munitions would probably have brought the Allies to heel. Their own factories were unable to supply the enormous demand of their armies for high explosives; the cutting off of supplies from America would have lost them the war. But Wilson and the State Department had no intention of taking a stand for neutral rights which, if persisted in, might land America in war on the side of autocracy, as had happened in 1812. So they chose the course of protest and persuasion in order to keep the record clear while avoiding the catastrophe of war. As a consequence, until the beginning of 1917, the British and French continued to violate neutral rights, while the State Department filed protests and the Germans fumed.

Faced with economic strangulation, Germany struck back with the only weapons at its disposal: mines and submarines. As early as August 1914 it began to mine the North Sea and the Irish Sea, and on 4 February 1915 it announced that all the waters around the British Isles constituted a war zone in which Allied vessels would be destroyed and warned neutral ships to keep out in order to preclude accidental attacks, which seemed highly likely. That the sinking of unarmed neutral ships was a clear violation of existing international law, Germany did not deny; but it insisted that its policy was justified by the equally lawless British blockade.

Wilson and most Americans distinguished between British and German violations of neutral rights. As Mr. Asquith said, 'Let the neutrals complain about our blockade and other measures taken as much as they may, the fact remains that no neutral national has ever lost his life as the result of it.' (To be sure, if the United States had insisted on full freedom of the seas, American lives might well have been lost to British mines in the North Sea.) But the U-boat warfare took a toll of 209 American lives on the high seas—twenty-eight of them on American ships. Damages to property entailed by Allied violations of American rights could be settled after the war; loss of lives could never be adequately indemnified.

Alarmed at the threat of submarine warfare,

Wilson informed the German government on 10 February 1915 that 'the United States would be constrained to hold the Imperial German Government to a strict accountability' for 'property endangered or lives lost.' Thereby the Wilson administration took the stand that must inevitably lead to war, unless either the United States or Germany backed down. Soon came a test of the meaning of 'strict accountability.' On 28 March 1915 an American citizen went down on a British ship; on 29 April a U.S. merchant vessel was attacked by a German airplane; and on 1 May an American tanker was torpedoed. Germany offered to make reparations for an 'unfortunate accident' but refused to abandon submarine warfare. Matters came to a head when on 7 May the Cunard liner *Lusitania* was torpedoed off the coast of Ireland with a loss of over 1100 lives, including 128 American citizens. Germany justified the sinking as one of the hazards of war: the *Lusitania* was a 'semiwarship' carrying munitions and troops, and passengers had been duly warned. Yet the sinking violated international law as it then stood, and it was a piece of criminal folly as well. Nothing except the invasion of Belgium did so much to inflame American sentiment against Germany. Leaders like Theodore Roosevelt clamored for war.

But the country was not yet mentally prepared for war, and Wilson refused to be stampeded. On 13 May he demanded that Berlin disavow the sinking of the *Lusitania*, 'make reparation so far as reparation is possible for injuries that are without measure, and take immediate steps to prevent the recurrence of anything so obviously subversive of the principles of warfare.' Germany, persuaded that Wilson was playing to the gallery, tried to drag out the issue by a series of technical objections. Impatient of procrastination, Wilson sent, on 9 June, a second peremptory note insisting upon a formal disavowal of the outrage.

Bryan, who felt that this protest was perilously close to an ultimatum, resigned from the cabinet rather than sign the note. His own solution was to renounce responsibility for the lives of Americans who chose passage on belligerent ships. 'Germany,' he said, 'has a right to prevent contraband from going to the Allies, and a ship carrying con-

The *Lusitania* tragedy, 1915. This was one of a series of cartoons by William A. Rogers of the New York *Herald,* who taunted Wilson with being too unwilling to go to war against Germany. For his efforts, Rogers received the French Legion of Honor. (*Library of Congress*)

traband should not rely upon passengers to protect her from attack—it would be like putting women and children in front of an army.' (Subsequently, this plausible argument was embodied in the Gore-McLemore Resolutions of 1916 refusing passports to American citizens who purposed to travel on the armed ships of belligerents. Wilson moved promptly to defeat the resolutions. 'Once accept a single abatement of right,' he wrote to Senator Stone, 'and many other humiliations would certainly follow, and the whole fine fabric of international law might crumble under our hands piece by piece.' As a result of executive pressure, the resolutions were defeated, and the 'whole fine fabric of international law' was saved—for the moment.)

Despite Bryan's misgivings, Wilson persisted in taking a stern line with the Germans, for he regarded the U-boat campaign as intolerable. On 19 August 1915, before the *Lusitania* controversy had been settled, the English liner *Arabic* was torpedoed with the loss of two American lives. A diplomatic rupture seemed inescapable, but Germany pledged that in the future 'liners will not be sunk by our submarines without warning and without safety of the lives of non-combatants,' and the crisis passed.

For six months American relations with Germany were undisturbed by any new U-boat sinkings, but this peaceful interlude was rudely shattered when in February 1916 the German government announced a renewal of submarine warfare on armed merchant vessels. On 24 March the unarmed channel steamer *Sussex* was torpedoed without warning. Outraged at this violation of the pledge which had been given after the *Arabic* affair, Wilson warned Germany that unless she immediately abandoned submarine warfare against freight and passenger vessels the United States would break off diplomatic relations. Faced with this threat, Berlin capitulated, promising, on 4 May, that henceforth no more merchant vessels would be sunk without warning, provided the United States held England also to 'strict accountability.' For the next nine months American relations with Germany were less disturbed than at any time since the *Lusitania* tragedy, and, in fact, during the summer and fall of 1916 the United States had sharper differences with England than with Germany.

The Coming of War

Despite this apparent settlement of the U-boat controversy, President Wilson became more and more persuaded that the only way in which the United States could avoid war was to end the war. So eager was Wilson to achieve peace that he went to the somewhat inconsistent extreme of suggesting he might fight for it. In February 1916 Lord Grey, after a series of conferences with the ubiquitous Colonel House, was able to assure his government that 'President Wilson was ready . . . to propose that a Conference should be summoned to put an end to the war. Should the Allies accept this proposal, and should Germany refuse it, the United States would probably leave the Conagainst Germany. . . . If such a Conference met, it would secure peace on terms not unfavorable to the Allies; and if it failed to secure peace, the United States would probably leave the Conference as a belligerent on the side of the Allies, if Germany was unreasonable.' But Grey did not take these overtures seriously; the British did not want to negotiate at a time when Germany held the upper hand, and like the French and Germans they wanted the spoils of an eventual victory.

Profoundly discouraged, Wilson turned early in 1916 toward a program of military preparedness, in part from conviction, in part from political expediency. A presidential campaign was in the offing, and the Democrats could not afford to permit their Republican opponents to capitalize on the popular issue of national defense. During the summer of 1916, the administration urged through Congress a series of measures strengthening military and naval forces. The National Defense Act enlarged the regular army, integrated the national guard into the National Defense system, and provided for an officers' reserve corps; the Naval Appropriation Act authorized the construction of new battleships and cruisers. To lessen the dependency on belligerent or Scandinavian merchantmen to carry exports, the United States Shipping Board Act appropriated $50 million for the purchase or construction of merchant ships. To co-ordinate industries and resources, Congress created a Council for National Defense.

Having thus made appropriate gestures toward the more militant elements, the President embarked upon a campaign for re-election under the slogan, 'He kept us out of war.' With the Republicans and the Progressives reunited behind Supreme Court Justice Charles Evans Hughes, all the portents indicated a Republican victory, but Hughes proved a disappointing candidate; Wilson's reforms were not forgotten; and hundreds of

'Berlin's Candidate.' This partisan cartoon by Rollin Kirby in the Democratic New York *World* shows the Kaiser, using 'hyphen paste,' posting a picture of the Republican candidate, Charles Evans Hughes. At a time when both parties were aware that German-Americans, Irish-Americans, and other groups designated with hyphens might determine the outcome of the 1916 election, publicists frequently charged their opponents with catering to the 'hyphenate' vote. During his years on the *World* (1913–21) Kirby was America's leading cartoonist and the recipient of three Pulitzer Prizes.

thousands of Socialists, more loyal to peace than to party, gave their votes to the candidate who had kept America out of war. By forging a new alliance of the South and West, Wilson overcame the massed strength of the reunited Republican party. But the future of this coalition rested on a precarious supposition: that the President could continue to keep the country out of war.

As soon as his re-election was assured, Wilson determined to renew his overture for a negotiated peace, but without success. Faced with intransigence on the part of the belligerents, and convinced that the time had come when the United States must cooperate in securing and maintaining world peace, Wilson, in a memorable speech on 22 January 1917, formulated the conditions upon which such co-operation might be extended. Those conditions, anticipating the subsequent 'Fourteen Points,' included government by the consent of the governed, freedom of the seas, limitation of armaments, and a League to enforce peace. Fundamental to all of these principles was the requirement that the settlement must be a 'peace without victory,' an appeal that fell upon

deaf ears. Increasingly, Wilson came to feel that only if America was a belligerent would he be able to win attention for his ideas at the peace table.

Even before Wilson made his 'peace without victory' speech, Berlin had made a decision that would plunge America into war. The Germans decided to embark upon unrestricted submarine warfare, knowing full well this might bring the United States into the war. Wilson promptly severed diplomatic relations, and though he still hoped that Germany would not commit the supreme folly of aggressive acts against the United States, the nation prepared for war. Wilson himself took the first step in this direction by calling upon Congress for authority to arm American merchant vessels. A Senate filibuster, led by La Follette and what Wilson described as 'a little group of willful men,' prevented congressional action until the adjournment of 4 March, when the President discovered a piracy statute of 1819 that authorized him to act. But events moved so rapidly that this controversy was soon irrelevant. Late in February the British secret service gave Washington a copy of the 'Zimmermann note' in which the German government proposed that, if the United States declared war, Mexico conclude an offensive alliance with Germany and Japan; Mexico to have Texas, New Mexico, and Arizona for its share of the loot. This note, released to the press on 1 March, immensely strengthened the popular demand for war. On the 17th came news that a revolution in Russia had overthrown the Tsar and established a provisional republican government; the last taint of autocracy in the Allied cause disappeared. When, also during March, German submarines torpedoed five American merchant vessels, Wilson decided that Germany was warring upon the United States.

So on 2 April 1917, the President appeared before Congress and read his message asking for a declaration of war:

It is a fearful thing to lead this great peaceful people into war, into the most terrible and disastrous of all wars, civilization itself seeming to be in the balance. But the right is more precious than peace, and we shall fight for the things which we have always carried nearest our hearts,—for democracy, for the right of those who submit to authority to have a voice in their own Government, for the rights and liberties of small nations, for a universal dominion of right by such a concert of free peoples as shall bring peace and safety to all nations and make the world itself at last free. To such a task we can dedicate our lives and our fortunes, everything that we are and everything that we have, with the pride of those who know that the day has come when America is privileged to spend her blood and her might for the principles that gave her birth and happiness and the peace which she has treasured. God helping her, she can do no other.

In the small hours of Good Friday morning, 6 April 1917, Congress passed a joint resolution declaring war on the German Empire.

Industrial and Financial Mobilization

'It is not an army that we must shape and train for war,' said President Wilson, 'it is a nation.' At a time when German submarine warfare was succeeding beyond all expectations and the Allies were almost at the end of their tether, the United States not only had to raise an army but provide clothing, arms, ammunition and explosives, build

a 'bridge' across the Atlantic, set up dockage facilities and arrange transportation in France, string thousands of miles of telephone wires, create a vast medical and nursing corps, and construct hundreds of hospitals in the United States and overseas. No task of similar magnitude had ever been attempted before by this country.

Spurred by necessity, Congress conferred upon the President extensive powers to commandeer essential industries and mines, requisition supplies, control distribution, fix prices, and take over and operate the entire system of transportation and communication. The President in turn delegated these powers to a series of boards, under the Council for National Defense. These boards mobilized America's industrial, agricultural, and even intellectual resources for war purposes, and gave the country an experience in government planning that went far beyond anything the pre-war reformers had contemplated.

To mobilize the nation's industrial resources, the Council set up a War Industries Board in the summer of 1917, but not until the economy verged on collapse did the WIB get the sweeping powers it needed. In March 1918 Wilson made a Wall Street broker, Bernard Baruch, virtual economic dictator. Under Baruch, the board regulated all existing industries that produced war materials, developed new industries, enforced efficiency, fixed prices, determined priorities of production and delivery, and managed all war purchase for the United States and the Allies. The production of some 30,000 articles came under minute supervision. Baby carriages were standardized, and traveling salesmen were limited to two trunks. It was such a regimentation of the economy as had never before been known, and it later served as a model for the New Deal mobilization of 1933.

The United States Shipping Board Act of 1916 had already called into existence an organization to cope with the task of providing ships to replace the vessels which the submarines were destroying at the rate of over half a million tons monthly. In April 1917 Congress authorized the creation of a subsidiary of the Shipping Board, the Emergency Fleet Corporation, to build ships. This operation moved at a snail's pace; the first vessel from the

PROVIDE THE SINEWS OF WAR
BUY LIBERTY BONDS

Liberty bond poster, 1918, by Joseph Pennell. After studying briefly under Eakins, Pennell (1857–1926) became an expatriate, living much of his life in London, where he moved in the circles of Whistler and the pre-Raphaelites. When World War I broke out, Pennell, an outstanding etcher, made lithographs of British munitions-workers which the War Ministry sponsored, and was invited by the French government in the spring of 1917 to make drawings for them. But the first-hand experience of the Western front unnerved him. Pennell fled to the United States, where he regained his emotional stability by contributing more than 100 posters to the American cause and by serving as vice-chairman of a division of the Creel Committee. (*Library of Congress*)

enormous shipyard at Hog Island in the Delaware river was not delivered until after the armistice. But by seizing interned German ships, commandeering or buying neutral vessels, taking over all private shipping, and by a modest amount of new construction, the Shipping Board succeeded in increasing the available tonnage from one million to ten million and overcoming the submarine danger.

The administration also had to reorganize transport within the United States, for under the impact of war orders and troop movements the railroad system broke down. In December 1917 the government took it over, and proceeded to operate the railroads as a unified system, guaranteeing adequate compensation to the owners. Secretary of the Treasury William G. McAdoo resigned to become Director-General of the railroads. By consolidating terminal facilities, standardizing equipment, shutting down little-used lines, spending millions on sorely needed improvements, discouraging passenger traffic, and coordinating freight traffic, he succeeded in bringing the railroads to a peak of effectiveness heretofore unknown. But this experiment cost the government $714 million. During the war the government also took over other agencies of transportation and communication, including warehouses and telephone, telegraph, and cable lines.

The Food Administration really brought the war home to the American people. Under Herbert Hoover it displayed extraordinary ingenuity in stepping up production and decreasing consumption of food so that the Allies might have enough. Hoover fixed the price of wheat, established a grain corporation to buy and sell it, organized the supply and purchase of meat, and bought the entire Cuban and American sugar crop and resold it. A systematic campaign persuaded the American people to observe 'Wheatless Mondays,' 'Meatless Tuesdays,' and 'Porkless Thursdays.' As a result of 'Hooverizing,' the United States was able to export in 1918 approximately three times the normal amounts of breadstuffs, meats, and sugar.

The war spawned a great many other agencies. A fuel administration, under the direction of Harry A. Garfield, president of Williams College, introduced daylight saving and 'Fuelless Mondays,' banned electric displays, and closed down non-essential plants in order to conserve coal. A war trade board licensed exports and imports and blacklisted firms suspected of trading with the enemy. A war finance corporation supervised all security issues of $100,000 or over and in addition was empowered to underwrite loans to war industries.

The war produced unprecedented changes in the government's relationship to labor unions. A War Labor Policies Board under Felix Frankfurter standardized wages and hours and for the first time gave the government a national labor policy. A newly created United States Employment Service placed nearly four million workers in vital war jobs. But the most important new agency was the War Labor Board, headed by former President Taft and the brilliant labor lawyer, Frank P. Walsh. Many of the prewar progressives had frowned on unions as monopolies which denied equality of opportunity and threatened middle-class interests, but the WLB threw the power of government behind the right of workers to organize and bargain collectively. When the Smith & Wesson Arms plant rejected a WLB decision, the board boldly commandeered the plant. The various labor boards also made progress in imposing the eight-hour day and in protecting women and children from exploitation. When the Supreme Court overturned the Child Labor Act of 1916, Congress quickly enacted a new law using the taxing power to discourage the employment of child labor. As a result of all of these actions and of the insatiable manpower demand, the A.F. of L. gained more than a million members; hours of labor declined sharply; and real wages rose 20 per cent.

The government had to find money not only for its own but for Allied expenses. During and immediately after the war the United States Government lent some $10 billion to the Allies and associated governments, practically all of which was spent in this country. These loans, direct war expenditures of $26 billion, and indirect costs like pensions brought the total cost of the war to well over $42 billion by 1936. The country financed approximately one-third of the war cost by taxation, two-thirds by loans. To avoid a repetition of the unhappy experience of Cleveland's negotiations with Wall Street, Congress insisted that bonds be sold through popular subscription. The five loans which were floated between May 1917 and May 1919—four Liberty loans and one Victory loan—were all handsomely oversubscribed. The war also demonstrated the potential of the steeply graduated income tax as an instrument for distributing costs more equitably. In the Revenue Act of 1918 Congress not only raised the excess profits tax to 65 per cent but increased the surtax so that the total levy on the

Samuel Gompers (1850–1924). In this unusual photograph, he is togged out in an aviator's helmet looking for all the world like a war ace. The picture indicates the indefatigable support the head of the American Federation of Labor gave to America's participation in World War I at a time when the IWW and many other working-class groups opposed the war. (*Office of War Information, National Archives*)

wealthy reached 77 per cent. Although the war created new millionaires and resulted in swollen profits in some instances, it also showed that in a time of crisis the government can impose its will on the rich in a way that is rarely possible in peacetime.

Notwithstanding the many achievements, the war mobilization fell short. Despite the enormous upsurge of production, the American army depended heavily on Allied arms and supplies. By the end of the war American factories had produced only 64 tanks, the Liberty aviation engine was just getting into production, field artillery relied almost exclusively on French 75 mm. field guns, and more doughboys went to Europe in British transports than in American vessels.

Mobilizing Public Opinion

When Congress declared war, a sizable minority objected and a very large part of the public was indifferent to the issues. Millions of Americans—anti-war Socialists, German, Irish, and other ethnic groups, pacifists, 'Wobblies,' many progressives—opposed American intervention. In Oklahoma's 'Green Corn Rebellion,' tenant farmers, including Indians and Negroes, burned bridges and cut pipelines in protest against participation in the war. Anti-war progressives charged that the poor people of the country had been dragooned into war by greedy profiteers. 'We are going into the war,' George Norris asserted, 'upon the command of Gold.' Furthermore, many who did not oppose the conflict had little ideological commitment. Consequently, Congress established a Committee on Public Information, whose chairman, George Creel, undertook to mobilize the mind of America as Baruch was mobilizing industry. Creel enlisted artists, advertisers, poets, historians, photographers, and educators, who inundated the country with a flood of propaganda. Creel distributed over 100 million pieces of 'literature,' while 75,000 'four-minute men' let loose a barrage of oratory which all but paralyzed the intelligence of the country. Motion pictures displayed to horrified audiences the barbarities of the 'Hun'; pamphlets written by learned professors proved to the more skeptical that the Germans had always been a depraved people; and thousands of canned editorials taught the average man what to think about the war. School children learned to lisp the vocabulary of hatred, and foreigners were taught to be ashamed that they had not arranged to be born in America.

The administration directed its propaganda toward international opinion too. Charges by radicals that the war was being fought for imperialistic aims encouraged Wilson to enunciate a declaration of principles. He sought two ends: to establish a moral basis for peace upon which all belligerents—including the Allies—must agree, and to sow dissatisfaction among the peoples of Germany and Austria-Hungary. To achieve these goals Wilson announced, on 8 January 1918, the Fourteen Points upon which it would be possible to formulate terms of peace. They included the principle of 'open covenants openly arrived at,' freedom of the seas, the reorganization of much of Europe on the basis of self-determination, and the creation of a 'general association of nations.' Wilson's statement, assiduously circulated throughout Germany, eventually helped to drive a wedge between the people and the government, and, at the end, led to negotiations for an armistice upon the basis of the Fourteen Points.

The Wilson administration also took steps, frequently drastic ones, to deal with internal dissension. The Espionage Act of 1917 fixed a maximum penalty of a $10,000 fine and 20 years' imprisonment for anyone who interfered with the draft or encouraged disloyalty, and empowered the Postmaster General to deny the mails to any materials he thought seditious. The Sedition Act of 1918 extended these penalties to anyone who should obstruct the sale of United States bonds, incite insubordination, discourage recruiting, 'wilfully utter, print, write or publish any disloyal, profane, scurrilous or abusive language about the form of government of the United States, or the Constitution, or the flag, or the uniform of the Army or Navy, or bring the form of Government... or the constitution... into contempt... or advocate any curtailment of production of anything necessary to the prosecution of the war.' In addition a Trading-with-the-Enemy Act of 1917 gave the President authority to censor all international communications, and the Postmaster General power over the foreign-language press in the United States. Under these harsh laws the government instituted widespread censorship of the press and banned two Socialist newspapers from the mails. A film-producer was sentenced to ten years in jail for producing a film on the American Revolution called *The Spirit of Seventy-six*, because it was thought that it might excite anti-British sentiments; a Vermont minister was sentenced to fifteen years' imprisonment for citing Jesus as an authority on pacifism; and South

Dakota farmers went to jail for petitioning for a referendum on the war and on the payment of war costs through taxation. A drive against conscientious objectors, who were theoretically excluded from the draft, netted 4000 men, of whom more than 400 were hurried to military prisons.

Altogether, the government carried out 1500 prosecutions under the Espionage and Sedition laws. Among those convicted, the two most distinguished were Eugene V. Debs and Victor Berger. Debs, four times a candidate for the presidency of the United States, was sentenced to 20 years in jail for a speech which was held to have a tendency to bring about resistance to the draft, though there was no evidence to prove that it did. Berger, Congressman from Milwaukee, also received a 20-year sentence for editorials in his newspaper branding the war a capitalist conspiracy. Twice re-elected by his constituents he was twice refused his seat. C. T. Schenck, General Secretary of the Socialist party, was convicted on the same charge; Justice Holmes's opinion sustaining the conviction is memorable because it announced for the first time the 'clear and present danger' test as a safeguard for freedom of speech. 'The question in every case,' wrote Holmes,

is whether the words are used in such circumstances and are of such a nature as to create a clear and present danger that they will bring about the substantive evils that Congress has a right to prevent. It is a question of proximity and degree.

Holmes's standard was not adhered to in a more controversial case where a miserable garment-worker, Jacob Abrams, was sentenced to twenty years' imprisonment for distributing a pamphlet calling on the workers of the world to rise against the American military expedition to Siberia—an expedition conceived in folly, conducted in vain, and abandoned in disorder.[1] The decision of the Court in 1919 evoked from Justice Holmes the most moving of his many eloquent dissents:

1. A token force of Americans fought in the Archangel-Murmansk campaign of 1918–19 and another in an Allied expedition in Siberia that terminated in 1920. Though some historians have interpreted these interventions as attempts to destroy Bolshevism, or to check the Japanese, they appear to have been motivated largely by military concerns, which turned out to be quite ill-founded.

When men have realized that time has upset many fighting faiths, they may come to believe even more than they believe the very foundations of their own conduct that the ultimate good desired is better reached by free trade in ideas—that the best test of truth is the power of the thought to get itself accepted in the competition of the market, and that truth is the only ground upon which their wishes can be safely carried out. That at any rate is the theory of our Constitution. It is an experiment, as all life is an experiment. Every year if not every day we have to wager our salvation upon some prophecy based upon imperfect knowledge. While that experiment is part of our system I think that we should be eternally vigilant against attempts to check the expression of opinions that we loathe and believe to be fraught with death, unless they so imminently threaten immediate interference with the lawful and pressing purposes of the law that an immediate check is required to save the country.

No less disturbing than this official crusade against sedition was the unofficial witch-hunting. The war offered a great opportunity to bring patriotism to the aid of personal grudges and neighborhood feuds. A non-conformist was lucky if he did not have flashes from his shaving mirror reported as signals to U-boats. German-Americans, the vast majority of them loyal to the United States, were subjected to all sorts of indignities. Schools dropped German from their curricula; Frederick Stock, distinguished conductor of the Chicago Symphony Orchestra, was deprived of his baton; and some universities revoked degrees they had conferred on distinguished Germans, thus giving academic sanction to the doctrine of retroactive guilt.

Naval and Military Operations

'Force to the utmost, force without stint or limit' had been Wilson's promise, yet neither the Germans nor the Allies expected much military and naval contribution from the United States. In fact, it was fully a year after the declaration of war before American soldiers arrived in sufficient numbers to affect the military situation on the Western front, and the Germans confidently expected to win the war in less than a year. When American military aid did come, it was decisive. But even before American troops turned the tide

'The Draftee.' In World War I the draft was the main supplier of recruits for the Army, but through most of the conflict the Navy, as well as the Marines, relied upon voluntary enlistment. Not until the last three months of the war did the selective service system embrace sailors and marines too. This picture is by Lewis W. Hine (1874–1940), who succeeded Jacob Riis as the most important photographer of the New Immigrants in the urban slums. (*George Eastman House Collection*)

at Château-Thierry, the navy had cooperated to destroy the effectiveness of German submarines.

General Joffre early assured American officials that half a million soldiers was the largest number the Allies expected the United States to send to France, but the government organized its military machine upon a far more ambitious basis. Within eighteen months the United States created an effective army of 4 million men, transported over 2 million to France, and placed 1.3 million on the firing line. This was a result of the organizing genius of Newton D. Baker, who, despite pacifist inclinations, proved himself one of the ablest of all secretaries of war. Even before the actual declaration of war, Baker had been convinced of the need to raise an army by conscription rather than by the volunteer system. Under the Selective Service Act of 1917, 2,810,296 men were inducted into the army. The regular army, national guard, navy, and marine corps continued to be recruited by voluntary enlistment. Including these and 'minor branches of service,' the armed forces totalled nearly five million.

The United States Navy got into the thick of the action much sooner than the army, but only after a bad start. Although Secretary Daniels and his Assistant Secretary, Franklin D. Roosevelt, had done a great deal to build up the morale and efficiency of the fleet, new construction was still mostly in the blueprint stage. The Chief of Naval Operations had no war plan ready when war was declared, and the one he promulgated on 11 April envisioned a considerable Pacific Fleet to watch Japan—an ally! Fortunately, the President had been prevailed upon to send the gifted and energetic Rear Admiral William S. Sims to London a few days ahead of the declaration of war; and Sims's pungent dispatches described a situation so appalling that the navy almost completely altered its plans. Sims reported that England had only a three weeks' supply of grain on hand, the U-boats were increasingly devastating, and if something was not done promptly to repair the life line, the Allies would have to throw in the sponge before the end of the year.

Under Sims's influence, the Allies adopted the convoy system of operating merchant ships in groups so that they could be protected from submarine attack by an escort of cruisers and destroyers, and the convoy system enabled American troops and supplies to cross the Atlantic safely. Sims also persuaded the navy to send as many destroyers as it could spare to Ireland to be operated for escort-of-convoy and anti-submarine patrol under the British. The new convoy tactics and aggressive patrolling reduced Allied monthly shipping losses from 881,000 tons (April) to 289,000 tons (November), and these losses were more than replaced by new construction; submarine operations became very hazardous and the United States could send troops and supplies abroad with confidence that they would arrive. Not one loaded transport was lost. Finally, it was the U.S. Navy that laid the colossal mine barrage across the North Sea which, beginning in June 1918, practically closed that exit to enemy submarines. Without the work by the U.S. Navy, the

Allies might have been defeated before American ground forces could have arrived. Nevertheless, it was the American Expeditionary Force which, in conjunction with the Allied armies, secured victory.

Late in 1917 the military situation turned radically against the Allies. In October the Italian army cracked at Caporetto and the Allies had to hurry troops from the Western front to stem the Austrian tide. Two months later negotiations by the new Soviet government at Brest-Litovsk released hundreds of thousands of German soldiers for the Western front. By the spring of 1918 the Germans had a clear numerical superiority in the West, and their high command prepared with confidence for a drive on Paris that would end the war.

A Macedonian cry went up for American troops, and there began a 'race for France.' Could the United States speed up her troop shipments sufficiently to redress the balance between the Allies and the Central Powers? 'Would she appear in time to snatch the victor's laurels from our brows?' asked Hindenburg. 'That, and that only was the decisive question! I believed I could answer it in the negative.' Altogether, during the critical months from March to October 1918, 1,750,000 American soldiers landed in France. 'America,' wrote German Commander-in-Chief Ludendorff, 'thus became the decisive power in the war.'

The great German offensive began on 21 March 1918, and by early June, after capturing well over 100,000 prisoners, the Germans, standing on the right bank of the Marne, threatened Paris. At this crisis of the war Pershing, who wanted the American army in France to form an independent unit, temporarily waived this claim and placed all his forces at the disposal of the new supreme commander, General Foch, who dispersed them among the Allied armies where, at engagements like Belleau Wood, they made an incalculable contribution to Allied morale. On 15 July came the fourth and last phase of the German offensive, the Second Battle of the Marne. The Germans launched their heaviest attack at the Château-Thierry salient; had they broken through, Paris could not have been saved. American troops, 275,000 strong, supported the French in stemming a tide which at first seemed irresistible. In

(*West Point Museum*)

three days the German offensive was exhausted, and on 18 July, without giving the enemy an opportunity to consolidate, Foch called upon the 1st and 2nd American and the First French Morocco Divisions to spearhead a counterattack, which was brilliantly executed. The German Chancellor later confessed that 'at the beginning of July 1918, I was convinced . . . that before the first of September our adversaries would send us peace proposals. . . . That was on the 15th. On the 18th even the most optimistic among us knew that all was lost. The history of the world was played out in three days.'

With the passing of the crisis on the Marne, Pershing won approval of his cherished plan for an independent American army. In September the new American force wiped out the strategically important St. Mihiel salient in two days, and in the Meuse-Argonne battle, which cost 117,000 American casualties, played an important role in breaking the Hindenburg line. On 3 October Prince Max of Baden addressed to President Wilson the first overture for peace—on the basis of the Fourteen Points. Wilson handled these negotiations with a skill that belied his reputation as an impractical idealist. After a month of diplomatic fencing, in which the Germans were worsted, the Allied governments instructed Foch to negotiate for an armistice. On 9 November the Kaiser fled across the border to Holland. Two days later an armistice was officially proclaimed, and the greatest and most costly war that the world had yet known came to an end.

The Peace Conference, the Treaty, and the League

Wilson was to discover that it was easier to win a war than to make a peace. The only statesman representing a major power who combined intelligence and magnanimity, he nevertheless bore some of the responsibility for creating a situation in which vindictiveness and greed would have free play. He had acquiesced in the suppression of freedom of expression in the United States; he had supported Creel's campaign to inoculate Americans with the germs of hatred for the Central Powers; and he had encouraged utopian expecta-

tions about the outcome of the war. Furthermore, it should be recognized that if no other statesman had Wilson's breadth of vision, he was not altogether disinterested, for his aims were congruent with America's stake in a stable international order in which liberal capitalism would prosper.

Even before the armistice Wilson determined to shatter precedent by taking personal charge of the peace negotiations. On 24 October 1918 he had appealed to the American electorate for a vote of confidence: 'If you have approved of my leadership and wish me to continue to be your unembarrassed spokesman in affairs at home and abroad, I earnestly beg that you will express yourselves unmistakably to that effect by returning a Democratic majority to both the Senate and House of Representatives.' Two weeks later the voters chose a majority of Republicans for both houses of Congress. By winning control of the Senate by two votes, the Republicans were able to place Henry Cabot Lodge in the chairmanship of the critically important Senate Foreign Relations Committee.

Well before the election Republican leaders like Roosevelt and Lodge had opposed Wilson's plans for a postwar association of nations. Roosevelt, who had long had an intense hatred of Wilson, was a bitter partisan who believed that casualty lists were being suppressed in order to hide the fact that two-thirds of the American war dead were Republicans. The former President insisted that the United States had gone to war strictly to seek vengeance for insults to American honor, and he demanded that the peace be dictated by 'hammering guns' instead of 'clicking . . . typewriters.' Lodge, who regarded himself as a Scholar in Politics, resented the renown Wilson had won in the same field. (In fact, Senator Depew's remark is to the point: Lodge had a mind like the New England landscape—'naturally barren, but highly cultivated.') Though the Democratic setback in 1918 resulted less from resentment at the President's appeal than from Western grievances over price regulation, Wilson left himself open to the Republican claim that, after drawing the line on foreign policy, he had been rejected. When on 13 December the President sailed for France, Roosevelt

'Signing of the Treaty of Versailles,' by John C. Johansen. The ceremony took place on 28 June 1919 which, by an odd coincidence, marked the fifth anniversary of the slaying of the Archduke Francis Ferdinand at Sarajevo, and it was held in the Hall of Mirrors in Louis XIV's palace of Versailles. The Germans, who were compelled to sign, were unreconciled. 'We must never forget it is only a scrap of paper,' said the Berlin *Vorwärts*. 'Treaties based on violence can keep their validity only so long as force exists. Do not lose hope. The resurrection day comes.' (*Smithsonian Institution*)

warned 'our allies, our enemies and Mr. Wilson himself' that 'Mr. Wilson has no authority whatever to speak for the American people at this time. His leadership has just been emphatically repudiated by them.'

In the preliminary armistice negotiations with the Allies, Wilson had been made painfully aware of the conflict in war aims between the United States and the Allied powers. Though he had clung tenaciously to his Fourteen Points, he had been forced to admit qualifications with respect to the important items of 'freedom of the seas' and reparations. Aware of the existence of secret treaties which in part nullified the Fourteen Points, he persuaded himself to ignore their significance. These secret treaties had been concluded between the major Allies and powers like Japan, Italy, and Romania, in order to induce them to join the Allied side. The treaties were contrary to the principle of self-determination, and Wilson should have tried to obtain abrogation or modification of them before sending American troops to Europe.

In the Peace Conference, which held its first formal session 18 January 1919, all the Allied and associated powers were represented, but the 'Big Four'—Britain, France, Italy, and the United States—made the important decisions. Like the conference at Brest-Litovsk, this one gave the defeated powers no part in the negotiations; they were merely called in when the treaty was ready and ordered to sign. Moreover, the jingo atmosphere of Paris and the personalities of leaders made a just peace exceedingly difficult to attain. David Lloyd George, the British prime minister, had won a general election since the armistice on the slogans 'Hang the Kaiser' and 'Make Germany Pay.' Georges Clemenceau, the 'tiger' of French politics, regarded Wilsonian liberalism with complete skepticism and assailed it with mordant wit: 'Mr. Wilson bores me with his Fourteen Points; why, God Almighty has only ten!' Many Europeans regarded Wilson as little short of a new Saviour come to bring peace on earth. But too many had been outraged, impoverished, and wounded by a war which they regarded as entirely Germany's fault to support the sort of peace that Wilson wanted. In the end Wilson was forced to agree to many compromises, but he imposed upon his colleagues something of his own ideas of a 'just' peace and wrung from them some concessions. Perhaps no one could have done more.

The Treaty of Versailles, to which the Germans affixed their signature on 28 June, was not as drastic as France wanted, nor harsh enough to keep Germany down. It required Germany to admit her war guilt, stripped her of all colonies and commercial rights in Africa and the Far East, of Alsace-Lorraine, Posen, and parts of Schleswig and Silesia, confiscated the coal mines of the Saar basin, imposed disarmament upon her, saddled her with an immediate indemnity of $5 billion and a future reparation bill of indeterminate amount, and placed practically the whole of her economic system under temporary Allied control. The Versailles treaty and collateral agreements also sanctioned the creation of a number of new states, including Czechoslovakia, Yugoslavia, and Poland. Wilson successfully resisted some of the more extreme demands of the Allies. He prevented France from detaching the entire Rhineland from Germany; denied Fiume to Italy, an action which caused Orlando to withdraw from the conference in a huff; persuaded Japan to evacuate Shantung; and refused to permit the Allies to charge Germany with the whole cost of the war. And, finally, he wrote into the treaty the covenant of the League of Nations, which, he felt, was the part that justified the whole.

The League of Nations gave every member nation an equal vote in the Assembly, which was a deliberative body, while the United States, Great Britain, France, Italy, and Japan were permanent and four other nations temporary members of the Council, which was more largely an executive body. An independent Permanent Court of International Justice was established at The Hague. The members of the League pledged themselves to 'respect and preserve as against external aggression the territorial integrity and existing political independence of all Members of the League' (Art. X); to give publicity to treaties and to armaments; to submit to inquiry and arbitration all disputes threatening international peace, breaches of treaties, and questions of international law, and refrain from war until three months after the award by the arbiters; to refrain from war with the nations complying with the award of the League;

and to employ, on the recommendation of the League Council, military, naval, financial, and economic sanctions against nations resorting to war in disregard of their covenants under the League. The Council was further authorized to exercise mandates over the former colonies of Germany and Turkey and oversee conditions of labor, traffic in women and children, drugs, arms, and munitions, and the control of health. The covenant specifically recognized 'the validity of . . . regional understandings like the Monroe Doctrine.'

The President called Congress into special session to consider the treaty and the League of Nations, but when he returned to the United States, early in June, 1919, he found the Senate in an ugly mood. Opposition to the League was compounded of diverse elements: hostility to Wilson, partisanship, and senatorial pique; resentment at the fact that the American delegation to Versailles included no senator and no prominent Republican; indignation of German-Americans who felt that their country had been betrayed, Italian-Americans angry over Fiume, and Irish-Americans stirred up against England, then engaged in trying to suppress the Sinn Fein revolution; conservative disapproval of what was alleged to be leniency toward Germany, liberal disapproval of severity toward Germany; and a general feeling that Wilson and America had been tricked, and that the country should avoid future European entanglements. In the Senate three groups could be discerned. At one extreme stood the 'irreconcilables'—Borah, Johnson, La Follette, and others who were determined to undo the whole of Wilson's handiwork; at the other extreme were the President's faithful followers who were ready to ratify the treaty as it stood. In between a large number favored reservations to protect American interests. At all times, during the prolonged debate over the treaty, more than three-fourths of the Senate was ready to accept membership in the League in some form or other.

Both opposition to the League and support of it broke on party lines. Of the 47 Democrats in the Senate, only four were outright opponents of the treaty, a remarkable record of party solidarity. With Democratic votes Wilson could easily overcome the irreconcilables like Borah. His crucial problem was how to cope with the pivotal group of Republican reservationists, especially the powerful faction of strong reservationists led by Lodge who were not only jealous of American sovereignty but wanted to deny the Democrats the opportunity to go to the country in 1920 as the party which had led the nation not only through a victorious war but to a successful peace. Lodge insisted on altering the treaty proposal so that it no longer bore Wilson's stamp; if this failed, he preferred to see it die.

Wilson, unwilling to accept any but the mildest 'interpretations,' showed himself almost as stubborn as the irreconcilables. Failing to make headway against the senatorial clique, he resorted to a direct appeal to the people. On 4 September he set out on a speaking tour which carried him through the Middle West and Far West. He spoke with passionate conviction. In Omaha, he warned: 'I tell you, my fellow citizens, I can predict with absolute certainty that within another generation, there will be another world war if the nations of the world do not concert the method by which to prevent it.' But against the rising tide of isolationism and illiberalism he made little headway, and much of the effect of his speeches was spoiled by the counter-arguments of the irreconcilables who stalked him relentlessly from city to city. On 25 September he suffered a physical collapse. And with his collapse went all the hopes of ratification.

On 19 November 1919, the Treaty of Versailles went down to defeat in the Senate, both with and without reservations. Yet a large majority of Senators favored ratification with some kind of reservations, as did a large majority of the American people. Senator Lodge would not budge; neither would Wilson. He instructed Senate Democrats to vote down the treaty with reservations, and half of them heeded him. When the treaty came up for reconsideration again on 19 March 1920, twenty-three Democrats joined the twelve Republican irreconcilables to defeat ratification with reservations by a vote of 49 to 35, seven votes less than the required two-thirds. Thus was sacrificed the fairest prospect for world order which had yet been opened to mankind.

Like a British prime minister with a balky Parliament, Wilson waited for the next general elec-

Ben Shahn, 'Bartolomeo Vanzetti and Nicola Sacco.' This is one of a number of *gouaches* that brought the painter Ben Shahn (1898–1969) into the public eye in 1932. Shahn was to become the most important social commentator in twentieth-century art in America. 'Ever since I could remember I'd wished I'd been lucky enough to be alive at that great time—when something big was going on, like the Crucifixion,' he said. 'And suddenly I realized I was. Here I was living through another crucifixion. Here was something to paint!' (*Museum of Modern Art, Gift of Abby Aldrich Rockefeller*)

tion to vindicate his policies and give him a more malleable legislature. The 1920 election, he declared, should be 'a solemn referendum' on American membership in the League of Nations. But the League question was obfuscated in the campaign, and it never again figured as a vital issue in a national election. As early as 1922 the United States began to send 'unofficial observers' to League conferences, but it never took a direct part in the League's peace-keeping machinery.

Aftermath

No sooner had the war ended than the country moved precipitately to erase all evidence of the war experience, especially the experiment of an enhanced role for government. Wilson called for a rapid liquidation of governmental activities, and legislation returning the railroads to private operation and promoting a privately owned merchant marine was enacted after the war. Nonetheless, the government continued to affect the structure of the transportation industry. The Esch-Cummins Transportation Act of 1920 differed from previous railroad regulation in that it sought to encourage rather than discourage consolidation, but with small success. More consequential were a series of actions by federal, state, and local governments which built up rivals of the railroads—trucks, buses, private cars, and airplanes. In the half-century after the experiment with federal operation of the railways in World War I, the government, instead of managing the railroads in the public interest, chose to subsidize highways which scarred the countryside and spewed traffic into crowded cities, while the railroads, which in other lands were the basis of an efficient transportation system, faced extinction.

Another legacy of the war roiled the waters of international affairs. America's efforts to collect more than $10 billion in debts from its former Allies involved it in a series of abortive enterprises in which financiers like Charles G. Dawes and Owen D. Young attempted to develop a viable relation between the debts and German reparations. The insistence by the United States that the debts be repaid proved to the Europeans that 'Uncle Shylock' was heartless, and by June 1933 only Finland was meeting its obligations in full. The whole business addled American politics and poisoned relations with Europe for more than a decade.

World War I had a still more venomous consequence: a residue of pent-up violence that found expression in a number of ugly forms. Between 1917 and 1925, some 600,000 blacks moved north, thereby jeopardizing the pattern of racial segregation in America, and black soldiers returned from the war less willing to accept second-class citizenship. Southern whites responded by using violence and intimidation to compel the Negro to acquiesce in the rituals of white supremacy. In the first year after the war, seventy Negroes were lynched, some still wearing their army uniforms. In Washington, D.C., on a sultry Sunday in the summer of 1919, gangs of whites, many of them restless unemployed ex-servicemen, set upon isolated blacks and beat them; two Negroes were mauled right in front of the White House. The next day, blacks struck back, firing shots into crowds of whites, attacking a streetcar, emptying their guns at random at whites in the street. One Negro explained: 'We have been through war and gave everything, even our lives, and now we are going to stop being beat up.'

That same year the government itself contributed to the postwar acrimony by playing an active role in the Red Scare, in which Wilson's Attorney General, A. Mitchell Palmer, tried to make political capital by persecuting alien radicals. Using private spies and *agents provocateurs*, Palmer conducted a series of lawless raids on private houses and labor headquarters, rounded up several thousand aliens, and subjected them to drumhead trials. Some five hundred aliens were deported, many of them illegally. State governments also persecuted dissenters. In 1920 the Empire State distinguished itself by expelling five Socialist members from the state legislature. It was not alleged that the party was illegal or that the Socialist members were guilty of any crime, but merely that socialism was 'absolutely inimical to the best interests of the State of New York and of the United States.' The distinguished Charles Evans Hughes, later to be elevated to the chief justiceship, was one of many to protest against this palpable violation of elementary constitutional rights, but his call for sanity fell on deaf ears.

Hostility to radicals, antipathy to foreigners, and a jealous protection of the status quo were revealed in the most sensational murder trial since that of the Haymarket anarchists—the Sacco-Vanzetti case (1920–27). Nicola Sacco and Bartolomeo Vanzetti, foreigners and philosophical anarchists, were accused of murdering a paymaster at South Braintree, Massachusetts. When they were convicted and sentenced to death there was a widespread belief that the jury had been moved more by their radical views and their evasion of military service than by the evidence. For seven years men and women of all shades of opinion and in almost every country labored to obtain a retrial, and the governor of Massachusetts appointed an investigating committee consisting of two college presidents and a judge of probate. Although this committee found the trial judge guilty of 'grave breach of official decorum,' it reported that justice had been done. When Sacco and Vanzetti were electrocuted on 23 August 1927, a cry of horror went up around the world. Citizens of Massachusetts who loved justice remembered John Adams and the Boston Massacre case and Judge Sewall's retraction in the case of the Salem witches and hung their heads in shame.

29

American Society in Transition

1910–1940

The New Society

In the interwar decades American society underwent far-reaching changes, many of which were foreshadowed in the years before the United States entered World War I. As early as 1908 the photographer Alfred Stieglitz had hung Matisse canvases in his Fifth Avenue gallery. In 1909 Sigmund Freud came over to lecture at Clark University, and by 1916 some 500 psychoanalysts were already practicing in New York. At Mabel Dodge's salon in Greenwich Village, writers, artists, and revolutionaries discussed the ideas of Henri Bergson and Georges Sorel, of Nietzsche and Shaw and those insurgent thinkers who stressed spontaneity, instinct, emotion, and movement, and assaulted nineteenth-century conceptions of morality and decorum. In 1913 a dance craze swept the country, symbol of a growing sense of sexual liberation. Disturbed by the intimacy of movement, Columbia University stipulated that six inches must separate the dancers. By 1915 H. L. Mencken had identified the new American woman as 'the Flapper.' In intellectual circles at least, there was a quickening awareness of taking part in an insurrection against the old order, and a vivid anticipation of the coming of great events.

The prewar rebels, for all their earthshaking manifestos, lived in an exuberant age of confidence, an era that World War I shattered beyond repair. Too many had known the young men who, in Ezra Pound's words, 'walked eye-deep in hell / believing in old men's lies,' or, as e.e. cummings wrote, had heard 'death's enormous voice,' which left 'all the silence / filled with vivid noiseless boys.' The war blighted the immense sense of promise of the Progressive period and left a sense of outrage at the killing and maiming. Hemingway caught much of the spirit of the postwar years in his story of the Oklahoma boy who returned from the war 'much too late' and who 'did not want any consequences ever again.' Although some of the old progressives remained faithful to earlier ideals, many rejected public involvement for a preoccupation with self. Like the 'Hamlet' of Archibald MacLeish, they would 'Cry I! I! I! forever.' This private vision inspirited the literature of the 1920's but impoverished the politics.

Portrait of Gertrude Stein (1874–1946) by Pablo Picasso. 'Three generations of young writers have sat at her feet,' wrote Carl Van Vechten. Writers were deeply affected by her experiments with prose style in works like *Three Lives* (1909) and *The Autobiography of Alice B. Toklas* (1933) and even more by the shelter and stimulus she provided at her salon at 27 rue de Fleurus, Paris. 'It was like one of the best rooms in the finest museum,' recalled Ernest Hemingway, 'except there was a big fireplace and it was warm and comfortable and they gave you good things to eat and tea.' (*Metropolitan Museum of Art, Bequest of Gertrude Stein, 1946*)

The socialist Norman Thomas protested: 'The old reformer has become the Tired Radical, and his sons and daughters drink at the fountain of the *American Mercury*. They have no illusions but one. And that is that they can live like Babbitt and think like Mencken.'

George Babbitt, the protagonist of Sinclair Lewis's novel, personified the materialistic aspirations of this period. During the piping years of the 'twenties, population grew by 17 millions in a decade, and the growth in national wealth was equally noteworthy. The wealth of the nation was unevenly distributed: 25 million families—over 87 per cent of the population—had incomes of less than $2500, while only about a million families—less than 3 per cent—had incomes of over $5000. Yet since advertising looked to a mass market, a large proportion of the nation was able to find more gratification of its wants. Business cooperated with these desires by providing easier credit, and the public responded by buying what it wanted on the installment plan. No longer inclined to regard thrift as a virtue, Americans speculated avidly on the stock market or in Florida real estate.

These changes contributed to significant alterations in the national character, for as Joseph Gusfield has noted, 'In an easygoing, affluent society, the credit mechanism has made the Ant a fool and the Grasshopper a hero.' The nation was swiftly moving toward a society in which styles of consumption would determine status. The New Middle Class—from the white collar clerk to the Madison Avenue executive—was captivated by the plethora of novel consumer products. In Montgomery Ward catalogues, toasters and irons made their first appearance in 1912, vacuum cleaners in 1917, the electric range in 1930, the refrigerator in 1932.

These new products first found their way in an urban market, for rural America still lacked electricity, and in this period America was becoming a predominantly urban nation. In 1890 the population was 65 per cent rural; in 1930 it was 56 per cent urban. Many cities, especially in Florida and California, grew tenfold during these years, while increases in the larger cities of the older parts of

the country were spectacular.[1] Nearly half the population of the country lived within easy access of cities of 100,000 inhabitants or more; these cities became the shopping, entertainment, and cultural centers of the nation. The city promised excitement and adventure. In a Floyd Dell novel, the protagonist has a recurring image of a map at the depot 'with a picture of iron roads from all over the Middle West centering in a dark blotch in the corner. . . . "Chicago!" he said to himself.'

To this process of urbanization the automobile especially contributed. At the close of World War I there were some 9 million motor cars in use; a decade later, 26 million. The automobile broke down isolation and provincialism, promoted standardization, accelerated the growth of cities at the expense of villages and then of suburbs at the expense of cities, created a hundred new industries and millions of new jobs. It also required the destruction of large parts of the country to make way for roads, and took an annual toll of life and limb as high as that exacted by the First World War.

The radio, like the automobile, began as a plaything and became a necessity and a promoter of social change. The first broadcasting station opened at Pittsburgh in 1920; within a decade there were almost 13 million radios in American homes, and by 1940 there were close to 900 broadcasting stations and 52 million receiving sets. From the beginning radio was privately owned, not—as in Europe—in public hands, and a few great networks controlled most of the wavelengths. Government regulation was tardy, feeble, and fragmentary; not until 1927 did Congress

1. Thus, in thousands:

	1890	1930
Atlanta, Ga.	65	270
Detroit, Mich.	205	1568
Grand Rapids, Mich.	60	170
Hartford, Conn.	60	150
Indianapolis, Ind.	105	305
Kansas City, Mo.	130	400
Minneapolis, Minn.	164	464
Pittsburgh, Pa.	238	669
Rochester, N.Y.	130	320
Syracuse, N.Y.	88	209
Toledo, Ohio	81	290
Washington, D.C.	189	487

establish a Federal Radio Commission to license stations, assign wave-lengths, and supervise policies. In 1934 this commission gave way to the Federal Communications Commission, which was authorized to require that all broadcasts conform to the 'public interest, convenience and necessity,' a stipulation interpreted so loosely as to be almost meaningless.

Second only to the radio as diversion were the 'movies.' Invented by the resourceful Thomas Edison at the turn of the century, the motion picture grew steadily in popularity. David Griffith's *The Birth of a Nation*, shown to rapt audiences in 1915, introduced the spectacle film which another producer, Cecil B. de Mille, shortly made his peculiar property. Stars of the silent screen supplanted luminaries of the 'legitimate' stage: Mary Pickford, 'America's sweetheart'; Charles Chaplin, greatest of comedians; Douglas Fairbanks, handsome and acrobatic; Bill Hart, always in cowboy costume; Pearl White, whose endless escapades left her audience palpitating each week for the next installment. Sound, introduced in 1927, greatly expanded film potentialities, and the development of the cartoon movie by Walt Disney, creator of Mickey Mouse and Donald Duck, delighted adults as well as children. By 1937 the motion-picture business was eleventh in assets among the industries of the nation, and some 75 million persons visited the movies each week, while millions more were attracted to sporting events.

Few phenomena attracted so much attention as the 'emancipation' of women, though, in fact, there was less change than many thought. Woman suffrage was written into the Constitution in 1920, and increasing numbers of women took part in public life; a generation that observed Jane Addams and Eleanor Roosevelt could not seriously believe women less competent than men in public affairs. During the manpower shortage in World War I, so many women crowded into factory and office that it appeared a major shift had occurred in the position of women. In fact, patterns of employment in the 1920's remained essentially unaltered. More enduring changes came in the social and psychological realms. Labor-saving appliances liberated millions of women from the stove and the wash-tub, and knowledge of birth control from the demands of large families. As women won greater independence, they had some success, too, in replacing the old double standard of morality.

The institution of the family faced a difficult adjustment. In 1890 out of every one hundred marriages, six ended in divorce; forty years later, eighteen of every one hundred marriages were thus terminated, and that year some 200,000 couples were legally separated. In other respects, too, family life seemed less stable. Those who continued to live in the town where they were born became objects of curiosity, and the shift from roomy Victorian houses to city flats made it difficult for large families—grandparents and maiden aunts—to live together. For many Americans the Depression was to reveal that

Home is the place where when you have to go there,
They have to take you in.[2]

For many it was that, and nothing more. Yet for all the vicissitudes, the family continued to adapt, and to endure.

Literary Interpretations

In the 'lyric years' before the war almost everything was 'new': the new poetry, the new criticism, the new art, the 'New Freedom,' the 'New Nationalism,' the new history. Herbert Croly established the *New Republic*; the Armory Show of 1913 exploded traditional art; the Provincetown Players welcomed young Eugene O'Neill; and William C. Handy composed the 'Memphis Blues.' 'The fiddles are tuning up all over America,' wrote John Butler Yeats.

So they were, but it was in Chicago that Harriet Monroe whipped them together into a kind of orchestra. In 1912 she launched *Poetry: A Magazine of Verse*, and within six years almost all the poets who would dominate the literary scene for the next fifty years made their bow, most of them in the pages of this little magazine: the

2. Robert Frost, 'Death of the Hired Man.'

'The Leaguers.' This depiction of members of the League of Women Voters is almost certainly the first (and perhaps the only) example of a painting of women in politics by a prominent artist. It is even more surprising that it should come from the brush of Guy Pène du Bois (1884–1958), one of the leading spirits behind the Armory Show, who concentrated on painting café society. 'His canvases,' it has been noted, 'often show two or three simplified figures in frozen motion, like mannequins caught in a spotlight.' (*Goldfield Galleries, Los Angeles*)

'prairie' poets, Carl Sandburg and Vachel Lindsay; the imagists, Amy Lowell and Conrad Aiken; the lyricists, Edna St. Vincent Millay and Elinor Wylie; Freudians like Edgar Lee Masters; and Robinson Jeffers, who went his own way. In England three Americans—Ezra Pound, T. S. Eliot, and Robert Frost—were publishing their first books. Not since New England's golden day had there been anything like it.

When Carl Sandburg published 'Chicago' in *Poetry*:

Hog Butcher for the World,
Tool Maker, Stacker of Wheat,

Player with Railroads and the Nation's Freight Hand-
ler;
Stormy, husky, brawling,
City of the Big Shoulders

a jaundiced critic wrote that 'the typographical arrangement for this jargon creates a suspicion that it is intended to be taken as some form of poetry.' And so it was. A disciple of Whitman, Sandburg thought nothing too undignified for poetry. Born of Swedish parents, Sandburg was as authentically American as Lincoln, whose biography he later wrote in six huge volumes. Like Lincoln he was instinctively democratic; his most important collection of poetry is called *The People, Yes.*

Another son of Illinois, Vachel Lindsay, wandered from town to town preaching the 'Gospel of Beauty,' and 'trading his rhymes for bread.' In 1913 he brought out *General Booth Enters Heaven* with its moving tribute to Governor Altgeld, the 'Eagle Forgotten,' and thereafter the 'Congo' and 'The Chinese Nightingale.' His verse, made to be chanted rather than read, led Lindsay to a career on the lecture circuit which laid a heavy toll on his energy, and in December 1931 he took his own life.

Imagism was altogether more sophisticated, closer to abstract painting and modern music than to the kind of poetry being written by Vachel Lindsay. A revolt against the verbose pretentiousness of late nineteenth-century rhymesters, it valued the intense, concrete image. Ezra Pound, who led the movement, explained that there was to be 'no Tennysonianness of speech; nothing— nothing that you couldn't in some circumstance, in the stress of some emotion, actually say.' When Pound wearied of it, Amy Lowell assumed leadership of the group and aggressively promoted *vers libre.* The 'Amygists,' as Pound called them, not only encouraged free verse, but sought to write 'hard and clear' poetry and sometimes succeeded.

Ezra Pound and T. S. Eliot were both in London when Harriet Monroe launched *Poetry;* Pound became its London editor, and Eliot contributed to it his first important poem, 'The Love Song of J. Alfred Prufrock.' Impetuous and scholarly, adventurous and reactionary, Pound poured out a steady stream of translations, criticisms, and original verse—notably the endless series of *Cantos* composed with brilliant and calculated obscurity. Where Pound dissipated his talents, Eliot became one of the commanding figures of his age. Like Henry James he lived by preference in London, and eventually became a British citizen; like James, too, he became increasingly the champion of traditionalism. Equally distinguished as a poet, a dramatist, and a critic, Eliot did as much to change modern poetry as had Wordsworth and Whitman in earlier generations, and his *The Waste Land* (1922), subtle and profound, became the *vade mecum* of a whole generation. Yet some

rebelled against the imagery of disintegration and sterility. 'After this perfection of death,' concluded Hart Crane, 'nothing is possible but a motion of some kind.'

American traditionalists looked to Henry James rather than to Eliot for inspiration, notably the three intrepid women who bridged the gap between the realism of Howells and the social protest of Dos Passos: Edith Wharton, Ellen Glasgow, and Willa Cather. In a series of novels from *The House of Mirth* (1905) to *Hudson River Bracketed* (1929), Mrs. Wharton presented complex social problems against a background of fashionable New York where Civil War profiteers and the new rich were crashing the gates of society, shattering old standards of elegance and taste, and calling in question old moralities. She was fascinated by the moral implications of the clash of cultures, and though she began as a rebel against the traditional social standards, she ended as something of an apologist for them. Ellen Glasgow, too, began by writing with ironic detachment about an old social order that she subsequently came to treat with 'sympathetic compassion.' By the 'twenties she perceived the threat to the values she cherished came less from the sentimentality of the Old South than from the absence of tradition in the New. Beginning with *Barren Ground* (1925), she expressed a mounting distaste for the emptiness of the new day and a grudging appreciation of the older virtues; with *The Sheltered Life* (1932) the appreciation was ardent; and *Vein of Iron* (1935) was an open appeal for the re-creation of the older values. Similarly, Willa Cather's novels and stories—those of the Arcadian Virginia of her childhood, the golden Nebraska of her youth, the shimmering Southwest of Bishop Latour, the Quebec of the Ursulines—were animated by a single theme: the superiority of the moral values of the past over the material interests of the present. The American West, she wrote, had been settled

by dreamers, great hearted adventurers who were unpractical to the point of magnificence; a courteous brotherhood strong in attack but weak in defence, who could conquer but could not hold. . . .

All this now was gone; industry, business, and

speculation had destroyed it: that was the moral of the most nearly perfect of her books, *A Lost Lady*, and of *The Professor's House*.

The most popular serious poet of this generation was both traditionalist and innovator. Robert Frost made his first appearance just as the fiddles were tuning up, but he belonged to no school, took part in no movement, fitted into no pattern. For half a century he went his own way, developing a philosophy deceptively homespun and a style deceptively simple. Born in San Francisco, he was unmistakably a New Englander; raised in cities, he was a countryman to the marrow; authentically American, he did not gain recognition until he expatriated himself to England, where he published his first two volumes of poetry: *A Boy's Will* (1913), and *North of Boston* (1914), with 'Mending Wall,' 'Death of the Hired Man,' 'Home Burial'—poems not surpassed in our literature for beauty and insight. Through the 'twenties and 'thirties, Frost turned out book after book: *New Hampshire*, *West Running Brook*, *A Further Range*, until by the end of this period he was the grand old man of American letters, and with yet another quarter-century of honors ahead of him.

If the second decade of the new century had been one of affirmation, the decade of the 'twenties was one of disillusionment. The most vociferous critic of his generation, Henry L. Mencken of Baltimore, made it his special business to expose bourgeois complacency and his 'Americana' column in the *American Mercury* recorded with melancholy faithfulness the fatuousness and vulgarity of American life. His views were almost all malicious, for Mencken was catholic in his dislikes: he disapproved of the rich and the poor, the ignorant and the intelligent, the mob and the elite, fundamentalism and advanced thought, devotion to the past and confidence in the future. Still, Mencken made some positive contributions: a magazine that attracted the brightest writers of the day; an irreverent style that went far to liberate writing from pedantic pretentiousness; and three learned volumes on *The American Language*.

The 'revolt from the village' found its bards in Edgar Lee Masters and Sherwood Anderson. In *The Spoon River Anthology* (1915) Masters recorded, in the mode of the Greek Anthology, the drab existence of some two hundred victims of life in a little Illinois town, where dreamers were always defeated and idealists ended as cynics. Sherwood Anderson's grotesques revealed the unhinging experience of alienation and loneliness. *Winesburg, Ohio* (1919) was a declaration of war against the small town, the factory, industry, the ties of marriage and of family; and almost all other conventions. It was Sinclair Lewis, however, whose *Main Street* (1920) and *Babbitt* (1922) made the revolt against the small town and against business a popular preoccupation. Lewis satirized the dullness and provincialism of Gopher Prairie and Zenith City, but, like Mark Twain, he was very much a part of the world he repudiated, and he had a grudging affection for the characters he ridiculed.

American poetry ranged widely in the interwar period. Elinor Wylie and Edna St. Vincent Millay mastered the traditional sonnet form. Wallace Stevens wrote sensual, elegant poems distinguished by the vivid hues of their imagery: 'pungent oranges and bright, green wings,' 'porcelain chocolate and pied umbrellas,' and 'a dove with an eye of grenadine.' In *The Bridge* Hart Crane attempted to create an ambitious synthesis of American experience; and although he failed, his brilliant employment of symbol and myth made his failure a greater achievement than lesser men's successes. Robinson Jeffers revealed a preoccupation with violence, depravity, and death. William Carlos Williams wrote poetry spare in form, conversational in idiom, like 'The Red Wheelbarrow,' and Marianne Moore peopled 'imaginary gardens with real toads.'

The 'Harlem Renaissance' produced in quick succession Countee Cullen's *Color* in 1925, Langston Hughes's *The Weary Blues* in 1926, and James Weldon Johnson's *God's Trombones* in 1927. (Cullen's moving poem, 'Heritage,' reflected a fascination with the Negro's African origins which prompted Marcus Garvey to lead an abortive back-to-Africa movement in the 1920's.) 'I can never put on paper the thrill of the underground ride to Harlem,' Hughes wrote. 'I went up the steps and out into the bright September sun-

Langston Hughes (1902–67). This pastel by Winold Reiss was done about 1925, a year before the publication of *The Weary Blues*, the volume of poems that brought Hughes to artistic prominence. Over the next generation, Hughes published other works of poetry, including *Fine Clothes to the Jew* and *Shakespeare in Harlem*, as well as novels, short stories, drama, witty essays, and an autobiography. (*National Portrait Gallery, Smithsonian Institution*)

light. Harlem! I stood there, dropped my bags, took a deep breath and felt happy again.' The exuberant 'Negro Renaissance' resulted not only in poems but novels, plays, and social analyses by writers such as Claude McKay, Jean Toomer, Alain Locke, and E. Franklin Frazier. Yet the Harlem Renaissance often burdened the black writer with unrealistic expectations, and the white world's celebration of 'exotic' Harlem gave a distorted image of the 'laughing, swaying' black and glossed over the grim reality of slum life.

The most significant and most widely read writers of this period were those who confessed that theirs was a 'lost generation.' F. Scott Fitzgerald's *This Side of Paradise* (1920) became a guidebook to the new generation 'grown up to find all Gods dead, all wars fought, all faiths in man shaken.' Fitzgerald depicted the world of Princeton and the St. Regis roof, the Riviera and the Ritz bar in Paris, West Egg and Hollywood, of ambition that cannot be gratified, of wealth that in the end makes no difference, of pleasures that bring ennui and passion that cannot achieve lasting love. 'My millionaires,' he wrote, 'were as beautiful and damned as Thomas Hardy's peasants.' Still, his characters do not experience the nightmare that broods over the novels of a Kafka or a Camus; they differ little from the denizens of Gopher Prairie or Zenith City, and *The Great Gatsby* (1925), a melancholy account of Jay Gatsby, who put his life at 'the service of a vast, vulgar and meretricious beauty,' is a counterpart of Willa Cather's *A Lost Lady*.

The year after the appearance of *The Great Gatsby*, the 28-year-old Ernest Hemingway published his first novel, *The Sun Also Rises*. In this book, and in subsequent works like *A Farewell to Arms*, set against the background of the Italian retreat after Caporetto, Hemingway sought to work out his preoccupation with senseless, violent injury, especially the wound he had received in the war, and to develop a code whereby a man may live with honor in the face of violence and annihilation. Hemingway lived the flamboyant life which was the stuff of his novels and stories—he drove an ambulance in war-torn Italy, was a correspondent in the Spanish Civil War, and hunted big game in Africa. But his great influence came not from his manner of living but from his literary style: direct, pithy, nervous, idiomatic. No other quite mastered it, but almost every writer of his generation imitated it.

A third major literary figure of the 1920's, Eugene O'Neill, has the distinction of being the first American dramatist to approach the kind of fame accorded Ibsen, Chekhov, and Shaw. Very much a child of his age, he reflected almost all the intellectual currents of the day, responding—as he put it—to the 'discordant, broken, faithless rhythms of our time.' He indulged himself in naturalism in his early plays of the sea like *Anna Christie*; participated in the revolt from the village—particularly the New England village—in *Desire Under the Elms*; shot his arrows at Babbitry in *The Great God Brown*; confessed a brief nostalgia for a homespun past he had never known in the charming *Ah, Wilderness!*; experimented with expressionism in *Lazarus Laughed*; immersed himself in Freudianism in *Strange Interlude* and in *Mourning Becomes Electra*, where he boldly invited comparison with the Agamemnon trilogy of Aeschylus. When he died he left a searing autobiographical drama, *Long Day's Journey into Night*, which, like *The Iceman Cometh*, returned to naturalism. A note of desperation resounds in this the best of O'Neill's plays, which recapitulate his painful childhood memory of his intimidating father, his drug-addicted mother, and his alcoholic elder brother; and in his final autobiographical *cri du cœur* there is a sense of hopelessness and of doom.

The fourth major figure to emerge during these postwar years, William Faulkner, wrote of the disintegration of the values of the Old South and the failure of the New, on such eternal themes as the conflict of freedom and necessity and Man's quest to liberate himself from the burden of history. Beginning with *The Sound and the Fury* (1929), and including such masterpieces as *Light in August, As I Lay Dying,* and *The Hamlet,* Faulkner traced the pathology of the South, Old and New—the collapse of standards, the ineffectiveness of the old families—like his own Falkners— and the irredeemable vulgarity and corruption of the new—like the Snopeses and the Sutpens. The greatest of American literary experimenters, a writer of dazzling virtuosity, Faulkner had learned something from Proust, something from

James Joyce, but his use of the stream of consciousness technique, the flashback, interior monologues, tortured syntax, and jumbled time sequences is all his own.

A host of lesser writers addressed themselves to the crises that bedeviled the postwar years and made a powerful impression on their own generation. John Dos Passos's sprawling *U.S.A.* trilogy, a profoundly pessimistic work, portrays a society that is rootless and disintegrated, hurrying to wealth and pleasure without faith or purpose. James T. Farrell, Dreiser's most faithful disciple, in his *Studs Lonigan* series depicts the Chicago of the 'twenties with unrelenting bitterness. Thomas Wolfe, the promise of whose *Look Homeward, Angel* (1929) was never wholly fulfilled in his later and more popular books, belongs only marginally to this group. Gargantuan, tempestuous, capable of both bathos and beauty, Wolfe was something of a genius and something of a charlatan. John Steinbeck's early books—*Tortilla Flat, In Dubious Battle,* and the enchanting *Red Pony*—revealed a high technical skill and a deep understanding of the Mexican Americans and the migratory workers of California. His *Grapes of Wrath* (1939), a moving saga of the trek of the Joad clan from their dust-blown Oklahoma farm to the promised land of California, was the one great story to come out of the depression that caught the tragedy of the Dust Bowl, the gallantry as well as the meanness of the rural proletariat.

Painting and Music

A new chapter in American art began when the Armory Show opened its doors in February 1913. In the next month or so more than 100,000 people crowded into the vast hall in New York City to gaze at paintings by Impressionists and post-Impressionists, Fauvists and Cubists. Here for the first time Americans could see the paintings of Cézanne and Matisse, Van Gogh and Picasso as well as that forever baffling 'Nude Descending a Staircase' by Marcel Duchamp. The new sculptors were there too—figures by Epstein and Maillol and Brancusi as well as by the newly Americanized Gaston Lachaise.

Yet the triumph of the Modernists still lay well ahead, and preoccupation with the social scene became the most pronounced feature of American painting. In 1936 the artist George Biddle, reviewing an exhibition of contemporary American and French painting, found that while among the French pictures there was not one that was concerned with social problems, among the American works 'seventy-four dealt with the American scene or with a social criticism of American life; six with strikes or with strikebreakers; six with dust, sand, erosion, drought, and floods. There were no nudes, no portraits, and two still lifes. Out of the hundred not one could be said to enjoy, reflect, participate in our inherited democratic-capitalist culture.'[3] Biddle himself was preoccupied with the social scene. So, too, were those abler artists, Charles Burchfield and Edward Hopper. Burchfield spread before us a panorama of ugliness—the ugliness of the small town in Ohio or Indiana, of the factory in that Buffalo where he chose to live, of rain-swept nights on dreary streets. He set himself, writes Sam Hunter, 'the task of exploring in humble visual metaphors the failures behind the American success story, the corruption of the landscape that followed in the wake of industrial progress and which most Americans had managed to ignore.'[4] Edward Hopper painted the poignant isolation of people in the great cities, while social criticism is to be found in the political cartoons of William Gropper; in Reginald Marsh's gaudy pictures of Coney Island, the Bowery, and other gathering places of those who have nowhere to go; and in Ben Shahn's Daumier-like commentaries. Better disposed toward American institutions were the regionalists: Thomas Hart Benton, who transcribed the social history of the Mississippi, of the South and the West; John Steuart Curry, who celebrated the plains of Kansas and the cottonfields of Dixie; Grant Wood, who bathed the rolling hills and the gimcrack houses of Iowa in rich color and sentiment, though in such paintings as 'American Gothic' and 'Daughters of the Revolution' he showed that he, too, could indulge in social criticism.

In the meantime the Modernists were rebelling against representational art. During a brief transi-

3. *An American Artist's Story,* p. 292.

4. *Modern American Painting and Sculpture,* p. 111.

'The Bridge' by Joseph Stella, 1922. Born in Italy, Stella (1880–1946) came to America in 1900 and first exhibited as an Italian Futurist, but by the 1920's he was identified with American Precisionists like Charles Sheeler and Charles Demuth who were fascinated by the structures of an industrial civilization. Of the Brooklyn Bridge, which also captivated the poet Hart Crane, Stella said: 'To realize this towering imperative vision, I lived days of anxiety, torture and delight alike, trembling all over with emotion. . . . Upon the swarming darkness of the night, I rung all the bells of alarm with the blaze of electricity scattered in lightnings down the oblique cables, the dynamic pillars of my composition. . . .' (*Newark Museum*)

tion period, craftsmen like Jonas Lie and John Marin moved into new experiments in the use of color or—as with Charles Sheeler—in geometric designs. They were succeeded by modernists such as Marsden Hartley, Stuart Davis, and the brilliant Georgia O'Keeffe. And, after them, the pure abstractionists like Jackson Pollock were just around the corner.

American music was not as advanced as American art. With the notable exceptions of folk music and Negro spirituals, America had always imported its music and musicians, and the most determined efforts to cultivate a 'native' music had failed. Edward MacDowell's sonatas and concertos were applauded on two continents, but most of the music of this generation now seems second-rate and derivative. More vitality appeared in the generation of composers that came to maturity after World War I—Virgil Thomson, John Alden Carpenter, Roy Harris, and Aaron Copland. Influenced by modernists like Stravinsky and Schönberg, Carpenter and Copland explored the symphonic possibilities of jazz and translated into music the nervous and explosive character of our mechanical civilization, while George Gershwin's *Rhapsody in Blue* and *Porgy and Bess* and Jerome Kern's *Show Boat* raised popular music to an art form. America's musical genius was best revealed in folk melodies and their modern equivalents, ragtime, jazz, blues, and swing. The Negro carried jazz from New Orleans to Chicago, and by 1915, the year W. C. Handy wrote 'St. Louis Blues,' jazz had reached Harlem. In the ensuing years Benny Goodman and Duke Ellington and Louis Armstrong won a loyal following among millions of Americans ranging from 'bobby-soxers' to musical sophisticates. The totalitarian terror recruited to American shores some of the most distinguished of contemporary European composers—Stravinsky, Hindemith, Bartók, Schönberg, to mention only a few. Musical conservatories like the Juilliard flourished, and great foundations like the Guggenheim stood ready to give such patronage to budding genius as Mozart and Schubert never knew.

Science

Tocqueville had observed that 'in America the purely practical part of science is admirably understood, and careful attention is paid to the theoretical portion which is immediately requisite to application . . . but hardly any one in the United States devotes himself to the essentially theoretical and abstract portion of human knowledge.' That was still true a century later; yet by then not only universities but industry were liberally underwriting research in pure science. What is more, the United States greatly benefited from the migration of European scientists which set in with the advent of Hitler to power in 1933. Einstein was the most famous of hundreds of physicists, chemists, and medical men who found in America refuge from oppression and an opportunity to pursue their researches in the most favorable circumstances. The most striking advances came in astronomy and physics. Working with the giant telescope of Mt. Wilson Observatory, which enabled them to plot thousands of new galaxies, astronomers postulated an expanding universe. Physicists, meantime, invented the cyclotron to break down the composition of the atom and held out the hope that some elements—uranium, for example—might yield fabulous amounts of energy.

Throughout this postwar generation doctors and chemists and bacteriologists, working in the laboratories of universities, the Federal Government, or the great foundations, waged war against diseases that had baffled medical science for centuries. The results were spectacular. In the first third of the century, infant mortality declined in the United States by two-thirds and life expectancy increased from 49 years to 59 years. The death rate for tuberculosis dropped from 180 to 49 per 100,000, for typhoid from 36 to 2, for diphtheria from 43 to 2, for measles from 12 to 1. Yellow fever and smallpox were practically wiped out, the battle against malaria, pellagra, hookworm, and similar diseases was brilliantly successful, and insulin cut the death rate of diabetes from over 700 to 12 per 1000 cases. The most sensational development came in the fight against coccus infections. Sulfanilamide and its numerous derivatives were used with stunning success against a host of coccal infections—streptococcus, meningitis, gonorrhea, gangrene, pyelitis, and, above all, pneumonia.

Nevertheless, the general health of the American people was not a matter for complacency. Infant mortality was still higher than in countries such as Norway and Sweden, and the draft statistics of the early 'forties revealed that an alarmingly large proportion of American men suffered from ailments caused by poverty or neglect, and that the incidence of venereal disease was shockingly high, especially in the rural counties of the South. The clear correlation between health and income suggested the desirability of government support to public health comparable with that given to public education, a goal that America did not even begin to take seriously until the 1960's and has yet to achieve.

30

The New Era and the Old Order

1920–1929

Return to 'Normalcy'

In the decade after the First World War, the dominant Republican party avowed a philosophy of laissez faire, but in practice made government an instrument of large corporations. The decade saw a florid but badly distributed industrial prosperity accompanied by agricultural distress and succeeded by acute and prolonged depression. It was characterized by a decline in liberalism and an ardent nationalism. And it moved into the future with its eyes fixed on the past; as the post-Civil War decade looked back to ante-bellum days, the 1920's sought to preserve the rural values of nineteenth-century America from the rude intrusion of the great city.

After years of playing second fiddle to strong leaders like Theodore Roosevelt within their own party and to a strong-minded Democratic President, the Republican Old Guard in 1920 was determined to nominate a pliable candidate, one who would not attempt to dictate to the Senate. They had such a man in the undistinguished Senator from Ohio, Warren Harding, who announced that the country needed a return to 'not heroism but healing, not nostrums but normalcy . . . not experiment but equipoise, not submergence in internationality but sustainment in triumphant nationality.' For the party's vice-presidential nominee, the delegates selected Calvin Coolidge. Fame had recently thrust herself upon Governor Coolidge when, in the course of a Boston police strike, he declared that there was 'no right to strike against the public safety by anybody, anywhere, anytime.' This resounding declaration caught the imagination of a public jittery about the 'Red menace.'

The Republicans exploited the national mood of weariness with the tensions and discord of the Wilson years—the war, the draft, the meatless days, and Spartan life of the war economy, the League fight, the Red Scare. Since much of this dissatisfaction found a personal target in Wilson, many of the Republicans directed their fire not against the Democratic presidential nominee, Governor James Cox of Ohio, but against the President. At the Republican convention, Lodge cried: 'Mr. Wilson and his dynasty, his heirs and assigns, or anybody that is his, anybody who with bent knee has served his purposes, must be driven

Franklin D. Roosevelt accepts the vice-presidential nomination of his party, 9 August 1920. On the platform with him at his Hyde Park, New York, home are his wife, Eleanor, and his 'Chief' when he was Assistant Secretary of the Navy, Josephus Daniels, in white suit and black string tie. In his acceptance speech, at a time when Harding was enunciating isolationist themes, FDR said, 'Modern civilization has become so complex and the lives of civilized men so interwoven with the lives of other men in other countries as to make it impossible to be in this world and not of it.' Compared to Harding's performance, observed the Harvard economist F. W. Taussig, Roosevelt's acceptance address was 'like Hyperion to a satyr.' (*Franklin D. Roosevelt Library*)

from all control, from all influence upon the Government of the United States.' The Democrats, who were hurt by the difficulties of operating a war economy which splintered their coalition into antagonistic interest groups, also bungled the transition from war to peace, which resulted in severe economic dislocations. The middle class was angered by the post-war inflation, labor by the cut in take-home pay after the war and the suppression of strikes. The administration, which had lost the support of many conservatives who disliked Wilson's progressive measures, was now blamed by liberals for the Palmer raids, the compromises at Versailles, and the increasingly conservative orientation of the government.

In the 1920 election the Republicans won a crushing victory which restored them as the majority party, a position they would hold for the next twelve years. With the electorate swollen by millions of new women voters, Harding won over 61 per cent of the vote, the largest proportion ever achieved in a presidential contest up to that time. He received 16 million votes to Cox's 9 million, and took 404 electoral votes to Cox's 127 by capturing the entire North and West and breaking the Solid South by carrying Tennessee. (The Socialist Eugene V. Debs received slightly under a million votes, although he was serving a term in the federal penitentiary at Atlanta.) Harding swept every borough in New York City, and Cox won but one county in all New England and lost every county on the Pacific Coast. Although the League issue had been muddled, isolationists claimed Harding's landslide victory as a triumph for their views. Even more emphatically, the election marked an end to an era of political intensity and discouraged the forces of reform.

Save for the Washington arms conference and

the creation of the Bureau of the Budget, Harding's administration was barren of accomplishment and tarnished by scandal. If Harding found room in his cabinet for Charles Evans Hughes as Secretary of State and Herbert Hoover as Secretary of Commerce, he dismayed conservationists by naming Albert B. Fall to the Department of the Interior. Fall, with the acquiescence of Secretary of the Navy Denby, entered into a corrupt alliance with the Doheny and Sinclair interests to give them control of immensely valuable naval oil reserves. The Elk Hills reserve in California was leased to Doheny's company; the Teapot Dome reserve in Wyoming to Sinclair's; in return Fall got at least $100,000 from Doheny and $300,000 from Sinclair. Investigations conducted by Senator Thomas Walsh of Montana forced the resignations of Denby and Fall; civil prosecutions in the federal courts brought the cancellation of the oil leases; criminal prosecutions sent Fall and Sinclair to prison. Colonel Charles R. Forbes, director of the Veterans' Bureau, was charged with the corrupt sale of government property, liquor, and narcotics, and misconduct in office, and was sentenced to a term in the federal penitentiary. Colonel Thomas W. Miller, the alien-property custodian, who sold valuable German chemical patents for a song, was dismissed from office and convicted of a criminal conspiracy to defraud the government. The President's close friend Attorney-General Harry Daugherty, who had been Harding's campaign manager, was found guilty by a Senate committee of various malpractices, but on a criminal trial he escaped conviction.

Harding seems to have been innocent of participation in or profit from this orgy of corruption, but he could not have been entirely unaware of it or of the consequences when the inevitable exposures began to come shortly before his death in office on 2 August 1923. Eight years later, at the belated dedication of the Harding Memorial at Marion, Ohio, President Hoover said, 'Warren Harding had a dim realization that he had been betrayed by a few men whom he trusted, by men whom he had believed were his devoted friends. It was later proved in the courts of the land that these men had betrayed not alone the friendship and trust of their staunch and loyal friend, but they

had betrayed their country. That was the tragedy of the life of Warren Harding.'

When Vice-President Coolidge succeeded Harding, Republicans breathed a sigh of relief. For Calvin Coolidge, whatever his limitations, represented probity and economy; if he displayed little zeal in tracking down the malefactors who had wrecked the Harding administration, he did not permit a continuation of their malpractices. A person of respectable mediocrity, Coolidge had little to his credit in the way of constructive legislation or political ideas and equally little to his discredit. So completely negative a man never before lived in the White House; it is characteristic that Coolidge is best remembered for his vetoes and his silence. 'Mr. Coolidge's genius for inactivity is developed to a very high point,' observed Walter Lippmann. 'It is far from being an indolent inactivity. It is a grim, determined, alert inactivity which keeps Mr. Coolidge occupied constantly.'

Yet this dour, abstemious, and unimaginative figure became one of the most popular of all American Presidents. For his frugality, unpretentiousness, and taciturnity gave vicarious satisfaction to a generation that was extravagant, pretentious, and voluble. To people who had pulled up their roots and were anxiously engaged in 'keeping up with the Joneses,' there was something comforting about the fact that Coolidge had been born in a village named Plymouth, that his first name was Calvin, that he had been content with a modest law practice and half of a two-family house in a small Massachusetts city, and that the oath of office which inducted him into the presidency had been administered in a Vermont farmhouse by his aged father, and by the light of a kerosene lamp. Actually Coolidge's frugality indicated no distrust of wealth; his taciturnity no philosophic serenity; his simplicity no depth. Coolidge lacked such Yankee traits as a desire to make the world better. Consequently, although 'Silent Cal' had a moral integrity wanting in his predecessor, his administration, more fully even than Harding's, represented a return to 'normalcy.'

Throughout this period, these conservative regimes held the progressives at bay. Even before the war some of the progressives had dropped by the way, and the war, although it brought such achievements as government labor boards, deeply divided the reformers. The aftermath was even more costly, for progressives disagreed with one another about the League, and some of them played an active role in the Red Scare. In the early 1920's a progressive element took part in the attempt to build a farmer-labor party, but the effort failed, chiefly because both farmers and workers were on the defensive throughout the decade.

During most of the 1920's, farmers were in distress, and the government did little of value to help them out. High war prices had persuaded farmers to expand, with an increase in borrowings and mortgage indebtedness, but farm prosperity did not last long enough to enable them to liquidate their debts. Even more important was the collapse of the foreign market. For a brief period, farmers took effective steps to meet their difficulties. During the Wilson administration the Non-Partisan League, organized in North Dakota, spread into fifteen states of the West. In 1916 the League captured control of the government of North Dakota and in the ensuing years enacted a far-reaching program: state-owned warehouses and elevators, a state bank, exemption of farm improvements from taxation, creation of a hail-insurance fund, a Home Building Association to encourage home ownership, and the establishment of an industrial commission to organize state-owned and state-financed industries. After the war, the more conservative American Farm Bureau Federation came to dominate farm politics. In the Harding regime a bipartisan 'farm bloc' pushed agrarian legislation through Congress. But by the Coolidge era the Non-Partisan League had disintegrated, and the farm bloc had lost much of its power. When farm leaders came up with schemes to enlist government support for agriculture as the tariff engaged its support for industry, they ran into a stone wall.

Union labor fared little better. Labor's time of troubles came right after the war when the return of millions of veterans, the threat of cheap labor and cheap products from abroad, and the cancellation of wartime contracts led to industrial unrest. More than 3000 strikes involving over 4 million workers erupted in 1919, and almost as many the following year. Business, and some elements in

'The Temple of Ceres,' Salina, Kansas. In this conceptualization, F.B. Bristow likens grain elevators on the Great Plains to a shrine of the Roman goddess of agriculture. The photograph is similar in design to that of Precisionist painters like Sheeler and Demuth. (*Smithsonian Institution*)

the government, made a concerted effort to establish the 'open shop' and to break the power of the unions, once and for all. During the 'twenties the position of organized labor deteriorated steadily; membership in unions declined from 5.1 million in 1920 to 3.6 million in 1929.

A series of spectacular strikes in steel, coal, railways, and textiles marked the beginning and the end of this decade of 'normalcy.' The most dramatic of the 1919 strikes came in the steel industry. One-third of all steel workers still labored twelve hours a day, seven days a week, and most of the rest worked a ten-hour day; when the steel workers demanded an eight-hour day, Judge Gary of the U.S. Steel Corporation refused even to discuss the matter with them. A commission of the Federal Council of Churches reported that the grievances of labor were acute: 'the average week of 68.7 hours . . . and the underpayment of unskilled labor, are all inhumane. The "boss system" is bad, the plant organization is military, and the control autocratic.' But the Steel Corporation managed to portray the strike as the entering wedge of communism, and it collapsed.

The coal industry had long been sick. The toll of accidents and deaths in the underground pits was appalling; many miners could count on only two or three days' work a week; and miners who lived in company-owned towns could call neither their homes nor their souls their own. When in 1919 West Virginia miners went out on strike, President Wilson pronounced the walkout a violation of wartime regulations, and the governor of West Virginia used state militia to smash it. Three years later another and more widespread strike exploded in the 'massacre' of imported strikebreakers at Herrin, Illinois. So devastated was the United Mine Workers by these strikes, and by hard times in the mines, that between 1920 and 1932 it declined from half a million to 150,000 members.

In 1922, to avert a slash in wages, railway shopmen, 400,000 strong, went out on strike. Harding set up a mediation board whose terms were accepted by the shopmen but rejected by the railway operators, or the bankers who controlled them, and the strike continued. At this juncture Attorney-General Daugherty invoked the law, not against the operators but against the strikers;

he obtained a sweeping injunction which outlawed any word or gesture that aided the strike in any way. The injunction was probably unconstitutional, but the strike ended before this could be determined.

The textile industry, like coal mining, had chronic difficulties. Originally centered in New England, it was now shifting to the South where there was less agitation about limitations on hours of work or child labor. Southern textile companies owned not only their mills but the mill villages, and usually the local sheriffs and politicians as well. A strike in 1927, in Elizabethton, Tennessee, where girls worked 56 hours a week for 18 cents an hour, was broken by a combination of local vigilantes, company militia, and state troops. In 1929 the union tried to organize the textile workers of North Carolina and Virginia, but once again vigilantes and police smashed both strike and strikers.

Throughout this period, the government, including the courts, threw its weight to the side of management. The Supreme Court held two child-labor laws unconstitutional, struck down a minimum wage law for women, sustained yellow-dog contracts, assessed triple damages against an unincorporated union, and threw out an Arizona anti-injunction law. Not until 1932 did the Norris-LaGuardia law erect effective safeguards against the misuse of the injunction in labor disputes and against the yellow-dog contract.

Both labor unions and farm organizations looked increasingly toward the national government to redress their grievances, but both major parties turned their backs. In 1924 the Republicans nominated Coolidge for a full term at a convention dominated by eastern business elements. The leading candidate for the Democratic nomination, William McAdoo, had been besmirched by the oil scandals. Not only did this make it difficult for the Democrats to make the most of the Republican scandals but the party became a national laughing stock when it took 103 ballots to choose a presidential nominee. After the convention deadlocked between McAdoo and Governor 'Al' Smith of New York, the Democrats tried to compete with the Republicans by nominating an ultraconservative, John W. Davis. 'I have a fine list of clients,' Davis declared. 'What lawyer wouldn't want them? I have J. P. Morgan and Company, the Erie Railroad, the Guaranty Trust Company, the Standard Oil Company, and other foremost American concerns on my list. I am proud of them.' The choice of Charles W. Bryan, brother to the 'Great Commoner,' as Davis's running mate did little to remove the taint of Wall Street. 'How true was Grant's exclamation,' observed Hiram Johnson, 'that the Democratic Party could be relied upon at the right time to do the wrong thing!'

Despairing of both major parties, labor and farm leaders joined with Socialists and old Bull Moosers to run a third ticket headed by 'Fighting Bob' La Follette. For their vice-presidential nominee the Progressives chose Senator Burton K. Wheeler, Montana Democrat, who declared: 'When the Democratic party goes to Wall Street for its candidate I must refuse to go with it.' The Progressive platform stressed the ancient issue of anti-monopoly but also advocated public ownership of water power, farm relief, abolition of the injunction in labor disputes, a federal child labor amendment, the election of all federal judges, legislation permitting Congress to override a judicial veto, the abolition of conscription, and a popular referendum on declarations of war.

At a time of boom prosperity most of the nation was satisfied enough with Republican policies to give Coolidge a lopsided victory with more than 54 per cent of the vote to Davis's less than 29 per cent, the least ever registered by a Democratic presidential candidate. Davis, with 136 electoral votes to Coolidge's 382, won only 12 states, all in the South. La Follette ran ahead of Davis in much of the West, and with nearly 5 million votes (better than 16 per cent) he made a respectable showing. But his failure to win any state but his own Wisconsin shattered the movement for a farmer-labor party, and his death the following year deprived the Progressives of their commander.

Businessmen responded more ebulliently to the returns; they interpreted Coolidge's victory as a ratification of the 'New Era' in which a benevolent capitalism would develop the economy in the national interest. In the Coolidge years the nation reaped the benefits from the application of electric-

ity to manufacturing and the adoption of the scientific management theories of Frederick Winslow Taylor. In 1914, electricity operated only 30 per cent of American factory machinery; by 1929, it sparked 70 per cent. The war nurtured a chemical industry, and the electrochemical revolution drastically altered factory procedures and improved output in industries like petroleum and steel. As a consequence of all these changes, the productivity of the worker increased rapidly and the real income of each person gainfully employed rose from $1308 in 1921 to $1716 in 1929, though prosperity was less widely diffused than many thought.

These achievements added to the stature of the businessman and encouraged Republican administrations to heed his demands, such as tax reduction. Instead of liquidating the public debt of $24 billion left by the war, Secretary of the Treasury Andrew Mellon, an aluminum magnate who held this post under all three Republican Presidents, sought to reduce taxes, especially the steep war levies. For a few years, an alliance of Democrats and Republican progressives balked him, but after the 1924 landslide Democratic conservatives outdid the Coolidge administration in urging lower taxes for the well-to-do. A series of revenue acts wiped out excess profit levies, drastically reduced surtaxes, granted rebates on 'earned income' and refunds to corporations of over $3.5 billion. Yet notwithstanding these reductions, the national debt was lowered by 1930 to $16 billion. No wonder the business community asserted that Andrew W. Mellon was 'the greatest Secretary of the Treasury since Alexander Hamilton.'

This policy of tax reduction, however, was not maintained with respect to one critical tax—the tariff. The Underwood tariff had never really been tried under normal conditions, for the war afforded protection to American manufactures and fostered the establishment of new industries. On conclusion of the war these 'infant' industries like chemicals clamored for protection. Fearful that the United States would be inundated with the produce of depressed European labor, a Republican Congress, in March 1921, pushed through an emergency tariff bill which Wilson promptly vetoed. 'If we wish to have Europe settle her debts, governmental or commercial, we must be prepared to buy from her,' he said. But this elementary logic failed to sink in.

Within a month of Harding's accession to the presidency, Congress enacted the emergency tariff of 1921, with prohibitive agricultural schedules which, though affording no relief to farmers with surplus crops to sell, did commit them to the principle of protection. More important was the Fordney-McCumber tariff of 1922, which established rates higher than ever before. The law also authorized the President to raise or lower duties as much as 50 per cent, but Harding and Coolidge used this authority only thirty-seven times. Thirty-two of these changes, involving items such as pig iron, were upward; the five articles on which duties were reduced were mill feed, bobwhite quail, paint-brush handles, cresylic acid, and phenol, but there was no Mr. Dooley to see the joke. The Fordney-McCumber act provoked a tariff war which cut seriously into our foreign trade, persuaded many manufacturers to establish branch plants abroad, and inspired among some large manufacturers and bankers their first serious misgivings about the wisdom of protection. Nonetheless, no sooner was Hoover inaugurated than he summoned Congress in special session to consider farm relief and 'limited changes in the tariff.' The Hawley-Smoot tariff bill represented increases all along the line. Objections from the American Bankers Association and from industries with foreign markets were brushed aside and a vigorous protest from 1028 economists had no effect on President Hoover, who signed the bill in June 1930. Within two years twenty-five countries established retaliatory tariffs, and American foreign trade slumped further.

Yet Republican administrations could not be impervious to considerations of foreign markets, raw materials, and investments. During the First World War the United States had changed from a debtor to a creditor nation. American private investments abroad, less than $3 billion before the war, increased to $14 billion by 1932. Part of this investment reflected the determination of American industry to control its own sources of raw material, and in this policy the government cooperated, just as governments had cooperated in the mercantilism of the seventeenth and eighteenth centuries. It encouraged foreign trade associations, discovered new trade opportunities abroad, and helped American oil interests obtain concessions in Latin America and in the Middle East.

Characteristically, the neo-mercantilists of the 1920's fostered large-scale combinations. Herbert Hoover, as Secretary of Commerce, inaugurated a policy of 'alliance with the great trade associations.' His sense of engineering efficiency was outraged at the spectacle of competition with its inevitable waste, and he proposed modifying the Sherman Act to permit business organizations to combine for certain purposes. He placed his department at the disposal of business, and under his auspices trade associations not only pooled information, advertising, insurance, traffic, and purchases, but drew up codes of fair practice. 'We are passing,' said Hoover, 'from a period of extreme individualistic action into a period of associational activities.'

In part as a result of this official encouragement, concentration of control grew apace. The decade from 1919 to 1929 saw 1268 combinations in manufacturing and mining, involving the merging of some 4000 and the disappearance of some 6000 firms. The same process took place in other fields. In the eight years after the war 3744 public utility companies disappeared through merger. In 1920 there were 30,139 banks; fifteen years later the number had been reduced by failures and mergers to 16,053. In 1920 the twenty largest banking institutions held about 14 per cent of all loans and investments; ten years later, 27 per cent. Chain stores ate heavily into the business of the independent shopkeeper. As the inevitable result of this process, in 1933 some 594 corporations, each capitalized at $50 million or more, owned 53 per cent of all corporate wealth in the country; the other 387,970 owned the remaining 47 per cent.

In few fields had concentration gone further than in hydroelectric power, but not without challenge. In the years after World War I the electric light and power industry grew with extraordinary rapidity, and largely through the holding-company device, control was concentrated in the

Charles Sheeler, 'Classic Landscape.' In 1912 Sheeler (1883–1965), whose paintings appeared in the controversial Armory Show of 1913 in New York, turned to photography, and this 1931 oil is based on photographs he had taken of the Ford Motor Works at River Rouge in 1927. Sheeler's paintings have the sharply defined order characteristic of the Precisionists, who adapted Cubism to American edifices like skyscrapers and grain elevators, as well as the ascetic attitude toward color and light that led critics to describe Sheeler and Charles Demuth as 'Immaculates.' (*Collection Mrs. Edsel B. Ford, Dearborn, Mich.*)

hands of six giant financial groups. Senators Walsh of Montana, La Follette of Wisconsin, and the indomitable Norris of Nebraska led the most important contest in this sphere—for government operation of the water-power dams at Muscle Shoals on the Tennessee river, which had been constructed to furnish power for nitrate plants during World War I. After the war, conservatives wanted to turn them over to private companies, and President Coolidge vetoed a bill providing for government operation of the dams. But in 1931 Congress once more passed the Norris bill, calling for the construction of a second dam on the Tennessee river and for government manufacture and sale of fertilizer and power. President Hoover vetoed the measure. 'I am firmly opposed to the Government entering into any business the major purpose of which is competition with our citizens,' he stated. 'That is not liberalism, it is degeneration.' This *ex cathedra* statement as to the nature and purposes of government did not settle the matter. Two years later, with the creation of the Tennessee Valley Authority, the Roosevelt administration entered jauntily upon the course of 'degeneration.'

The Quest for Peace

Although all three Republican administrations followed a generally isolationist course, they cooperated with other governments for purposes like disarmament. In his first year of office Harding, pursuant to a resolution sponsored by Senator Borah, called a conference of the nine powers with interests in the Pacific area, and in November 1921 delegates heard Secretary Hughes propose an itemized plan for scrapping warships and limiting naval armaments to prevent a naval race. The United States, Great Britain, Japan, France, and Italy agreed upon maintenance of a battleship and carrier ratio of 5-5-3 for the first three countries and 1.7 for the others, the scrapping of designated ships, and a ten-year naval holiday in the construction of capital ships. At the time, this Washington Treaty of 1922 and the London Naval Treaty of 1930, which extended its provisions to other classes of ships, were regarded as outstanding victories for peace. Yet few well-meaning reforms of the twentieth century proved so disappointing as naval limitation. Despite concessions to the Japanese which rendered the defense of Guam, Singapore, and the Philippines virtually impossible, Japan was insulted rather than appeased; their militarists used the slogan '5-5-3' to discredit the liberal government which had accepted limitation, and to get into power. When that had been accomplished, at the end of 1934 Japan denounced the naval-limitation treaties and started a frenzied building program which, by the time war broke out in the Pacific, rendered the Japanese navy more powerful in every type of ship than the United States and British Pacific and Asiatic fleets combined.

The Washington conference was designed not only to achieve arms limitation but to avoid conflict in the Far East where the Japanese had been extending their power. Japan had profited greatly from World War I by seizing the German islands in the North Pacific and the German concessions in Shantung, and, taking advantage of the involvement of the European powers and the isolation of the United States, consolidating its position in Manchuria and browbeating China. Early in 1915 the Japanese government presented to China Twenty-one Demands that would establish a practical protectorate over China. The ultimatum was a clear violation of the Root-Takahira agreement of 1908 to maintain the independence and territorial integrity of China and the 'open door' for commerce. Bryan protested, but he acted from a position of weakness, for it was just at this time that California, contemptuously rejecting President Wilson's plea for moderation, forbade Japanese to own land in the state. Such discriminatory legislation outraged the Japanese, who found it difficult to distinguish between action by the United States government and an affront from one of its sovereign states. In 1917 the Wilson administration conceded Japan's 'paramount' interest in China. Though the Lansing-Ishii Agreement reaffirmed the 'open door,' pledged both nations to respect the independence and territorial integrity of China, and disclaimed any desire for 'special rights or privileges,' it specifically recognized that 'territorial propinquity creates special relations, and that Japan has special interests in China, particularly in that part to which her possessions are contiguous.' At the Paris Peace Conference Japan also succeeded in legalizing her claims to Shantung and the former German islands in the Pacific.

At the Washington Conference, the American government sought to make the best of a bad situation by converting bilateral into multilateral understandings, thus freeing the United States from sole responsibility for a policy which it could not in any event enforce. By the Four Power Treaty (1921) the United States, Great Britain, France, and Japan engaged mutually to 'respect their rights in relation to their insular possessions in the region of the Pacific Ocean' and pledged themselves to confer about any controversy that

The changing of the guard. In 1925, when this photograph was taken, Frank B. Kellogg (1856–1937) succeeded Charles Evans Hughes (1862–1948), Secretary of State under Harding and Coolidge. In 1930, the bearded Hughes became Chief Justice of the United States, a position appropriate to his Jove-like appearance. (*Library of Congress*)

might arise over these rights. By the Nine Power Treaty (1922) the same powers, plus Italy, Belgium, the Netherlands, Portugal, and China, agreed to respect China's sovereignty, independence, and territorial and administrative integrity, maintain the principle of the 'open door,' and refrain from creating 'spheres of influence,' seeking privileges or concessions, or abridging therein the rights and privileges of citizens of friendly states. The Four Power Treaty buried the Anglo-Japanese alliance, and the Nine Power pact gave treaty form to the open door. But these agreements had one serious weakness: they set up no machinery for enforcement.

Lack of enforcement machinery was also the glaring weakness of the Pact of Paris (or Kellogg-Briand Pact). When in 1927 the French foreign minister, Aristide Briand, proposed a bilateral treaty to the United States for the outlawry of war, Secretary of State Frank B. Kellogg countered with the suggestion of a multilateral treaty of the same character. In the Pact of Paris of 1928, adhered to eventually by 62 nations, the contracting powers renounced war 'as an instrument of national policy.' The most thoroughgoing commitment to peace the great powers ever made, the Pact of Paris may fairly be called an attempt to keep peace by incantation. Little more than three years after the Pact of Paris was negotiated, Japanese militarists riddled its pretensions. World War II in the Far East really began on 18 September 1931 when General Hayashi moved his army into Manchuria and overran that great Chinese province. The Japanese government, which had not authorized this 'Manchuria Incident,' was forced to acquiesce under threat of assassination, and in 1932 Japan declared Manchuria the independent kingdom of Manchukuo, under a puppet monarch. This course violated the Nine Power Treaty, the Kellogg Pact, and the Covenant of the League of Nations, by each of which Japan was bound.

Secretary of State Henry L. Stimson met the Japanese aggression by enunciating the Stimson doctrine of refusing to recognize forceful acquisitions of territory, and he edged the United States closer to cooperation with the League, which proved to be impotent throughout the crisis. Stimson was uncertain about what else to do, and Hoover, who viewed the Kellogg Pact and the Nine Power Treaty as 'solely moral instruments,' opposed both military and economic sanctions. By 1932 little remained of the treaty structure of the 1920's.

In Latin America the outlook was more promising, despite the fact that here, too, Wilson had left his successors a heritage not only of fine principles but of tough problems, especially in Mexico. Article 27 of the Constitution of 1917 had vested in the Mexican nation ownership of all mineral and oil resources, and limited future concessions to Mexican nationals. If Article 27 should be interpreted as retroactive, American investments in mining and oil amounting to about $300 million would be confiscated. Under Harding war threatened over the possibility of a retroactive interpretation, and under Coolidge the conflict deepened when the Mexican government promoted agrarian laws that jeopardized American land investments and ecclesiastical legislation that affronted Roman Catholics. But Secretary of State Kellogg was unable to enlist popular support for an aggressive defense of American oil interests, and in January 1927 the Senate voted unanimously to arbitrate the controversy.

Sobered by this rebuke, Coolidge appointed as ambassador to Mexico his Amherst classmate, Dwight W. Morrow, a member of the House of Morgan who had publicly declared opposition to 'dollar diplomacy.' Through a remarkable combination of character, intelligence, shrewdness, and charm, Morrow succeeded in repairing most of the damage that his predecessors in Mexico City and his superiors in Washington had done. In response to Mexican Supreme Court rulings, oil and mineral legislation was modified in line with American objections, while Morrow obtained an adjustment of land issues, claims, and the Church

question. Throughout the 1930's this new understanding remained undisturbed, while in the United States a widespread admiration for Mexican culture (especially the paintings of Rivera and Orozco) and a growing appreciation of the social ideals of the Mexican revolution made a good base for the future.

Elsewhere in the Caribbean the United States showed more reluctance to pick up the 'big stick' that Theodore Roosevelt, Taft, and Wilson had brandished. American opinion was impatient with 'dollar diplomacy,' the Caribbean countries manifested a greater sense of order, and American investors wielded so much influence on the local governments that the old cry 'Send the Marines!' was unnecessary. In 1924 the Dominican flag displaced the American in that distracted republic. In 1925 United States Marines returned to Nicaragua to put down a revolution and supervise elections, but the acrimonious criticism which greeted this brief revival of intervention led to a more circumspect policy and eventually to a final withdrawal in 1933. Indeed, it was upon the foundation of the Latin American policy of Herbert Hoover that Franklin Roosevelt built his Good Neighbor Policy.

Nineteenth-Century America's Last Stand

In the years after World War I the older America of the Protestant, old-stock culture felt deeply threatened by the values of the burgeoning city and erected barriers against change. The census of 1920 revealed that for the first time most Americans lived in urban areas, broadly defined, a frightening statistic for those on the farms and in small towns whose way of life had prevailed for three centuries. They attributed to the metropolis all that was perverse in American society: the revolution in morals, the corner saloon, the control of municipal government by urban immigrants, and the modernist skepticism of the literal interpretation of the Bible.

Religious fundamentalism took an aggressive form after the war. Under the leadership of William Jennings Bryan, crusader for religious orthodoxy, several southern states enacted laws forbidding the teaching of evolution. In 1925 the whole country became caught up in the fun-

John Steuart Curry, 'Baptism in Kansas,' 1928. This painting is the best known of a series of Midwestern subjects by Curry (1897–1946) that helped set the style of 'regionalism.' In an age of urban-rural tension when New York City art circles responded to the latest fashion from Europe, the Kansas-born Curry, along with Grant Wood and Thomas Hart Benton, established a rival power center in the Midwest that cultivated indigenous American painting. (*Whitney Museum of American Art*)

damentalist controversy when a high-school biology teacher, John T. Scopes, was tried for violating a Tennessee statute forbidding the teaching of evolution. To Dayton, Tennessee, swarmed armies of reporters to watch Clarence Darrow, the iconoclastic attorney, subject Bryan, who joined the prosecution, to a savage examination that revealed the ignorance of the Commoner. Within a few days after his ordeal, Bryan was dead, and

with him died much of the older America. The judge found Scopes guilty,[1] and the anti-evolution laws remained on the statute books. But the fundamentalist crusade no longer had the same force.

The impulse to use coercion to preserve the

1. A higher court subsequently reversed the conviction on a technicality.

589

The Ku Klux Klan. This KKK gathering took place in Beckley, W. Va., on 9 August 1924. (*Library of Congress*)

values of the older America took a much uglier form in the creation of the Ku Klux Klan. An organization of white, native-born Protestants, the Klan was aggressively anti-Negro, but its chief target was not the Negro but the Catholic. (The chief organ of the KKK in Illinois advertised '12 red hot anti-Catholic postcards, all different.') The Klan was also anti-Semitic and anti-foreign-born. Although the Klan was founded in Georgia, it had its greatest strength not in the Deep South but in the Midwest, where the dominant figure was the Grand Dragon of the Realm of Indiana, David Stephenson. In its war against 'metropolitan morality' the Klan opposed all the forces turning cities into 'modern Sodom and Gomorrahs.' To compel adherence to its moral code, the KKK employed social ostracism against individuals judged guilty of moral infractions, but it also sometimes resorted to violence—church burnings, lynchings, mutilations, and whippings.

Wherever it had strength, the Klan reached out for political power. In some states the KKK was so potent that elections were held in Klaverns before the regular primaries. The Klan infiltrated both major parties. In 1924 in Colorado it elected a governor, one house of the legislature, several judges and sheriffs, and the Denver chief of police. In Alabama, it ended the career of the veteran Senator Oscar Underwood, whom it denounced as the 'Jew, jug, and Jesuit candidate,' and replaced him with Hugo Black, who accepted a life membership in the KKK. In the 1924 presidential campaign it silenced the Republicans and fractured the Democrats, who voted not to mention the Klan by name, 543³/20 to 542³/20. No longer did the KKK hide in the shadows. On 8 August 1925, in a brazen assertion of strength, more than 50,000 Klansmen marched for 3½ hours down Pennsylvania Avenue in the nation's capital.

But the Klan declined even more rapidly than it rose to power. It was fought by the various ethnic groups it attacked; by liberals and old-stock conservatives; by corruptionists and bootleggers; and by courageous southern governors and mayors. In Indiana in 1925, after a sordid episode, Stephenson was convicted of second-degree murder and sentenced to life imprisonment. When the governor refused to come to his aid, Stephenson made public the corruption and violence in the order. Within a year, the Klan was headed downhill, and by the end of the decade only small pockets of power remained.

Many who abhorred the Klan shared the order's conviction that the older Americans of Anglo-Saxon stock owned the United States and its fear that republican institutions were being undermined by the tidal wave of European immigrants. During the 'twenties Congress enacted laws which drastically limited immigration and set up a quota system that discriminated in favor of the 'old' and against the 'new' immigration. As a result of this legislation and, even more, of the Great Depression, immigration from the Old World fell to about 35,000 during the 1930's, while during that decade almost 100,000 more aliens returned to their homes than came to America.

At the very outset of the decade rural America had scored an emphatic victory when the Eighteenth Amendment, forbidding the 'manufacture, sale or transportation of intoxicating liquors,' went into effect in January 1920. Prohibition permitted the Protestant countryside to coerce the newer Americans in the city. One 'dry' asserted: 'Our nation can only be saved by turning the pure stream of country sentiment and township morals to flush out the cesspools of cities and so save civilization from pollution.' In the cities opposition to prohibition, once strongest among foreign-born workingmen, spread through every class of society, and the thirst for liquor was sublimated into a philosophy of 'personal liberty.' Mencken claimed that prohibition had caused suffering comparable only to that of the Black Death and the Thirty Years War, and the president of the Carnegie Institute of Technology told a Senate committee that rum was 'one of the greatest blessings that God has given to men out of the teeming bosom of Mother Earth.' States with large urban populations sabotaged prohibition laws just as Northern states had once nullified the fugitive slave acts. Agents of the Prohibition Bureau entered into corrupt alliances with bootleggers like Chicago's vicious Al Capone, and there was a breakdown not only of law but of respect for the law.

Both political parties tried to evade the troublesome issue, but without success. The Republicans, strongest in rural, Protestant communities, were inclined to stand behind what Hoover called 'an experiment noble in motive and far-reaching in purpose.' The Democrats were in a quandary. Their strength came in almost equal proportions from southern and western rural constituencies which were immovably dry and northern industrial constituencies which were incurably wet. In the Northeast Democratic leaders reflected the rage of foreign-born and second-generation Americans at the moralistic attitudes of the drys. 'The government which stands against the founder of Christianity cannot survive,' declared Senator David I. Walsh of Massachusetts. If Christ came back to earth and performed the Cana miracle again, 'he would be jailed and possibly crucified again.' But Democratic leaders like Bryan found their Methodist followers no less intensely in favor of prohibition. This division almost split the party in 1924 and deeply affected the outcome of the 1928 election.

In 1928 the Democrats, impaled on the urban-rural split four years earlier, decided to ride with the forces of urbanism by nominating Alfred E. Smith, the able governor of New York and *beau ideal* of the newer Americans from the slums of the great cities. A product of the 'Sidewalks of New York,' he was a Tammany brave, wringing wet, and the first lifetime city-dweller to receive the presidential designation of a major party. The *New Republic* observed: 'For the first time, a representative of the unpedigreed, foreign-born, city-bred, many-tongued recent arrivals on the American scene has knocked on the door and aspired seriously to the presiding seat in the national Council Chamber.'

Since the Democrats were as solicitous as the Republicans of business interests in 1928, they erased any real difference on economic issues between the candidates, permitting much of the campaign to revolve around a single fact: that for the first time in American history a major party had nominated a Roman Catholic for President. Smith's detractors whispered that if he were elected all Protestant children would be declared bastards. When bigots were not claiming that Smith's election would make the White House an outpost of the Vatican, they were depicting the election of a wet like Smith as a religious affront to rural Protestants. If 'the Christian vote' did not go to the polls, warned the *Christian Endeavor World*, 'we shall see our towns and villages rum-ridden in the near future and a whole generation of our children destroyed.' Finally, the assault on Smith was closely linked to an attack on the foreign-born in the northern cities. 'Elect Al Smith to the presidency,' declared one southern churchman, 'and it means that the floodgates of immigration will be opened, and that ours will be turned into a civilization like that of continental Europe. Elect Al Smith and you will turn this country over to the domination of a foreign religious sect, which I could name, and Church and State will once again be united.'

The objection to Smith expressed not simply anti-Catholicism but a pervasive anti-urbanism that embraced antagonism to his religion, his views on liquor, his tie to Tammany Hall, his identification with the new immigrants, and his

association with the city itself. On the other hand, Smith's opponent, Herbert Hoover, had the advantage of being able to summon up the image of a pristine America. He wrote of boyhood memories of gathering walnuts in the fall, carrying grain to the mill, fishing for catfish and sunnies, and finding 'gems of agate and fossil coral' on the Burlington track. His family, he recalled, had woven its own carpets, made its own soap, preserved 'meat and fruit and vegetables, got its sweetness from sorghum and honey.'

Hoover won decisively, with over 58 per cent of the popular vote to Smith's less than 41 per cent. Whereas Cox had taken eleven states and Davis twelve, Smith took only eight. For the first time since Reconstruction, the Republicans cut deeply into the Solid South. Smith, who received a much higher proportion of the popular vote than Davis or Cox had, ran well in the large cities inhabited by newer Americans; in Irish wards in South Boston, he got as much as 90 per cent of the vote. Hoover won because he ran as a candidate of the majority party at a time of boom prosperity, but Smith's background also proved costly. 'America is not yet dominated by its great cities,' concluded a Minnesota newspaper after the election. 'Main Street is still the principal thoroughfare of the nation.'

Collapse

Herbert Hoover entered the White House with the brightest of reputations. His successful management of relief organizations in Belgium, Russia, and the Mississippi valley had earned him the sobriquet of great humanitarian; his vigorous administration of the Commerce Department won him the confidence of business, if not of Wall Street. Innocent of any previous elective office, Hoover seemed to be a new type of political leader: a socially minded efficiency expert, a world-famous mining engineer. Hoover, in short, carried into the White House with him all of the shining promises of the New Era. 'We in America are nearer to the final triumph over poverty,' he proclaimed during the campaign, 'than ever before in the history of any land. . . . We have not reached the goal, but, given a chance to go forward with the policies of the last eight years,

Thomas Hart Benton, 'City Activities with Subway.' This panel, one of a series of murals Benton was commissioned to paint for the New School for Social Research in Greenwich Village in 1930, conveys both the frenetic energy and the fragmentation of the big city. In the subjects he chooses—a prize fight, a burlesque show, a tabloid, a Salvation Army street band—and in his depiction of raw sexuality, Benton also conveys a sense of a metropolitan way of life alien to the pristine society of the American heartland that he and the other 'regionalists' were portraying. In Benton's view, 'the great cities,' dominated by Marxists and homosexual aesthetes, were 'dead.' (*New School for Social Research*)

we shall soon with the help of God be in sight of the day when poverty will be banished from this nation.'

Hoover's election was the signal for a boom on the Stock Exchange. The average value of common stocks soared from 117 in December 1928 to 225 the following September. Inspired by dazzling gains, brokers increased their borrowings from $3.5 billion in 1927 to $8.5 billion two years later,

and in the single month of January 1929 no less than a billion dollars' worth of new securities were floated. Factory employment, freight car loadings, construction contracts, bank loans, almost all the indices of business, showed a marked upward swing.

Yet even as Hoover announced in his inaugural address that 'in no nation are the fruits of accomplishment more secure,' shrewd investors were pulling out of the market. The Federal Reserve Board did little to reverse the policy of easy credit it had inaugurated in 1927, but there were many reasons for concern. The world economic situation was discouraging. War debts were uncollectable, foreign trade had declined precipitously, and the interest on billions of dollars of private investments was in default. Agriculture was depressed, and industries such as coal and textiles had not shared in the general well-being. Much of the new wealth had gone to the privileged few; 5 per cent of the population enjoyed one-third of the income. Business plowed a disproportionate amount of the gains in productivity into new plants or passed them on as dividends rather than wages. So long as industry turned out mountains of goods but denied workers the purchasing power to buy them, a breakdown was inevitable. Meantime public and private debts had mounted to staggering sums; by 1930 the total debt burden was estimated at approximately one-third the national wealth. Too many Americans were living on the future. When confidence in the future disappeared, the system collapsed.

The crash came in October 1929. In less than a month stocks suffered an average decline of 40 per cent. At the outset many assumed that the Wall Street crash, although devastating, was only the latest of those familiar financial panics that America had experienced before. In fact, it helped bring about a depression which would leave an enormous fault line in the United States. 'The stock market crash,' wrote the literary critic Edmund Wilson, 'was to count for us almost like a rending of the earth in preparation for the Day of Judgment.' Before the Great Depression ended, some thirteen years later, it would alter the whole landscape of American society, terminate the long reign of the Republicans as the majority party, cut short the political career of Herbert Hoover, and bury in its ruins the bright prospects of the New Era.

31

The Great Depression
and the New Deal

1929–1939

The Depression and the Hoover Response

The stock market crash of 1929 confronted the United States with its greatest crisis since the Civil War. Factories slashed production; construction practically ceased; millions of investors lost their savings; over 5000 banks closed their doors in the first three years of the depression. Between 1920 and 1932 total farm income declined from $15.5 billion to $5.5 billion. 'Wheat on the Liverpool market,' noted one observer, 'fetched the lowest price since the reign of Charles II.' Foreign trade declined in three years from $9 billion to $3 billion. One writer observed: 'We seem to have stepped Alice-like through an economic looking-glass into a world where everything shrivels. Bond prices, stock prices, commodity prices, employment—they all dwindle.'

As the depression wore on, unemployment mounted to staggering levels, and suffering became intense. Of New England's 280,000 textile millhands, 120,000 had no work a year after the crash. New Bedford was bankrupt; Lowell and Lawrence seemed like ghost towns. By 1933 the number of jobless was variously estimated at from 12 to more than 15 million, as factory payrolls fell to less than half the level of 1929. In a country of some 120 million people, probably more than 40 million were either unemployed or members of a family in which the main breadwinner was out of work. Blacks learned the cruel truth of the saying that they were the 'last to be hired, first to be fired.' Those who did have jobs often worked for a pittance. Young girls got $1.10 a week for sweatshop labor in progressive Connecticut, and grown men worked for 5 cents an hour in sawmills. Yet this desperate deprivation came at a time when orchards were heavy with fruit, granaries bulging with grain. Miners froze in the midst of mountains of coal, while their children lived on weeds and dandelions.

The depression seriously impaired confidence in business leadership. Nowhere else in the world had the titans of finance and the moguls of industry enjoyed such prestige, but by 1932 businessmen who in the 1920's had taken credit for prosperity now found themselves saddled with the blame for hard times. One economist wrote: 'It is easier to believe that the earth is flat than to believe that private initiative alone will save us.'

The Great Depression, Fulton Street, New York City. (*National Archives*)

Yet business leaders became discredited not merely because they were judged accountable for the depression and proved unable to restore prosperity but because so many revealed themselves to be socially irresponsible. The public learned with astonishment that the dignified House of Morgan kept a 'preferred list' of customers and influential public men to whom it sold securities below the market price. 'The belief that those in control of the corporate life of America were motivated by ideals of honorable conduct was completely shattered,' observed the millionaire Joseph P. Kennedy.

The crisis in confidence produced by the depression went far beyond a disaffection with business leadership. Throughout the Western world, men brooded over whether the great society of the West which had grown in strength since the days of Charlemagne had not begun to disintegrate. The British historian Arnold Toynbee wrote: 'The year 1931 was distinguished from previous years—in the "post-war" and in the "pre-war" age alike—by one outstanding feature. In 1931, men and women all over the world were seriously contemplating and frankly discussing the possibility that the Western system of Society might break down and cease to work.' If in Europe men wondered whether the Western world had not reached the stage of the Roman empire after Theodosius, most Americans were of a more optimistic frame of mind. Yet even in the United States the cold fear that the world Americans had known might be at a terminus could not easily be overcome.

The Hoover administration discounted the seriousness of the depression, for those who had guided the destinies of the nation through the 1920's believed that the economy was fundamentally sound and that prosperity would return as soon as there was a restoration of confidence. To this end President Hoover urged industrial leaders to maintain employment and wages and, in speech after speech, exhorted the nation to keep a stiff upper lip. But he did more than this. Assuming responsibilities no President had ever taken on before, he stepped up public works; announced a tax cut; and, through the Federal Reserve System, encouraged an easy credit policy. To support crop prices, the Federal Farm Board purchased vast quantities of wheat and cotton.

Yet these measures were largely nullified by other policies. Committed to budget-balancing, Hoover took away with one hand what he gave with the other. The increase in federal spending for public works was so modest that it was more than offset by the drastic cut in state and local spending. Although he insisted that the source of America's troubles lay overseas, he agreed to the Hawley-Smoot tariff which raised new barriers to international trade. Above all, he persisted in relying on voluntary agreements even when this faith proved misplaced.

Nothing demonstrates so well the inadequacy of voluntarism as the sad experience of Hoover's Federal Farm Board. Despite the Board's activities, cotton prices skidded from 17½ cents in October 1929 to less than 8 cents in 1930. The program failed because the Board was attempting to support crop prices without restricting production, and it was swamped by surpluses. In summer 1931, faced by a glut of millions of bales of cotton, the chairman of the Board wired cotton state governors 'to induce immediate plowing under of every third row of cotton now growing.' But Hoover continued to hold out against controls. By June 1932 cotton prices had slumped to 4.6 cents. The Board had financed the removal of 3½ million bales from the market only to see ten million bales added to the surfeit. After the collapse of these voluntary price stabilization operations, Hoover had nothing more to offer. The farmer faced ruin, and because of his importance to the economy of agrarian states, he threatened to pull the nation's banks down with him.

Despite mounting evidence of the breakdown of his program for recovery, Hoover spurned appeals for more vigorous federal action. He shared the common belief that federal spending would prolong the depression by discouraging investment and inviting inflation. A man touted as a Great Engineer, he brought to government none of the engineer's insistence on testing theories by their results. One who prided himself on his willingness to consult experts, he ignored advice which ran counter to his preconceptions. In vain did progressives like La Follette, Costigan, and Cutting plead for a large-scale program of public works, financed directly by federal funds. In vain did they present statistics proving the breakdown of private charity and the inability of municipal and state authorities to carry the burden any longer.

In 1931 European financial squalls struck the United States in full force. In June Hoover braved the displeasure of isolationists by proposing a one-year moratorium on reparations and war debt payments, a constructive move which failed to save the day. The European panic caused a fresh financial crisis in America. In August, 158 banks failed, in September, 305, in October, 522. When the Federal Reserve Board raised the rediscount rate sharply, it halted the flow of gold abroad but did untold damage. As credit tightened, production fell off, stocks plummeted, and a typhoon of bank failures swept areas that had been hardly touched before: New England, the Carolinas, the Pacific Northwest.

Hoover responded first by encouraging bankers to set up their own credit organization, and then by asking Congress for an eight-point program intended chiefly to shore up the great financial institutions. In December 1931 he called on Congress to establish a Reconstruction Finance Corporation, which was the old War Finance Corporation in new guise. The RFC, chartered by Congress in 1932, was authorized to lend money to banks, railroads, and other institutions. Congress also approved most of the rest of Hoover's requests in 1932, including the creation of such institutions as the Federal Home Loan Banks to discount mortgages.

Yet Hoover's new program proved no more successful than his original efforts, and for the same reasons: he acted on too small a scale and put too much faith in voluntarism. The RFC made so little use of its power that it frustrated the intent of Congress. The Federal Home Loan Banks neither averted collapse of the mortgage market nor helped the distressed homeowner. The credit organization fell apart when bankers refused to cooperate. As Hoover himself later wrote: 'After a few weeks of enterprising courage, the bankers' National Credit Association became ultraconservative, then fearful, and finally died. It had not exerted anything like its full possible strength. Its members—and the business world—threw up their hands and asked for government action.'

This same misplaced faith in voluntarism marked Hoover's approach to relief for the unemployed. Despite widespread hardship, Hoover claimed that federal relief was not needed, and that the traditional sources—private charity and local government—would meet the needs of the unfortunate. But neither private agencies nor municipal governments could hope to meet distress in a city like Cleveland where 50 per cent of the work force were jobless, or in Akron or East St. Louis when unemployment reached 60 per cent, or Toledo where it mounted to 80 per cent. By the spring of 1932 the country confronted a

relief crisis. New York City, where the average family stipend for relief was $2.39 a week, had 25,000 emergency cases on its waiting list. Houston, Texas, announced: 'Applications are not taken from unemployed Mexican or colored families. They are being asked to shift for themselves.' In Chicago, families were separated, and husbands and wives sent to different shelters. On 25 June 1932, Philadelphia ran out of funds—private, municipal, state—and suspended aid to some 52,000 families. But Hoover, doggedly, stubbornly, continued to insist that he had the situation well in hand.

The failure of Hoover to liquidate the depression placed the Republicans in an extremely vulnerable position, and brightened the expectations of the Democrats who chose as their presidential candidate in 1932 the governor of New York, Franklin D. Roosevelt. A distant connection of T. R., and married to the former President's niece, Franklin D. Roosevelt was born to wealth and position, and as a child had learned a patrician's conviction of *noblesse oblige*. He rose rapidly in the Democratic party, served as Assistant Secretary of the Navy under Wilson, and in 1920 was nominated as Cox's running mate. The following year his promising political career was apparently ended by a severe case of infantile paralysis, but during the next seven years, he fought his way back, though he remained permanently crippled. In 1928 the voters of New York elected him governor when they rejected Smith for President, and in 1932, after a closely fought contest, he was picked as his party's presidential nominee. Running safely ahead, FDR straddled a number of important questions and was silent on others, and scolded Hoover as a spendthrift, but he also made clear that he favored unemployment relief, farm legislation, and 'bold and persistent experimentation' to give a 'new deal' to the 'forgotten man.' Furthermore, he showed a willingness to turn to the universities for counsel, since his 'Brain Trust' of speech writers and advisers included three Columbia University professors: Raymond Moley, Rexford Guy Tugwell, and Adolf A. Berle, Jr.

Hoover, laboring under the dead weight of hard times, faced a hopeless task. He made matters still worse when in the summer of 1932 he resorted to

The routing of the bonus army, 1932. The shanties of World War I veterans encamped in Washington go up in flames in sight of the Capitol dome. (*National Archives*)

force to rout a 'bonus army' that had marched on Washington to demand immediate payment of the bonuses voted to veterans of World War I. Swords in hand, cavalrymen rode down the marchers and their wives and children, burning their hovels and scattering their pitiful possessions. The smouldering ruins of Anacostia flats served to confirm the impression that the President was hostile to the dispossessed, and that the country needed a change. Roosevelt received almost 23 million votes, to fewer than 16 million votes for Hoover, and his victory was even more decisive in the Electoral College, where he carried every state but six. Hoover, with less than 40 per cent of the vote, sustained the worst defeat ever inflicted on a Republican presidential nominee in a two-party race. The Democrats also won their greatest majority in the House since 1890 and their largest margin in the Senate since before the Civil War. The Great Depression had ended the reign of the Republicans as the nation's majority party and fastened on the G.O.P. the unwelcome reputation of the party of hard times.

Franklin Roosevelt would not take office for another four months, since the Twentieth Amendment, the 'lame duck' proposal advanced by Senator George Norris, had not yet been ratified. The harsh interregnum was a time of exaggerated worry over the peril of incipient revolution, as Iowa farm rebels recalled the insurrection of Daniel Shays, but it was even more a time of lassitude and of fear. Charles M. Schwab of Bethlehem Steel was quoted as saying: 'I'm afraid, every man is afraid.' The premonitions of disaster seemed well founded when, on the eve of Roosevelt's inauguration, banks shut their doors in every section of the country and on the morning of inauguration day the Stock Exchange closed

The inauguration of Franklin D. Roosevelt, 4 March 1933. In this fanciful and highly stylized depiction of the event, the Mexican illustrator Miguel Covarrubias shows the Chief Justice of the United States, Charles Evan Hughes, placing a wreath on the President's head while the new First Lady, Eleanor Roosevelt, looks on. The tableau, which appeared in *Vanity Fair*, is in the manner of David's 'Coronation of Napoleon' and foreshadowed those observers who were soon to see in Roosevelt's reign manifestations of imperial Rome. The two men to the left of FDR in the picture are the pudgy, high-collared outgoing President, Herbert Hoover, with a high hat, and the incoming Vice President, John Nance Garner, in wrinkled trousers and carrying the Stetson cowboy hat of his native Texas. *(Copyright © 1933 (renewed 1961) by Condé Nast Publications).*

down. As the financial system collapsed, all eyes looked toward Washington.

Wall Street and Washington

When Roosevelt took the oath of office on 4 March 1933, he declared, 'This nation asks for action, and action now!' If it proved necessary, he said in his electrifying inaugural address, he would ask Congress for 'broad Executive power to wage a war against the emergency as great as the power that would be given me if we were in fact invaded by a foreign foe.' Roosevelt's first task was to rehabilitate the nation's banks. In the Treasury, lights burned all through the night as Hoover and Roosevelt lieutenants worked to-

Franklin D. Roosevelt signs the Emergency Banking Act, 9 March 1933. Behind him are the United States flag and the presidential flag and two naval prints. Some of the progressives who admired FDR's domestic policies were uneasy about the fact that he was a 'big navy man.' (*UPI (INS)*)

gether in a spirit of wartime unity to cope with the financial crisis. On the day after his inauguration, the President issued two edicts: one summoned Congress into special session; the other halted transactions in gold and proclaimed a national bank holiday. When Congress convened on 9 March, it took only seven hours to pass Roosevelt's banking bill which validated presidential powers over banks and facilitated the reopening of liquid banks under proper regulation. Three days later, in the first of his radio 'fireside chats,' the President told his listeners it was safer to 'keep your money in a reopened bank than under the mattress'; when the bank holiday ended the next morning in Federal Reserve cities, deposits exceeded withdrawals. The crisis had been ended. Although the powers of government had been greatly enhanced, the nation's financial institutions remained in private hands.

The historic 'Hundred Days' had begun. From 9 March until Congress adjourned on 16 June, Roosevelt sent fifteen different proposals to Congress and saw all fifteen adopted. In quick succession, he followed up his banking message with proposals for government economy and to amend the Volstead Act to legalize light wine and beer.[1] Within two weeks after FDR took office, the country seemed to have regained a large share of its sense of purpose, a recapture of morale, said Walter Lippmann, comparable only to the news of the second battle of the Marne.

Yet the weight of Roosevelt's early actions was deflationary, and he recognized that he must experiment with ways to raise prices, in order to alleviate the debt burden and speed recovery. In a bold series of actions, he took the United States off the gold standard.[2] That fall, the President tried to raise prices through buying gold, and he later bowed to the demand of Mountain State senators

1. Before the year was out, the Twenty-first Amendment repealing the Eighteenth (Prohibition) Amendment had been ratified.

2. A Joint Resolution of 5 June canceled the gold clauses in all government and private obligations and made all debts payable in legal tender. When the resolution was challenged in the courts, the Supreme Court in a 5–4 decision sustained congressional power over legal tender and held that though the cancellation of gold clauses in government contracts was both illegal and immoral the plaintiff had suffered no damage and had no grounds for suit.

to undertake silver purchases; however, currency manipulation did not effect any appreciable increase in commodity prices. In January 1934 the President obtained authority to devalue the dollar, which he fixed at 59.06, and the nation returned to this modified gold standard. Though the goal of controlled inflation had been carried through with utmost caution, the country had taken a big stride toward a managed currency.

Roosevelt also dealt with the debt burden directly. Foreclosures of rural properties had become so numerous that in some sections farmers banded together to intimidate prospective purchasers, close courts, and terrorize judges; in late April 1933 a mob dragged an Iowa judge off his bench and came close to lynching him. The following month Congress authorized the creation of a new Farm Credit Administration which within eighteen months had refinanced a fifth of all farm mortgages in the United States. Congress also came to the aid of the distressed home owner, in the cities as well as in the country. In June 1933 it established a Home Owners' Loan Corporation to refinance small mortgages on privately owned homes; within a year this corporation had approved almost a billion dollars in loans.

Roosevelt, who had a patrician's distrust of Wall Street and a Wilsonian's memory of the machinations of the 'money trust,' was determined to discipline the financiers. The congressional investigation of banking and securities practices directed by Ferdinand Pecora, which revealed conditions characterized as 'scandalous,' and the banking collapse of 1932–33 dramatized the need and furnished the opportunity for reform. The Glass-Steagall Act of June 1933 separated commercial and investment banking, severely restricted the use of bank credit for speculative purposes, and expanded the Federal Reserve System. To prevent a recurrence of the epidemic of bank failures, the act set up a Federal Deposit Insurance Corporation to insure bank deposits up to a fixed sum. Roosevelt accepted this proposal with reservations, and the American Bankers Association denounced it as 'unsound, unscientific, unjust and dangerous,' but it turned out to be one of the most constructive devices of the New Deal era. Bank failures, which had averaged a thousand a year in the previous decade, became almost non-existent. During the 'Second Hundred Days'

William Gropper, 'The Senate,' 1935. Called 'the American Daumier,' Gropper, the son of a sweatshop worker, left high school to work at odd jobs like dishwasher, scraped enough cash together to study with the artists Robert Henri and George Bellows, became an illustrator for the radical *New Masses*, and on his return from a trip to Soviet Russia with Theodore Dreiser and Sinclair Lewis in 1927, put out a book of drawings. Like so many other painters in the Great Depression, Gropper found employment on the Federal Art Project. In this bitter satire, a balding, pot-bellied U.S. Senator declaims to a largely empty chamber while one solon dozes and another reads a newspaper. (*Museum of Modern Art, Gift of A. Conger Goodyear*)

of the summer of 1935, Congress put the final stone in the new structure of government regulation of banking with the Banking Act of 1935 which expanded the powers of the reorganized and newly named Board of Governors of the Federal Reserve System.

The New Deal also brought the marketing of stocks and bonds under federal control. The Securities Act of 27 May 1933 stipulated that new securities must be registered with a government agency, subsequently the Securities and Exchange Commission; that every offering should contain full information to enable the prospective purchaser to judge its value; corporation officials were to be criminally liable for any misrepresentation. The following year came legislation to curb malpractices on the Stock Exchange. An act of June 1934 created a Securities and Exchange Commission and instituted regulation of stock exchanges. Joseph P. Kennedy, financier and speculator, was appointed chairman of the SEC because, Roosevelt said, he knew the tricks of the trade. Much of this legislation reflected the influence of the followers of Justice Brandeis—Felix Frankfurter of the Harvard Law School, Benjamin Cohen, Thomas Corcoran. In the Second Hundred Days, the Brandeisians scored their greatest triumph when Congress enacted legislation to level the public-utility holding company pyramids and to place these companies, too, under the SEC.

Although the New Deal left the system of private control of credit and investment intact, it markedly altered the relationship between government and finance. As early as 1934 one writer noted: 'Financial news no longer originates in Wall Street. . . . The pace of the ticker is determined now in Washington, not in company board-rooms, or in brokerage offices.' The new securities and banking legislation, the reorientation of the Reconstruction Finance Corporation under the Houston banker Jesse Jones, the enhanced powers of the Federal Reserve System, and the accelerated rate of government spending gave Washington a significantly new position as senior partner in the management of the nation's finances.

Farm Relief

In consultation with national farm leaders, Roosevelt's Secretary of Agriculture Henry A. Wallace prepared a farm relief plan of unexpected boldness. On 12 May 1933 Congress passed the Agricultural Adjustment Act, in order to reestablish 'parity' between agriculture and industry by raising the level of commodity prices and easing the credit and mortgage load. Its most important provisions authorized the Secretary of Agriculture to make agreements with staple farmers whereby, in return for government subsidies, they undertook to reduce production. Costs of payments to growers were to be met from

taxes on the processing of the products involved. The Secretary could also negotiate marketing agreements for commodities like citrus fruits and dairy products. Subsequent programs made available Commodity Credit Corporation loans on crops and authorized compulsory marketing quotas for cotton and tobacco. In part because of crop reduction, in part because of government payments, and in part because of the devaluation of the dollar, farm income increased from $5,562,000,000 in 1932 to $8,688,000,000 in 1935.

On 6 January 1936 in a 6 to 3 decision the Supreme Court invalidated the AAA's processing tax as an improper exercise of the taxing power and an invasion of the reserved rights of states. 'This is coercion by economic pressure,' said Justice Owen Roberts, who conjured up the terrifying consequences that would flow from unbridled national power. Justice Harlan Fiske Stone, in his powerful dissenting opinion, protested, pointing out that 'the present levy is held invalid, not for any want of power in Congress to lay such a tax . . . but because the use to which its proceeds are put is disapproved' and observed, with some asperity, that 'courts are not the only agency of government that must be assumed to have capacity to govern.'

The Court's decision in the Butler case compelled the administration to piece together a stopgap measure: the Soil Conservation and Domestic Allotment Act of 1936. This law subsidized farmers for increasing acreage of soil-conserving crops and reducing acreage of soil-depleting crops, which, conveniently, were the surplus staples; it financed this program directly, rather than through the outlawed processing tax. Although this act speeded the development of soil conservation, it proved unsatisfactory as a price-raising device since the government had no way to compel compliance. In 1938 Congress adopted a second AAA which embraced a number of earlier programs in addition to such new approaches as the 'ever normal granary' and crop insurance; furthermore, it extended the coercive principle, which a chastened Supreme Court was now willing to sanction.

The administration also took steps to cope with

YEARS OF DUST

RESETTLEMENT ADMINISTRATION
Rescues Victims
Restores Land to Proper Use

Dust Bowl blues, 1936. In 1935 the Resettlement Administration sent Ben Shahn on a three-month photographic assignment in the South and Southwest. A much admired painter who had studied with Diego Rivera, Shahn had no training with a camera, but he returned with a portfolio of photographs that were valuable in themselves and also served as the basis for murals and posters. 'Shahn,' F. Jack Hurley has written, 'had an ability few could match for capturing the torture in the body of a farm wife, old before her time, or the terror in the eyes of a drought-scarred child.' (*Museum of Modern Art*)

A family of 'Okies.' In this portrait of drought refugees from Oklahoma in Blythe, California, in 1936, Dorothea Lange demonstrates the stark candor, combined with a sense of dignity and compassion, that was characteristic of her work. In 1935 Roy Stryker, impressed by her pictures of the rural poor on the West Coast, had hired her for the historical section of the Resettlement Administration (later absorbed by the FSA), and in 1939 she and her husband Paul Taylor brought out the splendid *American Exodus* which drew on this experience. *(Library of Congress)*

the long-range problems of agriculture and assist the disadvantaged farmer. In 1935 the President set up a Resettlement Administration which, under the guidance of Rexford Tugwell, removed from cultivation some 10 million acres of marginal land; gave financial aid to 635,000 farm families; and built model suburban 'greenbelt' developments. The Farm Security Administration, which succeeded the Resettlement Administration in 1939, lent tenants almost $260 million to purchase farms and over $800 million in rehabilitation loans; helped organize co-operatives, including medical co-ops; and built camps for migratory workers, like the Joads of Steinbeck's *The Grapes of Wrath*. But as the spokesman for the poorer farmers, the FSA incurred the opposition of the powerful Farm Bureau Federation, and its funds were never large enough to meet the need. World War II did more than the New Deal to bail out the tenant farmer. In 1935, two-fifths of the farmers in the country were tenants; by 1950 only one state—Mississippi—reported more than half of her farms held by tenants; in the nation as a whole the figure had dropped to one-fourth.

Like the New Deal's financial operations, its agricultural program expanded the power of government while leaving property relationships essentially undisturbed. AAA subsidies gave disproportionate benefits to large farmers, and the crop reduction campaign even drove some of the tenants and sharecroppers off the land. Furthermore, the New Deal remained perpetually embarrassed by its scarcity economics, even though the plow-up of cotton and the slaughter of the little pigs were only emergency measures restricted to 1933. Yet, for all its shortcomings, the New Deal's farm program marked a great improvement on the single-interest government of the 1920's. Though net farm income in 1939 still fell well under that of 1929, the administration rescued the farmer from his desperate plight of the late Hoover period. The New Deal sent out millions of subsidy checks; saved large numbers of rural families from foreclosure; extended participatory democracy to involve thousands of local volunteers in the administration of the AAA; gave Southern Negro farmers the opportunity to vote in national crop referenda; and made at least a start toward helping the forgotten men of American agriculture.

Industry and Labor Under the New Deal

The New Deal's program for industrial recovery had multiple origins. Business groups like the U.S. Chamber of Commerce wanted government sanction for trade associations to draft agreements exempt from anti-trust prosecution. Planners such as Tugwell sought centralized direction of the economy. Labor leaders like John L. Lewis wanted guarantees for workers. Progressive senators led by 'Young Bob' La Follette had been pressing for massive public works spending. When the President told advocates of these different proposals to lock themselves in a room and stay there until they had reached agreement, they came out with an omnibus measure that had something for everybody.

The National Industrial Recovery Act of June 1933 authorized businessmen to organize their industries by drafting codes, exempt from the anti-trust laws but requiring government approval. Section 7(a) of the statute guaranteed labor the right to collective bargaining. The Recovery Act also set up a Public Works Administration with an appropriation of $3.3 billion, and the President designated his Secretary of the Interior, Harold Ickes, to head the PWA. Under the prodigiously energetic Recovery Administrator, General Hugh Johnson, administrators were familiar only with the general principles of the new program, businessmen and their legal advisers were familiar with all the details; the inevitable result was that big business generally imposed its own codes upon both government and small business. Yet out of the welter of conference and debate there emerged a pattern of industrial organization that met many of the requirements laid down by the act. To rally support, Johnson hit on the Blue Eagle as a symbol of compliance with the wage and hour provisions of the codes, and for a short time the Blue Eagle was almost as popular as the flag. Within a year some 500 codes had been adopted and some 200 more were in process of formulation. Under the NRA, industry reabsorbed unemployed workers, adopted hundreds of codes setting minimum wages and maximum hours, and went far toward abolishing child labor and the sweatshop.

But the NRA overextended itself in trying to regulate small enterprises, and it could not muster enough power to discipline the big corporations, which raised prices and persisted in monopolistic practices. During 1934 and 1935 the NRA was assailed with increasing bitterness from all sides: by large businessmen who resented government control of their labor relations; by small businessmen dismayed at the growth of monopoly; by liberals who feared the long-range consequences of a 'planned economy' dominated by business; by consumers outraged at price increases; by labor disappointed in the practical results of the codes.

The NRA was breaking down of its own weight when in May 1935 the Supreme Court destroyed it by undermining its legal foundations in a unanimous decision, the Schechter case. The Recovery Act, said the Court, involved an illegal delegation of legislative power to the Executive. Furthermore, it constituted an improper exercise of the commerce power and an invasion by the Federal Government of the realm reserved to the states, for 'if the commerce clause were construed to reach all enterprises and transactions which could be said to have an indirect effect upon interstate commerce, the federal authority would embrace practically all the activities of the people and the authority of the state over its domestic concerns would exist only by sufferance.' Never again would big business play so large a role in the New Deal, but neither would the planners like Tugwell ever have so promising, but illusory, an opportunity to impose centralized planning on the economy.

The framers of the Recovery Act hoped, too, that the $3.3 billion appropriation for public works would be an important lever for industrial recovery. However, Roosevelt, pledged to budget-balancing, was skeptical of the value of public works and repeatedly raided the grant for other projects, while Ickes, worried about the possibility of another Teapot Dome, insisted on reviewing every word of every PWA contract. The industrious, sardonic Ickes won himself the reputation of 'Honest Harold,' but neither he nor the President realized the economic potentialities of public works spending.

On the other hand, Roosevelt's labor policy, despite a period of uncertainty, proved much more successful. His appointment of Frances Perkins, the first woman cabinet member, to the post of Secretary of Labor augured well for the workingman, and Section 7(a) of the National Industrial Recovery Act showed some responsiveness to the aspirations of union leaders. Under the impetus of the NRA, organized labor more than recovered all the losses which it had suffered in the preceding decade. Using the magic name of FDR, John L. Lewis launched an organizing drive in the coal fields in the summer of 1933 which gained the United Mine Workers 300,000 members in two months, and by the tens of thousands workers signed union cards in industries that had long been resistant to organization—rubber, automobiles, textiles.

But 1934 proved considerably more troublesome. By manipulating the device of the company union, industrialists complied with the letter of the Recovery Act while keeping organizers out of their plants. At the same time the craft union leaders of the A.F. of L., hostile or indifferent to the unskilled recruits flocking to the Federation, treated their new members with such disdain that many tore up their union cards. In 1934 an epidemic of strikes by industrial workers under radical sponsorship hit cities such as Minneapolis. Most failed; in San Francisco a general strike was smashed by the militia and by self-constituted vigilantes. The Roosevelt administration, dismayed by strikes that impeded its recovery effort, fumbled for a labor policy. It antagonized employers, who resented any kind of intervention, and industrial unionists, who protested that government labor boards were powerless to cope with employer defiance. While the executive branch temporized, congressional liberals stepped in to replace the New Deal's makeshifts with legislation of a more permanent character.

In 1935, Congress, led by Senator Robert Wagner, gave labor an emphatic victory with the National Labor Relations Act, better known as the Wagner Act. This measure, which secured Roosevelt's last-minute endorsement, not only embraced some of the provisions of the recently invalidated Recovery Act but also significantly

The Memorial Day massacre, South Chicago, 1937. Philip Evergood's 'The American Tragedy' shows club-wielding police mauling workers and firing pistols at the backs of unarmed demonstrators at Tom Girdler's Republic Steel plant. For radicals, the episode amply demonstrated the brutality of the employer class, but proletarians in flight, even from overwhelming force, left an inappropriate impression; hence, Evergood also depicts, in the foreground, a heroic worker shielding his pregnant wife from officers of the law gone berserk. Though Evergood, a New Yorker who painted for the WPA's Federal Art Project, affected the crude style of an untrained dauber from the working class, he had in fact gone to Eton and Cambridge and studied art in Paris and London. (*Coll. Mrs. Gerrit Pieter Van de Bovenkamp*)

expanded the government's powers. It set up an independent National Labor Relations Board authorized to conduct plant elections and issue 'cease and desist' orders against unfair practices, including coercion of employees, discrimination against union members, and refusal to bargain collectively with employees. By stipulating that a majority of workers should have exclusive bargaining rights, the law all but destroyed the divisive tactic of the company union.

Under the umbrella of government protection, organized labor carried out a dramatic recruiting drive. In 1935 Lewis led a secession from the A.F. of L. of unions impatient with the resistance of the Federation's leadership to organizing factory workers. The C.I.O., first known as the Committee for Industrial Organization and later as the Congress of Industrial Organizations, sometimes employed the novel technique of the 'sit-down,' seizing possession of a plant and refusing to leave until demands had been granted. In February 1937 General Motors agreed to a settlement after a forty-four-day sit-down, and before the year was out such giants as U.S. Steel, Chrysler, and General Electric had surrendered, too. The C.I.O. insurrection also awakened the A.F. of L., which emerged even more powerful than its upstart rival.

The New Deal had helped make possible one of the most important developments of twentieth-century America: the unionization of the mass production industries. The benevolent neutrality of the administration (including Roosevelt's refusal to countenance force to oust the sit-down strikers), the sympathy of local leaders like Governor Frank Murphy of Michigan, and the aid of congressional liberals such as Wagner and La Follette, who headed a Senate committee that exposed employer violence, all proved immensely beneficial to the unions. By World War II even Henry Ford had recognized the worker's right, long granted in other industrial nations, to unionize and to bargain collectively.

Conservation and the TVA

No part of the New Deal was more imaginative than that which looked at the conservation of natural resources. The initial step was the creation

(March 1933) of the Civilian Conservation Corps, to give work relief to jobless young men from 17 to 25. In the eight years of its existence the CCC enlisted almost 3 million young men, who, under the direction of army officers and foresters, added over 17 million acres of new forest land, checked forest fires, fought plant and animal diseases, stocked hatcheries with over a billion fish, built 6 million check dams to halt soil erosion, and by mosquito control helped stamp out malaria.

Of more lasting importance was the dramatic Tennessee Valley Authority, a vast experiment in regional reconstruction. The TVA acquired or constructed some 25 dams for flood control, nitrate production, and the generation of electric power; to these it eventually added a series of stream generator plants. The government built some 5000 miles of transmission lines and sold surplus power to nearby communities at rates low enough to ensure widespread consumption. In 1932 only two farms out of one hundred in the valley were electrified; five years later the proportion was one out of seven, and by 1960 electrification was well-nigh complete. The TVA also resettled marginal farmers, promoted public health, and encouraged local industry, all in close cooperation with the people of the valley, for the TVA was dedicated to decentralized administration. Too often, decentralized administration meant that decisions were made by wealthy white farmers and the TVA bowed to the local pattern of racial segregation. But the TVA also left a substantial record of achievement. Within a few years millions of abandoned acres were restored to cultivation, industry returned to the valley, vacationers crowded its artificial lakes, and the river, navigable now over its entire length from Knoxville to the Ohio river, was one of the busiest streams in the country. The TVA itself became a model which attracted the emulation of the whole world.

The Roosevelt administration initiated a host of new enterprises in conservation and electric power. It not only disciplined the utility-holding companies and strengthened the Federal Power Commission but set up the Rural Electrification Administration which radically changed life on the farm. At the outset of the New Deal, only one out

Moses Soyer, 'Artists on WPA,' 1936. The art projects of the New Deal helped foster a cultural nationalism that esteemed native American subjects. But Soyer, one of three brothers who were artists, warned against being 'misled by the chauvinism of the 'Paint America' slogan. Yes, paint America, but with your eyes open. Do not glorify Main Street. Paint it as it is—mean, dirty, avaricious. Self glorification is artistic suicide. Witness Nazi Germany.' Soyer's statement revealed not only the righteous provincialism of New York artists but the ubiquitous anxiety about fascism in the 1930's. (*Smithsonian Institution*)

of nine American farms had electricity; by the end of the Roosevelt era, eight out of nine enjoyed electric power. In the Pacific Northwest, construction of the Grand Coulee Dam, and of Bonneville Dam in the lower Columbia river basin, developed some 2.5 million kilowatts of electric power and made possible the irrigation and reclamation of over a million acres of farm land. The alarming spread of the 'dust bowl' on the high plains inspired the planting of a 100-mile-wide shelter belt of trees, stretching from Texas to Canada. To stop soil erosion the government enlisted one-fourth of the nation's farmers. The New Deal found a home for the brilliant head of the Soil Conservation Service, Hugh H. Bennett; for the thoughtful planner, Morris Llewellyn Cooke, who turned out landmark reports on the nation's resources; for John Collier, who, as Indian Commissioner, sought to save the Indians' lands at the same time that he preserved their culture; and Pare Lorentz, who produced such film epics as *The River* and *The Plough That Broke the Plains.* Not even in Uncle Teddy's day had the conservation movement enjoyed such brilliant leadership.

The Welfare State

Roosevelt had promised during his campaign that no one should starve, and during the Hundred Days of 1933, Congress responded to his recommendations for the unemployed by creating the Civilian Conservation Corps and setting up the Federal Emergency Relief Administration to make grants to state and local governments for public projects and, where necessary, direct grants to the needy. Under the experienced social-work administrator, Harry Hopkins, the FERA in the next two years disbursed $4 billion for relief, three-fourths from federal and one-fourth from local funds.[3] By 1934 more than twenty million people—one out of every six Americans—were receiving public assistance. In addition the Public Works Adminis-

3. When Roosevelt realized that not even the FERA would get the country through the first New Deal winter of 1933–34, he named Hopkins to head a temporary Civil Works Administration, and the resourceful Hopkins quickly put four million jobless on federal projects.

tration under Ickes was putting men to work on construction projects which helped change the face of the land. The PWA burrowed Chicago's new subway, built the Skyline Drive in Virginia, and constructed the carrier *Yorktown;* in the six years of its existence it helped build two-thirds of all new school buildings in the nation and one-third of the new hospitals.

In January 1935 Roosevelt proposed that a distinction to be made between employables and unemployables, that more satisfactory provision be made for the former, and that the burden of supporting the latter be transferred to the states. In response, Congress appropriated nearly $5 billion, and the President established a Works Progress Administration to disburse most of this huge sum. The WPA was wasteful, and the government never provided for all who were in need. Yet by 1943 when the WPA terminated its activities, it had given work to over 8 million unemployed, who were responsible for 600,000 miles of highways, 125,000 public buildings, 8000 parks, 850 airport landing fields, and thousands of hospitals, municipal power plants, and school buildings, and the achievement of the imaginative Federal Arts Project. The Federal Theatre produced the classic works from Euripides to Ibsen; offered the plays of contemporaries like Eugene O'Neill; and sponsored vaudeville troupes, marionettes, and circuses. The Federal Writers' Project gave jobs to established writers like Conrad Aiken, unknown men such as John Cheever and Richard Wright, and, mercifully, jobless historians. It turned out a thousand publications, including the immensely useful series of state guides. The Federal Music Project put together three orchestras—the Buffalo Philharmonic, the Oklahoma Symphony, and the Utah State Symphony—which became the established orchestras in their communities, while the Federal Arts Project supported such painters as Jackson Pollock and sponsored the influential *Index of American Design.* Another progeny of the relief act of 1935, the National Youth Administration, found part-time jobs for more than 600,000 college and 1.5 million high-school students, and 2.5 million who were out of school.

The New Deal's housing program joined together a number of separate aims: to create public works projects to employ the jobless; to revive the construction business; and to provide better dwellings. In 1934 Congress set up the Federal Housing Administration which insured mortgages to encourage the repair and building of private homes. Of benefit chiefly to the middle class, the FHA had by 1945 financed more than one-third of all privately constructed homes, and proved a boon to builders and savings and loan associations. On a much more modest scale the PWA constructed low-rent public housing, but the New Deal moved so slowly that, as Charles Abrams wrote, 'a great opportunity to rebuild many of America's decayed urban centers was lost.' Roosevelt was much more interested in bootless schemes to return city-dwellers to the land than in massive urban housing projects; not until 1937 did he commit himself to the public housing measure Senator Wagner had been sponsoring. With FDR's support, Congress in 1937 created the U.S. Housing Authority to assist local communities in slum clearance and the construction of low-cost housing. The USHA eventually built 165,000 family units. If the New Deal failed to take full advantage of the opportunity that housing offered, both as a humanitarian enterprise and as a lever for recovery, it did establish a new principle: federal responsibility for clearing slums and housing the poor.

As early as 1934 the President had called for a broad program of old-age and unemployment insurance. 'There is no reason,' he told Secretary Perkins, 'why every child from the day he is born, shouldn't be a member of the social security . . . cradle to grave—they ought to be in a social insurance system.' Pressure for an old-age pension scheme was also exerted by advocates of the Townsend Plan. Dr. Francis Townsend of California agitated for monthly payments of $200 to all persons over 60 years of age, on the sole proviso that they retire from work and spend the money; Dr. Townsend's plan was championed by Townsend Clubs claiming close to a million members. In August 1935 Congress enacted the Social Security law, an omnibus measure which provided for old-age insurance, unemployment insurance, benefit payments to the handicapped, aid to dependent children and their mothers, pensions to needy aged, and extensive appropriations for public health.

The United States still had a long way to go to provide adequately for the impoverished and the handicapped, but the New Deal had taken giant strides in that direction. It not only engaged in an unprecedented range of activities—vast relief programs, slum clearance, aid to tenant farmers, curbs on the sweatshop and child labor, minimum labor standards, a social security system—but had established the principle of federal responsibility for society's victims. 'Government has a final responsibility for the well-being of its citizenship,' Roosevelt declared. 'If private co-operative endeavor fails to provide work for willing hands and relief for the unfortunate, those suffering hardship from no fault of their own have a right to call upon the Government for aid; and a government worthy of its name must make fitting response.'

The Roosevelt Coalition

The Great Depression made a deeper impact on American politics than any event since the Civil War. By identifying the Republican party with the collapse, the voters in 1932 had given the Democrats an opportunity to establish themselves as the majority party for the next generation, and Roosevelt made the most of it. By 1936 he had forged a new party coalition which would prevail not only in his lifetime but for many years thereafter. From 1930 to 1976 the Republicans would win control of the House in only two elections.

The Roosevelt coalition centered in lower income groups in the great cities. In 1936 FDR captured all but two of the 106 cities of 100,000 population or more. The New Deal's urban appeal was especially marked among labor and ethnic groups. John L. Lewis, who had endorsed Hoover in 1932, opened his union treasury to Roosevelt in 1936, and voting broke sharply on class lines. A variety of ethnic elements were grateful for New Deal measures and for recognition. In 1932 the Negro had still given his allegiance to the party of Lincoln, and in the early years of the New Deal, black leaders were distressed by racial discrimination in agencies like the CCC. However, attitudes

Eleanor Roosevelt and Alice Hamilton. Mrs. Roosevelt made the most of her opportunity as First Lady to accord recognition to individuals of singular achievement who had been battling for social justice for decades before the advent of the New Deal. Alice Hamilton (1869–1970) overcame prejudice against women in medicine and against female reformers to become an outstanding authority on industrial toxicology. In the progressive era, she investigated occupational diseases and industrial poisons for the state of Illinois and the U.S. Department of Labor, and her service as assistant professor of industrial medicine at Harvard, which began just after World War I, continued into the age of FDR. *Exploring the Dangerous Trades* is a fascinating account of the long and useful career of a woman who lived to be a centenarian. (*Schlesinger Library, Radcliffe College*)

changed in response to the fact that Negroes received a lion's share of relief jobs; got one-third of the federal housing units; and won appointments to important national posts. Although the President refused to antagonize Southern committee chairmen by pressing civil rights legislation, Eleanor Roosevelt intervened repeatedly on behalf of the blacks. By 1934 Negro voters were switching to the Democrats in large numbers, and in 1936 they rolled up big majorities for FDR.

In his bid for re-election Roosevelt faced a dual challenge from the Republicans and from a third party. The G.O.P. chose as its nominee Alfred M. Landon of Kansas, who had been a fairly progressive governor. But Landon was embarrassed by the Hoover wing of the party which took the campaign away from him. His only hope lay in the possibility that a third-party candidate would draw enough votes away from FDR to let a Republican slip in. For a time Louisiana's Senator Huey Long, advocate of a popular share-the-wealth scheme, raised the formidable threat of an alliance of his forces with those of Dr. Townsend and Father Coughlin, the rabble-rousing radio priest. But in September 1935 Long was assassinated and the Union party ticket, fielded by dissidents in 1936, attracted little support.

On 2 November Roosevelt's campaign manager, Postmaster General Jim Farley, wrote the President: 'I am still definitely of the opinion that you will carry every state but two—Maine and Vermont.' Farley hit it right on the button. With 523 votes to Landon's 8, Roosevelt won the greatest electoral margin of any presidential candidate since Monroe. Never before had a major party suffered so overwhelming a defeat as the Republicans had sustained. Buoyed by this impressive vote of confidence, Roosevelt began his second term in office with high hopes.

The Constitutional Revolution

Outnumbered in Congress, humiliated at the polls, the Republicans lifted their eyes to the Supreme Court. The G.O.P. 'retired into the judiciary as a stronghold, and from that battery all the works of republicanism were to be beaten down and erased.' So Jefferson had said of the Federalists over a century earlier, and his successor in the White House had reason to echo the bitter charge. Never before had the Supreme Court worked such havoc with a legislative program as it did in 1935 and 1936 with that of the New Deal. It overthrew the NRA in part on the novel ground of improper delegation of power. It struck down the AAA through what a dissenting justice called a 'tortured construction of the Constitution,' while the Bituminous Coal Act was invalidated because the Court, in the Carter case, insisted that mining was a purely local business. It nullified the Municipal Bankruptcy Act on the assumption that such legislation invaded the domain of the states—even though the Act required state consent, which many states had already given. The Federal Government had long been denied the power to enact minimum-wage legislation; when in the Tipaldo case the Court denied this power to the states as well, it created a no-man's-land where neither federal nor state power might be applied.

What was Roosevelt to do? The process of constitutional amendment was slow and uncertain, and in the past the judiciary had been brought to acquiescence in majority will only by the process of new appointments. But Roosevelt was the first President in more than a century to serve a full term without having the opportunity to choose at least one new justice, although six of the judges were over seventy years of age. If the trouble lay not in Constitution but in the Court, that could be remedied by appointing new members. So at least Roosevelt thought, and this was the crucial part of the proposal he submitted to a startled Congress on 5 February 1937. The President proposed to obtain the 'addition of younger blood' by the appointment of one new judge, up to a maximum of six, for every justice of the Supreme Court who, having passed the age of seventy and served for ten years, failed to retire.

For months the nation reverberated to protests against the scheme as an attempt to 'pack' the Supreme Court and subvert the judiciary, but in the end it was the strategic retreat of the Court that brought about the defeat of the plan. For abruptly and unpredictably, the Court found ways of making the constitutional sun shine on legislation which had heretofore been under a judicial cloud. Nine months after the Court had struck down the New York minimum-wage law, it sustained a similar act of the state of Washington. Two weeks later came five decisions, all upholding various provisions of the National Labor Relations Act. A month later, and the controversial Social Security law was vouchsafed judicial blessing. In all but one of these decisions, the conservative 'Four Horsemen'—McReynolds, Sutherland, Butler, and Van Devanter—took an adamant stand, but they now constituted a minority, because Justice Roberts had joined the liberal triumvirate of Brandeis, Cardozo, and Stone, together with Chief Justice Hughes, whom many credited with frustrating the President by marshalling the Court in support of new interpretations. At the same time that the Court approved New Deal laws, it spiked the 'court packing' scheme, for many saw no point in altering the judiciary now that the reform legislation had been validated. As one commentator quipped: 'A switch in time saved nine.' Although the fight continued into the month of July, the opponents prevailed. The President, at the height of his power, had suffered a stinging rebuke.

Roosevelt claimed that though he had lost the battle, he had won the war. Even while the Court debate was under way, Justice Van Devanter announced his retirement, and before the President left office he would be able to name eight of the nine justices and elevate Justice Stone to the chief justiceship. Since 1937 the Court has not invalidated a single congressional statute in the realm of regulation of business, and very few laws, national or state, in any realm. In a series of decisions it swept away any lingering doubts about the power of the Federal Government over manufacturing and farming and removed the limitation imposed upon congressional spending in the Butler case. In addition the Court took a sympathetic attitude toward the exercise of police power by the states. Finally, the 'Roosevelt Court' continued even more assiduously than the Court had before 1937 to throw new safeguards around civil liberties, although even in the 1920's important gains had been made in protecting the rights of minorities. It had long been assumed that the Bill of Rights limited only the national Congress. Be-

ginning, however, with *Gitlow v. New York* in 1925, the Court intimated that the rights of 'life, liberty and property,' guaranteed against state impairment by the Fourteenth Amendment, might be presumed to embrace many of those rights set forth in the first ten amendments. This dictum, at first only cautiously advanced, was within a decade incorporated into constitutional law.

In its decisions on property rights even more than on civil liberties, the Court had wrought a constitutional revolution that appeared to justify Roosevelt's claims that he had won the war; yet in another sense he lost the war. The Supreme Court fight, together with such other developments in 1937 as the recession and resentment at the sit-down strikes, cost the President much of his middle-class following and dealt a heavy blow at the Roosevelt coalition. The Court struggle helped weld together a bipartisan coalition of anti-New Deal legislators who soon held a pivotal position. If Roosevelt's Court proposal secured the legitimization of a vast expansion of the power of government, it also played an important role in the untimely end of the New Deal.

The End of the New Deal

Middle-class enthusiasm for Roosevelt owed much to the fact that the President appeared to be leading the country out of the depression, for in the spring of 1937 the nation had finally achieved 1929 levels of production, but in August the economy suddenly slumped. From September 1937 to June 1938, in a decline of unparalleled severity, industrial output fell 33 per cent. Middle-class support for the President, already shaken by the Supreme Court and sit-down episodes, was now even more seriously tried, for no longer did FDR seem a magic-maker who had a formula for ending the depression. Yet, ironically, the recession had been produced by Roosevelt's acquiescence in the most cherished of middle-class prescriptions for recovery: balancing the budget. Denounced as a wild spender, the President had, in fact, always viewed federal deficits with regret. As Tugwell later reflected: 'Roosevelt felt just as much convicted of sin when the budget was unbalanced as Hoover had been.' When early in 1937 the econ-

Defense industry town. Jack Delano's photograph of a Pittsburgh mill district in the winter of 1941 was taken for the historical section of the Farm Security Administration. Under the direction of Roy Stryker, this New Deal unit nurtured the talents of artists like Delano, John Vachon, and John Collier, Jr., and assisted the brilliant young black photographer Gordon Parks. Increasingly in 1941 the section turned its attention toward portraying a country preparing for war. (*Library of Congress*)

617

omy continued to show steady improvement, Roosevelt concluded that he could safely return to more conservative fiscal policies; the Federal Reserve Board contracted credit, and government spending was radically slashed. Since it had been the deficit spending that had been largely responsible for the gains of Roosevelt's first term, his abrupt reversal produced a convulsive reaction.

Through the winter of 1937–38, Roosevelt's advisers belabored him with conflicting advice. Secretary of the Treasury Henry Morgenthau, Jr. urged him to commit himself to orthodox finance to win business 'confidence.' But men like Harry Hopkins and Federal Reserve Chairman Marriner Eccles argued that when private investment fell off, the government should step up spending. 'In other words,' Eccles insisted, 'the Government must be looked upon as a compensatory agency in the economy to do just the opposite to what private business and individuals do.' In addition, these New Dealers believed that the government should curb monopoly, on the grounds that the inflexible 'administered' price practices of the monopolies were prolonging the depression. Some of these ideas reflected the influence of the British economist, John Maynard Keynes, but Keynes made rather little impact on Roosevelt; he served chiefly to reinforce views which the New Dealers already held.

In the early spring of 1938 the liberals won out, for Roosevelt had concluded that the recession was taking too great a toll of the unemployed and that he must spend. He asked Congress to approve a large-scale 'lend-spend' program, and Congress responded by voting nearly a billion for public works and almost three billions more for other federal activities. The President gave his liberal advisers something else to cheer about when he asked Congress for a full-dress investigation of the concentration of economic power, which led to the creation of the Temporary National Economic Committee, and when he appointed Thurman Arnold of Yale Law School to be Assistant Attorney-General in charge of the Antitrust Division. That same year Congress established the second AAA and passed a Fair Labor Standards Act which reduced child labor and put a floor under wages and a ceiling on hours for workers in industries engaged in interstate commerce. In the re-

mainder of Roosevelt's second term, the economy painfully climbed up toward its earlier levels, but the New Dealers could not escape the fact that whatever they had done had not been sufficient to avert the recession, and that in 1939 there were still ten million unemployed. Never before had any administration been so responsive to the nation's social needs or built so many useful economic institutions, but it would require the coming of World War II to restore the country's prosperity.

After the passage of the Fair Labor Standards Act in 1938, Congress did not adopt any other reform legislation for the rest of the decade. The impetus of the New Deal came to an end not only because it failed to bring recovery, but because the forces opposed to further change were too powerful. The informal conservative bipartisan coalition forged during the Court fight showed its strength in the special session of Congress in the fall of 1937 when the President could not gain approval of a single measure. In 1938 Democratic insurrectionists joined with Republicans to bury Roosevelt's plan for executive reorganization.[4] That same spring the House set up a Committee on Un-American Activities which, under the chairmanship of the Texas Democrat Martin Dies, became a forum for right-wing forays against the Roosevelt administration. 'Stalin baited his hook with a "progressive" worm,' Dies said, 'and New Deal suckers swallowed bait, hook, line, and sinker.'

This series of setbacks exasperated New Dealers who recalled that many of the Democrats who were now attacking Roosevelt had come in on the President's coattails only a short time before. Liberal Democrats, convinced that Roosevelt still had the country with him, persuaded the President to attempt to 'purge' a number of legislators in the 1938 Democratic primaries, in particular Senators Walter George of Georgia, 'Cotton Ed' Smith of South Carolina, and Millard Tydings of Maryland. The President succeeded in eliminating a Tammany congressman, but George, Smith, and Tydings all won handily, leaving the party's con-

---

4. Congress did, however, approve a modified program to revamp the executive branch in 1939, the same year that it adopted the Hatch Act to restrict the political activities of government employees.

Roosevelt as captain of the ship of state. This little-known painting by the Norwegian-American artist Gulbrand Sether conveys the enthusiasm for the New Deal in FDR's first months in office. The two women in the picture are Secretary of Labor Frances Perkins and the First Lady, Eleanor Roosevelt. The figures in cap and gown may be intended to suggest the influence of the Brain Trust on the Roosevelt administration. By the end of FDR's second term, the naval craft depicted here had become increasingly important as the issues of World War II overwhelmed those of the New Deal. (*Library of Congress*)

servatives more cocksure than ever. That fall, the Republicans picked up 81 seats in the House, 8 in the Senate, and 13 governorships; all but given up for dead two years before, they introduced to the national spotlight that year such new faces as Thomas Dewey and Robert Taft.

Without enough votes to carry his program through Congress before the election, the President now faced a greatly bolstered conservative alliance. Resigned to the inevitable, Roosevelt in his annual message to Congress in January 1939 for the first time advanced no new measures. 'We have now passed the period of internal conflict in the launching of our program of social reforms,' he told Congress. 'Our full energies may now be released to invigorate the processes of recovery in order to preserve our reforms.' As an innovating force, the New Deal was at an end, and the President henceforth directed most of his attention to the critical problems of foreign policy.

The New Deal: An Evaluation

Critics of the New Deal, at the time and subsequently, have argued that it should have done more, that it should have done less, and that it should have done things differently. They emphasize that the Roosevelt administration failed in its fundamental assignment—bringing the country out of the depression, for recovery came only with the tocsins of war. In the 1970's both Right and Left have seen in the New Deal the breeding place of the 'Imperial Presidency' of the Watergate era. There can be no doubt that the New Deal was deficient in a number of respects.

Nevertheless, the accomplishments of the New Deal seem more impressive than its shortcomings. At the very outset, it brought the country through the crisis that Roosevelt had inherited, and it did a whole lot to ameliorate the worst hardships of the depression. As a result of the legislation of the Hundred Days, farm families were safeguarded from foreclosure of their lands and debt-ridden city families from dispossession of their homes. Throughout the 1930's, work was found for millions of unemployed in a series of projects from the FERA to the WPA, and the government took pains to provide rewarding jobs for novelists and essayists, muralists and sculptors, circus clowns and symphony composers. It showed particular concern for the young—from subsidizing hot lunches for grade school pupils to making it possible for college students to continue their education.

In contrast to the largely single-interest government of the 1920's, the New Deal extended benefits to groups that had been neglected, or short-changed, in the past. It encouraged unionization of factories and curbed sweatshops and child labor by stipulating minimal working conditions. AAA checks sustained millions of staple farmers, and the government made it possible for tenants to own farms and built camps for migrant workers, albeit on a modest scale. Though, unhappily, some agencies persisted in discrimination, blacks made unprecedented gains and the New Deal provided the American Indian with new opportunities for self-government. Eleanor Roosevelt and Frances Perkins gave visible evidence of the enhanced role of women in government, and the 'Brain Trust' meant a new welcome by Washington to university graduates.

The New Deal vastly expanded the scope of government in America. It fostered the Welfare State with old-age pensions, unemployment insurance, and aid for dependent children; engaged in multifarious housing ventures; created the nation's first state theater; and shot documentary films. It inaugurated ambitious regional enterprises like the TVA and the Columbia river projects, brought electricity to rural America, set up the Soil Conservation Service, dispatched the CCC boys into the forests, and, in countless other ways, changed the American landscape. For the first time, in the 1930's Wall Street was compelled to accept federal regulation, and national authority was extended to business units like public-utility holding companies. Before the decade was over, this enlargement of the orbit of government had been legitimized by the Constitutional Revolution of 1937 and the 'Roosevelt Court.'

Most significant of all was the maintenance of a democratic system in a world swept by totalitarianism. 'The only sure bulwark of continuing liberty,' Roosevelt had observed, 'is a government strong enough to protect the interests of the people, and a people strong enough and well enough informed to maintain its sovereign control over its government.' The proof that in the United States it was possible for such a government to exist and such a people to flourish was of fateful significance. For in the 'thirties it became doubtful whether liberty or democracy could survive in the modern world. It was of utmost importance to the peoples of the world that American democracy had withstood the buffetings of depression and that the American people were refreshed in their faith in the democratic order.

32

Gathering Storm

1933–1941

The Pacifist Mood

If there was one principle upon which the vast majority of the American people agreed in 1937, it was that what was happening in Europe was no concern of theirs; and that if Europe were so wicked or stupid as to get into another war, America would stay out of it. Yet at a time when the Fascist powers were planning to pounce on the democratic states and when the system of collective security was breaking down, it was not clear that pacifism and isolation would bring peace. Edna St. Vincent Millay wrote:

Longing to wed with Peace, what did we do?—
Sketched her a fortress on a paper pad;
Under her casement twanged a love-sick string;
Left wide the gate that let her foemen through.[1]

Such admonitions fell on deaf ears. They sounded too much like the slogans of World War I, now recalled with bitter resentment. Ostensibly fought to preserve democracy, the war had left Europe a continent where democracy appeared to

1. *Make Bright the Arrows*, Harper & Brothers, 1942, copyright 1939, 1940 by the author.

have only the barest chance to survive. In 1925, Prime Minister Stanley Baldwin had asked: 'Who in Europe does not know that one more war in the West and the civilization of the ages will fall with as great a shock as that of Rome?' In America, fifteen years later, thousands of grim reminders of that conflict still lay in veterans' hospitals.

Many thought the greatest danger of war came not from Hitler but from war-mongering internationalists who would attempt to embroil the United States, an attitude that received official sanction in 1934 from a Senate investigation under Gerald Nye. The Nye committee concluded that America had intervened in World War I not to defend its own interests, nor for the altruistic purpose of saving the world for democracy, but as a consequence of the intrigues of financiers and armament interests. If Europeans had to fight, Nye scolded, 'let them pay for their own wars. If the Morgans and other bankers must get into another war, let them do it by enlisting in the Foreign Legion.' Although the Nye committee failed to prove anyone's responsibility for the war, it did reveal scandalously high profits, and, along with historians like Charles A. Beard and journalists like Colonel McCormick of the Chicago *Tribune*, converted much of the nation to the naïve view that America had been stampeded into war in order to make money for 'merchants of death,' and that the United States could go its own way oblivious of the rest of the world.

Watchfully Waiting

On the very day Roosevelt took the oath of office, the Japanese marched into the provincial capital of Jehol in China, and on the following day the last free elections in Germany consolidated the power of Adolf Hitler. Roosevelt recognized the perils of the breakdown of the world order, but isolationist and pacifist opinion left him little room to maneuver, and the crisis of the Great Depression persuaded him he must concentrate his energies on domestic affairs. 'I shall spare no effort to restore world trade by international economic readjustments,' he said in his inaugural address, 'but the emergency at home cannot wait on that accomplishment.'

In his first months in office Roosevelt encouraged the world to believe that he held out high hopes for the international economic conference scheduled for London in June. But by the time the delegates convened, he had come to fear that France and the other gold bloc countries were seeking to commit him to a policy that would destroy his efforts at price-raising at home. He not only killed a currency stabilization agreement but sent the conference a harsh message scolding the delegates for succumbing to the 'old fetishes of so-called international bankers.' Some like Keynes thought that the President was 'magnificently right,' but Roosevelt's 'bombshell message' undoubtedly reinforced the isolationists and persuaded Europe it could not count on the United States.

Despite this initial setback, Roosevelt's Secretary of State, Cordell Hull, unsympathetic to economic nationalism, persisted in exploring the possibilities for the recapture of foreign markets through reciprocity agreements. Under the terms of the Trade Agreements Act of June 1934, Hull negotiated a series of unconditional most-favored-nation reciprocity treaties. He hoped that the new commercial policy would not only operate for economic improvement but would advance international understanding. In fact, these agreements failed to have important economic consequences but did serve to win political good will. Even more illusory as a panacea for improved trade was the recognition of the Soviet Union in 1933, an event which twenty years later would be denounced as a treasonable act perpetrated by New Deal liberals. The truth of the matter is that recognition was widely applauded by businessmen avid for Russian markets, and Roosevelt's decision simply brought American practice in line with that of most of the rest of the world.

Roosevelt had the greatest leeway in foreign affairs when he sought to liquidate American commitments. 'In the field of world policy,' he said in his inaugural address, 'I would dedicate this Nation to the policy of the good neighbor.' The 'Good Neighbor policy' soon became the term for FDR's willingness to disavow America's intention to intervene in the internal affairs of Latin American nations. In 1934 the United States agreed to abrogate the Platt Amendment, thereby giving up its right to intervene at will in Cuba, and that same year it pulled the last marines out of Haiti, recognized a revolutionary government in El Salvador, and established the Export-Import Bank which extended credit to Latin American republics. Before the decade was over, the administration had ended financial controls in the Dominican Republic and resisted pressures to prevent Mexico from expropriating American oil. On the other side of the world, the Philippines won a promise of independence in 1946 when Congress passed the Tydings-McDuffie Act of 1934.

But such actions defined the limits of Roosevelt's power, for when he sought to use his influence in European affairs Congress would have none of it. In 1933 isolationists warned the President away from a proposal to co-operate in League sanctions against an aggressor, and in 1935 the Senate killed a measure to permit the United States to join the World Court. That year, too, Congress passed the first of a series of neutrality measures which prohibited private loans or credits to belligerent nations, embargoed shipments of arms or munitions to belligerents, and stipulated 'cash and carry' for any other articles. That is, belligerents who wanted to buy nonmilitary goods had to pay for them on delivery and haul them away in their own vessels or those of some country other than the United States. As Italy marched into Ethiopia in 1935 and Germany reclaimed the Rhineland the following year, Roosevelt found himself powerless to do anything effective. 'I am "watchfully waiting,"' he wrote one of his envoys, 'even though the phrase carries us back to the difficult days from 1914 to 1917.'

By August 1936, when the President spoke at Chautauqua, he appeared to have capitulated to the pacifist mood. 'We shun political commitments which might entangle us in foreign wars; we avoid connection with the political activities of the League of Nations,' he asserted. He added:

I have seen war. I have seen war on land and sea. I have seen blood running from the wounded. I have seen men coughing out their gassed lungs. I have seen the dead in the mud. I have seen cities destroyed. I have seen two hundred limping, exhausted men come out of line—the survivors of a regiment of one thousand that went forward forty-eight hours before. I have seen children starving. I have seen the agony of mothers and wives. I hate war.

When in July 1936 anti-republican forces plunged Spain into a 'civil war' that Hitler and Mussolini soon made a testing ground for World War II, Roosevelt outdid the isolationists in his plea that Congress impose an arms embargo. Most of the nation approved, secure in the belief that the United States, by this series of steps, was avoiding the mistakes that had led to its unhappy involvement in the First World War. Claude Bowers, Roosevelt's ambassador to Spain, was unconvinced. 'My own impression,' he wrote in July 1937, 'is that with every surrender beginning long ago with China, followed by Abyssinia and then Spain, the fascist powers, with vanity inflamed, will turn without delay to some other country—such as Czechoslovakia—and that with every surrender the prospects of a European war grow darker.'

In signing the Neutrality Act of 1937, Roosevelt seemed to be endorsing all the assumptions of the isolationists; in fact, he was a troubled man. By 1937 Roosevelt's alarm at the actions of Hitler and Mussolini in Europe was matched by concern over the ambitions of the Japanese in the Far East. That year, Japan engaged in hostilities in China with a barbarity, as in the bombing of Shanghai and the sack of Nanking, that appalled American opinion. Roosevelt was still committed to peace, but he looked for some way to build a concert of powers to curb the expansion of Germany, Italy, and Japan.

In October 1937 in Chicago, the isolationist capital, the President warned that, if aggression triumphed elsewhere in the world, 'let no one imagine that America will escape, that America may expect mercy, that this Western Hemisphere will not be attacked.' Roosevelt noted that 'the epidemic of world lawlessness' was spreading, and he added: 'When an epidemic of physical disease starts to spread, the community approves and joins in a quarantine of the patients in order to protect the health of the community against the spread of the disease.' The President's 'quarantine' speech was interpreted as a new departure in Roosevelt's foreign policy—the abandonment of isolation for collective security, and advance notice to Tokyo of sanctions against Japan. Actually, Roosevelt had not yet committed himself to any project to contain the Axis powers, and though public response to the quarantine speech was generally favorable, the nation resolutely opposed any commitment of American forces abroad. On 12 December 1937 a small river gunboat of the American navy's Yangtze river patrol, U.S.S. *Panay*, was bombed and sunk by Japanese planes. When the Japanese government apologized and offered to pay indemnity to the victims, a sigh of relief passed over the length and breadth of America. In a January 1938 poll, 70 per cent of those with an opinion on the subject favored complete withdrawal from China—Asiatic Fleet, marines, missionaries, medical teams, and all.

By 1938 the Fascist powers were on the march. Hitler called Austrian Chancellor Kurt von Schuschnigg to his retreat in Berchtesgaden to bully him into submission. 'Perhaps I shall be suddenly overnight in Vienna, like a spring storm,' he warned. 'Do you want to turn Austria into another Spain?' On 11 March 1938 Schusch-

Ernest Hemingway (1898–1961). The publication of *For Whom the Bell Tolls*, centering on the Spanish Civil War, which appeared in 1940, was as much a political as a literary event. Hemingway's longest novel was hailed as a reaffirmation of democratic values by a novelist identified with the disillusionment of the post-World War I era, and the title, derived from John Donne, became a text for internationalists who argued that Americans should be as much concerned with the erosion of liberty abroad as at home, for the cause of humanity was indivisible. (*National Archives*)

nigg resigned. Immediately afterwards, Nazis swarmed into Vienna's Kärntnerstrasse; they ripped badges off Austrian officials, broke the shop windows of Jewish merchants, ran up the swastika over the Chancellery. The next morning, German tanks and troops poured over the border and, to the pealing of church bells and deafening cheers from Nazi followers, Adolf Hitler entered Austria at Braunau. In Vienna the following night, the Gestapo arrested no fewer than 76,000 people. Yet when at Munich in September 1938 Britain and France succumbed to Hitler's demand that Czechoslovakia be dismembered and the Sudetenland incorporated in the Reich, Americans had an overwhelming feeling of relief, coupled with the conviction that the European democracies were concerned only with self-interest. The New York *Post* commented: 'If this transcendental sellout does not force the Administration at Washington to return to our policy of isolation—then Heaven help us all!' Two months later, the Nazis carried out an appalling pogrom. Numbers of German and Austrian Jews came to America, but the United States, shamefully, refused to lower immigration barriers in any substantial way. Many who were denied visas later died in Hitler's gas chambers.

In September 1938, Hitler had said that once the Sudeten problem was settled, there would be 'no further territorial problem in Europe.' He added: 'We want no Czechs.' But less than six months later, on the Ides of March, Germany gobbled up most of Czechoslovakia. On the night of 15 March 1939 the Gestapo roved the streets of Prague making mass arrests; no Jewish shops opened the next day. The Fuehrer had, in a single stroke, destroyed any pretext that his ambitions were restricted to the desire to reunite Germans; had exposed appeasement as a failure; and had rendered general war all but inevitable.

At an off-the-record conference with newspaper editors in April 1939, the President confided that informants had told him that there was now an even chance of war in Europe and that it was even money on which side would win. If the totalitarian countries triumphed, Roosevelt said, the United States would face serious economic problems just as this country would have 'if Napoleon Bonaparte had won out that time that he organized the fleet to invade England.' The President concluded: 'We are not going to send armies to Europe. But there are lots of things, short of war, that we can do to help maintain the independence of nations who, as a matter of decent American principle, ought to be allowed to live their own lives.'

Roosevelt did all that he could, 'short of war.' He asked Congress for larger appropriations to rebuild the army, which in 1933 ranked seventeenth in the world, and got approval for a Naval Expansion Act. He solidified friendship with Canada by promising in August 1938 at Kingston, Ontario, 'that the people of the United States will not stand idly by if domination of Canadian soil is threatened by any other Empire.' On 14 April 1939 he sent a personal message to Hitler and Mussolini asking them to promise not to attack some twenty small countries in Europe. Hitler made an insulting reply and then bullied some of the countries (which he was about to swallow) into assuring Roosevelt that they had no cause to fear good neighbor Germany. To strengthen his hand, the President asked Congress to repeal the Neutrality Act. But on 11 July 1939 the Senate Foreign Relations Committee voted, 12–11, to postpone such action, in part out of the conviction that there would be no war. Less than two months later, on 1 September 1939, Germany attacked Poland and brought the 'Long Armistice' to an end.

And the War Came

Three weeks after the outbreak of war, the President asked Congress, called into special session, to repeal the arms embargo. He said of the Neutrality law: 'I regret that the Congress passed that Act. I regret equally that I signed that Act.' Roosevelt preferred no neutrality legislation at all, but isolationist sentiment was still too strong. 'If you try that you'll be damn lucky to get five votes in my committee,' Senator Pittman told him. The President was forced to compromise on a bill continuing the principle of cash-and-carry, and even this brought forth violent denunciations from isolationists. But after six weeks of heated debate, Congress repealed the arms embargo and applied the cash-and-carry requirement to munitions as well as raw materials. Events in Europe had moved America another step toward war. Yet the anti-war forces were still strong enough to include a provision forbidding American ships to sail to belligerent ports and, if the President stipulated, to combat zones. The Neutrality Act of 1939 abandoned the doctrine of freedom of the seas that had been maintained since the days of the Napoleonic wars and the incursions of the Barbary pirates.

The nation still did not feel that its own security

was at stake in Europe—and, so long as it did not, further commitments were stoutly opposed. Not even Russia's attack on Finland in November shook this determination. The war in the West settled down to a long siege; some Americans even complained about the lack of excitement in the 'bore' war. Since the war seemed so unreal, there was little to shake the conviction that Hitler would be defeated in a war of attrition, and the United States, without danger to itself, could be the quartermaster for the Allied forces.

Early in April 1940, the 'phony war' came to a dramatic end. Without warning Germany moved into Denmark, a nation with whom Hitler had recently concluded a non-aggression pact, and then into Norway. Denmark fell within hours, Norway in less than two months. One month later, on 10 May, the German army invaded the Low Countries. In five days the Netherlands was conquered; three days later Antwerp fell. Already the German Panzer (armored) divisions had crashed through the Ardennes Forest, enveloped a French army, and smashed ahead toward the Channel ports. On 21 May—only eleven days after the attack on Holland—the Germans reached the English Channel, cutting off the British expeditionary force which had been rushed to the aid of Belgium and France. A week later Belgium surrendered, and the British were left to their fate. Their evacuation has well been called 'the miracle of Dunkirk.' Every available warship, yacht, power boat, fisherman, barge, and tug, to the number of 848, was pressed into service; and with a suicide division holding the front and the Royal Air Force screening, 338,000 men were transported to England. But they did not bring their weapons, and evacuations do not win wars.

The German army now swung south, and in two weeks cut the French army to pieces. On 10 June 1940 Mussolini entered the war. Five days later Paris fell, and Premier Reynaud, in desperation, appealed to Roosevelt for 'clouds of planes.' But Roosevelt could give only sympathy, and a hastily formed French government under the aged Marshal Pétain sued for peace. Hitler exacted a savage price. He occupied half of France, leaving the southern part to be ruled, from Vichy, by Pétain and Premier Laval, who were forced to collaborate with the victors, even to recruit

workers for German war industry and to deliver French Jews to torture and death. In one month Hitler's mechanized armies had done what the forces of William II had been unable to accomplish in four years.

The Nazi *Blitzkrieg* had shattered America's illusions about the outcome of the European war and its own impregnability. France had capitulated, Britain might soon go under. Walter Lippmann wrote: 'Our duty is to begin acting at once on the basic assumption that the Allies may lose the war this summer, and that before the snow flies again we may stand alone and isolated, the last great Democracy on earth.' For the moment even Roosevelt's severest critics rallied to him as the nation's leader in a time of crisis. Within a year after the invasion of the Low Countries, Congress appropriated $37 billion for rearmament and aid to the Allies— more than the total cost to the United States of World War I. To take advantage of the support by elements in both parties for his foreign policy, Roosevelt replaced the colorless Secretaries of War and of the Navy in his cabinet with two prominent Republicans—the 72-year-old Henry Stimson, who had been Secretary of War under Taft and Secretary of State under Hoover, and Frank Knox, the G.O.P. vice-presidential candidate in 1936.

At Charlottesville, Virginia, on 10 June the President pledged to 'extend to the opponents of force the material resources of this nation,' but Congress was less willing to approve aid to Britain than to agree to strengthening American defenses. Only 30 per cent of the country still thought the Allies would triumph, and the President's military and naval advisers warned that, with America's own stocks below the safety point, stepped-up aid to Britain would be highly precarious. If the United States extended such aid, and Britain surrendered, leaving the United States, stripped of its arms, to face an Axis invasion, Roosevelt would be hard put to justify his decision. Nonetheless, Roosevelt made available to the Allies planes, supplies of arms, and ammunition. He went even further by concluding a swap with Britain which was, as Churchill later observed, 'a decidedly unneutral act,' which by 'all the standards of history' would have 'justified the German Government in declaring war' on

Peter Blume, 'The Eternal City.' In this powerful satire of the corruption of Fascist Italy, Blume depicts a jack-in-the-box Mussolini in the ruins of Rome's once proud city. Blume, called 'the most sophisticated of /the/ practitioners of Magic Realism,' explained, 'Since I am concerned with the communication of ideas I am not at all ashamed of "telling stories" in my paintings, because I consider this to be one of the primary functions of the plastic arts.' (*Museum of Modern Art, Mrs. Simon Guggenheim Fund*)

America. In early September the President announced an arrangement whereby the United States transferred to Britain 50 World War I destroyers and received in return 99-year leases on a series of naval and air bases in the British West Indies.[2]

2. The Argentia (Newfoundland) and Bermuda bases were free gifts. The U.S. Navy also transferred ten Coast Guard cutters to Britain.

By the time the destroyer-bases deal was announced, Congress was in the closing stages of a bitter wrangle over a proposal to conscript men for military service in time of peace. Mail to Congressmen ran 90 per cent against the bill, and on Capitol Hill angry women hanged internationalist Senator Claude Pepper in effigy. But as the Nazis poised to strike across the English Channel, polls revealed a rapid shift of opinion in favor of selective service. In mid-September, Congress voted to draft men between the ages of twenty-one and thirty-five. A month later, Secretary Stimson, blindfolded, plucked from a fishbowl the first of the numbers which would determine the order men would be called into uniform.

The Election of 1940

In the midst of a heated debate over Roosevelt's foreign policy came the presidential election. The German *Blitzkrieg* made it inadvisable for the Republicans to chose an isolationist for their presidential candidate, and this gave an opportunity to a political maverick, Wendell Willkie, a Wall Street lawyer and a life-long Democrat, who had become the utility interests' most articulate critic of the New Deal and a frank proponent of aid to the Allies. When the Republican convention met in June, seasoned politicians could not hold back the rising tide of Willkie sentiment, although as late as April he had not had a single delegate. Events in Europe also assured FDR the Democratic nomination for a third term. Roosevelt, who had long since parted company with Garner, brought pressure on the delegates to accept the much more liberal Henry Wallace, a former Republican, as his running mate. The President demonstrated convincingly to people who thought he had lost control in the purge of 1938 that he still dominated the Democratic party.

Willkie looked forward to a personal battle with FDR, but the President refused to recognize him; instead, he played his role as commander in chief to the hilt. One Republican Congressman complained: 'Franklin Roosevelt is not running against Wendell Willkie. He's running against Adolf Hitler.' In such a contest, Willkie was at a decided disadvantage, especially because he shared Roosevelt's outlook on foreign policy. In his acceptance speech, Willkie warned: 'We must face a brutal but terrible fact. Our way of life is in competition with Hitler's way of life.' To be sure, before the campaign was over, both candidates had succumbed to the temptation to make extravagant appeals. Willkie said that if Roosevelt were elected 'you may expect war in April 1941,' and the President asserted, 'I have said this before, but I shall say it again and again and again. Your boys are not

going to be sent into any foreign wars.' But the isolationists knew that neither candidate was their man, and the conviction that the nation had never had a fair choice between war and peace in 1940 was to poison American politics for many years to come.

In the November election Roosevelt received 449 electoral votes, Willkie only 82, but FDR's share of the popular vote had fallen to less than 55 per cent. He continued to run very well in lower income districts. In an analysis of the election, Samuel Lubell wrote: 'The New Deal appears to have accomplished what the Socialists, the I.W.W. and the Communists never could approach. It has drawn a class line across the face of American politics.'

Year of Decision

The President interpreted re-election as an endorsement of his policies. When Congress met early in January 1941 he appealed to it for support of nations who were fighting in defense of what he called the Four Freedoms—freedom of speech, freedom of religion, freedom from want, freedom from fear. Four days later he submitted a program which was the result of an urgent message the President received a month after his election to an unprecedented third term. Prime Minister Churchill had written that Britain was in 'mortal danger' and that it was fast reaching the point when it would not be able to pay cash for the vast quantities of American arms it needed. As a consequence Roosevelt unveiled a new proposal: to lend arms directly on the understanding that they would be returned, or replacements for them provided, when the war ended. 'What I am trying to do,' he explained, 'is to eliminate the dollar sign.'

The lend-lease plan aroused fierce opposition. 'Lending war equipment is a good deal like lending chewing gum,' Senator Taft grumbled. 'You don't want it back.' Montana's Senator Wheeler called lend-lease the 'New Deal's "triple A" foreign policy—to plow under every fourth American boy.' (Roosevelt told newspapermen two days later: 'That really is the rottenest thing that has been said in public life in my generation.') However, by mid-January 1941, aid to Britain even at

'Vandenberg, Dewey, and Taft' by Ben Shahn, 1941. A year earlier it had appeared all but certain that one of this trio—Senator Arthur H. Vandenberg of Michigan, New York's district attorney Thomas E. Dewey, Senator Robert A. Taft of Ohio—would be the Republican presidential nominee in 1940. But as it turned out, the G.O.P. chose a newcomer, Wendell Willkie, to contest Franklin D. Roosevelt's bid for a third term. (*Museum of Modern Art, Gift of Lincoln Kirstein*)

the risk of war was favored by 70 per cent of those polled; and when the rolls were called in March, Congress voted passage of the Lend-Lease Act by sizable margins. The law authorized the President to 'sell, transfer, exchange, lease, lend,' any defense articles 'to the government of any country whose defense the President deems vital to the defense of the United States.' It also made available to such nations the facilities of American shipyards. By the end of the month Congress had voted the staggering sum of $7 billion, and this would be only the first installment in a mammoth program to arm the Allies that would total more than $50 billion.

Events now moved speedily. A few weeks after the enactment of lend-lease, the United States seized all Axis shipping in American ports. In April 1941 it took Greenland under protection and announced that the navy would patrol the sea lanes in defense zones. In May, after the sinking of an American freighter by a U-boat, Roosevelt proclaimed an 'unlimited national emergency.' In June the United States froze all Axis assets in this country and closed all Axis consulates. And on 24 June the President announced that lend-lease would be extended to a new ally—Russia. For on 22 June, Hitler broke his 1939 pact and set out to conquer that vast country, a colossal mistake which gave England and France an ally capable of pinning down the bulk of the German army on an eastern front. The Communist party in the United States, which had been denouncing the 'imperialist war,' now demanded American participation in a 'crusade.'

Roosevelt, like Wilson a generation earlier, moved to obtain a statement of war aims from the Allies. On 14 August 1941 he and Winston Churchill met afloat in Argentia Bay, Newfoundland, and there drew up the Atlantic Charter. Its principles included the already proclaimed Four

Freedoms, renunciation of territorial aggrandizement, a promise to restore self-government to those deprived of it, and a pledge of equal access to trade and raw materials.

The Atlantic also appeared likely to be the place where the United States would be drawn into World War II. On 4 September a German submarine attacked the United States destroyer *Greer* in the waters off Iceland, where American troops had been stationed some weeks earlier. The President ordered the navy to 'shoot on sight' these 'rattlesnakes of the Atlantic,' and stated indignantly: 'I tell you the blunt fact that the German submarine fired first upon this American destroyer without warning, and with deliberate design to sink her.' The President was being less than frank. The *Greer* had not only informed a British plane of the presence of the U-boat but had pursued the sub and broadcast its position for three and a half hours. During this period, the British plane had dropped four depth charges. Only then had the U-boat fired at the *Greer*. Two days after the shoot-on-sight speech, the Atlantic Fleet was ordered to protect all vessels on the run between North America and Iceland, even convoys which numbered no American ships. Since the Fleet had also been instructed to destroy any Nazi ship it sighted, the order of 13 September brought the United States Navy into all-out, even though undeclared, war in the Atlantic.

On 9 October, the President asked Congress to repeal the 'crippling provisions' of the Neutrality Act of 1939. Isolationists organized for a protracted struggle to defeat the President, but they failed to reckon on the impact of events in the North Atlantic. On 17 October, news arrived that the destroyer *Kearny* had been torpedoed southwest of Iceland; eleven sailors were lost. Three days later, the destroyer *Reuben James* became the first armed American vessel to be sunk by Germany; ninety-six officers and men lost their lives. Within two weeks Congress had voted to repeal restrictive sections of the neutrality law; henceforth, the President could arm merchantmen and send ships directly into combat areas. Little wonder that the nation's attention was focused on these reverberations of the war in Europe. But when war came to America, it would come not as the result of developments in the

Atlantic but as a consequence of even more momentous events in the Pacific.

For over a year, tension had been mounting in the Far East. After the German victories of May–June 1940, it became more difficult for moderate elements in Japan to restrain the militarists. With France and Holland conquered, Indo-China and the Netherlands East Indies were ripe for the picking; Malaya, Burma, and even India looked inviting. Japan wrested permission to build airfields in Indo-China from the helpless Vichy government of France, and added Tokyo to the Rome-Berlin Axis when it signed a Tripartite Pact with the European Fascist powers. The United States struck back with a loan to China and a partial embargo on exports to Japan.

In 1941 events moved toward a final crisis. In July, Japan occupied Indo-China. President Roosevelt responded by appointing General Douglas MacArthur to command all army forces in the Far East, and froze Japanese assets in the United States; Great Britain and the Netherlands followed suit. Japan was now cut off from its American market and such vital commodities as rubber, scrap metal, oil, and aviation fuel. The Japanese war lords decided to make war on these three countries within four months unless the flow of strategic supplies was restored, for the armies had to have fuel or evacuate China and Indo-China, which the military would not countenance. The subsequent negotiations were a sparring for time by two governments that considered war all but inevitable. Japan would not get out of China, and the United States would settle for nothing less. The American government wanted to stall off war, for its armed forces were not ready, but by late autumn Tokyo's plans had hardened. On 26 November 1941 a Japanese striking force of six big carriers with 353 battle-ready planes, two battleships, two heavy cruisers, and eleven destroyers sortied for Pearl Harbor.

The Japanese carried out the covert operation with devastating effect. Oahu was in a relaxed Sunday morning mood at 7:55 a.m. 7 December, when the bombs began to drop. Despite a war warning message of 27 November, Admiral Kimmel had not canceled week-end leave; General Short had his army planes parked wing-to-wing, fearing only danger from sabotage. At the end of

(*Library of Congress*)

this sad and bloody day, 2403 American sailors, soldiers, marines, and civilians had been killed, and 1178 more wounded; 149 planes had been destroyed on the ground or in the water; battleship *Arizona* was sunk beyond repair; *Oklahoma* shattered and capsized; *Tennessee*, *West Virginia*, and *California* were resting on the bottom; *Nevada* run aground to prevent sinking; other vessels destroyed or badly damaged. Although MacArthur's Far Eastern command had ample notice of the attack on Pearl Harbor, a Japanese bomber assault from Formosa caught the army air force grounded on fields near Manila and all but wiped it out—a major disaster. Next day Congress declared a state of war with Japan; on 11 December Germany and Italy, faithful to their tripartite pact with Japan, declared war on the United States. Pacifism and isolationism had been strong enough to keep America at peace for more than two years after the invasion of Poland in September 1939, but in the end the United States, too, was embroiled in the Second World War.

33

World War II

*

1941–1945

Mobilization

Franklin D. Roosevelt led America into war, not as an Associated Power as in World War I, but as a full-fledged member of the 'United Nations,' a grand alliance that would ultimately embrace forty-six countries. In collaboration with Prime Minister Churchill, the President involved himself directly in working out military strategy and in supervising war operations. The two countries had already established one critical priority: they would concentrate first on winning the war in Europe. This concept had been arrived at because the Rome-Berlin Axis had a greater war potential than Japan, a consideration that became the more pressing after Hitler attacked Russia; for if Germany prevailed the geopolitical 'heartland' would be Hitler's dominion, from Finisterre to Vladivostok and from the North Cape to the bulge of Africa. The informal Anglo-American understanding thus formed continued throughout the war. Meeting together, the American Joint Chiefs of Staff (as the heads of army, navy, and army air force shortly became) and the British Chiefs of Staff were called the Combined Chiefs of Staff.

They, under President Roosevelt and Prime Minister Churchill, initiated strategy, drafted plans, allocated forces, and directed the war.

A war of this magnitude required a massive mobilization and considerable sacrifice. All men between 18 and 45 were made liable to military service. Including voluntary enlistments, over 15 million people served in the armed forces during the war; 10 million in the army, 4 million in the navy and coast guard, 600,000 in the marine corps. About 216,000 women served as nurses, and in the auxiliary 'Waves' and 'Wacs' or as marines. There were 970,000 American casualties, including 254,000 dead and 66,000 missing.

Although at the time of Pearl Harbor only 15 per cent of industrial production was going to industrial needs, the United States truly became the 'arsenal of democracy' after entering the war. When the Allies launched their cross-Channel invasion in 1944, the armies 'lurched forward,' wrote Allan Nevins, 'like a vast armed workshop; a congeries of factories on wheels with a bristling screen of troops and a cover of airplanes.' The mobilization gave an enormous impetus to aluminum and magnesium production, enlarged

'Naval Recruiting Station, No. 1.' In 1942, Mitchell Jamieson's watercolor won a competition sponsored by the Section of Fine Arts, one of a number of New Deal experiments mobilized to serve martial purposes during World War II. (*National Archives*)

electricity output to nearly half again as much as in 1937, increased machine tool production seven-fold, and turned out more iron and steel than the whole world had produced a short time before. In 1939 America's airplane industry employed fewer than 47,000 persons and produced fewer than 6000 planes; in the peak year of 1944, the industry employed 2,102,000 workers and rolled out more than 96,000 planes. Medium tank production advanced so rapidly that it had to be cut back. By the beginning of 1944 the industrial output of America was twice that of all the Axis nations.

The genius of ship construction, Henry J. Kaiser, trimmed the time for turning out merchant ships from 105 days to 46, then 29, then 14. In mid-November 1942, Kaiser's Richmond, California, yard launched 'Hull 440,' the *Robert E. Peary*, in 4 days, 15½ hours. It went down the ways fitted out with life belts, coat hangers, electric clocks, and ink wells. By the middle of 1942, Kaiser was building one-third of the government's vessels, and his pace-setting rec-

ords fixed the standard the Maritime Commission demanded of other firms. As a consequence, merchant shipping construction, which amounted to only one million tons in 1941, surpassed 19 million only two years later.

In January 1942 the President set up the War Production Board to direct the mobilization. Donald Nelson, the WPB administrator, did not have the personal force to impose priorities, and not until 1943 was an effective system of allocation developed. As a consequence of Nelson's failings, the President named 'czars' to handle the critical problems of oil and rubber, and in October 1942 appointed Supreme Court Justice James F. Byrnes to head an Office of Economic Stabilization. In May 1943 he gave Byrnes, who proved an able administrator, still greater authority as director of the Office of War Mobilization.

To curb inflation, the government not only stepped up taxes and sold nearly $100 billion in war bonds but controlled prices directly through the Office of Price Administration which

Women welders, Todd Erie Basin drydock. 'Females had demonstrated that they could do a man's work and do it well, and, as the war progressed, more and more men in the factory started treating their women co-workers as equals,' William H. Chafe has written of World War II. 'A Women's Bureau official noted after an extensive tour of a California shipyard that men barked orders at women, refused to pick up their tools when dropped. . . . After witnessing the extent to which females had become assimilated into the formerly male-dominated industries of the Connecticut Valley, Constance Green observed that "presenting a tool chest to a little girl need no longer be dubbed absurdly inappropriate."' (*Library of Congress*)

Roosevelt had set up in August 1941 under Leon Henderson, an ebullient New Deal economist. After experimenting with selective controls of prices and rents, Henderson imposed a general price freeze in April 1942. The OPA also rationed scarce commodities like meat, gasoline, and tires. But the agency ran into trouble from businessmen who resented controls, from the farm bloc which insisted on 110 per cent of parity, and from union labor which protested that even the War Labor Board's formula of a 15 per cent wage increase did not meet the rising cost of living. In 1943, to counter a strike by John L. Lewis's mine workers, the government took over the coal mines; at the same time, it rolled back food prices. By the middle of 1943, prices had reached a plateau, and for the rest of the war, the OPA, under the advertising executive Chester Bowles, held the increase in the cost of living to less than 1.5 per cent, one of the remarkable achievements of the war.

Mighty as America's effort was, it did not add up to total war. There was no firm control over manpower, no conscription of women. A few edibles were rationed, but most Americans ate more heartily than before. Gasoline and tires were rationed, but hundreds of thousands of cars managed to stay on the road for purposes remotely connected with the war. As prices of most essentials were kept down, the standard of living rose. The country was never invaded, except by U-boats penetrating the three-mile limit, and a large measure of the 'blood, sweat and tears' that Churchill promised his countrymen was spared his country's ally. Yet even for Americans it was a grim, austere war. In contrast to the Creel Committee in World War I, the Office of War Information, under the sensible newspaperman, Elmer Davis, presented the war not as a utopian struggle, but, in the President's words, simply as 'the survival war.' For the American fighting forces there were no brass bands or bugles, no 'Over There' or marching songs, no flaunting colors; not even a ship's bell to mark the watches.

Social Consequences of the War

World War II had a profound impact on American society, for good or evil. Of the many changes, none had more immediate importance than the termination of the Great Depression. The demands of the armed services and the war industries brought to an end more than a decade of unemployment. Indeed, there quickly developed a shortage of workers which gave women opportunities in aircraft plants and shipyards. Women accounted for one-third of all workers on the B-29's. Moreover, unlike World War I, the Second World War resulted in a permanent increase in the proportion of women in the labor force. The war brought unparalleled prosperity to millions of Americans. The farmers' net cash income more than quadrupled between 1940 and 1945, and the weekly earnings of industrial workers rose 70 per cent.

Wartime full employment, together with progressive tax legislation, resulted in a redistribution of income that had not been achieved in the halcyon days of the New Deal. Although tax laws hit millions of Americans for the first time, through the new device of 'withholding,' the top 5 per cent of income receivers were soaked more than at any time in our history. Their share of disposable income dropped from 26 per cent in 1940 to 16 per cent in 1944, as the federal income levy reached a maximum of 94 per cent of total net income. With a corporation income tax as high as 50 per cent and an excess profits tax stepped up to 95 per cent, few corporations enjoyed 'swollen profits.' Net corporation income in 1945 was less than in 1941.

World War II reshuffled more Americans than had any internal migration over the same span in the nation's history. During the war years, the West showed a net gain of 1,200,000 people, three-fourths of them from the South. Within a few months after Pearl Harbor, the Pacific Coast states were building one-fourth of the nation's war planes, one-third of its ships. Southern California, which ranked second only to Akron as a rubber manufacturing center, even boasted a steel plant. A nation in which 27 million people moved during the war counted the social costs of this upheaval: a critical housing shortage, lack of civic facilities in jerry-built war plant towns, and a conspicuous rise in juvenile delinquency occasioned by the uprooting of families.

'Negro Soldier,' by Thomas Hart Benton. During World War II, a half-million blacks saw service overseas. Twenty-two Negro combat units, including nine field artillery battalions and two tank battalions, fought in Europe, and eighty-two black pilots received the Distinguished Flying Cross. (*State Historical Society of Missouri*)

During the war, 60,000 Negroes moved from the Deep South to Detroit, 100,000 to Chicago, 250,000 to the West Coast, and wherever they went they encountered discrimination. When they gave their blood to the Red Cross, it was segregated from that of whites. When war plants advertised for more help, black applicants were rejected. When they got jobs, as in the Mobile shipyards, white workers organized 'hate strikes' against them. Although not confined to labor battalions, as they largely had been in World War I, blacks were generally segregated in barracks and mess halls, and often confined to menial tasks.[1]

But Negroes fought with increased militance for their rights. From 1940 to 1946 NAACP membership grew ninefold. Dismayed by the reluctance of employers to hire black labor even in boom times, A. Philip Randolph, president of the Brotherhood of Sleeping Car Porters, issued a call for 50,000 Negroes to march on Washington in protest. Randolph cancelled the call only after Roosevelt had issued Executive Order 8802 on 25 June 1941. The President's edict forbade discrimination in work under defense contracts and established a Fair Employment Practices Committee. In part as a result of the FEPC's activities, but more because of the critical labor shortage, the Negro's share of jobs in war industries increased from 3 to 8 per cent of the whole, while the number of black employees in the Federal Government jumped from 40,000 to over 300,000.

Despite such brutal episodes as a race riot in

1. However, 7000 blacks were commissioned as officers. The all-Negro 99th Fighter Squadron won distinction in Europe, and a combat team of the 93rd Infantry Division at Bougainville.

Detroit in which 25 Negroes and nine whites were killed, World War II resulted in marked advances for black Americans and for relations between the races. Georgia repealed the poll tax; the Supreme Court outlawed the white primary in Texas; and in Atlanta in 1944, Negro and white leaders sat down together to organize the Southern Regional Council. The doctrine of white supremacy met a formidable intellectual challenge. Gunnar Myrdal's *An American Dilemma* offered an imposing scholarly analysis, and Lillian Smith's novel, *Strange Fruit*, found a wide audience.

Although America's performance on civil liberties was generally better than in World War I, one dreadful blot stained this record: the relocation and internment of Japanese-Americans. The Roosevelt administration attempted to quiet demands for the evacuation of the 112,000 Japanese or Americans of Japanese descent (*Nisei*) from the West Coast, but it was overwhelmed by the outcry against them. Even men long regarded as friends of civil liberties beat the drums for evacuation: Senator Hiram Johnson, California's Attorney-General Earl Warren, Walter Lippmann. On 19 February 1942, Roosevelt, yielding to the hysteria, approved an edict surrendering control to the army, which ordered the ouster of every 'Japanese' (more than two-thirds were American citizens) from the western parts of Washington, Oregon, and California and the southern quarter of Arizona. Thousands of United States citizens were expelled from their homes and herded into relocation centers in the western deserts and the Arkansas swamplands. No such action was taken against German or Italian aliens, let alone Americans of German or Italian descent. Much of the justification for the expulsion rested on fears of sabotage. Yet in Hawaii, where people of Japanese birth were much more concentrated than on the West Coast (and where they were not interned), not one act of sabotage was committed. Nonetheless, the Supreme Court sanctioned the government's action in the Korematsu case, although Justice Murphy commented that the evacuation of Japanese-Americans bore 'a melancholy resemblance' to the Nazis' treatment of the Jews. When the army reversed its policy and recruited *Nisei*, they proved to be the toughest of all fighters in the Italian campaign. But when

Japanese-Americans returned to the West Coast after the war, they still encountered gross discrimination and personal indignities.

Retreat and Resurgence in the Pacific

In the Far East in the days after Pearl Harbor, the news was calamitous. Thailand surrendered to the Japanese, who promptly began a relentless march on the British base at Singapore. On 10 December the Rising Sun flag was hoisted on Guam, which had been bravely but pitifully defended by a few hundred Americans and Chamorros. Other Japanese task forces captured Hong Kong and the Borneo oilfields. On Wake Island, lonely outpost in the Central Pacific, a small marine defense force was overwhelmed. In the Philippines, General MacArthur evacuated Manila on 27 December, and withdrew his army to the Bataan Peninsula. On 9 April the 'battling bastards of Bataan,' about 12,500 Americans and over 60,000 Filipinos, had to surrender unconditionally. Only a couple of thousand escaped to the island fortress of Corregidor before the ranks of the prisoners were thinned by the infamous 65-mile 'death march' from Bataan to Japanese prison camps. A month earlier, on orders of President Roosevelt, MacArthur had left the Philippines and set up headquarters in Australia; he vowed to return, as he did. On 6 May, General Jonathan M. Wainwright was forced to surrender Corregidor together with its 11,000 defenders, and a Philippine army of over 50,000 on the Visayas and Mindanao. There had been no such capitulation in American history since Appomattox.

In the meantime the Japanese had won all their objectives in Southeast Asia. The great naval base of Singapore, on which Britain had lavished millions of pounds, fell on 15 February. On 9 May 1942 Java surrendered. Rangoon, capital and chief seaport of Burma, had been occupied by the Japanese the day before. The Japanese now ruled East Asia, west to British India and south to the waters adjacent to Australia and Fiji. India, as threatened by nationalists within as by enemies without, and Australia trembled that their turn might come next. Never in modern history has there been so quick and valuable a series of conquests; even Hitler's were inferior. The prestige

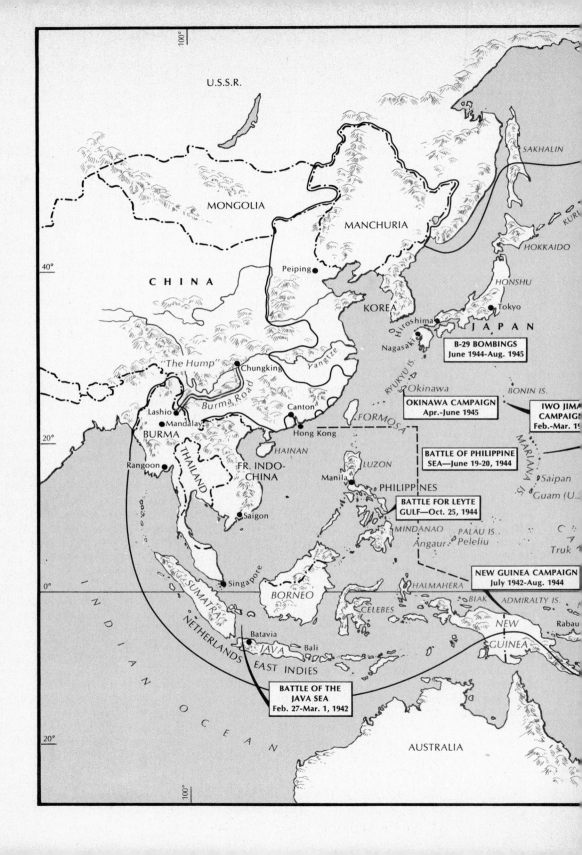

U.S.S.R.

MONGOLIA

MANCHURIA

CHINA

Peiping ●

KOREA

SAKHALIN

HOKKAIDO

HONSHU

Tokyo ●

JAPAN

Hiroshima ○
Nagasaki ●

B-29 BOMBINGS
June 1944-Aug. 1945

"The Hump"

Chungking ●

Yangtze

Burma Road

Lashio ●
Mandalay ●

BURMA

Canton ●

Hong Kong ●

HAINAN

RYUKYU IS.

Okinawa

OKINAWA CAMPAIGN
Apr.-June 1945

BONIN IS.

**IWO JIMA
CAMPAIGN**
Feb.-Mar. 19

FORMOSA

THAILAND

Rangoon ●

FR. INDO-
CHINA

Saigon ●

Manila ●

LUZON

PHILIPPINES

**BATTLE OF PHILIPPINE
SEA—June 19-20, 1944**

MARIANA IS.

Saipan ●

Guam (U.

**BATTLE FOR LEYTE
GULF—Oct. 25, 1944**

MINDANAO

PALAU IS.

Angaur ● Peleliu

C A

Truk ●

Singapore ●

BORNEO

HALMAHERA

BIAK

NEW GUINEA CAMPAIGN
July 1942-Aug. 1944

ADMIRALTY IS.

NEW

Rabau

SUMATRA

NETHERLANDS

Batavia ●

JAVA

Bali

EAST INDIES

CELEBES

GUINEA

INDIAN

OCEAN

**BATTLE OF THE
JAVA SEA**
Feb. 27-Mar. 1, 1942

AUSTRALIA

100°

40°

20°

0°

20°

100°

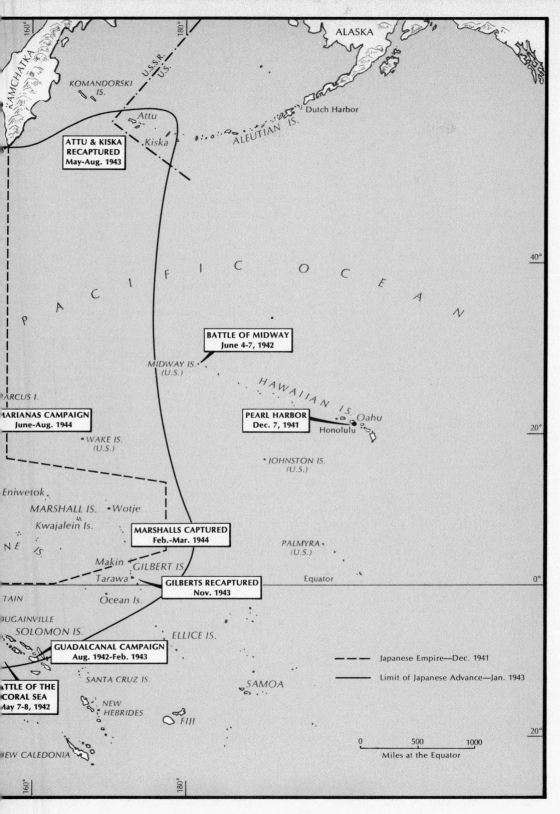

The Pacific Theater of War, 1941–45

Within the figure, the following labels appear:

ALASKA

KAMCHATKA

KOMANDORSKI IS.

U.S.S.R.
U.S.

Attu

Kiska

Dutch Harbor

ALEUTIAN IS.

ATTU & KISKA RECAPTURED
May–Aug. 1943

PACIFIC OCEAN

40°

BATTLE OF MIDWAY
June 4–7, 1942

MIDWAY IS.
(U.S.)

HAWAIIAN IS.

Oahu

PEARL HARBOR
Dec. 7, 1941

Honolulu

20°

MARCUS I.

MARIANAS CAMPAIGN
June–Aug. 1944

WAKE IS.
(U.S.)

JOHNSTON IS.
(U.S.)

Eniwetok

MARSHALL IS.

Wotje

Kwajalein Is.

MARSHALLS CAPTURED
Feb.–Mar. 1944

PALMYRA
(U.S.)

NE IS.

Makin

GILBERT IS.

Tarawa

Equator

0°

GILBERTS RECAPTURED
Nov. 1943

Ocean Is.

TAIN

BOUGAINVILLE

SOLOMON IS.

ELLICE IS.

GUADALCANAL CAMPAIGN
Aug. 1942–Feb. 1943

SANTA CRUZ IS.

SAMOA

BATTLE OF THE CORAL SEA
May 7–8, 1942

NEW HEBRIDES

FIJI

NEW CALEDONIA

20°

- - - - Japanese Empire—Dec. 1941

——— Limit of Japanese Advance—Jan. 1943

0   500   1000

Miles at the Equator

160°   180°   160°   180°

of the white races fell so low that even victory over Japan could not win it back; and the areas that the Japanese conquered, though no longer Japanese, are now also independent of Europe.

However, instead of consolidating their new conquests to make their country invincible, the Japanese succumbed to what one of their admirals after the war ruefully called 'victory disease.' They decided to wrest more Pacific territory from the Allies, and Admiral Yamamoto wished to provoke a major sea battle. A good prophet, he pointed out that the United States Navy must be annihilated, if ever, in 1942, before American productive capacity replaced the Pearl Harbor losses. But even in 1942 American forces proved to be more formidable than the Japanese anticipated.

The Battle of the Coral Sea (7–8 May 1942) frustrated the first forward lunge in the new Japanese offensive to capture Port Moresby, a strategic base in Papua, New Guinea. This was the first naval battle in which no ship of either side sighted one of the other; the fighting was done by carrier plane against carrier plane, or carrier plane against ship. Each side in this new sort of naval warfare made mistakes, but the Japanese made more; and although their losses were inferior, they dared not press on to occupy Port Moresby. For Australia, Coral Sea was the decisive battle, saving her from possible invasion.

In the next and more vital Japanese offensive, Yamamoto went all-out. Personally assuming command, he deployed almost every capital ship of his navy. His first objective was to capture Midway, a tiny atoll at the tip end of the Hawaiian chain, 1134 miles northwest of Pearl Harbor, where the United States had an advanced naval and air base, but his dearest object was to force Admiral Nimitz to give battle with his numerically inferior Pacific Fleet. He had his wish, but the battle did not go to the strong. On 4 June 1942, a Japanese four-carrier force, advancing undetected under a foul-weather front, was near enough Midway to batter the air base, but American carrier-based planes destroyed all four of the best Japanese carriers and Yamamoto had to order his vast fleet to retire. He had sustained the first defeat to the Japanese navy in modern times.

After this glorious Battle of Midway, the Joint Chiefs of Staff decided to breach the island barrier to an Allied advance toward Japan by invading the mountainous, jungle-clad Solomon Islands. On 7 August 1942, the 1st Marine Division landed at Tulagi and Guadalcanal, surprised the enemy, and seized the harbor of the one island and the airfield on the other. There then began the prolonged and bloody struggle for Guadalcanal; an island worthless in itself, like the battlefield of Gettysburg in 1863, but even more violently contested. Seven major naval battles were fought, until Iron Bottom Bay, as American sailors named Savo Island Sound, was strewn with the hulls of ships and the bodies of sailors. Every few nights the Japanese ran fast reinforcement echelons, the 'Tokyo Expresses,' down the central channel, the Solomons' 'Slot'; every few days American reinforcements came in, and daily air battles became routine. On shore, the marines, reinforced by army divisions, fought stubbornly and, in the end, successfully. On 9 February 1943, six months after the landings, the Japanese evacuated Guadalcanal. In this campaign American soldiers found that the supposedly invincible Japanese foot-soldiers, who had overrun half of Eastern Asia, could be beaten, and after this deadly island had been secured, the navy won every battle with the Japanese fleet. In the meantime the western prong of this Japanese offensive had been stopped on the north coast of Papua, New Guinea, by American and Australian troops. The fighting, in malaria-infested mangrove swamps against a trapped and never-surrendering enemy, was the most horrible of the entire war, but by early 1943 the defensive period in the war with Japan had finally come to an end, at the very time when the Allies were carrying out ambitious new designs in a more vital area of concern—the European theater.

From North Africa to Italy

While Winston Churchill was conferring with Roosevelt at the White House in June 1942, news came of the German capture of Tobruk in North Africa. Churchill confessed that he was the most miserable Englishman in America since the surrender of Burgoyne. For the fall of Tobruk opened a German road into Egypt and beyond. If Alexan-

DETACH HERE

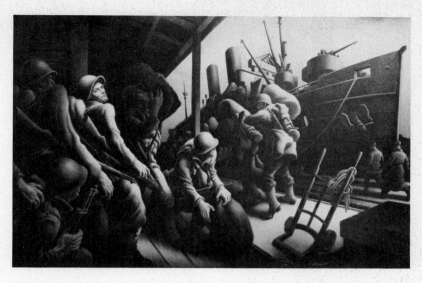

Thomas Hart Benton, 'Prelude to Death.' Benton's painting is based on sketches he made at the loading docks in Brooklyn of the first contingent of American troops departing for the North African front. It was intended as a contribution to the war propaganda program, but government officials rejected it because, Benton explained, 'the central character is looking back home instead of "forward to duty."' (*State Historical Society of Missouri*)

dria and the Suez Canal fell, nothing short of a miracle could keep the Axis out of India, on whose eastern frontier the Japanese were already poised.

Meeting at the White House the Allied leaders debated the time and place for the first combined military operation against the Axis. The Americans wanted a cross-Channel operation in France, a beachhead in 1942 and the big invasion in 1943. The British opposed any such attempt before the Allies had overwhelming force, lest it be thrown back with heavy loss. Roosevelt was deeply impressed with the need for a second front in Europe to prevent Russia's being overrun. Something had to be done in 1942—Churchill and Roosevelt could not stand the obloquy of fighting another 'phony war.' They decided, overriding most of their military advisers, on an occupation of French North Africa. Oran and Algiers on the Mediterranean, and Casablanca on the Atlantic coast of Morocco, were selected as the three strategic harbors to be seized by amphibious forces

under General Dwight D. Eisenhower, who, as he later wrote, was to occupy 'the rim of a continent where no major military campaign had been conducted for centuries.'

On 23 October 1942 General Sir Bernard Montgomery launched the second battle of El Alamein against Rommel, and on the same day Rear Admiral H. Kent Hewitt, commanding the Western Naval Task Force, sailed from Hampton Roads. Never before had an amphibious operation been projected across an ocean, but the complex operation went like clockwork. By midnight 7–8 November all three task forces (the two for Oran and Algiers under British command) had reached their destinations, unscathed and unreported. Admiral Hewitt had to fight a naval battle with the French fleet off Casablanca, and sink most of it, in order to get General Patton's troops ashore safely, but there was little resistance from the French army. Admiral Darlan, second to Marshal Pétain in the Vichy government, was so impressed by the

At the headquarters of Lieutenant-General George S. Patton, the four-star general Dwight D. Eisenhower studies a map of the Tunisian campaign. At one point in the bitter fighting in North Africa, Patton, disappointed that a certain general had twice failed to take a hill, noted in his diary: 'I believe that he is a coward. Therefore, I have ordered him to ride in the lead attack vehicle tomorrow. This will make him either a corpse or a man.' The general took the hill, and Patton concluded, 'I feel I can now put full confidence in this officer.' (*Library of Congress*)

strength of the Anglo-American landings that Eisenhower was able to persuade him to issue a cease-fire order to all French forces in North Africa on 11 November. Defended as a military expedient, this 'Darlan deal' was denounced by liberals as capitulation to a Nazi collaborator. Darlan was assassinated on Christmas eve, but not until October 1944 did the United States recognize Charles de Gaulle as the leader of the French nation.

Early in January 1943 Roosevelt and Churchill and the Combined Chiefs of Staff met at Casablanca to plan future operations. For the first time Allied prospects seemed favorable; this was, as Churchill said, 'the end of the beginning.' The Russians had turned the tide at the decisive battle of Stalingrad; the British had saved Egypt; Mussolini could no longer call the Mediterranean *mare nostrum*. Allied chiefs at Casablanca decided to invade Sicily as soon as Tunisia was secured, gave America the green light to start an offensive against the Japanese, and promised 'to draw as much weight as possible off the Russian armies by engaging the enemy as heavily as possible at the best selected point.' And they made the momentous announcement that the war would end only with 'unconditional surrender.' That formula, borrowed from General Grant's declaration before Fort Donelson, was prompted by the failure of the armistice of 1918 to eliminate the German menace, and a desire to reassure Russia that it would not be let down. The formula was subsequently criticized as helping Hitler to persuade his people to fight to the bitter end, but it is not clear that it actually had much effect.

While Roosevelt and Churchill were discussing grand strategy, the war took a critical turn. For a time Rommel's Afrika Korps threatened to cut the Allied armies in two. But this proved to be Rommel's last offensive. Hammered front and rear, pounded by a devastating aerial attack, Rommel retreated northward into Tunisia. The Allied armies, now half a million strong, closed in for the kill. As Montgomery broke the German lines in the south and raced for Tunis, Omar Bradley smashed into Bizerte. Both cities fell on 7 May 1943. Cornered, the German army, still 275,000 strong, surrendered on 13 May. It was the greatest victory that British and American arms had yet won. North Africa was cleared of the enemy, the spliced lifeline of the British Empire to India through Suez made it possible to reinforce Russia via the Persian Gulf, and the way was open at last for a blow at what Churchill mistakenly called 'the soft underbelly' of Europe.

D-day for the Anglo-American attack on Sicily was 10 July. In the biggest amphibious assault of the war, 250,000 British and American troops landed simultaneously, eight divisions abreast, and in black darkness. The 350,000 Italian and German defenders of Sicily were surprised and thrown off balance. The American Seventh Army swept across Sicily; on 22 July General Patton made a triumphal entry into Palermo and set up headquarters in the ancient palace of the Norman kings. By 17 August the great island was in Allied hands.

Italy, though not mortally wounded, was heartily sick of the war. On 25 July, six days after Allied air forces had delivered a 560-plane bombing raid on Rome, King Victor Emmanuel III summoned up enough courage to force Mussolini to resign. Marshal Badoglio, who told the king that the war was *perduto, perdutissimo* (absolutely and completely lost), now headed the government and began to probe for peace. While negotiations dragged along until 3 September, the Germans had time to rush reinforcements into Italy and to seize key points such as Rome. In early September 1943 the American Fifth Army, commanded by General Mark W. Clark, with two British and two American infantry divisions in the assault, took off from a dozen ports between Oran and Alexandria to invade the Italian mainland. En route to the objective the familiar voice of General 'Ike' was heard broadcasting news of the Italian surrender, so all hands expected a walk-over. They had a bitter surprise. Some very tough and uncooperative Germans were at the beach at Salerno on D-day, 9 September. After a week of vicious fighting, the beachheads were secured, and as the Germans started an orderly retirement northward, the Fifth Army on 1 October entered Naples.

Here the Italian campaign should have been halted. But the British contended that the battle of Italy pinned down and used up German divisions which might resist the Normandy landing in

The Yanks in Tunisia. When American troops entered a North African town, the first to greet them were swarms of Arab boys asking for candy and cigarettes. In this scene, photographed by Robert Capa, a sergeant from Mississippi and a corporal from Connecticut are besieged in their jeep by boys crying 'bon-bon' and 'shoon-gum.' (*Robert Capa—Magnum*)

1944. Actually the Italian campaign failed to draw German reserves from France, and by June 1944 the Allies were deploying in Italy double the number of the Germans in that area. Marshal Kesselring, fighting a series of delaying operations along prepared mountain entrenchments, exploited natural advantages to the full. From Naples to Rome is but a hundred miles; yet the Allies, with numerical superiority on land and in the air, and with control of adjacent waters, took eight months to cover that ground. In the mud and frost of that miserable campaign, wrote the war correspondent Ernie Pyle, GI's 'lived like men of prehistoric times, and a club would have become them more than a machine gun.' Not until midnight of 4 June 1944 did the Fifth Army enter Rome. For one brief day the American troops in Italy held the attention of the world. Then, on 6 June, came the news that the Allies had landed on the coast of Normandy, and the soldiers in Italy, their brief share of the limelight quickly ended, plodded on to meet the Germans at the Gothic line another 150 miles to the north.

The Battle of the Atlantic

Before the Allies could launch the long-awaited cross-Channel invasion, they first had to win control of the Atlantic. The Atlantic sea lanes had to be kept open for supplies and to build up a United States army in England for the eventual assault on the Continent. During the first eleven months of 1941 almost a thousand Allied or neutral merchantmen, totaling over 3.6 million tons, had been lost by enemy action, half of it by U-boats, and in 1942 Admiral Doenitz moved his wolf-packs to the American east coast, where he rightly anticipated rich pickings from non-convoyed tankers and merchantmen. The U-boat offensive opened on 12 January 1942 off Cape Cod, and frightful destruction was wrought by the submarines in coastal shipping lanes. During January–April 1942, almost 200 ships were sunk in North American, Gulf, and Caribbean waters, or around Bermuda. Doenitz then shifted his wolf-packs to the Straits of Florida, the Gulf of Mexico, and the Caribbean; and in those waters 182 ships totaling over 751,000 tons were sunk in May and June.

Vessels were torpedoed 30 miles off New York City, within sight of Virginia Beach, off the Passes to the Mississippi, off the Panama Canal entrance. Since tourist resorts from Atlantic City to Miami Beach were not even required to turn off neon signs until April 1942, hapless freighters and tankers passing them were silhouetted to the benefit of the U-boats.

Fortunately Admiral Ernest J. King, commander in chief of the United States fleet, was taking energetic measures to combat the submarine menace. To supply small escort vessels, the slogan 'sixty vessels in sixty days' was nailed to the mast in April 1942, and 67 vessels actually came through by 4 May, when a second 60–60 program was already under way. Scientists were mobilized to find more efficient means of tracking and sinking U-boats (British scientists had already contributed radar and would soon give America sonar); inshore and offshore patrols were organized into a 'Hooligan Navy' of converted yachts, and an interlocking convoy system was worked out. In the second half of 1942 coastal convoys lost only 0.5 per cent of their ships; transatlantic convoys lost only 1.4 per cent in a whole year.

The crucial period in the Battle of the Atlantic came in the first half of 1943, when the Germans more than doubled the number of U-boats operating in the Atlantic. A fresh German blitz in March 1943 accounted for 108 merchant ships aggregating over 625,000 tons. These sinkings, occurring at the worst season in the North Atlantic when the temperature of the water hovers around 30° F, were accompanied by heavy loss of life. And although the United States Navy, which escorted transatlantic troop transports, lost none of those going to and from Great Britain or the Mediterranean, it lost three army transports en route to Greenland and Iceland; one of these, the *Dorchester*, on 3 February 1943, with great loss, including four army chaplains. By April, though, the Allies were definitely ahead. The increased number of convoys and escorts, improved devices and training, and the work of scientists and technicians were getting results, and merchant ship new construction was now well ahead of losses. But throughout the war the Germans were able, on

'Emmitsburgians in Service.' This photograph by Marjory Collins of a window display in a general store in Emmitsburg, Maryland, in February 1943 indicates the pervasive impact of World War II on American communities. The array of pictures includes 'boys in the service' of a wide range of ages and ranks, Army and Navy, and near the center a woman commissioned second lieutenant in the U.S. Army Nursing Corps, Camp Meade, Md. (*Library of Congress*)

occasion, to send wolf-packs full cry after transatlantic traffic; the Battle of the Atlantic did not end until Germany surrendered.

Forward in the Pacific

In the same months that the Allies were clearing the Atlantic of the U-boat menace in preparation for the assault on the Continent, the war on the other side of the globe was entering its climactic phase. Before Japan could be invaded, positions had to be taken within air-bombing distance. But how to get there? The short northern route, via the Aleutians, was ruled out by bad flying weather. In the Central Pacific, hundreds of atolls and thousands of islands—the Gilberts, Marshalls,

Carolines, Marianas, and Bonins—plastered with airfields and bristling with defenses, sprawled across the ocean like a maze of gigantic spider webs. South of the equator, Japan held the Bismarck Archipelago, the Solomons north of Guadalcanal, and all New Guinea except its slippery tail. General MacArthur wished to advance by what he called the New Guinea-Mindanao axis; but Rabaul, planted like a baleful spider at the center of a web across that axis, would have to be eliminated first. And as long as Japan held the island complex on MacArthur's north flank, she could throw air and naval forces against his communications at will. So it was decided that Admiral Nimitz must take a broom to the Gilberts, the Marshalls, and the Carolines, while MacArthur and Halsey cleaned out the Bismarcks. All could then join forces for a final push into the Philippines and on to the coast of China.

Accordingly the plans for mid-1943 to mid-1944 began with preliminary operations to sweep up enemy spider webs. The central Solomons were the first objective. After three sharp naval actions up the Solomons' Slot in July and a number of motor torpedo boat actions (in one of which John Fitzgerald Kennedy distinguished himself), the United States Navy won control of surrounding waters, and in New Guinea and on New Britain, amphibious operations secured the main passage from the Coral Sea through the Bismarcks barrier into the Western Pacific. Japan could now be approached in a series of bold leaps instead of a multitude of short hops. The essence of the 'leap-frogging' strategy was to by-pass the principal Japanese strongpoints like Truk and Rabaul, sealing them off with sea and air power, leaving their garrisons to 'wither on the vine,' while the Allies constructed a new air and naval base in some less strongly defended spot several hundred miles nearer Japan. By 25 March 1944 the Bismarcks barrier to MacArthur's advance was decisively breached, and almost 100,000 Japanese troops were neutralized at Rabaul.

Meantime, Allied forces had moved into the Gilberts and Marshalls in the first full-scale amphibious operations in the Pacific. Some 200 sail of ships, carrying 108,000 soldiers, sailors, marines, and aviators converged on two coral atolls of the Gilbert group. Makin, where the enemy had no great strength, was taken methodically, but Tarawa, a small, strongly defended position behind a long coral-reef apron, cost the lives of almost a thousand marines and sailors in disposing of 4000 no-surrender Japanese on an islet not three miles long. The Gilberts became bases from which aircraft helped to neutralize the Japanese air bases in the Marshalls, which were invaded early in 1944 at Kwajalein and Eniwetok. The Japanese troops, as usual, resisted to the last man; but the Marshalls cost many fewer casualties than tiny Tarawa. Another leap-frogging operation scored important victories in New Guinea in the spring of 1944, while an offensive against the Marianas, of which the principal islands were Saipan, Tinian, and Guam, threatened Japan's inner line of defense. When the Japanese attempted to beat back the American offensive by deploying a huge naval force, they lost over 345 planes and three carriers in the Battle of the Philippine Sea (19 June 1944). Thereafter the conquest of the Marianas proceeded apace. On 6 July, the Japanese general and his staff committed suicide, and the rest of his army jumped off cliffs or holed up in caves. By 1 August 1944 three big islands of the Marianas were in American possession, and by fall, Marianas-based B-29's were bombing southern Japan.

The more sagacious Japanese now knew they were beaten; but they dared not admit it, and nerved their people to another year of bitter resistance in the vain hope that America might tire of the war when victory was within grasp in Asia and the Allies were on the offensive in Europe.

From Normandy to the Rhine

While waiting for an appropriate moment to launch the cross-Channel invasion of Hitler's 'Fortress Europe,' the R.A.F., in conjunction with the United States Army Air Force, was doing its best to render invasion unnecessary by bombing Germany into submission. Largely British, but assisted by B-17's of the Eighth Army Air Force, was the most destructive air bombing of the European war—the series of attacks on Hamburg in July-August 1943, which, by using incendiary

D-Day, 6 June 1944. At Utah Beach, near Cherbourg, members of an American landing party help ashore soldiers whose craft was sunk by enemy action. These survivors of the Normandy invasion made their way through rough seas in a life raft to this stony beach. (*U.S. Army Photograph*)

bombs, wiped out over half the city, killed 42,600, and injured 37,000 people. This strategic air offensive never succeeded as an alternative to land invasion. The bombing almost nightly by the R.A.F. and every clear day by the A.A.F. did not seriously diminish Germany's well-dispersed war production and conspicuously failed to break civilian morale. It was also frightfully expensive. In

six days of October 1943, culminating in a raid on the ball-bearing plants at Schweinfurt, deep in the heart of Germany, the Eighth lost 148 bombers and their crews, mostly as a result of battles in the air.

Yet the Allied bombing raids, much more effective in 1944, did deny many hundreds of aircraft to the enemy when he needed them most. By the spring of 1944 the Allied air forces had established a thirty-to-one superiority over the German air force. On D-day, 'Ike' told his troops, 'If you see fighting aircraft over you, they will be ours,' and so they were. The air war in Europe cost the lives of some 158,000 British, Canadian, and American aviators. In this new dimension of warfare, many mistakes were made; but the Germans made even more. Without victory in the air there could have been no victory anywhere, no expectation of success in that enormously risky continental invasion on which hinged all hopes for a final triumph in the war.

Never before in modern times had an invading army crossed the English Channel against opposition, and Hitler's coastal defenses were formidable: underwater obstacles and mines, artillery emplacements, pill boxes, wire entanglements, tank traps, land mines, and other hazards, and behind these defenses were stationed 58 divisions. Yet the Allies had reason for confidence. For six weeks Allied air forces had been smashing roads and bridges in northern France, reducing the transportation system to chaos. The Allied force of soldiers, sailors, aviators, and service amounted to 2.8 million men, all based in England. Thirty-nine divisions and 11,000 planes were available for the initial landings, and the Allied supporting fleet was overwhelmingly superior to anything the Germans could deploy; the U-boats had been so neutralized by the Allied navies that not one of the thousands of vessels engaged in the invasion was torpedoed.

The Allied command selected as target a 40-mile strip of beach along the Normandy coast. The eastern sector was assigned to the British, the western to the Americans. Shortly after midnight 5 June three paratroop divisions were flown across the Channel to drop behind the beaches. During the night the invasion fleet of 600 warships and 4000 supporting craft, freighted with 176,000 men from a dozen different ports, moved over to the Norman coast. Before naval bombardment ended, landing craft, lowered from transports over ten miles from shore, began their approach. It was D-day, 6 June.

The first assault troops, who touched down at 6:30, achieved tactical surprise. On the American right—designated Utah Beach—VII Corps got ashore against light opposition, but 1st and 29th Divisions, landing on four-mile Omaha Beach, found the going tough. Soldiers were wounded in a maze of mined underwater obstacles, then drowned by the rising tide; those who got through had to cross a 50-yard-wide beach, exposed to cunningly contrived cross-fire from concrete pill boxes. Men huddled for protection under a low sea wall until company officers rallied them to root the defenders out of their prepared positions. The numerically superior British assault force had a somewhat less difficult landing, but it bore the brunt of the next week's fighting. All in all, the D-day assault on that memorable 6th of June was a brilliant success. In a single week the Allies landed 326,000 men, 50,000 vehicles, and over 100,000 tons of supplies. 'The history of war,' said Marshal Stalin, in one of his rare compliments to his allies, 'does not know any undertaking so broad in conception, so grandiose in scale, and so masterly in execution.'

It required less than three months to reach the French capital. By early August the Allied armies had conquered Normandy and overrun Brittany, and on 15 August they invaded southern France. Toulon and Marseilles were soon taken by the French, while General Patch's Seventh American Army rolled up the Rhone valley and captured Lyons; by mid-September Patch had linked up with Patton. 'Liberate Paris by Christmas and none of us can ask for more,' said Churchill to Eisenhower. General Hodges's First Army raced for the Seine; Patton's Third boiled out onto the open country north of the Loire and swept eastward. Paris rose against her hated masters, and, with the aid of General Leclerc's 2nd Armored Division, was liberated on 25 August, four months ahead of Churchill's request. General Charles de Gaulle entered the city in triumph and assumed the presidency of a French provisional government.

With Paris freed, the Allied armies drove relentlessly toward the Rhine. Patton's spearheads reached the Marne on 28 August, pushed through Château-Thierry, overran Rheims and Verdun. To the north, Montgomery's British and Canadians drove along the coast into Belgium. By 11

General George Patton, General Omar Bradley, and General Sir Bernard L. Montgomery, France, July 1944. The two Americans confer with 'Monty' in the month following the Normandy invasion. (*Library of Congress*)

September the American First Army had liberated Luxembourg and near Aachen crossed the border into Germany. Within six weeks all France had been cleared of the enemy, and from there to Switzerland Allied armies stood poised for the advance into Germany.

On other fronts, the German position was becoming equally bad. By the spring of 1944 the Red armies had reached the Dnieper in the north and the Carpathians in the south. On 23 June Stalin launched a new offensive along an 800-mile front. In five weeks the Russians swept across the Ukraine and Poland and up to the gates of Warsaw where, despicably, they paused instead of helping Polish patriots to liberate their capital; they hoped to reduce Poland to a satellite state, and they did. Romania threw in the sponge when another Red

Army crossed her borders, and by October the Russians had linked up with Tito forces in Yugoslavia. Yet in the east as well as in the west the Germans were still strong enough to force another winter's campaign on their enemies.

Political Interlude

As the Allied armed forces fought ahead, another presidential election came up—the first in wartime since 1864 although in no war had the United States ever suspended elections. In World War II America's energies were devoted not only to winning the struggle against the Axis but to political and ideological battles at home. In some respects, the war was a boon to the New Dealers. TVA, Grand Coulee, and the other public power projects

650

proved indispensable; private utility spokesmen who had claimed there would never be a market for so much power had to eat their words. Under the approving eye of the War Labor Board, union membership rose to nearly 15 million by 1945. Inevitably, the war enhanced the powers of the President and accelerated the aggrandizement of Federal bureaus. The war resulted, too, in a revolutionary change in fiscal policy. Total Federal spending in the war years soared above $320 billion—twice the total of Federal expenditure in all the previous history of the republic. When in 1936 the government outlay totaled eight billion dollars, critics had cried that the New Deal was risking national bankruptcy. When the government spent $98 billion in 1945, few were concerned, for the country was enjoying boom prosperity. The war amply demonstrated the Keynesian hypothesis: with mounting deficits, unemployment disappeared.

Yet in other respects the war tilted politics in a more conservative direction. The President frankly confessed that 'Dr. New Deal' had given way to 'Dr. Win-the-War.' Roosevelt and aides like Hopkins became preoccupied with the grand design of military strategy and diplomatic alliances. In 1942, the Republican Congressional candidates received more votes than Democrats for the first time since 1928, and conservatives interpreted the outcome as a mandate for their policies. Ever since 1937 the coalition of conservative Southern Democrats and Republicans had been gaining power, and in World War II this alliance was cemented. The next session of Congress set out to dismantle the New Deal and drive liberals out of war agencies, and it had considerable success in both aims. As the New Deal lost its momentum, political power shifted perceptibly to what Samuel Lubell has called the 'border state Democrats': men like Jimmie Byrnes and Fred Vinson. Respected by Congress as tough legislative tacticians who were unlikely to advance 'visionary' ideas, the 'border state Democrats' headed the crucial war agencies and fixed the boundaries of what Roosevelt could hope to achieve in domestic affairs. When the 'visionary' Henry Wallace, who in 1942 proclaimed 'the century of the common man,' brawled with the

business-minded Jesse Jones, Roosevelt resolved the conflict by awarding victory to the Jones faction.

In 1944 organization Democrats insisted that Roosevelt drop Vice-President Wallace as his running mate and choose instead Missouri's Senator Harry S. Truman whose able management of a Defense Investigating Committee (the 'Truman committee') had won him a national reputation. Another 'border state Democrat,' Truman satisfied the demand for a candidate who would be acceptable both to the New Dealers and the party bosses; the New York *Times* dubbed him 'the new Missouri Compromise.' With no need this time for a 'draft,' Roosevelt won his party's presidential nomination for a fourth term on the first roll call. The Chicago *Daily News* commented: 'If he was good enough for my pappy and my grandpappy, he is good enough for me.'

While the Democrats were using the vice-presidential nomination as a contest for party control, the Republican party was carrying on a similar struggle between its internationalist and isolationist wings for the G.O.P. presidential nomination in 1944. Leader of the internationalist wing was Wendell Willkie who in 1943 published an account of a trip around the globe, *One World*, that proved enormously popular. Yet isolationism was still powerful enough to drive Willkie out of the race. With Willkie out, the contest for the Republican nomination in 1944 proved a runaway for New York's competent but colorless Governor Thomas E. Dewey, a moderate.

Dewey, wanting the personal charm that made Willkie and FDR so formidable, was a poor campaigner, and the issue was never in doubt. Although the President had less than 53 per cent of the vote, his following in the big cities swung large states with big blocks of electoral votes. Roosevelt carried 36 states with 432 electoral votes; Dewey, 12 states with 99 electoral votes. Isolationists like Gerald Nye went down to defeat, and internationalists such as J. William Fulbright arrived in the Senate to strengthen the forces favoring world organization. The election marked the end of isolationism as a potent political factor, though it would re-emerge in new guises after the war.

The New Deal goes to war. From 1942 to 1945 the Tennessee Valley Authority built Fontana Dam on the Little Tennessee river in North Carolina bordering the Great Smokies. The highest concrete dam east of the Rockies, Fontana Dam generated 225,000 kilowatts. Not only the TVA but installations like Grand Coulee and Bonneville powered munitions industries in World War II. (*Tennessee Valley Authority*)

Victory in Europe,
September 1944–May 1945

While Americans at home were going to the polls, GI's in Europe were trying to increase the momentum of their campaign against the Germans. In the confused fighting that stretched from October to mid-December 1944, the war settled down to what General Eisenhower called 'the dirtiest kind of infantry slugging.' At a heavy cost in casualties, the Canadians took logistically important Antwerp, and Americans seized the ancient capital of Charlemagne, Aachen, the first German city to fall to the Allies; reached the Roer river;

captured Metz; plunged into the Saar; and drove into Alsace. By mid-December the Allied armies were poised all along the border from Holland to Switzerland, ready to plunge into Germany.

Then came a dramatic change of fortune: a German counteroffensive through the Ardennes Forest. Because bad weather prevented Allied air reconnaissance, the Germans achieved surprise and success along a 50-mile front on 16 December. They concentrated on the center of the Allied line, and as they thrust toward the Meuse, maps of the Western front showed a marked 'bulge' to indicate their advance. But at Bastogne they were checked. This little Belgian town, headquarters of General Troy Middleton's VIII Corps, was a center of a network of roads essential to the Germans, and Middleton decided to hold it at all costs. For six days the enemy hurled armor and planes at them, while foul weather prevented aerial reinforcement of the defenders. On 22 December the American situation appeared hopeless, and the Germans presented a formal demand for surrender, to which General 'Tony' McAuliffe of the 101st Airborne replied 'Nuts!' Next day the weather cleared, and planes began dropping supplies; by Christmas Eve, with bomber and fighter support, the situation looked more hopeful. Meantime, Patton's Third Army had started pell-mell north to the rescue of the besieged garrison; on 26 December it broke through the German encirclement and Bastogne was saved. The Battle of the Bulge was not over, but by 15 January 1945 the original lines of mid-December had been restored. Hitler had held up the Allied advance by a full month, but at a cost of 120,000 men, 1600 planes, and a good part of his armor. Never thereafter were the Germans able to put up an effective defense.

At the end of January, Eisenhower resumed the advance toward the Rhine, while the Russians, moving off on a thousand-mile front, crossed the Vistula, and swept toward Germany in a gigantic pincer movement that inflicted over a million German casualties. The 7th of March 1945 was one of the dramatic days of the war. On that day a detachment of the 9th Armored Division of the First Army captured the bridge over the Rhine at Remagen, just as the Germans were about to blow it up. And on 22 March Patton began crossing the Rhine at Oppenheim. Moving at breakneck speed—the 3rd Armored Division covered 90 miles in a single day—Hodges's First Army swung north, Simpson's Ninth turned south, and a giant pincer closed on the Ruhr, trapping some 400,000 Germans. Encircled, pounded on all sides, hammered day and night by swarms of bombers, the German armies caught in the pocket disintegrated. Montgomery now drove toward Bremen and Hamburg, Patton raced for Kassel, and Patch sped through Bavaria toward Czechoslovakia.

As the Allied armies drove deep into Germany, Austria, and Poland, they came upon one torture camp after another—Buchenwald, Dachau, Belsen, Auschwitz, Linz, Lublin—and what they reported sickened the whole Western world. These atrocity camps had been established in 1937 for Jews, gypsies, and anti-Nazi Germans and Austrians; with the coming of war the Nazis used them for prisoners of all nationalities, men, women, and children, and for Jews rounded up in Italy, France, Holland, and Hungary. In these camps, hordes of prisoners had been scientifically murdered; other multitudes had died of disease, starvation, and maltreatment. The total number of civilians done to death by Hitler's orders exceeded 6 million. And the pathetic story of one of the least of these, the diary of the little Jewish girl Anne Frank, has probably done more to convince the world of the hatred inherent in the Nazi doctrine than the solemn postwar trials.

As German resistance crumbled and victory appeared certain, the Western world was plunged into mourning by the news that a great leader had died. President Roosevelt, returning from the Yalta conference of the Combined Chiefs of Staff in February a sick man, went to his winter home in Warm Springs, Georgia, to prepare for the inauguration of the United Nations at San Francisco, which he hoped would usher in a new era of peace and justice. On 12 April, as he was drafting a Jefferson Day address, he died suddenly. The last words he wrote were an epitome of his career: 'The only limit to our realization of tomorrow will be our doubts of today. Let us move forward with strong and active faith.'

The end was now in sight for Hitler's Germany. The Western Allies were rolling unopposed to the Elbe; the Russians were thrusting at Berlin. Ad-

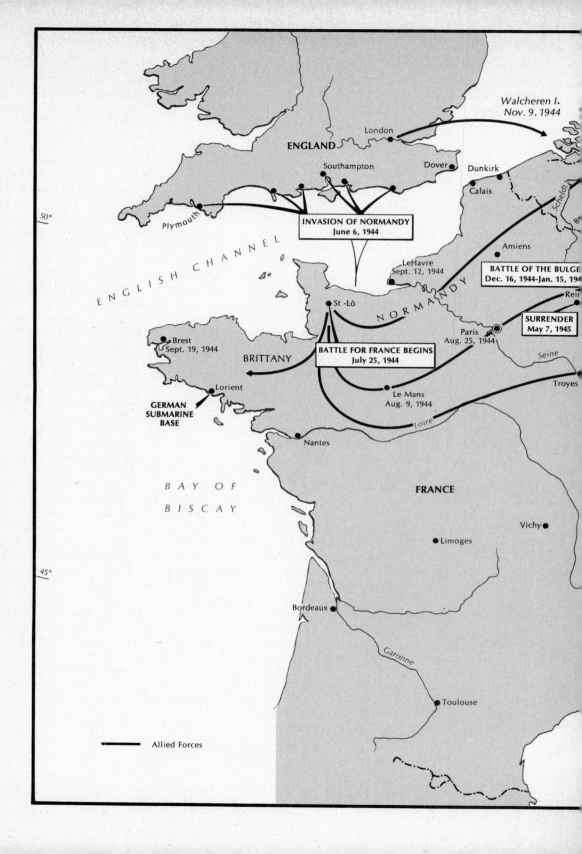

Walcheren I.
Nov. 9, 1944

ENGLAND

London

Southampton   Dover   Dunkirk

Calais

INVASION OF NORMANDY
June 6, 1944

Plymouth

ENGLISH CHANNEL

Amiens

LeHavre
Sept. 12, 1944

BATTLE OF THE BULGE
Dec. 16, 1944-Jan. 15, 194

NORMANDY

St -Lô

Reir

SURRENDER
May 7, 1945

Brest
Sept. 19, 1944

BRITTANY

BATTLE FOR FRANCE BEGINS
July 25, 1944

Paris
Aug. 25, 1944

Seine

Troyes

Lorient

Le Mans
Aug. 9, 1944

GERMAN
SUBMARINE
BASE

Loire

Nantes

BAY OF

BISCAY

FRANCE

Limoges

Vichy

Bordeaux

Garonne

Toulouse

Allied Forces

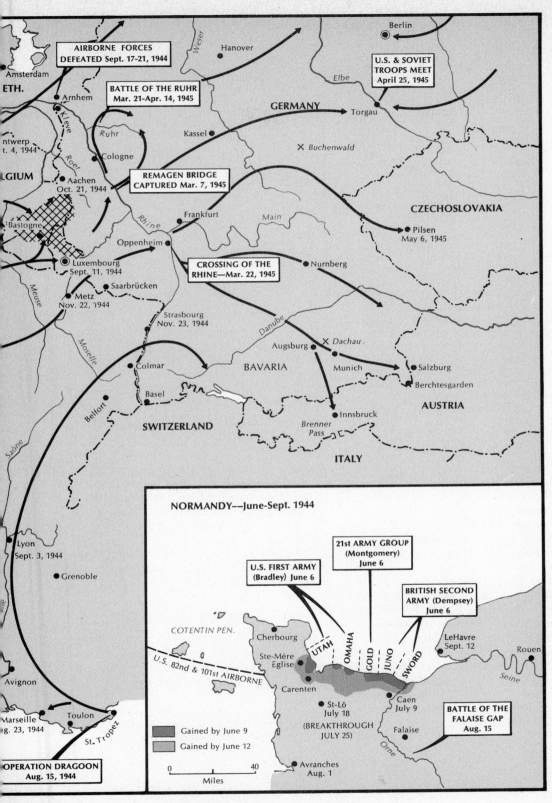

The Conquest of Germany, 1944–45

'Warsaw 1943.' Two decades later, Ben Shahn commemorated the heroic resistance of the remnants of the Jewish community in the Polish capital to the Nazis. The Hebrew inscription comes from the thirteenth-century 'ten martyrs' prayer' for Yom Kippur based on the legend of the execution of ten Jews by the Roman emperc Hadrian. The prayer begins, 'These martyrs I well remember, and my soul is melting with secret sorrow. Evil men have devoured us, and eagerly consumed us.' (*New Jersey State Museum Collection, Trenton*)

vance detachments of the two armies met at Torgau on 25 April, severing Germany. On the last day of April, Hitler died a coward's death, killing first his mistress and then himself in a bombproof bunker under Berlin. On 4 May General Mark Clark's Fifth Army, which had fought all the way up the boot of Italy, met, at the Brenner Pass, General Patch's Seventh, coming down through Austria, and next day German resistance in Italy ceased. Italian partisans had already captured and killed Mussolini. Thus ended, in ruin, horror, and despair, the Axis that pretended to rule the world and the Reich which Hitler had boasted would last a thousand years. Admiral Doenitz, Hitler's designated heir, tried desperately to arrange a surrender to the Western Allies instead of Russia, but loyalty to our Eastern ally caused General Eisenhower sternly to decline these advances. On 7 May General Jodl signed an unconditional surrender.[2] Bradley, awakened by a telephone call from Eisenhower with the news, opened his mapboard and smoothed out the tabs of the 43 divisions under his command.

'With a china-marking pencil, I wrote in the new date: D day plus 335.'

'I walked to the window and ripped open the blackout blinds. Outside the sun was climbing into the sky. The war in Europe had ended.'

Victory Over Japan

On the other side of the globe the war had entered its final phase. In the fall of 1944 MacArthur launched his cherished plan to return to the Philippines. After a three-day 'knock-down,

2. V-E Day is celebrated on 8 May because the surrender became effective at 2301 that day, Central European Time.

Franklin Delano Roosevelt, 12 April 1945. Lucy Mercer Rutherfurd, with whom FDR had conducted a long-term affair, commissioned Elizabeth Shoumatoff to paint this watercolor of the President as a gift to her daughter. As Madame Shoumatoff sketched on that April afternoon at Roosevelt's retreat in Warm Springs, Ga., Lucy watched. But the portrait was never finished, for near the end of the session, the President said, 'I have a terrific headache' and slumped over; in a short while, he was pronounced dead. (*Franklin D. Roosevelt Warm Springs Memorial Commission*)

drag-out fight,' as Halsey described it, over the Ryukyus and Formosa destroyed more than 500 planes, the Central Pacific forces and the Southwest Pacific forces were combined in one massive thrust. On 20 October 1944 General MacArthur and President Osmeña of the Philippines splashed ashore from a landing craft. MacArthur announced: 'I have returned. By the grace of Almighty God our forces stand again on Philippine soil.... Rally to me.... Let no heart be faint.'

At Tokyo the war lords decided that now was the time to commit the entire Japanese fleet, defeat American forces afloat, and isolate MacArthur, so that he would be virtually back at Bataan. From that decision there resulted, on 25 October, the battle for Leyte Gulf, greatest sea fight of this or of any other war. The Japanese divided their fleet into three forces. In a night encounter in Surigao Strait, the American navy devastated the Japanese Southern Force and killed Admiral Nishimura. A short time later, in the critical central sector, there ensued the bloodiest naval action in American history—1130 Americans killed, 913 wounded—in which, off Samar, a fleet more than ten times as powerful as the Americans in gunfire power was defeated. Up north, off Cape Engaño, all four Japanese carriers (including the last survivor of those which had struck Pearl Harbor) were sunk. This three-part battle for Leyte Gulf left the United States Navy in complete command of Philippine waters; never again could the Japanese navy offer a real threat. But months of fighting ashore were required against the no-surrender Japanese infantry before the archipelago was liberated.

After the landings at Leyte the Allies concentrated on securing island bases for a final assault on Japan. On 19 February 1945 marines landed on Iwo Jima, a desolate little island of coal-black lava, which could serve as a halfway house on the 1500-mile bomber run to Tokyo. Even before organized resistance ceased on 14 March, B-29's began using the Iwo airfields; and it is estimated that by this means thousands of American lives were saved. But Iwo, which cost the navy and marine corps some 28,000 casualties, was remembered with a special kind of horror, for the island seemed too small for all the killing it absorbed.

Two weeks after Iwo fell, four American divisions went ashore on Okinawa on Easter Sunday, 1 April. The Japanese put up a desperate resistance, exacting a heavy toll of American lives, before the island was finally conquered late in June. In the meantime the navy, which had to cover the operation and furnish fire support, took a terrific beating from the self-sacrificing kamikaze planes. Twenty-seven ships were sunk, and sixty-one others so badly damaged as to be out of the war; casualties were heavy even on the ships that survived—the carriers *Franklin*, *Wasp*, and *Bunker Hill* between them lost 2211 men killed and 798 wounded. The total cost to the United States of the invasion of Okinawa was over 12,500 killed and over 62,500 wounded; but the island as a base proved indispensable.

While the Allies were conducting amphibious operations on islands like Okinawa, they were also waging a war of attrition against Japan. The navy and the army air force redoubled the fury of their attacks on the Japanese home islands, where B-29 bombing raids directed by General LeMay of the Air Strategic Command burned large parts of Tokyo and other industrial cities. Meanwhile Allied naval forces were destroying the Japanese merchant fleet. Japan, with 10 million tons of merchant shipping by conquest and new construction, ended up with only 1.8 million tons, mostly small wooden vessels in the Inland Sea. United States forces alone sank 2117 Japanese merchant vessels of almost 8 million tons during the war, and 60 per cent of this was done by submarines, of which 50 were lost in action.

The Combined Chiefs of Staff, meeting at Quebec in September 1944, figured that it would take eighteen months after the surrender of Germany to defeat Japan. Actually, the war in the Pacific ended with a terrific bang only three months after V-E Day. President Truman and Winston Churchill, meeting with the C.C.S. at Potsdam, presented Japan with an ultimatum on 26 July 1945. The surrender must be complete, and must include a temporary Allied occupation of Japan and the return of all Japanese conquests since 1895 to their former owners. The alternative was 'prompt and utter destruction.' If Tokyo had made up its mind promptly to accept the Potsdam declaration as a basis for peace, there would have been no atomic bomb explosion over Japan. But the government was more afraid of Japanese militarists than of American power.

The fearful consequences resulted from experimentation in atomic fission. In 1939 Albert Einstein, Enrico Fermi, Leo Szilard, and other physicists who had sought refuge in the United States from tyranny in their native countries warned President Roosevelt of the danger of Germany's obtaining a lead in uranium fission. In the summer of 1940 Fermi, assisted by members of Columbia's football team, began to build an atomic pile. Using a mighty cyclotron, or 'atom smasher,' Dr. Ernest Lawrence of the University of California solved the problem of turning out fissionable material in sufficient quantities. The President assigned responsibility for further developments to the Office of Scientific Research and Development, set up in May 1941 under the direction of Vannevar Bush and James B. Conant.[3] By December Fermi and others, working in the squash court at the University of Chicago's Stagg Field, achieved the first self-sustaining nuclear chain reaction, halfway mark to the atomic bomb. Army engineers under General Leslie Groves then took over, under the code name 'Manhattan District,' and built small cities at Oak Ridge, Tennessee, and Hanford, Washington, to make plutonium. As research progressed, a special laboratory was erected at Los Alamos, New Mexico, for which J. Robert Oppenheimer was responsible.

On 16 July 1945, scientists and military men gathered before dawn on the New Mexico desert, their eyes covered with dark glasses, their faces with anti-sunburn cream, some of the young scientists unnerved by the tension, Oppenheimer holding onto a post to steady himself. With the word, 'Now!' the bomb was detonated. A blinding flash illuminated the desert, and an enormous fireball, changing colors from deep purple to orange to 'unearthly green' erupted skyward. Following the fireball, a great column rose from the ground, eventually taking the mushroom shape that was to symbolize the new age; pushing through the clouds, it reached a height of 41,000 feet. Then came a wave of intense heat and a thunderous roar; the ground trembled as though shaken by an earthquake. Oppenheimer was reminded of the passage from the *Bhagavad-Gita*: 'I am become Death, the shatterer of worlds.' Another scientist commented: 'This was the nearest to doomsday one can possibly imagine. I am sure that at the end of the world—in the last millisecond of the earth's existence—the last man will see something very similar to what we have seen.'

President Truman's committee of high officials and top atomic scientists recommended that atomic bombs be exploded over Japan at once, and without warning. At 9:15 a.m., 6 August, the bomb was toggled out over Hiroshima, the second most important military center in Japan. The bomb wiped out the Second Japanese Army to a man, razed four square miles of the city, and killed 60,175 people including the soldiers. That morning the dreadfully-burned survivors moved through the city, eerily silent, holding their arms out before them to prevent the burned surfaces from touching, hoping in vain that someone could ease their pain. Of the 1780 nurses in the city, 1654 had been killed instantly or were too badly hurt to work; most of the doctors were dead or wounded. That afternoon people who seemed to have escaped unharmed died, the first signs of the effects of radiation. At about noon 9 August, a few hours after Russia declared war on Japan, a second atomic bomb was exploded over Nagasaki, killing 36,000 more.

Should the United States have used this most terrible of weapons? Having revealed its dreadful potentialities over Hiroshima, should America have used it a second time over Nagasaki? These are

3. The OSRD supervised such developments in military technology as the proximity fuse and short-range rockets, notably the 'bazooka.' The government also fostered the achievement of the 'miracle drug,' penicillin, soon to be followed by streptomycin. DDT also proved effective during the war. The development of sulfa drugs and penicillin, the use of plasma, and new techniques reduced the death rate from wounds to less than half that of World War I.

questions men will ask for a hundred years, if the atomic weapon allows mankind another hundred years. On the one hand it can be said that if Japan had not been brought to its knees by this awful display of power, the war might have dragged on for another year, with incomparably greater loss of lives, both Japanese and American; for Japan still had more than 5000 planes with kamikaze pilots, and a million ground troops prepared to contest every beachhead and every city. The explosion over Hiroshima caused fewer civilian casualties than the repeated B-29 bombings of Tokyo, and those big bombers would have had to wipe out one city after another if the war had not ended in August. On the other hand it is asserted that destruction of the Japanese merchant marine and the blockade had brought Japan to the verge of defeat, that the empire could have been strangled without invasion. Long-range considerations are likewise surrounded by uncertainty. It is, however, fairly certain that if the war in the East had lasted six months longer, Russia would have oc-cupied the northern part of Japan and would still be there; and that the costs in blood and bitterness of an Allied invasion of the Japanese mainland are incalculable. Honorable and humane men made the fateful decision to drop the two atomic bombs; honorable and humane men may, in time, conclude that it was the most mistaken decision in the history of warfare.

Even after the two atomic bombs had been dropped, and the Potsdam declaration had been clarified to assure the Japanese that they could keep their emperor, the surrender was a very near thing. Hirohito had to override his two chief military advisers, and take the responsibility of accepting the Potsdam terms. That he did on 14 August. Even thereafter, a military *coup d'état* to sequester the emperor, kill his cabinet, and continue the war was narrowly averted. Yet the gloom of the postwar years owed not a little to the awareness that a liberal, democratic government had not scrupled to unleash a weapon which might mean the end of mankind.

34

Cold War and Fair Deal

1945–1952

Organization for Peace

We seek peace—enduring peace. More than an end to war, we want an end to the beginnings of all wars—yes, an end to this brutal, inhuman and thoroughly impractical method of settling the differences between governments.... We are faced with the pre-eminent fact that, if civilization is to survive, we must cultivate the science of human relationships—the ability of all peoples, of all kinds, to live together and work together in the same world, at peace.... Today, as we move against the terrible scourge of war—as we go forward toward the greatest contribution that any generation of human beings can make in this world,—the contribution of lasting peace—I ask you to keep up your faith.

These were among the last words Franklin Roosevelt wrote, and they were eloquent of a concern that possessed him throughout the war years. Roosevelt's interest in peace went back to his service in the Wilson administration during World War I. That he had been impressed by Wilson's idealism is clear; that he was determined not to repeat Wilson's mistakes is equally clear. 'The tragedy of Wilson,' wrote Robert Sherwood, 'was always somewhere within the rim of his consciousness.'

Harsh experience had taught Roosevelt a lesson denied to Wilson of the importance of a sturdy economic foundation for the postwar world. A decade of depression had preceded World War II and had been an important cause of that war. Furthermore, the depression had undermined democratic institutions and aspirations in countries like Germany. Roosevelt recognized that foreign as well as domestic policies could be directed toward averting another collapse in the United States, and that economic aid could be used as an American weapon toward achieving an international arrangement in which Western conceptions would prosper. During the war he brushed aside ideological objections to collaboration with the Kremlin and approved a program of aid to the USSR that eventually totaled $11 billion. Yet in one respect he was as 'Wilsonian' as his predecessor, for, like the World War I President, he favored a global economic order in which American and other goods would flow freely, and this attitude would lead to discord with both the Russians and the British.

While the war was still being fought, the United States took steps both to foster a stable postwar economy and to sustain the millions of victims of the war. As early as 1944 a United Nations Monetary and Financial Conference at Bretton Woods, New Hampshire, had set up two new agencies: an International Monetary Fund to stabilize currencies and an International Bank for Reconstruction and Development to make credit available for international trade and investment. Even before that the United States had taken the lead in creating the United Nations Relief and Rehabilitation Administration (UNRRA) in 1943. Under the leadership of Herbert Lehman and Fiorello LaGuardia, UNRRA distributed food, clothing, seed, fertilizer, livestock, machinery, and medicine where the need was greatest. In four years UNRRA spent some $4 billion, of which the United States gave $2.75 billion. In addition, the U.S. Army fed large areas of occupied Europe, lend-lease continued to pour foodstuffs and other supplies into Allied countries, and private gifts and CARE supplemented governmental contributions on a generous scale. Yet if America did much for relief, it did less than its resources permitted.

Unlike Wilson, Roosevelt did not wait until the war was over to join other nations in taking first steps toward creating a new international organization designed to keep the peace. He made more effort than Wilson had to cultivate the support of prominent Republican senators, but it is also true that he benefited as Wilson had not from a change of outlook that led commentators to speak of the 'conversion' of prewar isolationists like Senator Arthur Vandenberg. Pearl Harbor, Vandenberg said later, 'drove most of us to the irresistible conclusion that world peace is indivisible. We learned that the oceans are no longer moats around our ramparts. We learned that mass destruction is a progressive science which defies both time and space and reduces human flesh and blood to cruel impotence.' Allied leaders engaged in drafting proposals for a postwar international organization, and in August 1944 their representatives met at Dumbarton Oaks, in Washington, D.C., and drew up the blueprint for the Charter of the United Nations.

All prospects for the success of this legatee of the League of Nations hinged on whether the two powers that would dominate the postwar world—the United States and the Soviet Union—could reach an accommodation. Roosevelt saw clearly the importance of Russian co-operation to assure peace after the defeat of the Axis; he did not see so clearly the forces militating against such co-operation. During the war, American publicists depicted Stalin as a lovable pipe-smoking uncle; in fact, he united, as one knowledgeable Communist said, 'the senselessness of a Caligula with the refinement of a Borgia and the brutality of a Czar Ivan the Terrible.' Still, even the most benign Russian leader might well have insisted on safeguarding his nation's western border from another German assault, and here lay the seeds of future conflict with the West. At times Roosevelt appeared to accept the idea of a Soviet sphere of influence in eastern Europe. When the leaders of the Big Three powers met at Teheran in 1943, Roosevelt told Stalin that he 'did not intend to go to war with the Soviet Union' over its subjugation of the Baltic nations, and also agreed that Russia's Polish boundary should be shifted westward. On the other hand, Roosevelt persisted in believing that the peoples of eastern Europe should also have the right to their own governments, freely chosen. Furthermore, Roosevelt had to bear in mind the possibility of a backlash at his party from voters of eastern European extraction if he made too many concessions to Stalin. The Russians, on the other hand, could not comprehend why, when America could roam all the rest of the world, it begrudged the USSR a small sphere on its borders, or why the West claimed the right to meddle in eastern Europe when it barred the Soviet Union from Italy. Roosevelt hoped that these frictions would yield to the emollient of wartime comradeship, and that particular misunderstandings could be cleared up by personal consultations, and to this end he went to Teheran and to Yalta.

The Yalta Conference of February 1945 in the Crimea appeared to have achieved the end to which Roosevelt so ardently looked. Of primary importance was Russia's agreement to enter the war against Japan 'within two or three months' of the defeat of Germany. In return the USSR was promised the Kurile Islands, the southern half of Sakhalin, and privileges in Manchuria and at Port Arthur and Dairen. Stalin acquiesced in the American formula for the admission of Latin

American states to the United Nations, withdrew his preposterous demand for 16 votes in the General Assembly, agreed to permit France a zone of occupation in Germany, accepted the reparation figure as tentative only, and—presumably—left open to further negotiation the reorganization of the Polish government. Roosevelt and Churchill conceded the Curzon line as Russia's western boundary, accepted a tentative reparations figure far beyond what they thought proper, promised the USSR three votes in the General Assembly, and left open for future negotiation such thorny questions as Soviet rights in the Dardanelles and in Iran, the future of the Baltic countries, and the disposition of Italian colonies. 'We really believed in our hearts,' said Roosevelt's aide Harry Hopkins, 'that this was the dawn of the new day we had all been praying for and talking about for so many years.'

Yet, in truth, Yalta had revealed the rudiments of much of the discord that would bedevil the postwar world. Later Yalta came to be regarded as a sellout to the Kremlin by a sick Roosevelt manipulated by pro-Communist advisers, but in reality the West conceded nothing substantial that Russian armies could not have taken anyway. Roosevelt's fault lay rather in leading the American people to expect that fundamental difficulties had been readily resolved. Eastern Europe remained a bleeding sore, especially after the Polish government in exile in London charged, with good reason, that the Russians had murdered thousands of Polish officers whose bodies were found in the Katyn Forest, and had permitted the courageous Warsaw underground fighters to be slaughtered by the Nazis when Soviet forces could have gone to their aid. Though Stalin promised 'free and unfettered elections' in Poland, he had no intention of tolerating an open choice in the eastern European nations. As he later said, 'A freely elected government in any of these countries would be anti-Soviet, and that we cannot allow.' In April 1945, shortly before his death, Roosevelt expressed to Stalin his 'astonishment,' 'anxiety,' and 'bitter resentment' over Russia's 'discouraging lack of application' of the Yalta protocols.

Roosevelt died on 12 April, but invitations had already gone out for a United Nations Conference to meet at San Francisco to draft a charter for the new organization, and late in that month delegates from 50 nations gathered at that city whose very choice suggested the new importance of the Pacific area. The conference, which lasted for two months, was marked by many sharp disagreements over such matters as the Polish delegation, but it ended on a note of surface harmony with all 50 nations signing the Charter.

The United Nations Charter provided for a General Assembly in which each nation had one vote, and whose functions were largely deliberative, and a Security Council of five permanent and six elected members, which alone had power to act in international disputes. It permitted any one of the five great powers (the United States, Britain, Russia, France, and China) to exercise a veto on any but procedural questions, and it authorized the use of force against aggressor nations.[1] So far had the United States moved away from traditional isolationism that the Senate ratified the document on 28 July 1945 with only two votes in opposition.

Launched with high hopes, the United Nations soon ran into the dangerous waters of the East-West conflict. Nonetheless, in the first few years of its existence it had some accomplishments to its credit. It succeeded in settling—after a fashion—three major disputes: that between Russia and Iran, the problems connected with the emergence of Israel as a nation, and the inflammable Indonesia issue. Furthermore, it served—in Senator Vandenberg's phrase—as a 'town meeting of the world,' and such agencies as the International Labor Organization performed useful services. Yet the United Nations unquestionably disappointed those who had hoped that it would succeed where the League had failed. The ostensible difficulty was the veto; designed for use only in

1. The Charter also created a number of other agencies: an International Court of Justice with powers comparable to those formerly exercised by the World Court; an Economic and Social Council to promote social and cultural welfare and human rights; a trusteeship system to replace the unsatisfactory mandate system of the old League; a permanent Secretariat. Under the Economic and Social Council there was a proliferation of special agencies—UNESCO, a Food and Agriculture Organization, an International Labor Organization, a World Health Organization, and eventually many others of a technical character.

President Harry S. Truman at Mackinac Island in a typically jaunty posture. (*Elliot Erwitt—Magnum*)

emergencies, it was invoked by Russia some fifty times in the first four years, often for purposes that were trivial. But the real difficulty of the United Nations was not mechanical but substantial: the division of the world into hostile camps led by the United States and the Soviet Union. For within an ominously brief period after the end of World War II, the two great powers had come to a total impasse.

Truman and the Cold War

When, on 12 April 1945, Franklin D. Roosevelt died and the Vice-President took the oath of office as President, there were some who affected to ask, 'Who is Harry S. Truman?' just as a century earlier some had asked, 'Who is James K. Polk?' Yet if Truman lacked the renown and the imposing presence of FDR, he came to the presidency with longer experience in politics than Theodore Roosevelt, Woodrow Wilson, or Herbert Hoover, and as Chief Executive revealed a continuing capacity for growth. He frequently spoke, and acted, impulsively, a quality that caused him grief in the handling of crises both at home and abroad. Intensely loyal to his friends, he was inclined to overlook even their more flagrant shortcomings. Too often he surrounded himself with men unsympathetic to the cause he espoused. But these failings were matched by corresponding virtues: boldness, decisiveness, and courage. Truman's domestic record, which seemed modest by comparison with that of his predecessor, came to seem more respectable when compared with that of his successor, and few Presidents did so much to shape American foreign policy as did this unassuming man from Missouri.

Truman came to power just as Soviet-American distrust was congealing, and he was determined to prove himself a strong President who would brook no nonsense from the Kremlin. Within a day after he entered the White House, he was telling his Secretary of State, 'We must stand up to the Russians at this point and not be easy on them.' Before the month was out, he was chewing out Molotov for not keeping pledges. 'I have never been talked to like that in my life,' said the Russian foreign minister. 'Carry out your agreements,' Truman replied, 'and you won't get talked to like that!' By January 1946 Truman was writing his Secretary of State: 'Unless Russia is faced with an iron fist and strong language another war is in the making. Only one language do they understand—"how many divisions have you?" . . . I'm tired of babying the Soviets.' Two months later he accompanied Sir Winston Churchill to Fulton, Missouri, where the former Prime Minister declared: 'From Stettin in the Baltic to Trieste in the Adriatic, an iron curtain has descended across the Continent.'

Much of the disagreement between the USSR and the West centered on policy toward their defeated enemy, Germany, despite elaborate efforts to agree on a common course. Wartime meetings of the Allies had worked out the basic principles for the treatment of Germany after the war: the destruction of German militarism and military potential; the dissolution of the Nazi party and the punishment of war criminals;[2] creation of occupation zones; readjustment of Germany's eastern border to compensate Poland for territory lost to Russia; and the payment of reparations 'to the greatest extent possible.' At the Potsdam Conference, held in July 1945, Truman, Stalin, and Clement Attlee—who had replaced Churchill as spokesman for the British government—decided that notwithstanding the division into occupation zones, Germany should be treated as an economic unit; but also provided that each occupying power should take reparations from its own zone and that, in addition, the USSR might receive reparations in the form of industrial equipment from the Western sectors in exchange for food and other products from its zone. Eastern Germany was assigned to Russia; northwestern Germany to Britain; southwestern Germany to the United States; while France received two smaller areas, Baden and the Saar. Austria, too, was carved up into four occupation zones, and both Berlin and Vienna were parceled out to the victors.

The principle of treating Germany as an economic unit broke down almost immediately. The

---

2. Postwar trials before an International Military Tribunal at Nuremberg resulted in death sentences for twelve high Nazi officials, including Goering and Ribbentrop, and the sentence of death was pronounced at trials of lesser Nazi leaders too.

Russians stripped their own zone and made heavy demands for factories, power plants, rolling stock, and tools in the British and American zones. But the Potsdam declaration had included a precautionary clause to the effect that the conquerors 'should leave enough resources to enable the German people to subsist without external assistance.' If Britain and the United States permitted their zones to be gutted, Germany would become a permanent burden on their taxpayers. Furthermore, if the industrial potential of the Ruhr and the Saar were destroyed, the consequences for European recovery generally would be disastrous. On 3 May 1946, almost exactly one year after the German surrender, General Lucius Clay, deputy American commander in Germany, announced an open break between the victors when he halted delivery of reparations to the Soviet zone. To the Russians it seemed unreasonable that when their country had been bled by the war (in Leningrad alone, 600,000 civilians had starved to death during a prolonged siege) the United States, which had emerged more prosperous than ever, should hamper their drive for economic reconstruction. Furthermore, the Russians were alarmed that the West was deliberately rebuilding the economy, and hence the war-making potential, of their hereditary Teutonic foe. To the West it was no less unsettling that Stalin was violating the spirit and the letter of wartime agreements, creating a permanent Communist regime in his temporary zone of occupation, and insisting on leaving Germany so impoverished that the prospects for a thriving world economy were seriously jeopardized.

In a speech at Stuttgart in September 1946, Secretary of State Byrnes enunciated the Truman administration's 'get tough' policy. Although he offered the USSR a forty-year security treaty, Byrnes plainly implied that he no longer contemplated agreement with the Russians over Germany. The United States, which had started out determined to reduce Germany's industrial potential, would henceforth seek to spur the country's economic revival. To that end, the British and American zones were fused on 1 January 1947. So within less than two years after the defeat of Hitler's Reich, Germany was being divided into two nations, one owing its allegiance to Russia, the other to the West.

In these same months, another East-West dispute erupted over the atomic bomb. Truman recognized the fact that the United States monopoly of 'the ultimate weapon' gave it a decided diplomatic advantage. Nonetheless, American officials were fully cognizant of the menace to peace that the A-bomb constituted, and were prepared to share control. In March 1946, the United States put forth a plan, formulated by two committees headed by Dean Acheson and David Lilienthal. It called for the creation of an International Atomic Development Authority, which should have exclusive control over raw materials such as uranium and over every stage of the production of atomic energy throughout the world, and should act as custodian of atomic weapons and stockpiles of fissionable materials. At its first session the General Assembly of the United Nations had created an Atomic Energy Commission to consist of representatives from all eleven members of the Security Council plus Canada. President Truman appointed Bernard Baruch as American representative on this commission, and in June 1946 Baruch presented a proposal that incorporated the main features of the Acheson-Lilienthal Plan plus provision for rigid international inspection and for the elimination of the veto in cases involving illegal manufacture of atomic bombs. Under the Baruch Plan, the proposed International Atomic Development Authority, which would control the whole field of atomic energy, would concern itself not only with the prevention of the manufacture of atomic weapons but with the production of atomic energy for peaceful purposes. If this program were adopted, the United States stood ready to destroy its stock of atom bombs, stop further manufacture of bombs, and share its scientific knowledge with the rest of the world.

The United Nations Atomic Energy Commission endorsed the American plan by a vote of 10–0; the USSR and Poland abstained. Russia rejected it for several reasons: inspection would be an intolerable invasion of national sovereignty, and the suspension of the veto would destroy the unanimity principle that was the basis of the Security Council. They also objected that the plan would give the United States the advantage of knowing how to make an atomic bomb while restricting experimentation by other countries. Fur-

Bikini, 25 July 1946, the world's first underwater blast of a nuclear weapon. Though the explosion sent up a towering column of water, neither this test nor one a few weeks earlier at the Pacific atoll seemed as awe-inspiring as had been expected. Only afterwards did scientists realize how widely dispersed was the radioactive debris. 'The most improbable objects turned out to be thoroughly charged—a ship's bell of brass, some chemicals from a first-aid locker on a deck, a bar of soap that had been caught in a stream of neutrons,' Eric Goldman has written. 'Rocks miles away were found tainted by fission products. Fish that had been near the fleet area and fish that had eaten the deadly fish spread over huge areas of the Pacific. On the ships themselves, nothing—soap, scrubbing, the best of Navy profanity—nothing short of sandblasting off the whole outer surface got rid of the deadly material.' (*U.S. Air Force Photo*)

Albert Einstein (1879–1955) and J. Robert Oppenheimer (1904–67), by Alfred
Eisenstaedt. Both Einstein, whose 1905 equation $E = mc^2$ provided the theoretical
foundation for nuclear fission, and Oppenheimer, who as director of the Los
Alamos Science Laboratory was known as 'the father of the atomic bomb,'
expressed misgivings over the race to build bigger and bigger nuclear devices.
Eisenstaedt was already an established photographer in Europe before he came to
America in 1935, when he almost immediately joined the staff of the new picture
magazine *Life*. Although Eisenstaedt was not, as he is often said to be, 'the father
of photojournalism,' a description that better fits earlier artists like Lewis Hine, he
did contribute to *Life* close to two thousand picture stories, many of distinction.
(*Alfred Eisenstaedt LIFE Magazine* © *Time Inc.*)

thermore, the United States would almost certainly control the international atomic agency. Gromyko proposed instead the immediate destruction of all atom bombs and the prohibition of the manufacture of atomic weapons. Such a scheme was unacceptable to the West, for it required the surrender by the United States of its advantage, and, in the absence of inspection, gave no corresponding assurance that Russia would not proceed secretly to make atomic weapons. With the great powers unable to agree, the United Nations Atomic Energy Commission suspended its deliberations.

When the Russians detonated an atomic device in September 1949, and the United States, a few months later, announced plans for a hydrogen bomb, a thousandfold as powerful as the atomic bomb, the quest for effective international control assumed a new urgency. Speaking with deep solemnity, the venerable philosopher-scientist Albert Einstein, who had originally called President Roosevelt's attention to the potentialities of nuclear fission, warned the world,

The armament race between the U.S.A. and the U.S.S.R., originally supposed to be a preventive measure, assumes hysterical character. On both sides, the means to mass destruction are perfected with feverish haste, behind respective walls of secrecy. The H-bomb appears on the public horizon as a probably attainable goal. . . . If successful, radio-active poisoning of the atmosphere and hence annihilation of any life on earth has been brought within the range of technical possibilities. The ghost-like character of this development lies in its apparently compulsory trend. Every step appears as the unavoidable consequence of the preceding one. In the end, there beckons more and more clearly general annihilation.

Although the differences over weapons control and over policy toward Germany had serious repercussions, the first actual showdowns between Russia and the West took place in the Mediterranean and the Near East. In March 1946, the United States forced Russia to withdraw its troops from oil-rich Iran, but within a year there was a new crisis in Greece where Communist guerillas supported by Soviet satellites, were threatening a conservative monarchy backed by the British, and in Turkey where the USSR was exerting pressure

on the Dardanelles. On 24 February 1947 the British informed the American government that they could no longer carry the burden and proposed to pull out. Rarely in history had there been so dramatic a moment when one nation turned over responsibilities of empire to another.

On 12 March, Truman sent a message to Congress embodying not only a request for appropriations for Greece and Turkey, but what came to be known as the Truman Doctrine: 'that it must be the policy of the United States to support free peoples who are resisting attempted subjugation by armed minorities or by outside pressures.' Congress voted the money—eventually close to $700 million—and American power moved into the vacuum created by Britain in the Near East. After prolonged fighting the Greek guerillas were beaten, Turkish defenses were strengthened, and the situation in the Mediterranean was stabilized. But a perilous precedent had been established—that the United States would arm any regime, no matter how reactionary, that was threatened by Communists or by forces thought to be Communist. Even more troublesome were the implications of Truman's speech—that the menace of Communism was global and that the United States was prepared to intervene anywhere in the world.

In July 1947 *Foreign Affairs* published an article under the enigmatic signature of 'X' which took a hard-headed view of Russian-American relations. 'X,' shortly revealed to be one of the State Department's veteran Russian experts, George Kennan, warned that, at least for some time to come, there could 'never be on Moscow's side any sincere assumption of a community of aims between the Soviet Union and powers which are regarded as capitalist.' In enunciating what came to be known as the 'containment' policy, Kennan argued that it must be made clear to the USSR that expansion beyond a given perimeter would be met with force. Kennan stressed:

The United States has it in its power to increase enormously the strains under which the Soviet policy must operate, to force upon the Kremlin a far greater degree of moderation and circumspection than it has had to observe in recent years, and in this way to promote tendencies which must eventually find their outlet in

The Cold War: Soviet version. In this Russian cartoon, an armed, filthy-rich American soldier overwhelms a European continent pockmarked with U.S. bases. In his hip pocket an American propagandist, waving an olive branch at the same time that yet another American base is being established in Greece, spouts hypocritical slogans. (*Library of Congress*)

The Cold War: American version. In this cartoon by Milt Morris for the Associated Press, an avaricious Russian bear, a red star on his cap, salivates as he paws the entire globe. (*Wide World*)

either the breakup or the gradual mellowing of Soviet policy.[3]

Kennan, who thought the Truman Doctrine too negative an application of the containment doctrine, made an important contribution to a more imaginative development in American foreign policy: the Marshall Plan. In 1947 a policy-planning staff headed by Kennan recommended short-term aid to halt deterioration of the European economy and a long-range program looking to European economic integration. Speaking at a Harvard Commencement in June, Secretary of State Marshall advanced these recommendations by advising Europe to work out a joint plan for reconstruction and pledging full co-operation by the United States.

Marshall's speech came at a time when much of western Europe approached economic breakdown. By 1947 the world owed the United States $11.5 billion for goods it had acquired but could not pay for. Europe needed everything but was able to buy nothing; the United States had—or was capable of producing—almost everything, but could sell nothing to a bankrupt Europe. If the European economy collapsed, the American economy would take a tailspin. Moreover, if the United States stood idly by while western Europe plunged into economic chaos, it would be faced, in a few years, with a Soviet-dominated continent. Truman's abrupt and ill-considered termination of lend-lease in 1945 had precipitated a serious economic crisis in Britain, whose resources had been drained by the war. To ward off a catastrophe, Congress voted a substantial loan which, it was hoped, would carry Britain through the next five years. But despite heroic efforts, the money ran out in two years, and by 1947 Britain again confronted economic disaster. In March 1947, as UNRRA came to an end just when Europe was buffeted by a vicious winter, the people of western Europe faced starvation. So critical was the coal shortage in England that, for hours every day, London shut off electric power. The financial editor of Reuter's wrote: 'The biggest crash since the fall of Constantinople—the collapse of the heart of an

Empire—impends.' The political consequences of the impending disaster would be as serious as the economic cost. Europe, wrote Churchill, was 'a rubble heap, a charnel house, a breeding ground of pestilence and hate.'

The invitation from Marshall found an instantaneous response. The Prime Ministers of Britain and France promptly issued an invitation to 22 nations, including Russia, to meet at Paris the following month to draw a blueprint for European recovery. Though Molotov came to Paris to discuss preliminaries, the Kremlin decided it was unwise to take part in a project that would extend American influence in Europe. Molotov withdrew, and all the Soviet satellites followed. In the end representatives of 16 nations, under the leadership of the Oxford philosopher Sir Oliver Franks, drafted an elaborate plan for European recovery, which fixed new production targets and set other economic goals.

In December 1947 President Truman asked Congress to further these ambitious aims by appropriating $17 billion over a four-year period. Opposition to the proposal, led by Senator Taft, came chiefly from those who felt that the American economy could not stand so heavy a burden. Liberals of both parties as well as powerful business, farm, and labor organizations rallied to the bill, whose leading senatorial champion was Arthur Vandenberg, architect of the bipartisan foreign policy. What finally turned the tide was not so much economic arguments as the Communist coup in Czechoslovakia in March 1948, together with new Russian demands on Finland and the fear of Communist success in the forthcoming Italian elections. A program to halt the advance of Communism appealed to many who were immune to an appeal on economic or humanitarian grounds, and the Foreign Assistance Act—providing an immediate grant of $5.3 billion for European recovery plus $463 million for China and $275 million for Greece and Turkey—passed both houses of Congress by big majorities and became law on 3 April 1948.

The Marshall Plan mounted the most effective counterattack on poverty, despair, and disintegration in modern history. Altogether Congress voted some $12 billion to carry it out. Critics had

3. *Foreign Affairs*, July 1947.

The Marshall Plan, Berlin. The German signboard announces that Marshall Plan aid is supporting the city's Emergency Works Program (*Berliner Notprogramm*). The photograph was taken in the early spring of 1952, seven years after American planes reduced much of the former German capital to rubble. (*National Archives*)

predicted that the enterprise would bankrupt the United States; instead the country enjoyed unparalleled prosperity, in part because Marshall Plan funds, like almost every cent of subsequent 'foreign aid,' had to be spent in the United States for American products. Moreover, by 1951 the administration could point to an over-all increase of production in Marshall-aid countries of 37 per cent. As the economy rebounded, so did the confidence of the peoples of western Europe, not only in their ability to fend for themselves but in their democratic institutions.

However, if the Marshall Plan succeeded in reviving western Europe, it also served to deepen divisions between the United States and Russia. In April 1947, in a speech at Columbia, South Carolina, Bernard Baruch had declared: 'Let us not be deceived—today we are in the midst of a cold war.' Increasingly, American institutions—the government, the corporation, the university, the foundation—were called into the service of the Cold War, and economic aid, too, came chiefly to be a weapon in that war. At the outset, Congress stipulated that not one penny of Marshall Plan aid was to be used for military purposes. In less than three years the United States was informing Europe that every cent of aid would be allotted so as to contribute to Western defenses.[4]

This new military posture resulted in large part from concern over Soviet aggressiveness in Germany. The Russians had been disturbed when the French fused their zone with the British and the American zones to create a 'Trizonia' with the richest industrial resources in Germany and a population of 50 million which outstripped the Soviet zone's 17 million. In the spring of 1948 the Western powers alarmed the Kremlin by inviting the Germans to elect delegates to a convention to create a new government for West Germany. (Subsequently, in May 1949, the German Federal Republic was established at Bonn.) When in June 1948 the Allies carried out a drastic currency reform that triggered a remarkable economic revival for western Germany, the Russians retaliated on 24 June by clamping a tight blockade around Berlin. Through some inexplicable oversight the Western powers had not guaranteed access to their zones of Berlin, and as a result the Russians were able to cut all land communication by erecting road blocks and stopping railroad trains.

Confronted with the alternatives of mass starvation for the 2 million Germans of the western zones of Berlin or an ignominious evacuation of that city, the American and British governments rejected both. They also spurned the temptation to ram an armored train through the Russian blockade, for this might have precipitated general war. Instead they embarked upon an 'airlift' operation to supply the beleaguered capital not only with food but with coal and other necessities. To the consternation of the Russians the airlift was a spectacular success: American and British planes dropped 2.5 million tons of provisions into the city. On 12 May 1949, outwitted by the West, Russia ended the blockade.

The Berlin crisis and the Czech coup prompted

4. When the United States set up 'Point Four' (named after the fourth point of Truman's inaugural address of 1949), the program began as a modest venture in providing technological aid to underdeveloped nations, but by 1951 had been brought under the Mutual Security Act as another weapon in the Cold War arsenal.

negotiations for a military alliance that would weld western Europe into a unified military force. The Brussels Pact of 1948, joining Britain, France, and the Benelux nations in a defensive alliance, provided the springboard. In April 1949 the North Atlantic Treaty brought together the United States, Canada, and ten nations of western Europe in an alliance against aggression; eventually it embraced other nations as well. The treaty pledged that an armed attack against any one member would be considered an attack upon them all. Never before had the United States gone so far in a practical surrender of part of its sovereign power, or so clearly recognized that its frontier henceforth lay overseas along the lines that divided non-Communist nations from the Soviet Union.

A military assistance program gave the North Atlantic Treaty Organization (NATO) authority to spend over a billion dollars on military needs. From 1945 to 1950 the armed services had been reduced from 12 million to well below one million. But in 1946 a peacetime draft had been instituted temporarily, and in 1948 it became a regular feature of American life. The NATO pact encouraged an increase in the size of America's armed forces, and United States troops were stationed in Europe. In 1950 the first American shipments of arms reached Europe, and within a few years West Germany's armed forces were integrated into the NATO army. Not surprisingly, Russia looked upon the creation of NATO as a declaration of hostility and upon the re-arming of Germany as an act of defiance.

Reconversion, Reaction, and Reform

Truman not only had to lead the country in the final months of the war but guide it through the difficult transition from war to peace. Fortunately, reconversion presented fewer problems than had been anticipated, and the postwar depression many had feared never materialized. Nor was there a re-enactment of the Harding melodrama. However, the political stalemate that had begun with the waning of the New Deal in 1938 persisted in the era of the Cold War and the age of affluence.

Unlike the aftermath of World War I, the Tru-

The Berlin airlift, 1948. German children watch from a hillside as a U.S. plane approaches Tempelhof airport. A Berlin clerk wrote: 'Every two minutes a plane arrives from West Germany, loaded with food for West Berlin! The sound of engines can be heard constantly in the air, and is the most beautiful music to our ears. One could stand for hours on the Tempelhof elevated station platform and watch the silver birds landing and taking off.' Forty-eight men were killed in the joint American-British effort to provision a city which little more than three years before had been the capital of the Third Reich and the object of relentless Allied bombing. 'When the first victims of the combined airlift were reported, we grieved about these young men as much as if they had been our own,' reflected a Berliner. 'Nobody wanted to mention that perhaps it had been the same boy who had presented us with a quite different variety of cargo a few years before, and whom we then quietly cursed.' (*National Archives*)

man years saw a continuation and expansion of wartime prosperity. In the five years after the war, national income increased from $181 billion to $241 billion. In 1935 over one-half the workers of the country earned less than $1000; by 1950 only one-tenth of the workers were in this unhappy category. Farmers, too, continued to enjoy unprecedented prosperity. Total farm income in 1948 was over $30 billion as compared with $11 billion in 1941 and $5.5 billion in 1933. As a consequence, farm tenancy fell to the lowest point in the twentieth century. In 1935 only 6 per cent of American families enjoyed an income of over $3000 a year; by 1950 half of all families earned over $3000 a year, though, to be sure, a sharp increase in the cost of living qualified these statistics.

What was the explanation of this phenomenon of postwar prosperity? It was, in part, the pent-up demand for goods after five years of war; in part, the market for American surpluses assured by the program of relief and reconstruction abroad; in part, the explosive increase in private investment; in part, the continuation of heavy government spending. At the depth of the depression the Federal Government had spent about $9 billion; five years after the war the Federal budget ran over $40 billion. The government cushioned the shock of the transition from the armed services to civilian life by providing mustering-out pay, unemployment pay for one year, civil-service preferment, insurance and loans for home building and the purchase of farms or businesses. Eventually some 12 million veterans took advantage of the education subsidies of the 'G.I. Bill of Rights.'

Yet if reconversion went more smoothly than had been expected, Truman nonetheless faced one grievous problem: inflation. Manufacturers and farmers, who had bridled at wartime controls, wanted to exploit a sellers' market, and consumers, their pockets bulging, demanded goods that had been denied them during the war. The President was expected both to get rid of controls and prevent inflation, and he could anticipate political reprisals if he failed to achieve this impossible assignment. While Roosevelt in the depression years had been able to distribute benefits to interest groups as a part of his recovery program,

Truman had to discipline interest groups at the very time when peace encouraged them to expect new gains. When Truman sided with John Snyder, a conservative Missouri banker whom he had named director of the Office of War Mobilization and Reconversion, against Chester Bowles, the OPA administrator who represented the consumer, he antagonized New Deal liberals who wanted to keep a tight lid on prices. FDR's followers had been impressed when in September 1945 Truman outlined a twenty-one point program of far-reaching reforms, but they were dismayed by Truman's support of Snyder and his appointment of other conservatives to his cabinet and the Supreme Court. Before long, Roosevelt stalwarts like Harold Ickes had fled the government in protest.

However, when Truman did take a firmer stand against inflation, he added to his difficulties with the liberal wing of his party because he ran into a head-on conflict with union labor. After the war, fear of rising costs of living and the prospect of a return to the 40-hour week with consequent loss of overtime pay brought a demand for substantial wage increases. Within a month after victory over Japan half a million workers were out on strike, while 1946 saw a loss of 116 million man-days of work. On 1 April 1946 John L. Lewis led 400,000 coal miners out of the pits, and for forty days the strike cut off the nation's supply of fuel and threatened European recovery. On 21 May, after a brief truce, the government took over the mines. When Lewis refused to order his men back to work, a Federal court slapped the union with a fine of $3.5 million, later reduced to $700,000. Nonetheless, Lewis eventually won almost all of his demands. If Truman did not find some way to call a halt, wages and prices threatened to chase one another up to the sky.

When in the midst of the coal crisis railway union leaders threatened the first total strike on the roads since 1894, the President seized the railroads to head it off. But in defiance of the President the rail workers walked out, marooning 90,000 passengers and stopping 25,000 freight cars, many of them loaded with perishables. On 25 May, Truman went before Congress to ask for authority to draft strikers into the army. Since the strike was settled that day, he never had an opportunity to carry out this threat, but he had shocked liberals and severed his ties with union leaders. Yet when Congress enacted a milder labor measure, Truman irked conservatives by vetoing it. The politics of inflation was costing the President support at both ends of the political spectrum.

Five weeks after Truman's threat to draft the rail strikers, he confronted a showdown on price control, for on 1 July 1946 the authority of the OPA would expire. When just before the deadline Congress passed a bill which eviscerated the OPA, Truman vetoed it, although this left the nation temporarily with no controls. In two weeks prices jumped 25 per cent, more than in the previous three years. After Congress enacted a new measure, stockmen held back their cattle, and meat all but disappeared. Truman's popularity fell from a peak of 87 per cent to 32 per cent, and Republicans jeered at 'Horsemeat Harry.' On 14 October the President announced he had no alternative but to take off controls on meat, but when meat returned to the butcher's counter, housewives were incensed to find that it commanded sharply increased prices.

At the height of national annoyance over the price control controversy, the country went to the polls in the 1946 elections. Exasperated by high prices and shortages, voters gave the Republicans their first majority in Congress since 1930. They sent to the Senate for the first time that year such conservatives as John Bricker of Ohio and the little known Joseph McCarthy, who toppled the La Follette dynasty in Wisconsin, and to the House young Richard Nixon. The election was interpreted as a brutal repudiation of Truman's leadership. Democratic Senator William Fulbright of Arkansas advised the President to name a Republican successor and resign from office. Truman rejected this gratuitous advice, but four days after the election he removed most of the remaining controls.

The 1946 elections gave the Republicans an opportunity to demonstrate that they were a party of moderation, but the 80th Congress misinterpreted the vote, which reflected a momentary impatience over reconversion, as a mandate reaction. It not only rejected Truman's recom-

mendations to raise the minimum wage and extend social security coverage but turned down modest proposals by Republican Senator Robert Taft of Ohio for Federal action in education and housing. Bricker complained: 'I hear the Socialists have gotten to Taft.' While performing creditably on foreign affairs, the 80th Congress antagonized farmers by failing to provide adequate crop-storage facilities, Westerners by slashing funds for power and reclamation, and ethnic groups by enacting an anti-Semitic, anti-Catholic displaced persons law. When the lifting of controls resulted in a price rise from 1946 to 1947 greater than in all of World War II, people on fixed incomes were caught in the inflationary squeeze.

If Senator Taft differed with the Bricker wing of his party on some welfare measures, he shared their determination to curb organized labor. The Taft-Hartley Act of 1947 outlawed the closed shop and the secondary boycott; made unions liable for breach of contract or damages resulting from jurisdictional disputes; required a 60-day cooling-off period for strikes; authorized an 80-day injunction against strikes that might affect national health or safety; forbade political contributions from unions, featherbedding, and excessive dues; required union leaders to take a non-Communist oath; and set up a conciliation service outside the Labor Department, which was suspected of being too friendly to labor. When Truman vetoed the bill, Congress re-enacted it by thumping majorities. The Taft-Hartley law drove organized labor back into Truman's arms, and in 1948 union members returned to private life many Republican supporters of the act, including Representative Hartley.

The Republicans muffed an even more promising opportunity to capitalize on Democratic vulnerability when they failed to enact civil rights legislation and chose instead to coalesce with Southern Democrats to block reforms. It was President Truman who seized the initiative, in part because he understood that at a time when the United States was competing with Soviet Russia for the allegiance of the uncommitted nations events in Mississippi and Alabama were watched closely in Beirut and Karachi. In response to protest against a number of racial murders in the

South in 1946, Truman appointed a President's Committee on Civil Rights which in October 1947, after ten months of study, issued an historic report, 'To Secure These Rights.' In February 1948 Truman asked Congress to implement part of this report by approving a ten-point program which embraced a permanent Civil Rights Commission, a Federal Fair Employment Practices Act, and laws to protect the right to vote, do away with poll taxes, and prevent lynching. Spurned by the 80th Congress, Truman refused to back down. He increased the pace of desegregation of the armed forces and issued an executive order which stipulated that there was to be no discrimination in Federal employment. No President in at least seventy-five years had done so much for the cause of civil rights. Yet by his actions Truman infuriated Southern whites who feared that their social system was collapsing at a time when the Supreme Court was ruling restrictive covenants unenforceable and when Jackie Robinson was breaking the color line in baseball. The President appeared to have ensured his defeat in the 1948 election.

Only in the area of governmental reorganization did the 80th Congress make important contributions, and here, too, Truman played an important role. The Presidential Succession Act of 1947 provided that the Speaker of the House and the President pro tempore of the Senate should be next in line of presidential succession after the Vice-President. That same year Congress adopted a proposed Twenty-second Amendment limiting Presidents to two terms; the amendment was ratified in 1951, an indication of growing concern over presidential power. In 1947 Congress also established a commission which, headed by Herbert Hoover, pointed the way toward more effective governmental administration. Yet another act of 1947 unified the army, navy, and air force under a Secretary of Defense. The National Security Act also set up a National Security Council, a Central Intelligence Agency, and a National Security Resources Board, and gave legal status to the Joint Chiefs of Staff. That same year Congress created the Atomic Energy Commission.

The Truman years marked a transition from the informal personal presidency of the Roosevelt era to the institutionalized White House of Eisenhower. By 1947 the President was filing three separate messages to Congress: State of the Union, Budget, and Economic Report, the latter as a consequence of the Employment Act of 1946 which established a three-man Council of Economic Advisers. Although the main responsibility for economic decision-making was left in private hands, this law recognized a degree of government responsibility for the health of the economy, and in subsequent years the reports of the Council helped educate the country in the new economics. However, this innovation came only after the 80th Congress had gutted the original legislation.

Despite the generally dismal performance of the 80th Congress, the Republican victory in 1946 and subsequent rifts in the Democratic party convinced almost everyone that Truman could not win in 1948. When, over the opposition of the administration, which sought to unite the party on a moderate civil rights plank, the Democratic convention adopted a strong civil rights plank sponsored by Hubert Humphrey, the young mayor of Minneapolis, Mississippi and Alabama delegates, waving the battle flag of the Confederacy, marched out. Within a week the 'Dixiecrats' had organized a States Rights party with Governor J. Strom Thurmond of South Carolina as their presidential nominee.

At the same time that the Dixiecrats were cutting off one flank of the Democratic party, opponents of Truman's foreign policy were severing another. In September 1946 the President had dropped Henry Wallace from his cabinet because he had become too vocal a critic of the administration's Cold War tactics. In July 1948 his followers organized the Progressive party with Wallace as their candidate. Although the platform of the new party included such demands as the nationalization of basic industries, it centered its fire at the President's foreign policy. The party's uncritical attitude toward Soviet Russia deprived it of much of its potential support, but observers reckoned that Wallace would cut heavily into Truman's vote in the North.

The Republicans felt so confident as to nominate a former loser, Thomas E. Dewey, with the liberal governor of California, Earl Warren, as his

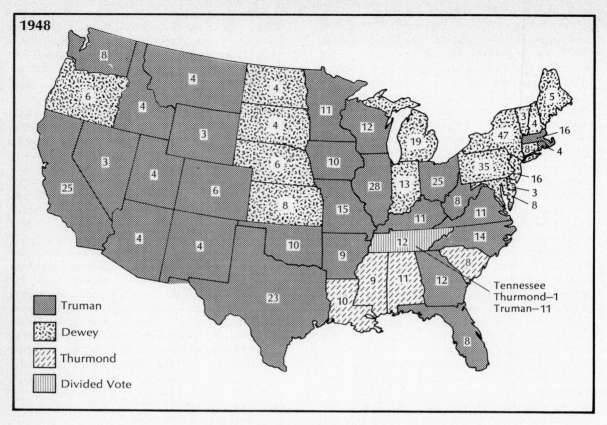

1948

Truman
Dewey
Thurmond
Divided Vote

Tennessee
Thurmond—1
Truman—11

Presidential Election, 1948

running mate. Dewey ran a deliberately cautious campaign, during which he made such startling observations as 'We need a rudder to our ship of state and . . . a firm hand at the tiller,' 'Our streams should abound with fish,' and 'Our future lies before us.' Truman, on the other hand, made full use of the powers of his office to wage a vigorous campaign to remould the Roosevelt coalition. Throughout the election year he fired a series of messages to Congress calling for specific reforms, and that summer he summoned Congress back into a special session on 26 July, the day turnips are planted in Missouri. When the 'turnip Congress' did nothing, Truman was well on his way to making the issue of the campaign not Dewey's

record but the performance of the 'do-nothing, good-for-nothing' 80th Congress. On a 22,000-mile 'give-em hell, Harry' whistle-stop tour, the President met an enthusiastic response. Still, almost every political expert, and pollsters like Gallup and Roper, predicted defeat for Truman.

To the astonishment of both prognosticators and the nation, Truman scored the biggest political upset of the century.[5] Thurmond captured four

5. The vote was:

	Popular	Per Cent	Electoral College
Truman	24,179,345	49.6	303
Dewey	21,991,291	45.1	189
Thurmond	1,176,125	2.4	39
Wallace	1,157,326	2.4	0

Southern states, and Wallace, while winning no electoral votes, deprived Truman of New York, Michigan, and Maryland. But the President ran well among workers, blacks, and farmers, many of whom resented the 80th Congress. Dewey had 'snatched defeat out of the jaws of victory,' while Truman, running as the candidate of the majority party in an election with a low turnout, got enough of the party faithful to the polls to prevail. The party also recaptured control of both houses of Congress; to the Senate came Humphrey of Minnesota, Estes Kefauver of Tennessee, and, by the tiny margin of 87 votes, Lyndon Johnson of Texas. The Roosevelt coalition, which had seemed shattered two years before, had taken a new lease on life.

The 81st Congress, which met for the first time in January 1949, enacted more liberal legislation than any Congress since 1938. It extended social security benefits; raised the minimum wage; expanded public power, rural electrification, soil conservation, and flood control projects; approved a more generous, but still inadequate, Displaced Persons Act; set up a National Science Foundation; and granted the President powers to cope with inflation. By adroitly exploiting middle-class dissatisfaction with the housing shortage, Truman put through a law which authorized new public housing for the slum-dweller. The National Housing Act of 1949 provided for the construction of 810,000 subsidized low-income housing units over the next six years, as well as grants for slum clearance and rural housing.

However, most of this legislation represented only extensions of New Deal measures; and when Truman tried to break new grounds for his 'Fair Deal,' he had little success. Congress bowed to the American Medical Association's campaign against the President's proposal for national health insurance, rejected a new approach to farm subsidies, and filibustered an FEPC bill to death. Federal aid to education was lost in an unhappy squabble over whether such aid should go to private and parochial schools. Truman also fought losing battles to extend the TVA principle to the Columbia and the Missouri river valleys, and was able to carry out no more than a delaying action to preserve for the United States the immensely valuable oil reserves

under the 'tidelands.' He also vetoed a bill which would have raised the price of natural gas, even though the measure was supported by powerful elements in his own party.

Truman's troubles with Congress resulted largely from the insurmountable obstacles he faced, but also owed something to his own shortcomings as a legislative leader. Although genuinely interested in achieving change, he never could arouse the kind of popular enthusiasm for his proposals that a Roosevelt did. 'Alas for Truman,' wrote one commentator, 'there is no bugle note in his voice.' Nor did Truman take pains enough to cultivate good will among Congressmen. Much more significant, though, was the powerful opposition he confronted, especially the rural-based, bipartisan conservative coalition entrenched in the committee structure in Congress. In his final months in office Truman, his program frustrated, was reduced to fighting a rearguard action against those who wished to repeal the New Deal and was overwhelmed by an explosion of ill feeling that was fueled by irritation at an undeclared war in a part of the world to which most of the nation had given little heed.

The Korean War

While Americans were preoccupied with the problems of Europe, the Far East burst into flames. When Truman took over, he continued the Roosevelt policy of regarding China as the mainstay of American interests in Asia and of supporting the Nationalists against the Communists. However, the Chiang Kai-shek regime, corroded by corruption and without strong popular support, proved wholly unable to stem the tide of Chinese Communism. Efforts by the United States to reform and strengthen the Nationalist regime and to force some settlement of the Chinese civil war proved abortive. Early in 1946 General Marshall arranged a truce between the Nationalists and the Communists, but it was speedily violated by both sides. Exasperated with both factions, Marshall withdrew most of the American troops from China and washed his hands of the whole muddle. Though the United States continued to send military and financial aid to Nationalist China, Truman would not make a massive commitment to the Nationalists because he and his advisers did not believe that Chiang could be salvaged. By the end of 1949 the Communists had swept the whole of the mainland, and Chiang, with the remnant of his forces, had fled to the island of Formosa (Taiwan).

The 'fall' of China had a number of momentous consequences. By allying the 500 million Chinese with the Russians, it shifted the balance of power in the Cold War in Asia. It led to a fierce attack on the Truman administration from Republican 'Asia-firsters' and publicists like the Luce empire, fostered anxiety about subversion, helped bring the twenty-year reign of the Democrats to an end, and served to lock American policy in Asia in the matrix of an inflexible anti-Communism. The Democrats were vulnerable to criticism, for Roosevelt had led the country to believe that Nationalist China was a major power and some diplomats had misconceived the nature of the Communist threat. Yet, as John King Fairbank pointed out, 'The illusion that the United States could have shaped China's destiny assumes that we Americans can really call the tune if we want to, even among 475 million people in the inaccessible rice paddies of a subcontinent 10,000 miles away.' The administration, shocked by indignities to American consular officials and sensitive to criticism of its Asia policy, refused to recognize Red China and blocked attempts to admit Mao Tse-tung's government to the United Nations. And the 'loss' of China resulted in a dramatic reversal of American policy toward Japan.

At the end of World War II, the United States had but one aim in Japan: to make certain that the Japanese would never again constitute a military threat in Asia. To this end the American occupation authorities sought both to democratize Japan and to reduce that country to a second-rate power. Within a short time after the surrender, General MacArthur in co-operation with liberal elements in Japan destroyed Japanese military potential and inaugurated drastic reforms. Meantime an International Tribunal tried the leading war criminals and sentenced Prime Minister Tojo and a dozen of the leading generals to death for their part in war crimes and atrocities, while, as a result of action by local tribunals, no fewer than 720 high-ranking officers of the army and navy were executed. A new Diet, elected under a law permitting woman suffrage, drafted a democratic constitution that provided for popular sovereignty and parliamentary government, reduced the Emperor to a figurehead, and included a bill of rights. The United States took special pride in one provision of the constitution, written in part by Americans, which stipulated that 'the Japanese people forever renounce war as a sovereign right of the nation.'

With the fall of China, American policymakers did a complete about face. The United States now came to value Japan as a military counterweight against Red China. As a consequence, it took steps to help the Japanese win industrial supremacy in Asia. No longer did the Americans press Tokyo for a permanent renunciation of war; and when in 1951 the United States signed a treaty which formally ended World War II and the occupation, it put through another which permitted America to maintain troops and air bases on the Japanese islands.

The United States little reckoned that the focus of its attention would shortly become neither Japan nor China but Korea. After World War II that nation, which was annexed to Japan in 1910, had been divided temporarily along the 38th parallel into zones of occupation: the United States in the more populous south, and Russia in the north. All efforts at unification proved vain; the Russians set up a Communist regime in North Korea, while the Americans threw their support to the conservative Syngman Rhee, a kind of Korean Chiang Kai-shek, who in 1948 was elected President of a new republic in South Korea. However, even after the American military occupation came to an end, the nation continued to be a heavy drain on the American taxpayer, and in January 1950 when Secretary of State Acheson outlined a 'defensive perimeter' vital to national security, he included neither Korea nor Formosa.

On 25 June 1950, just five months after Acheson's 'perimeter' speech, North Korean troops launched a full-scale attack upon the South, and within three days they had seized the capital at Seoul and threatened to overrun the entire country. Once again, as at the time of the threat to

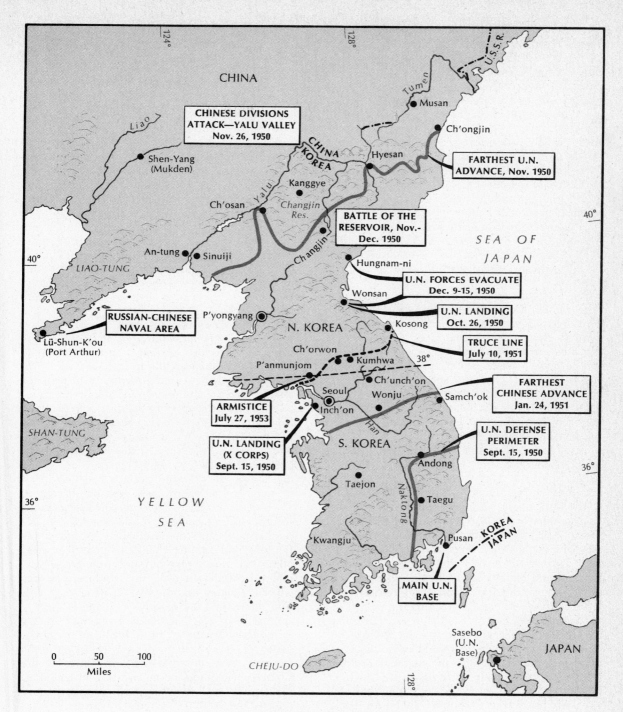

The Korean War, 1950–53

CHINA

CHINESE DIVISIONS
ATTACK—YALU VALLEY
Nov. 26, 1950

FARTHEST U.N.
ADVANCE, Nov. 1950

Shen-Yang
(Mukden)

CHINA
KOREA

Musan

Ch'ongjin

Hyesan

Kanggye

Ch'osan

Changjin
Res.

BATTLE OF THE
RESERVOIR, Nov.-
Dec. 1950

An-tung   Sinuiji

LIAO-TUNG

Changjin

Hungnam-ni

SEA OF
JAPAN

40°

U.N. FORCES EVACUATE
Dec. 9-15, 1950

Wonsan

P'yongyang

U.N. LANDING
Oct. 26, 1950

40°

RUSSIAN-CHINESE
NAVAL AREA

N. KOREA

Kosong

Lü-Shun-K'ou
(Port Arthur)

Ch'orwon

TRUCE LINE
July 10, 1951

P'anmunjom

Kumhwa

38°

Ch'unch'on

Seoul

Wonju

Samch'ok

FARTHEST
CHINESE ADVANCE
Jan. 24, 1951

ARMISTICE
July 27, 1953

Inch'on

Han

U.N. DEFENSE
PERIMETER
Sept. 15, 1950

U.N. LANDING
(X CORPS)
Sept. 15, 1950

S. KOREA

Andong

36°

SHAN-TUNG

Taejon

Naktong

Taegu

36°

YELLOW

SEA

Kwangju

Pusan

KOREA
JAPAN

MAIN U.N.
BASE

0   50   100

Miles

CHEJU-DO

Sasebo
(U.N.
Base)

JAPAN

128°

The Korean War, 1950–53

Berlin, Truman reacted decisively. The President reflected: 'I recalled some earlier instances: Manchuria, Ethiopia, Austria. I remembered how each time that the democracies failed to act it had encouraged the aggressors to go ahead. . . . If this was allowed to go unchallenged, it would mean a third world war.' On 27 June he announced that he was sending American air and naval forces to the aid of the South Koreans. That same day the United Nations Security Council—with Russia momentarily absent on a boycott—called on member nations to repel aggression in Korea, and before long the UN banner waved over a motley world army—the first of its kind in history. But since the United States sent more than five times as many troops as the rest of the world combined, most Americans regarded the conflict as a U.S. war.

For nearly six weeks North Korean armies advanced down the peninsula driving the outnumbered South Korean and American forces before them to the southernmost tip of Korea. There they held firm while reinforcements poured into the harbor of Pusan and General MacArthur, commander in chief of the United Nations forces, built up naval and air support. In mid-September, MacArthur carried out a daring amphibious landing at Inchon, the first engagement in a well-conceived counteroffensive that drove the North Koreans in full retreat to the north. On 26 September Seoul was once more in South Korean hands, and the United Nations armies were pounding on the North Korean border.

The United States had gone to war when North Koreans crossed the 38th parallel; would China go to war when South Koreans—and Americans—crossed it in the other direction? From the beginning, Truman had insisted that the intervention in Korea would be limited; he had no intention of getting bogged down in a land war in Asia, or in a direct conflict with Russia or China. Exponents of containment like George Kennan now argued that the UN had achieved its objective of expelling the North Koreans; the UN should consolidate its lines along the 38th parallel and negotiate a settlement. But MacArthur, buoyed by his success, was convinced that the only way to end the war, and unite Korea, was to conquer the North. For a

brief interval both Truman and Acheson, as well as the UN, were persuaded. In the teeth of a Chinese warning that they might enter the war, the UN General Assembly authorized MacArthur to cross the parallel.

So concerned was Truman with the threat of Chinese intervention that in mid-October he flew to Wake Island to confer with MacArthur. The General assured him that the Chinese would not attack, and if they did 'there would be the greatest slaughter.' On this advice, Truman approved an advance to within a few miles from the Chinese border on the Yalu river. MacArthur predicted that enemy resistance would be ended by Christmas, and for a time it seemed he might be right. On 20 October the North Korean capital of Pyongyang fell to UN forces, and by the end of the month MacArthur was approaching the Manchurian border. Yet even as Truman and MacArthur spoke, masses of Red Chinese soldiers were streaming across the Yalu into Korea. On the night of 25 November Mao's 'volunteers' unleashed a ferocious assault. Three days later MacArthur issued a chilling communiqué: 'We face an entirely new war.' An army of more than a quarter-million Chinese drove MacArthur's armies out of all the territory they had won in North Korea and sent them reeling back across the 38th parallel. That winter saw some of the cruelest warfare in American history, with shocking cold and blinding storms, a rugged terrain of jagged mountains, treacherous swamps and unbridged streams, and an enemy who gave no quarter.

MacArthur, who in September had been lauded for the Inchon success, found himself by December under fire for miscalculating Chinese intentions and for deploying his troops poorly. Never one to take reproof lightly, the proud general turned increasingly to issuing statements which intimated that the real blame lay not with him but with Washington's decision to fight a limited war. He proposed bombing China's 'privileged sanctuary' in Manchuria, pursuing MIGs across the Yalu into China, a blockade of the Chinese coast, air attacks on the cities of the Chinese mainland, and an invasion of China by the armies of Chiang Kai-shek. Truman firmly rejected these ideas. Chastened by its costly flirta-

Truman and MacArthur at Wake Island, 15 October 1950. For press photographers, the President and the General made a show of cordiality, but Truman has offered a saucy version of what took place at their private meeting, the details of which are in dispute. To Truman's dismay, MacArthur was not at the airfield to greet him. 'So, I just sat there,' Truman told Merle Miller. 'I'd have waited until hell froze over, if I'd had to. I wasn't going to have one of my generals embarrass the President of the United States. Finally, the son of a bitch walked out of one of the buildings . . . wearing those damn sunglasses of his and a shirt that was unbuttoned and a cap that had a lot of hardware. I never did understand . . . an old man like that and a five-star general to boot, why he went around dressed up like a nineteen-year-old second lieutenant.' When they were alone, he admonished the General, 'I don't give a goddamn what you do or think about Harry Truman, but don't you ever again keep your Commander-in-Chief waiting.' (*Brown Brothers*)

tion with a liberation policy, the administration returned to the policy of containment. It did not want MacArthur to lead the United States into the 'gigantic booby trap' of an all-out war with Red China. Moreover, the military situation in Korea in early 1951 offered new hope for peace. UN forces under General Matthew Ridgway blunted the Chinese offensive, and in March recaptured

Seoul for the second and last time and recrossed the 38th parallel. With the Republic of Korea cleared of Communist soldiers, Truman and the UN believed the time had come to press for negotiations.

The General would have none of it. Although he had been warned repeatedly not to make statements which conflicted with UN policy, on 24

March 1951 he defiantly threatened China with an attack, a declaration which Truman believed killed any hope for an early truce. On 5 April, on the floor of the House, Republican minority leader Joseph Martin read a letter MacArthur had written him on 19 March criticizing the President and insisting, 'There is no substitute for victory.' This arrogant challenge to civilian authority was intolerable, and Truman peremptorily dismissed General MacArthur from command. He came home to receive tumultuous ovations. Herbert Hoover saw MacArthur as 'a reincarnation of St. Paul into a great General of the Army who came out of the East,' and when this new apostle addressed Congress, Republican Congressman Dewey Short declared that he had seen 'a great hunk of God in the flesh.' But enthusiasm for MacArthur died down after it was revealed that all three Chiefs of Staff backed Truman against the General. If MacArthur's counsel had been followed, the President's military advisers declared, the United States would have won the enmity of all Asia, wrecked the coalition of free nations, and diverted its strength to a costly struggle with China while Russia, which had instigated the North Korean invasion, would have been unscathed. MacArthur's policy, General Bradley observed, 'would involve us in the wrong war, at the wrong place, at the wrong time, and with the wrong enemy.'

Yet if Truman survived the MacArthur episode, the Korean War cost him and his party dearly. The President made the decision to intervene without seeking the approval of Congress, for, by treating the conflict as a 'police action,' he hoped to avoid a major war. However, this strategy deprived Congress of its constitutional authority to declare war, and proved unwise politically; when the fighting went badly, the President had to bear sole responsibility for intervention. By the spring of 1951 the Korean conflict was deadlocked; and when in June the Soviet delegate to the United Nations suggested an armistice with mutual withdrawal behind the 38th parallel, Washington welcomed the proposal. But discussions looking to an armistice dragged on interminably, and the bloodletting did not stop. When the country went to the polls in November 1952, this unpopular war still had not ended, and it was inevitable that the President's party would pay the price.

The Korean War mobilization hurt Truman in yet another way. When steel workers threatened to strike in the midst of the war, the Wage Stabilization Board recommended an increase of 18 cents an hour without corresponding rises in steel prices. The operators rejected this solution; the union called a walkout; and Truman on 8 April 1952 seized the mills. One of the mills—the Youngstown Sheet and Tube Company—challenged the constitutionality of the President's act, and the Supreme Court struck down the presidential order on the ground that it constituted executive lawmaking. The Court's decision, and the President's helplessness in the face of the ensuing 54-day strike, further impaired Truman's prestige.

The combat in Korea had other and deeper consequences. It accelerated the pace of desegregation of the armed forces. It tied American interests more closely to those of Chiang on Formosa and to the French in Indochina, and thereby moved the country a fateful step toward the subsequent disaster in Southeast Asia. It resulted in a vast increase in the military budget, which underwrote the prosperity of America in the 1950's but also occasioned alarm over whether the United States was becoming a 'Warfare State.' And it nurtured a nasty period of xenophobia rivaling the Red Scare of 1919.

The Politics of Subversion

Although the Cold War with Russia and the hot war in Korea provided most of the fuel for the era of 'McCarthyism,' anxiety over subversion preceded World War II, and although Republicans were the main agents of this new Red Scare, Democrats, including Truman and his appointees, played an important part. As early as 1938 the House established a committee on un-American activities, but HUAC was so irresponsible that its allegations were discounted. However, when a raid in 1945 on the magazine *Amerasia* turned up quantities of classified State Department documents, another House committee began a study which resulted in Truman's issuing Executive Order 9835 in March 1947. Though this order to investigate the loyalty of civil servants set up procedural safeguards, it also embraced the doctrines of guilt by intention and by association.[6] Of the 3 million persons passed on, only a few thousand were actually investigated. Of these, 212 were dismissed, but none, apparently, had committed offenses serious enough to warrant prosecution. Potentially the most ominous feature of the executive order was the one authorizing the Attorney-General to prepare lists of subversive organizations and giving these lists a quasi-legal character. 'If there is any fixed star in our constitutional constellation,' Justice Jackson had said, 'it is that no official, high or petty, can prescribe what shall be orthodox in politics, nationalism, religion or other matters of opinion, or force citizens to confess by word or act their faith therein.'

Even the executive order did not free the Truman administration from charges of being 'soft on communism,' and on 20 July 1948 it precipitately took steps to indict the eleven top Communists on the charge of violating the Smith Act of 1940, which made it a crime to conspire to 'advocate and teach' the violent overthrow of government. In the Dennis case the Supreme Court accepted Judge Learned Hand's modification of the 'clear and present danger' test: 'in each case courts must ask whether the gravity of the evil, discounted by its improbability, justifies such invasion of free speech as is necessary to avoid the danger'—and concluded that the Smith Act was constitutional and that the Communists were in fact guilty of conspiracy to advocate the overthrow of government.

The outcome of the 1948 election left the Republicans embittered (to be beaten by Roosevelt was disappointing but familiar; to be rejected in favor of Truman seemed intolerable) and shortly after the election came two prodigious events: the Communist takeover in China and the Soviet detonation of an atomic bomb. On top of this came the Korean War. How did it happen? How did we 'lose' China, and the atomic monopoly all at once, and then come close to losing the Korean War as well? To many it was unthinkable that Com-

munism could win on its own and incredible that Soviet scientists were as clever as American or British. The answer must lie elsewhere—in subversion and treachery, perhaps by intellectuals and 'one-worlders' in the State Department who were secret sympathizers with Russia. For Republicans seeking a promising political issue, such an assumption was especially attractive. Yet though the Communists did, in fact, control a number of 'fronts' and perhaps one-third of the C.I.O., and though there were Communist cells in Washington, no hard evidence was adduced to link an important government official to actual espionage.

Then came the Hiss case. In August 1948 Whittaker Chambers, onetime editor of *Time* magazine, accused Alger Hiss, who had been a State Department official before becoming president of the Carnegie Endowment for International Peace, of having been a Communist. Since Chambers produced nothing convincing to sustain his charge, Truman decried the affair as a 'red herring' aimed at distracting the public from the failures of the 80th Congress. But in December 1948 Chambers produced microfilms of classified State Department documents—out of a pumpkin!—and asserted that Hiss had not only been a party member but a spy. When Hiss denied these allegations, a New York grand jury indicted him for perjury; since the statute of limitations had expired, Hiss could not be indicted for espionage, but everyone understood that it was treason that was really at issue. After two trials Hiss was found guilty and sentenced to five years in jail. Though Hiss was not a key policy-maker, he had been with Roosevelt in a minor capacity at Yalta where, it was contended, American interests had been 'sold out' to the Russians. Moreover, Hiss was tailormade for the role of a villain: a graduate of the Harvard Law School, a New Dealer, a friend of Secretary Acheson, who said he would not turn his back on him, an international 'do-gooder'; even his name suggested perfidy! Two weeks after Hiss's conviction came disquieting news from England—Klaus Fuchs, an atomic physicist who had worked at the Los Alamos laboratory, had been found guilty of systematically feeding atomic information to the Russians.

This series of events provided the background for that phenomenon known as McCarthyism.

6. A supplementary executive order in April 1951 authorized the firing of Federal employees even if there was only 'reasonable doubt' as to their loyalty. That same month Julius and Ethel Rosenberg were sentenced to death for conspiring to transmit secret information on the atomic bomb to Soviet Russia.

AFTER GENERAL EISENHOWER HANGS UP HIS UNIFORM, WILL HE DON —

AN 'ABE LINCOLN' — A 'TEDDY ROOSEVELT' — A 'WOODROW WILSON' — A 'HERBERT HOOVER' — AN 'F.D.R' — OR A 'HARRY TRUMAN'?

The fungible candidate. So popular was Eisenhower that elements in both major parties wanted to nominate him even though they knew little about what course he would follow, as this panel by the British cartoonist, Vicky, in the *News Chronicle* suggests. (*Associated Newspapers Group, Ltd., London*)

Senator McCarthy himself was a finished demagogue: brutal, unscrupulous, and cunning; his methods were wild charges, fake evidence, innuendoes and lies, appeals to ignorance, prejudice, hatred, and fear. On 9 February 1950 he alleged that he had the names of 205—or was it 57?—'card-carrying Communists' in the State Department. Five months later, a Senate committee under Senator Tydings reported that McCarthy's charges were 'a fraud and a hoax perpetrated on the Senate of the United States and on the American people. They represent perhaps the most nefarious campaign of half-truth and untruth in the history of the Republic.' Nothing daunted, McCarthy moved on to larger game. 'It was Moscow,' he cried, 'which decreed that the United States should execute its loyal friend, the Republic of China. The executioners were that well-defined group headed by Acheson and George Marshall.'

Out of the panic aroused by such accusations emerged the McCarran-Nixon Internal Security Act of 1950. This law required all Communist-front organizations to register with the Attorney-General, excluded Communists from employment in defense plants, made it illegal to *conspire* to perform any act that would 'substantially contribute' to the establishment of a dictatorship, debarred from the United States anyone ever affiliated with a totalitarian organization, or with organizations looking to the revolutionary overthrow of government, authorized deportation for aliens involved in suspect organizations, denied passports to Communists, provided for the internment of subversives in the event of war, and set up a Subversive Activities Control Board. Truman vetoed the bill, alleging that it was 'worse than the Sedition Act of 1798,' but Congress passed it over his veto by acclamation.

The subversion issue highlighted the 1950 elections in which the Republicans picked up five seats in the Senate and twenty-eight in the House. McCarthy, who received more invitations from Republican senators to speak in their states than all other senators combined, received credit for the defeat of Governor Bowles in Connecticut and of Senator Tydings in Maryland, where a fraudulent composite photograph was used. In California,

Richard Nixon, who emphasized McCarthyite issues, won a Senate seat. Actually, voters were less concerned with the Communist question than politicians believed. Nonetheless, the 1950 elections not only sealed the fate of the Fair Deal but encouraged the Republicans to anticipate that the same tactics would win them the White House in 1952.

By the spring of 1952 Americans were ready to listen to the Republicans' contention that it was 'time for a change' from twenty years of Democratic administration. Prices were too high; there was a 'mess in Washington'; anxiety about subversion was rife; and the war in Korea was at a stalemate. The Republicans also had an attractive candidate. Though right wing Republicans rallied behind Senator Taft, the more moderate, internationalist wing of the G.O.P. secured the nomination for the popular General Dwight D. Eisenhower, Supreme Commander of NATO on leave from the presidency of Columbia University, with Senator Nixon as his running mate. The Democrats faced the necessity of choosing a candidate not too closely identified with the Truman administration, which was blemished by scandals involving such agencies as the RFC. Senator Kefauver of Tennessee had won a large following by his investigation of organized crime, the first political event to attract an avid television audience, but the convention turned instead to Governor Adlai Stevenson of Illinois, a man of wit, intelligence, and eloquence, who, nonetheless, was overmatched.

Eisenhower captivated the nation in 1952. At first the General showed himself unwilling to repudiate policies of the Truman administration which he had helped to shape, but after a momentous meeting with Taft, he began to give aid and comfort to the right wing of his party. He accepted the support of demagogues like McCar-

thy, denounced the Truman administration for harboring subversives, and poured scorn on the 'eggheads' who had rallied to Stevenson. To no avail did Stevenson remind the country: 'No one is running on a pro-corruption ticket or in favor of treachery.' With ample funds at their command, the Republicans exploited to the full the possibilities of television which, for the first time, was important in a presidential campaign. Thus when Nixon was revealed to have been subsidized by a secret fund subscribed by California millionaires, he converted the liability into an asset by a dramatic television appearance, which critics denounced as 'soap opera' but to which the public responded favorably. However, the greatest advantage that the Republicans enjoyed was neither control of the mass media, the smoke screen of 'subversion,' nor the corruption issue, but 'Ike' himself. 'The crowd is with him,' wrote one correspondent. 'Idolatry shows in their solemn, upturned faces.' Moreover, at a time when casualties were mounting in Korea, Eisenhower struck a popular chord when he promised he would go to Korea to bring the deadlocked war to an early end.

General Eisenhower won with more than 55 per cent of the popular vote and captured 39 states with 442 electoral votes, while Stevenson carried only 9 states with 89 votes in a contest marked by a sharply increased turnout. Eisenhower even won four states of the no longer Solid South. The personal nature of this triumph was apparent when contrasted with the congressional vote. In spite of all their advantages, the Republicans barely carried the House and managed only a tie in the Senate. Clearly the election was less a triumph for the Republican party than a vote of confidence in Eisenhower; and if the support of the people is the secret of presidential power, the new President could be expected to be one of the strongest of American executives.

35

The Eisenhower Era: Tranquility and Crisis

✳

1953–1960

Dynamic Conservatism

Dwight Eisenhower's conception of his office suited the mood of many Americans in the 1950's, a mood the President himself helped to set. In the 1952 campaign some backed Eisenhower because they hoped he would lead the nation in new ventures, while others did so because they wished him to repeal the past. Yet many, perhaps most, who voted for him did so because they anticipated that the General would give the country a respite from a generation of unrelieved crises: a disastrous depression, a world war, a cold war, an enervating limited war. Kept in a constant state of tension by two activist Presidents, they had reached a point of weariness with the intrusion of public issues into their lives. They expected Eisenhower not to solve problems but somehow to charm them away.

The country demanded too much of the new President; and, since he was asked to do contradictory things, he was bound to disappoint some of his followers. Those who thought the General would lead the country in new directions were quickly disillusioned, and those who favored a sharply conservative turn had to accommodate themselves to the fact that most of what the New Deal had wrought could not be undone. For a time he satisfied those who hoped he would bring a new spirit of quiescence, until the eruption of crises at home and abroad disrupted the sense of tranquility. Even then, however, Eisenhower continued to hold the affection of most of the nation.

Eisenhower belonged to the McKinley-Taft rather than the Roosevelt-Wilson tradition of the presidency. He thought of the President less as party leader or chief legislator than as a combination chief of staff, mediator, and father of his people. To be sure, Eisenhower was more active in mobilizing his party in support of his objectives, especially in foreign affairs, than many recognized at the time. But he repudiated the 'left-wing theory that the Executive has unlimited powers' and adopted the Whig view that the prerogatives of his office should be used as little as possible. His general outlook, noted Walter Johnson, was: 'What will we refrain from doing now?' Thoroughly American as 'Ike' was, he nevertheless conceived his role to be somewhat like that of a constitutional monarch: he was to be a symbol above the battle.

Dwight David Eisenhower (1890–1969). Ike's enormous popularity owed much to his self-deprecating manner, a quality not always associated with victorious generals. In the years after World War II, he spurned efforts to draft him as a presidential candidate. 'I don't believe a man should ever try to pass his historical peak,' he told reporters. 'I think I pretty well hit my peak in history when I accepted the German surrender in 1945.' Of his election to the presidency in 1952 he later wrote, 'Remembering my beginnings, I had to smile. . . . The . . . old saw had proved to be true: in the United States, any boy *can* grow up to be President.' (*Dwight D. Eisenhower Library*)

Eisenhower's long military experience predisposed him toward a staff system, which he had used successfully in Europe. He preferred to work through subordinates who would shelter him from demands on his time and protect him from personal involvement in the hurly-burly of politics. He was not disposed to probe deeply into any subject; and he liked to have every problem, even the most complex, summarized for him on a single sheet of paper. Because he insulated himself from public affairs, he was often taken by surprise on learning things that almost everyone knew— such as book burning by Department of State underlings in overseas libraries or sit-ins by black students in the South.

As his special assistant Eisenhower chose one of his original backers, Governor Sherman Adams of New Hampshire. This dour Yankee, who became a kind of unofficial alter-ego of the President, wielded a power out of all proportion to his official position. Under the Eisenhower staff system he decided who could see the President and selected letters and papers to be submitted. Increasingly, as the President took refuge on his Gettysburg farm from routine demands, the burden of running the presidential office fell on the hard-working 'Governor.' He was to Eisenhower what Colonel House had been to Wilson, who also took office after a long reign by the opposition party.

The 1952 election marked the return of the Republican party to power after twenty years; many Republicans looked forward to a complete reversal of Democratic policies which, their platform asserted, led toward socialism and the wrecking of the free enterprise system. Yet, once in power, the Republicans found they could do little more than modify past practices, for the country had become irretrievably committed to many elements of the Welfare State. In the 1952 campaign Eisenhower had displayed sympathy with the Taft conservatives; and when he took office he aimed to remove 'the Left-Wingish, pinkish influence in our life.' In his first year he fired 200,000 government workers and boasted of having 'instituted what amounts almost to a revolution' in the national government by 'finding things it can stop doing rather than new things for it to do.' But the

new President also wanted to demonstrate that his party was responsible. Eisenhower's two favorite phrases were 'middle of the road' and 'dynamic conservatism.' His administration turned out to be more conservative than dynamic, but when he left office federal employment was the same as when he came in, and it was apparent that the President had not moved far from the middle of the road.

Eisenhower kept to the middle of the road mostly because the political situation left him little choice. The Democrats erased the slim Republican margin in Congress in 1954, and for six of his eight years in office Eisenhower had to work with a Congress controlled by the opposing party, a circumstance that served to modify his conservative predilection. In 1956 he once again trounced Adlai Stevenson, polling 35,590,000 votes (57.4 per cent) and sweeping 41 states with a total electoral vote of 457 to Stevenson's 26,023,000 votes (42 per cent) and only 73 electoral votes from 7 states, none in the North or West. Yet, astonishingly, despite Eisenhower's one-sided triumph, the Democrats held control of both houses of Congress. Not since Zachary Taylor had a President been elected without carrying at least one house of Congress for his party. The Eisenhower era, noted one political scientist, 'was one of almost unprecedented ambiguity in regard to partisan responsibility for the conduct of the government,' and both conservatives and liberals had to settle for a government of the center which was in keeping with the quiescent spirit of the 'fifties.

At the outset, however, Eisenhower appeared to have free rein to give government a conservative stamp. He named to his first cabinet six prominent businessmen, several of whom were multimillionaires. Secretary of Defense Charles E. Wilson, who had been head of the General Motors Corporation, achieved a kind of immortality by his statement that 'what was good for our country was good for General Motors, and vice versa.' Arthur Summerfield, also of General Motors, distinguished himself as Postmaster-General by trying to put the department on a 'businesslike footing,' regardless of the impact on postal service,

Harry Truman and Eleanor Roosevelt, 1956. One would not guess from the affectionate look the 72-year-old former President bestows on his 72-year-old companion that she has just clobbered him at a press conference. In 1956 Truman, opposed to the renomination of Adlai Stevenson, insisted that the party required a 'fighting' candidate. But, in what was called 'an adroit and ruthless performance,' the former First Lady demolished this argument at a session in which she told reporters that Stevenson was 'better equipped' in foreign affairs than Truman had been when he succeeded her husband. (*Cornell Capa—Magnum*)

while Secretary of the Interior Douglas MacKay, a third product of General Motors, had a long record of hostility to conservation and public power. Secretary of Commerce Sinclair Weeks, a Massachusetts manufacturer, began his administration by firing the head of the Bureau of Standards because he was oblivious to 'the business point of view.' Both Secretary of the Treasury George Humphrey, president of Mark Hanna's old firm, and Secretary of Agriculture Ezra Taft Benson had strong convictions about the dangers of Federal centralization. Attorney-General Herbert Brownell, a prominent New York lawyer, represented the Dewey wing of the party as did the leader of the cabinet, John Foster Dulles, the new Secretary of State. Dulles employed his energies chiefly in foreign affairs, but as a Wall Street lawyer he, too, weighted the cabinet on the conservative side. In this atmosphere it is little wonder that Secretary of Labor Martin Durkin, a Stevenson Democrat and union official, felt thoroughly out of place and resigned before the year was out; his post was filled by James P. Mitchell, a former personnel manager.

Nowhere did the conservatism of the Eisenhower administration express itself more emphatically than in its attitude toward natural resources. Truman had twice vetoed bills giving the states control of the underseas oil deposits lying off their shores, but within a few months of Eisenhower's accession he signed a Submerged Lands Act, put through by Republicans and Southern Democrats, which assigned Federal rights to the off-shore oil to the seaboard states. In the realm of atomic energy private interests also gained. The Atomic Energy Act of 1954 provided for government financing of atomic research but farmed out the operation of the new atomic energy plants to General Electric and Union Carbide. In addition, the Eisenhower administration cut the budget of Federal power administrations and jettisoned a plan for a federally built and controlled dam at Hell's Canyon on the Snake river in favor of a project of the Idaho Power Company.

Early in his administration, Eisenhower cited the TVA as an example of that 'creeping socialism' against which he so insistently warned his countrymen, and he even indicated he would like to sell the TVA to private industry. Between 1952 and 1960 appropriations for the TVA fell from $185 million to $12 million. It was the administration's reluctance to expand this enterprise that led in 1954–55 to the Dixon-Yates fiasco. To serve the needs of the Memphis area, the Atomic Energy Commission signed a juicy contract with two private utilities, represented by Edgar Dixon and Eugene Yates, to build a generating plant. However, a congressional investigation revealed that the contract had been written by a consultant to the Bureau of the Budget who, by an odd coincidence, was also vice-president of the corporation which would finance the operation; and the AEC had to void the contract. When Dixon-Yates sued to recoup its losses, the administration was placed in the awkward position of claiming that the contract, in which it had taken such pride, had been illegal and 'contrary to the public interest' from the very beginning.

Devotion to private enterprise, and suspicion of public, persisted throughout the Eisenhower administration. Shortly after assuming office the President ended all price and rent controls and did away with the Reconstruction Finance Corporation. He vetoed a school construction bill which he thought interfered unduly with local autonomy, acquiesced in a sharp reduction in Federal aid to public housing, and opposed medical insurance amendments to social security bills. In general, he subscribed to the Republican orthodoxy that an unbalanced budget was the road to ruin.

But he soon discovered that it was one thing to preach the virtues of economy and another to practice them, as the intractable farm question demonstrated. Disturbed by the cost of government subsidies, Eisenhower embraced Secretary Benson's recommendation for flexible agricultural price supports, but Benson's program proved a costly failure. Farm income fell drastically, surpluses mounted. In 1954 Senator Humphrey revived Henry Wallace's idea of paying farmers to take their land out of production. This 'soil bank' scheme was at first rejected by Eisenhower, but in 1956 he came around to it, and even persuaded Congress to adopt it. Although the Republican platform of 1952 had charged the Democrats with using 'tax money to make farmers dependent upon government,' federal expenditures for agriculture multiplied during Eisenhower's two terms. Indeed, overall, in only three of its eight years did the administration achieve a balanced budget.

The Eisenhower administration stayed in the 'middle of the road' not only by maintaining a significant, if restrained, role for government in the economy but by balancing conservative policies in fields like natural resources with more liberal responses in other areas. Congress extended reciprocal trade agreements; enlarged social security to embrace some ten million additional persons; raised the minimum wage; pushed through two civil-rights bills; established a new Department of Health, Education, and Welfare; admitted Hawaii and Alaska to statehood in 1959; appropriated some $887 million for student loans and the support of science and language teaching under the National Defense Education Act; provided for the admission of an additional 214,000 refugees outside the normal immigration quotas; and authorized the construction of the Great Lakes-St. Lawrence seaway, which Hoover, Roosevelt, and Truman had all urged in vain and which Canada and the United States completed within the decade. In short, Eisenhower, partly by intent, partly by inadvertence, pursued a course of moderation in domestic affairs that much of the country seemed to approve.

Liquidation of McCarthyism

For one of the long-needed accomplishments in Washington, the Senate rather than the President deserves credit: the liquidation of Senator McCarthy as an effective force. Yet in truth both performed ingloriously. Only a rare senator like Herbert Lehman dared to stand up to McCarthy, and the administration at times seemed bent on diverting the Wisconsin mountebank by outdoing him. Shortly after taking office Eisenhower extended the security system to all agencies of the government, replaced the earlier criterion of 'loyalty' with a broader and vaguer criterion of 'security risk,' and authorized the discharge of any person whose employment was not 'clearly consistent with the interests of national security.' Be-

tween May 1953 and October 1954 no fewer than 6926 'security risks' were 'separated' from their government jobs. Very few of these were even charged with subversion, and not one had committed any crime or breach of duty for which he was brought to trial in a court of law. Secretary Dulles appointed a McCarthyite as the State Department's security officer and sacrificed valued officials to appease the Senator. In December 1953 the Atomic Energy Commission, on orders from Eisenhower, withdrew security clearance from the 'father of the atomic bomb,' J. Robert Oppenheimer.

All this display of zeal, however, failed to assuage McCarthy, who now trained his guns on the administration itself. McCarthy objected to Eisenhower's new ambassador to Russia, Charles Bohlen, because he had been at Yalta, and he sent to Europe two bumbling assistants to track down and destroy 'subversive' literature (such as the works of Emerson and Thoreau) in libraries of the U.S. Information Service—a usurpation of State Department authority in which Dulles readily acquiesced. Early in 1954, McCarthy seized on the case of an obscure army dentist, a major who had been given a routine promotion and an honorable discharge from the army notwithstanding a suspicion of Communist sympathies. In the course of an investigation of this trivial episode of the 'pink dentist' McCarthy browbeat the major's superior, General Zwicker, and then turned on Robert Stevens, Secretary of the Army, who allowed himself to be cowed into signing a 'memorandum of agreement' with the Senator.

But on 11 March 1954 the army struck back with the charge that McCarthy had demanded preferential treatment in the army for one of his aides who had been drafted. The Senator counterattacked with forty-six charges against the army, and the war was on. The hearings to determine the facts were televised nationally, and the whole country watched with a kind of horrified fascination the spectacle of McCarthy as bully. Thereafter the tide of opinion turned against McCarthy. No sooner was the investigation concluded than Republican Senator Ralph Flanders moved that the Senate formally censure McCarthy for improper conduct. A Senate committee

Earl Warren (1891–1974). Appointed Chief Justice of the United States in 1953, he rapidly used his gifts as a harmonizer to achieve unanimity of the Court in the historic school desegregation decision the following year. Not regarded as a great technician, Warren nonetheless moved the judiciary onto a number of new paths by posing the question, 'Is this fair and just?' Throughout his tenure he had to cope with 'Impeach Earl Warren' placards, but when he left the bench in 1969 he was widely regarded as the most influential Chief Justice since John Marshall. This picture is by the noted photographer Karsh. (© *Karsh, Ottawa*)

headed by Watkins of Utah, another Republican, recommended censure, and on 2 December 1954 the Senate formally 'condemned' McCarthy by a vote of 67 to 22, with Republicans casting all the opposition votes. Thereafter McCarthy's influence declined rapidly. On 2 May 1957 he died, his force largely spent, his name an 'improper noun' for a guiltily-remembered episode.

Yet if McCarthy was gone, McCarthyism left as a heritage a large body of laws and practices based on the notion that there were litmus tests for Americanism, and that it was the business of governments to apply these tests to all who served in any public capacity. The elaborate apparatus improvised in the 'forties now hardened as a permanent engine of the American security system. To the Smith Act of 1940 and the Internal Security Act of 1950 was added the Communist Control Act of 1954 outlawing the Communist party. Just as in pre-Civil War days Southern hostility to abolition gradually became hostility to all liberal nineteenth-century ideas, so now hostility to 'subversion' became also a bitter opposition to those who championed the rights of Negroes, favored recognition of Communist China, and supported medical care for the aged, or even—as Arthur Schlesinger said—those who believed in the income tax, the fluoridation of water, and the twentieth century.

Constitutional questions raised by security programs sharply divided the Supreme Court, with Justice Frankfurter speaking for one group—usually the majority—and Justices Black or Douglas or Chief Justice Earl Warren for the other. The Frankfurter wing tended to support the right of the legislature to qualify or suspend some of the guarantees of the First Amendment where it felt that the security of the commonwealth was at stake; it believed that in a democratic society, popularly elected legislatures, not judicial tribunals, should strike the balance between liberty and security. The Black group believed that the constitutional prohibition against the abridgment of free speech was an absolute, and that legislatures should not be permitted to plead the necessity of security as a justification for overriding constitutional guarantees. In the Dennis case of 1951 the Court had found the balance of interest to be on the side of security, but after 1954 there was

a shift toward stronger emphasis on the guarantees of the First Amendment. In 1957 alone, *Yates v. United States* curtailed the scope of the Dennis opinion and of the Smith Act by holding that even advocacy of forcible overthrow of government was not illegal if it confined itself to mere advocacy; *Watkins v. United States* curbed the authority of the Un-American Activities Committee to punish uncooperative witnesses at will; and in *Kent v. Dulles* and *Dayton v. Dulles*, the Court deprived the State Department of the right to deny passports arbitrarily. However, with the sharpening of the Cold War after 1958 there was a perceptible shift to the side of security, and the Court sustained the activities of legislative investigating committees even when these were palpably bent on exposure rather than on acquiring information.

The Civil Rights Revolution

If the Supreme Court failed to speak with a clear voice on civil liberties, it acted emphatically on behalf of blacks who, as the centenary of the Emancipation Proclamation approached, were still second-class citizens. In the South, black children were fobbed off with schools that were not only segregated but inferior, and black youths were denied entrance to the state universities they helped to support by taxation. When Negroes traveled they were forced to use segregated waiting rooms and sections of buses. They were not permitted to sit with white people in theaters, movies, restaurants, or at lunch counters; even in many churches. Their right to vote was flouted by various devices, and they were tried by Jim Crow juries. In the North urban blacks met various kinds of discrimination and were confined to slum dwellings in black ghettos. Yet changes were in the wind. Between 1940 and 1960 blacks in the North increased from 2.8 to 7.2 million, thereby markedly increasing their political leverage in a region where they could freely exercise the vote. Furthermore, the conscience of the nation had been deeply disturbed by what the great Swedish sociologist, Gunnar Myrdal, called the American Dilemma—the dilemma of commitment both to equality and to white superiority.

After a series of antidiscrimination rulings in

fields like housing and public transportation, the Supreme Court struck a heavy blow against white supremacy in the 1954 school segregation case, *Brown v. Board of Education of Topeka.* In 1896 the Supreme Court had held that the Fourteenth Amendment did not require that blacks and whites share all public facilities and that it was not illegal for such facilities to be 'separate' as long as they were 'equal.' In the Brown case a unanimous Court, speaking through Chief Justice Warren, reversed this decision and held that 'separate educational facilities are inherently unequal.' It followed this ruling with another in May 1955 which required that desegregation of the schools proceed 'with all deliberate speed'—in short, gradually but with a 'prompt and reasonable start.'

Deliberateness became more apparent than speed. In the border states, except Virginia, desegregation encountered only sporadic resistance, but in the Deep South, segregationists organized White Citizens' Councils, and whipped up opposition sentiment to fever pitch. Georgia made it a felony for any school official to spend tax money for public schools in which the races were mixed; Mississippi made it a crime for any organization to institute desegregation proceedings in the state courts; North Carolina withheld school funds from any school district which integrated its public schools. In February 1956, when Autherine Lucy became the first black to register at the University of Alabama, a howling mob of students drove her from the campus.

Out of patience with resistance in the Deep South, where not a single child attended a desegregated school at the beginning of Eisenhower's second term, a Federal court ordered a start of desegregation in the schools of Little Rock, Arkansas, a city known for racial progress, in the fall of 1957. But Governor Orval Faubus responded by creating an atmosphere of violence and then calling out the National Guard, not to protect the black children in their right to attend the public schools but to deny them that right. When these troops were withdrawn on order of a Federal district judge, a mob blocked Negro students from entering Central High School. President Eisenhower, who had not lifted a finger to enforce the Brown decision, now confronted an act of de-

fiance that could not be permitted to go unchallenged. On 24 September he dispatched Federal troops to Little Rock. However, Faubus, re-elected to the governorship, persisted in his tactics of obstruction, and not until the Supreme Court handed down yet another decision in September 1958 was even token integration accomplished.

If desegregation was to be achieved, the President and Congress would have to assume some of the lonely burden of the Federal judiciary. But Eisenhower spurned suggestions that he use his immense prestige to educate the country on civil rights. He did take effective action in areas like the District of Columbia where Federal authority was unquestioned. But even after the Little Rock episode, he observed: 'I have never said what I thought about the Supreme Court decision—I have never told a soul.' Congress proved somewhat more responsive. In 1957, under the leadership of Lyndon Johnson of Texas, the Senate Majority Leader, it enacted the first civil rights law in 82 years. Although weakened by amendments, it provided a degree of Federal protection for Negroes who wanted to vote and set up a Civil Rights Commission. A second statute in 1960 authorized the appointment of Federal referees to safeguard the right to vote and stipulated that a threat of violence to obstruct a Court order was a Federal offense. However, Congress did nothing effective to speed enforcement of the Court's decisions. Six years after the Court had called for desegregation with 'all deliberate speed,' not a single school was integrated in South Carolina, Georgia, Alabama, Mississippi, or Louisiana.

The brightest spark for the civil rights revolution came not from the President or Congress, not even from the Supreme Court, but from the blacks themselves. The pathbreaking Court decisions would not have been possible without the carefully developed strategy of black and white attorneys in the National Association for the Advancement of Colored People under the astute leadership of Roy Wilkins. They would have had no meaning if there had not been black children with the courage to brave the wrath of ugly mobs and withstand the taunts of their fellow students.

Yet in the long run more important still may have been an occurrence on a Montgomery,

Martin Luther King (1929–1968). On the wall hangs a picture of Gandhi. From his first acquaintance at Boston University with the Mahatma's teachings through his time of testing in the Montgomery bus boycott to his climactic visit to India in 1959, King grew ever more deeply committed to the doctrines of nonviolent resistance and *Satyagraha* (soul force) and to the need to set an example of physical suffering by inviting imprisonment. In confrontations in Georgia and Alabama in the 1960's, King would recall Gandhi's experiences in Punjab and at Ahmadabad. The Negro, King wrote, must reach the point where he could say to his white brother: 'We will not hate you, but we will not obey your evil laws. We will soon wear you down by pure capacity to suffer.' (*Bob Fitch–Black Star*)

697

Alabama, bus on 1 December 1955. Late that day Rosa Parks, a middle-aged black seamstress riding home from work, refused to give up her seat to a white man. When she was arrested for violating the city's Jim Crow statutes, the blacks of Montgomery boycotted the buses. Led by a twenty-five-year-old Baptist minister, the Reverend Martin Luther King, Jr., who had been influenced by Gandhi and Thoreau, they employed non-violent resistance in a campaign that eventually resulted in desegregation of the city's buses. King, whose home was bombed and who was arrested (one of thirty jailings in his career) said:

If we are arrested every day, if we are exploited every day, if we are trampled over every day, don't let anyone pull you so low as to hate them. We must use the weapon of love. We must have compassion and understanding for those who hate us. . . .

Out of this experience Dr. King emerged a national leader, and his new organization, the Southern Christian Leadership Conference, would be in the vanguard of many protests in the 1960's.

A similar small incident toward the end of Eisenhower's reign touched off a movement that shook Southern society to its foundations. On 1 February 1960, four freshmen at a black college in North Carolina sat down at a lunch counter in downtown Greensboro; when the waitress refused to serve them, they remained in their seats. Within a few weeks the sit-in movement had swept the South and soon took such forms as 'wade-ins' in motel and municipal swimming pools and 'kneel-ins' in churches. In the North the Congress of Racial Equality (CORE), which had employed the tactic of passive resistance as early as the 1940's, organized demonstrations to break racial barriers. Other blacks and whites joined in 'freedom rides' to desegregate interstate transportation. Within a brief period Northern hotels and restaurants ended their subtle forms of discrimination, Southern department stores and lunch counters were desegregated, and WHITE and COLORED signs were pulled down from waiting rooms in hundreds of Southern rail, air, and bus terminals.

The New Look and the Old View

In domestic affairs Eisenhower set the tone for his administration, but in foreign policy the dominant figure was his Secretary of State, John Foster Dulles. Grandson of one secretary of state and nephew of another, he had been a secretary at the Hague Peace Conference of 1907 and an adviser to the United States delegation at Versailles. One of the architects of the United Nations, Dulles, like Eisenhower, had been so closely identified with the programs of the outgoing administration that it seemed probable that there would be substantial continuity in policy. Yet Eisenhower had won election on a platform which attacked 'the negative, futile and immoral policy of containment' and Dulles denounced the Truman-Acheson approach as 'treadmill policies which, at best, might perhaps keep us in the same place until we drop exhausted.'

Dulles advanced as alternatives to containment a series of policies which would permit the United States to seize the initiative in world affairs. A prominent Protestant layman with a moralistic view of America's responsibilities, he objected that containment abandoned 'countless human beings to a despotism and Godless terrorism' and proposed the 'liberation' of the captive peoples of eastern Europe. The satellites were to be liberated not by force but by the intensity of our moral indignation. The mere announcement by the United States 'that it wants and expects liberation to occur would change, in an electrifying way, the mood of the captive peoples,' Dulles claimed. 'Never before,' noted one writer, 'had the illusion of American omnipotence demanded so much of American diplomacy.'

At the same time that Eisenhower and Dulles would roll back the Iron Curtain and 'unleash' Chiang to assault the Chinese mainland, they would reduce the armed forces. They shared the fear of men like Senator Taft that America's security was threatened less from abroad than by inflationary spending to meet foreign commitments. Under what Admiral Radford, chairman of the Joint Chiefs of Staff, called the 'New Look' policy, the United States cut back on expensive ground troops and placed more reliance on

John Foster Dulles (1888–1959). This photograph shows the peripatetic Secretary of State in a characteristic action—in full stride after alighting from an aircraft. (*Wide World*)

nuclear bombs, which the air force would deliver. The New Look responded to America's pride in air power and its revulsion from trench warfare. Although it reduced military spending, the administration insisted it was providing greater security by getting 'more bang for a buck.'

In January 1954 Dulles announced that henceforth the United States would rely more on 'the deterrent of massive retaliatory power . . . a great capacity to retaliate instantly, by means and at times of our own choosing.' The doctrine of 'massive retaliation' reflected the irritation of much of the country with limited war, as a result of the Korean experience. The United States, declared Secretary Humphrey, had 'no business getting into little wars.' If the country had to intervene, he said, 'let's intervene decisively with all we have got or stay out.' But the trouble with the massive retaliation doctrine was that it escalated every dispute into an occasion for a war of annihilation, and, if carried to its logical conclusion, left the country with no alternative save surrender or a nuclear holocaust. Moreover, since the threat of

nuclear retaliation had not proved effective even when the United States held an atomic monopoly, it seemed even less likely to work now that Russia had its own nuclear arsenal.

In the end the Eisenhower foreign policies differed from those of Truman more in style than in substance. The President shared Dulles's faith in 'personal' diplomacy; not only was everything to be talked out in front of microphones and television lights but the participants should be principals, not subordinates. Eisenhower preferred to negotiate 'at the summit'; while Dulles, flitting from continent to continent, turned out to be the most traveled Secretary of State in American history prior to Kissinger. But despite the bustle, the new administration learned that it had far less room for maneuver in the conduct of foreign affairs than it imagined.

Elected on a platform which charged the Democrats with waging war in Korea 'without the will to victory' and with 'ignominious bartering with our enemies,' Eisenhower quickly scored one of the most important achievements of his administration by bartering with the enemy to secure a peace without victory in Korea. In obtaining a cease-fire in that stricken country, the President fixed the pattern for the remainder of his years in office: warlike rhetoric would yield to deeds of peace. The war had cost the United States some 30,000 dead and over 100,000 wounded and missing; Korean and Chinese casualties probably totalled more than two million. Korea, divided absurdly at the waist, faced an uncertain and gloomy future. It was threatened hourly by the 'People's Republic' on its northern boundary and by Communist China and Russia on its flanks; lacking a sound economic basis, it subsisted largely on the vast sums poured in by the United States, which was committed to come to its aid. Syngman Rhee, who grew more and more dictatorial with the passing years, was eventually ousted by a popular rebellion, only to be succeeded by the equally dictatorial General Park. Still, if the outcome was less than satisfactory, Eisenhower had fulfilled his pledge to go to Korea, and the fighting had stopped.

In 1954 the revolution against colonialism in Asia and Africa presented another test of administration doctrines. For almost seven years Communist guerillas known as the Viet-Minh had been waging war against the French in the jungles of Indochina. By the summer of 1953 they had overrun much of the northern half of Vietnam, largest of the three states comprising French Indochina, and threatened the neighboring state of Laos. Fearful that the Communist wave might engulf the whole of southeastern Asia, and eager to take pressure off the French so that they could fulfill their obligations toward the European Defense Community, Truman had sent a military mission to Saigon and stepped up aid. By 1954 America was paying almost four-fifths of the cost of the war. When the French position became critical that spring, Dulles insisted that Indochina could not be permitted to fall; Admiral Radford proposed an air strike to save the beleaguered jungle fortress of Dienbienphu; and Vice-President Nixon favored, if necessary, 'putting our boys in.' But the British as well as elements in America, including military advisers and such Democratic leaders as Lyndon Johnson, opposed

action which might lead to another Korea. Eisenhower believed that the United States had a vital stake in Vietnam. 'You have a row of dominoes set up,' he explained. 'You knock over the first one, and what will happen to the last one is that it will go over very quickly.' But despite his attraction to this 'domino theory,' he was persuaded to veto the plan to intervene. When the United States permitted Dienbienphu to fall on 7 May, the doctrine of massive retaliation died an early death. As a consequence of a conference at Geneva of the great powers, the Kingdoms of Cambodia and Laos emerged as nominally independent new nations, while Vietnam was divided provisionally in two along the 17th parallel until free elections could be held.

To counter Communist influence in this region, Dulles took steps to create an Asiatic defense community that would parallel NATO. In November 1954, Pakistan, Thailand, and the Philippines joined with the United States, Britain, France, Australia, and New Zealand to set up a Southeast Asia Treaty Organization (SEATO). Unlike NATO, however, SEATO existed largely on paper; the signatories had no obligation save to consult, although in the 1960's it would be falsely argued that the United States was compelled by its SEATO commitment to intervene militarily in Vietnam.

At the same time that Dulles was negotiating the SEATO pact, he was fostering liberation illusions on Formosa—now called Taiwan—whither Chiang Kai-shek and the Chinese Nationalists had betaken themselves when driven by the Reds from the mainland in 1949. With the encouragement of Taft's successor as Republican leader in the Senate, William Knowland, 'the Senator from Formosa,' Dulles nurtured the unrealistic notion that Chiang, representing the true and rightful government of all China, would eventually recross the Formosa Strait and reconquer the mainland. Chiang multiplied the dangers of the Formosan problem by occupying a group of small islands— Quemoy, Matsu, and the Tachens—close to the Chinese mainland. On his accession to the presidency, Eisenhower had announced that he was lifting Truman's 'blockade' of Taiwan by the U.S. Seventh Fleet, thus 'unleashing' Chiang Kai-shek

President Eisenhower greets the Prime Minister of India, Jawaharlal Nehru, in the north portico of the White House as journalists make notes and snap pictures. In the 1950's relations between the two leaders were made more difficult by the pro-Chinese attitudes of India's supercilious special envoy, Krishna Menon, and by the hardshelled hostility to neutralism of America's sanctimonious Secretary of State, John Foster Dulles. (*Library of Congress*)

for an attack upon the mainland, an enterprise that existed largely in the minds of men like Senator Knowland, for Chiang lacked the strength to carry it out. When, in the summer of 1954, the Communists began a heavy bombardment of the off-shore islands, the President told the Congress that 'in the interest of peace the United States must remove any doubt regarding our readiness to fight.' Congress responded with a somewhat ambiguous resolution authorizing the President to

use the armed force of the nation 'as he deems necessary' to defend this region, one of the few times in history that Congress formally gave the Executive power to involve the nation in war at his discretion. But Eisenhower once again pulled back from a war of liberation, and Chiang gave up the Tachens to the Communists.

In August 1958 the problem flared up again when the Communists opened another and heavier bombardment of the islands. Dulles promptly asserted that the United States stood ready to repel any attack, and the Seventh Fleet escorted troops which Chiang rushed to garrison the beleaguered islands. But public opinion at home and abroad reacted sharply to the threat of war over these islands, which were almost as close to the Chinese mainland as Staten Island is to Manhattan. Were they really worth an atomic war—or even a 'conventional' war? On 30 September, Dulles executed a stunning reversal. He stated that Chiang had been 'rather foolish' and declared that the United States had 'no commitment to help Chiang back to the mainland'; Eisenhower, who had recklessly committed himself to the ambitions of the Nationalists, now said that Chiang's build-up of troops on the offshore islands was 'a thorn in the side of peace.' On 23 October, Dulles 'releashed' Chiang by compelling him to renounce publicly the use of force to regain control of the mainland of China. So ended another experiment in 'liberation.'

In a magazine interview Dulles offered an explanation of his approach which gave birth to a new term: 'brinkmanship.' He stated:

You have to take chances for peace, just as you must take chances in war. Some say that we were brought to the verge of war. Of course we were brought to the verge of war. The ability to get to the verge of war without getting into the war is the necessary art. If you cannot master it, you inevitably get into wars. If you try to run away from it, if you are scared to go to the brink, you are lost. We've had to look it square in the face—on the question of enlarging the Korean War, on the question of getting into the Indo-China war, on the question of Formosa. We walked to the brink and we looked it in the face.

Critics not only disputed the accuracy of Dulles's account of these incidents but asked whether, in a world of nuclear terror, such an attitude was not irresponsibly provocative.

However, the administration matched these bellicose gestures with more pacific ones, and at times, especially midway through Eisenhower's first term, the new administration displayed a more conciliatory attitude. By 1955 a series of events combined to bring about a mild thaw in the Cold War: the death of Stalin, truce in Korea, a cease-fire in the Formosa Strait, a compromise peace in Vietnam. Eisenhower himself had become a symbol of peace. In a dramatic gesture before the United Nations Assembly in December 1953 he had proposed that the major scientific nations of the world jointly contribute to a United Nations pool of atomic power to be used exclusively for peaceful purposes. On four crucial occasions—Korea, Taiwan, Indochina, and in negotiations with China over prisoners—he had thrown the weight of his influence to the side of peace. The European defense community was now a reality. A wave of prosperity surged through Western Europe, greatly diminishing fear of Communist subversion or aggression. Russia, having detonated a hydrogen bomb, showed signs of a more reasonable relationship with the West. As if to dramatize the new spirit, the Soviet Union in May 1955 ended its long and harsh occupation of Austria.

Thus the stage was set for the 'summit' conference at Geneva in mid-summer 1955, at which Eisenhower proposed a disarmament plan that caught the popular imagination. He called upon Russia and the United States to:

give each other a complete blueprint of our military establishments, from beginning to end, from one end of our countries to the other; lay out the establishments and provide the blueprints to each other. Next to provide within our countries facilities for aerial photography to the other country, ample facilities for aerial reconnaissance where you can make all the pictures you choose and take them to your own country to study, you to provide exactly the same facilities for us, and we to make these examinations, and by this step to convince the world that we are providing as between ourselves against the possibility of great surprise attack, thus lessening danger and relaxing tension.

'What I propose,' he added, 'would be but a beginning.' As Moscow would not even consider Eisenhower's generous offer, nothing came of the Geneva conference. But the 'spirit of Geneva' still seemed to many to symbolize the change in mood that Eisenhower epitomized—from the rancorous 'thirties and 'forties to the more tranquil 'fifties.

Affluence and Apprehension

Tocqueville had predicted that American society in achieving equality would preserve the same civilization, habits, and manners. In the Eisenhower years, it appeared that this prophecy had been fulfilled. To some, this was a source of pride; to others, an occasion for dismay; while still others were more impressed by the persistence of inequality. The nineteen-fifties would be remembered as a period of placidity typified by the genial Eisenhower. But this was also a decade of discord and strife as well as dissatisfaction with a culture which conveyed the dreary sense, in the words of the novelist John Updike, of 'a climate of time between, of standoff and day-by-day.' Mobility and affluence opened greater opportunities to millions of Americans, but before Eisenhower's reign was over an accumulation of problems—the decline of the central city and the countryside, the vicissitudes of the economy, the impairment of national prestige in the 'space race', and the complacency of political leadership—would lead to questioning of whether the United States had not lost its sense of 'national purpose.'

The 'affluent society' derived from the phenomenal expansion of the economy in the postwar era. By 1955 the United States, with only 6 per cent of the world's population, was turning out half the world's goods. From 1945 to 1967 the gross national product increased from $213 billion to $775 billion a year; even when adjusted for inflation, this was an astonishing gain. In the twenty years after 1940 electrical energy surged from 150 to 800 trillion kilowatt hours. The economy was sparked by the emergence of new industries like plastics and electronics and by the huge investments of business and government in research. Not content with the vast home market, American corporations bought control of great automobile, drug, and electrical companies overseas, and economists expressed concern about the vast power of the 'multinational corporation.'

This prodigious economic growth brought a sharp rise in national income and a remarkable expansion of the middle class. From 1945 to 1970, a time when 22 million people, including a sizable segment of women, were added to the labor force, real weekly earnings of factory workers increased 50 per cent and the proportion of Americans defined as living in poverty was cut almost in half. Even more striking is the fact that the proportion of families and unattached individuals receiving an annual income of at least $10,000 (measured in 1968 dollars) had soared from 9 per cent in 1947 to 33 per cent in 1968.

The most impressive social development was the advance, rather than the decline, of equalitarianism. The expansion of the middle class, the cessation of large-scale immigration, the advent of all but universal high school education and the enormous increment in college and university enrollments, the standardization of consumer products—all of these developments tended to make American society at mid-twentieth century more equalitarian. The gap between native and foreign-born, Protestant, Catholic, and Jew, narrowed, and representatives of newer stocks like Governor DiSalle and Governor Rosellini, Secretary Ribicoff and Secretary Goldberg, moved into the seats of power. With 95 per cent of the population native-born, American society became more homogeneous, though racial distinctions remained painfully significant.

America was the first country in modern history where each generation had more education than its forebears—an elementary consideration which goes far to explain that child-centered society which puzzled foreign observers. The familiar process of enlarging both the base and the height of the educational pyramid was greatly accelerated in the years after the Second World War. Prosperity, the G.I. Bill of Rights, the urgent demands for expertise—all of these combined to give a powerful impetus to education. By 1960 the college occupied about the same position in the educational enterprise as the high school in 1920 and the junior college in 1940. Between 1920 and 1960, the total number of students at institutions of higher education grew from less than 600,000 to 3.6 million, a critical development in the enlargement of the middle class.

Automation in industry, mechanization on the farm, and labor-saving devices in the home combined to add to the hours of leisure. For thousands of years most men and women, and many children too, had worked from sun-up to sun-down; now, abruptly, the work day was cut to seven hours and the work week to five days or occasionally even less, with paid holidays and more extended vacations. Industries catering to leisure flourished: boating, golf, skiing, camping, touring, and swimming pools, and as the work ethic evaporated America became increasingly a society dedicated to play. Television, which absorbed many leisure hours each day, was in almost no homes at the start of the postwar era, became widespread in the 1950's, and was virtually universal in the 'sixties. It affected the political process, was a strong nationalizing influence, and carried the pervasive consumer culture into every section of the country.

As fewer farmers and workers were needed to produce the food and goods for an affluent society, the service industries swiftly became central to the economy, a development which also helped to obliterate class lines. In 1956 for the first time white collar workers outnumbered blue collar employees. Between 1947 and 1957, the number of factory operatives declined 4 per cent while clerical workers increased 23 per cent and the salaried middle class 61 per cent. The proportion of self-employed dropped sharply, and an increasing number of Americans spent their lives in a world of organizations, a phenomenon which many found alarming. In W. H. Whyte, Jr.'s *The Organization Man*, C. Wright Mills's *White Collar*, Vance Packard's *The Status Seekers*, and Sloan Wilson's *The Man in the Gray Flannel Suit*, a bureaucratized society discouraged the free-wheeling individual and placed a premium on conformity, and in John Hersey's *The Child Buyer* a pupil is marked down as a troublesome deviate because he scores poorly in 'followership.' The 'other-directed man' described by David Riesman, whose aptly titled *The Lonely Crowd* was the prophetic book of this generation, engaged in 'smooth, unruffled manipulation of the self' to satisfy an 'irrational craving for indiscriminate approval.'

The economy of the second half of the century created a new type of employee whose talents lay primarily in adaptability and team work rather than independence and ingenuity; and it discour-

aged dominant personalities, even at the top. Just as the academic system no longer produced strong presidents like Eliot, Butler, and Harper, so the new economy rarely brought to the fore new Rockefellers, Carnegies, McCormicks, and Morgans. Yet if there was social loss in the failure of innovative and strong-willed leaders to emerge, few deplored the passing of the type represented by George Baer, Tom Girdler, or Sewell Avery; if leadership was blander, it was also more responsive.

Even in organized labor, where the tradition of personal leadership was strong, warriors like John L. Lewis and idealists like Eugene Debs gave way to bureaucrats who ran large and flourishing organizations from comfortable and well-staffed offices. In the postwar years unions achieved both prosperity and stability. In 1955 when the A. F. of L. and the C.I.O. merged, they boasted a joint membership of 17 million; still only one-fourth of the entire labor force, it was well over one-half of blue collar workers who had always been the core of labor strength. By then organized labor generally had secured the 40-hour week, vacations with pay, and welfare benefits. As labor prospered, it became increasingly conservative. European union officials claimed that the only way they could tell the difference between businessmen and labor leaders in America is that the union chieftains dressed better and drove bigger cars.

Social critics who had long been disturbed by the inequalities in American life now expressed their anxiety about the trend toward a homogenized society. They drew a dismaying picture of the American suburb which displayed the same 'ranch houses' on single or split levels, with picture windows, television antennae, and a two-car garage; the same well-manicured back gardens with little swimming pools; the same country clubs and shopping centers and supermarkets, all built to a pattern. Almost all the men commuted to nearby cities, society was matriarchal, and the well-protected young gravitated from the local high or country-day school to the state university or the Ivy League college of the East.

But American society had more variety than such a portrait suggests. To be sure, in the Eisenhower years, many observers sensed that

'Office in a Small City' by Edward Hopper, 1953. 'In the inhuman surfaces of urban life,' the art critic Sam Hunter has written, Hopper 'has found metaphors for spiritual vacancy and imprisonment. . . . He is an artist of American ennui and loneliness. . . . His atmosphere . . . is stifling and curiously unreal, with a strange anxiety hovering at its edges. . . . The result of his combination of bald literalism and dramatic heightening by a mysterious alchemy of light, is to give a mood of impenetrable monotony the quality of a dream.' (*Metropolitan Museum of Art, George A. Hearn Fund, 1953*)

'the bland were leading the bland,' and the college generation of the 1950's seemed exceptionally passive. Still, not even the suburbs were uniform: in New York's Westchester County blacks in the river streets of Ossining lived different lives from bankers on Scarsdale estates, as the world of Cicero differed from that of Oak Park, and Daly City from Tiburon. No doubt standardization and conformity are tributes that a mobile, equalitarian society is often compelled to pay, but this same movement toward equality opened up new opportunities for many Americans.

Nevertheless, mobility exacted a heavy toll, and increasingly social observers asked whether the pace of change, affecting every type of community from metropolis to village, was not moving too fast. The census of 1960 revealed what had long been foreseen—the erosion of the great cities: eight of the ten largest cities had fewer people in 1960 than in 1950. The movement to the suburbs began well before the war, but after 1945 it became something like a mass migration. Driven by the urge for space and privacy, better schools and recreation facilities, by concern about status, and sometimes by the lure of all-white communities, some 40 or 50 million Americans had by 1960 found refuge in suburbia or, as the fringes came to be called, 'exurbia.' The well-to-do led the exodus to outlying areas, thus depriving the central cities of much of their tax base; city residential districts deteriorated into ghettos of the poor. As population fled to the suburbs, newcomers from the cotton fields of Mississippi, the mountains of West Virginia, and the teeming villages of Puerto Rico poured in to fill some of the void. A few cities, such as New Haven, had some success in arresting the erosion that was eating them away, but for the most part the efforts of cities to stop decay were like those of Alice in her race with the Red Queen: they found that they had to run at least twice as fast if they expected to get anywhere.

Many came to question whether the American city was governable. Efforts to raze slums through 'urban renewal' often resulted in sterile housing projects which destroyed the old neighborhoods. Strikes of municipal employees crippled essential services for weeks at a time; white policemen and black residents viewed one another with mutual suspicion; and by 1968 the welfare population of New York City had passed 900,000, with one person on welfare for every three employed in private industry. Lewis Mumford wrote mordantly: 'Lacking any sense of an intelligent purpose or a desirable goal, the inhabitants of our great American cities are simply "waiting for Godot."'

The automobile not only made it possible to live in the suburbs, or far out in the country, and do business in the city, but also, by creating insoluble traffic problems, ruining public transportation, devouring space for parking lots (two-thirds of central Los Angeles has been given over to streets, freeways, parking lots, and garages) and filling the air with noxious fumes, made it disagreeable to live in the central city. Intended as a vehicle for quick mobility, the automobile no longer served this function in many cities. In 1911 a horse and buggy paced through Los Angeles at 11 m.p.h.; in 1962 an auto moved through the city at rush hour at an average of 5 m.p.h. Yet while commuter railroads received little government aid, federal and local governments poured money into highways which funneled yet more traffic into the city.

As metropolitan areas wrestled with the problems of growth, the countryside became citified. Nearly 70 per cent of the population lived in and near cities in 1970, when the total farm population was less than in 1830. For generations farmers had taken pride in sending their children to agricultural colleges; now these schools dropped the word 'agricultural' from their names, and the students turned to everything except tilling the soil.

While some fretted about the transformation of rural and urban society, others worried about what the swift pace of change was doing to the economy, for if growth continued, so did concentration. The giant corporation came to be more and more gigantic, and the ten years after 1948 saw no fewer than 2191 mergers and combinations of corporations worth over $10 million. Between 1940 and 1960 bank deposits increased fourfold, but the number of banks declined by over one thousand and branch banking came to be almost as common in the United States as in Great Britain. Three great corporations—General Motors, Ford, and Chrysler—dominated the automobile industry, although in the 'fifties a fourth, American Motors, entered the competition. Three networks all but monopolized the air; six tobacco companies fed the insatiable appetite of Americans for cigarettes. Even in the realm of news the process seemed inexorable. In 1910 almost 700 cities and towns in the United States had competing daily newspapers; by 1967 the number had fallen to 64, and 17 states were without any locally competing newspapers. In many cities newspaper publishers held a news monopoly by owning the radio and television stations as well.

Automation increased apace, as computers stored and used information to control, adjust, and correct complex operations. Walter Reuther wrote:

I went to work in the automotive industry back in 1927. At that time, it took us about twenty-four hours to take a rough engine block, as it was cast in the foundry, and to machine that block, ready for assembly. . . . We kept making progress. We cut it down to 18 hours, and then 14 hours, then 12, then 9 hours. If you'll go through the Cleveland Ford engine plant, which is fully automated, you will see a Ford V-engine, 8 cylinders—a very complicated piece of mechanism—in which the rough castings are automatically fed into this automated line, and in fourteen and six-tenths minutes later, it is fully machined, without a human hand touching it. . . . There are acres and acres of machines, and here and there you will find a worker standing at a master switchboard, just watching green and yellow lights blinking off and on, which tell the worker what is happening in the machine.[1]

1. Walter P. Reuther, *Selected Papers*, Henry M. Christman (ed.), pp. 178, 180.

'Supermarket' by Ben Shahn, 1957. In the postwar era, painters like Shahn and Andy Warhol, as well as poets such as Allen Ginsberg and Randall Jarrell, were captivated by the consumer culture. Shahn called this serigraph of shopping baskets, one of several works commissioned by CBS, 'among the abiding symbols of American life, to be celebrated and brought into awareness.' (*Philadelphia Museum of Art, the Print Club Permanent Coll.*)

Automation presented labor with the menace of falling employment—and industry with the peril of declining purchasing power among workers; made inevitable the shorter working day, week, and year; and gave rise to an urgent demand for the annual wage. At a time when the numbers of young and old were growing at the expense of the numbers in between, it denied employment to the young and retired the old, thus putting on the 20- to 55-year-olds an ever increasing burden of support for the rest of the community. Since the new technology raised skill requirements for jobs, the school 'dropout' was at a disadvantage, and educational opportunities assumed increased urgency.

America had never known an economy of scarcity in the Old World sense of the term, but in the past it had always been able to dispose of its abundance by a steady rise in the standard of living and by exports. Now the capacity of farm and factory to produce far more than could normally be consumed created a new series of problems. Four responses were adopted in whole or in part. One was to build obsolescence into the product itself, thus making reasonably sure that there would be a continuous demand for new models. A second was to create new consumer wants: this task was the special responsibility of the advertisers, who rose to so prominent a position that the term 'Madison Avenue' came to take on some of the connotations that 'Wall Street' had held a generation earlier. A third technique was to dump vast quantities of surplus goods abroad—to give wheat or airplanes, dynamos or books, to 'needy' nations. The fourth, government expenditures in the public area—highways, airports, the military, the exploration of outer space—helped keep the economy going.

Though the nation's space enterprise owed something to the desire to stimulate the economy, it owed more to concern about the country's prestige, and also about the state of American society. In October 1957 the Russians startled Americans by putting a satellite in orbit around the globe; a month later Sputnik II, more than six times heavier and carrying a live dog, orbited the earth;

Edward Hopper, 'Western Motel, 1957. Lloyd Goodrich, the leading authority on
Hopper, has written: '*Western Motel* with its awful interior in decorator's green,
beige, and crimson, its hard-faced blonde, its bright green automobile, and its bare
desert landscape under a burning sun, is one of his toughest pictures of any period.
It makes no concessions to accepted ideas of what is artistically admissible. Its
garish colors are unsoftened by grays. It captures the quintessence of that most
American of institutions, the motel. In a purely naturalistic style it is as firsthand
an exposé of our mass culture as pop art.' (*Yale University Art Gallery*)

and in 1959 they fired a rocket past the moon.
These achievements led to self-searching examination to explain how the Soviet Union had managed to get ahead of the United States in the 'space
race.' In particular, publicists took a hard look at
the American educational system. They found
that Russia was spending a larger proportion of its
income on education than was the United States,
and Russian and Western European students who
left school at eighteen were better educated than
the average American of college age. Not a few
blamed the inadequacies of American schools on
progressive education, which valued 'adjustment'
more than intellectual discipline. One consequence of the furor was that the national government became much more willing to grant funds to
colleges, often to good effect but also with the less
desired result of shaping the curriculum to the
needs of the Department of Defense. The 'Sputnik
crisis' also led to far-ranging, and often tenden-
tious, discussion of whether the country did not
have a distorted sense of values, a matter which,
from a very different perspective, was also disturbing American men of letters.

The literature of these years reflected the anxiety of 'the lonely crowd.' The leader of the postwar poets, Robert Lowell, in *Lord Weary's Castle*, voiced the same absorbed interest in the quest for identity that characterized novels like Saul Bellow's *The Adventures of Augie March* and the writings of J. D. Salinger, who, one critic observed, presented 'madness as the chief temptation of modern life, especially for the intelligent young.' Salinger's *The Catcher in the Rye*, which sold almost two million copies, became the special favorite of adolescents in the 1950's. Writers persistently sounded the theme of loneliness, isolation, and the inability of people to communicate with one another. In one of Tennessee Williams's plays a character says, 'We're all of us sentenced to solitary confinement inside our own skins for life.' If America's mobile society permitted unparalleled freedom, it also cut people off from tradition and a sense of community, a rootlessness which concerned almost all of these writers. In Truman Capote's *Other Voices: Other Rooms*, one character protests, 'We go screaming round the world, dying in our rented rooms, nightmare hotels, eternal homes of the transient heart.'

In the early nineteen-fifties very few writers expressed their foreboding about the path America had taken, but in Eisenhower's second term a hornet's nest of troubles swarmed around him, and pundits raised an outcry about the country's lack of a sense of 'national purpose.' Late in 1957 a severe recession brought an abrupt and unanticipated end to the 'Eisenhower prosperity.' With the country reeling from the shock of the highest unemployment rate since 1941, it learned that Eisenhower's 'crusade' for decency in government had also turned out unhappily. 'Not one appointee of this Administration has been involved in scandal or corruption,' the President had boasted. But in his second term a series of scandals rocked the administration. The worst blow fell in September 1958 when Sherman Adams had to resign as confidential assistant to the President after a congressional committee had exposed his indiscreet relations with an industrial promoter. As a consequence of these developments, American voters in 1958 handed the Republicans their third consecutive congressional defeat, an event un-

precedented in the history of a party that controlled the executive branch. The Democrats swelled their margin in the Senate from a one-seat advantage to almost 2–1 and gained the largest proportion in the House that any party had won since Roosevelt's landslide in 1936.

In the last two years of Eisenhower's tenure a conflict between the President and liberal Democrats in Congress created a virtual deadlock in Washington. Eisenhower, convinced that the Democrats were leading the country down the road to socialism, set himself obdurately against proposals for Federal action in areas like education and housing; liberal Democrats knew that they could enact such legislation only if they were able to muster a two-thirds vote to override the President's veto, an unlikely circumstance. On the other hand, Eisenhower could not impose his will on Congress since he confronted the largest opposition majority in the twentieth century. In such a situation an unusual share of the responsibility for leadership fell to such moderates as Majority Leader Lyndon B. Johnson and Speaker Sam Rayburn, both veteran Texas Democrats who pursued a course of compromise with the administration. In vain, liberal Democrats protested that the Johnson-Rayburn strategy of slicing appropriations to escape vetoes blurred the party's identity and surrendered crucial legislation to the President's 'reckless frugality spree.' Despite the large Democratic majorities, accomplishments were meager.

A World in Turmoil

In Eisenhower's last years in office he took even more direct responsibility for the conduct of foreign affairs than for domestic policy. In April 1959 Dulles, fatally ill, resigned; his successor, Christian Herter, was much less self-assertive, and, with both Dulles and Adams gone, the President grasped the reins more firmly. In the next year he made trips which rivaled Dulles's peregrinations: a 22,000-mile journey to eleven countries from Spain to India and a good-will tour of Latin America. 'There is no place on this earth to which I would not travel, there is no chore I would not undertake, if I had any faintest hope that by so doing, I would promote the general cause of world peace,' Eisenhower said. On these travels, as at the conference in Geneva, the President's personal commitment to avoid a nuclear war was unmistakable. In India people showered him with flowers until he stood a foot deep in them, and he was hailed with signs: 'WELCOME PRINCE OF PEACE.' Yet well before then he had been taught that dedication was not enough and that the world was rapidly spinning out of control.

Even before Eisenhower's first term was over, the 'spirit of Geneva,' which had inspired such high hopes, had evaporated. At the celebration of the Twentieth Communist Party Congress in February 1956, Nikita Khrushchev, the new leader of the USSR, startled the world by a fierce attack on his predecessor, Stalin; that kind of savage leadership, he implied, was a thing of the past. Seven months later the festering discontent of the Poles broke out into the open; and under the leadership of Wladyslaw Gomulka, the Poles demanded freedom from Soviet bayonets and autonomy within the Communist system. When Khrushchev accepted these demands, it looked like the dawn of a new and better day. But when that same autumn the long-suffering Hungarians rose up against Communist misrule, Khrushchev sent two hundred thousand soldiers and thousands of tanks, and while the West looked on in despair, this heroic revolt was ruthlessly stamped out. These events revealed the hollowness of 'massive retaliation' and 'liberation' when Eisenhower refrained from intervening.

The crisis in the Middle East, which erupted the very same week the Hungarian revolt was put down, had been building since World War II. Syria and Lebanon had asserted their independence; and in 1948 the British gave up their mandate in Palestine, the Israelis struck for freedom and, when invaded by the combined forces of Egypt, Lebanon, Jordan, and Syria, broke the invaders and won independence. In 1952 the King of Egypt was driven into exile, and two years later Colonel Gamal Abdel Nasser took over the government, as Arab nationalism surged through the whole Moslem world.

Into this extraordinarily complex situation Dulles jumped with both feet. When he attempted to create a regional defense against Soviet penetration, the result was the Baghdad Pact of 1954 to which Turkey, Iraq, Iran, and Pakistan adhered, but not the United States! The Pact did not in fact intimidate the Soviets; it did, however, antagonize Nasser, who saw it as a deliberate attempt to undermine his own leadership and to split the Moslem world. Nasser struck back by negotiating for the withdrawal of all British troops from the Suez Canal zone by 1956; forming a close military alliance with Syria, Jordan, and Saudi Arabia; swinging a deal with Czechoslovakia for arms, presumably to use against the Israelis; and launching a war of nerves—and of attrition—against Israel by denying Israeli ships passage through the Suez Canal, by subversion, and by ceaseless threats of destruction. Finally, he entered on the dangerous game of inviting the United States and the USSR to bid against each other for the privilege of financing a vast dam and irrigation system at Aswan on the Upper Nile. Dulles first offered to help Egypt build the dam, then abruptly withdrew the offer.

On 26 July 1956, one week after Dulles's about-face, Nasser precipitated a serious world crisis by seizing the Suez Canal in clear violation of treaty agreements. Faced with the prospect of being cut off from essential Middle East oil supplies, the British and French determined to use force to recover control of the Canal. This provided Israel with an opportunity to launch its own offensive against Egypt. On 29 October, as Russian tanks were rumbling into the streets of Budapest, Israeli troops invaded the Sinai peninsula, scattered a much larger Egyptian army, and within a few days were on the banks of the Canal. When Britain and France joined in hastily with aerial attacks, Nasser responded by sinking enough ships in the Canal to close it to traffic indefinitely. Here were the makings of another major war, for India and the Soviet bloc threatened to pile in unless there was an immediate cease-fire. A possibly fatal rift between East and West was avoided when the United Nations, too, denounced the war as aggression and the United States supported the UN position. But though hostilities ended, the Suez affair had driven a wedge between the United States and her allies, while playing into the hands of Nasser, who now presented himself as the very symbol of Arab nationalism in its struggle against Western imperialism. The peaceful settlement was a victory for Eisenhower; a few more such victories and the Western alliance would be in ruins.

The Suez dispute had created a situation favorable to the expansion of Communist influence throughout the Middle East, and in January 1957 Eisenhower asked for authority to extend economic assistance to Middle Eastern countries and to use the armed forces to protect any nation 'threatened by aggression from any country controlled by international communism.' On 9 March Congress authorized some $200 million for economic and military aid to implement this 'Eisenhower Doctrine.' When in the spring of 1958 nationalists threatened the pro-Western government of Lebanon, there was some doubt about the applicability of the Eisenhower Doctrine, but Eisenhower immediately ordered the Sixth Fleet to steam into the eastern Mediterranean and dispatched marines to Lebanon. By October the crisis had eased, but Russia hurriedly announced that it would help finance Egypt's Aswan dam, and henceforth the United States would have to cope with the fact that the Soviet Union was in the Middle East to stay.

Preoccupied with affairs across the sea, the United States failed to take note of what was happening in the Western hemisphere. The abrupt cessation of wartime purchases dealt a heavy blow to Latin American economies; the population explosion pressed implacably on existing resources which were exploited by foreign capital; the gap between rich and poor grew wider. Latin American friendship was taken for granted. Down to 1951 all the Latin American republics together had received about the same amount of foreign aid as Greece; and in the next ten years Latin America received only $3.4 billion out of a total of some $80 billion in aid: that was less than Taiwan got.

Events in Guatemala shocked the United States out of its complacency. For years that little Central American state had groaned under the dictatorship of General Jorge Castañeda; in 1954 he was overthrown and the government came under the control of Jacobo Arbenz, sympathetic to Communism. He and his followers carried through a wholesale confiscation of land, dominated the labor unions, ran the government-owned newspapers, and obtained arms from Poland. Alive to the proximity of Guatemala to the Panama Canal, Dulles shipped arms to Guatemalan rebels gathering along the Honduras border, and in June these forces, with American support, invaded Guatemala, overthrew the Arbenz government, and set up a new regime led by ultra-conservatives. What Secretary Dulles cheered as a triumph for constitutionalism, most Latin Americans, with greater logic, condemned as old-fashioned intervention in the same year that Eisenhower presented the Legion of Merit to the dictators of Venezuela and Peru. When in 1958 Vice-President Nixon visited South America on a good will tour he was showered with anti-American pamphlets in Uruguay, stoned in Peru, mobbed in Venezuela. Only tardily did the United States apply itself to mending its Latin American fences by stepping up economic aid.

Cuba provided a hard test for the new departure. In January 1959 a rebellion led by Fidel Castro succeeded in overthrowing the cruel dictatorship of General Batista. Influenced by his Argentine Communist economic adviser, 'Che' Guevara, Castro apparently planned to turn the 'Pearl of the Antilles' into the first Communist country in the New World. This was not evident for some time. Castro made a triumphant tour of eastern America in 1959, and in Washington was promised economic aid. But when Castro returned to Cuba, he dispensed with elections, threw thousands of Cubans who opposed his regime into jail, and expropriated plantations and major businesses. When the United States protested, Castro became overtly hostile and moved ever closer to the USSR, which for the first time had a foothold in the Western hemisphere.

At the same time that Eisenhower bridled at the establishment of a Communist beachhead in the Caribbean, he approached a potentially even more explosive confrontation with the Kremlin over Berlin. Under the auspices of Russia, the Communists had sought to make East Germany a showpiece of Communism which would win over the hesitant neighbors in the West. To their in-

Paul Cadmus, 'Night in Bologna,' 1958. In the cold war years large numbers of Americans, military and civilian, were stationed at posts thousands of miles from home. Cadmus's painting of an American soldier in Italy conveys a sense of yearning and foreboding in an alien land. (*Sara Roby Foundation, New York*)

tense mortification, every week thousands of East Germans escaped into West Germany, which prospered beyond any other European state, and it was West Berlin, a glittering jewel in the drab fabric of East Germany, that was the showpiece. A thriving rearmed West Germany, its economy united with that of France and other nations in the European Economic Community, its NATO forces possibly equipped by the United States with nuclear weapons, raised a threat which the Communist bloc regarded with grave misgivings. In 1958 Khrushchev delivered an ultimatum to Berlin and the Germanies: either negotiate a settlement within six months, recognizing the permanent partition of Germany, or Russia would make a separate treaty with East Germany, giving it control of East Berlin and the air lanes into West Berlin. Committed to the defense of West Germany, and of Berlin as an outpost of freedom, and dependent on West Germany's contribution to the European defense system and to the economy of the Western world, the United States refused to back down. For the rest of Eisenhower's term, the Berlin controversy smoldered.

Yet at the same time Khrushchev showed an interest in conciliation, and Eisenhower was more than willing to meet him halfway. In September 1959, at the President's invitation, Khrushchev made his first visit to the United States; he wound up his tour at Eisenhower's rural retreat, Camp David, where the two leaders appeared to get on famously. The 'spirit of Camp David' supplanted the defunct 'spirit of Geneva' as the Western world prepared for a summit meeting to resolve the problems of Berlin and nuclear weapons. Not since the beginning of the Cold War had hopes for a peaceful world run so high.

Once again everything went wrong. On 5 May 1960, only eleven days before the summit conference was to have convened in Paris, Khrushchev announced that the Russians had shot down an American U-2 reconnaissance plane in the heart of Russia. After trapping the administration in a lie, the premier gave further details: they had captured the pilot, Francis Powers, who admitted that he was employed by the U.S. Central Intelligence Agency and engaged in aerial photographic espionage. Khrushchev chose to use this incident as

an excuse to wreck the summit conference, and, in a deliberate insult, withdrew his invitation to the President to visit the USSR. American 'aggressors,' he cried, should be treated as a boy handled an erring cat: 'We would catch such a cat by the tail and bang its head against the wall.' A month later, the Russians broke up the ten-nation disarmament conference in Geneva. Eisenhower's hopes for a *détente* had been shattered.

Within less than two months of the U-2 fiasco, the friendly nation of Japan told Eisenhower it would be unsafe for him to visit their country; relations with Castro's Cuba fell to a new low; and Africa burst into flame. In the vast area of tropical Africa, one former colony after another won its independence, sometimes with a minimum of unpleasantness and a maximum of co-operation. But in the Congo (as well as in Algeria) prolonged violence attended the transfer of power. When the Belgians pulled out of the Congo, civil war erupted. Under the leadership of the intrepid Secretary-General, Dag Hammarskjöld, the United Nations raised an international military force to maintain the peace. But to extend Soviet influence south of the Equator, Khrushchev disrupted the work of the UN. In the same year that Soviet Russia penetrated the Western hemisphere for the first time, the Communists made their presence felt in the jungles of Africa. Soviet bloc technicians infiltrated the Congolese government, and Red China used Guinea as a base of operations in other African countries. The UN eventually brought the war under control and set the Congo on the road to nationhood, but the negotiations cost Hammarskjöld his life, and the Congo crisis provided a dreadful example of how Cold War rivalries might envelop the whole world.

The session of the United Nations which opened in September 1960 revealed the tumultuous changes that had taken place in the Eisenhower years. When Eisenhower took office, the West dominated the UN; now the Afro-Asian nations were the largest voting bloc, and African states that did not exist in 1953—countries like Upper Volta—each had parity with the United States in the General Assembly. To New York came a group of prominent leaders none of whom held power in 1953, all antagonistic to the United

States: Khrushchev, Nasser, Castro, as well as spokesmen for the revolution of rising expectations like Sukarno of Indonesia and Nkrumah of Ghana. As Khrushchev banged his shoe on a table to show his boorish displeasure, Castro assaulted the delegates with an interminable harangue, and American blacks stormed the chambers to protest the murder of the Congolese leader, Patrice Lumumba, it seemed that the winds of violence from every quarter of the globe were racing through the sheltered corridors of the pristine buildings on the East river, once fraught with hopes for peace.

Eisenhower: An Assessment

Eisenhower's place in history will probably rest less on what he did than on what he did not do. He gave the nation a chance to consolidate past gains, take stock of itself, and renew its spirits for future struggles. The querulous partisanship of the late Truman years had been mitigated, the acerbity of the national temper had been sweetened. Yet these achievements came at a price. By the very nature of his role as a moderator of differences, he could not risk dividing the country by raising new questions. Moreover, he had a limited interest in such matters and, at times, limited strength. One writer observed: 'When he leaves office in January 1961, the foreign policies and the domestic policies of the past generation will be about where he found them in 1953. No national problem, whether it be education, housing, urban revitalization, agriculture, or inflation, will have been advanced importantly toward solution nor its dimensions significantly altered.' Critics like the Harvard economist John Kenneth Galbraith charged that America's preoccupation with the output of consumer goods was starving the public sector, and Adlai Stevenson protested that the United States had become a society characterized by the 'contrast of public squalor and private opulence.' A country with a half-trillion dollar economy permitted crowded classrooms and hospital wards, antiquated transportation systems and festering slums. If America was more tranquil, the uneasy peace in the South had been bought at the expense of the blacks. None could doubt that Eisenhower had made an important contribution toward unifying the nation, but not a few asked whether the price that had been paid was too high.

In foreign policy it seems likely that Eisenhower's place in history will rest largely on what he did not do. Above all he did not go to war: he achieved peace in Korea and resisted the temptation to intervene in Vietnam and Quemoy, in Hungary and Suez. Even the Lebanon episode was quickly ended. Elected on a platform of denouncing containment, he had gone beyond the Truman-Acheson policies to explore the possibility of peaceful coexistence with the Communist world. And he ended his tenure by warning against 'the acquisition of unwarranted influence, whether sought or unsought, by the military-industrial complex.' Yet it could fairly be asked whether Eisenhower and Dulles had not, by rhetoric and deed, often contributed to the atmosphere of violence and to the recurrent crises which brought the world to the 'brink' of war. Even in his last days in office the President was heading toward a collision with the Russians in Laos and promoting an invasion of Castro's Cuba. He went out of office with his hopes for peace unfulfilled and with America's world prestige diminished, and he left to his successor a legacy of difficulties—in Berlin, in Cuba, in the Middle East, in Southeast Asia—which might, at any moment, bring on that war of annihilation that he so conscientiously sought to prevent.

36

From Camelot to Watergate

1960–1976

John Fitzgerald Kennedy

In 1960, as the elderly Eisenhower prepared to leave office, both major parties turned to younger men, each of whom had been identified with the unadventurous politics of the 1950's. The Republicans named the Vice-President, Richard Nixon; the Democrats the senator from Massachusetts, John F. Kennedy, who, to the dismay of liberals, persuaded Lyndon Johnson, the middle-of-the-road Majority Leader, to take second place on the ticket. Neither candidate aroused much enthusiasm among those who had been critical of America's failure to develop a strong sense of national purpose under Eisenhower. Nixon, who had been an ardent supporter of McCarthy, was manipulative and unimaginative. By failing to take a stand against McCarthy, Kennedy, who had won a Pulitzer Prize for his book *Profiles in Courage*, opened himself to the taunt that he should have shown less profile and more courage. But in his acceptance speech delineating a 'New Frontier,' Kennedy gave indications that his critics may have misjudged him, for he began to elaborate the theme of his campaign: the need for sac-

rifice, imagination, and boldness to 'get the country moving again.'

Senator Kennedy ran under a formidable handicap: he was a Roman Catholic, and Al Smith's defeat was well remembered. He met this issue directly by addressing the Greater Houston Ministerial Association and answering frankly any question the ministers chose to ask. He declared:

I believe in an America where the separation of Church and State is absolute—where no Catholic prelate would tell the President (should he be a Catholic) how to act, and no Protestant minister would tell his parishioners for whom to vote—where no church or church school is granted any public funds or political preference—and where no man is denied public office merely because his religion differs from the President who might appoint him or the people who might elect him.

By his forthrightness he succeeded in muting, if not eliminating, the religious issue.

Polls still showed Nixon running ahead of his rival when he agreed to a series of four nationally televised debates in late September and October. Nixon, who had used television skillfully in 1952,

At a White House press conference the youthful President, John Fitzgerald Kennedy, radiates charm. (*National Archives*)

thought he would improve his advantage, but he was outpointed in the crucial first debate in which Kennedy displayed a poise and maturity that erased the impression that he was a callow upstart lacking the experience of Nixon, who had actually held the reins of government during Eisenhower's illnesses. Kennedy also improved his standing with black voters, who had been cool toward him. When, on 19 October, Martin Luther King was sentenced on a technicality to four months' hard labor in a Georgia penitentiary, from which many feared he would not emerge alive, Kennedy phoned Dr. King's wife to express concern; and Kennedy's brother, Robert, secured the minister's release. This act appears to have swung large numbers of Negro voters to Kennedy, and black ballots provided the margin of victory in several critical states.

Kennedy won, but in the closest race in this century. He gained a popular majority of only 118,000 out of a total of some 68 million votes, a mere two-tenths of 1 per cent, though he had a more comfortable majority of 303 to 219 in the Electoral College. Yet, by however small a margin, Kennedy and Johnson had ended eight years of Republican rule despite the handicaps of youth, Catholicism, a discontented South, and the immense popularity of Eisenhower.

Ten weeks later, as blustery winds and snow flurries swept across Washington, the new President announced:

Let the word go forth from this time and place, to friend and foe alike, that the torch has been passed to a new generation of Americans—born in this century, tempered by war, disciplined by a hard and bitter peace, proud of our ancient heritage, and unwilling to witness or permit the slow undoing of those human rights to which this Nation has always been committed.

He called upon his generation

to bear the burden of a long twilight struggle, year in and year out, 'rejoicing in hope, patient in tribulation'—a struggle against the common enemies of man: tyranny, poverty, disease and war itself.

And he concluded with an affirmation of confidence and of faith:

And so, my fellow Americans: ask not what your country can do for you—ask what you can do for your country.

Kennedy, who so deliberately made himself the spokesman for 'a new generation of Americans,' put together an administration notable for its youth. His cabinet, which included his thirty-five-year-old brother Robert as Attorney-General, was ten years younger than Eisenhower's. The youngest man ever elected to the presidency, he appointed to key positions still younger men, who were, as one observer said, the junior officers of World War II now come to power. By the youth and 'vigor' of his administration, Kennedy contributed to that change in the national mood which saw the 'Silent Generation' of the 1950's give way to the deeply committed young people of the 'sixties.

From the very first day in the brilliant winter sunshine of the inauguration, at which Robert Frost read a poem, Kennedy gave a tone to the White House which not only contrasted sharply to that of the Eisenhower years but differed from anything Washington had seen. Kennedy and his circle developed a style that reminded some of the Whig society of early nineteenth-century Britain, others only of the 'jet set' of Palm Beach and St. Tropez. Led by a President who quoted Madame de Staël on television, Kennedy's world found a place for both Oleg Cassini gowns and Pablo Casals at the White House, even for a Postmaster-General who had published a novel.

In contrast to the Eisenhower era, in which the 'egghead' was an object of contempt, the new administration welcomed the contributions of men of ideas to public affairs. Kennedy made a point of honoring Nobel Prize winners at a White House dinner; with characteristic felicity he greeted them as 'the most extraordinary collection of talent, of human knowledge, that has ever been gathered together at the White House, with the possible exception of when Thomas Jefferson dined alone.' He also sought to encourage the arts, and to improve the appearance of Washington he invited architects like Mies van der Rohe to design Federal buildings, while his wife Jacqueline, born into the Newport plutocracy, refurbished the White House to make it a cherished 'national object.' Increasingly, Washington commentators talked of 'the Kennedy style.'

Yet no one was more impatient than Kennedy with the notion that the success of a presidency

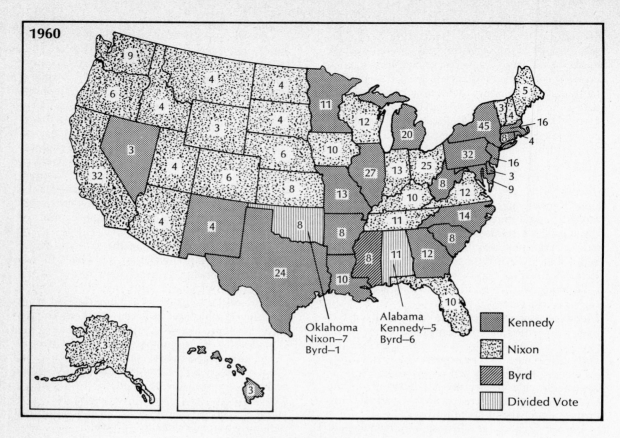

1960

Oklahoma
Nixon—7
Byrd—1

Alabama
Kennedy—5
Byrd—6

Kennedy

Nixon

Byrd

Divided Vote

Presidential Election, 1960

could be measured by style. The real test of his administration, he knew, would be whether he could achieve significant substantive changes. 'I run for the Presidency,' he had declared, 'because I do not want it said that the years when our generation held political power . . . were the years when America began to slip. I don't want historians writing in 1970 to say that the balance of power . . . began to turn against the United States and against the cause of freedom.' He approached this task full of hope, yet soberly, and the reference to 'balance of power' gave an ominous hint of what was to be his chief preoccupation.

The End of the Postwar World

At the same time that Kennedy sought to explore the 'New Frontier' of American society, he faced the formidable task of shaping a foreign policy which would accommodate to a world in flux. The Cold War had entered its sixteenth year, yet the situation in 1961 seemed to differ dramatically from that of 1945 and commentators spoke of 'the end of the postwar world.' The bipolar alignment of 1945 was breaking apart in both East and West. Within the Communist camp, the Soviet Union confronted the rivalry of Red China. In the West a prosperous Europe no longer recognized the United States as the unchallenged leader of the free world. The emerging nations of three continents, comprising more than half of the world's population, often found the East-West conflict irrelevant to their own needs.

Kennedy comprehended these changes, but he did not respond consistently to them. Weary of Dulles's chiliastic rhetoric, the new President reminded the American people that

the United States is neither omnipotent nor omniscient—that we are only six per cent of the world's population—that we cannot impose our will upon the other ninety-four per cent of mankind—that we cannot right every wrong or reverse every adversity—and that therefore there cannot be an American solution to every world problem.

It was a just observation but one he himself often forgot. He had charged during the campaign that under Eisenhower the United States had lost its 'position of pre-eminence,' and he intended to regain that position at the earliest opportunity. His choice for Secretary of State, Dean Rusk, shared some of Dulles's unfortunate quality of moralistic rigidity, and on more than one occasion the President's own rhetoric suggested that he anticipated a showdown with the Kremlin. For all of his emphasis on restraint, he was destined, in a number of fearful episodes, to carry brinkmanship farther than Dulles had dared, or Eisenhower permitted.

After his election, Kennedy learned the startling news that plans were far advanced for an invasion of Cuba to overthrow Fidel Castro. Since the spring of 1960 the CIA had been secretly training and arming hundreds of anti-Castro exiles in Florida and Guatemala. Kennedy gave the bizarre scheme his reluctant approval. On 17 April 1961 the invaders landed at the Bay of Pigs on the swampy southern coast of Cuba. In short order Castro's forces overwhelmed the rebels, who lacked adequate air cover. The United States was denounced for trying to destroy the government of a weaker nation and jeered for botching the attempt. The fiasco badly impaired the prestige of the Kennedy regime and put an end to the euphoria of the young administration.

Six weeks later, in a grim confrontation with Kennedy in Vienna, Khrushchev threatened to extinguish Western rights of access to Berlin. That summer the menace of nuclear war mounted dangerously. In response to appeals from Kennedy, Congress authorized the calling up of reserves and passed huge military appropriations, and a frenzy of air-raid shelter building swept the country. At border points in Berlin, American tanks eyed Soviet tanks. In August the crisis reached its peak when East Germany sealed the Berlin border and erected an ugly wall of concrete and barbed wire to halt the flow of refugees into West Berlin, a tacit admission of the Communist world's inability to compete with the West in Germany. To reassure West Berliners that the United States would not be driven out of the old German capital, Kennedy ordered a battle force of American troops down the 100-mile Autobahn from Western Germany through the Communist zone into Berlin. In another move in the war of nerves, the USSR that fall exploded some fifty nuclear devices, including a bomb nearly 3000 times more powerful than the one which had leveled Hiroshima.

By the end of the year the crisis had eased. Fallout shelter companies went bankrupt, and civil defense units folded. Critics charged that Kennedy, after behaving provocatively in Cuba, had over-reacted in Berlin. Yet just as he had resisted demands for full-scale American intervention in Cuba after the Bay of Pigs debacle, he had shown restraint as well as firmness in Berlin. In particular he had rejected counsel to smash through the Berlin Wall, for he recognized the danger of a nuclear exchange. The President told the country, 'In the thermonuclear age, any misjudgment on either side about the intentions of the other could rain more devastation in several hours than has been wrought in all the wars of human history.'

The Berlin experience reinforced Kennedy's determination to expand and diversify America's military forces. Whereas Dulles had relied inordinately on nuclear power, Kennedy and his Defense Secretary, Robert McNamara, developed a more balanced fighting capability. Kennedy won from Congress the biggest military and naval build-up in the country's history, one which increased the nuclear arsenal but placed more emphasis on mobile Polaris submarines than on overseas missile sites. The administration stressed

Adlai Stevenson and Eleanor Roosevelt at the United Nations, 2 March 1961. On Stevenson's recommendation, President Kennedy named Mrs. Roosevelt to the United States delegation to the Special Session of the General Assembly. Illness limited her service, but at a time when episodes like the Bay of Pigs elicited international distrust for American representatives, she remained a popular figure. When she dropped by the Human Rights Commission, the delegates broke into applause and the chairman invited her to speak. Near the end of the General Assembly session, she wrote the President, 'I don't think I have been very useful but I think I accomplished what Adlai wanted in just appearing at the UN.' (*The New York Times*)

The Berlin Wall. In February 1962 Robert F. Kennedy, seen here with Mayor Willy Brandt, addressed an enthusiastic crowd of 120,000 West Germans. The Wall, he told them, was a 'snake across the heart of your city.' (*Keystone Press Agency*)

the importance of conventional forces that could fight limited conflicts and special forces trained for jungle and guerilla warfare.

Even the exploration of space became implicated in the Cold War. From the moment on 20 February 1962 when Lt. Col. John Herschel Glenn, Jr., began the first of three orbits of the earth through Astronaut Gordon Cooper's landing in May 1963 'right on the money' after twenty-two orbits, the United States, which had once known little but bitter failure in its space efforts, scored a series of spectacular successes in the 'space race' with the Russians. In May 1961, Kennedy announced plans to land a man on the moon 'before this decade is out,' and Congress responded with huge appropriations for 'Project Apollo.'

In the fall of 1962 the United States came to the very brink of nuclear war. That summer, ships displaying the hammer and sickle had steamed boldly past the American base at Guantánamo, Cuba, and had unloaded missiles, patrol boats, and MIG fighters, as well as Russian technicians and instructors. This was no more than the United States had done for years in Turkey, Greece, and elsewhere, but the very fact that the Russian move was unprecedented gave it an ominous character. Hard-pressed to take action against this Soviet build-up, the President refused to risk a calamitous war so long as photographic reconnaissance showed no evidence of offensive missiles. On 16 October, however, he received shocking news: an Air Force U-2 had spotted Russian medium-range missiles in place, and the USSR, despite solemn assurances to the contrary, was rushing launching pads to completion. Missiles from these sites could deliver hydrogen warheads to targets as distant as Minneapolis.

Kennedy responded with a combination of determination and restraint. He would not permit the USSR to shift the balance of power by establishing a missile base only ninety miles from America's shores. Instead, on 22 October he quarantined arms shipments to Cuba and issued orders to intercept Russian vessels headed for the island. He warned the Kremlin that a nuclear attack from Cuba on any nation in the Western hemisphere would require a 'full retaliatory response on the Soviet Union' by the United States. Yet he rejected the advice of all his military advisers, many of his civilian aides, and even Senator Fulbright that he order an air strike, for this might lead to general war. Nonetheless, as Soviet vessels headed toward Havana where U.S. ships of war awaited them, the world shuddered at the imminence of Doomsday.

But the President's firm stand prevailed. At the end of two weeks, Kennedy, confronted by two letters from Khrushchev offering conflicting replies, chose to acknowledge the more acceptable one. Russia agreed to remove all offensive weapons and accept international inspection if the United States promised not to invade Cuba; the President consented, and the crisis ended. After a time the bases were dismantled and the missiles crated and withdrawn. Kennedy had won the war of nerves. Yet he took pains not to humiliate Khrushchev, for he recognized there were limits to 'eyeball to eyeball' diplomacy.

The missiles crisis had the ironic consequence of improving hopes for peace and permitting the President to direct his attention to more constructive programs, many of which he had initiated earlier. Kennedy appointed envoys sympathetic to the aspirations of the emerging nations in the Southern Hemisphere; expanded Food for Peace shipments of farm surpluses to almost $1.5 billion each year; and shifted the emphasis of foreign aid from military to economic assistance. The newly created Peace Corps, under the President's brother-in-law, R. Sargent Shriver, sent enthusiastic volunteers to offer educational or technical services to underdeveloped regions. Kennedy abandoned the Dulles attitude of condemning neutralism as immoral and gave his support to the attempt of the UN to build a central government in the Congo which would resist both Communist-oriented elements and right-wing secessionists. In August 1961 he proposed an ambitious program for Latin America: the Alliance for Progress. Upon agreement to basic reforms of their social structure to end the grievances Castroism might exploit, Latin American nations would be eligible for a ten-year, $20 billion program of aid, half of it provided by the United States. But the *Alianza* got off to a poor start, and in the end its contributions were negligible.

When on the morning before his inauguration Kennedy met with Eisenhower at the White House, the outgoing President pointed to a map of Southeast Asia and said: 'This is one of the problems I'm leaving you that I'm not happy about. We may have to fight.' In Laos, Kennedy, recognizing that the conservative regime backed by Eisenhower lacked popular support, abandoned the idea of an anti-Communist crusade and by an adroit use of force and diplomacy achieved his aim of 'a neutral and independent Laos, tied to no outside power,' and, at least for a time, removed from the Cold War.

Elsewhere in Southeast Asia, Kennedy showed less prudence. The Geneva settlement of 1954, which ended the Indochinese war, had stipulated the calling of free elections to unify Vietnam, but the elections were never held, and the United States backed Ngo Dinh Diem, who rapidly established authoritarian rule in the Republic of South Vietnam. When the Communist dictatorship of Ho Chi Minh in North Vietnam gave aid to the Viet Cong, the Communist guerillas of South Vietnam, Kennedy stepped up his support of Diem and sent military 'advisers' to assist the Saigon regime. In the spring of 1963 the Diem government took harsh repressive measures against dissidents, a policy which aroused the indignant opposition of many Americans to the Diem regime. In vain Kennedy urged Diem to undertake reforms to win the loyalty of landless peasants, and he expressed doubts about the extent of America's commitment to the South Vietnamese. However, he also believed that he could not afford a defeat like that of the French at Dienbienphu, and his advisers assured him that a military victory was within grasp. On 1 November 1963 the situation entered a new phase when, with the tacit approval of the American government, a military junta deposed Diem and murdered him and his brother; the United States promptly recognized the new government. At that point the American contingent in Vietnam was still less than 16,000, but Kennedy had planted the grapes of wrath which the next administration would nurture and harvest.

In Europe, President Kennedy sought to re-create the transatlantic community fractured by the independence of France's premier, Charles de Gaulle. The 'Grand Design' aimed to tie the United States into a European Common Market which would also admit the British. To make this possible, Kennedy secured from Congress the Trade Expansion Act of 1962 which empowered the President to lower tariff barriers in return for trade concessions. But when in January 1963 de Gaulle vetoed the admission of Britain to the Common Market, he ended Kennedy's dream of an 'Atlantic Partnership,' and when he insisted on developing an independent nuclear force, he jeopardized the unity of NATO. No longer could the United States count on getting its way in the Western world.

During his 1960 campaign Kennedy promised 'a supreme effort to break the log jam on disarmament and nuclear tests,' because 'the world was not meant to be a prison in which man awaits his executioner.' Though for more than two years the Russians balked, Kennedy persisted in his efforts toward achieving a test ban and a *détente* with the USSR. In June 1963 in a remarkable address at American University he stated that the United States should not see 'only a distorted and desperate view of the other side,' and urged: 'Let us reexamine our attitude toward the Soviet Union.' The President, observed one commentator, 'spoke at times of the cold war as if it hardly existed any longer.' As a consequence of Kennedy's appeal, and perhaps even more of the growing breach between the USSR and Red China, the Russians agreed to enter into negotiations toward a limited test ban in environments where physical inspection would not be required. At Moscow in July 1963 the United States, Great Britain, and the USSR signed a pact banning atmospheric and underwater testing of nuclear devices. It was a small step, but for the first time the powers had made a start, as the President said, toward getting 'the genie back in the bottle.' By the summer of 1963 there was renewed optimism about a thaw in

the Cold War. The Kremlin agreed to the installation of a 'hot line' which would connect it with the White House by telephone in the event of a future crisis that might result in nuclear war, and the President approved a big sale of wheat to Russia. Yet fundamental disagreements persisted, and in Southeast Asia the Vietnam war was a running sore.

The New Frontier

The Kennedy circle hoped that the first session of Congress in 1961 would rival Roosevelt's Hundred Days, but the young President quickly found that in domestic legislation as in foreign policy he could score only limited gains. The conservative coalition of Southern Democrats and Northern Republicans which had blocked almost all innovative social reform measures for a generation had no interest in moving America toward new frontiers. Congress turned down Kennedy's pleas for medical care for the aged (Medicare) and for a Department of Urban Affairs and Housing, while Federal aid to education was blocked once again because of an inability to resolve the issue centering on the demand of Roman Catholic bishops for grants to parochial schools.

Kennedy's critics deplored his failure to take advantage of his great popularity to win support for administration measures, and his lack of finesse in dealing with congressmen. They conceded that the conservative coalition posed difficulties, but pointed out that he had top-heavy Democratic majorities in both houses and complained that the President was too unwilling to risk defeat. Kennedy, doubtful that direct appeals to the nation would find an effective response, recalled that when in Shakespeare's *Henry IV, Part I*, Owen Glendower boasts, 'I can call spirits from the vasty deep,' Hotspur retorts:

Why, so can I, or so can any man;
But will they come when you do call for them?

Moreover Kennedy could point to a number of accomplishments. By a narrow margin he won a tough fight to dislodge conservatives from control of the Rules Committee. He pushed through legislation which raised the minimum wage,

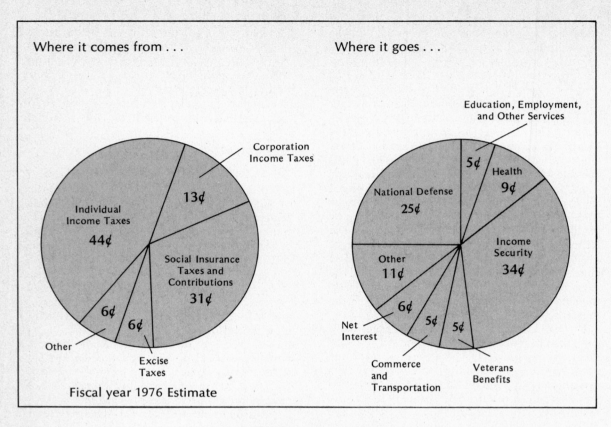

Where it comes from . . .

Corporation Income Taxes — 13¢

Individual Income Taxes — 44¢

Social Insurance Taxes and Contributions — 31¢

Other — 6¢

Excise Taxes — 6¢

Fiscal year 1976 Estimate

Where it goes . . .

Education, Employment, and Other Services — 5¢

Health — 9¢

National Defense — 25¢

Income Security — 34¢

Other — 11¢

Net Interest — 6¢

Commerce and Transportation — 5¢

Veterans Benefits — 5¢

The Federal Government Dollar

liberalized social security benefits, extended emergency unemployment compensation, appropriated funds for mental health, provided new housing, and funneled public-works money into depressed areas. Kennedy won approval for a Federal Water Pollution Control Act, and Congress established three national seashores, one of them at the President's favorite vacation place, Cape Cod.

Kennedy played an important part, too, in sparking an economic revival, although at the outset he moved too cautiously. He came to office at a time when nearly 7 per cent of the working force was unemployed in the fourth recession since World War II. Some of the President's liberal ad-

visers urged him to stimulate the economy through social spending, but in a period of near-crisis in the international balance of payments, Kennedy feared that massive expenditures might accelerate the gold drain and augment inflation. Instead, he adopted a more modest program which included easier credit. Together with stepped-up military and highway spending, these measures lifted the country out of the recession.

To preserve these gains, Kennedy emphasized the importance of maintaining the price level. The President was delighted when steel workers were persuaded to accept a non-inflationary wage contract. Ten days later he received the unwelcome news from Roger M. Blough, chairman of the

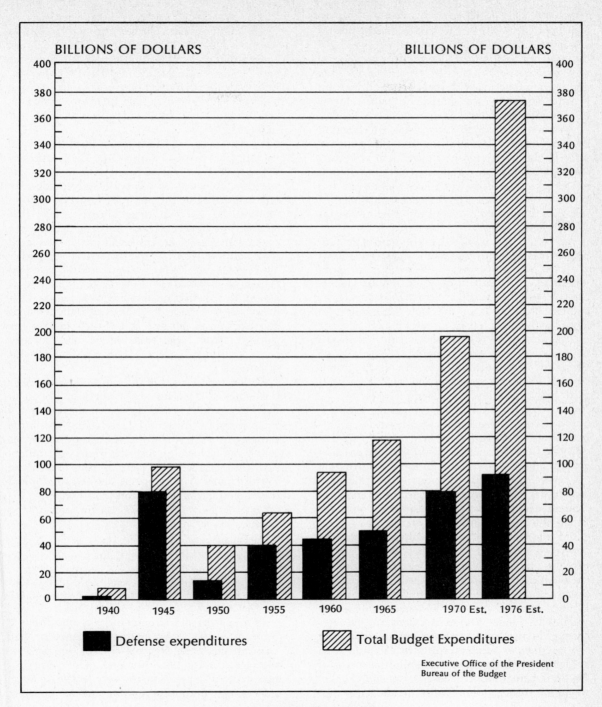

BILLIONS OF DOLLARS

BILLIONS OF DOLLARS

■ Defense expenditures

▨ Total Budget Expenditures

Executive Office of the President
Bureau of the Budget

National Spending 1940–1976

board of U.S. Steel, that his company was raising prices six dollars a ton; other steel firms quickly followed. Believing he had been betrayed by the steel corporations, Kennedy denounced the rise angrily in public and with more vivid language in private. To compel the companies to back down, the President mobilized the power of the Federal government: anti-trust suits, a tax investigaton by the Treasury, an FTC inquiry into collusive price-fixing, a Defense Department boycott. Within 72 hours steel capitulated. After Blough surrendered, Kennedy was asked what he had said to the steel magnate. The President responded: 'I told him that his men could keep their horses for the spring plowing.'

Although Kennedy's skillful management helped promote an upturn, the President recognized the need for further measures to create more jobs, and under the tutelage of Walter Heller, chairman of the Council of Economic Advisers, he embraced the ideas of the New Economics. In keeping with the New Economics heresy that the government should deliberately create deficits at a time when indices were climbing, Kennedy asked Congress for a multibillion dollar tax cut to encourage consumer spending and business investment and thus stimulate economic growth. The President did not live to see the tax cut adopted, but the Kennedy years mark a watershed in thinking about the economy.

In the field of civil rights, too, Kennedy at first moved slowly. He sought to avoid jeopardizing the rest of his program by antagonizing Southern Democrats over civil rights legislation, and consequently relied instead on executive action to advance civil rights. Unlike Eisenhower, he left no doubt that he supported the Brown decision. He appointed a number of Negroes to high places, notably Thurgood Marshall, general counsel of the NAACP, to the United States Circuit Court, Robert Weaver to head the Housing and Home Finance Agency, and Carl Rowan as ambassador to Finland. Under Robert Kennedy the Department of Justice acted far more vigorously than in the Eisenhower administration in bringing suits on denial of voting rights. When in the spring of 1961 Alabama mobs mauled 'freedom riders' traveling through the South to challenge Jim

Crow bus terminals and bombed and set afire a 'freedom bus,' the young Attorney-General dispatched hundreds of Federal marshals. Later that year, at the goading of the Department of Justice, the ICC ordered bus companies to desegregate interstate buses and to stop only at restaurants and terminals that took down their WHITE and COLORED signs.

When James H. Meredith, a black Air Force veteran, was denied admission to the University of Mississippi, a United States Circuit Court issued an injunction to compel his acceptance, an order sustained by the Supreme Court on 10 September 1962. Meredith tried to register later that month, but Governor Ross Barnett, defying the courts, physically interposed himself and used state police to rebuff Meredith. On 30 September 1962 President Kennedy sent several hundred Federal marshals to escort Meredith to the campus at Oxford. That night a howling mob engulfed the marshals, and Kennedy dispatched Federal troops and federalized national guardsmen; before the rioting ended, two were killed and seventy wounded. Under Federal bayonets, Meredith was registered.

Though the actions of the administration made the names of 'the Kennedy brothers' anathema in the Deep South, civil rights leaders castigated them for not acting more forcefully. During the campaign the President had said that discrimination in public housing could be wiped out 'tomorrow' with a stroke of the pen; but pens flooded the White House mail before he decided to act, and then administrative interpretation weakened his order of 20 November 1962. Martin Luther King stated:

This Administration has outstripped all previous ones in the breadth of its civil rights activity. Yet the movement, instead of breaking out into the open plains of progress, remains constricted and confined. A sweeping revolutionary force is pressed into a narrow tunnel.

In the spring and summer of 1963, one hundred years after the Emancipation Proclamation had been effected, the Negro's cry for equality resounded throughout the land. Dr. King announced: 'We're through with tokenism and gradualism and see-how-far-you've-comeism.

We're through with we've-done-more-for-your-people-than-anyone-elseism. We can't wait any longer. Now is the time.' North and South, blacks came out on the streets. In one week they carried out sixty separate demonstrations. That spring in Birmingham, where King led massive protests, civil rights marchers were met with snarling police dogs, electric cattle prods, and high-pressure fire hoses that sent demonstrators sprawling; and the police commissioner, Eugene 'Bull' Connor, crowded the jails with hundreds of young marchers. But they continued to sing their freedom anthem:

> Black and white together
> We shall overcome some day.

The combination of passive resistance—'Refrain from violence of fist, tongue or heart'—and the latent threat of violence won speedy results. In the first two weeks of June 1963 all the leading hotels and motels of Nashville agreed to desegregate; Atlanta announced plans to integrate its swimming pools; and blacks teed off on the municipal golf course in Jackson, Mississippi.

By 1963 only one state in the Union, Alabama, had no Negro attending any state-supported school with white students. When in June two young blacks sought to register at the University of Alabama, Governor George C. Wallace stood in the doorway to bar their way. But it was only a charade. After the President ordered the Alabama National Guard into Federal service, the Governor submitted. In 1956 Eisenhower had done nothing to help Autherine Lucy, but seven years later Kennedy threw the full weight of Federal power behind the black students. One week after the tawdry melodrama in the doorway, the President delivered a notable message calling for far-reaching Federal legislation to curb discrimination and segregation. He said:

Surely, in 1963, 100 years after Emancipation, it should not be necessary for any American citizen to demonstrate in the streets for the opportunity to stop at a hotel, or to eat at a lunch counter in the very department store in which he is shopping, or to enter a motion picture house, on the same terms as any other customer.

Other American Presidents, notably Harry Truman, had spoken out against discrimination, but Kennedy will go down in history as the first President to identify himself with the elimination of racial segregation.

Yet Kennedy's eloquence failed to move Congress to enact civil rights legislation that year, and his last months in office saw a rising tide of ugly rhetoric and violent deeds. A white racist murdered Medgar Evers, the head of the Mississippi NAACP, and in Jackson police used clubs, tear gas, and dogs against marchers who sought to pay tribute to their slain leader. A bomb in a Birmingham church killed four little Negro girls while they attended Sunday school. To win passage of Kennedy's comprehensive civil rights bill 200,000 people, 'black and white together,' took part in a 'March on Washington,' but it was clear that Congress would not pass the bill at that session, and on 12 November the New York Times wrote: 'Rarely has there been such a pervasive attitude of discouragement around Capitol Hill and such a feeling of helplessness to deal with it. This has been one of the least productive sessions of Congress within the memory of most of the members.'

Ten days later, on 22 November 1963, the President arrived in Dallas, recently the scene of displays of violence by the radical right. As the motor caravan of open cars moved through the streets of the city, the wife of Texas's governor, John Connally, remarked to Kennedy: 'You can't say that Dallas isn't friendly to you today.' An instant later the President was struck twice by rifle bullets; within minutes he was pronounced dead. Over that frightful weekend, yet another act of violence stunned a grief-stricken nation. Before a national television audience, the President's assassin, Lee Harvey Oswald, who had once expatriated himself to Russia, was murdered in a corridor of the city jail by Jack Ruby, the operator of a sleazy night club. A commission under Chief Justice Warren subsequently concluded that the assassination of the President was the work of Oswald, acting alone. The commission's findings have frequently been challenged, and though no substantial evidence of a conspiracy has been adduced, doubts remain.

Within a short time after the painful mourning

A Kennedy era retrospective. In 'Buffalo II' (1964), Robert Rauschenberg displays not only the late President at a press conference, but an American eagle, an army helicopter, an astronaut descending from outer space, and symbols of the consumer culture like a Coca-Cola sign, all caught in a swirl of paint indicative of a globe spinning out of control. Rauschenberg, born in Port Arthur, Texas, in 1925, had his first one-man show in New York in 1951, and is thought of as a New York City artist. He has adapted the Cubist innovation of collage to incorporate 'found objects' and photographs on a canvas of brushed and spilled paint reminiscent of the Abstract Expressionists. (*Coll. Mrs. Robert B. Mayer and the Estate of Robert B. Mayer*)

over the President's death, writers began to debate the meaning of his life. Some said that a President must be judged by his accomplishments, and that Kennedy's were small. Others granted that the achievements of ·his administration had been meager, but insisted that Kennedy, if he had lived, would have achieved much more. Kennedy, one writer observed, was a Prince Hal who died before Agincourt. Many, however, concluded that he was a man of greatness less for what he did than for what he was. They recalled his gallantry in the face of an intimate acquaintance with death and misfortune, and remembered his disarming wit: When asked how he became a wartime hero, he retorted, 'It was involuntary. They sank my boat.' At the time of his death, *Le Figaro* wrote: 'What remains as the loss . . . is a certain feeling of possibilities, of an *élan*, and—why not say it?—of an impression of beauty. These are not political qualities, but surely they are enduring legendary and mythological qualities.' It is the legend that built swiftly—of the young prince brutally dispossessed from Camelot.

But still others contended there was more to Kennedy's short presidency than the gossamer of legend. Arthur Schlesinger, Jr., who served on Kennedy's staff, wrote:

Yet he had accomplished so much: the new hope for peace on earth, the elimination of nuclear testing in the atmosphere and the abolition of nuclear diplomacy, the new policies toward Latin America and the third world, the reordering of American defense, the emancipation of the American Negro, the revolution in national economic policy, the concern for poverty, the stimulus to the arts, the fight for reason against extremism and mythology. . . . He re-established the republic as the first generation of our leaders saw it—young, brave, civilized, rational, gay, tough, questing, exultant in the excitement and potentiality in history.

Both critic and admirer tended in retrospect to be more sympathetic toward Kennedy's reluctance to divide the nation to achieve his goals. In the summer before his death he read to White House visitors the speech of Blanche of Castile from *King John*:

The sun's o'ercast with blood; fair day, adieu!
Which is the side that I must go withal?
I am with both: each army hath a hand;

And in their rage, I having hold of both,
They whirl asunder and dismember me.

No legacy of John F. Kennedy is more important than his championing of reason against the anarchy of Right and Left and his understanding that liberty is possible only in an ordered society. But in the end the whirling forces of violence, pulling the nation asunder, dismembered him.

The Great Society

At 2:38 p.m. on 22 November 1963, in the plane bearing the late President's body back to Washington, Lyndon Baines Johnson took the oath of office as President of the United States. A self-made man from the Texas hill country, Johnson quickly imprinted the LBJ brand on the White House. At fifty-five he was only a decade older than his predecessor; yet they seemed a generation apart, for Johnson had first come to Washington while Kennedy was a student at Choate. Intimidating, irascible, egocentric, he radiated a lust for power. 'The President,' wrote an English observer, 'comes into a room slowly and warily, as if he means to smell out the allegiance of everyone in it.' As Kennedy's patrician grace gave way to Johnson's country manners, the Eastern 'Establishment' so deplored the change in style that it frequently refused to give the new President his due.

For as chief legislator Johnson had infinitely greater experience than Kennedy. A veteran of twenty-three years in Congress, he had served in both houses and had risen to Majority Leader of the Senate, where he had won renown for his skill as a legislative tactician. Liberals, recalling his role as a moderate in the 1950's, feared he had only a lukewarm commitment to the Kennedy reforms; but Johnson, who came out of a Populist background and had been a protégé of Franklin Roosevelt's, had known hard times and the direct benefits of government as Kennedy had not, and he was determined to be a national, not a sectional, leader.

Johnson came to power at a time when political scientists were bewailing 'the deadlock of democracy,' but in short order he broke the log jam of Kennedy legislation. Within a month of his acces-

730

sion to office, Congress had voted $1.2 billion for college construction projects. He quickly secured assent for a mass transit bill and legislation to protect wilderness areas. By giving an impression of fiscal responsibility, he consolidated business interests behind liberal measures and induced congressmen to approve an $11.5 billion tax cut. The economy responded immediately; in 1964 gross national product soared $38 billion over the previous year.

The first resident of a Southern state to enter the White House since Andrew Johnson a century earlier, the new President urged Congress to enact the civil rights bill as a memorial to Kennedy. With the cooperation of the Democratic whip, Senator Hubert Humphrey, and Republicans like Senator Everett Dirksen, he dislodged the bill from the House Rules Committee and broke the Southern filibuster in the Senate. The Civil Rights Act of 1964, the most sweeping since Reconstruction, and the most effective, prohibited discrimination in places of public accommodation; authorized the Attorney-General to bring suits to speed school desegregation; strengthened voting rights statutes; set up an Equal Opportunity Commission to wipe out job discrimination; and empowered Federal agencies to withhold funds from state-administered programs that discriminated against Negroes.

Johnson not only won approval for proposals that had been stymied under Kennedy but began to enunciate his own program. His State of the Union Message in January 1964 announced: 'This Administration today, here and now, declares unconditional war on poverty in America.' Starting with the Economic Opportunity Act of 1964, Congress in the next two years voted funds for such anti-poverty projects as VISTA, the domestic peace corps; a Job Corps for dropouts; Upward Bound, to encourage bright slum children to go to college; a Neighborhood Youth Corps for jobless teenagers; Operation Head Start, to give pre-school training; and a Community Action Program to permit 'maximum feasible participation' of the poor. In an address at Ann Arbor in the spring of 1964, Johnson emphasized that he wanted to achieve a 'Great Society,' which he described as 'a place where the city of man serves not

LBJ in the shadow of FDR. Lyndon B. Johnson's attitude toward Franklin D. Roosevelt was ambivalent. On the day Roosevelt died, Johnson said, 'He was a daddy to me, always,' and Johnson's Great Society clearly owed a large debt to the New Deal. Yet Johnson was not content to emulate the hero of his youth; he sought to outdo him, to have History record him as a President who had achieved more than FDR. Furthermore, Roosevelt's reign provided not only an example to be followed but a failure to be avoided. Johnson carried a vivid memory of the fact that a Chief Executive may win in a landslide, as Roosevelt did in 1936, and be in deep trouble within a year—for Johnson first entered Congress in a special election in the spring of 1937 in the midst of FDR's abortive 'Court-packing' struggle. In 1964 Johnson triumphed by an even greater margin than FDR had, and within a year discord over Vietnam was pulling his coalition apart. (Wally McNamee, *The Washington Post*) only the needs of the body and the demands of commerce but the desire for beauty and the hunger for community.'

In the 1964 campaign the credo of the Great Society faced a sharp challenge from a new kind of Republican candidate, not a man of the center but of the Right, Barry Goldwater of Arizona. The Right had long argued that outside the Northeast there was a vast silent vote—conservative and isolationist—which had never been drawn to the polls. By offering 'a choice not an echo,' the Arizona senator, it was claimed, would command a huge support which 'Me Too' Republicans like Willkie had never been able to attract.

Certainly Goldwater seemed to offer a clear choice. He appealed to all those elements who were frustrated by modern America. At a time when the country was deeply troubled by extremists, he told the Republican convention, 'Extremism in the defense of liberty is no vice.' In Cleveland, a scene of racial strife, Goldwater, who had voted against the civil rights bill, exploited white 'backlash' by speaking for the freedom not to associate. In the Tennessee valley, he suggested the sale of the TVA to private interests. To the old folks of St. Petersburg he criticized social security. Such statements permitted Johnson to campaign both as the liberal candidate and as the 'safe' candidate.

In foreign affairs Goldwater, who raised uneasy feelings about whether he could be trusted with The Bomb, denounced the administration's 'no win' policy in Vietnam, which he promised to reverse. But Johnson took much of the sting out of this charge when in August he ordered air raids against North Vietnam in response to an attack by North Vietnamese gunboats on American destroyers in the Gulf of Tonkin. (Subsequently a Senate inquiry disclosed that the order for 'retaliation' had been prepared long before the Tonkin Gulf incident, and indicated that the whole 'incident' had been deliberately designed and fraudulently publicized to provoke a military response which could be used as justification for bombing North Vietnam.) The President seized advantage of the occasion to secure from Congress the 'Tonkin resolution' authorizing him 'to take all necessary measures to repel any armed attack against the forces of the United States and to prevent future aggression.' The resolution was so ambiguously worded that it could be interpreted as a blank check authorization for escalating the war, yet only two Senators, Morse of Oregon and Gruening of Alaska, had the courage to vote against it. At the same time Johnson appealed to the nation as the peace candidate. When Goldwater advocated enlarging the war, Johnson stated: 'We are not going to send American boys nine or ten thousand miles away from home to do what Asian boys ought to be doing for themselves.'

Goldwater's appeal received a sharp rebuke. The electorate exploded the theory of the silent vote and gave Lyndon Johnson a record-breaking popular majority. With 43 million votes (61.1 per cent) to Goldwater's 27 million (38.5 per cent), Johnson captured 44 states and the District of Columbia which, as a consequence of the Twenty-third Amendment ratified in 1961, voted in the national election. Negroes, once a mainstay of the G.O.P., voted better than 90 per cent for Johnson, and the Irish supported the President more strongly than they had Kennedy. The Republicans had the electoral votes only of Goldwater's Arizona and five Deep South states which backed him on the race issue. In Congress, so sizable was the Democratic margin that for the first time since 1938 the bipartisan conservative coalition would not hold the balance of power.

When the 89th Congress convened in January 1965, Johnson fired a fusillade of messages, and before Congress recessed in October he had gotten almost everything he had asked. Among the new measures were a number long deferred, including Medicare, to provide medical care for the aged under the social security system, Federal aid for elementary and secondary education, and the creation of a cabinet-level Department of Housing and Urban Development. Congress also expressed the Great Society's concern for 'quality' with the Highway Beautification Act. Throughout 1965 the United States witnessed a new national rite: the pageant of presidential bill-signing. Johnson signed the Voting Rights Act of 1965 in the President's Room of the Capitol where exactly 104 years before Lincoln had signed a bill freeing slaves impressed into the Confederate service. He

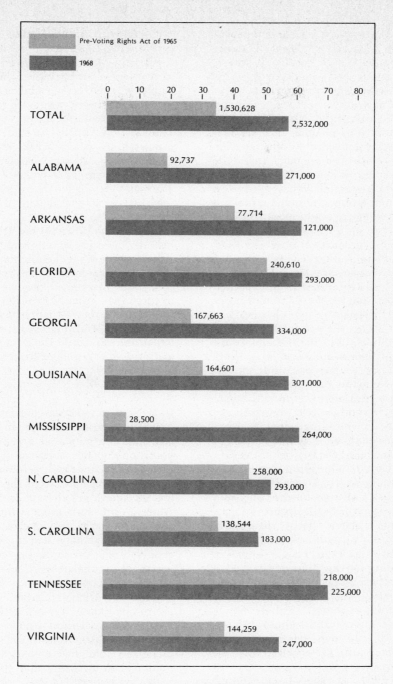

	0	10	20	30	40	50	60	70	80

TOTAL — 1,530,628 / 2,532,000

ALABAMA — 92,737 / 271,000

ARKANSAS — 77,714 / 121,000

FLORIDA — 240,610 / 293,000

GEORGIA — 167,663 / 334,000

LOUISIANA — 164,601 / 301,000

MISSISSIPPI — 28,500 / 264,000

N. CAROLINA — 258,000 / 293,000

S. CAROLINA — 138,544 / 183,000

TENNESSEE — 218,000 / 225,000

VIRGINIA — 144,259 / 247,000

Per Cent of Black Voting Age Population Registered

put his name to a Federal aid to elementary education bill at the one-room schoolhouse in Texas he had attended as a child. At the National Institutes of Health in Bethesda, Maryland, he signed a measure authorizing a multimillion-dollar program for medical research. On a bright autumn day in the Rose Garden of the White House, attended by such luminaries as Agnes de Mille, Ben Shahn, and Katherine Anne Porter, he affixed his name to a Federal-aid-to-the-arts bill. And in the shadow of the Statue of Liberty, facing Ellis Island, he signed into law the bill which ended racist restrictions on immigration, although for the first time it placed a ceiling on immigration from the Western Hemisphere. In 1965 and 1966, the 89th Congress, the most productive since the New Deal, adopted such innovations as legislation for rent subsidies, demonstration cities, a teacher corps, regional medical centers, 'vest pocket' parks, a rescue operation for the economically depressed region of 'Appalachia,' and Medicaid to provide medical care for the poor.

The Voting Rights Act of 1965 resulted from a series of demonstrations organized by Martin Luther King early in 1965 to point out the obstacles to voting by blacks that persisted despite civil rights statutes. In Dallas County, Alabama, where Negroes of voting age outnumbered whites, there were 28 whites registered for every one black. A series of violent responses to King's demonstrations, including the murder of the Rev. James J. Reeb, a Unitarian minister from Boston, in Selma, the county seat of Dallas County, led the President to ask Congress for sweeping new legislation. He also gave Federal support to a massive civil rights march from Selma to Montgomery, the state capital, which it reached on 25 March. That August the President approved a new law providing for direct Federal intervention. In districts where 50 per cent or more of the voting-age population was unregistered, Federal examiners would enroll voters.

Together with Supreme Court decisions based on the principle of 'one man, one vote,' which struck at malapportionment (starting with the 1962 landmark case of *Baker v. Carr*), and the ratification in 1964 of the Twenty-fourth Amendment, which curbed the use of the poll tax to abridge suffrage, the Voting Rights Act of 1965 took another long stride toward democratizing American politics. In the next three years Federal voting examiners registered more than 150,000 Negroes in five Deep South states. Mississippi, with 6.7 per cent of voting-age blacks registered in November 1964, had 59.8 per cent by the spring of 1968. In 1967 a major city chose a black mayor for the first time when Carl B. Stokes triumphed in Cleveland, and Mississippi elected a black legislator. That same year the President elevated Thurgood Marshall to the Supreme Court; he was the first Negro to be appointed to the highest tribunal.

Returned to office by the greatest landslide in history, Lyndon Johnson could take pride in the achievements of the 'fabulous 89th' which opened up prospects for a new era of reform and of Democratic domination for the next generation. But in these same months Johnson had made fateful commitments in Vietnam which would snuff out hopes for reform, undo much of the work of the 89th Congress, topple the Democrats from power, and drive the President from the White House.

The Vietnam Quagmire

In his State of the Union message in January 1965 President Johnson found the international picture so bright that he was able to place his main emphasis on domestic concerns. To be sure, Southeast Asia remained troublesome, but as the President began his new term there were still only 23,000 American 'advisers' in Vietnam. In Latin America, prospects seemed the most hopeful in years. The world rejoiced that in the recent election the United States had emphatically rejected a reckless Cold Warrior and given decisive backing instead to a candidate who had scoffed at the 'illusion that the United States can demand resolution of all the world's problems and mash a button and get the job done.' Yet before the new term was four months old the President had taken initiatives in Latin America that caused world-wide apprehension and had embarked on a course in Southeast Asia that would embroil the United States in the fourth largest war in its history and the longest.

In April 1965 civil strife erupted in the Dominican Republic, which had failed to find stability after the assassination of the ruthless dictator Trujillo. From the outset the American embassy and the State Department sided with conservative generals against the forces loyal to Juan Bosch, a democratic reformer. Claiming that Bosch's movement had been taken over by Communists, Johnson, without consulting with Latin American republics, landed more than 20,000 marines on the island. Critics at home and abroad deplored Johnson's misjudgment, for there was scant evidence that Communists controlled the movement, and denounced the President's usurpation of power and his heavy-handed, unilateral action that revived memories of gunboat diplomacy. The Dominican venture ended in a compromise solution, but it raised disquieting doubts about Johnson's ability to use power with discrimination.

Some months before the Dominican affair the President had made a much more critical decision about Vietnam. Even as he was denouncing Goldwater for his belligerency, he was listening to advisers who warned him that if he did not step up America's military contribution the anti-Communist forces in South Vietnam would be overwhelmed. Prudence might have suggested a reconsideration of America's commitment if after more than a decade of U.S. aid the army of the Saigon government could not overcome the Viet Cong forces it outnumbered six to one. But Johnson was not prudent and refused to admit 'defeat' or withdraw. Two days after he took office he had told the U.S. ambassador to Saigon, Henry Cabot Lodge, 'I am not going to lose Vietnam. I am not going to be the President who saw Southeast Asia go the way China went.'

On 7 February 1965 when a mortar attack by the Viet Cong on an American camp at Pleiku killed eight Americans and wounded 108 others, Johnson retaliated by ordering carrier-based air strikes against North Vietnam, for he viewed the Viet Cong in the South only as agents of Hanoi. So quickly did the President respond that it seemed clear that the administration had planned such a strike well in advance. On 7 March two battalions of marines, the first U.S. combat units,

landed in Vietnam, and by 28 June they had moved into battle in the land war on the Asian continent against which almost every military expert had warned. Month by month the war reeled farther out of control. Like the generals in World War I who thought 'one more push' on the Western front would terminate the war, the administration was confident that 'one more step' would bring an early victory; in each case it served only to raise the cost of the war. The Pentagon found it hard to believe that a little more firepower would not overcome these miserable guerillas, clad in black pajamas and supplied with ammunition carried over jungle trails on the backs of old women. As a result the war steadily became Americanized. During some weeks in the spring of 1966, U.S. casualties were greater than those of the South Vietnamese. By the middle of 1968 the total of U.S. forces had passed half a million, and by the end of the year American casualties exceeded 30,000 dead and 100,000 wounded.

The bombing, too, found new justifications. In April 1965 the President offered to begin 'unconditional discussions' to end the war and pledged a $1 billion investment in Southeast Asia including North Vietnam. When the Communists replied with a demand that the United States get out of Vietnam altogether, the administration expanded the bombing raids on the grounds that only additions to 'the quotient of pain' in North Vietnam would bring Hanoi to the bargaining table. By the end of 1968 the United States had dropped more tons of bombs on Vietnam than fell on Germany and Japan in World War II.

In the face of sharpening criticism Johnson and his associates asserted that they must persist, for if Vietnam went Communist, all Southeast Asia would tumble, the Pacific would become a 'Red Sea,' and America's defense line would fall back to California. They insisted that the Vietnamese conflict was not a civil war but a scheme by 'the Sino-Soviet military bloc' and more particularly by Red China to expand into Southeast Asia through its agents, the Communist regime of Ho Chi Minh in Hanoi and the Viet Cong. The Vietnam war represented the crucial test of the feasibility of 'wars of national liberation'; a Communist victory would lead Southeast Asian

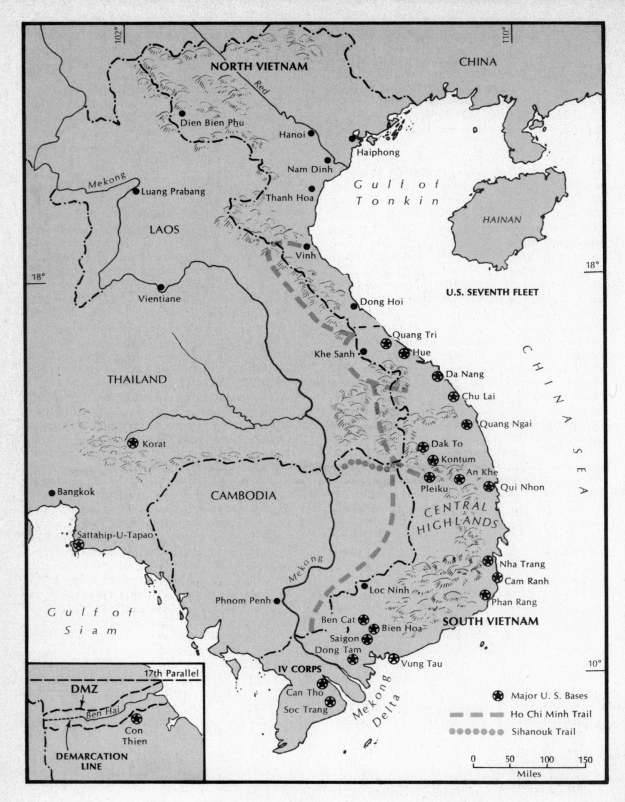

Vietnam

Vietnam, 1967. Men of the 1st Infantry Division, dropped from helicopters near Phuoc Vinh, dash for cover. (*U.S. Army Photograph*)

nations to turn to China as Balkan countries had sought out Nazi Germany after Munich. 'I'm not the village idiot,' Rusk said. 'I know Hitler was an Austrian and Mao is Chinese.... But what is common between the two situations is the phenomenon of aggression.'

Critics of Johnson's policy mounted a formidable assault on the administration's arguments. 'Hawks,' especially strong among conservative Republicans, urged the President to be even more bellicose; and as late as the spring of 1967 polls showed that a preponderance of opinion favored strong measures. More dangerous to the administration were the objections of the 'doves,' embracing both those who wanted to end the bombing in order to encourage negotiations and those who favored withdrawal, for the 'doves' threatened to disrupt the Johnson coalition. In the Senate the 'dove' faction, which in 1965 consisted of only a few mavericks, came by 1967 to include such respected Democratic leaders as the chairman of the Senate Foreign Relations Committee, J. William

Fulbright, Robert Kennedy of New York, Eugene McCarthy of Minnesota, and George McGovern of South Dakota.

The 'doves' denied that the United States was advancing the cause of democracy in Asia. The corrupt, repressive regime of Air Marshal Nguyen Cao Ky made a mockery of Washington's claim that it was defending the right of the Vietnamese to govern themselves. They viewed the Vietnam conflict as primarily a civil war in which the Viet Cong were an indigenous force, and they denied that the North Vietnamese, with a long history of distrusting the Chinese, were pawns of Peking. They scoffed at the Munich analogy and the domino theory; General David M. Shoup, former commandant of the Marine Corps, thought it 'ludicrous' to believe that if the Communists won in Vietnam, they would 'soon be knocking at the doors of Pearl Harbor.' Many of America's allies, it was noted, deplored the attempt of the United States to set itself up as judge, jury, and executioner for mankind, and Afro-Asian nations resented the bombing of non-white populations. Finally, the 'doves' pointed out that even if this dirty war, in which the United States employed napalm, and the South Vietnamese (as well as the Viet Cong) tortured prisoners, could be 'won,' Vietnam would be destroyed in the process, its countryside defoliated and gutted by bomb craters, its society shattered.

Such criticism fell on deaf ears. As Johnson jeered at 'nervous Nellies,' and Dean Rusk at 'the gullibility of educated men,' administration critics escalated their activities too, from 'teach-ins' on campuses and demonstrations at which draft cards were burned to more violent confrontations with authority. Johnson's policies, by reversing the apparent mandate of the 1964 election, soured many Americans, especially young people, on a political system which appeared to give them so little effective voice and put enormous strains on the bonds that held American society together. 'Our Saigon expedition,' warned Archibald MacLeish, 'may well turn out to have played the part in our ultimate destiny which the Syracusan expedition played in the destiny of Athens.'

As early as April 1965 Senator Wayne Morse predicted that Johnson's policy in Vietnam would send him 'out of office the most discredited President in the history of this nation'; but few doubted that Johnson, after his unprecedented victory in 1964, would win another four-year term in 1968. When on 30 November 1967 Senator Eugene J. McCarthy announced he would enter Democratic primaries to challenge the President over the issue of Vietnam, his decision was viewed as quixotic, for Johnson's control of his party appeared unshakable. However, liberal Democrats had become increasingly disenchanted with a war that, by draining money and energy from critical domestic problems, had brought to an abrupt halt the most promising reform movement in a generation, and, by overheating the economy, sent prices and interest rates soaring. With stunning rapidity the tide of events overwhelmed the President. On 23 January 1968 four North Korean gunboats seized U.S.S. *Pueblo*, a Navy intelligence-gathering ship (and held its officers and crew captive for the next eleven months). One week later, on 30 January, as Vietnam began to celebrate the Tet (lunar New Year) holiday, the Communists launched a massive assault on thirty provincial capitals, overran the ancient city of Hué, and in Saigon even held a portion of the American embassy compound for several hours. By demonstrating that after years of effort the United States and South Vietnam could not even safeguard Saigon, the Tet offensive shook the faith in Johnson's policy of some of the President's most stalwart supporters.

On 12 March 1968, Senator McCarthy surprised the nation by rolling up 40 per cent of the vote in the New Hampshire primary. Four days later Robert Kennedy plunged into the race for the Democratic nomination. Polls now indicated that McCarthy would carry Wisconsin against the administration (which he did), and showed only 26 per cent approved Johnson's handling of the Vietnam situation. On 31 March Johnson told a national television audience that he was restricting the areas of North Vietnam to which bombing missions would be sent and invited Hanoi to discuss a settlement, an invitation that was quickly accepted. He concluded his address with a statement that jolted the country: 'I shall not seek and I will not accept the nomination of my party for a

The President shows his scar. The ebullient LBJ created a minor ruckus when he raised his shirt and showed reporters the evidence of a recent operation. Some thought that such behavior on the part of a President of the United States was in poor taste. The episode also spawned an outrageous pun; Johnson, it was said, was the Abdominal Showman. In this 1966 caricature, David Levine has cleverly made use of the incident to suggest that the scar that the President has revealed is in the shape of the map of Vietnam, a jagged wound from which Johnson never recovered. (*The New York Review of Books*)

second term as your President.' The war in Vietnam, which had claimed so many victims, had now consumed Lyndon Johnson's ambitions too.

A Divided Nation

In the last years of Johnson's tenure, spasms of violence rocked the nation as bitterness over Vietnam, racial strife, and a series of assassinations raised doubts about the stability of American society. 'The rage to demolish,' in John Gardner's phrase, threatened the most venerable institutions and symbols; antiwar radicals rampaged through college campuses and burned the American flag. Even movements dedicated to peaceful change turned to the use of force. The Student Nonviolent Coordinating Committee chose as its leaders young men who urged blacks to use arms against whites, while in San Francisco's Haight-Ashbury, once the haunt of the flower children of the 'counter culture,' love posters were taken down and violent crime increased sharply.

On 11 August 1965, just five days after President Johnson signed the Voting Rights Act of 1965, which appeared to take the civil rights struggle out of the streets, the worst race riot in the nation's history erupted in the Watts community of Los Angeles. Six turbulent days left 34 dead, 856 injured, far more serious than any of the disturbances that had troubled Northern cities in 1964. In 1966 riots broke out in the Negro districts of Cleveland, Chicago, and other cities, and racial insurrections in 1967 took 26 lives in Newark and 43 in Detroit, where black militants set fires and sniped at police. Northern Negroes, who had long exercised such rights as the suffrage, complained that civil rights statutes did almost nothing to alleviate the hardships of the urban ghetto: unemployment, inferior education, slum housing, and hostile police.

In 1966 Negro rioters chanted a new slogan: 'black power,' which could mean anything from an expression of pride ('black is beautiful') to a determination to play the same kind of ethnic politics that groups like the Irish had found profitable, to hatred of whites, reliance on violent confrontations, or a rejection of integration in favor of separate black institutions. Black nationalism

Ben Shahn, 'I Think Continually of Those Who Were Truly Great.' Beneath the dove are the words of Stephen Spender's poem, and above are inscribed the names of those who died in the cause of civil rights or were the victims of wanton racial violence. Among the names that may be discerned are those of Jimmie Lee Jackson, a 26-year-old black youth slain in Marion, Ala.; the Rev. James J. Reeb, a white Unitarian minister from Boston clubbed to death in Selma, Ala.; Carol Robertson, 14, one of four Negro girls killed by a bomb while attending Sunday School at a church in Birmingham, Ala.; Viola Gregg Liuzzo, a white civil rights worker from Detroit, murdered on an Alabama highway on the night of the Selma-Montgomery march; Virgil Wade, a 13-year-old black boy killed as he rode his bicycle on the outskirts of Birmingham; and William L. Moore, a white postal worker who set out to walk alone from Chattanooga, Tenn., to Jackson, Miss., to show that peaceful protest against segregation was possible, and who, near Attalla, Ala., was shot to death. When Shahn was asked what his subjects were, he answered there were only three: 'aloneness, the impossibility of people to communicate, and the indestructible spirit of man.' (*Kennedy Galleries, New York*)

had long been espoused by the Black Muslim movement, most recently by the eloquent Malcolm X. In 1964 he defected from the organization, only to be murdered by three Black Muslims the next year. Many of his ideas, however, were taken up by the new leaders of SNCC, Stokely Carmichael and his even more militant successor, H. Rap Brown, and by such guerilla groups as the Black Panthers. Martin Luther King commented on this movement: 'In advocating violence it is imitating the worst, the most brutal, and the most uncivilized value of American life.' However, President Johnson's National Advisory Commission on Civil Disorders, headed by Governor Otto Kerner of Illinois, put the main blame for the riots on 'white racism,' and issued a grim warning: 'Our nation is moving toward two societies, one black, one white—separate and unequal.'

Reviled by vindictive racists, hounded by

J. Edgar Hoover and the FBI, and regarded as a compromiser by black extremists, Dr. Martin Luther King still hoped to bridge the gulf between the two societies. As the leading apostle of non-violence, he had been honored with the award of the Nobel Peace Prize, but in the United States he had made little headway in his recent efforts on behalf of the poor of all races. He met rebuff both in Chicago, where techniques of passive resistance encountered obdurate hostility, and in Memphis, where he came to the aid of striking garbage collectors. In the early evening of 4 April 1968, as he stood on the balcony of a Memphis motel, Dr. King was shot and killed. James Earl Ray, a white man who was an escaped convict, was imprisoned for the crime.

The nation grieved for the slain leader who in his thirty-nine years had contributed so much, but it reacted to his death in the same ambiguous

MICHAEL SCHWERNER

Ben Shahn

The civil rights martyrs. On 21 June 1964 James Earl Chaney, a 21-year-old black from Meridian, Miss., Andrew Goodman, a 20-year-old white from New York who was a student at Queens College, and Michael Henry Schwerner, a 24-year-old white from Brooklyn, all of whom were taking part in a project to register Negro voters in Mississippi, disappeared. On 4 August their bullet-ridden bodies were unearthed; before Chaney was murdered, he had been subjected to an 'inhuman beating.' These lithographs are by Ben Shahn. (*Philadelphia Museum of Art, Given by the Lawyers Constitutional Defense Fund of the American Civil Liberties Union.*)

way it had responded to his life. The death of a man who had so often cautioned against violence triggered race riots in a hundred cities, at the cost of thirty-nine lives. On 10 April 1968, a day after Dr. King was buried, the House of Representatives passed a 'fair housing' bill designed to ban racial discrimination in 80 per cent of housing in the United States. Yet even King's death failed to move 171 Congressmen who voted in opposition. The act also set penalties for activities in interstate commerce aimed at encouraging riots.

With King gone many looked toward Robert Kennedy as the one national leader who had the confidence of the poor of both races. A Kennedy campaign aide, Charles Evers, brother of the murdered Medgar Evers, later called him 'the only white man in this country I really trusted.' Kennedy won in Indiana, but when McCarthy upset him in Oregon, he had to capture the California

primary of 5 June 1968 if he was to stay in the race. A little after midnight it became clear that Kennedy had won California and South Dakota on the same day. As he walked through a kitchen passageway at the Ambassador Hotel in Los Angeles, he was shot and fatally wounded by a Jordanian immigrant, Sirhan Bishara Sirhan, who resented Kennedy's support of Israel. At the age of forty-two, Robert Francis Kennedy was buried beside his brother in the hillside plot at Arlington National Cemetery.

The anguish over the deaths of Robert Kennedy and Martin Luther King raised probing questions about the nature of American society. Their deaths recalled other recent murders: John Kennedy, Medgar Evers, Rev. James Reeb, Malcolm X, the four Negro girls killed by a bomb in a Birmingham church, the three young men—James Chaney, Andrew Goodman, and Michael

Schwerner—brutally murdered by enemies of civil rights in Mississippi, and too many more. The rising crime rate, the casual merchandising of slaughter on television, the resort to coercion by students at Berkeley, Columbia, and other universities, and the lobbying by the National Rifle Association against effective gun control legislation caused many to ask whether violence was not the American way of life. Such assessments were often ill-balanced, for the United States had achieved notable success in developing peaceful solutions to social crises; yet in the context of the continuing warfare in Vietnam, the events of the spring of 1968 could not help but be disturbing.

The winds of violence whistled through the chinks in the American political structure in the 1968 campaign, but the party system withstood the buffeting. To the Democratic convention city of Chicago that summer came the youthful idealists of Senator McCarthy's 'Children's Crusade.' To Chicago, too, came itinerant revolutionists bent on provoking a violent confrontation. In most respects the convention was exceptionally democratic; it suspended the unit rule, seated black delegates from states like Mississippi, and provided for full debate on Vietnam. But the McCarthy enthusiasts believed the will of the people had been flouted when the presidential nomination went to Vice-President Hubert Humphrey, whose delegates had been chosen at party meetings rather than in primaries. Bitter exchanges marred the convention proceedings while in the streets anti-war demonstrators clashed with Mayor Richard J. Daley's police, some of whom ran amok. Televised accounts of the party warfare and the mayhem in the streets placed an enormous handicap on Humphrey's campaign.

Millions of Americans felt that in being asked to choose between Humphrey and the Republican nominee Richard Nixon they were offered no real choice, since both men had been identified with a 'hard' line in Vietnam and with the politics of the older generation. Humphrey countered by pointing to his outstanding record as leader of the Senate liberals and spokesman for civil rights. Moreover, he had made a fortunate move when he picked Senator Edmund S. Muskie to be his running mate. On the other hand, Nixon had selected for his vice-presidential candidate Governor Spiro T. Agnew of Maryland, who, by racial slurs and chauvinistic invective, tempted Democratic dissidents to return to the fold.

Still other Americans expressed a different kind of dissatisfaction with the presidential choices in 1968 by building the most formidable third party in a generation. Governor George Wallace's American Independent party appealed chiefly to those who resented gains for the Negro, especially in the South but also among many white workingmen in the Northern cities. Wallace's plea for 'law and order,' although largely a euphemism for racial discrimination, also struck a chord among those who blamed the upsurge of crime and the violence of college students and anti-war demonstrators on men in authority, especially 'permissive' Supreme Court justices. To exploit the sentiment of those who criticized Johnson for not prosecuting the war more unrestrainedly, Wallace chose as his running mate General Curtis Le May, former Air Force Chief of Staff who was known for his strident advocacy of bombing North Vietnam back to the Stone Age. But Le May's complaint about the country's 'phobia' concerning the use of nuclear weapons drove still more Democratic defectors back into the arms of their party.

Humphrey, who started out far behind, almost pulled even in the final five days of the campaign after Johnson announced he was halting the bombing of North Vietnam, but Nixon scored a narrow victory. With 31.8 million votes (43.4 per cent) Nixon gained a 301–191 margin in the Electoral College. Humphrey, with 31.3 million votes (42.7 per cent), continued to draw most of his support from the 'Roosevelt coalition' of lower-income voters in the big cities, including 85 per cent of the non-white vote. But his share of the ballots of manual workers fell off sharply, and the once-Solid South was so shattered that he captured only one Southern state, Texas. Wallace polled 9.9 million votes (13.5 per cent) and 46 electoral votes, all in the South. The Vietnam war and social disruption had cost the Democrats dearly. In four years a plurality of 16 million votes on the presidential line had evaporated, and for the first time a party that won a landslide victory lost control of the White House at the subsequent election.

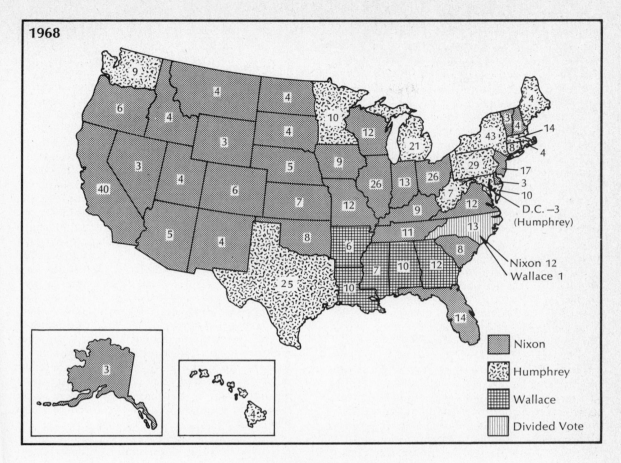

Presidential Election, 1968

As the grim year of 1968 drew to an end the country found excitement in a majestic voyage that dramatized the potentialities of American society. In Christmas week Col. Frank Borman, Capt. James A. Lovell, Jr., and Col. William A. Anders of Apollo 8 became the first mortals to see the dark side of the moon. Many wondered why the United States, capable of so spectacular an achievement in outer space, could not approach its problems on earth with the same dedication and resourcefulness. As President Johnson prepared to turn over the reins of office to a successor known neither for his imagination nor his scruples, few could be sanguine about the prospects.

The Nixon Melodrama

The outcome of the 1968 election set the ill-fated course of the Nixon presidency. Despite all that had befallen the Democratic administration, Nixon had won only a narrow triumph, with the smallest percentage of the popular vote of any victor since 1912. Long thought of as a 'born loser,' he was determined to win re-election in 1972—and by a landslide. To do so he adopted a number of strategies: moderation to appeal to the Center, divisiveness to attract the followers of George Wallace, and exploitation of the issues of cultural politics that were troubling 'Middle

America.' In the end, the Nixon 'team,' not content with these expedients, did not scruple at adopting methods that would reduce the presidency morally to its lowest point in the nation's history and bring about a crisis of confidence in the democratic process.

When analysts sifted through the 1968 returns, they found that voters were more concerned about 'law and order' than any other problem, even the Vietnam war, and Nixon made the most of this. The country had been shaken by five consecutive summers of rioting in the black ghettos; by campus violence; and by a sharp rise in crime, including assaults upon persons. In his inaugural address, the President declared:

America has suffered from a fever of words; from inflated rhetoric that promises more than it can deliver; from angry rhetoric that fans discontents into hatreds; from bombastic rhetoric that postures instead of persuading.
We cannot learn from one another until we stop shouting at one another—until we speak quietly enough so that our words can be heard as well as our voices.

Nixon had some initial success in portraying himself as a promoter of domestic peace. The ghetto turbulence abruptly ended, to a certain extent because Nixon, by raising few expectations, created less possibility of disappointment. The bloodletting in Vietnam continued (one-third of American deaths in the war would occur under Nixon), but in the process of taking as long to end the war as Lincoln had required to fight the Civil War, he did reduce United States troop levels, which had peaked at 543,000 in 1968 to 39,000 on 1 September 1972. Furthermore, a reform of the draft diminished anxiety for registrants with higher numbers. In part as a consequence of these developments, the mood of protest on college campuses became muted, if only for a time.

However, Nixon's role as a builder of bridges over troubled waters proved less congenial than that of capitalizing on apprehension about social change. Millions of Americans strongly disapproved of the ideology of the 'counter culture,' which denigrated respected institutions and values, notably the work ethic. Dislike of the counter culture was especially marked among lower in-

come voters, long the ballast of the Democratic party. In the Johnson years the 'greening of America' had taken a bewildering variety of forms, including experimentation with psychedelic drugs, uninhibited sexual behavior, and the vogue of 'acid' rock music, a volatile mixture which in Nixon's first year in office drew hundreds of thousands of young people to the Woodstock Music and Art Fair.

At the same time the counter culture was assailing American folkways, the women's liberation movement was raising challenges to traditional perceptions of sex roles and the structure of the family. In the 1960's two-thirds of new jobs went to women, and by 1970 43 per cent of adult women were in the labor force. Advocates of equal opportunity, who succeeded in securing legislation like the Civil Rights Act of 1964 which forbade discrimination in employment on the basis of sex, sometimes asked only that women receive equal pay for equal work. But increasingly, they advanced other demands—for child care centers, an end to restrictions on abortion, and sex quotas in hiring—that defied orthodox conceptions of woman's 'place' and the nuclear family. These innovations seemed especially unsettling in a period when the stability of the family was shaken by an 80 per cent rise in the number of divorces between 1960 and 1972.

Into this highly controverted arena of cultural politics barged the Nixon administration, led by the lubberly Spiro Agnew who took to the stump to deplore the erosion of time-honored American values. 'We have gone through a debilitating, enervating age of indulgence,' the Vice-President said. Agnew barnstormed less on the old issues of economic policy than on the latest disputes about life style, although he linked the two when he blamed changing attitudes on 'a political hedonism that permeates the philosophy of the radical liberals' and when he excoriated Dr. Benjamin Spock, author of an immensely popular manual on child-rearing and an outspoken foe of the Vietnam war. Nixon, too, berated the 'Spock-marked generation,' attacked 'abortion on demand,' and denounced the latitudinarian conclusions of the Federal Commission on Obscenity and Pornography.

The disintegration of the consumer culture. Probably the best known work of 'pop art' is Andy Warhol's silk-screen of a bright array of Campbell's soup cans in cheerful order on a supermarket shelf. Such a painting could be perceived either as indifferent to the banality of its subject or even as a celebration of consumer goods. Warhol's 'Campbell's Soup Can with Peeling Label,' however, implies the decay of a consumer-oriented society. (*Kunsthaus, Zürich*)

Many of the new manifestations converged on the Supreme Court. In invalidating the censorship of *Lady Chatterley's Lover* in 1959, the Court stated that the First Amendment 'protects advocacy of opinion that adultery may sometimes be proper, no less than advocacy of socialism or the single tax,' and in defense of *Fanny Hill* in 1966, the justices ruled that a book could not be proscribed unless it was found 'to be utterly without redeeming social value.' During the same years when it was ending virtually all restrictions on pornography, the Warren Court stirred up an even sharper controversy by outlawing Bible-reading and prayer in public schools as a violation of the First Amendment. 'They've put the Negroes in the schools,' expostulated an Alabama Congressman, 'and now they've driven God out.' Many of the same people who were exercised about these decisions deplored the rulings of the Court in cases such as *Escobedo v. Illinois* (1964), which stipulated that a suspect must be informed of his right to remain silent and to have counsel present when he was interrogated. Though civil libertarians applauded decisions like *Gideon v. Wainwright* (1963), which stipulated that the state must provide a pauper charged with a felony with an attorney at public expense, others, frequently unreasonably, blamed the Warren Court for the dramatic rise in crime in the cities, and in the climactic *Miranda* case of 1966, which broadened the 'due process' requirement of the Fourteenth Amendment, the four dissenting justices warned against returning 'a killer, a rapist or other criminal to the streets . . . to repeat his crime whenever it pleases him.'

When Nixon took office, he set out to reverse this jurisprudence by appointing law-and-order judges who would be 'strict constructionists,' and he was soon given the opportunity to fill several vacancies. In 1969, Chief Justice Warren retired, and the President chose a federal judge, Warren Burger, to replace him. That selection occasioned little comment, but when he and his maladroit Attorney-General, John Mitchell, attempted to elevate judges from Southern circuits to the High Court they were twice rebuffed by the Senate, a humiliation that had not been visited on an American President in this century. Nixon and Mitchell then came up with two more names that were so unacceptable that they did not submit them. All of this greatly distressed a Republican Senator from Nebraska who said of one of Nixon's nominees: 'There are lots of mediocre judges and people and lawyers. They are entitled to a little representation aren't they?... We can't have all Brandeises and Frankfurters and Cardozos and stuff like that there.'

In the end Nixon, by more respectable though still conservative appointments, did succeed in modifying the stance of the Court but not nearly to the extent he desired. In a number of decisions the 'Burger Court' softened the position of the Warren Court. Nonetheless, it also broadened the orbit of cultural politics and extended the safeguards of civil liberties and civil rights. The Court elaborated the right of a woman to an abortion during the first three months of pregnancy, curbed the imposition of the death penalty, repudiated the Attorney-General's arrogant claim that he could utilize wiretaps on domestic dissenters without a court order, and held that the government could not restrain publication of the 'Pentagon Papers,' a detailed examination of Vietnam policy which a Pentagon expert, Daniel Ellsberg, leaked to the press. In a unanimous opinion in April 1971, the Court, in a Charlotte, North Carolina, case, sustained the busing of pupils out of their neighborhoods in order to foster racial integration.

The Nixon administration found this last decision especially galling, for it had been pursuing a 'Southern strategy' to wean George Wallace's followers away from him. The aborted attempt to name a South Carolina judge to the Supreme Court had been aimed at pleasing that state's archconservative senator, Strom Thurmond, who regarded Agnew as the greatest Vice-President America had ever had, save only for Calhoun. Toward blacks the administration pursued a policy of 'benign neglect,' in the words of Nixon's ad-

viser Daniel Patrick Moynihan. Sometimes 'benign neglect' implied continuing to foster racial gains but doing it surreptitiously so as not to antagonize the Wallaceites. At other times it meant outright hostility to programs of the Kennedy-Johnson era, as when Mitchell's Department of Justice opposed extension of the Voting Rights Act of 1965. When the administration asked a federal court to delay the desegregation of Mississippi schools, the NAACP asked to have the United States named a defendant, for 'it no longer seeks to represent the rights of Negro children.'

The accent on 'benign neglect' came in an era when other groups besides blacks were insisting on their rights. So substantial was the migration from the Caribbean islands in the quarter-century after World War II that there were more Puerto Ricans in New York than in San Juan, and by 1970 nearly a quarter of a million Cubans in Florida's Dade County; both groups wanted greater recognition. Over one-fourth of Mexican-Americans lived below the poverty line; cultural nationalists furthered the cause of these 'Chicanos,' and Cesar Chavez led strikes of migrant workers in the vineyards and lettuce fields of California that evoked sympathy among liberal Democrats. However, the Nixon administration showed no understanding of the aspirations of Spanish-American groups or of the afflictions of American Indians who, with a rapidly growing population, had a life expectancy of only 46 years, compared with the national average of 69, and the country's highest rate of infant mortality. The increasing militance of Indian groups, beginning with an occupation of Alcatraz Island in San Francisco Bay and running through the ransacking of the Bureau of Indian Affairs headquarters in Washington, reached a climax in the Nixon period in a bloody confrontation on the Sioux reservation at Wounded Knee.

The hard-shelled indifference of the Nixon administration reflected the composition of its leadership. 'Richard Nixon's White House is a controlled, antiseptic place, not unlike the upper tier of a giant corporation,' observed an American journal, while a British commentary referred to the Nixon cabinet as 'a steering committee of the conformist middle class triumphant.' Dominating

Nixon the hardhat. On 8 May 1970 construction workers wearing 'hardhats' and shouting 'All the way USA' and 'Love it or leave it' beat up student antiwar demonstrators in New York City. 'Once the defender of economic and social justice, in the vanguard of progressive movements, we now find the AFL-CIO endorsing the war in Vietnam,' said one union official ruefully. 'It has totally alienated our youth and antagonized others as well.' By donning a hardhat, President Nixon identified himself both with the prowar stance of the construction workers and with their tactics. (*National Archives*)

the White House staff were two former 'advance men,' Harry R. Haldeman and John Ehrlichman who, with their Prussian haircuts and no-nonsense comportment, seemed so much alike that they were called the 'Rosencrantz and Guildenstern' of the administration. The President for his part frequently isolated himself behind the 'Berlin Wall' erected by his two main advisers on domestic policy.

In foreign affairs, too, despite all of the buncombe about bringing the nation together, Nixon launched periodic forays that provoked paroxysms of rage. Although Nixon had claimed during the 1968 campaign that he had a plan to move the Vietnam conflict to a speedy end, the war went on,

year in, year out. In 1969 massive antiwar demonstrations shook Washington, but to no avail. The President detonated an even greater explosion in 1970 when he sent American troops and bombers into Cambodia and sought to justify the invasion by saying, 'We will not be humiliated. We will not be defeated.... If when the chips are down, the world's most powerful nation ... acts like a pitiful, helpless giant, the forces of totalitarianism and anarchy will threaten free nations and free institutions throughout the world.' Nixon's expansion of the fighting ignited campuses from coast to coast. Martial law was proclaimed in a number of states, including Ohio, where Kent State demonstrators firebombed the ROTC building. The situation became more inflamed when on 4 May National Guardsmen shot to death four students at Kent State and, in an unrelated incident on 15 May, Mississippi troopers killed two students at Jackson State College. In protest, indignant students, faculty, and administrators shut down scores of colleges, some for the rest of the semester.

The unmistakable evidence that he had miscalculated caused Nixon to back-track momentarily by pulling out of Cambodia, but he soon resumed a more bellicose line, in part in order to appeal to those who favored a hawkish foreign policy. When New York's mayor, John Lindsay, ordered the flag at City Hall lowered to half-staff in respect for the Kent State victims, hard-hatted construction workers rampaged through the financial district bludgeoning long-haired students and ran the flag up again. Nixon deliberately cultivated both these 'hard hats' and the disciples of George Wallace by intervening in the case of Lt. William L. Calley, Jr., convicted of slaughtering several hundred defenseless civilians at the South Vietnamese hamlet of Mylai. In 1971 the President incited new outbursts by invading Laos, and in 1972 he risked a confrontation with Russia by saturation bombing of North Vietnam and by mining harbors used by Soviet vessels there.

Yet though Nixon embarked on inflammatory adventures in foreign policy, he also undertook initiatives which lent credence to his claim to be a sponsor of *détente*. In 1969 he proclaimed a 'Nixon Doctrine,' which implied willingness to forego any more interventions like Vietnam. He appointed as his National Security Adviser a Harvard professor, Henry Kissinger, who was regarded as a 'realist' in foreign affairs, and in 1972 the President flew to Moscow to negotiate a treaty limiting strategic missiles. He also ended the production of biological weapons. But Nixon created the greatest sensation by flying to Peking in February 1972 to confer with Premier Chou En-lai. A man who had built a career on relentless animosity to the Communist world had become the first President to contrive an opening to the People's Republic of China.

Nixon also gained stature from an extraordinary event toward which he had made no

Man on the Moon. The astronaut Col. Edwin E. 'Buzz' Aldrin, Jr. is photographed walking on the lunar surface. In Aldrin's visor are reflected the photographer, Neil A. Armstrong, civilian commander of Apollo II, and the lunar landing vehicle, *Eagle*. Notice the American flag patch, emblem of U.S. victory in the 'space race.' Aldrin's 73-year-old father, a veteran aviator who was a friend of Orville Wright and Charles Lindbergh, suggested as the text for their mission Psalm 8: 'When we behold the heavens, the work of Your fingers, the moon and the stars which You set in place; what is man that You should be mindful of him, or the son of man that You should care for him.' On 20 July 1976, on the seventh anniversary of this extraordinary event, an American spacecraft made the first successful landing on Mars, more than 212 million miles from Earth. (*NASA*)

contribution—man's first voyage to the moon. On 20 July 1969, four days after they blasted off from earth, two members of the crew of Apollo 11—Neil A. Armstrong and Col. Edwin E. Aldrin, Jr.—became the first men ever to walk on the moon. While Lt. Col. Michael Collins maneuvered their spaceship, Armstrong and Aldrin placed on the surface of the moon a plaque signed by the crew and President Nixon that read: '*Here men from the planet earth first set foot upon the moon July 1969, A.D. We came in peace for all mankind.*' Some complained that the country's resources would be better spent in coping with terrestrial problems, but more were impressed by the achievement, and Nixon, sharing the television screen with the astronauts, profited from the approbation for the journey to the Sea of Tranquility.

The President's domestic policies, too, sometimes departed from the conservatism of Mitchell's 'Southern strategy.' The proportion of pupils in all-black schools fell precipitously from 68 per cent in 1968 to 18 per cent in 1970, in large part because of longtime trends, some of which Nixon resisted, but also because of positive steps as when the administration sued the entire state of Georgia to end dual educational systems. A series of statutes starting with the National Environmental Policy Act of 1969 improved the quality of air and water, and the Environmental Protection Agency, created in 1970, enforced higher standards on the automobile industry and on municipalities and corporations. Frequently initiatives came not from the White House but from the Democratic Congress, as when plans to construct supersonic transport aircraft were frustrated. Still, either because of or despite the attitude of the White House, social advances continued in the Nixon years. Social security benefits increased more than 50 per cent from 1969 to 1972, and federal expenditures for education and health soared. Though these developments were offset by other moves in a reactionary direction, liberals found them a welcome surprise. 'Everybody is saying that Mr. Nixon is doing better than they expected,' noted James Reston, 'which proves the success of past failures.'

Nixon also showed more flexibility than antici-pated in coping with the main domestic issue he confronted—the ailing economy. From Lyndon Johnson he had inherited an economy overstimulated by spending on the Vietnam war, and soon he had to deal with an unpropitious combination that liberal economists had not envisaged: skyrocketing prices accompanied by rapidly mounting unemployment. The President started out by prescribing conventional nostrums, but when these failed, he turned to deficit spending. 'I am now a Keynesian,' he said; as one commentator remarked, that was 'a little like a Christian crusader saying, "All things considered, I think Mohammed was right."' But Nixon continued to resist more direct intervention. 'Controls, Oh my God, no!' he expostulated in 1969. However, when in 1971 prices continued to rise, and the nation experienced its first trade deficit since 1893, he ordered a temporary freeze on wages, prices, and rents and devalued the dollar. Nixon's new policies enjoyed only moderate success. Nonetheless, he was able to make his bid for re-election at a time when many Americans were enjoying the benefits of the world's first trillion-dollar economy.

In the 1972 campaign Nixon had the decisive advantage of prevailing over both the Right and the Center sectors of the electorate. His main worry from the Right ended on 15 May 1972 when George Wallace, who showed conspicuous strength among blue-collar workers in Democratic primaries, was shot and so badly wounded that he had to withdraw from the presidential race. Nixon appropriated the Center when the Democrats chose as their Presidential nominee a factionalist, Senator George McGovern. An antiwar liberal who had made an admirable record, McGovern won the nomination as the result of changes in party procedure that alienated union chieftains and big city organizations and left the erroneous impression that he was the candidate of the counter culture. He had the further misfortune of picking as his running mate Senator Thomas Eagleton of Missouri and, after it came out that Eagleton had been treated for mental illness, dropping him from the ticket. Nixon overwhelmed McGovern with 47.2 million votes (60.7 per cent) to 29.2 million and a 520 to 17 triumph in the Electoral College; McGovern carried only Massachusetts and the predominantly black District of Columbia. Especially disappointing to McGovern was the performance of young people; an act of Congress and the Twenty-sixth Amendment, ratified in 1971, had given eighteen-year-olds the right to vote, but the majority of them did not trouble to go to the polls.

On the eve of the election Henry Kissinger had marshaled votes for Nixon by stating, 'Peace is at hand.' This welcome announcement proved premature, for in the month after his re-election the President celebrated the Christmas season by approving a merciless bombing of North Vietnam, especially of heavily populated Hanoi, that dismayed and disgusted large numbers of Americans and brought worldwide censure. However, Nixon did finally achieve a cease-fire in Vietnam in January 1973 and by the end of March the last United States troops had been withdrawn from the stricken country. In addition, the government proclaimed the end of the draft. Nixon boasted that he had achieved 'peace with honor.' In fact, the agreement acknowledged an unmitigated defeat and the term 'honor' was totally irrelevant. The war had cost 57,000 American lives, more than 300,000 wounded; had inflicted over one million casualties on Asians; had absorbed billions of dollars in resources; and had done incalculable damage to American society and to the effectiveness of the United States in world affairs.

Returned to office by one of the most convincing margins in history, Nixon gave up all pretense of being a man of the Center and immediately veered sharply to the Right. He had hardly begun his second administration when he precipitated a serious constitutional crisis. He flaunted the authority of Congress by dismantling the Office of Economic Opportunity that administered the War on Poverty, impounded funds Congress had appropriated for social purposes, and defied requests from Capitol Hill for information on the behavior of civil servants. Increasingly Nixon's aides, who supervised a White House staff over two-and-a-half times larger than that with which Roosevelt had run World War II, behaved less like servants of the people in a democratic republic and more like a Praetorian Guard. Nixon, wrote a British

journalist, was asserting 'Robespierre's claim to personify the general will,' while other critics likened him to de Gaulle, a refractory ruler convinced that history was on his side, contemptuous of the legislature, and isolated from those he governed.

Concern about abuse of power became the leitmotif of the second Nixon administration. In the spring of 1973 the United States Attorney for Maryland launched a criminal investigation into allegations that Spiro Agnew, while county executive of Baltimore and governor of Maryland, had accepted bribes. On 10 October the Vice-President, faced with a possible prison term, pleaded *nolo contendere* (no contest) to a charge of filing a 'false and fraudulent' tax return, and resigned. A federal court fined Agnew $10,000 and sentenced him to probation for three years. Though the Department of Justice halted prosecution, it released an extensive account of Agnew's malefactions which, it stated, continued during the period when he was 'only a heartbeat away' from becoming President of the United States. Never before had so high an office in the republic been so disgraced. Under the terms of the Twenty-fifth Amendment, ratified in 1967, Nixon named as Agnew's successor the Republican Minority Leader, Representative Gerald R. Ford of Michigan, a conservative who had never been suspected of originality. But neither had he aroused suspicions of dishonesty, and so far had the reputation of the American government sunk that this qualification, which should have been taken for granted, was regarded as an exceptional mark of distinction.

Agnew's resignation occurred in a season of mounting public indignation over a matter of far graver purport: 'the Watergate affair.' On 17 June 1972 a security guard came upon intruders in the Democratic National Committee headquarters. Though the culprits, who were quickly tried and convicted, were employees of the Committee to Re-elect the President (CREEP), Nixon dismissed the burglary as a 'bizarre incident,' and for a time it seemed that no more would come of the episode. But neither Judge John J. Sirica of the U.S. District Court nor reporters for the *Washington Post* were content with this explanation, and by the

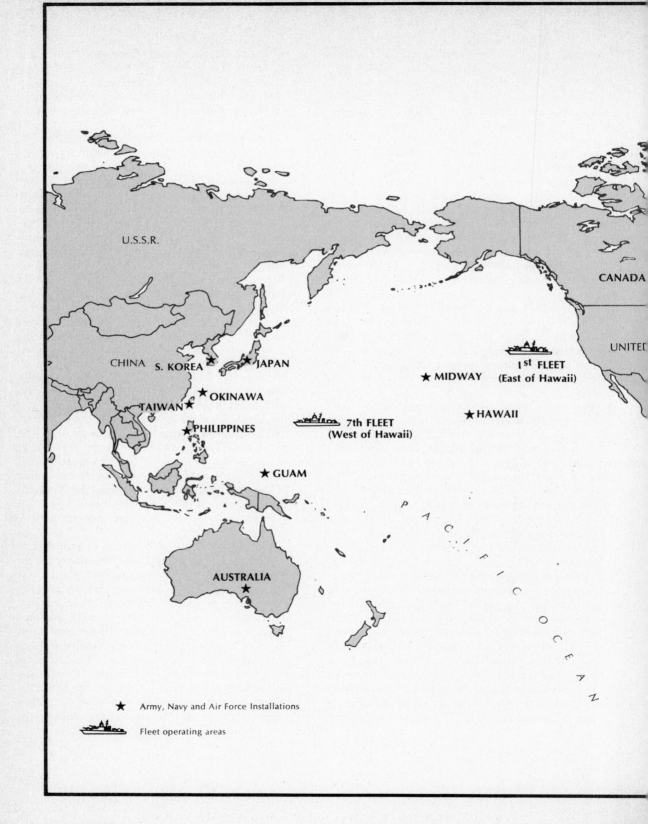

U.S.S.R.

CANADA

UNITED

CHINA

S. KOREA ★ ★ JAPAN

★ MIDWAY   1ˢᵗ FLEET
(East of Hawaii)

★ OKINAWA

TAIWAN ★

7th FLEET
(West of Hawaii)

★ HAWAII

★ PHILIPPINES

★ GUAM

PACIFIC OCEAN

AUSTRALIA
★

★   Army, Navy and Air Force Installations

Fleet operating areas

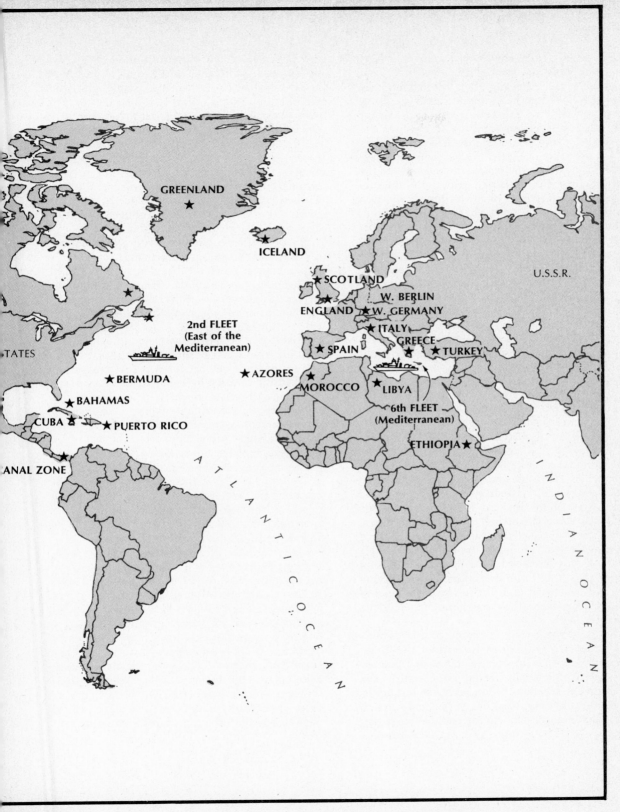

Major Concentrations of U.S. Armed Forces Overseas

spring of 1973 the Nixon administration had become enmeshed in a web of duplicity and deceit.

Investigation disclosed that wrongdoing had not been limited to the Watergate break-in. Campaign officials had engaged in political sabotage and other 'dirty tricks' in New Hampshire and Florida, and the White House had connived in rifling the office of Daniel Ellsberg's psychiatrist. Both businessmen and politicians had violated the laws governing campaign contributions, and corporations were accused of subverting the election process not only in America but in Chile and other countries. Most damaging of all was the report that some of the President's closest advisers had been involved in suborning perjury and paying 'hush money' to cover up the Watergate scandal.

A Senate investigation headed by Sam Ervin, Jr., of North Carolina, shook the Nixon administration to its foundations. When, to forestall interrogation by the Senate inquiry, Nixon sought to cloak his assistants with a mantle of Executive prerogative, Ervin responded that 'divine right went out with the American Revolution and doesn't belong to White House aides.' Under pressure from the Ervin committee, John W. Dean, III, counsel to the President, confessed to having taken part in an elaborate conspiracy to conceal the Watergate transgressions, and he implicated others. L. Patrick Gray, III, acting director of the FBI, admitted that he had deliberately destroyed documents. He resigned under fire, as on 30 April 1973 did Dean, Haldeman, Ehrlichman, and Attorney-General Richard Kleindienst. Former Attorney-General Mitchell, the champion of law and order, conceded that he had attended three meetings at which bugging the Democratic headquarters was discussed. But the most startling disclosure of the Ervin committee hearings came when it developed that Nixon had been surreptitiously tape recording discussions and telephone conversations.

The tapes spelled Nixon's doom. Until this revelation, no one had demonstrated that the President himself was culpable, though such pointed questions had been asked about his tax returns and government expenditures on his lavish residences in Florida and California that he felt compelled to say, 'I am not a crook.' (In the end, he had to pay the government nearly half a million dollars in back taxes and interest.) If he had nothing to hide about his role in the Watergate imbroglio, the tapes should clear him. But Nixon refused to turn over the tapes, even to a special prosecutor, Archibald Cox of Harvard Law School, to whom he had pledged full cooperation. When Cox went to court to obtain the tapes, Nixon ordered Attorney-General Elliot Richardson to fire him, but, to their credit, both Richardson and his assistant, William Ruckelshaus, resigned instead on 20 October 1973. The solicitor general then obliged the President by discharging Cox.

This 'Saturday night massacre,' as Washington called it, led to widespread demands for Nixon's impeachment. When the President, at bay, agreed to surrender tapes to Judge Sirica, it turned out that critical conversations were missing and that a crucial portion of one tape had been 'accidentally' erased. On 30 April 1974, to still the outcry against him, Nixon made available edited, and inaccurate, transcripts of some of the tapes, but this self-serving move backfired. The transcripts shocked the country by exposing the President's naked insensitivity to the national interest and his crude language; overnight 'expletive deleted' became a catchphrase. Cox's successor, unpersuaded by White House subterfuges about the separation of powers, subpoenaed tapes and documents of 64 additional conversations, and on 24 July, in *U.S. v. Richard M. Nixon*, the Supreme Court, while accepting the President's contention that he might invoke a claim of Executive privilege in the national security sphere, ruled unanimously that in this instance he must comply 'forthwith.'

One week later, after nationally televised deliberations impressive for the evidence they gave of conscientiousness and probity, the House Judiciary Committee voted three articles of impeachment. The President was charged with betraying his oath of office by lying, obstructing justice, and manipulating the Internal Revenue Service and other agencies to breach the Constitutional rights of citizens. In desperation, Nixon played his final card. He released the transcripts of three conversations with Haldeman and, in essence, threw himself on the mercy of the Senate. But since the transcripts further incrimi-

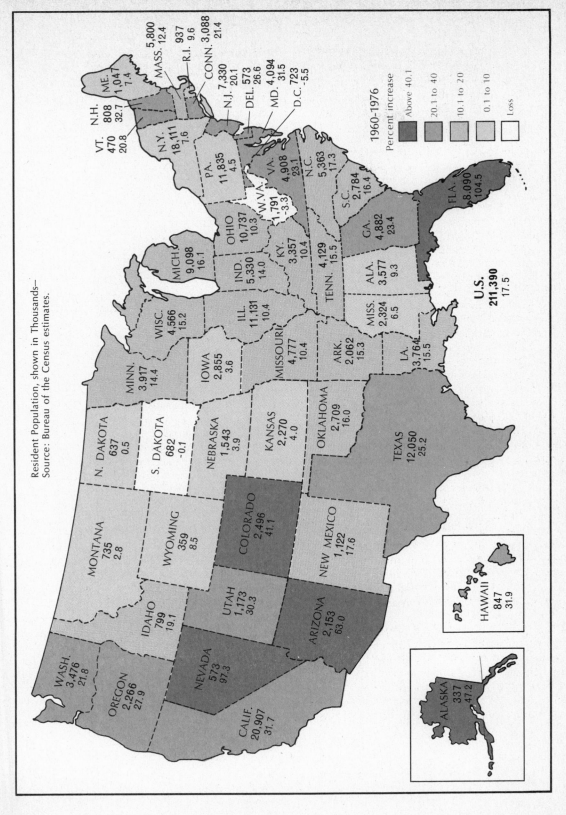

Resident Population, shown in Thousands—
Source: Bureau of the Census estimates.

Population of the United States, 1976

1960-1976
Percent increase

- Above 40.1
- 20.1 to 40
- 10.1 to 20
- 0.1 to 10
- Loss

ME. 1,047 7.4
N.H. 808 32.7
VT. 470 20.8
MASS. 5,800 12.4
R.I. 937 9.6
CONN. 3,088 21.4
N.Y. 18,111 7.6
N.J. 7,330 20.1
DEL. 573 26.6
MD. 4,094 31.5
D.C. 723 -5.5
PA. 11,835 4.5
VA. 4,908 23.1
N.C. 5,363 17.3
S.C. 2,784 16.4
W.VA. 1,791 -3.3
OHIO 10,737 10.3
MICH. 9,098 16.1
IND. 5,330 14.0
KY. 3,357 10.4
TENN. 4,129 15.5
GA. 4,882 23.4
ALA. 3,577 9.3
FLA. 8,090 104.5
WISC. 4,566 15.2
ILL. 11,131 10.4
MISS. 2,324 6.5
MINN. 3,917 14.4
IOWA 2,855 3.6
MISSOURI 4,777 10.4
ARK. 2,062 15.3
LA. 3,764 15.5
N. DAKOTA 637 0.5
S. DAKOTA 682 -0.1
NEBRASKA 1,543 3.9
KANSAS 2,270 4.0
OKLAHOMA 2,709 16.0
TEXAS 12,050 25.2
MONTANA 735 2.8
WYOMING 359 8.5
COLORADO 2,496 41.1
NEW MEXICO 1,122 17.6
IDAHO 799 19.1
UTAH 1,173 30.3
ARIZONA 2,153 63.0
WASH. 3,476 21.8
OREGON 2,266 27.9
NEVADA 573 97.3
CALIF. 20,907 31.7

U.S. 211,390 17.5

HAWAII 847 31.9

ALASKA 337 47.2

Robert Indiana, 'The Golden Future of America.' It has been said that the work of Indiana, who named himself after his native state, 'both celebrates and chides the signs and sights of Middle America.' This 1976 serigraph captures the ambivalent attitude of many Americans as the nation marked the two hundredth anniversary of its independence in the aftermath of Watergate. At first glance the work appears to be an exultant paean to the U.S.A. But closer examination reveals that the painting contains both a verbal and a visual pun: 'The "Ayes" Have It' and the three eyes, which also represent the letter 'I.' When each of the eyes is interpreted as a letter 'I' and combined with block letters in the circles, they spell out CIA, FBI, and IRS (Internal Revenue Service), all of which were implicated in the Watergate scandals. (*Trans World Art Corp., New York*)

nated him, he lost the last remnants of his support among right-wing Republicans. With no other recourse left, Richard Nixon, on 8 August 1974, brought the sordid affair to a climax by writing, 'I hereby resign the Office of President of the United States.' 'For 25 years,' wrote Bill Moyers, 'the man had massaged the baser instincts of politics.' Now he was gone, and with him went fifty-six men convicted of Watergate-related offenses, including twenty former members of the cabinet, the White House staff, and CREEP.

On the day after Nixon submitted his resignation, Gerald Ford succeeded to the presidency, the first man ever to become Chief Executive by the appointment route. Ford began with a large reservoir of good will which he quickly dissipated. On 8 September 1974 he stunned the nation by announcing that he was pardoning Nixon for all federal crimes he 'committed or may have committed or taken part in' while President. White House Press Secretary J. F. ter Horst resigned immediately as a matter of 'conscience,' and amidst a clamor of disapproval of Ford's action, which smacked of the exercise of the royal prerogative, public support for the new President dropped precipitately.

In most respects Ford's administration differed little from Nixon's. To be sure there appeared to be much less of the knavery of the Watergate era. But when Senate investigators revealed that the FBI had been involved for over a quarter of a century in more than two hundred 'black bag jobs' against 'domestic security targets' and that the CIA had not only contravened its charter by spying on American citizens but had recruited the Mafia to assassinate Fidel Castro, Ford responded not with moral outrage but by endeavoring to suppress the evidence and punish those who wished to bring it to light. He continued to rely on Kissinger in foreign affairs and, despite the lesson of Vietnam, to contemplate intervention in the civil war in Angola. In domestic matters, Ford was more reactionary and less imaginative than Nixon. At a time of tenacious unemployment and 'double-digit' inflation, he persisted in shopworn economic policies, and repeatedly vetoed legislation for public housing, federal aid to education, health care, and other social purposes. He asked regulatory agencies to give 'maximum freedom to private enterprise' and told industrialists that he wanted Washington 'out of your business, out of your lives, out of your pockets and out of your hair.' Early in 1976 a poll found that overwhelmingly the American people thought he was 'a nice guy,' but by a large margin, too, they had concluded that 'he does not seem to be very smart about the issues the country is facing.' No one summed up his performance better than the President himself when he said, disarmingly but truthfully, 'I am a Ford, not a Lincoln.'

As a consequence of the lacerating experiences it had undergone in the past decade, the nation entered its bicentennial year in a chastened mood. The 200th birthday of the United States of America seemed less an occasion for self-congratulation than for sober introspection. Pundits raised searching questions about whether the values that had served the republic well in the beginning were any longer appropriate. For much of their history Americans had been buoyed by the conviction that they dwelt in a Zion settled by Chosen People, that they were citizens of, in Jefferson's words, 'the only monument of human rights and the sole depository of the sacred fire of freedom and self-government,' from which was 'to be lighted up . . . other regions of the earth.' But critics now asked whether the myth of America's uniqueness had not led to an arrogance toward the rest of the world that culminated in imperial misadventures like Vietnam. They inquired, too, whether America's faith in perpetual progress was salutary in an era when dwindling resources and the aspirations of the Third World made it imperative to nurture the environment, discipline technology, and curb population growth, and whether the United States should not accept a sense of limits. 'For the first time in the nearly four centuries of the American experiment, America as a nation is encountering failure, the final frontier of every civilization,' commented a European observer. 'It has reached the termination of boundless potentiality.'

Yet America has repeatedly shown its capacity for self-renewal. It has created a nation; peopled deserts and built great cities; cut the bonds of the black slave and made its industrial system more

Bicentennial Quilt. Though some Americans took a jaundiced view of the nation's 200th birthday, millions of others participated in observances from Maine to Hawaii. In many communities, women sewed bicentennial quilts. This especially fine example was a cooperative enterprise of the Friends of the Library of Dobbs Ferry, N.Y. The quilt details the history of a Hudson River village that was the staging area for the battle of Yorktown in the American Revolution and grew from a section of a great Dutch manor in the seventeenth century to a modern suburb in the twentieth century. (*Photo Cathleen Polgreen*)

humane; resolved the baffling problem of federalism; devised political forms to permit majority rule but protect the rights of dissenters; and fostered an economic order which, for all its failings, has provided more abundance than any other in history. As the United States moved toward the year 2000, it still had the resources of character and spirit to make an important contribution to the problems confronting the world.

Perhaps no one stated the realities that loomed in the last third of this century so well as John Kennedy. In his moving talk to the Irish parliament, he said: 'Across the gulfs and barriers that now divide us, we must remember that there are no permanent enemies. Hostility today is a fact, but it is not a ruling law. The supreme reality of our time is our indivisibility as children of God and our common vulnerability on this planet.' Yet no one knew better than Kennedy how difficult was the road to peace, at home as well as abroad. In the last speech he ever gave, at Fort Worth on 21 November 1963, he warned: 'This is a dangerous and uncertain world. . . . No one expects our lives to be easy—not in this decade, not in this century.'

Bibliography

GENERAL WORKS

1. Journals, Encyclopedias, and Reference Books

The American Historical Review (1895–   ); The Mississippi Valley Historical Review (1915–   ), now The Journal of American History; U.S. Bureau of the Census, Historical Statistics of the United States; Colonial Times to 1970, and Statistical Abstract of the United States (annual); F. Freidel & R. K. Showman (eds.), Harvard Guide to American History; A. Johnson & D. Malone (eds.), The Dictionary of American Biography (22 vols.), and supplementary volumes; R. B. Morris, Encyclopedia of American History.

2. Collections of Documents and Other Sources

H. S. Commager, Documents of American History; R. Leopold, A. Link, and S. Coben (eds.), Problems in American History; M. Meyers et al., Sources of the American Republic (2 vols.); R. B. Morris (ed.), Documentary History of the United States.

CHAPTER 19

1. General

P. H. Buck, The Road to Reunion; J. A. Carpenter, Sword and Olive Branch: Oliver Otis Howard; A. Conway, The Reconstruction of Georgia; E. M. Coulter, The South During Reconstruction; A. Craven, Reconstruction; C. Crowe (ed.), The Age of Civil War and Reconstruction; R. Cruden, The Negro in Reconstruction; R. O. Curry, Radicalism, Racism, and Party Realignment; D. Donald, The Politics of Reconstruction, 1863–1867; W. A. Dunning, Reconstruction, Political and Economic; R. F. Durden, James Shepherd Pike; J. H. Franklin, Reconstruction; H. M. Hyman (ed.), New Frontiers of the American Reconstruction; A. Nevins, The Emergence of Modern America; E. P. Oberholtzer, History of the United States since the Civil War, vol. i; O. H. Olsen, Carpetbagger's Crusade: The Life of Albion Winegar Tourgee; R. W. Patrick, The Reconstruction of the Nation; J. G. Randall & D. Donald, The Civil War and Reconstruction; J. F. Rhodes, History of the United States, vol. v; R. P. Sharkey, Money, Class, and Party; K. M. Stampp, The Era of Reconstruction, 1865–1877; A. W. Trelease, White Terror; I. Unger, The Greenback Era; F. G. Wood, The Era of Reconstruction, 1863–1877.

2. The Negro as Freedman

P. A. Bruce, The Plantation Negro as Freedman; G. W. Cable, The Negro Question (Arlin Turner, ed.); W. J. Cash, The Mind of the South; H. H. Donald, The Negro Freedman; W. E. B. Du Bois, Black Reconstruction, and The Souls of Black Folk; F. A. Logan, The Negro in North Carolina, 1876–1894; R. W. Logan, The Negro *in American Life and Thought, 1877–1901*; W. S. McFeely, *Yankee Stepfather*; J. M. McPherson, *The Struggle for Equality*; B. Mathews, *Booker T. Washington*; A. Meier, *Negro Thought in America, 1880–1915*; G. Myrdal, *An American Dilemma* (2 vols.); W. Peters, *The Southern Temper*; B. Quarles, *Lincoln and the Negro*; A. Raper, *Preface to Peasantry*; J. M. Richardson, *The Negro in the Reconstruction of Florida, 1865–1877*; O. Singletary, *Negro Militia and Reconstruction*; S. R. Spencer, Jr., *Booker T. Washington and the Negro's Place in American Life*; C. E. Synes, *Race Relations in Virginia, 1870–1902*; G. B. Tindall, *South Carolina Negroes, 1877–1900*; B. T. Washington, *Up from Slavery*; C. H. Wesley, *Negro Labor in the United States, 1850–1925*; V. Wharton, *The Negro in Mississippi*; J. Williamson, *After Slavery: The Negro in South Carolina During Reconstruction, 1861–1877*; C. G. Woodson, *A Century of Negro Migration*.

3. Presidential Reconstruction

H. Beale, *The Critical Year*; L. & J. H. Cox, *Politics, Principle, and Prejudice: 1865–1866*; J. Dorris, *Pardon and Amnesty under Lincoln and Johnson*; W. B. Hesseltine, *Lincoln's Plan of Reconstruction*, and *Lincoln and the War Governors*; C. McCarthy, *Lincoln's Plan of Reconstruction*; E. McKitrick, *Andrew Johnson and Reconstruction*; G. F. Milton, *The Age of Hate*; J. G. Randall, *Constitutional Problems under Lincoln*; W. L. Rose, *Rehearsal for Reconstruction: The Port Royal Experiment*.

4. Congressional Reconstruction

T. B. Alexander, *Political Reconstruction in Tennessee*; M. L. Benedict, *A Compromise of Principle*; G. Bentley, *A History of the Freedmen's Bureau*; W. R. Brock, *An American Crisis: Congress and Reconstruction*; W. M. Caskey, *Secession and Restoration in Louisiana*; W. L. Fleming, *Civil War and Reconstruction in Alabama*; J. W. Garner, *Reconstruction in Mississippi*; W. Gillette, *The Right To Vote: Politics and the Passage of the Fifteenth Amendment*; R. Shugg, *Origins of Class Struggle in Louisiana*; F. B. Simkins & R. H. Woody, *South Carolina during Reconstruction*; D. Y. Thomas, *Arkansas in War and Reconstruction*; C. M. Thompson, *Reconstruction in Georgia*; H. L. Trefousse, *Benjamin Franklin Wade*.

5. Reconstruction and the Constitution

H. Hyman, *A More Perfect Union*, and *The Era of the Oath*; J. B. James, *The Framing of the Fourteenth Amendment*; S. Kutler, *Judicial Power and Reconstruction Politics*; J. M. Mathews, *Legislative and Judicial History of the Fifteenth Amendment*; J. Ten Broek, *Antislavery Origins of the Fourteenth Amendment*; C. Warren, *The Supreme Court in United States History*, vol. ii.

6. Radical Reconstruction

M. L. Benedict, *The Impeachment and Trial of Andrew Johnson*; F. Brodie, *Thaddeus Stevens*; R. N. Current, *Old Thad Stevens*; D. Donald, *Charles Sumner and the Rights of Man*; W. R. Gillette, *The Right to Vote*; H. Hyman & B. P. Thomas, *The Life and Times of Lincoln's Secretary of War*; R. Korngold, *Thaddeus Stevens*; H. L. Trefousse, *Impeachment of a President*, and *The Radical Republicans*; H. White, *Life of Lyman Trumbull*.

7. Grant and Domestic Politics

H. Adams, *The Education of Henry Adams*; D. C. Barrett, *Greenbacks and the Resumption of Specie Payments*; W. A. Cate, *L. Q. C. Lamar*; M. Duberman, *Charles Francis Adams*; W. B. Hesseltine, *Ulysses S. Grant, Politician*; H. Larson, *Jay Cooke, Private Banker*; R. S. Mitchell, *Horatio Seymour of New York*; A. B. Paine, *Thomas Nast, His Period and His Pictures*; E. D. Ross, *The Liberal Republican Movement*; J. Schafer, *Carl Schurz, Militant Liberal*.

8. Foreign Affairs

S. F. Bemis (ed.), *The American Secretaries of State and Their Diplomacy*, vol. vii; J. M. Callahan, *The Alaska Purchase*; C. L. Jones, *Caribbean Interests of the United States*; A. Nevins, *Hamilton Fish*; C. C. Tansill, *The United States and Santo Domingo 1789–1873*.

9. The Election of 1876

H. Barnard, *Rutherford B. Hayes and His America*; H. J. Eckenrode, *Rutherford B. Hayes*; A. C. Flick, *Samuel Jones Tilden*; P. L. Haworth, *The Hayes-Tilden Disputed Election of 1876*; A. Nevins, *Abram S. Hewitt: With Some Account of Peter Cooper*; J. F. Rhodes, *History of the United States*, vol. vii; L. B. Richardson, *William E. Chandler, Republican*; C. R. Williams, *Life of Rutherford B. Hayes* (2 vols.); C. V. Woodward, *Reunion and Reaction*.

CHAPTER 20

1. General

R. Andreano (ed.), *New Views on American Economic Development*; A. D. Chandler, Jr., *Giant Enterprise* and *Strategy and Structure*; V. S. Clark, *History of Manufactures in the United States 1860–1914*; S. Coben & F. G. Hill (eds.), *American Economic History*; T. Cochran & W. Miller, *The Age of Enterprise*; R. Fels, *American Business Cycles, 1865–1897*; M. Friedman and A. J. Schwartz, *A Monetary History of the United States*; S. P. Hays, *The Response to Industrialism*; E. C. Kirkland, *A History of American Economic Life* and *Industry Comes of Age*; S. Kuznets, *National Income*; L. Mumford, *Technics and Civilization*; W. N. Parker (ed.), *Trends in the American Economy in the Nineteenth Century*; S. Ratner, *American Taxation as a Social Force*; R. Robertson, *History of the American Economy*.

2. Special Industries and Industrial Leaders

F. L. Allen, *The Great Pierpont Morgan*; S. Buder, *Pullman*; R. A. Clemen, *American Live Stock and Meat Industry*; A. H. Cole, *The American Wool Manufacture* (2 vols.); R. Current, *The Typewriter and the Men Who Made It*; P. de Kruif, *Seven Iron Men*; P. Giddens, *The Birth of the Oil Industry* and *The Standard Oil Company of Indiana*; R. and M. Hidy, *Pioneering in Big Business: The Standard Oil Company of New Jersey*; W. T. Hutchinson, *Cyrus McCormick* (2 vols.); M. Jacobstein, *The Tobacco Industry*; M. James, *Alfred I. DuPont*; H. Larson, *Jay Cooke*; S. E. Morison, *The Ropemakers of Plymouth*; A. Nevins, *John D. Rockefeller* (2 vols.) and *Abram Hewitt: With Some Account of Peter Cooper*; A. Nevins & F. E. Hill, *Henry Ford* (3 vols.); H. C. Passer, *The Electric Manufacturers*; C. C. Rister, *Oil*; P. Temin, *Iron and Steel in Nineteenth Century America*; H. F. Williamson & A. H. Daum, *The American Petroleum Industry*; F. P. Wirth, *Discovery and Exploitation of the Minnesota Iron Lands*.

3. Trusts and Trust Regulation

J. D. Clark, *Federal Trust Policy*; J. R. Commons, *Legal Foundations of Capitalism*; E. Jones, *The Trust Problem in the United States*; D. Keezer & S. May, *Public Control of Business*; O. W. Knauth, *The Policy of the United States Towards Industrial Monopoly*; H. W. Laidler, *Concentration of Control in American Industry*; G. W. Nutter, *Extent of Enterprise Monopoly*; W. Z. Ripley, *Trusts, Pools, and Corporations*; H. R. Seager & G. A. Gulick, *Trust and Corporation Problems*; H. B. Thorelli, *Federal Anti-Trust Policy*; A. Walker, *History of the Sherman Law*.

4. Big Business and Its Philosophy

C. Barker, *Henry George*; F. B. Copley, *Frederick Taylor*; S. Diamond, *The Reputation of the American Businessman*; J. Dorfman, *Economic Thought in American Civilization*, vol. 3; S. Fine, *Laissez Faire and the General-Welfare State*; R. Hofstadter, *Social Darwinism in the United States*; E. C. Kirkland, *Business in the Gilded Age*; R. G. McCloskey, *American Conservatism in the Age of Enterprise*; I. Wyllie, *The Self-Made Man in America*.

CHAPTER 21

1. General

D. Brody, *Butcher Workmen* and *Steelworkers in America*; R. Christie, *Empire in Wood*; J. R. Commons *et al.*, *History of Labor in the United States* vols. 3 and 4; G. Grob, *Workers and Utopia*; A. L. Harris, *The Black Worker*; H. Harris, *American Labor*; H. Pelling, *American Labor*; M. Perlman, *The Machinists*; S. Perlman, *History of Trade Unionism in the United States* and *A Theory of the Labor Movement*; P. Taft, *The A.F. of L. in the Time of Gompers*; L. Ulman, *The Rise of the National Trade Union*; N. J. Ware, *Labor Movement in the United States 1860–1895*; C. H. Wesley, *Negro Labor in the United States 1850–1925*; L. Wolman, *Growth of American Trade Unions 1880–1923*.

2. Labor Leaders and Leadership

C. Barker, *Henry George*; H. Barnard, *Eagle Forgotten* (Altgeld); C. R. Geiger, *The Philosophy of Henry George*; R. Ginger, *The Bending Cross* (Debs); E. Glück, *John Mitchell*; S. Gompers, *Seventy Years of Life and Labor* (2 vols.); J. Grossman, *William E. Sylvis*; R. E. Harvey, *Samuel Gompers*; B. Mandel, *Samuel Gompers*; A. E. Morgan, *Edward Bellamy*; T. Powderly, *The Path I Trod*; L. Reed, *Philosophy of Gompers*.

3. Labor Conflicts and Industrial Violence

L. Adamic, *Dynamite*; P. W. Brissenden, *The I.W.W.*; W. G. Broehl, Jr., *The Molly Maguires*; J. R. Brooks, *American Syndicalism*; R. Bruce, *1877: Year of Violence*; J. W. Coleman, *The Molly Maguire Riots*; J. R. Commons *et al.*, *History of Labor in the United*

States, vol. 4; H. David, *History of the Haymarket Affair*; M. Dubofsky, *We Shall Be All*; C. Goodrich, *The Miner's Freedom*; A. Lindsey, *The Pullman Strike*; B. S. Mitchell, *Textile Unionism in the South*; B. Rastall, *Labor History of the Cripple Creek District*; T. Tippett, *When Southern Labor Stirs*.

4. *Labor Legislation and the Courts*
E. Abbott, *Women in Industry*; E. Berman, *Labor and the Sherman Act*; J. R. Commons & J. B. Andrews, *Principles of Labor Legislation*; J. R. Commons *et al.*, *History of Labor in the United States*, vol. 3; F. Frankfurter & N. V. Greene, *The Labor Injunction*; E. Freund, *The Police Power*; G. G. Groat, *Attitude of American Courts on Labor Cases*; C. E. Jacobs, *Law Writers and the Courts*; M. Karson, *American Labor Unions and Politics*; A. T. Mason, *Organized Labor and the Law*; E. E. Witte, *The Government in Labor Disputes*; I. Yellowitz, *Labor and the Progressive Movement in New York*.

5. *Immigration*
H. S. Commager (ed.), *Immigration and American History*; J. R. Commons, *Races and Immigrants in America*; O. Handlin, *Boston's Immigrants*, *The Uprooted*, and *Immigration as a Factor in American History*; M. Hansen, *The Atlantic Migration* and *The Immigrant in American History*; M. A. Jones, *American Immigration*; M. Rischin, *Promised City*; C. Wittke, *We Who Built America*.

6. *Special Groups*
K. C. Babcock, *Scandinavian Element in the United States*; G. Barth, *Bitter Strength*; R. Berthoff, *British Immigration to Industrial America 1790–1850*; K. O. Bjork, *West of the Great Divide: Norwegian Migration to the Pacific Coast*; T. C. Blegen, *Norwegian Migration to America* (2 vols.); T. Capek, *The Czechs in America*; J. Davis, *The Russian Immigrant*; A. De Conde, *Half Bitter, Half Sweet* (Italians); A. B. Faust, *German Element in the United States* (2 vols.); R. Foerster, *The Italian Emigration of Our Times*; M. Gamio, *Mexican Immigration to the United States*; E. F. Hirshler (ed.), *Jews from Germany in the United States*; F. E. Janson, *The Background of Swedish Immigration 1846–1930*; H. S. Lucas, *Netherlanders in America 1789–1950*; W. Mulder, *Homeward to Zion: Mormon Migration from Scandinavia*; H. Nelli, *Italians in Chicago, 1880–1930*; H. Pochmann, *German Culture in America*; C. C. Qualey, *Norwegian Settlement in the United States*; T. Saloutos, *The Greeks in*

the *United States* and *They Remember America*; A. Schrier, *Ireland and the American Emigration 1850–1900*; B. Lee Sung, *Mountain of Gold: The Story of the Chinese in America*; W. I. Thomas & F. Znaniecki, *The Polish Peasant in Europe and America*; C. Wittke, *The Irish in America*.

7. *Immigration Restriction*
M. T. Bennett, *American Immigration Policies*; W. Bernard (ed.), *American Immigration Policy—A Reappraisal*; J. P. Clark, *Deportation of Aliens from the United States to Europe*; J. Higham, *Strangers in the Land*; R. Paul, *The Abrogation of the Gentlemen's Agreement*; B. Solomon, *Ancestors and Immigrants*.

CHAPTER 22

1. *General*
R. G. Athearn, *High Country Empire*; R. Billington, *Westward Expansion*; H. E. Briggs, *Frontiers of the Northwest*; E. Dick, *The Sod House Frontier, 1854–1890*; G. W. Fite, *The Farmer's Frontier*; E. W. Hollon, *The Southwest*; P. Horgan, *Great River*; J. G. Malin, *The Grassland of North America*; E. Pomeroy, *The Pacific Slope*; R. E. Riegel & R. G. Athearn, *America Moves West*; F. A. Shannon, *The Farmer's Last Frontier*; W. P. Webb, *The Great Plains* and *The Great Frontier*.

2. *Railroads*
G. D. Bradley, *Story of the Santa Fe*; S. Daggett, *Chapters on the History of the Southern Pacific*; J. P. Davis, *The Union Pacific Railroad*; C. R. Fish, *Restoration of the Southern Railroads*; P. Gates, *The Illinois Central Railroad and Its Colonization Work*; J. Grodinsky, *Jay Gould* and *Transcontinental Railway Strategy*; E. Hungerford, *The Story of the Baltimore and Ohio Railroad* (2 vols.); G. Kennan, *Life of E. H. Harriman* (2 vols.); E. C. Kirkland, *Men, Cities and Transportation, 1820–1900* (2 vols.); W. Lane, *Commodore Vanderbilt*; O. Lewis, *The Big Four*; J. Moody, *The Railroad Builders*; E. H. Mott, *Between the Ocean and the Lakes*; J. G. Pyle, *James J. Hill* (2 vols.); E. L. Sabin, *Building the Pacific Railway*; E. Smalley, *History of the Northern Pacific Railroad*; J. F. Stover, *American Railroads*; G. R. Taylor & I. D. Neu, *The American Railroad Network*; N. Trottman, *History of the Union Pacific*.

3. Railroads and the West

T. Cochran, *Railroad Leaders, 1845–1890*; T. Donaldson, *The Public Domain*; R. W. Fogel, *Railroads and American Economic Growth* and *The Union Pacific Railroad*; L. H. Haney, *Congressional History of Railways, 1850–1887*; J. B. Hedges, *Henry Villard and the Railways of the Northwest*; R. C. Overton, *Burlington West*; J. R. Perkins, *Trails, Rails and War*; G. C. Quiett, *They Built the West*; R. E. Riegel, *The Story of the Western Railroads*; R. L. Thompson, *Wiring a Continent*.

4. Indians

American Heritage Book of Indians; E. D. Branch, *The Hunting of the Buffalo*; D. Brown, *Bury My Heart at Wounded Knee*; J. Collier, *Indians of the Americas*; C. A. Fee, *Chief Joseph*; G. Foreman, *The Five Civilized Tribes*; G. B. Grinnell, *The Story of the Indian* and *The Cheyenne Indians* (2 vols.); W. T. Hagan, *American Indians*; H. H. Jackson, *A Century of Dishonor*; J. P. Kinney, *A Continent Lost, a Civilization Won*; E. P. Priest, *Uncle Sam's Stepchildren 1865–1887*; P. Radin, *The Story of the American Indian*; R. N. Richardson, *The Comanche Barrier to the South Plains Settlement*; F. W. Seymour, *Indian Agents of the Old Frontier*; W. P. Webb, *The Texas Rangers*.

5. The Mining Frontier

H. H. Bancroft, *Popular Tribunals* (2 vols.); D. De Quille, *The Big Bonanza*; R. R. Elliott, *Nevada's Twentieth Century Mining Boom*; C. W. Glasscock, *Gold in Them Hills*, *The War of the Copper Kings*, and *The Big Bonanza*; W. T. Jackson, *Treasure Hill*; N. P. Langford, *Vigilante Days and Ways*; O. Lewis, *Silver Kings*; G. D. Lyman, *Saga of the Comstock Lode*; E. M. Mack, *Nevada, a History of the State*; W. P. Morrell, *The Gold Rushes*; R. Paul, *California Gold* and *Mining Frontiers of the Far West*; T. A. Rickard, *The History of American Mining*; C. H. Shinn, *Mining Camps*; C. C. Spence, *British Investments and the American Mining Frontier, 1860–1901*; W. J. Trimble, *The Mining Advance into the Inland Empire*.

6. Cattle Kingdom

A. Adams, *The Log of a Cowboy*; L. Atherton, *The Cattle Kings*; E. D. Branch, *The Cowboy and His Interpreters*; M. Burlingame, *The Montana Frontier*; R. Cleland, *Cattle on a Thousand Hills*; E. E. Dale, *Cow Country* and *The Cattle Range Industry*; J. F. Dobie, *A Vaquero of the Brush Country*; J. B. Frantz & J. Choate, *The American Cowboy*; G. R. Hebard & E. A. Brininstool, *The Bozeman Trail* (2 vols.); S. Henry, *Conquering Our Great American Plains*; E. Hough, *The Story of the Cowboy*; W. Kupper, *The Golden Hoof*; E. S. Osgood, *The Day of the Cattlemen*; O. B. Peake, *The Colorado Cattle Range Industry*; L. Pelzer, *The Cattleman's Frontier, 1850–1890*; S. P. Ridings, *The Chisholm Trail*; P. A. Rollins, *The Cowboy*; J. T. Schlebecker, *Cattle Raising on the Plains, 1900–61*; F. Shannon, *The Farmer's Last Frontier*; C. W. Towne & E. N. Wentworth, *Shepherd's Empire*; W. Webb, *The Great Plains*; P. I. Wellman, *The Trampling Herd*; E. Wentworth, *America's Sheep Trails*.

7. Passing of the Frontier and Organization of the West

L. J. Arrington, *Great Basin Kingdom*; R. G. Athearn, *William Tecumseh Sherman and the Settlement of the West*; M. Austin, *The Land of Little Rain*; H. E. Briggs, *Frontiers of the Northwest*; R. Cleland, *California* (2 vols.); E. Dick, *Vanguards of the Frontier*; P. W. Gates, *Frontier Landlords and Pioneer Tenants*; J. Ise, *Sod and Stubble*; M. James, *Cherokee Strip*; R. Lillard, *Desert Challenge*; J. C. Malin, *Winter Wheat in the Golden Belt of Kansas*; J. C. Parish, *The Persistence of the Westward Movement*; R. N. Richardson, *Texas, the Lone Star State*; R. Robbins, *Our Landed Heritage*; F. J. Turner, *Significance of the Frontier in American History*.

CHAPTER 23

1. General

H. Agar, *The Price of Union*; J. Bryce, *The American Commonwealth* (2 vols.); J. Dorfman, *Economic Mind in American Civilization*, vol. 3; H. U. Faulkner, *Politics, Reform and Expansion 1890–1900*; S. Fine, *Laissez Faire and the General-Welfare State*; J. Garraty, *The New Commonwealth, 1877–1890*; E. Goldman, *Rendezvous with Destiny*; S. Hirshson, *Farewell to the Bloody Shirt*; J. R. Hollingsworth, *The Whirligig of Politics*; R. Jensen, *The Winning of the Midwest*; M. Josephson, *The Politicos*; P. Kleppner, *The Cross of Culture*; R. D. Marcus, *Grand Old Party*; H. Merrill, *Bourbon Democracy in the Middle West 1865–1896*; H. W. Morgan, *From Hayes to McKinley*; R. B. Nye, *Midwestern Progressive Politics 1870–1950*; D. Rothman, *Politics and Power*; L. D. White, *The Republican Era 1865–1900*; W. A. White, *Masks in a Pageant*.

2. Reform

G. Blodgett, *The Gentle Reformers*; C. R. Fish, *The Civil Service and the Patronage*; H. F. Gosnell, *Boss Platt and the New York Machine*; A. Hoogenboom, *Fighting the Spoilsmen*.

3. Biographies

H. Barnard, *Eagle Forgotten: Life of John P. Altgeld*; J. A. Barnes, *John G. Carlisle*; H. Bass, *'I Am a Democrat'*; H. Croly, *Marcus Alonzo Hanna*; C. Fuess, *Carl Schurz*; M. A. Hirsch, *William C. Whitney*; G. Hoar, *Autobiography of Seventy Years*; G. F. Howe, *Chester A. Arthur*; M. Leech, *In the Days of McKinley*; A. Nevins, *Grover Cleveland*; W. A. Robinson, *Thomas B. Reed*; H. J. Sievers, *Benjamin Harrison*; T. C. Smith, *Life and Letters of James A. Garfield* (2 vols.); N. W. Stephenson, *Nelson Aldrich*; F. Summers, *William L. Wilson and Tariff Reform*; J. F. Wall, *Henry Watterson*; C. R. Williams, *Life of Rutherford B. Hayes* (2 vols.).

4. Railroad Regulation

C. F. Adams, *Railroads*; S. J. Buck, *The Granger Movement*; E. G. Campbell, *The Reorganization of the American Railroad System 1893–1900*; F. A. Cleveland & F. W. Powell, *Railway Promotion and Capitalization*; J. B. Crawford, *The Credit Mobilier of America*; F. Frankfurter, *The Commerce Clause under Marshall, Taney and Waite*; W. Larrabee, *The Railroad Question*; F. Merk, *Economic History of Wisconsin*; I. L. Sharfman, *The Interstate Commerce Commission* (5 vols.).

CHAPTER 24

1. General

L. H. Bailey, *Cyclopedia of American Agriculture* (4 vols.); O. E. Baker (ed.), *Atlas of American Agriculture*; M. Benedict, *Farm Policies of the United States 1790–1950*; E. L. Bogart, *Economic History of American Agriculture*; A. Bogue, *From Prairie to Corn Belt* and *Money at Interest*; B. H. Hibbard, *A History of Public Land Policies*; E. L. Peffer, *The Closing of the Public Domain*; W. Range, *A Century of Georgia Agriculture*; R. Robbins, *Our Landed Heritage*; A. Sakolski, *The Great American Land Bubble*; J. Schafer, *Social History of American Agriculture* and *History of Agriculture in Wisconsin*; F. A. Shannon, *The Farmer's Last Frontier*; C. C. Taylor, *The Farmers' Move-*

ment, 1620–1920; U.S. Dept. of Agriculture, *Yearbook, 1940: American Agriculture, the First Three Hundred Years*; R. Vance, *Human Geography of the South*; W. P. Webb, *The Great Plains*; H. Wilson, *The Hill Country of Northern New England*; C. V. Woodward, *Origins of the New South*.

2. Farm Problem and Agrarian Revolt

A. M. Arnett, *Populist Movement in Georgia*; L. Benson, *Merchants, Farmers, and the Railroads*; R. P. Brooks, *The Agrarian Revolution in Georgia*; S. J. Buck, *The Granger Movement* and *The Agrarian Crusade*; J. B. Clark, *Populism in Alabama*; E. Dick, *The Sod House Frontier*; E. Ellis, *Henry Moore Teller*; N. Fine, *Labor and Farmer Parties in the U.S.*; P. R. Fossum, *The Agrarian Movement in North Dakota*; P. Gates, *Fifty Million Acres*; M. Harrington, *Populist Movement in Georgia*; F. E. Haynes, *James Baird Weaver* and *Third Party Movements Since the Civil War*; J. D. Hicks, *The Populist Revolt*; O. M. Kile, *Farm Bureau Movement*; S. Noblin, *L. L. Polk*; M. Ridge, *Ignatius Donnelly*; T. Saloutos, *Farmer Movements in the South, 1865–1933*; T. Saloutos & J. D. Hicks, *Agricultural Discontent in the Middle West*; R. Shugg, *Origins of the Class Struggle in Louisiana*; C. V. Woodward, *Tom Watson*.

3. The Money Question and the Panic of 1893

J. A. Barnes, *John G. Carlisle*; D. R. Dewey, *Financial History of the United States*; M. Gresham, *Life of Walter Q. Gresham* (2 vols.); M. D. Hirsch, *William C. Whitney*; D. L. McMurray, *Coxey's Army*; S. Ratner, *American Taxation*; I. Unger, *The Greenback Era*; A. Weinstein, *Prelude to Populism*; M. S. Wildman, *Money Inflation in the United States*.

4. The Populist Revolt

A. M. Arnett, *The Populist Movement in Georgia*; H. Barnard, *Eagle Forgotten: John Peter Altgeld*; J. B. Clark, *Populism in Alabama*; J. D. Hicks, *The Populist Revolt*; A. D. Kirwan, *Revolt of the Rednecks*; W. T. K. Nugent, *The Tolerant Populists*; R. B. Nye, *Midwestern Progressive Politics*; N. Pollack, *The Populist Response to Industrial America*; F. A. Shannon, *The Farmer's Last Frontier*; W. D. Sheldon, *Populism in the Old Dominion*; F. Simkins, *The Tillman Movement in South Carolina*.

5. Bryan and the Election of 1896

W. J. Bryan, *Memoirs* and *The First Battle*; P. E. Coletta, *William Jennings Bryan*, vol. 1: *Political Evan-*

gelist 1860–1908; H. Croly, Marcus Alonzo Hanna; R. F. Durden, The Climax of Populism; E. Ellis, Henry Teller; P. W. Glad, The Trumpet Soundeth and McKinley, Bryan and the People; P. Hibben, W. J. Bryan; S. Jones, The Presidential Election of 1896; H. W. Morgan, McKinley and His America; M. R. Werner, Bryan; W. Williams, William Jennings Bryan.

CHAPTER 25

1. Philosophy and Religion

A. I. Abell, American Catholicism and Social Action and The Urban Impact on American Protestantism; P. Carter, The Spiritual Crisis of the Gilded Age; H. S. Commager, The American Mind; M. Curti, The Growth of American Thought; J. T. Ellis, American Catholicism; C. H. Hopkins, The Rise of the Social Gospel, 1865–1915; H. F. May, The End of Innocence and The Protestant Churches and Industrial America; T. Maynard, The Story of American Catholicism; R. B. Perry, The Thought and Character of William James (2 vols.); S. Persons (ed.), Evolutionary Thought in America and American Minds; G. Santayana, Character and Opinion in the United States and Winds of Doctrine; H. Schneider, A History of American Philosophy and Religion in Twentieth Century America; A. P. Stokes, Church and State in the United States (3 vols.); H. Townsend, Philosophical Ideas in the United States; P. Weiner, Evolution and the Founding of Pragmatism; M. G. White, Social Thought in America.

2. Social and Legal Thought

S. Chuggerman, Lester Ward; J. R. Commons, Legal Foundation of Capitalism; B. Crick, The American Science of Politics; C. M. Destler, American Radicalism 1865–1901; J. Dorfman, Thorstein Veblen and His America; F. Frankfurter, Mr. Justice Holmes and the Supreme Court; R. Hofstadter, Social Darwinism in America; M. DeW. Howe, Justice Oliver Wendell Holmes: The Proving Years; W. Jordy, Henry Adams: Scientific Historian; M. Lerner (ed.), The Mind and Faith of Justice Holmes; H. Odum (ed.), American Masters of Social Science; E. Samuels, Henry Adams: The Middle Years; H. E. Starr, William Graham Sumner; B. Twiss, Lawyers and the Constitution.

3. Literature

H. Adams, The Education of Henry Adams; G. N. Bennett, William Dean Howells; V. W. Brooks, New England: Indian Summer, Howells: His Life and World, The Ordeal of Mark Twain, and The Confident Years; E. H. Cady, William Dean Howells; O. Cargill, Intellectual America and The Novels of Henry James; E. Carter, Howells and the Age of Realism; H. H. Clark (ed.), Transitions in American Literary History; M. Cowley, After the Genteel Tradition; B. DeVoto, Mark Twain's America; D. Dudley, Forgotten Frontiers: Theodore Dreiser and the Land of the Free; L. Edel, Henry James; M. Geismar, Ancestors and Rebels; A. Kazin, On Native Grounds; F. O. Matthiessen, The James Family and Henry James: The Major Phase; E. Neff, Edwin A. Robinson; V. L. Parrington, Beginnings of Critical Realism in America; R. E. Spiller et al., Literary History of the United States, vol. 2; W. Taylor, The Economic Novel in America; Y. Winters, E. A. Robinson.

4. Journalism

W. G. Bleyer, Main Currents in the History of American Journalism; G. Britt, Forty Years, Forty Millions: A Biography of Frank Munsey; O. Carlson, Hearst: Lord of San Simeon; H. S. Commager (ed.), The St. Nicholas Anthology; E. Davis, The New York Times; G. Johnson, An Honorable Titan: Adolph Ochs; J. M. Lee, History of American Journalism; F. L. Mott, American Journalism and History of American Magazines, vol. 3; D. Seitz, Joseph Pulitzer; W. A. Swanberg, Citizen Hearst; J. Tebbel, George Horace Lorimer and the Saturday Evening Post; B. A. Weisberger, The American Newspaperman.

5. Education

L. Cremin, The Transformation of the School; E. P. Cubberley, Public Education in the United States; M. Curti, Social Ideas of American Educators; C. W. Dabney, Universal Education in the South (2 vols.); H. Hawkins, Pioneer: A History of the Johns Hopkins University; R. Hofstadter & W. Metzger, Academic Freedom in the United States; H. James, Charles W. Eliot (2 vols.); E. Krug, Charles W. Eliot and Popular Education; T. LeDuc, Piety and Intellect at Amherst College; R. D. Leigh, The Public Library in the United States; P. Monroe (ed.), Cyclopedia of Education (5 vols.); S. E. Morison, Development of Harvard University 1869–1929; A. Nevins, The Land Grant Colleges; G. Pierson, Yale; E. D. Ross, Democracy's College; R. J. Storr, Harper's University; T. Veblen, The Higher Learning in America; L. Veysey, The Emergence of the American University.

6. Art and Architecture

W. Andrews, *Architecture in America* and *Architecture, Ambition, and Americans*; V. Barker, *American Painting*; C. Beaux, *Background with Figures*; J. Burchard & A. Bush-Brown, *The Architecture of America*; A. Burroughs, *Limners and Likenesses*; H. S. Commager, *The American Mind*; R. Cortissoz, *Augustus St. Gaudens* and *John La Farge*; W. H. Downes, *John Singer Sargent*; J. M. Fitch, *American Building*; S. Giedion, *Space, Time and Architecture*; I. Glackens, *William Glackens and the Ashcan Group*; L. Goodrich, *Albert Ryder*, *Winslow Homer*, and *Thomas Eakins*; T. Hamlin, *The American Spirit in Architecture*; J. Kouwenhoven, *Made in America*; O. Larkin, *Art and Life in America*; R. McKinney, *Thomas Eakins*; C. H. Moore, *Daniel H. Burnham*; L. Mumford, *Roots of Contemporary Architecture*, *The Brown Decades*, *Sticks and Stones*, and *The South in Architecture*; J. Myers, *Artist in New York*; E. P. Richardson, *Painting in America*; M. Ryerson (ed.), *The Art Spirit: Robert Henri*; M. Schuyler, *American Architecture* (2 vols.); F. Sherman, *Albert Pinkham Ryder*; L. Taft, *History of American Sculpture*; W. Walton, *Art and Architecture at the World's Columbian Exposition* (3 vols.); F. L. Wright, *Autobiography*, *Modern Architecture*, and *Writings and Buildings*.

CHAPTER 26

1. General

J. B. Brebner, *The North Atlantic Triangle*; F. R. Dulles, *The Imperial Years* and *America in the Pacific*; L. Gelber, *The Rise of Anglo-American Friendship 1898–1906*; A. W. Griswold, *The Far Eastern Policy of the United States*; G. F. Kennan, *American Diplomacy*; W. La Feber, *The New Empire*; H. W. Morgan, *William McKinley and His America* and *America's Road to Empire*; R. E. Osgood, *Ideals and Self-Interest in America's Foreign Policy*; D. Perkins, *Hands Off! A History of the Monroe Doctrine*; D. W. Pletcher, *The Awkward Years*; A. K. Weinberg, *Manifest Destiny*; A. Whitaker, *The Western Hemisphere Idea: Its Rise and Decline*; B. M. Williams, *Economic Foreign Policy of the United States*; W. A. Williams, *The Roots of the Modern American Empire* and *The Tragedy of American Diplomacy*.

2. Rise of Imperialism and Manifest Destiny in the 'Nineties

H. C. Allen, *Great Britain and the United States*; H. K. Beale, *Theodore Roosevelt and the Rise of America to World Power*; E. J. Carpenter, *America in Hawaii*; P. E. Corbett, *The Settlement of Canadian-American Disputes*; T. Dennett, *Americans in Eastern Asia*; W. Livezey, *Mahan on Sea Power*; F. Merk, *Manifest Destiny and Mission in American History*; A. Nevins, *Henry White*; G. O'Gara, *Theodore Roosevelt and the Rise of the Modern Navy*; E. S. Pomeroy, *Pacific Outpost: American Strategy in Guam*; W. D. Puleston, *Admiral Mahan*; G. H. Ryden, *The Foreign Policy of the United States in Relation to Samoa*; H. & M. Sprout, *The Rise of American Naval Power*; S. K. Stevens, *American Expansion in Hawaii 1842–1898*; R. West, *Admirals of American Empire*.

3. The Spanish War

F. R. Chadwick, *Relations of the United States and Spain: The War* (2 vols.); F. Freidel, *The Splendid Little War*; W. Millis, *The Martial Spirit*; B. A. Reuter, *Anglo-American Relations During the Spanish American War*; J. Wisan, *The Cuban Crisis as Reflected in the New York Press*.

4. Imperialism and Anti-Imperialism

R. Beisner, *Twelve Against Empire*; R. Cortissoz, *Life of Whitelaw Reid* (2 vols.); M. Curti, *Bryan and World Peace*; T. Dennett, *John Hay*; E. Ellis, *Henry Teller*; M. Leech, *In the Days of McKinley*; E. R. May, *Imperial Democracy* and *American Imperialism*; A. S. Pier, *American Apostles to the Philippines*; J. Pratt, *Expansionists of 1898*.

5. The Open Door

M. J. Bau, *Open Door Doctrine in Relation to China*; J. M. Callahan, *American Relations in the Pacific and in the Far East*; C. Campbell, Jr., *Special Business Interests and the Open Door Policy*; H. Chung, *The Oriental Policy of the United States*; P. H. Clements, *The Boxer Rebellion*; T. Dennett, *Americans in Eastern Asia* and *John Hay*; A. L. P. Dennis, *Adventures in American Diplomacy*; J. W. Pratt, *America's Colonial Experiment*; P. A. Varg, *Open Door Diplomat—The Life of William W. Rockhill* and *Missionaries, Chinese, and Diplomats*; M. Young, *The Rhetoric of Empire*.

6. Foreign Affairs in the Progressive Era

T. A. Bailey, *Theodore Roosevelt and the Japanese-American Crisis*; H. K. Beale, *Theodore Roosevelt and the Rise of America to World Power*; C. S. Campbell, *Anglo-American Understanding 1898–1903*; T. Dennett, *John Hay, Roosevelt and the Russo-Japanese War*, and *Americans in Eastern Asia*; L. E. Ellis, *Reci-*

procity, 1911; R. Esthus, *Theodore Roosevelt and Japan*; L. M. Gelber, *The Rise of Anglo-American Friendship*; A. W. Griswold, *The Far Eastern Policy of the United States*; D. Miner, *The Fight for the Panama Route*; C. Vevier, *The United States and China 1906–1913*.

CHAPTER 27

1. General

D. Aaron, *Men of Good Hope*; J. D. Buenker, *Urban Liberalism and Progressive Reform*; J. R. Chamberlain, *Farewell to Reform*; L. A. Cremin, *The Transformation of the School*; R. Daniels, *The Politics of Prejudice*; C. M. Destler, *American Radicalism 1865–1901*; J. Dorfman, *Economic Mind in American Civilization*, vol. 3, and *Thorstein Veblen and His America*; R. Ginger, *Age of Excess*; S. Haber, *Efficiency and Uplift*; S. Hays, *The Response to Industrialism 1885–1914*; R. Hofstadter, *The Age of Reform* and *The Progressive Historians*; G. Kolko, *The Triumph of Conservatism* and *Railroads and Regulation, 1877–1916*; C. Lasch, *The New Radicalism in America*; A. Mann, *Yankee Reformers in the Urban Age*; E. E. Morison, *Turmoil and Tradition* (Stimson); D. W. Noble, *The Paradox of Progressive Thought*; R. B. Nye, *Midwestern Progressive Politics*; R. Wiebe, *Businessmen and Reform*; R. Wilson, *In Quest of Community*; C. V. Woodward, *Origins of the New South, 1877–1913*.

2. Political Reform and Era of the Muckrakers

R. M. Abrams, *Conservatism in a Progressive Era*; C. Barker, *Henry George*; W. E. Bean, *Boss Reuf's San Francisco*; H. F. Bedford, *Socialism and the Workers in Massachusetts*; C. Bowers, *Beveridge and the Progressive Era*; J. Braeman, *Albert J. Beveridge*; D. M. Chalmers, *The Social and Political Ideas of the Muckrakers*; D. D. Egbert & S. Persons (eds.), *Socialism and American Life* (2 vols.); E. Ellis, *Mr. Dooley's America*; L. Filler, *Crusaders for American Liberalism*; E. A. Fitzpatrick, *McCarthy of Wisconsin*; D. Grantham, *Hoke Smith and the Politics of the New South*; F. E. Haynes, *Third Party Movements in the United States*; F. C. Howe, *Confessions of a Reformer*; I. Kipnis, *The American Socialist Movement 1897–1912*; A. D. Kirwan, *The Revolt of the Rednecks*; A. S. Kraditor, *The Ideas of the Woman Suffrage Movement, 1890–1920*; B. C. and F. La Follette, *Robert M. La Follette* (2 vols.); E. R. Lewinson, *John Purroy Mitchel*; P. Lyon, *Success Story* (McClure); R. S. Maxwell, *La Follette and the*

Rise of Progressives in Wisconsin; G. E. Mowry, *The California Progressives* and *The Era of Theodore Roosevelt*; R. E. Noble, *New Jersey Progressivism before Wilson*; C. W. Patton, *The Fight for Municipal Reform*; H. Quint, *The Forging of American Socialism*; C. C. Regier, *The Era of the Muckrakers*; D. A. Shannon, *The Socialist Party of America*; L. Steffens, *Autobiography*; H. L. Warner, *Progressivism in Ohio*; A. & L. Weinberg (eds.), *The Muckrakers: An Anthology*; Brand Whitlock, *Forty Years of It*.

3. Humanitarian Reform

G. Adams, Jr., *Age of Industrial Violence*; J. Addams, *Forty Years at Hull House*; R. H. Bremner, *From the Depths*; A. F. Davis, *Spearheads for Reform*; J. C. Farrell, *Beloved Lady* (Jane Addams); G. P. Geiger, *Philosophy of Henry George*; J. R. Gusfield, *Symbolic Crusade*; R. M. Lubove, *The Progressives and the Slums* and *The Struggle for Social Security, 1900–1935*; A. E. Morgan, *Edward Bellamy*; W. L. O'Neill, *Divorce in the Progressive Era*; J. Riis, *The Battle with the Slum* and *How the Other Half Lives*; L. Wade, *Graham Taylor*; L. Wald, *The House on Henry Street* and *Windows on Henry Street*; S. B. Wood, *Constitutional Politics in the Progressive Era*.

4. The Struggle for Negro Rights

W. J. Cash, *The Mind of the South*; L. Dinnerstein, *The Leo Frank Case*; W. E. B. DuBois, *Dusk of Dawn*, *The Philadelphia Negro, Color and Democracy*, and *The Souls of Black Folk*; J. H. Franklin, *From Slavery to Freedom*; T. F. Gossett, *Race: The History of an Idea in America*; L. Harlan, *Booker T. Washington*; A. Locke, *The New Negro*; A. Meier, *Negro Thought in America*; A. Meier & E. M. Rudwick, *From Plantation to Ghetto*; S. Redding, *The Lonesome Road*; S. M. Scheiner, *Negro Mecca: A History of the Negro in New York City, 1865–1920*; A. H. Spear, *Black Chicago: The Making of a Negro Ghetto, 1890–1920*; C. V. Woodward, *Strange Career of Jim Crow*.

5. The Progressive Era

J. Blum, *The Republican Roosevelt*; C. Bowers, *Beveridge and the Progressive Movement*; H. U. Faulkner, *The Decline of Laissez Faire*; J. S. Garraty, *Henry Cabot Lodge* and *Right-Hand Man* (George W. Perkins); E. Goldman, *Rendezvous with Destiny*; W. H. Harbaugh, *Power and Responsibility* (Roosevelt); J. Holt, *Congressional Insurgents and the Party System, 1907–1916*; P. Jessup, *Elihu Root* (2 vols.); W. Johnson, *William Allen White's America*; R. M. Lowitt, *George Norris*; M. N. McGeary, *Gifford Pinchot*;

G. E. Mowry, *The Era of Theodore Roosevelt* and *Theodore Roosevelt and the Progressive Movement*; H. F. Pringle, *Theodore Roosevelt* and *Life and Times of William Howard Taft* (2 vols.); N. W. Stephenson, *Nelson W. Aldrich*.

6. *The Extension of Government Regulation*

S. Fine, *Laissez Faire and the General-Welfare State*; S. P. Hays, *Conservation and the Gospel of Efficiency 1890–1920*; A. Martin, *Enterprise Denied*; A. T. Mason, *Bureaucracy Convicts Itself: The Ballinger-Pinchot Controversy*; J. Penick, Jr., *Progressive Politics and Conservation*; E. R. Richardson, *The Politics of Conservation*; H. B. Thorelli, *The Federal Anti-Trust Policy*.

7. *Woodrow Wilson*

R. S. Baker, *Woodrow Wilson: Life and Letters* (8 vols.); H. C. Bell, *Woodrow Wilson and the People*; J. M. Blum, *Woodrow Wilson and the Politics of Morality* and *Joe Tumulty and the Wilson Era*; W. Diamond, *Economic Thought of Woodrow Wilson*; C. Forcey, *The Crossroads of Liberalism*; J. A. Garraty, *Woodrow Wilson*; A. Link, *Woodrow Wilson* (5 vols.) and *Woodrow Wilson and the Progressive Era*; A. T. Mason, *Brandeis*; F. L. Paxson, *The Pre-War Years*; M. J. Pusey, *Charles Evans Hughes*; C. Seymour (ed.), *The Intimate Papers of Colonel House* (4 vols.); A. L. Todd, *Justice on Trial: The Case of Louis D. Brandeis*; M. I. Urofsky, *A Mind of One Piece* (Brandeis) and *Big Steel and the Wilson Administration*; O. G. Villard, *Fighting Years*; A. Walworth, *Woodrow Wilson* (2 vols.).

CHAPTER 28

1. *General*

A. Arnett, *Claude Kitchin and the Wilson War Policies*; R. S. Baker, *Woodrow Wilson: Life and Letters*, vols. 5 and 6; R. S. Baker & W. E. Dodd (eds.), *The Public Papers of Woodrow Wilson* (6 vols.); E. H. Buehrig, *Woodrow Wilson and the Balance of Power*; H. F. Cline, *The United States and Mexico*; J. Cooper, *The Vanity of Power*; C. H. Cramer, *Newton D. Baker*; R. W. Curry, *Woodrow Wilson's Far Eastern Policy*; M. Curti, *Bryan and World Peace*; B. J. Hendrick, *Life and Letters of Walter Hines Page* (3 vols.); T. Iyenage & K. Sato, *Japan and the California Problem*; A. S. Link, *Wilson the Diplomatist* and *Wilson* (5 vols.); V. S. Mamatey, *The United States and East Central Europe, 1914–1918*; E. R. May, *The World War and American Isolation, 1914–1917*; A. J. Mayer, *Political Origins of the New Diplomacy, 1917–1918*; A. Nevins (ed.), *The Letters and Journals of Brand Whitlock* (2 vols.); H. Notter, *Origins of the Foreign Policy of Woodrow Wilson*; R. E. Osgood, *Ideals and Self-Interest in America's Foreign Relations*; F. L. Paxson, *American Democracy and the World War*, vol. 1; R. Quirk, *An Affair of Honor*; C. Seymour, *American Neutrality, 1914–1917* and *American Diplomacy During the World War*.

2. *Struggle for Neutral Rights*

T. A. Bailey, *The Policy of the United States Towards Neutrals*; K. E. Birnbaum, *Peace Moves and U-Boat Warfare*; E. M. Borchard & W. P. Lage, *Neutrality for the United States*; D. M. Smith, *Robert Lansing and American Neutrality* and *The Great Departure*; C. Tansill, *America Goes to War*; B. Tuchman, *The Zimmermann Telegram*.

3. *Propaganda*

T. A. Bailey, *The Man in the Street: Impact of American Public Opinion on American Foreign Policy*; C. J. Child, *The German-American in Politics 1914–1917*; L. Gelber, *Rise of Anglo-American Friendship*; H. C. Peterson, *Propaganda for War*; A. Rappaport, *British Press and Wilsonian Neutrality*; C. E. Scheiber, *Transformation of American Sentiment Toward Germany 1898–1914*.

4. *Mobilization*

D. R. Beaver, *Newton D. Baker and the American War Effort*; G. B. Clarkson, *Industrial America at War*; B. Crowell & R. F. Wilson, *How America Went to War* (6 vols.); R. Cuff, *The War Industries Board*; S. W. Livermore, *Politics Is Adjourned*; F. L. Paxson, *American Democracy and the World War*, vols. 1 and 2; P. W. Slosson, *The Great Crusade and After*; H. Stein, *Government Price Policy During the World War*; G. S. Watkins, *Labor Problems and Labor Administration During World War* (2 vols.); W. F. Willoughby, *Government Organization in War Times and After*.

5. *Public Opinion and Civil Liberties*

Z. Chafee, *Free Speech in the United States*; D. Johnson, *The Challenge to American Freedoms*; J. R. Mock & C. Larson, *Words that Won the War*; H. C. Peterson & G. C. Fite, *Opponents of War, 1917–1918*; H. Scheiber, *The Wilson Administration and Civil Liberties*.

6. Military and Naval History

T. G. Frothingham, *Naval History of the World War* (3 vols.) and *American Re-enforcement in the World War*; L. Guichard, *The Naval Blockade 1914–1918*; E. Morison, *Admiral Sims and the Modern American Navy*; F. Palmer, *America in France* and *Bliss: Peacemaker*; D. Trask, *The United States in the Supreme War Council*.

7. Intervention in Russia

T. A. Bailey, *America Faces Russia*; W. S. Graves, *America's Siberian Adventure 1918–1920*; G. Kennan, *Russia Leaves the War* and *The Decision to Intervene*; C. Lasch, *The American Liberals and the Russian Revolution*; B. M. Unterberger, *America's Siberian Expedition 1918–1920*; W. A. Williams, *American-Russian Relations 1781–1947*.

8. The Treaty, the League, and the Peace

T. Bailey, *Woodrow Wilson and the Lost Peace* and *Woodrow Wilson and the Great Betrayal*; R. S. Baker, *Woodrow Wilson and World Settlement* (3 vols.) and *What Wilson Did at Paris*; P. Birdsall, *Versailles Twenty Years After*; A. Cranston, *The Killing of the Peace*; D. F. Fleming, *The United States and the League of Nations* and *The United States and the World Court*; J. Garraty, *Henry Cabot Lodge*; L. E. Gelfand, *The Inquiry*; W. S. Holt, *Treaties Defeated by the Senate*; J. M. Keynes, *Economic Consequences of the Peace*; N. Levin, *Woodrow Wilson and World Politics*; E. Mantoux, *The Carthaginian Peace*; D. H. Miller, *The Drafting of the Covenant* (2 vols.); H. Nicolson, *Peace Making, 1919*; K. F. Nowak, *Versailles*; H. R. Rudin, *Armistice, 1918*; G. Smith, *When the Cheering Stopped*; R. Stone, *The Irreconcilables*; H. W. V. Temperley *et al.*, *History of the Peace Conference* (6 vols.); S. P. Tillman, *Anglo-American Relations at the Paris Peace Conference of 1919*.

CHAPTERS 29–30

1. General

F. L. Allen, *Only Yesterday*; J. Braeman *et al.* (eds.), *Change and Continuity in Twentieth-Century America: The 1920's*; P. Carter, *The Twenties in America*; R. Crunden, *From Self to Society, 1919–1941*; J. D. Hicks, *The Republican Ascendancy*; G. H. Knoles, *The Jazz Age Revisited*; I. Leighton (ed.), *The Aspirin Age*; W. E. Leuchtenburg, *The Perils of Prosperity, 1914–32*; G. Ostrander, *American Civilization in the First*

Machine Age: 1890–1940; J. Prothro, *Dollar Decade*; G. Tindall, *The Emergence of the New South, 1913–1945*.

2. Politics

J. Allswang, *A House for All Peoples*; W. Bagby, *The Road to Normalcy*; J. L. Bates, *The Origins of Teapot Dome*; D. Burner, *The Politics of Provincialism*; C. Chambers, *Seedtime of Reform*; P. Coletta, *William Jennings Bryan*; O. Handlin, *Al Smith and His America*; W. Harbaugh, *Lawyer's Lawyer*; J. J. Huthmacher, *Massachusetts People and Politics, 1919–1933*; I. Katznelson, *Black Men, White Cities*; M. Keller, *In Defense of Yesterday*; B. C. & F. La Follette, *Robert M. La Follette* (2 vols.); L. Levine, *Defender of the Faith* (Bryan); R. Lowitt, *George W. Norris*; K. MacKay, *The Progressive Movement*; D. R. McCoy, *Calvin Coolidge*; A. T. Mason, *William Howard Taft: Chief Justice, The Supreme Court from Taft to Warren*, and *Harlan Fiske Stone*; E. Moore, *A Catholic Runs for President*; R. Murphy, *The Constitution in Crisis Times, 1918–1969*; R. Murray, *The Harding Era* and *The Politics of Normalcy*; B. Noggle, *Teapot Dome*; H. Quint & R. Ferrell, *The Talkative President*; F. Russell, *The Shadow of Blooming Grove*; E. E. Schattschneider, *Politics, Pressures and the Tariff*; A. Sinclair, *The Available Man*; W. A. White, *Puritan in Babylon*; H. Zinn, *La Guardia in Congress*.

3. Intolerance and Civil Liberties

J. W. Caughey, *In Clear and Present Danger*; Z. Chafee, *Free Speech in the United States*; S. Coben, *A. Mitchell Palmer*; H. S. Commager, *Freedom, Loyalty, and Dissent*; R. Cushman, *Civil Liberties in the United States*; T. Draper, *The Roots of American Communism*; R. L. Friedheim, *The Seattle General Strike*; E. M. Morgan & G. L. Joughin, *The Legacy of Sacco and Vanzetti*; P. Murphy, *The Meaning of Freedom of Speech*; R. Murray, *Red Scare*; W. Preston, *Aliens and Dissenters*; E. M. Rudwick, *Race Riot at East St. Louis*; F. Russell, *Tragedy in Dedham*; D. Shannon, *The Socialist Party of America*.

4. Political Fundamentalism

C. C. Alexander, *The Ku Klux Klan in the Southwest*; D. M. Chalmers, *Hooded Americanism*; V. Dabney, *Dry Messiah*; N. Furniss, *The Fundamentalist Controversy, 1918–1931*; W. B. Gatewood, Jr., *Preachers, Pedagogues, & Politicians*; R. Ginger, *Six Days or Forever?*; K. T. Jackson, *The Ku Klux Klan in the City*; D. Kirschner, *City and Country*; J. M. Mecklin, *The Ku Klux Klan*; R. Miller, *American Protestantism and So-*

cial Issues, 1919–1939; A. Sinclair, Prohibition: The Era of Excess; J. Timberlake, Prohibition and the Progressive Movement, 1900–1920; J. Weinstein, The Decline of Socialism in America, 1912–1925.

5. Foreign Affairs

S. F. Bemis, The Latin American Policy of the United States; D. Borg, American Policy and the Chinese Revolution 1925–1928; H. Cline, The United States and Mexico; R. Current, Secretary Stimson; A. De Conde, Herbert Hoover's Latin American Policy; L. Ellis, Republican Foreign Policy, 1921–1933; J. K. Fairbank, The United States and China; H. Feis, Diplomacy of the Dollar 1919–1932; R. H. Ferrell, Peace in Their Time; D. F. Fleming, United States and World Organization 1920–1933; B. Glad, Charles Evans Hughes and the Illusions of Innocence; A. W. Griswold, The Far Eastern Policy of the United States; H. Nicolson, Dwight Morrow; R. W. Paul, The Abrogation of the Gentlemen's Agreement; D. Perkins, The United States and the Caribbean and Hands Off! A History of the Monroe Doctrine; M. Pusey, Charles Evans Hughes (2 vols.); E. O. Reischauer, The United States and Japan; S. Smith, The Manchurian Crisis 1931–32; H. L. Stimson & M. Bundy, On Active Service in Peace and War; J. Tulchin, The Aftermath of War; J. C. Vinson, The Parchment Peace; B. H. Williams, Economic Foreign Policies of the United States; J. Wilson, American Business and Foreign Policy, 1920–1933.

6. The Economy

A. A. Berle & G. C. Means, Modern Corporation and Private Property; A. R. Burns, The Decline of Competition; C. Chapman, Development of American Business and Banking Thought; J. K. Galbraith, American Capitalism and The Great Crash; S. Giedion, Mechanization Takes Command; M. Heald, The Social Responsibilities of Business; H. Jerome, Mechanization in Industry; S. Kuznets, The National Income and Its Composition 1919–1938; H. W. Laidler, Concentration of Control in American Industry; W. W. Leontief, The Structure of American Economy 1919–1929; A. Nevins & F. E. Hill, Ford: Expansion and Challenge 1915–1933; G. W. Nutter, Extent of Enterprise Monopoly 1899–1931; O. Pease, The Responsibilities of American Advertising; The President's Committee, Recent Economic Changes in the United States (2 vols.); R. Sobel, The Big Board and The Great Bull Market; G. Soule, Prosperity Decade; E. R. Wicker, Federal Reserve Monetary Policy, 1917–1933; R. Wik, Henry Ford and Grass-roots America; T. Wilson, Fluctuations in Income and Employment.

7. Labor and Agriculture

H. Barger & H. Landsberg, American Agriculture 1899–1939; M. R. Benedict, Farm Policies of the United States 1790–1950; D. Brody, Labor in Crisis: The Steel Strike of 1919; J. R. Commons et al., History of Labor, vol. 4; J. D. Durand, The Labor Force, 1890–1960; G. Fite, George Peek and the Fight for Farm Parity; T. Saloutos & J. D. Hicks, Agricultural Discontent in the Middle West; P. Taft, The A.F. of L. in the Time of Gompers; J. Weinstein, The Decline of Socialism in America, 1912–1925.

8. Social Developments

J. Burnham, Psychoanalysis and American Medicine: 1894–1918; W. Chafe, The American Woman; N. Hale, Freud and the Americans; D. Kennedy, Birth Control in America; J. Lemons, The Woman Citizen; R. and H. Lynd, Middletown; W. F. Ogburn (ed.), Recent Social Changes in the United States; W. O'Neill, Everyone Was Brave; G. Osofsky, Harlem.

9. Literature

C. Baker, Hemingway; V. W. Brooks, The Confident Years; H. M. Campbell & R. E. Foster, William Faulkner; O. Cargill, Intellectual America; R. Chase, The American Novel and Its Tradition; M. Cowley, After the Genteel Tradition and Exile's Return; B. Duffey, Chicago Renaissance in American Letters; C. A. Fenton, The Apprenticeship of Ernest Hemingway; L. Fiedler, Life and Death in the American Novel; M. Geismar, Rebels and Ancestors, The Last of the Provincials, and Writers in Crisis; R. Gilbert, Shine, Perishing Republic: Robinson Jeffers; D. Heiney, Recent American Literature; F. J. Hoffman, Freudianism and the Literary Mind and The Twenties; I. Howe, William Faulkner; N. Huggins, Harlem Renaissance; R. Jarrell, Poetry and the Age; M. Josephson, Portrait of the Artist as an American; A. Kazin, On Native Grounds; W. Manchester, Disturber of the Peace: H. L. Mencken; F. O. Matthiessen, The Achievement of T. S. Eliot; H. F. May, The End of American Innocence; A. Mizener, The Far Side of Paradise (Fitzgerald); H. J. Muller, Thomas Wolfe; E. Neff, Edwin Arlington Robinson; W. V. O'Connor, The Tangled Fire of William Faulkner; S. Persons, American Minds; L. C. Powell, Robinson Jeffers; M. Schorer, Sinclair Lewis; R. Sklar, F. Scott Fitzgerald; R. E. Spiller et al., Literary History of the United States, vol. 2; E. Wilson, The Shores of Light.

10. Art, Painting, and Music

J. Baur, Revolution and Tradition in American Art; M.

Brown, *American Paintings from the Armory Show to the Depression*; E. Cary, *George Luks*; M. Cheney, *Modern Art in America*; I. Glackens, *William Glackens and the Ashcan Group*; S. Hunter, *Modern American Painting and Sculpture*; S. Janis, *Abstract and Surrealist Art in America*; S. Kootz, *Modern American Painters*; N. Leonard, *Jazz and the White Americans*; C. Rourke, *Charles Sheeler*; J. T. Soby, *Contemporary Painters*.

CHAPTER 31

1. *General*

I. Berstein, *The Lean Years*; J. Braeman et al. (eds.), *Change and Continuity in Twentieth-Century America* and *The New Deal*; P. Conkin, *The New Deal*; W. Droze et al., *Essays on the New Deal*; M. Einandi, *The Roosevelt Revolution*; M. J. Frish & M. Diamond (eds.), *The Thirties*; O. L. Graham, Jr., *An Encore for Reform*; C. Kindleberger, *World in Depression, 1929–1939*; W. E. Leuchtenburg, *The Perils of Prosperity, 1914–32* and *Franklin D. Roosevelt and the New Deal, 1932–1940*; B. Mitchell, *Depression Decade, 1929–1941*; R. Moley, *After Seven Years*; R. H. Pells, *Radical Visions and American Dreams*; A. M. Schlesinger, Jr., *The Age of Roosevelt*, vol. 1: *The Crisis of the Old Order*, vol. 2: *The Coming of the New Deal*, and vol. 3: *The Politics of Upheaval*; R. J. Simon (ed.), *As We Saw the Thirties*; G. Tindall, *The Emergence of the New South, 1913–1945*; D. Wecter, *The Age of the Great Depression, 1929–1941*.

2. *The Hoover Administration*

W. S. Myers & W. H. Newton, *The Hoover Administration*; A. U. Romasco, *The Poverty of Abundance*; J. Schwarz, *The Interregnum of Despair*; R. L. Wilbur & A. M. Hyde, *The Hoover Policies*.

3. *Roosevelt and His Circle*

B. Bellush, *Franklin D. Roosevelt as Governor of New York*; J. M. Blum, *From the Morgenthau Diaries: Years of Crisis, 1928–1938*; J. M. Burns, *Roosevelt: The Lion and the Fox*; F. Freidel, *Franklin D. Roosevelt* (4 vols.) and *F.D.R. and the South*; D. R. Fusfeld, *The Economic Thought of Franklin D. Roosevelt and the Origins of the New Deal*; T. Greer, *What Roosevelt Thought*; T. K. Hareven, *Eleanor Roosevelt*; H. Ickes, *The Secret Diary of Harold L. Ickes* (3 vols.); J. Lash, *Eleanor and Franklin*; F. Perkins, *The Roosevelt I Knew*; A. Rollins, Jr., *Roosevelt and Howe*; E. Roosevelt, *This Is My Story* and *This I Remember*; S. Rosenman, *Working with Roosevelt*; R. Sherwood,

Roosevelt and Hopkins; R. Tugwell, *The Brains Trust* and *The Democratic Roosevelt*.

4. *Politics and Elections*

E. C. Blackorby, *Prairie Rebel* (Lemke); F. Broderick, *Right Reverend New Dealer: John A. Ryan*; R. Burke, *Olson's New Deal for California*; J. Farley, *Jim Farley's Story*; G. Q. Flynn, *American Catholics and the Roosevelt Presidency*; J. J. Huthmacher, *Senator Robert F. Wagner and the Rise of Urban Liberalism*; R. Ingalls, *Herbert H. Lehman and New York's Little New Deal*; F. Israel, *Nevada's Key Pittman*; D. B. Johnson, *The Republican Party and Wendell Willkie*; B. Karl, *Executive Reorganization & Reform in the New Deal*; D. R. McCoy, *Angry Voices* and *Landon of Kansas*; G. Mayer, *The Political Career of Floyd B. Olson*; Rev. A. Ogden, *The Dies Committee*; J. T. Patterson, *Congressional Conservatism and the New Deal* and *The New Deal and the States*; R. Polenberg, *Reorganizing Roosevelt's Government*; B. Stave, *The New Deal and the Last Hurrah*; C. J. Tull, *Father Coughlin and the New Deal*; F. A. Warren, *Liberals and Communism*; T. H. Williams, *Huey Long*; G. Wolfskill, *Revolt of the Conservatives*.

5. *Industry and Finance*

A. W. Crawford, *Monetary Management under the New Deal*; R. de Bedts, *The New Deal's SEC*; J. K. Galbraith & G. C. Johnson, *Economic Effects of Federal Works Expenditures, 1933–1938*; E. W. Hawley, *The New Deal and the Problem of Monopoly*; G. G. Johnson, *The Treasury and Monetary Policy 1933–1938*; H. Johnson, *The Blue Eagle, from Egg to Earth*; S. Kennedy, *The Banking Crisis of 1933*; D. Lynch, *The Concentration of Economic Power*; L. S. Lyon et al., *The National Recovery Administration*; J. R. Reeve, *Monetary Reform Movements*; K. D. Roose, *Economics of Recession and Revival*.

6. *Agriculture*

M. R. Benedict, *Farm Policies of the United States*; G. Fite, *George N. Peek and the Fight for Farm Parity*; R. S. Kirkendall, *Social Scientists and Farm Politics in the Age of Roosevelt*; E. G. Nourse et al., *Three Years of the AAA*; J. Shover, *Cornbelt Rebellion*.

7. *Relief, Social Security, and Labor*

A. J. Altmeyer, *The Formative Years of Social Security*; J. Auerbach, *Labor and Liberty*; I. Bernstein, *The New Deal Collective Bargaining Policy* and *Turbulent Years*; J. C. Brown, *Public Relief*; P. Conkin, *Tomorrow a New World*; D. E. Conrad, *The Forgotten*

Farmers; M. Derber & E. Young (eds.), Labor and the New Deal; S. Fine, The Automobile Under the Blue Eagle and Sit-Down; W. Galenson, The C.I.O. Challenge to the A.F. of L.; H. Harris, American Labor; A. Holtzman, The Townsend Movement; D. S. Howard, The WPA and Federal Relief Policy; R. Lubove, The Struggle for Social security; R. & H. Lynd, Middletown in Transition; J. Mathews, The Federal Theatre, 1935–1939; J. A. Salmond, The Civilian Conservation Corps; E. E. Witte, The Development of the Social Security Act.

8. The TVA and Conservation

W. H. Droze, High Dams and Slack Waters; W. E. Leuchtenburg, Flood Control Politics; D. E. Lilienthal, The TVA: Democracy on the March and Journals: The TVA Years; T. McCraw, TVA and the Power Fight, 1933–1939; C. H. Pritchett, The Tennessee Valley Authority; P. Selznick, TVA and the Grass Roots.

9. Supreme Court

L. Baker, Back to Back; D. Carter, Scottsboro; H. S. Commager, Majority Rule and Minority Rights; R. Cortner, The Wagner Act Cases; E. S. Corwin, The Twilight of the Supreme Court, Court Over Constitution, The Commerce Power vs. State Rights, and Constitutional Revolution, Ltd.; J. P. Frank, Mr. Justice Black; E. C. Gerhart, America's Advocate: Robert H. Jackson; S. Hendel, Charles Evans Hughes and the Supreme Court; R. Jackson, Struggle for Judicial Supremacy; S. Konefsky, The Legacy of Holmes and Brandeis, Justice Stone and the Supreme Court, and The Constitutional World of Mr. Justice Frankfurter; A. T. Mason, Harlan Fiske Stone; A. T. Mason & W. M. Beaney, The Supreme Court in a Free Society; J. Paschal, Mr. Justice Sutherland; C. H. Pritchett, The Roosevelt Court; M. J. Pusey, Charles Evans Hughes (2 vols.); B. Schwartz, The Supreme Court: Constitutional Revolution in Retrospect.

10. Documents

D. Congdon (ed.), The '30s; L. Filler (ed.), The Anxious Years; M. Keller (ed.), The New Deal; W. E. Leuchtenburg (ed.), The New Deal and Franklin D. Roosevelt; E. Nixon (ed.), Franklin D. Roosevelt and Conservation (2 vols.); F. D. Roosevelt & S. Rosenman (eds.), The Public Papers and Addresses of Franklin D. Roosevelt (13 vols.); J. Salzman & B. Wallenstein (eds.), Years of Protest; D. Shannon (ed.), The Great Depression; B. Sternsher (ed.), The New Deal; H. Swados (ed.), The American Writer and the Great Depression.

CHAPTERS 32–33

1. Roosevelt's Foreign Policy and the Coming of the War

C. A. Beard, American Foreign Policy in the Making, 1932–1940 and President Roosevelt and the Coming of the War, 1941; R. P. Browder, The Origins of Soviet-American Diplomacy; F. A. Cave et al., Origins and Consequences of World War II; M. Chadwin, The Hawks of World War II; W. S. Churchill, The Second World War (6 vols.); W. I. Cohen, The American Revisionists; W. S. Cole, America First and Senator Gerald P. Nye and American Foreign Relations; G. Craig & F. Gilbert (eds.), The Diplomats, 1919–1939; E. Cronon, Josephus Daniels in Mexico; R. N. Current, Secretary Stimson; R. Dallek, Democrat & Diplomat; R. A. Divine, The Illusion of Neutrality; D. Drummond, The Passing of American Neutrality; T. R. Fehrenbach, F.D.R.'s Undeclared War; H. Feis, The Road to Pearl Harbor; R. Ferrell, The Diplomacy of the Great Depression; L. Gardner, Economic Aspects of New Deal Diplomacy; E. D. Guerrant, Roosevelt's Good Neighbor Policy; W. H. Heinrichs, Jr., American Ambassador (Grew); C. Hull, Memoirs (2 vols.); M. Jonas, Isolationism in America, 1935–1941; T. Kase, Journey to the Missouri; W. L. Langer & S. E. Gleason, The Challenge to Isolation 1937–1940 and The Undeclared War 1940–1941; E. E. Morison, Turmoil and Tradition; A. D. Morse, While Six Million Died; J. W. Pratt, Cordell Hull (2 vols.); B. Rauch, Roosevelt from Munich to Pearl Harbor; E. O. Reischauer, The United States and Japan; P. W. Schroeder, The Axis Alliance and Japanese-American Relations; C. C. Tansill, Back Door To War; F. J. Taylor, The United States and the Spanish Civil War; H. L. Trefousse, Germany and American Neutrality; M. S. Watson, Chief-of-Staff: Prewar Plans and Preparations; J. E. Wiltz, In Search of Peace and From Isolation to War, 1931–1941; R. Wohlstetter, Pearl Harbor: Warning and Decision; B. Wood, The Making of the Good Neighbor Policy.

2. General

J. P. Baxter, 3rd, Scientists Against Time; A. R. Buchanan, The United States in World War II (2 vols.); Bureau of the Budget, The U.S. at War; V. J. Esposito (ed.), A Concise History of World War II; J. F. C. Fuller, The Second World War, 1939–45; K. R. Greenfield, World War II Strategy Reconsidered and (ed.), Command Decisions; R. Hewlett & O. Anderson, The New World; J. A. Isely & P. A. Crowl, The U.S. Marines and Amphibious War; G. H. Johnston, The Toughest

Fighting in the World; L. Lansing, *Day of Trinity*; W. Millis (ed.), *The War Reports of General George C. Marshall, General H. H. Arnold, and Admiral E. J. King*; S. E. Morison, *Strategy and Compromise* and *The Two Ocean War*; T. Roscoe, *U.S. Submarine Operations, World War II*.

3. Biographies and Memoirs

H. H. Arnold, *Global Mission*; General Omar Bradley, *A Soldier's Story*; A. Bryant, *The Turn of the Tide* and *Triumph in the West* (2 vols.); R. L. Eichelberger, *Our Jungle Road to Tokyo*; D. D. Eisenhower, *Crusade in Europe*; W. F. Halsey & J. Bryan, 3rd, *Admiral Halsey's Story*; E. J. King & W. Whitehill, *Fleet Admiral King*; S.L.A. Marshall, *Blitzkrieg, Bastogne, Island Victory*, and *Night Drop* (Normandy); Viscount Montgomery of Alamein, *The Memoirs*; R. Payne, *The Marshall Story*; F. Pogue, *George C. Marshall*; T. White (ed.), *The Stilwell Papers*.

4. Comprehensive Multi-Volume Histories

U.S. ARMY. K. R. Greenfield *et al.* (eds.), *The U.S. Army in World War II* and *The American Forces in Action*; W. F. Craven & J. L. Cate (eds.), *The Army Air Forces in World War II*. U.S. MARINE CORPS. *History of U.S. Marine Corps Operations in World War II*; *Marine Corps Monographs*. U.S. NAVY AND COAST GUARD. J. A. Furer, *Administration of the Navy Dept. in World War II*; S. E. Morison, *History of United States Naval Operations in World War II*; M. F. Willoughby, *The United States Coast Guard in World War II*.

5. Wartime Diplomacy

J. M. Blum (ed.), *From the Morgenthau Diaries: Years of War, 1941–1945*; R. Butow, *Japan's Decision To Surrender*; R. A. Divine, *The Reluctant Belligerent*; H. Feis, *The China Tangle, Churchill-Roosevelt-Stalin, The Potsdam Conference*, and *Japan Subdued*; T. Higgins, *Winston Churchill and the Second Front*; G. Kolko, *The Politics of War*; W. L. Langer, *Our Vichy Gamble*; R. Murphy, *Diplomat Among Warriors*; W. L. Neumann, *Making the Peace, 1941–1945*; C. F. Romanus & R. Sunderland, *Stilwell's Mission to China*; G. Smith, *American Diplomacy during the Second World War*; J. L. Snell, *Illusion and Necessity* and (ed.), *The Meaning of Yalta*.

6. Mobilization and American Society in Wartime

A. A. Blum, *Drafted or Deferred*; B. Catton, *War Lords of Washington*; L. V. Chandler, *Inflation in the United States, 1940–1948*; M. Clinard, *The Black Market*; R. H. Connery, *Navy and Industrial Mobilization in World War II*; E. S. Corwin, *Total War and the Constitution*; J. Dos Passos, *State of the Union*; H. Garfinkel, *When Negroes March*; J. Goodman (ed.), *While You Were Gone*; M. Grodzins, *Americans Betrayed*; H. D. Hall, *North American Supply*; W. Hassett, *Off the Record with FDR 1942–1945*; E. Janeway, *The Struggle for Survival*; U. Lee, *The Employment of Negro Troops*; F. Merrill (ed.), *Social Problems on the Home Front*; D. Novik *et al.*, *War-time Production Control*; W. F. Ogburn (ed.), *American Society in Wartime*; D. H. Riddle, *The Truman Committee*; J. Seidman, *American Labor from Defense to Reconversion*; H. M. Somers, *Presidential Agency: OWMR*; J. ten Broek *et al.*, *Salvage: Japanese American Evacuation and Resettlement*; G. Tindall, *The Emergence of the New South, 1913–1945*; War Production Board, *Industrial Mobilization for War*, vol. 1; R. Young, *Congressional Politics in the Second World War*.

CHAPTERS 34–35

1. General

Congressional Quarterly, *Congress and Nation*; C. Degler, *Affluence and Anxiety*; M. Gelfand, *A Nation of Cities*; E. Goldman, *The Crucial Decade*; A. Hamby, *Beyond the New Deal*; W. Johnson, *1600 Pennsylvania Avenue*; W. Leuchtenburg, *A Troubled Feast*; B. McKelvey, *The Emergence of Metropolitan America*; L. Wittner, *Cold War America*; H. Zinn, *Postwar America, 1945–1971*.

2. Foreign Affairs: General

J. F. Byrnes, *Speaking Frankly*; W. G. Carleton, *Revolution in American Foreign Policy*; J. Davids, *America and the World in Our Time*; L. J. Halle, *The Cold War as History*; G. F. Kennan, *The Realities of American Foreign Policy*; J. Lukacs, *A History of the Cold War*; H. Morgenthau, *Dilemmas of Politics* and *Politics Among the Nations*; R. Osgood, *Limited War*; W. Reitzel *et al.*, *United States Foreign Policy, 1945–1955*; W. W. Rostow, *The United States in the World Arena*; J. W. Spanier, *American Foreign Policy Since World War II*; R. P. Stebbins, *The United States in World Affairs* (annual volumes); H. B. Westerfield, *Foreign Policy and Party Politics: Pearl Harbor to Korea*.

3. Liquidating the War

R. Benedict, *The Chrysanthemum and the Sword*; V.

H. Bernstein, *Final Judgment: The Story of Nurem-berg*; W. Friedman, *Allied Military Government of Germany*; S. Glueck, *Nuremberg Trial and Ag-gressive War*; G. Herring, *Aid to Russia*; R. Jackson, *The Case Against the Nazi War Criminals*; E. H. Litch-field (ed.), *Governing Postwar Germany*; A. F. Reel, *The Case of General Yamashita*; E. Reischauer, *The United States and Japan*; D. Ross, *Preparing for Ulys-ses*; R. Woetzel, *Nuremberg Trials in International Law*; H. Zink, *American Military Government in Germany*.

4. Organization for Peace and the Control of Atomic Weapons

G. Alperovitz, *Atomic Diplomacy*; R. Batchelder, *The Irreversible Decision 1939–1950*; P. M. Blackett, *Fear, War and the Bomb*; D. Bradley, *No Place to Hide*; B. Brodie, *The Absolute Weapon*; H. Brown, *The Chal-lenge of Man's Future*; D. Clemens, *Yalta*; N. Cousins, *Modern Man Is Obsolete*; R. A. Dahl & R. S. Brown, *The Domestic Control of Atomic Energy*; P. Gallois, *The Balance of Terror*; G. Gamow, *Atomic Energy in Cosmic and Human Life*; J. M. Gavin, *War and Peace in the Space Age*; R. Gilpin, *American Scientists and Nuclear Weapons Policy*; R. G. Hewlett & O. E. An-derson, Jr., *The New World*; H. Kahn, *On Thermo-nuclear War*; G. Kennan, *Russia, the Atom and the West*; H. Kissinger, *Nuclear Weapons and Foreign Policy*; R. Lapp, *Atoms and Peace*; P. McGuire, *Ex-periment in World Order*; J. Muther, *History of the United Nations Charter*.

5. Relief and Recovery

D. A. Baldwin, *Economic Development and American Foreign Policy*; W. A. Brown, *American Foreign Assis-tance*; M. Curti & K. Birr, *Prelude to Point Four: American Missions Overseas*; S. Harris, *European Re-covery Program* and *Foreign Economic Policy for the United States*; J. M. Jones, *The Fifteen Weeks*; G. Woodbridge (ed.), *UNRRA* (2 vols.).

6. The Cold War

D. Acheson, *Present at the Creation*; C. Bohlen, *Wit-ness to History*; E. H. Carr, *Soviet Impact on the West-ern World*; W. P. Davison, *The Berlin Blockade*; R. Drummond & G. Coblenz, *Duel at the Brink*; H. Feis, *Between War and Peace*, *Contest over Japan*, *From Trust to Terror*, and *Potsdam*; H. Finer, *Dulles Over Suez*; D. L. Fleming, *The Cold War* (2 vols.); J. Gaddis, *The United States and the Origins of the Cold War, 1941–1947*; L. Gardner, *Architects of Illusion*; N.

Graebner, *The New Isolationism*; M. F. Herz, *Begin-nings of the Cold War*; T. Hoopes, *The Devil and John Foster Dulles*; B. H. Ivanyi & A. Bell, *The Road to Potsdam*; G. Kolko, *The Roots of American Foreign Policy*; W. H. McNeill, *America, Britain, and Russia*; R. E. Osgood, *NATO: The Entangling Alliance*; H. L. Roberts, *Russia and America*; A. A. Rogow, *James Forrestal*; G. Smith, *Dean Acheson*; E. Stillman & W. Pfaff, *The New Politics*; L. Wittner, *Rebels Against War*.

7. The Korean War

C. Berger, *The Korea Knot*; R. Caridi, *The Korean War and American Politics*; M. Clark, *From the Danube to the Yalu*; H. Feis, *The China Tangle*; L. M. Goodrich, *Korea*; T. Higgins, *Korea and the Fall of MacArthur*; R. T. Oliver, *Why War Came to Korea*; D. Rees, *Korea: The Limited War*; R. Rovere & A. M. Schlesinger, Jr., *The General and the President*; J. Spanier, *The Truman-MacArthur Controversy*; A. Whiting, *China Crosses the Yalu*; C. Whitney, *MacAr-thur*; C. A. Willoughby & J. Chamberlain, *MacArthur, 1944–1951*.

8. Latin America

R. Alexander, *Communism in Latin America*; D. M. Dozer, *Are We Good Neighbors?*; R. Schneider, *Com-munism in Guatemala*; A. P. Whitaker, *Argentine Upheaval* and *The United States and Latin America: The Northern Republics*.

9. Politics

S. G. Brown, *Conscience in Politics: Adlai Stevenson*; A. Campbell *et al.*, *The American Voter*; P. David *et al.*, *Presidential Nominating Politics in 1952*; K. S. Davis, *A Prophet in His Own Country*; H. Eulau, *Class and Party in the Eisenhower Years*; R. Garson, *The Democratic Party and the Politics of Sectionalism, 1941–1948*; V. O. Key, Jr., *Southern Politics in State and Nation*; S. Lubell, *The Revolt of the Moderates*; N. Markowitz, *The Rise and Fall of the People's Century*; H. J. Muller, *Adlai Stevenson*; J. Patterson, *Mr. Re-publican*; C. A. H. Thomson & F. M. Shattuck, *The 1956 Presidential Campaign*; D. B. Truman, *The Con-gressional Party*.

10. Truman and the Fair Deal

S. K. Bailey, *Congress Makes a Law*; E. R. Bartley, *The Tidelands Oil Controversy*; B. Bernstein (ed.), *Politics and Policies of the Truman Administration*; P. A. Brinker, *The Taft-Hartley Act After Ten Years*; J. G.

Burrow, *AMA*; J. Daniels, *The Man of Independence*; R. Davies, *Housing Reform During the Truman Administration*; R. S. Kirkendall (ed.), *The Truman Period as a Research Field* and *The Truman Period as a Research Field: A Reappraisal*; R. A. Lee, *Truman and Taft-Hartley*; A. J. Matusow, *Farm Policies and Politics in the Truman Years*; H. A. Millis & E. C. Brown, *From the Wagner Act to Taft-Hartley*; C. Phillips, *The Truman Presidency*; H. S. Truman, *Memoirs* (2 vols.).

11. *Civil Liberties*

J. Anderson & R. May, *McCarthy*; A. Barth, *The Loyalty of Free Men*; D. Bell (ed.), *The New American Right*; E. Bontecou, *The Federal Loyalty-Security Program*; R. Brown, *Loyalty and Security*; R. K. Carr, *Federal Protection of Civil Rights*, *The House Committee on Un-American Activities*, and *To Secure These Rights*; J. W. Caughey, *In Clear and Present Danger*; W. Chambers, *Witness*; H. W. Chase, *Security and Liberty*; H. S. Commager, *Freedom, Loyalty, Dissent*; A. Cooke, *A Generation on Trial*; C. Curtis, *The Oppenheimer Case*; T. Draper, *The Roots of American Communism*; O. D. Fraenkel, *Supreme Court and Civil Liberties*; R. Freeland, *The Truman Doctrine and the Origins of McCarthyism*; W. Gellhorn, *Security, Loyalty, and Science*, *The States and Subversion*, and *American Rights*; R. Griffith, *The Politics of Fear*; M. Grodzins, *The Loyal and the Disloyal*; L. Hand, *The Spirit of Liberty*; A. Harper, *The Politics of Loyalty*; A. Hiss, *In the Court of Public Opinion*; S. Hook, *Heresy, Yes—Conspiracy, No*; D. J. Kemper, *The Decade of Fear*; M. Konvitz, *The Constitution and Civil Rights*; E. Latham, *The Communist Controversy in Washington*; R. P. Longacker, *The Presidency and Civil Liberties*; D. McCoy & R. Ruetten, *Quiet and Response*; C. H. Pritchett, *Civil Liberties and the Vinson Court*; M. P. Rogin, *The Intellectuals and McCarthy*; R. Rovere, *Senator Joe McCarthy*; D. Shannon, *The Decline of American Communism*; E. A. Shils, *The Torment of Secrecy*; S. A. Stouffer, *Communism, Conformity and Civil Liberties*; A. Theoharis, *Seeds of Repression*; J. A. Wechsler, *The Age of Suspicion*.

12. *The Eisenhower Government*

S. Adams, *First-Hand Report*; M. Childs, *Eisenhower: Captive Hero*; E. L. Dale, *Conservatives in Power*; R. J. Donovan, *Eisenhower: The Inside Story*; E. J. Hughes, *The Ordeal of Power*; A. McAdams, *Power and Politics in Labor Legislation*; M. Merson, *The Private Diary of a Public Servant*; R. M. Nixon, *Six Crises*; H. Parmet, *Eisenhower and the American Crusades*; M. J. Pusey,

Eisenhower the President; G. Reichard, *The Reaffirmation of Republicanism*; R. Rovere, *The Eisenhower Years: Affairs of State*; J. L. Sundquist, *Politics and Policy*; A. Wildavsky, *Dixon-Yates*.

13. *Civil Rights*

N. Bartley, *The Rise of Massive Resistance*; M. Berger, *Equality by Statute*; R. Dalfiume, *Desegregation of the Armed Forces*; B. Daniel (ed.), *Black, White and Gray*; R. Harris, *The Quest for Equality*; A. Lewis et al., *Portrait of a Decade*; D. R. Matthews & J. W. Prothro, *Negroes and the New Southern Politics*; A. Meier and E. Rudwick, *CORE*; C. Mitau, *Decade of Decision*; W. F. Murphy, *Congress and the Court*; B. Muse, *Ten Years of Prelude*; A. M. Rose, *The Negro in Postwar America*; R. H. Sayler et al. (eds.), *The Warren Court*; D. Shoemaker (ed.), *With All Deliberate Speed: Segregation-Desegregation*; J. W. Silver, *Mississippi: The Closed Society*; F. E. Smith, *Congressman from Mississippi*; B. M. Ziegler, *Desegregation and the Supreme Court*; H. Zinn, *SNCC: The New Abolitionists*.

14. *The Warfare State*

M. Berkowitz & P. G. Bock, *American National Security*; D. Caraley, *The Politics of Military Unification*; P. Hammond, *Organizing for Defense*; S. Huntington, *The Common Defense* and *The Soldier and the State*; W. R. Kintner et al., *Forging a New Sword*; E. A. Kolodziej, *The Uncommon Defense and Congress, 1945–1963*; E. R. May (ed.), *The Ultimate Decision*; W. Millis, *Arms and the State*; C. Rossiter, *The Supreme Court and the Commander-in-Chief*; J. M. Swomley, *The Military Establishment*.

15. *Growth and the Economy*

W. Adams & H. M. Gray, *Monopoly in America*; F. M. Bator, *The Question of Government Spending*; S. Donaldson, *The Suburban Myth*; E. S. Flash, Jr., *Economic Advice and Presidential Leadership*; Editors of Fortune, *America in the Sixties*; J. K. Galbraith, *The Affluent Society* and *American Capitalism*; D. Hathaway, *Government and Agriculture*; A. E. Holmans, *United States Fiscal Policy, 1945–1959*; R. Lekachman, *Age of Keynes*; M. Lerner, *America as a Civilization*; D. E. Lilienthal, *Big Business*; A. Shonfield, *Modern Capitalism*; L. Soth, *Farm Trouble in an Age of Plenty*; C. E. Warne & K. W. Lumpkin et al., *Labor in Post War America*; R. Wood, *Suburbia*.

16. *Arts and Letters*

J. Aldridge, *After the Lost Generation*; I. H. Baur,

Revolution and Tradition in Modern American Art; H. Harper, Jr., *Desperate Faith*; R. Jarrell, *Poetry and the Age*; J. Kramer, *Allen Ginsberg in America*; L. Lipton, *The Holy Barbarians*; A. C. Ritchie, *Abstract Painting and Sculpture in America*; B. Rosenberg & D. M. White (eds.), *Mass Culture*; S. Stepanchev, *American Poetry Since 1945*.

CHAPTER 36

1. *JFK and LBJ*

R. Berman, *America in the Sixties*; D. Burner *et al.*, *A Giant's Strength*; J. M. Burns, *John F. Kennedy*; M. Davie, *LBJ*; A. Donald (ed.), *John F. Kennedy and the New Frontier*; H. Fairlie, *The Kennedy Promise*; H. Golden, *Mr. Kennedy and the Negroes*; D. F. Hadwiger & R. B. Talbot, *Pressures and Protests*; L. Heren, *No Hail, No Farewell*; H. Miller, *Rich Man, Poor Man*; B. Muse, *The American Negro Revolution*; W. O'Neill, *Coming Apart*; P. Salinger, *With Kennedy*; A. M. Schlesinger, Jr., *A Thousand Days*; H. Sidey, *John F. Kennedy: President*; T. Sorenson, *Kennedy*; J. L. Sundquist, *Politics and Policy*; T. Wicker, *JFK and LBJ*; B. H. Wilkins & C. B. Friday, *The Economists of the New Frontier*.

2. *Politics*

L. Chester *et al.*, *An American Melodrama*; B. Cosman & R. J. Huckshorn (eds.), *Republican Politics*; M. C. Cummings, Jr. (ed.), *The National Election of 1964*; G. F. Gilder & B. K. Chapman, *The Party That Lost Its Head*; H. Graham & T. Gurr, *Violence in America*; S. E. Harris, *Economics of the Kennedy Years*; R. D. Novak, *The Agony of the G.O.P. 1964*; R. H. Rovere, *The Goldwater Caper*; T. White, *The Making of the President, 1960*, *The Making of the President, 1964*, and *The Making of the President, 1968*.

3. *Foreign Affairs*

G. Allison, *Essence of Decision*; J. R. Boettiger (ed.), *Vietnam and American Foreign Policy*; C. Bowles, *Promises to Keep*; J. Buttinger, *Vietnam: A Dragon Embattled*; C. Cooper, *The Lost Crusade*; B. Fall, *The Two Vietnams* and *Viet-Nam Witness, 1953–66*; F. Fitzgerald, *Fire in the Lake*; J. W. Fulbright, *The Arrogance of Power*; J. Galbraith, *Ambassador's Journal*; P. L. Geyelin, *Lyndon B. Johnson and the World*; R. N. Goodwin, *Triumph or Tragedy*; D. Halberstam, *The Best and the Brightest*; R. Hilsman, *To Move a Nation*; K. Meyer & T. Szulc, *The Cuban Invasion*; M. G. Raskin & B. B. Fall (eds.), *The Viet-Nam Reader*; A. M. Schlesinger, Jr., *The Bitter Heritage*; R. Shaplen, *The Lost Revolution*; R. Stebbins, *The United States in World Affairs* (for appropriate years); R. Walton, *Cold War and Counter-Revolution*.

4. *Nixon and Ford*

C. Bernstein & R. Woodward, *All the President's Men*; H. Brandon, *The Retreat of American Power*; R. Evans & R. Novak, *Nixon in the White House*; H. Fairlie, *The Spoiled Child of the Western World*; S. Graubard, *Kissinger*; R. Harris, *Justice*; J. Hersey, *The President*; E. Kahn, Jr., *The American People*; D. Landau, *Kissinger*; F. Mankiewicz, *Perfectly Clear*; New York Times (ed.), *The End of a Presidency*; R. Reeves, *A Ford not a Lincoln*; R. Scammon & B. Wattenberg, *The Real Majority*; J. Schell, *The Time of Illusion*; L. Silk, *Nixonomics*; G. Wills, *Nixon Agonistes*.

Statistical Tables

Admission of States to the Union

Immigration by Country of Origin, 1820–1973

Population of the United States, 1870–1974

Urban and Rural Population, 1870–1970

Presidential Vote, 1876–1972

Justices of the United States Supreme Court

Distribution of Income, 1950–1974

ADMISSION OF STATES TO THE UNION

State	Entered Union	State	Entered Union	State	Entered Union	State	Entered Union
Alabama	1819	Indiana	1816	Nebraska	1867	South Carolina	1788
Alaska	1959	Iowa	1846	Nevada	1864	South Dakota	1889
Arizona	1912	Kansas	1861	New Hampshire	1788	Tennessee	1796
Arkansas	1836	Kentucky	1792	New Jersey	1787	Texas	1845
California	1850	Louisiana	1812	New Mexico	1912	Utah	1896
Colorado	1876	Maine	1820	New York	1788	Vermont	1791
Connecticut	1788	Maryland	1788	North Carolina	1789	Virginia	1788
Delaware	1787	Massachusetts	1788	North Dakota	1889	Washington	1889
Florida	1845	Michigan	1837	Ohio	1803	West Virginia	1863
Georgia	1788	Minnesota	1858	Oklahoma	1907	Wisconsin	1848
Hawaii	1959	Mississippi	1817	Oregon	1859	Wyoming	1890
Idaho	1890	Missouri	1821	Pennsylvania	1787		
Illinois	1818	Montana	1889	Rhode Island	1790		

IMMIGRATION BY COUNTRY OF ORIGIN, 1820-1973[1]

Countries	1820–1910	1911–1920	1921–1930	1931–1940	1941–1950	1951–1960	1961–1970	Total 154 yrs. 1820–1973
All Countries	27,918,992	5,735,811	4,107,209	528,431	1,035,039	2,515,479	3,321,517	46,320,181
Europe & U.S.S.R.								
Albania[11]				2,040	85	59	98	2,393
Austria[2,5]	3,172,461	453,649	32,868	3,563	24,860	67,106	20,621 } 5,401	4,309,625
Belgium	103,796	33,746	15,846	4,817	12,189	18,575	9,192	199,706
Bulgaria[10]	39,440	22,533	2,945	938	375	104	619	67,250
Czechoslovakia[11]		3,426	102,194	14,393	8,347	918	3,273	135,347
Denmark	258,053	41,983	32,430	2,559	5,393	10,984	9,201	362,037
Estonia[11]				506	212	185	163	1,093
Finland[11]		756	16,691	2,146	2,503	4,925	4,192	32,168
France	470,868	61,897	49,610	12,623	38,809	51,121	45,237	738,466
Germany[2,5]	5,351,746	143,945	412,202	114,058	226,578	477,765	190,796	6,941,061
Great Britain: England	2,212,071	249,944	157,420	21,756	112,252	156,171	174,452	3,115,677
Scotland	488,749	78,357	159,781	6,887	16,131	32,854	29,849	815,085
Wales	59,540	13,107	13,012	735	3,209	2,589	2,052	94,490
Not specified[3]	793,741					3,884	3,675	802,649
Greece	186,204	184,201	51,084	9,119	8,973	47,608	85,969	608,960
Hungary[2,5]		442,693	30,680	7,861	3,469	36,637		
Ireland	4,212,169	146,181	220,591	13,167	26,967	57,332	37,461	4,718,052
Italy	3,086,356	1,109,524	455,315	68,028	57,661	185,491	214,111	5,243,981
Latvia[11]				1,192	361	352	510	2,484
Lithuania[11]				2,201	683	242	562	3,751
Luxembourg[14]				565	820	684	556	2,723
Netherlands	175,943	43,718	26,948	7,150	14,860	52,277	30,606	354,539
Norway[4]	665,189	66,395	68,531	4,740	10,100	22,935	15,484	854,552
Poland[5]	165,182	4,813	227,734	17,026	7,571	9,985	53,539	495,684
Portugal	132,989	89,732	29,994	3,329	7,423	19,588	76,065	389,149
Romania[12]	72,117	13,311	67,646	3,871	1,076	1,039	2,531	163,738
Spain	69,296	68,611	28,958	3,258	2,898	7,894	44,659	239,057
Sweden[4]	1,021,165	95,074	97,249	3,960	10,665	21,697	16,506	1,268,825
Switzerland	237,401	23,091	29,676	5,512	10,547	17,675	18,453	345,124
U.S.S.R.[5,6]	2,605	1,888	49,064	5,835	1,576	8,225	20,381	98,214
Yugoslavia[10]		8,111	9,603	2,361	3,983	10,820	4,203	53,630
Other Europe	2,359,048	921,201	61,742	1,356	548	584	2,336	3,348,392
Asia[15]								
China[16]	326,060	21,278	29,907	4,928	16,709	9,657	34,764	468,564
India[7]	5,409	2,082	1,886	496	1,761	1,973	27,189	81,416
Japan[7]	158,344	83,837	33,462	1,948	1,555	46,250	39,988	381,174
Turkey	192,281	134,056	33,824	1,065	798	3,519	10,142	382,137
Other Asia	16,942	5,973	12,980	7,644	11,537	88,707	315,688	707,699

America								
Canada and Newfoundland[8]	1,230,501	742,185	924,515	108,527	171,718	377,952	413,310	4,024,813
Central America	10,365	17,159	15,769	5,861	21,665	44,751	101,780	243,302
Mexico[9]	77,645	219,004	459,287	22,319	60,589	299,811	453,937	1,777,536
South America	29,385	41,899	42,215	7,803	21,831	91,628	257,954	559,209
West Indies	233,146	123,424	74,899	15,502	49,725	123,091	470,213	1,279,768
Other America[13]			31	25	29,276	59,711	19,630	109,409
Africa	9,581	8,443	6,286	1,750	7,367	14,092	28,954	93,326
Australia & New Zealand	31,654	12,348	8,299	2,231	13,805	11,506	19,562	106,778
Pacific Islands (U.S. adm.)[15]	8,859	1,079	427	780	5,437	4,698	1,769	23,618
Countries not specified	252,691	1,147	228		142	12,493	3,884	273,530

[1]Since July 1, 1868, the data is for fiscal years ending June 30. Prior to fiscal year 1869, the periods covered are as follows: from 1820–31 and 1843–49, the years ended on September 30—1843 covers 9 months; and from 1832—42 and 1850–67, the years ended on December 31—1832 and 1850 cover 15 months. For 1868, the period ended on June 30 and covers 6 months.

[2]Data for Austria-Hungary was not reported until 1861. Austria and Hungary have been recorded separately since 1905. From 1938–45, Austria is included in Germany.

[3]Great Britain not specified. From 1901–51, included in other Europe.

[4]From 1820–68, the figures for Norway and Sweden are combined.

[5]Poland recorded as a separate country from 1820–98 and since 1920. From 1899–1919, Poland is included with Austria–Hungary, Germany, and Russia.

[6]From 1931–63, the U.S.S.R. is broken down into European U.S.S.R. and Asian U.S.S.R. Since 1964 total U.S.S.R. has been reported in Europe.

[7]No record of immigration from Japan before 1861.

[8]Prior to 1920, Canada and Newfoundland are recorded as British North America. From 1820–98, the figures include all British North American possessions.

[9]No record of immigration from Mexico from 1886–93.

[10]Bulgaria, Serbia, and Montenegro were first reported in 1899. Bulgaria has been reported separately since 1920; also in 1920, a separate enumeration was made for the Kingdom of Serbs, Croats, and Slovenes. Since 1922, the Serb, Croat, and Slovene Kingdom has been recorded as Yugoslavia.

[11]Countries added to the list since the beginning of World War I are included with the countries to which they belonged. Figures available since 1920 for Czechoslovakia and Finland and, since 1924, for Albania, Estonia, Latvia, and Lithuania.

[12]No record of immigration from Romania until 1880.

[13]Included with countries not specified to 1925.

[14]Figures for Luxembourg are available since 1925.

[15]Beginning with the year 1952, Asia includes the Philippines. From 1934–51 the Philippines are included in the Pacific Islands. Prior to 1934, the Philippines are recorded in separate tables as insular travel.

[16]Beginning with the year 1957, China includes Taiwan.

POPULATION OF THE UNITED STATES, 1870–1974
(in Thousands)

State	1870	1880	1890	1900	1910	1920	1930	1940	1950	1960	1970	(estimate) 1974
New England												
Maine	627	649	661	694	742	768	797	847	914	969	992	1,047
New Hampshire	318	347	377	412	431	443	465	492	533	607	738	808
Vermont	331	332	332	344	356	352	360	359	378	390	444	470
Massachusetts	1,457	1,783	2,239	2,805	3,336	3,852	4,250	4,317	4,691	5,149	5,689	5,800
Rhode Island	217	277	346	429	543	604	688	713	792	859	947	937
Connecticut	537	623	746	908	1,115	1,381	1,607	1,709	2,007	2,535	3,032	3,088
Middle Atlantic												
New York	4,383	5,083	6,003	7,269	9,114	10,385	12,588	13,479	14,830	16,782	18,237	18,111
New Jersey	906	1,131	1,445	1,884	2,537	3,156	4,041	4,160	4,835	6,067	7,168	7,330
Pennsylvania	3,522	4,283	5,258	6,302	7,665	8,720	9,631	9,900	10,498	11,319	11,794	11,835
South Atlantic												
Delaware	125	147	168	185	202	223	238	267	318	446	548	573
Maryland	781	935	1,042	1,188	1,295	1,450	1,632	1,821	2,343	3,101	3,922	4,094
Dist. of Columbia	132	178	230	279	331	438	487	663	802	764	757	723
Virginia	1,225	1,513	1,656	1,854	2,062	2,309	2,422	2,678	3,319	3,967	4,648	4,908
West Virginia	442	618	763	959	1,221	1,464	1,729	1,902	2,006	1,860	1,744	1,791
North Carolina	1,071	1,340	1,618	1,894	2,206	2,559	3,170	3,572	4,062	4,556	5,082	5,363
South Carolina	706	996	1,151	1,340	1,515	1,684	1,739	1,900	2,117	2,383	2,591	2,784
Georgia	1,184	1,542	1,837	2,216	2,609	2,896	2,909	3,124	3,445	3,943	4,590	4,882
Florida	188	269	391	529	753	968	1,468	1,897	2,771	4,952	6,789	8,090
South Central												
Kentucky	1,321	1,649	1,859	2,147	2,290	2,417	2,615	2,846	2,945	3,038	3,219	3,357
Tennessee	1,259	1,542	1,768	2,021	2,185	2,338	2,617	2,916	3,292	3,567	3,924	4,129
Alabama	997	1,262	1,513	1,829	2,138	2,348	2,646	2,833	3,062	3,267	3,444	3,577
Mississippi	828	1,132	1,290	1,551	1,797	1,791	2,010	2,184	2,179	2,178	2,217	2,324
Arkansas	484	803	1,128	1,312	1,574	1,752	1,854	1,949	1,910	1,786	1,923	2,062
Louisiana	727	940	1,119	1,382	1,656	1,799	2,102	2,364	2,684	3,257	3,641	3,764
Oklahoma			259	790	1,657	2,028	2,396	2,226	2,233	2,328	2,559	2,709
Texas	819	1,592	2,236	3,049	3,897	4,663	5,825	6,415	7,711	9,580	11,197	12,050
North Central												
Ohio	2,665	3,198	3,672	4,158	4,767	5,759	6,647	6,908	7,947	9,706	10,652	10,737
Indiana	1,681	1,978	2,192	2,516	2,701	2,930	3,239	3,428	3,934	4,662	5,194	5,330
Illinois	2,540	3,078	3,826	4,822	5,639	6,485	7,631	7,897	8,712	10,081	11,114	11,131
Michigan	1,184	1,637	2,094	2,421	2,810	3,668	4,842	5,256	6,372	7,823	8,875	9,098
Wisconsin	1,055	1,315	1,693	2,069	2,334	2,632	2,939	3,138	3,435	3,951	4,418	4,566
Minnesota	4	781	1,310	1,751	2,076	2,387	2,564	2,792	2,982	3,414	3,805	3,917
Iowa	1,194	1,625	1,912	2,232	2,225	2,404	2,471	2,538	2,621	2,758	2,824	2,855
Missouri	1,721	2,168	2,679	3,107	3,293	3,404	3,629	3,785	3,955	4,320	4,677	4,777
North Dakota	14	135	191	319	577	647	681	642	620	632	618	637
South Dakota			349	402	584	637	693	643	653	681	666	682
Nebraska	123	452	1,063	1,066	1,192	1,296	1,378	1,316	1,326	1,411	1,483	1,543
Kansas	364	996	1,428	1,470	1,691	1,769	1,881	1,801	1,905	2,179	2,247	2,270

Mountain												
Montana	21	39	143	243	376	549	538	559	591	675	694	735
Idaho	15	33	89	162	326	432	445	525	589	668	713	799
Wyoming	9	21	63	93	146	194	226	251	291	330	332	359
Colorado	40	194	413	540	799	940	1,036	1,123	1,325	1,755	2,207	2,496
New Mexico	92	120	160	195	327	360	423	532	681	951	1,016	1,122
Arizona	10	40	88	123	204	334	436	499	750	1,302	1,771	2,153
Utah	87	144	211	277	373	449	508	550	689	891	1,059	1,173
Nevada	42	62	47	42	82	77	91	110	160	285	489	573
Pacific												
Washington	24	75	357	518	1,142	1,357	1,563	1,902	2,379	2,853	3,409	3,476
Oregon	91	175	318	414	673	783	954	1,090	1,521	1,769	2,091	2,266
California	560	865	1,213	1,485	2,378	3,427	5,677	6,907	10,586	15,717	19,953	20,907
Alaska						64	55	59	73	226	300	337
Hawaii					154	192	256	368	423	633	769	847
Puerto Rico						1,300	1,544	1,869	2,211	2,350	2,712	
Total	38,558	50,156	62,948	75,995	92,228	107,322	124,747	132,154	151,319	179,311	203,212	211,390

Source: U.S. Bureau of the Census

URBAN AND RURAL POPULATION, 1870–1970

Census Year	Urban* Number (In Thousands)	Urban Per Cent of Total	Rural Number (In Thousands)	Rural Per Cent of Total
1870	9,902	25.7	28,656	74.3
1880	14,129	28.2	36,026	71.8
1890	22,106	35.1	40,841	64.9
1900	30,159	39.7	45,834	60.3
1910	41,998	45.7	49,973	54.3
1920	54,157	51.2	51,552	48.8
1930	68,954	56.2	53,820	43.8
1940	74,423	56.5	57,245	43.5
1950	96,847	59.0	54,479	41.0
1960	125,269	69.9	54,054	30.1
1970	149,235	73.5	53,887	26.5

*Urban: Includes all persons living in places of 2,500 or more and in densely settled urban fringe areas.
Source: U.S. Census of Population, 1970

PRESIDENTIAL VOTE, 1876–1972

Year	Candidate	Party	Popular Vote	Per Cent	Electoral Vote
1876	Tilden	Democratic	4,284,885	50.9	184
	Hayes	Republican	4,033,950	48.0	185
	Cooper	Greenback	81,740	1.0	
	Smith	Prohibition	9,522	.1	
	Walker	American	2,636	.0	
1880	Garfield	Republican	4,449,053	48.3	214
	Hancock	Democratic	4,442,035	48.2	155
	Weaver	Greenback	307,306	3.3	
	Dow	Prohibition	10,487	.1	
	Phelps	American	707	.0	
1884	Cleveland	Democratic	4,911,017	48.9	219
	Blaine	Republican	4,848,334	48.2	182
	St. John	Prohibition	151,809	1.5	
	Butler	Greenback	133,825	1.3	
1888	Cleveland	Democratic	5,540,050	48.7	168
	Harrison	Republican	5,444,337	47.8	233
	Fisk	Prohibition	250,125	2.2	
	Streeter	Union Labor	146,897	1.3	
	Cowdrey	United Labor	2,808	.0	
1892	Cleveland	Democratic	5,554,414	46.0	277
	Harrison	Republican	5,190,802	43.0	145
	Weaver	People's	1,027,329	8.5	22
	Bidwell	Prohibition	271,058	2.2	
	Wing	Socialist	21,164	.2	
1896	McKinley	Republican	7,035,638	50.9	271
	Bryan	Democratic	6,467,946	46.8	176
	Levering	Prohibition	141,676	1.0	
	Palmer	Nat. Democratic	131,529	1.0	
	Matchett	Socialist-Labor	36,454	.3	
	Bentley	National	13,969	.1	
1900	McKinley	Republican	7,219,530	51.7	292
	Bryan	Democratic	6,358,071	45.5	155
	Woolley	Prohibition	209,166	1.5	
	Debs	Socialist Democrat	94,768	.7	
	Barker	People's	50,232	.4	
	Malloney	Socialist-Labor	32,751	.2	
	Ellis	Union Reform	5,098	.0	
	Leonard	United Christian	518	.0	
1904	Roosevelt	Republican	7,628,834	56.4	336
	Parker	Democratic	5,084,401	37.6	140
	Debs	Socialist	402,460	3.0	
	Swallow	Prohibition	259,257	1.2	

Year	Candidate	Party	Popular Vote	Per Cent	Electoral Vote
1932	Roosevelt	Democratic	22,821,857	57.3	472
	Hoover	Republican	15,761,841	39.6	59
	Thomas	Socialist	884,781		
	Foster	Communist	102,991	3.1	
	Upshaw	Prohibition	81,869		
	Harvey	Liberty	53,425		
	Reynolds	Socialist-Labor	33,276		
	Coxey	Farm-Labor	7,309		
1936	Roosevelt	Democratic	27,751,612	60.7	523
	Landon	Republican	16,681,913	36.4	8
	Lemke	Union	891,858		
	Thomas	Socialist	187,342	2.9	
	Browder	Communist	80,181		
	Colvin	Prohibition	37,609		
	Aiken	Socialist-Labor	12,729		
1940	Roosevelt	Democratic	27,243,466	54.7	449
	Willkie	Republican	22,304,755	44.8	82
	Thomas	Socialist	99,557		
	Babson	Prohibition	57,812	.5	
	Browder	Communist	46,251		
	Aiken	Socialist-Labor	14,861		
1944	Roosevelt	Democratic	25,602,505	52.8	432
	Dewey	Republican	22,006,278	44.5	99
	Thomas	Socialist	80,518		
	Watson	Prohibition	74,758	2.7	
	Teichert	Socialist-Labor	45,336		
	Misc. Independent		216,289		
1948	Truman	Democratic	24,179,345	49.6	303
	Dewey	Republican	21,991,291	45.1	189
	Thurmond	States Rights	1,176,125		39
	Wallace	Progressive	1,157,326	5.3	
	Thomas	Socialist	139,572		
	Watson	Prohibition	103,900		
	Misc. Independent		46,267		
1952	Eisenhower	Republican	33,936,234	55.2	442
	Stevenson	Democratic	27,314,992	44.5	89
	Hallinan	Progressive	140,023		
	Hamblen	Prohibition	72,949	.3	
	Haas	Socialist-Labor	30,267		
	Hoopes	Socialist	20,203		
	MacArthur	Constitution	17,205		
	Dobbs	Socialist Workers	10,312		

Year	Candidate	Party	Popular Vote	%	Electoral
	Watson	People's	114,753	.9	
	Corregan	Socialist-Labor	33,724	.3	
	Holcomb	Continental	830	.0	
1908	Taft	Republican	7,679,006	51.6	321
	Bryan	Democratic	6,409,106	43.1	162
	Debs	Socialist	420,820	2.8	
	Chafin	Prohibition	252,683	1.7	
	Hisgen	Independence	83,562	.6	
	Watson	People's	28,131	.2	
	Gillhaus	Socialist-Labor	13,825	.1	
	Turney	United Christian	461	.0	
1912	Wilson	Democratic	6,286,214	41.8	435
	Roosevelt	Progressive	4,126,020	27.5	88
	Taft	Republican	3,483,922	23.2	8
	Debs	Socialist	897,011	6.0	
	Chafin	Prohibition	208,923	1.4	
	Reimer	Socialist-Labor	29,079	.2	
1916	Wilson	Democratic	9,129,606	49.3	277
	Hughes	Republican	8,538,221	46.1	254
	Benson	Socialist	585,113	3.2	
	Hanly	Prohibition	220,506	1.2	
	Reimer	Socialist-Labor	13,403	.0	
	Misc.		41,894	.2	
1920	Harding	Republican	16,152,200	61.0	404
	Cox	Democratic	9,147,353	34.6	127
	Debs	Socialist	919,799	3.5	
	Watkins	Prohibition	189,408	.7	
	Cox	Socialist-Labor	31,175	.1	
	Christensen	Farmer Labor	26,541	.1	
	Macauley	Single Tax	5,837	.0	
1924	Coolidge	Republican	15,725,016	54.1	382
	Davis	Democratic	8,385,586	28.8	136
	La Follette	Independent, Progressive, and Socialist	4,822,856	16.6	13
	Faris	Prohibition	57,551		
	Johns	Socialist-Labor	38,958		
	Foster	Workers'	33,361	.5	
	Nations	American	23,867		
	Wallace	Com. Land	2,778		
1928	Hoover	Republican	21,392,190	58.2	444
	Smith	Democratic	15,016,443	40.8	87
	Thomas	Socialist	267,420		
	Foster	Workers'	48,770		
	Reynolds	Socialist-Labor	21,603	1.0	
	Varney	Prohibition	20,106		
	Webb	Farm-Labor	6,390		

Year	Candidate	Party	Popular Vote	%	Electoral
1956	Eisenhower	Republican	35,590,472	57.4	457
	Stevenson	Democratic	26,022,752	42.0	73*
	Andrews	States Rights	111,178		
	Haas	Socialist-Labor	44,450		
	Holtwick	Prohibition	41,937	.6	
	Misc. Independent		216,119		
1960	Kennedy	Democratic	34,226,731	49.7	303
	Nixon	Republican	34,108,157	49.5	219
	Byrd				15†
	Faubus	National States Rights	44,977		
	Haas	Socialist-Labor	47,522		
	Decker	Prohibition	46,203	.8	
	Dobbs	Socialist Workers	40,165		
	Misc. Independent		324,464		
1964	Johnson	Democratic	43,129,484	61.1	486
	Goldwater	Republican	27,178,188	38.5	52
	Haas	Socialist-Labor	45,219		
	DeBerry	Socialist Workers	32,720		
	Munn	Prohibition	23,267	.4	
	Misc. Independent		235,632		
1968	Nixon	Republican	31,770,237	43.4	301
	Humphrey	Democratic	31,270,533	42.7	191
	Wallace	American Independent	9,906,141	13.5	46
	Blomen	Socialist-Labor	52,588		
	Gregory	New	47,097		
	Halstead	Socialist Workers	41,300		
	Cleaver	Peace & Freedom	36,385	.4	
	McCarthy	New	25,858		
	Misc. Independent		36,680		
1972	Nixon	Republican	47,169,911	60.7	520
	McGovern	Democratic	29,170,383	37.5	17
	Schmidz	American	1,099,482		
	Spock	Peoples	78,756		
	Jenness	Socialist Workers	66,677		
	Fisher	Socialist-Labor	53,814	1.8	
	Hall	Communist	25,595		
	Munn	Prohibition	13,505		
	Hospers	Libertarian	3,673		1
	Misc. Independent		36,758		

*In 1956 in Alabama one Democratic elector refused to vote for Stevenson and cast his ballot for Walter B. Jones.

†Six unpledged electors from Alabama, eight from Mississippi, and one Oklahoma Republican who refused to vote for Nixon.

Source: *America Votes, Statistical Abstract of the United States,* and the Elections Research Center, Washington, D.C.

Name and State Appointed from	Service		Name	Service	
Chief Justices in Italics	Term	Yrs.		Term	Yrs.
John Jay, N.Y.	1789–1795	6	Henry B. Brown, Mich.	1890–1906	16
John Rutledge, S.C.	1789–1791	2	George Shiras, Jr., Pa.	1892–1903	11
William Cushing, Mass.	1789–1810	21	Howell E. Jackson, Tenn.	1893–1895	2
James Wilson, Pa.	1789–1798	9	Edward D. White, La.	1894–1910	16
John Blair, Va.	1789–1796	7	Rufus W. Peckham, N.Y.	1895–1910	14
Robert H. Harrison, Md.	1789–1790	1	Joseph McKenna, Cal.	1898–1925	27
James Iredell, N.C.	1790–1799	9	Oliver W. Holmes, Mass.	1902–1932	29
Thomas Johnson, Md.	1791–1793	2	William R. Day, Ohio	1903–1922	19
William Paterson, N.J.	1793–1806	13	William H. Moody, Mass.	1906–1910	4
John Rutledge, S.C.	1795–1795		Horace H. Lurton, Tenn.	1910–1914	5
Samuel Chase, Md.	1796–1811	15	Charles E. Hughes, N.Y.	1910–1916	6
Oliver Ellsworth, Conn.	1796–1799	4	Willis Van Devanter, Wyo.	1910–1937	27
Bushrod Washington, Va.	1798–1829	31	*Edward D. White*, La.	1910–1921	11
Alfred Moore, N.C.	1799–1804	5	Joseph R. Lamar, Ga.	1911–1916	6
John Marshall, Va.	1801–1835	34	Mahlon Pitney, N.J.	1912–1922	10
William Johnson, S.C.	1804–1834	30	Jas. C. McReynolds, Tenn.	1914–1941	27
Brock. Livingston, N.Y.	1806–1823	17	Louis D. Brandeis, Mass.	1916–1939	23
Thomas Todd, Ky.	1807–1826	19	John H. Clarke, Ohio	1916–1922	6
Joseph Story, Mass.	1811–1845	34	*William H. Taft*, Conn.	1921–1930	9
Gabriel Duval, Md.	1811–1836	25	George Sutherland, Utah	1922–1938	16
Smith Thompson, N.Y.	1823–1843	20	Pierce Butler, Minn.	1922–1939	17
Robert Trimble, Ky.	1826–1828	2	Edward T. Sanford, Tenn.	1923–1930	7
John McLean, Ohio	1829–1861	32	Harlan F. Stone, N.Y.	1925–1941	16
Henry Baldwin, Pa.	1830–1844	14	*Charles E. Hughes*, N.Y.	1930–1941	11
James M. Wayne, Ga.	1835–1867	32	Owen J. Roberts, Pa.	1930–1945	15
Roger B. Taney, Md.	1836–1864	28	Benjamin N. Cardozo, N.Y.	1932–1938	6
Philip P. Barbour, Va.	1836–1841	5	Hugo L. Black, Ala.	1937–1971	34
John Catron, Tenn.	1837–1865	28	Stanley F. Reed, Ky.	1938–1957	19
John McKinley, Ala.	1837–1852	15	Felix Frankfurter, Mass.	1939–1962	23
Peter V. Daniel, Va.	1841–1860	19	William O. Douglas, Conn.	1939–1975	36
Samuel Nelson, N.Y.	1845–1872	27	Frank Murphy, Mich.	1940–1949	9
Levi Woodbury, N.H.	1845–1851	6	*Harlan F. Stone*, N.Y.	1941–1946	5
Robert C. Grier, Pa.	1846–1870	24	James F. Byrnes, S.C.	1941–1942	1
Benj. R. Curtis, Mass.	1851–1857	6	Robert H. Jackson, N.Y.	1941–1954	13
John A. Campbell, Ala.	1853–1861	8	Wiley B. Rutledge, Iowa	1943–1949	6
Nathan Clifford, Me.	1858–1881	23	Harold H. Burton, Ohio	1945–1958	13
Noah H. Swayne, Ohio	1862–1881	20	*Fred M. Vinson*, Ky.	1946–1953	7
Samuel F. Miller, Iowa	1862–1890	28	Tom C. Clark, Tex.	1949–1967	18
David Davis, Ill.	1862–1877	15	Sherman Minton, Ind.	1949–1956	7
Stephen J. Field, Cal.	1863–1897	34	*Earl Warren*, Cal.	1953–1969	16
Salmon P. Chase, Ohio	1864–1873	9	John M. Harlan, N.Y.	1955–1971	16
William Strong, Pa.	1870–1880	10	William J. Brennan, Jr., N.J.	1956–	
Joseph P. Bradley, N.J.	1870–1892	22	Charles E. Whittaker, Mo.	1957–1962	5
Ward Hunt, N.Y.	1872–1882	10	Potter Stewart, Ohio	1959–	
Morrison R. Waite, Ohio	1874–1888	14	Byron R. White, Colo.	1962–	
John M. Harlan, Ky.	1877–1911	34	Arthur J. Goldberg, Ill.	1962–1965	3
William B. Woods, Ga.	1880–1887	7	Abe Fortas, Tenn.	1965–1969	4
Stanley Matthews, Ohio	1881–1889	8	Thurgood Marshall, N.Y.	1967–	
Horace Gray, Mass.	1881–1902	21	*Warren E. Burger*, Minn.	1969–	
Samuel Blatchford, N.Y.	1882–1893	11	Harry A. Blackmun, Minn.	1970–	
Lucius Q. C. Lamar, Miss.	1888–1893	5	William H. Rehnquist, Ariz.	1972–	
Melville W. Fuller, Ill.	1888–1910	22	Lewis F. Powell, Jr., Va.	1972–	
David J. Brewer, Kan.	1889–1910	21	John Paul Stevens, Ill.	1975–	

DISTRIBUTION OF INCOME, 1950–1974

Year and Color	Income Level (Per Cent Distribution)											Median	
	Under $1,000	$1,000 to $1,999	$2,000 to $2,999	$3,000 to $3,999	$4,000 to $4,999	$5,000 to $5,999	$6,000 to $6,999	$7,000 to $9,999	$10,000 to $14,999	$15,000 to $24,999	$25,000 and over	Income	Index (1950 = 100)
All Families													
1950	11.5	13.2	17.8	20.7	13.6	9.0	5.2	5.8	3.3			3,319	100
1955	7.7	9.9	11.0	14.6	15.4	12.7	9.5	12.9	4.8	1.4		4,421	133
1960	5.0	8.0	8.7	9.8	10.5	12.9	10.8	20.0	10.6	3.7		5,620	169
1965	2.9	6.0	7.2	7.7	7.9	9.3	9.5	24.2	17.7	7.6		6,957	210
1970	1.6	3.0	4.3	5.1	5.3	5.8	6.0	19.9	26.8	22.3		9,867	297
1974	1.3	1.3	2.7	3.6	4.1	4.4	4.4	13.8	24.3	28.3	11.5	12,836	387
White Families													
1950	10.0	12.2	17.3	21.3	14.4	9.6	5.5	6.1	3.5			3,445	100
1955	6.6	8.7	10.4	14.3	16.0	13.4	9.9	13.9	5.3	1.5		4,605	134
1960	4.1	6.9	8.1	9.4	10.5	13.3	11.2	21.3	11.2	4.1		5,835	169
1965	2.5	5.2	6.3	6.9	7.6	9.3	9.8	25.5	18.8	8.3		7,251	210
1970	1.4	2.4	3.7	4.6	4.9	5.5	5.8	20.1	27.9	23.7		10,236	297
1974	1.1	1.0	2.2	3.1	3.7	4.2	4.2	13.5	25.1	29.7	12.4	13,356	388
Nonwhite Families													
1950	28.1	25.3	23.5	13.5	4.3	1.9	1.5	1.7	0.3			1,869	100
1955	19.0	20.7	17.6	17.2	11.1	5.8	4.8	3.1	0.6	(Z)		2,549	136
1960	13.4	18.3	14.8	14.0	10.4	8.7	6.7	8.7	4.3	0.6		3,233	173
1965	7.1	13.6	14.6	14.8	10.8	9.5	6.8	13.7	7.6	1.4		3,994	214
1970	3.4	7.7	9.0	8.8	8.2	9.0	7.4	18.2	17.3	10.9		6,516	349
1974	2.2	4.4	7.0	8.2	7.8	6.3	6.7	16.2	19.0	17.9	4.5	8,265	442

Z: Less than 0.05 per cent.
Source: Dept. of Commerce, Bureau of the Census, *Current Population Reports*.

The Constitution
of the United States

We the People of the United States, in order to form a more perfect union, establish Justice, insure domestic tranquility, provide for the common defence, promote the general Welfare, and secure the Blessings of Liberty to ourselves and our Posterity, do ordain and establish this Constitution for the United States of America.

ARTICLE I

Section 1. All legislative Powers herein granted shall be vested in a Congress of the United States, which shall consist of a Senate and a House of Representatives.

Section 2. The House of Representatives shall be composed of Members chosen every second Year by the People of the several States, and the Electors in each State shall have the Qualifications requisite for Electors of the most numerous Branch of the State Legislature.

No Person shall be a Representative who shall not have attained to the Age of twenty-five Years, and been seven Years a Citizen of the United States, and who shall not, when elected, be an Inhabitant of that State in which he shall be chosen.

Representatives and direct Taxes shall be apportioned among the several States which may be included within this Union, according to their respective Numbers, which shall be determined by adding to the whole Number of free Persons, including those bound to Service for a Term of Years, and excluding Indians not taxed, three fifths of all other Persons. The actual Enumeration shall be made within three Years after the first Meeting of the Congress of the United States, and within every subsequent Term of ten Years, in such Manner as they shall by Law direct. The Number of Representatives shall not exceed one for every thirty Thousand, but each State shall have at Least one Representative; and until such enumeration shall be made, the State of New Hampshire shall be entitled to chuse three, Massachusetts eight, Rhode-Island and Providence Plantations one, Connecticut five, New-York six, New Jersey four, Pennsylvania eight, Delaware one, Maryland six, Virginia ten, North Carolina five, South Carolina five, and Georgia three.

When vacancies happen in the Representation from any State, the Executive Authority thereof shall issue Writs of Election to fill such Vacancies.

The House of Representatives shall chuse their Speaker and other Officers; and shall have the sole Power of Impeachment.

Section 3. The Senate of the United States shall be composed of two Senators from each State, chosen by the Legislature thereof, for six Years; and each Senator shall have one Vote.

Immediately after they shall be assembled in Consequence of the first Election, they shall be divided as equally as may be into three Classes. The Seats of the Senators of the first Class shall be vacated at the Expiration of the second Year, of the second Class at the Expiration of the fourth Year, and of the third Class at the Expiration of the sixth Year, so that one-third may be chosen every second Year; and if Vacancies happen by Resignation, or otherwise, during the Recess of the Legislature of any State, the Executive thereof may make temporary Appointments until the next Meeting of the Legislature, which shall then fill such Vacancies.

No Person shall be a Senator who shall not have attained to the Age of thirty Years, and been nine Years a Citizen of the United States, and who shall not, when elected, be an Inhabitant of that State for which he shall be chosen.

The Vice President of the United States shall be President of the Senate, but shall have no Vote, unless they be equally divided.

The Senate shall chuse their other Officers, and also a President pro tempore, in the Absence of the Vice President, or when he shall exercise the Office of President of the United States.

The Senate shall have the sole Power to try all Impeachments. When sitting for that Purpose, they shall be on Oath or Affirmation. When the President of the United States is tried, the Chief Justice shall preside: And no Person shall be convicted without the Concurrence of two thirds of the Members present.

Judgment in Cases of Impeachment shall not extend further than to removal from Office, and disqualification to hold and enjoy any Office of honor, Trust or Profit under the United States: but the Party convicted shall nevertheless be liable and subject to Indictment, Trial, Judgment and Punishment, according to Law.

Section 4. The Times, Places and Manner of holding Elections for Senators and Representatives, shall be prescribed in each State by the Legislature thereof; but the Congress may at any time by Law make or alter such Regulations, except as to the Places of chusing Senators.

The Congress shall assemble at least once in every Year, and such Meeting shall be on the first Monday in December, unless they shall by Law appoint a different Day.

Section 5. Each House shall be the Judge of the Elections, Returns and Qualifications of its own Members, and a Majority of each shall constitute a Quorum to do Business; but a smaller Number may

adjourn from day to day, and may be authorized to compel the Attendance of absent Members, in such Manner, and under such Penalties as each House may provide.

Each House may determine the Rules of its Proceedings, punish its Members for disorderly Behavior, and, with the Concurrence of two thirds, expel a Member.

Each House shall keep a Journal of its Proceedings, and from time to time publish the same, excepting such Parts as may in their Judgment require Secrecy; and the Yeas and Nays of the Members of either House on any question shall, at the Desire of one fifth of those present, be entered on the Journal.

Neither House, during the Session of Congress, shall, without the Consent of the other, adjourn for more than three days, nor to any other Place than that in which the two Houses shall be sitting.

Section 6. The Senators and Representatives shall receive a Compensation for their Services, to be ascertained by Law, and paid out of the Treasury of the United States. They shall in all Cases, except Treason, Felony and Breach of the Peace, be privileged from Arrest during their Attendance at the Session of their respective Houses, and in going to and returning from the same; and for any Speech or Debate in either House, they shall not be questioned in any other Place.

No Senator or Representative shall, during the Time for which he was elected, be appointed to any civil Office under the Authority of the United States, which shall have been created, or the Emoluments whereof shall have been encreased during such time; and no Person holding any Office under the United States, shall be a Member of either House during his Continuance in Office.

Section 7. All Bills for raising Revenue shall originate in the House of Representatives; but the Senate may propose or concur with Amendments as on other Bills.

Every Bill which shall have passed the House of Representatives and the Senate, shall, before it becomes a Law, be presented to the President of the United States; If he approves he shall sign it, but if not he shall return it, with his Objections to that House in which it shall have originated, who shall enter the Objections at large on their Journal, and proceed to reconsider it. If after such Reconsideration two thirds of that House shall agree to pass the Bill, it shall be sent, together with the Objections, to the other House, by which it shall likewise be reconsidered, and if approved by two thirds of that House, it shall become a Law. But in all such Cases the Votes of both Houses shall be determined by Yeas and Nays, and the Names of the Persons voting for and against the Bill shall be entered on the Journal of each House respectively. If any Bill shall not be returned by the President within ten Days (Sundays excepted) after it shall have been presented to him, the Same shall be a Law, in like Manner as if he had signed it, unless the Congress by their Adjournment prevent its Return, in which Case it shall not be a Law.

Every Order, Resolution, or Vote to which the Concurrence of the Senate and House of Representatives may be necessary (except on a question of Adjournment) shall be presented to the President of the United States; and before the Same shall take Effect, shall be approved by him, or being disapproved by him, shall be repassed by two thirds of the Senate and House of Representatives, according to the Rules and Limitations prescribed in the Case of a Bill.

Section 8. The Congress shall have Power To lay and collect Taxes, Duties, Imposts and Excises, to pay the Debts and provide for the common Defence and general Welfare of the United States; but all Duties, Imposts and Excises shall be uniform throughout the United States;

To borrow Money on the credit of the United States;

To regulate Commerce with foreign Nations, and among the several States, and with the Indian Tribes;

To establish an uniform Rule of Naturalization, and uniform Laws on the subject of Bankruptcies throughout the United States;

To coin Money, regulate the Value thereof, and of foreign Coin, and fix the Standard of Weights and Measures;

To provide for the Punishment of counterfeiting the Securities and current Coin of the United States;

To establish Post Offices and post Roads;

To promote the Progress of Science and useful Arts, by securing for limited Times to Authors and Inventors the exclusive Right to their respective Writings and Discoveries;

To constitute Tribunals inferior to the supreme Court;

To define and punish Piracies and Felonies committed on the high Seas, and Offences against the Law of Nations;

To declare War, grant Letters of Marque and Reprisal, and make Rules concerning Captures on Land and Water;

To raise and support Armies, but no Appropriation of Money to that Use shall be for a longer Term than two Years;

To provide and maintain a Navy;

To make Rules for the Government and Regulation of the land and naval Forces;

To provide for calling forth the Militia to execute the Laws of the Union, suppress Insurrections and repel Invasions;

To provide for organizing, arming, and disciplining the Militia, and for governing such Part of them as may be employed in the Service of the United States, reserving to the States respectively, the Appointment of the Officers, and the Authority of training the Militia according to the discipline prescribed by Congress;

To exercise exclusive Legislation in all Cases whatsoever, over such District (not exceeding ten Miles square) as may, by Cession of particular States, and the Acceptance of Congress, become the Seat of the Government of the United States, and to exercise like Authority over all Places purchased by the Consent of the Legislature of the State in which the Same shall be, for the Erection of Forts, Magazines, Arsenals, dock-Yards, and other needful Buildings;—And

To make all Laws which shall be necessary and proper for carrying into Execution the foregoing Powers, and all other Powers vested by this Constitution in the Government of the United States, or in any Department or Officer thereof.

Section 9. The Migration or Importation of such Persons as any of the States now existing shall think proper to admit, shall not be prohibited by the Congress prior to the Year one thousand eight hundred and eight, but a Tax or duty may be imposed on such Importation, not exceeding ten dollars for each Person.

The Privilege of the Writ of Habeas Corpus shall not be suspended, unless when in Cases of Rebellion or Invasion the public Safety may require it.

No Bill of Attainder or ex post facto Law shall be passed.

No Capitation, or other direct, tax shall be laid, unless in Proportion to the Census or Enumeration herein before directed to be taken.

No Tax or Duty shall be laid on Articles exported from any State.

No Preference shall be given by any Regulation of Commerce or Revenue to the Ports of one State over those of another: nor shall Vessels bound to, or from, one State, be obliged to enter, clear, or pay Duties in another.

No Money shall be drawn from the Treasury, but in Consequence of Appropriations made by Law; and a regular Statement and Account of the Receipts and

Expenditures of all public Money shall be published from time to time.

No Title of Nobility shall be granted by the United States: And no Person holding any Office of Profit or Trust under them, shall, without the Consent of the Congress, accept of any present, Emolument, Office, or Title, of any kind whatever, from any King, Prince, or foreign State.

Section 10. No State shall enter into any Treaty, Alliance, or Confederation; grant Letters of Marque and Reprisal; coin Money; emit Bills of Credit; make any Thing but gold and silver Coin a Tender in Payment of Debts; pass any Bill of Attainder, ex post facto Law, or Law impairing the Obligation of Contracts, or grant any Title of Nobility.

No State shall, without the Consent of the Congress, lay any Imposts or Duties on Imports or Exports, except what may be absolutely necessary for executing its inspection Laws: and the net Produce of all Duties and Imposts, laid by any State on Imports or Exports, shall be for the Use of the Treasury of the United States; and all such Laws shall be subject to the Revision and Controul of the Congress.

No State shall, without the Consent of Congress, lay any Duty of Tonnage, keep Troops, or Ships of War in time of Peace, enter into any Agreement or Compact with another State, or with a foreign Power, or engage in War, unless actually invaded, or in such imminent Danger as will not admit of delay.

ARTICLE II

Section 1. The Executive Power shall be vested in a President of the United States of America. He shall hold his Office during the Term of four Years, and, together with the Vice President, chosen for the same Term, be elected, as follows

Each State shall appoint, in such Manner as the legislature thereof may direct, a Number of Electors, equal to the whole Number of Senators and Representatives to which the State may be entitled in the Congress: but no Senator or Representative, or Person holding an Office of Trust or Profit under the United States, shall be appointed an Elector.

The electors shall meet in their respective States, and vote by ballot for two Persons, of whom one at least shall not be an Inhabitant of the same State with themselves. And they shall make a List of all the Persons voted for, and of the Number of Votes for each; which List they shall sign and certify, and transmit sealed to the Seat of the Government of the United States, directed to the President of the Senate. The President of the Senate shall, in the Presence of the Senate and House of Representatives, open all the Certificates, and the Votes shall then be counted. The Person having the greatest Number of Votes shall be the President, if such Number be a Majority of the whole Number of Electors appointed; and if there be more than one who have such Majority, and have an equal Number of Votes, then the House of Representatives shall immediately chuse by Ballot one of them for President; and if no Person have a Majority, then from the five highest on the List the said House shall in like Manner chuse the President. But in chusing the President, the Votes shall be taken by States, the Representation from each State having one Vote; A quorum for this Purpose shall consist of a Member or Members from two thirds of the States, and a Majority of all the States shall be necessary to a Choice. In every Case, after the Choice of the President, the Person having the greatest Number of Votes of the Electors shall be the Vice President. But if there should remain two or more who have equal Votes, the Senate shall chuse from them by Ballot the Vice President.

The Congress may determine the Time of chusing the Electors, and the Day on which they shall give their Votes; which Day shall be the same throughout the United States.

No Person except a natural born Citizen, or a Citizen of the United States, at the time of the Adoption of this Constitution, shall be eligible to the Office of President; neither shall any Person be eligible to that Office who shall not have attained to the Age of thirty five Years, and been fourteen Years a Resident within the United States.

In Case of the Removal of the President from Office, or of his Death, Resignation or Inability to discharge the Powers and Duties of the said Office, the same shall devolve on the Vice President, and the Congress may by Law provide for the Case of Removal, Death, Resignation or Inability, both of the President and Vice President, declaring what Officer shall then act as President, and such Officer shall act accordingly, until the Disability be removed, or a President shall be elected.

The President shall, at stated Times, receive for his Services, a Compensation, which shall neither be encreased nor diminished during the Period for which he shall have been elected, and he shall not receive within that Period any other Emolument from the United States, or any of them.

Before he enter on the Execution of his Office, he shall take the following Oath or Affirmation:—"I do solemnly swear (or affirm) that I will faithfully execute the Office of President of the United States, and will to the best of my Ability, preserve, protect and defend the Constitution of the United States."

Section 2. The President shall be Commander in Chief of the Army and Navy of the United States, and of the Militia of the several States, when called into the actual Service of the United States; he may require the Opinion, in writing, of the principal Officer in each of the executive Departments, upon any Subject relating to the Duties of their respective Offices, and he shall have Power to grant Reprieves and Pardons for Offences against the United States, except in Cases of Impeachment.

He shall have Power, by and with the Advice and Consent of the Senate to make Treaties, provided two thirds of the Senators present concur and he shall nominate, and by and with the Advice and Consent of the Senate, shall appoint Ambassadors, other public Ministers and Consuls, Judges of the supreme Court, and all other Officers of the United States, whose Appointments are not herein otherwise provided for, and which shall be established by Law: but the Congress may by Law vest the Appointment of such inferior Officers, as they think proper, in the President alone, in the Courts of Law, or in the Heads of Departments.

The President shall have Power to fill up all Vacancies that may happen during the Recess of the Senate, by granting Commissions which shall expire at the End of their next Session.

Section 3. He shall from time to time give to the Congress Information of the State of the Union, and recommend to their Consideration such Measures as he shall judge necessary and expedient; he may, on extraordinary Occasions, convene both Houses, or either of them, and, in Case of Disagreement between them, with Respect to the Time of Adjournment, he may adjourn them to such Time as he shall think proper; he shall receive Ambassadors and other public Ministers; he shall take Care that the Laws be faithfully executed, and shall Commission all the Officers of the United States.

Section 4. The President, Vice President and all civil Officers of the United States, shall be removed from Office on Impeachment for, and Conviction of, Treason, Bribery, or other high Crimes and Misdemeanors.

ARTICLE III

Section 1. The judicial Power of the United States, shall be vested in one supreme Court, and in such inferior Courts as the Congress may from time to time ordain and establish. The Judges, both of the supreme and inferior Courts, shall hold their Offices during good Behaviour, and shall, at stated Times, receive for their Services, a Compensation, which shall not be diminished during their Continuance in Office.

Section 2. The judicial Power shall extend to all Cases, in Law and Equity, arising under this Constitution, the Laws of the United States, and Treaties made, or which shall be made, under their Authority;—to all Cases affecting Ambassadors, other public Ministers and Consuls;—to all Cases of admiralty and maritime Jurisdiction;—to Controversies to which the United States shall be a Party;—to Controversies between two or more States;—between a State and Citizens of another State;—between Citizens of different States,—between Citizens of the same State claiming Lands under Grants of different States, and between a State, or the Citizens thereof, and foreign States, Citizens or Subjects.

In all Cases affecting Ambassadors, other public Ministers and Consuls, and those in which a State shall be Party, the supreme Court shall have original Jurisdiction. In all other Cases before mentioned, the supreme Court shall have appellate Jurisdiction, both as to Law and Fact, with such Exceptions, and under such Regulations as the Congress shall make.

The Trial of all Crimes, except in Cases of Impeachment, shall be by Jury; and such Trial shall be held in the State where the said Crimes shall have been committed; but when not committed within any State, the Trial shall be at such Place or Places as the Congress may by Law have directed.

Section 3. Treason against the United States, shall consist only in levying War against them, or in adhering to their Enemies, giving them Aid and Comfort. No Person shall be convicted of Treason unless on the Testimony of two Witnesses to the same overt Act, or on Confession in open Court.

The Congress shall have Power to declare the Punishment of Treason, but no Attainder of Treason shall work Corruption of Blood, or Forfeiture except during the Life of the Person attainted.

ARTICLE IV

Section 1. Full Faith and Credit shall be given in each State to the public Acts, Records, and judicial Proceedings of every other State. And the Congress may by general Laws prescribe the Manner in which such Acts, Records and Proceedings shall be proved, and the Effect thereof.

Section 2. The Citizens of each State shall be entitled to all Privileges and Immunities of Citizens in the several States.

A person charged in any State with Treason, Felony, or other Crime, who shall flee from Justice, and be found in another State, shall on Demand of the executive Authority of the State from which he fled, be delivered up, to be removed to the State having Jurisdiction of the Crime.

No Person held to Service or Labour in one State, under the Laws thereof, escaping into another, shall, in Consequence of any Law or Regulation therein, be discharged from such Service or Labour, but shall be delivered up on Claim of the Party to whom such Service or Labour may be due.

Section 3. New States may be admitted by the Congress into this Union; but no new State shall be formed or erected within the Jurisdiction of any other State; nor any State be formed by the Junction of two or more States, or Parts of States, without the Consent of the Legislatures of the States concerned as well as of the Congress.

The Congress shall have Power to dispose of and make all needful Rules and Regulations respecting the Territory or other Property belonging to the United States; and nothing in this Constitution shall be so construed as to Prejudice any Claims of the United States, or of any particular State.

Section 4. The United States shall guarantee to every State in this Union a Republican Form of Government, and shall protect each of them against Invasion; and on Application of the Legislature, or of the Executive (when the Legislature cannot be convened) against domestic Violence.

ARTICLE V

The Congress, whenever two thirds of both houses shall deem it necessary, shall propose Amendments to this Constitution, or, on the Application of the Legislatures of two thirds of the several States, shall call a Convention for proposing Amendments, which, in either Case, shall be valid to all Intents and Purposes, as Part of this Constitution, when ratified by the Legislatures of three fourths of the several States, or by Conventions in three fourths thereof, as the one or the other Mode of Ratification may be proposed by the Congress; Provided that no Amendment which may be made prior to the Year One thousand eight hundred and eight shall in any Manner affect the first and fourth Clauses in the Ninth Section of the first Article; and that no State, without its Consent, shall be deprived of its equal Suffrage in the Senate.

ARTICLE VI

All Debts contracted and Engagements entered into, before the Adoption of this Constitution, shall be as valid against the United States under this Constitution, as under the Confederation.

This Constitution, and the Laws of the United States which shall be made in Pursuance thereof; and all Treaties made, or which shall be made, under the Authority of the United States, shall be the supreme Law of the Land; and the Judges in every State shall be bound thereby, any Thing in the Constitution or Laws of any State to the Contrary notwithstanding.

The Senators and Representatives before mentioned, and the Members of the several State Legislatures, and all executive and judicial Officers, both of the United States and of the several States, shall be bound by Oath or Affirmation, to support this Constitution; but no religious Test shall ever be required as a Qualification to any Office or public Trust under the United States.

ARTICLE VII

The Ratification of the Conventions of nine States, shall be sufficient for the Establishment of this Constitution between the States so ratifying the Same.

DONE in Convention by the Unanimous Consent of the States present the Seventeenth Day of September in the Year of our Lord one thousand seven hundred and Eighty seven and of the Independence of the United States of America the Twelfth. IN WITNESS whereof We have hereunto subscribed our Names.

G° Washington
Presid¹ and deputy from Virginia

AMENDMENTS
ARTICLE I

[THE FIRST TEN ARTICLES PROPOSED 25 SEPTEMBER 1789; DECLARED IN FORCE 15 DECEMBER 1791]

Congress shall make no law respecting an establishment of religion, or prohibiting the free exercise thereof; or abridging the freedom of speech, or of the press; or the right of the people peaceably to assemble, and to petition the Government for a redress of grievances.

ARTICLE II

A well regulated Militia, being necessary to the security of a free State, the right of the people to keep and bear Arms, shall not be infringed.

ARTICLE III

No Soldier shall, in time of peace, be quartered in any house, without the consent of the Owner, nor in time of war, but in a manner to be prescribed by law.

ARTICLE IV

The right of the people to be secure in their persons, houses, papers, and effects, against unreasonable searches and seizures, shall not be violated, and no Warrants shall issue, but upon probable cause, supported by Oath or affirmation, and particularly describing the place to be searched, and the persons or things to be seized.

ARTICLE V

No person shall be held to answer for a capital, or otherwise infamous crime, unless on a presentment or indictment of a Grand Jury, except in cases arising in the land or naval forces, or in the Militia, when in actual service in time of War or public danger; nor shall any person be subject for the same offence to be twice put in jeopardy of life or limb; nor shall be compelled in any Criminal Case to be a witness against himself, nor be deprived of life, liberty, or property, without due process of law; nor shall private property be taken for public use, without just compensation.

ARTICLE VI

In all criminal prosecutions, the accused shall enjoy the right to a speedy and public trial, by an impartial jury of the State and district wherein the crime shall have been committed, which district shall have been previously ascertained by law, and to be informed of the nature and cause of the accusation; to be confronted with the witnesses against him; to have compulsory process for obtaining Witnesses in his favor, and to have the Assistance of Counsel for his defence.

ARTICLE VII

In suits at common law, where the value in controversy shall exceed twenty dollars, the right of trial by jury shall be preserved, and no fact tried by a jury shall be otherwise re-examined in any Court of the United States, than according to the rules of the common law.

ARTICLE VIII

Excessive bail shall not be required, nor excessive fines imposed, nor cruel and unusual punishments inflicted.

ARTICLE IX

The enumeration in the Constitution, of certain rights, shall not be construed to deny or disparage others retained by the people.

ARTICLE X

The powers not delegated to the United States by the Constitution, nor prohibited by it to the States, are reserved to the States respectively, or to the people.

ARTICLE XI

[PROPOSED 4 MARCH 1794; DECLARED RATIFIED 8 JANUARY 1798]

The Judicial power of the United States shall not be construed to extend to any suit in law or equity, commenced or prosecuted against one of the United States by Citizens of another State, or by Citizens or Subjects of any Foreign State.

ARTICLE XII

[PROPOSED 9 DECEMBER 1803; DECLARED RATIFIED 25 SEPTEMBER 1804]

The Electors shall meet in their respective states, and vote by ballot for President and Vice-President, one of whom, at least, shall not be an inhabitant of the same state with themselves; they shall name in their ballots the person voted for as President, and in distinct ballots the person voted for as Vice-President, and they shall make distinct lists of all persons voted for as President, and of all persons voted for as Vice-President, and of the number of votes for each, which lists they shall sign and certify, and transmit sealed to the seat of the Government of the United States, directed to the President of the Senate;—The President of the Senate shall, in the presence of the Senate and House of Representatives, open all the certificates and the votes shall then be counted;—The person having the greatest number of votes for President, shall be the President, if such number be a majority of the whole number of Electors appointed; and if no person have such majority, then from the persons having the highest numbers not exceeding three on the list of those voted for as President, the House of Representatives shall choose immediately, by ballot, the President. But in choosing the President, the votes shall be taken by states, the representation from each state having one vote; a quorum for this purpose shall consist of a member or members from two-thirds of the states, and a majority of all the states shall be necessary to a choice. And if the House of Representatives shall not choose a President whenever the right of choice shall devolve upon them, before the fourth day of March next following, then the Vice-President shall act as President, as in the case of the death or other constitutional disability of the President. The person having the greatest number of votes as Vice-President, shall be the Vice-President, if such number be a majority of the whole number of Electors appointed, and if no person have a majority, then from the two highest numbers on the list, the Senate shall choose the Vice-President; a quorum for the purpose shall consist of two-thirds of the whole number of Senators, and a majority of the whole number shall be necessary to a choice. But no person constitutionally ineligible to the office of President shall be eligible to that of Vice-President of the United States.

ARTICLE XIII

[PROPOSED 31 JANUARY 1865; DECLARED RATIFIED 18 DECEMBER 1865]

Section 1. Neither slavery nor involuntary servitude, except as a punishment for crime whereof the party shall have been duly convicted, shall exist within the United States, or any place subject to their jurisdiction.

Section 2. Congress shall have power to enforce this article by appropriate legislation.

ARTICLE XIV

[PROPOSED 13 JUNE 1866; DECLARED RATIFIED 28 JULY 1868]

Section 1. All persons born or naturalized in the United States, and subject to the jurisdiction thereof, are citizens of the United States and of the State wherein they reside. No State shall make or enforce any law which shall abridge the privileges or immunities of citizens of the United States; nor shall any State deprive any person of life, liberty, or property, without due process of law; nor deny to any person within its jurisdiction the equal protection of the laws.

Section 2. Representatives shall be apportioned among the several States according to their respective numbers, counting the whole number of persons in each State, excluding Indians not taxed. But when the right to vote at any election for the choice of electors for President and Vice President of the United States, Representatives in Congress, the Executive and Judicial officers of a State, or the members of the Legislature thereof, is denied to any of the male inhabitants of such State, being twenty-one years of age, and citizens of the United States, or in any way abridged, except for participation in rebellion, or other crime, the basis of representation therein shall be reduced in the proportion which the number of such male citizens shall bear to the whole number of male citizens twenty-one years of age in such State.

Section 3. No person shall be a Senator or Representative in Congress, or elector of President and Vice President, or hold any office, civil, or military, under the United States, or under any State, who, having previously taken an oath, as a member of Congress, or as an officer of the United States, or as a member of any State legislature, or as an executive or judicial officer of any State, to support the Constitution of the United States, shall have engaged in insurrection or rebellion against the same, or given aid or comfort to the enemies thereof. But Congress may by a vote of two-thirds of each House, remove such disability.

Section 4. The validity of the public debt of the United States, authorized by law, including debts incurred for payment of pensions and bounties for services in suppressing insurrection or rebellion, shall not be questioned. But neither the United States nor any State shall assume or pay any debt or obligation incurred in aid of insurrection or rebellion against the United States, or any claim for the loss or emancipation of any slave; but all such debts, obligations and claims shall be held illegal and void.

Section 5. The Congress shall have power to enforce, by appropriate legislation, the provisions of this article.

ARTICLE XV

[PROPOSED 26 FEBRUARY 1869; DECLARED RATIFIED 30 MARCH 1870]

Section 1. The right of citizens of the United States to vote shall not be denied or abridged by the United States or by any State on account of race, color, or previous condition of servitude.

Section 2. The Congress shall have power to enforce this article by appropriate legislation.

ARTICLE XVI

[PROPOSED 12 JULY 1909; DECLARED RATIFIED 25 FEBRUARY 1913]

The Congress shall have power to lay and collect taxes on incomes, from whatever source derived, without apportionment among the several States, and without regard to any census or enumeration.

ARTICLE XVII

[PROPOSED 13 MAY 1912; DECLARED RATIFIED 31 MAY 1913]

The Senate of the United States shall be composed of two senators from each State, elected by the people thereof, for six years; and each Senator shall have one vote. The electors in each State shall have the qualifications requisite for electors of the most numerous branch of the State legislature.

When vacancies happen in the representation of any State in the Senate, the executive authority of such State shall issue writs of election to fill such vacancies: PROVIDED, That the legislature of any State may empower the executive thereof to make temporary appointments until the people fill the vacancies by election as the legislature may direct.

This amendment shall not be so construed as to affect the election or term of any senator chosen before it becomes valid as part of the Constitution.

ARTICLE XVIII

[PROPOSED 18 DECEMBER 1917; DECLARED RATIFIED 29 JANUARY 1919]

After one year from the ratification of this article, the manufacture, sale, or transportation of intoxicating liquors within, the importation thereof into, or the exportation thereof from the United States and all territory subject to the jurisdiction thereof for beverage purposes is hereby prohibited.

The Congress and the several States shall have concurrent power to enforce this article by appropriate legislation.

This article shall be inoperative unless it shall have been ratified as an amendment to the Constitution by the legislatures of the several States, as provided in the Constitution, within seven years from the date of the submission hereof to the States by the Congress.

ARTICLE XIX

[PROPOSED 4 JUNE 1919; DECLARED RATIFIED 26 AUGUST 1920]

The right of citizens of the United States to vote shall not be denied or abridged by the United States or by any States on account of sex.

The Congress shall have power, by appropriate legislation, to enforce the provisions of this article.

ARTICLE XX

[PROPOSED 2 MARCH 1932; DECLARED RATIFIED 6 FEBRUARY 1933]

Section 1. The terms of the President and Vice-President shall end at noon on the twentieth day of

January, and the terms of Senators and Representatives at noon on the third day of January, of the years in which such terms would have ended if this article had not been ratified; and the terms of their successors shall then begin.

Section 2. The Congress shall assemble at least once in every year, and such meeting shall begin at noon on the third day of January, unless they shall by law appoint a different day.

Section 3. If, at the time fixed for the beginning of the term of the President, the President-elect shall have died, the Vice-President-elect shall become President. If a President shall not have been chosen before the time fixed for the beginning of his term, or if the President-elect shall have failed to qualify, then the Vice-President-elect shall act as President until a President shall have qualified; and the Congress may by law provide for the case wherein neither a President-elect nor a Vice-President-elect shall have qualified, declaring who shall then act as President, or the manner in which one who is to act shall be selected, and such person shall act accordingly until a President or Vice-President shall have qualified.

Section 4. The Congress may by law provide for the case of the death of any of the persons from whom the House of Representatives may choose a President whenever the right of choice shall have devolved upon them, and for the case of the death of any of the persons from whom the Senate may choose a Vice-President whenever the right of choice shall have devolved upon them.

Section 5. Sections 1 and 2 shall take effect on the 15th day of October following the ratification of this article.

Section 6. This article shall be inoperative unless it shall have been ratified as an amendment to the Constitution by the legislatures of three-fourths of the several States within seven years from the date of its submission.

ARTICLE XXI

[PROPOSED 20 FEBRUARY 1933; DECLARED RATIFIED 5 DECEMBER 1933]

Section 1. The eighteenth article of amendment to the Constitution of the United States is hereby repealed.

Section 2. The transportation or importation into any State, Territory or possession of the United States for delivery or use therein of intoxicating liquors, in violation of the laws thereof, is hereby prohibited.

Section 3. This article shall be inoperative unless it shall have been ratified as an amendment to the Constitution by convention in the several States, as provided in the Constitution, within seven years from the date of the submission hereof to the States by the Congress.

ARTICLE XXII

[PROPOSED 21 MARCH 1947; DECLARED RATIFIED 3 MARCH 1951]

Section 1. No person shall be elected to the office of the President more than twice, and no person who has held the office of President, or acted as President, for more than two years of a term to which some other person was elected President shall be elected to the office of the President more than once. But this Article shall not apply to any person holding the office of President when this Article was proposed by the Congress, and shall not prevent any person who may be holding the office of President, or acting as President, during the term within which this Article becomes operative from holding the office of President or acting as President during the remainder of such term.

ARTICLE XXIII

[PROPOSED 17 JUNE 1960; DECLARED RATIFIED 3 APRIL 1961]

Section 1. The District constituting the seat of Government of the United States shall appoint in such manner as the Congress may direct:
A number of electors of President and Vice President equal to the whole number of Senators and Representatives in Congress to which the District would be entitled if it were a State, but in no event more than the least populous State; they shall be in addition to those appointed by the States, but they shall be considered, for the purposes of the election of President and Vice President, to be electors appointed by a State; and they shall meet in the District and perform such duties as provided by the twelfth article of amendment.

Section 2. The Congress shall have power to enforce this article by appropriate legislation.

ARTICLE XXIV

[PROPOSED 27 AUGUST 1962; DECLARED RATIFIED 4 FEBRUARY 1964]

Section 1. The right of citizens of the United States to vote in any primary or other election for President or Vice President, for electors for President or Vice President, or for Senator or Representative in Congress, shall not be denied or abridged by the United States or any State by reason of failure to pay any poll tax or other tax.

Section 2. The Congress shall have power to enforce this article by appropriate legislation.

ARTICLE XXV

[PROPOSED 6 JULY 1965; DECLARED RATIFIED 23 FEBRUARY 1967]

Section 1. In case of the removal of the President from office or of his death or resignation, the Vice President shall become President.

Section 2. Whenever there is a vacancy in the office of the Vice President, the President shall nominate a Vice President who shall take office upon confirmation by a majority vote of both Houses of Congress.

Section 3. Whenever the President transmits to the President pro tempore of the Senate and the Speaker of the House of Representatives his written declaration that he is unable to discharge the powers and duties of his office, and until he transmits to them a written declaration to the contrary, such powers and duties shall be discharged by the Vice President as Acting President.

Section 4. Whenever the Vice President and a majority of either the principal officers of the executive department or of such other body as Congress may by law provide, transmit to the President pro tempore of the Senate and the Speaker of the House of Representatives their written declaration that the President is unable to discharge the powers and duties of his office; the Vice President shall immediately assume the powers and duties of the office as Acting President.

Thereafter, when the President transmits to the President pro tempore of the Senate and the Speaker of the House of Representatives his written declaration that no inability exists, he shall resume the powers and duties of his office unless the Vice President and a majority of either the principal officers of the executive department or of such other body as Congress may by law provide, transmit within four days to the President pro tempore of the Senate and the Speaker of the House of Representatives their written declaration that the President is unable to discharge the powers and duties of his office. Thereupon Congress shall decide the issue, assembling within forty-eight hours for that purpose if not in session. If the Congress, within twenty-one days after receipt of the latter written declaration, or, if Congress is not in session, within twenty-one days after Congress is required to assemble, determines by two-thirds vote of both Houses that the President is unable to discharge the powers and duties of his office, the Vice President shall continue to discharge the same as Acting President; otherwise, the President shall resume the powers and duties of his office.

ARTICLE XXVI

[PROPOSED 23 MARCH 1971; DECLARED RATIFIED 30 JUNE 1971]

Section 1. The right of citizens of the United States, who are 18 years of age or older, to vote shall not be denied or abridged by the United States or any state on account of age.

Secton 2. The Congress shall have the power to enforce this article by appropriate legislation.

Index